**KU-120-855**

# Travel Discount Coupon

This coupon entitles you to special discounts
when you book your trip through the

**TRAVEL NETWORK**®
**RESERVATION SERVICE**

## Hotels ◆ Airlines ◆ Car Rentals ◆ Cruises
## All Your Travel Needs

Here's what you get: *

◆ A discount of $50 USD on a booking of $1,000** or
  more for two or more people!

◆ A discount of $25 USD on a booking of $500** or more
  for one person!

◆ Free membership for three years, and 1,000 free miles
  on enrollment in the unique Travel Network Miles-to-
  Go® frequent-traveler program. Earn one mile for
  every dollar spent through the program. Redeem
  miles for free hotel stays starting at 5,000 miles. Earn
  free roundtrip airline tickets starting at 25,000 miles.

◆ Personal help in planning your own, customized trip.

◆ Fast, confirmed reservations at any property
  recommended in this guide, subject to availability.***

◆ Special discounts on bookings in the U.S. and around
  the world.

◆ Low-cost visa and passport service.

◆ Reduced-rate cruise packages and special car rental
  programs worldwide.

Visit our website at http://www.travelnetwork.com/Frommer
or call us globally at 201-567-8500, ext. 55. In the U.S., call
toll-free at 1-888-940-5000, or fax 201-567-1838. In Canada,
call at 1-905-707-7222, or fax 905-707-8108. In Asia, call
60-3-7191044, or fax 60-3-7185415.

\* To qualify for these travel discounts, at least a portion of your trip must
  include destinations covered in this guide. No more than one coupon discount
  may be used in any 12-month period, for destinations covered in this guide.
  Cannot be combined with any other discount or promotion.
\*\*These are U.S. dollars spent on commissionable bookings.
\*\*\* A $10 USD fee, plus fax and/or phone charges, will be added to the cost of
  bookings at each hotel not linked to the reservation service. Customers must
  approve these fees in advance. If only hotels of this kind are booked, the traveler(s)
  must also purchase roundtrip air tickets from Travel Network for the trip.

Valid until December 31, 1998. Terms and conditions of the Miles-to-
Go® program are available on request by calling 201-567-8500, ext 55.

 ARI234

# Frommer's® 98

# Arizona

## by Karl Samson
### with Jane Aukshunas

Macmillan • USA

## ABOUT THE AUTHORS

**Karl Samson** likes to flee the soggy Northwest to dry out in the Arizona sun and has been exploring the state's deserts, mountains, cities, and towns for the past decade. He is also the author of several other Frommer guidebooks.

**Jane Aukshunas** enjoys experiencing the unique regional style of Arizona's hotels and restaurants, and is always interested in discovering more about the stimulating landscapes of prehistory and contemporary art she finds there.

## MACMILLAN TRAVEL

A Simon & Schuster Macmillan Company
1633 Broadway
New York, NY 10019

Find us online at **http:// www.frommers.com** or
on America Online at Keyword: **Frommers**

ISBN 0-02-861638-3
ISSN 1053-2471

Editor: Margot Weiss
Production Editor: Lori Cates
Design by Michele Laseau
Digital Cartography by Raffaele Degennaro
Page Creation by Tammy Ahrens, Toi Davis, Sean Decker, CJ East, Natalie Hollifield, Donna Martin, Heather Pope, Linda Quigley, Terri Sheehan, and Karen Teo

## SPECIAL SALES

Bulk purchases (10+ copies) of Frommer's and selected Macmillan travel guides are available to corporations, organizations, mail-order catalogs, institutions, and charities at special discounts, and can be customized to suit individual needs. For more information write to Special Sales, Macmillan General Reference, 1633 Broadway, New York, NY 10019.

Manufactured in the United States of America

# Contents

# List of Maps

## AN INVITATION TO THE READER

In researching this book, we discovered many wonderful places—hotels, restaurants, shops, and more. We're sure you'll find others. Please tell us about them, so we can share the information with your fellow travelers in upcoming editions. If you were disappointed with a recommendation, we'd love to know that, too. Please write to:

Karl Samson
*Frommer's Arizona '98*
Macmillan Travel
1633 Broadway
New York, NY 10019

## AN ADDITIONAL NOTE

Please be advised that travel information is subject to change at any time—and this is especially true of prices. We therefore suggest that you write or call ahead for confirmation when making your travel plans. The authors, editors, and publisher cannot be held responsible for the experiences of readers while traveling. Your safety is important to us, however, so we encourage you to stay alert and be aware of your surroundings. Keep a close eye on cameras, purses, and wallets, all favorite targets of thieves and pickpockets.

## WHAT THE SYMBOLS MEAN

✪ **Frommer's Favorites**

Our favorite places and experiences—outstanding for quality, value, or both.

The following abbreviations are used for credit cards:

| | | | |
|------|------------------|------|------------------|
| AE | American Express | EURO | Eurocard |
| CB | Carte Blanche | JCB | Japan Credit Bank |
| DC | Diners Club | MC | MasterCard |
| DISC | Discover | V | Visa |
| ER | enRoute | | |

## FIND FROMMER'S ONLINE

Arthur Frommer's Outspoken Encyclopedia of Travel (www.frommers.com) offers more than 6,000 pages of up-to-the-minute travel information—including the latest bargains and candid, personal articles updated daily by Arthur Frommer himself. No other Web site offers such comprehensive and timely coverage of the world of travel.

# The Best of Arizona

Planning a trip to a state as large and diverse as Arizona involves making lots of decisions (other than which resort to stay at or which golf clubs to take), so in this chapter we've tried to give you some direction. Below we've chosen what we feel is the very best the state has to offer—the places and experiences you won't want to miss. Most are written up in more detail elsewhere in this book; this chapter should give you an overview of Arizona's highlights and get you started planning your trip.

## 1 The Best Places to Experience the Desert

- **Desert Botanical Garden** (Phoenix): There's no better place in the state to learn about the plants of Arizona's Sonoran Desert and the many other deserts of the world. Displays at this Phoenix botanical garden explain plant adaptations and how indigenous tribes once used many of the wild plants of this region. The gardens stay open until after dark so you can see how the desert changes as it cools off. See chapter 5.
- **Arizona–Sonora Desert Museum** (Tucson): The name is misleading—this is actually more of a zoo and botanical garden than a "museum." Naturalistic settings house dozens of species of desert animals, including a number of critters you might hope *not* to meet in the wild (rattlesnakes, tarantulas, scorpions, black widows, and gila monsters). See chapter 10.
- **Saguaro National Park** (near Tucson): Lying both east and west of Tucson, this preserve is a literal forest of saguaro cacti. This is the very essence of the desert as so many people imagine it. You can hike it or you can drive it. See chapter 10.
- **Tucson Botanical Gardens** (Tucson): Though it's small, this garden has extensive cactus gardens and also has displays on what it takes to garden in the desert. One area grows rare crops that are in danger of disappearing from the botanical gene pool. See chapter 10.
- **Organ Pipe Cactus National Monument** (west of Tucson): The organ pipe cactus is a smaller, multitrunked relative of the giant saguaro and lives only along the Mexican border about 100 miles west of Tucson. This remote national monument has hiking trails, scenic drives, even a large natural spring. All that's missing are the crowds you may encounter at Saguaro National Park. See chapter 10.

# Arizona

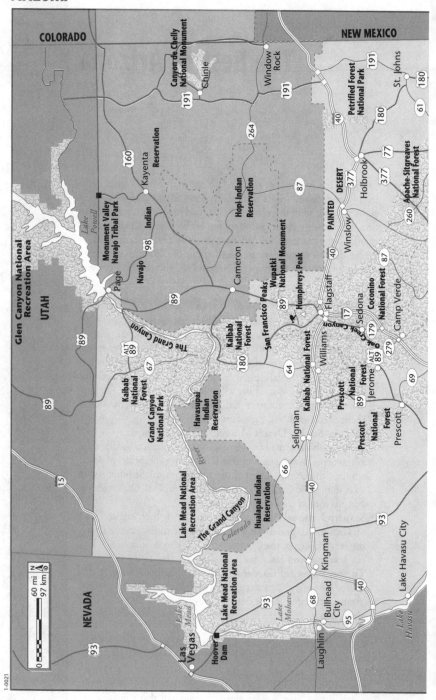

1-0021

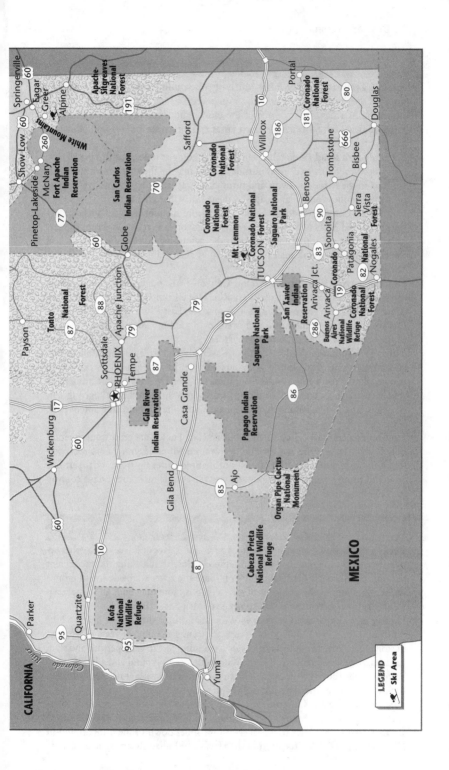

## 2 The Best Scenic Drives

- **Apache Trail** (east of Phoenix): Much of this winding road, which passes just north of the Superstition Mountains, is unpaved and follows a rugged route once ridden by Apaches. This is some of the most remote country you'll find in the Phoenix area, with far-reaching desert vistas and lots to see and do along the way. See chapter 5.
- **Schnebly Hill Road** (Sedona): It can be rough going at times, but this gravel road rising up through the red rocks outside Sedona may be the single most spectacular drive in the state. The twists and turns yield ever-changing perspectives on one of the most otherworldly landscapes in the country. See chapter 6.
- **Oak Creek Canyon** (Sedona): Slicing down from the pine country outside Flagstaff to the red rocks of Sedona, Oak Creek Canyon is a cool oasis. From the scenic overlook at the top of the canyon to the swimming holes and hiking trails at the bottom, this canyon road provides a rapid change in climate and landscape. See chapter 6.
- **Grand Canyon Rim Drives** (Grand Canyon): Although during the summer months you can't actually drive West Rim Drive from Grand Canyon Village, other times of year you can. Also at this time the East Rim Drive is still open to cars year-round. Together these two stretches of road provide easy access to some of the best views in the country. See chapter 7.
- **Through Monument Valley** (north of Kayenta): This valley of sandstone buttes and mesas is one of the most photographed spots in America and is familiar to people all over the world from the countless movies, TV shows, and commercials that have been shot here. A 17-mile dirt road winds through the park, giving visitors close-ups of such landmarks as Elephant Butte, the Mittens, and Totem Pole. See chapter 8.
- **Up Mount Lemmon** (Tucson): Sure the views of Tucson are great from the foothills to the north of the city, but the views from Mount Lemmon are even better. With a ski area at its summit, Mount Lemmon rises up from the desert like an island rising from the sea. Along the way the road climbs from cactus country to cool pine forests. See chapter 10.

## 3 The Best Active Vacations

- **Rafting the Grand Canyon:** Whether you go for 3 days or 2 weeks, no other active vacation in the state comes even remotely close to matching the excitement of a raft trip through the Grand Canyon. Sure the river is crowded with groups in the summer, but the grandeur of the canyon is more than enough to make up for seeing other adventurous souls during your trip. See chapter 7.
- **Hiking into the Grand Canyon:** Not for the unfit or the faint of heart, a hike down into the Grand Canyon is a journey through millions of years of time set in stone. This trip takes plenty of advance planning just to get a permit, and then requires some very strenuous hiking. With both a campground and a lodge at the bottom of the canyon, you can choose to make this trip with either a fully loaded backpack or just a light daypack. See chapter 7.
- **Hiking into Havasu Canyon:** Turquoise waters at the foot of cascading waterfalls, strange terraces formed by limestone deposits, and a cottonwood-shaded stream—that's what lures backpackers the 11 miles down to the campground in Havasu Canyon. This is the heart of the Havasupai Indian Reservation, and, aside

from the narrow ribbon of greenery along the canyon floor, is a landscape of sandstone and cacti. See chapter 7.

- **Hiking into Betatakin or Keet Seel:** Sure, you can drive right up to many of the Indian ruins in Arizona, but there's something much more rewarding about coming upon cliff dwellings after a long hike. These two ruins in Navajo National Monument in northern Arizona can be reached only on foot or on horseback: Betatakin is a day hike and Keet Seel an overnight trip. See chapter 8.

- **Riding the Range at a Guest Ranch:** Yes, Virginia, there are still cowboys. They ride ranges all over the state, and so can you if you book a stay at one of the many guest ranches (these used to be called dude ranches in the old days). You might even get to do the city slicker thing and move some cattle. After a long or short day in the saddle, you can usually soak in a hot tub, go for a swim, or play a game of tennis, before chowing down.

- **Staying at a Golf or Tennis Resort:** If horseback riding and cowboy cookouts aren't your thing, how about golf or tennis to your heart's content? The Phoenix/Scottsdale area has the greatest concentration of resorts in the country, and Tucson and Sedona add even more options to the mix. There's something very satisfying about swinging a racquet or club with the state's spectacular scenery in the background, and the climate means you can do it practically year-round.

- **Bird Watching in Southeastern Arizona:** Now, as an avid bird-watcher I know that this isn't the most active of sports, but a birder can get in a bit of walking when it's necessary (like, maybe to get to the nesting tree of an elegant trogon). The southeast corner of the state is one of the best birding regions in the whole country. See chapter 11.

## 4  The Best Golf Courses

- **The Boulders South Course** (Carefree, near Phoenix; ☎ 800/553-1717 or 602/488-9009): If you've ever seen a photo of someone teeing off beside a massive balancing rock and longed to play that same hole, then you've dreamed about playing The Boulders South Course. That tee of dreams is number 7 and is the single most photographed tee box in the state. The South Course, a desert-style design by Jay Morrish, plays around and through the jumble of massive boulders for which the resort is named. Now, you may not think rocks on fairways are such a good idea, but here at The Boulders, they're not just a challenge to your swing, but to your powers of concentration as well. See chapter 5.

- **The Wigwam Gold Course** (Litchfield Park, near Phoenix; ☎ 602/935-9414): If you're a traditionalist who eschews those cactus- and rattlesnake-filled desert target courses, you'll want to beg, borrow, or steal a tee time on the Wigwam Resort's Gold Course. This 7,100-yard resort course way out on the west side of the Valley of the Sun has long been an Arizona legend. You might want to work your way up to the Gold Course on the Blue and Red courses (the Wigwam is the only resort in America with three 18-hole courses). See chapter 5.

- **Gold Canyon Golf Club** (at Gold Canyon Ranch, Apache Junction, near Phoenix; ☎ 602/982-9090): Although it's out of the mainstream of Valley of the Sun resorts, the Gold Canyon Ranch offers superb golfing at the foot of the Superstition Mountains, where knocking wood takes on a whole new meaning. The back nine here are the truly memorable holes. They play across the foot of Dinosaur Mountain with the 11th, 12th, and 13th holes rated among the tops in the state. The latter of these plays straight at the Superstitions, and no matter how great your concentration, you'll be distracted when you tee off here. Try for a late-afternoon starting time. See chapter 5.

- **Troon North Golf Club** (Scottsdale; ☎ **602/585-5300**): Designed by Tom Weiskopf and Jay Morrish, this desert-style semiprivate course in north Scottsdale is named for the famous Scottish links that overlook both the Firth of Forth and the Firth of Clyde—but that's where the similarities end. Troon North now has two 18-hole courses, but the original, known as the Monument Course, is still the favorite. See chapter 5.

- **The Tournament Players Club (TPC) of Scottsdale** (at the Scottsdale Princess Resort, Scottsdale; ☎ **602/585-3600**): If you've always dreamed of playing where the pros play, then you may want to schedule a visit to the Scottsdale Princess and book a tee time on the Stadium Course, which is the site of the PGA Tour's Phoenix Open. Alternatively, you could play the resort's Desert Course. See chapter 5.

- **Sedona Golf Resort** (Sedona; ☎ **520/284-9355**): It's easy to think that all of Arizona's best courses are in the Phoenix and Tucson areas, but it just isn't so. Up in the red-rock country, at the mouth of Oak Creek Canyon, lies the fairly new Sedona Golf Resort, a traditional course that is among the best in the state. If you can keep your eye on the ball when facing all that gorgeous scenery, you're a better golfer than I am. Unfortunately, the course is rapidly being surrounded by luxury homes that are spoiling the views. See chapter 6.

- **The Lodge at Ventana Canyon** (Tucson; ☎ **520/577-4015**): Two Tom Fazio–designed courses, one a canyon course and the other a mountain course, are shared by two of the city's finest resorts. Both courses are desert-style and play through some of the most stunning scenery anywhere in the state. If I had to choose between the two, I'd go for the Canyon Course; even on an off day, I could enjoy the surroundings. See chapter 10.

- **Starr Pass Golf Club** (Tucson; ☎ **520/670-0300**): Where once stagecoaches rumbled through the desert, golfers now swing their clubs on a course designed by Robert Cupp and Craig Stadler. Built along an old stagecoach route just west of downtown, the Starr Pass course seduces players with its deceptively difficult 15th hole, which plays right through a narrow pass. This course has been the site of the PGA qualifying rounds for the past few years. See chapter 10.

- **Omni Tucson National Golf Resort and Spa** (Tucson; ☎ **520/297-2271**): With its wide expanses of grass, this course, often used as the site of the PGA Tour's Tucson Tournament (now known as the Tucson Chrysler Classic), is a traditional course that is both challenging and forgiving. The 18th hole of the Orange and Gold courses is considered one of the toughest finishing holes on the tour. See chapter 10.

- **Emerald Canyon Golf Course** (Parker; ☎ **520/667-3366**): While this municipal course way out on the bank of the Colorado River may not be the best course in the state, it certainly plays through some of the most astounding scenery. Canyons, cliffs, and ravines are the hazards you'll be avoiding on this very interesting course. See chapter 12.

## 5  The Best Day Hikes & Nature Walks

- **Camelback Mountain** (Phoenix): For many Phoenicians the trail up to the top of Camelback Mountain is a ritual, a Phoenix institution. Sure there are those who make this a casual but strenuous hike, but many more turn it into a serious workout by jogging to the top and back. We prefer a more leisurely approach, the better to enjoy the views. See chapter 5.

- **Picacho Peak State Park** (south of Casa Grande): The hike up this central Arizona landmark is short but strenuous, and from the top there are superb views out over the desert. The best time of year to make the hike is in spring when the peak comes alive with wildflowers. Picacho Peak is between Casa Grande and Tucson just off I-10. See chapter 5.
- **The Boynton Canyon Trail** (outside Sedona): Any walk among the red rocks around Sedona is rewarding, but the 6-mile round-trip hike into Boynton Canyon provides views as well as a chance to see ancient Sinagua ruins. See chapter 6.
- **Bright Angel Trail** (Grand Canyon South Rim): It's a human highway near the top, but this, the most popular trail into the Grand Canyon, offers everyone the chance to say that they've hiked the Grand Canyon. Despite its popularity, Bright Angel Trail is a strenuous hike even if you only go a mile or so down the trail. Remember, the trip back is all uphill. See chapter 7.
- **Hikes and Rambles in Petrified Forest National Park** (outside Holbrook): Few visitors to the Petrified Forest National Park venture far from their cars, which is understandable when you consider how much petrified wood there is to see near the road. More adventurous visitors, however, should venture farther afield (with plenty of water, of course). Back-country camping is also permitted here. See chapter 8.
- **The White House Ruins Trail** (Canyon de Chelly): There's only one Canyon de Chelly hike that the general public can do without a Navajo guide, and that's the $2^1/_2$-mile trail to White House Ruins. The trail leads from the canyon rim across bare sandstone, through a tunnel, and down to the floor of the canyon. Though it seems as though you've left the modern world behind, when you finally reach the ruins, you'll likely find quite a few four-wheel-drive vehicles parked near the ancient Anasazi cliff dwelling. See chapter 8.

## 6  The Best Swimming Holes

- **The Salt River** (east of Phoenix): When Phoenicians want to cool off on a scorching summer day, they head for the Salt River with inner tubes in tow. There are few better ways to beat the heat than lazing away the day floating downstream. See chapter 5.
- **Slide Rock State Park** (Sedona): Water is at a premium in the desert, and when it's available people take full advantage of it. Set on the banks of Oak Creek near Sedona, this park really does have a natural water slide, as well as a great little swimming hole. See chapter 6.
- **Havasu Canyon** (north of Peach Springs): Though it's an 11-mile hike to the turquoise waters and waterfalls of this swimming hole, thousands of people annually make the trek and camp out at the nearby campground. The contrast of turquoise waters and sandstone cliffs makes this one of the most striking settings in Arizona. See chapter 7.
- **Lake Powell** (near Page): This is Arizona's biggest "swimming hole," so big that it stretches all the way into Utah. Hundreds of miles of sandstone canyons are there to be explored by boat, with a quick dip right off the bow. See chapter 7.
- **Sabino Canyon** (Tucson): When the summer heats up, this is where Tucson cools off. With a cool stream running its length and forming pools and beaches, Sabino Canyon is an idyllic oasis (or at least it would be without the crowds). See chapter 10.

# 7  The Best Swimming Pools

- **Arizona Biltmore** (Phoenix; ☎ **800/950-0086** or 602/955-6600): The main pool here, which was added a few years back, mixes old and new with its private cabanas (available for a fee) and its Frank Lloyd Wright–inspired water-slide tower. See chapter 5.
- **The Buttes** (Tempe; ☎ **800/843-1986** or 602/225-9000): A lush stream cascading over desert rocks seems to feed this free-form pool; it's a desert oasis fantasy world unmatched in the state. A narrow canal connects the two halves of the pool, and tucked in among the rocks are several whirlpools. See chapter 5.
- **Hyatt Regency Resort at Gainey Ranch** (Scottsdale; ☎ **800/233-1234** or 602/991-3388): This Scottsdale resort boasts a 10-pool, 2¹/₂-acre water playground complete with sand beach, waterfalls, sports pool, lap pool, adult pool, three-story water slide, massive whirlpool, and lots of waterfalls. See chapter 5.
- **The Phoenician** (Scottsdale; ☎ **800/888-8234** or 602/941-8200): This system of seven pools is as impressive as the Hyatt's but has a much more sophisticated air about it. Waterfalls, a water slide, play pools, a lap pool, and, the crown jewel, a mother-of-pearl pool (actually opalescent tile) all add up to plenty of aquatic fun. See chapter 5.
- **The Pointe Hilton at Squaw Peak** (Phoenix; ☎ **800/876-4683** or 602/997-2626): They don't just have a pool here, they have a River Ranch, with an artificial tubing river, water slide, and a waterfall pouring into the large, free-form main pool. See chapter 5.
- **The Pointe Hilton Resort at Tapatio Cliffs** (Phoenix; ☎ **800/876-4683** or 602/866-7500): The Falls, a slightly more adult-oriented pool complex than that at sister property The Pointe Hilton Resort at Squaw Peak, includes two lagoon pools, a 40-foot waterfall, a 130-foot water slide, and rental cabanas. See chapter 5.
- **Enchantment Resort** (Sedona; ☎ **800/826-4180** or 520/282-2900): The pool itself here is nothing special, but the view you get while splashing around or swimming laps is nothing short of phenomenal. No where else in the state can you go for a swim with such views of red-rock canyon walls. See chapter 6.
- **Arizona Inn** (Tucson; ☎ **800/933-1093** or 520/325-1541): The pool here isn't large, but the private little courtyard that surrounds it is planted with jasmines, gardenias, and fragrant, flowering orange trees. The garden setting gives the pool a homey, old-Arizona feel. See chapter 10.

# 8  The Best Bird Watching

- **Madera Canyon:** The mountain canyons of southern Arizona tend to attract a variety of bird life, from species common in the lowland deserts to those that prefer thick forest settings. Madera is a good place to experience this variety. See chapter 10.
- **Patagonia:** With a year-round stream and a Nature Conservancy preserve on the edge of town, Patagonia is one of the best spots in the state for sighting various flycatcher species. See chapter 11.
- **San Pedro Riparian National Conservation Area:** With water such a scarce commodity in the desert, it tends to attract a lot of animal life, including more than 300 bird species. This is a life-list bonanza spot. See chapter 11.
- **Ramsey Canyon:** Nearly 200 species of birds—including 14 species of hummingbirds—frequent this canyon, making it one of the top birding hot spots in the country. See chapter 11.

- **Cave Creek Canyon:** Though there are other rare birds to be seen in this remote canyon, most people come in hopes of spotting the rare elegant trogon, which reaches the northernmost limit of its range here. See chapter 11.
- **Willcox Ponds:** Wading birds in the middle of the desert? You'll find them at the Willcox sewage-treatment ponds south of town. Avocets, sandhill cranes, and a variety of waterfowl all frequent these shallow bodies of water. See chapter 11.
- **Buenos Aires National Wildlife Refuge:** Gray hawks and masked bobwhite quails are among the refuge's rarer birds, but a wetland (cienaga), lake, and stream attract plenty of other birds. See chapter 11.

# 9  The Best Offbeat Travel Experiences

- **Taking a Vortex Tour in Sedona:** Crystals and pyramids are nothing compared to the power of the Sedona vortexes, which just happen to be in the middle of some very beautiful scenery. Organized tours shuttle believers from one vortex to the next. See chapter 6.
- **Touring Walpi Village:** Of the Hopi villages that stand atop the mesas of northeastern Arizona, only Walpi, one of the oldest, offers guided tours. The young Hopi guides share information on the history of the village and the Hopi culture. See chapter 8.
- **Sleeping in a Wigwam:** Back in the heyday of Route 66, the Wigwam Motel in Holbrook lured passing motorists with its unusual architecture—concrete wigwam-shaped cabins. Today this little motel is still a great place for anyone who appreciates retro style. See chapter 8.
- **Shake and Bake Tours into Canyon de Chelly:** There are only a few ways the public can visit this scenic canyon on the Navajo Reservation, and truck tours, known as "shake and bake" tours by the locals, are by far the least strenuous. See chapter 8.
- **Digging for Artifacts at Ravensite Ruin:** Looking at Anasazi ruins is all well and good, but how would you like to get your hands dirty digging for ancient artifacts? At the White Mountain Archaeological Center near St. Johns, you can—for a fee—participate in an ongoing archaeological dig. See chapter 8.
- **Gazing at the Stars:** Insomniacs and stargazers will find plenty to keep them sleepless in the desert as they peer at the stars through telescopes at Lowell Observatory in Flagstaff or Kitt Peak National Observatory near Tucson. In the town of Benson, you can even stay at a B&B that doubles as an astronomical observatory. See chapters 7 and 10.
- **A Visit to Biosphere 2:** This giant terrarium, in which humans are the residents, is a research center for understanding how the earth's ecosystems operate. The giant greenhouses in the middle of the desert are straight out of post-apocalyptic sci-fi. See chapter 10.
- **Touring the Queen Mine in Bisbee:** You can descend deep into the earth outside Bisbee and see how copper was once mined in the Copper State. Beginning in the late 1800s, copper mines turned Bisbee into the wildest boom town this side of New Orleans. This is also where Bisbee blue turquoise was once mined. See chapter 11.
- **Walking Across the London Bridge:** The famous bridge *was* falling down until a far-sighted (perhaps slightly daft) developer transported it to the middle of the Arizona desert. You'll find the bridge in Lake Havasu City and, if it's not too blazingly hot, you can stroll across it and admire all the surrounding pseudo-Tudor architecture. See chapter 12.

- **Visiting a Quartzsite Gem and Mineral Show:** Every winter, the community of Quartzsite becomes a sea of RVs as tens of thousands of rock hounds flock to the area for the many gem and mineral shows. These shows include hundreds of vendors selling everything from uncut geodes to beautiful jewelry. See chapter 12.

## 10  The Best Family Experiences

- **Tubing down the Salt River** (near Phoenix): If an aquatic amusement park is just too contrived for you and your family, how about a relaxing float down the Salt River? There are tube-rental companies and shuttle buses to make this an easy and fun outing. See chapter 5.
- **Pioneer Arizona Living History Museum** (north of Phoenix): This museum features old buildings and costumed interpreters who show and tell what life was like for Arizona pioneers 100 years ago. See chapter 5.
- **Wild West Restaurants:** No family should visit Arizona without spending an evening at a "genuine" cowboy steakhouse. With gunslingers and gimmicks (one will cut off your necktie, another has a slide from the bar to the dining room), cowboy bands, and false-fronted buildings, these Arizona eateries are all entertainment and loads of fun. See chapters 5 and 10.
- **Riding the Grand Canyon Railway:** Not only is this train excursion a fun way to get to the Grand Canyon, but it also lets you avoid the parking problems and congestion that can prove so wearisome. Shoot-outs and train robberies are to be expected in this corner of the Wild West. See chapter 7.
- **A Week on a Houseboat:** Renting a floating vacation home on lakes Powell, Mead, Mohave, or Havasu is a summer tradition for many Arizona families. With a houseboat, you aren't tied to one spot and can cruise from one scenic beach to the next. See chapters 7 and 12.
- **Arizona–Sonora Desert Museum** (Tucson): This is actually a zoo featuring the animals of the Sonoran Desert. There are rooms full of snakes, a prairie dog town, mountain goats, mountain lions, an aviary full of hummingbirds, even the best zoo restaurant we've ever eaten at. Kids and adults love this place. See chapter 10.
- **Shoot-outs at the O.K. Corral:** Tombstone may be "the town too tough to die," but poor Ike Clanton and his buddies the McLaury boys have to die over and over again at the frequent reenactments of the famous gunfight. See chapter 11.

## 11  The Top Architectural Landmarks

- **Arizona Biltmore** (Phoenix): Though Frank Lloyd Wright was not the official architect of this historic hotel, his influence and work can be seen throughout—in the distinctive concrete-block walls, in the stained glass in the lobby, and in the sculptures by the front door. See chapter 5.
- **Taliesin West** (Scottsdale): This was Frank Lloyd Wright's winter home and desert architecture school. The buildings are classic examples of Wright's work and tours are offered. See chapter 5.
- **Chapel of the Holy Cross** (Sedona): Built upon the rocks outside Sedona, this nondenominational chapel is an intriguing work of devotion that melds with its surroundings. See chapter 6.
- **Arcosanti** (Cordes Junction): This funky, futuristic city in the middle of the desert is the brainchild of a former student from Frank Lloyd Wright's Taliesin West. Organically shaped poured-concrete structures sprout from the desert like so many giant fungi. See chapter 6.

- **Mission San Xavier del Bac** (Tucson): Known as the "White Dove of the Desert," this 18th-century Spanish church is a primitive yet amazingly detailed building and is considered the finest mission church in the United States. See chapter 10.

## 12  The Best Art Communities

- **Scottsdale:** Only New York and Santa Fe have more art galleries than Scottsdale, which has become one of the nation's centers for Western and Native American art. Bronzes and large paintings are most popular here. With street after street lined with almost nothing but art galleries, the art aficionado will need plenty of time for a visit to Scottsdale. See chapter 5.
- **Jerome:** Perched high on the slopes of Cleopatra Hill on Mingus Mountain, Jerome is a former mining town that has become one of Arizona's most popular artists' communities. The streets are lined with interesting galleries, and the views are some of the best in the state. See chapter 6.
- **Sedona:** This was Arizona's original artists' community and today is second only to Scottsdale in number of galleries. Artists came, and still come, for the breathtaking scenery that has found its way onto countless canvases. See chapter 6.
- **Tubac:** This is the oldest town in Arizona and dates from 1691 when the Spanish founded this northern outpost of New Spain. Today the many old adobe homes in Tubac have been turned into art galleries, studios, and shops selling Southwestern crafts. See chapter 11.
- **Bisbee:** Once the largest town between New Orleans and San Francisco, Bisbee made its fortune on copper. When the copper ran out, the town was almost left to the ghosts. Today, Bisbee is once again making a name for itself, but this time as southern Arizona's liveliest arts community. Galleries and shops line the narrow, winding streets. See chapter 11.

## 13  The Best Museums

- **Heard Museum** (Phoenix): This is one of the nation's premier museums devoted to Native American cultures. In addition to historical exhibits, a huge kachina collection, and an excellent museum store, there are annual exhibits of contemporary Native American art as well as dance performances and demonstrations of traditional skills. See chapter 5.
- **Phoenix Art Museum** (Phoenix): A major expansion and renovation completed in late 1996 added acres of wall space to this already large art museum. There is an outstanding collection of contemporary art as well as a fascinating exhibit of miniature rooms. See chapter 5.
- **Museum of Northern Arizona** (Flagstaff): The geology, ethnography, and archaeology of this region are all explored in fascinating detail at this Flagstaff museum, and throughout the year there are excellent special exhibits and festivals focusing on the region's different tribes. See chapter 7.
- **University of Arizona Museum of Art** (Tucson): This collection ranges from the Renaissance to the present, with a set of 15th-century Spanish religious panels the focus of the collection. Georgia O'Keeffe and Pablo Picasso are among the artists whose works are on display here. See chapter 10.
- **Amerind Foundation Museum** (west of Willcox): Though located in the remote southeast corner of the state near Willcox, this museum and research center houses a superb collection of Indian artifacts. Displays focus on tribes of the Southwest, but other tribes are also represented. See chapter 11.

## 14 The Best Places to Discover the Old West

- **Rodeos:** Any rodeo, and this state has plenty, will give you a glimpse of the Old West, but Arizona has two that claim title to being the oldest in the country. Whether you head for the rodeo in Prescott or the one in Payson, you'll see plenty of bronco-busting, bull riding, and beer drinking. See chapters 6 and 8.
- **Monument Valley** (north of Kayenta): John Ford made it the hallmark of his Western movies, and today the starkly beautiful and unbelievably shaped buttes and mesas of this valley are the quintessential Western landscape. You'll recognize it the moment you see it. See chapter 8.
- **Old Tucson Studios** (Tucson): Though many of the original movie sets burned in a 1995 fire, this combination back lot and amusement park provides visitors with a glimpse of the most familiar Old West—the Hollywood West. Sure the shoot-outs and cancan reviews are silly, but it's all in good fun, and everyone gets a thrill out of seeing the occasional film crew in action. See chapter 10.
- **Tombstone:** This is the *real* Old West—Tombstone is a real town, unlike Old Tucson. However, "the town too tough to die" long ago was reincarnated as a major tourist attraction with gunslingers in the streets, stagecoach rides, and shoot-outs at the O.K. Corral. See chapter 11.
- **Guest Ranches:** The Old West lives on at guest ranches all over the state, where rugged wranglers lead city slickers on horseback rides through desert scrub and mountain meadows. Campfires, cookouts, and cattle are all part of the experience.

## 15 The Best Native American Ruins to Visit

- **Tonto National Monument** (east of Phoenix): Located east of Phoenix on the Apache Trail, this is one of the only easily accessible cliff dwellings in Arizona that you can still visit; you don't have to just observe from a distance. See chapter 5.
- **Besh Ba Gowah Archaeological Park** (Globe): These reconstructed ruins have been set up to look the way they might have appeared 700 years ago, providing a bit more cultural context than other ruins in the state. See chapter 5.
- **Casa Grande Ruins National Monument** (west of Florence): Unlike most of the other ruins in the state, this large and unusual structure is built of packed desert soil. Inscrutable and perplexing, Casa Grande seems to rise from nowhere. See chapter 5.
- **Montezuma Castle, Camp Verde:** Located just off I-17, this is the most easily accessible cliff dwelling in Arizona, though it cannot be entered. Nearby Montezuma's Well also has some small ruins. See chapter 6.
- **Wupatki** (north of Flagstaff): Not nearly as well known as the region's Anasazi cliff dwellings, these ruins are set on a wide plain. A ball court similar to those found in Central America hints at cultural ties with the Aztecs. See chapter 7.
- **Canyon de Chelly:** Small cliff dwellings up and down the length of Canyon de Chelly can be seen from overlooks. A trip into the canyon itself offers a chance to see some of these ruins close up. See chapter 8.
- **Keet Seel/Betatakin** (west of Kayenta): Although both of these ruins, located in Navajo National Monument, are at the end of long hikes, their size and state of preservation make them among the finest examples of Anasazi cliff dwellings. See chapter 8.

## 16 The Best Guest Ranches

- **Merv Griffin's Wickenburg Inn** (Wickenburg; ☎ 800/942-5362 or 520/684-7811): So maybe you like to ride horses, but your spouse prefers tennis, your daughter lives for ponies, and your son wants to see rattlesnakes. No problem. The Wickenburg Inn, a combination guest ranch and tennis resort that doubles as a nature preserve, should keep the whole family happy. See chapter 6.
- **Aspen Meadow Ranch** (Eagar; ☎ 520/521-0880 or 520/333-2717): Not every dude ranch in Arizona is studded with cactus and too hot for ridin' in the summer. This one, with its log cabins, is set high in the White Mountains of eastern Arizona and is the ideal choice for a summertime guest-ranch vacation. See chapter 9.
- **Tanque Verde Inn** (Tucson; ☎ 800/234-DUDE or 520/296-6275): Though other guest ranches might be more luxurious, no other choice offers such a superb setting, authentic ranch feel, creature comforts, and excellent food. See chapter 10.
- **Rancho de la Osa** (Sasabe; ☎ 800/872-6240 or 520/823-4257): Set on a historic 200-year-old ranch in a remote stretch of grasslands near the Mexican border, this guest ranch still has a feel of the Old West in its adobe buildings and remote location. See chapter 11.
- **Circle Z Ranch** (Patagonia; ☎ 888/854-2525 or 520/394-2525): In business since 1925 and the oldest working cattle ranch in the state, the Circle Z is set on the banks of Sonoita Creek and surrounded by national forest and a Nature Conservancy preserve. This all adds up to lots of places to ride. See chapter 11.
- **Grapevine Canyon Ranch** (Pearce; ☎ 800/245-9202 or 520/826-3185): If you already know a heifer from a steer and can keep a horse under control even when it smells the barn, then maybe you're ready to help with the spring cattle roundup at this ranch in southeastern Arizona. See chapter 11.

## 17 The Best Luxury Hotels & Resorts

- **Arizona Biltmore Resort & Spa** (Phoenix; ☎ 800/950-0086 or 602/955-6600): Combining discreet service and the architectural styling of Frank Lloyd Wright, the Arizona Biltmore has long been one of the most popular resorts in the state. Recent renovations have done much to improve the quality of the rooms, and a new pool is a big hit with families. See chapter 5.
- **The Boulders** (Carefree; ☎ 800/553-1717 or 602/488-9009): Taking its name from the massive blocks of eroded granite that are scattered about the grounds of this resort, the Boulders is among the most exclusive and expensive resorts in the state. Pueblo architecture fits seamlessly with the landscape, and the golf course is the most breathtaking in Arizona. See chapter 5.
- **Hyatt Regency Scottsdale Resort at Gainey Ranch** (Scottsdale; ☎ 800/233-1234 or 602/991-3388): Contemporary desert architecture, dramatic landscaping, a water playground with its own beach, a staff that's always at the ready to assist you, several good restaurants that aren't overpriced, and even gondola rides—it all adds up to a lot of fun at one of the most smoothly run resorts in Arizona. See chapter 5.
- **Marriott's Camelback Inn** (Scottsdale; ☎ 800/24-CAMEL or 602/948-1700): This is one of the few Scottsdale resorts that retains an old Arizona atmosphere

without sacrificing comfort or modern conveniences. A full-service spa caters to those who crave pampering, while two golf courses provide plenty of challenging fairways and greens. See chapter 5.

- **The Phoenician** (Scottsdale; ☎ **800/888-8234** or 602/941-8200): This Xanadu of the resort world is brimming with marble, crystal, and works of art. With staff seemingly around every corner, the hotel offers its guests impeccable service. Two of the resort's dining rooms are among the finest restaurants in the city, and the views are hard to beat. See chapter 5.

- **Scottsdale Princess** (Scottsdale; ☎ **800/344-4758** or 602/585-4848): The Moorish styling and numerous fountains and waterfalls of this Scottsdale resort create a setting made for romance. Two superb restaurants—one serving Spanish cuisine and one serving gourmet Mexican fare—top it off. See chapter 5.

- **Enchantment Resort** (Sedona; ☎ **800/826-4180** or 520/282-2900): A dramatic setting in a red-rock canyon outside Sedona makes this the most stunningly situated resort in the state. Guest rooms are for the most part quite large and are constructed in a pueblo architectural style. If you want to feel as if you're vacationing in the desert, this place fills the bill. See chapter 6.

- **Arizona Inn** (Tucson; ☎ **800/933-1093** or 520/325-1541): This Tucson resort dates from Arizona's earliest days as a vacation destination and prides itself on its personal service. The gardens are a fragrant and colorful oasis. This is a low-key operation and the only historic resort in the state. See chapter 10.

- **Loews Ventana Canyon Resort** (Tucson; ☎ **800/234-5117** or 520/299-2020): With the Santa Catalina Mountains rising up in the backyard of this resort and an almost-natural waterfall only steps away from the lobby, this is Tucson's most dramatic resort. Contemporary styling throughout makes constant reference to the desert setting. See chapter 10.

- **Sheraton El Conquistador Resort & Country Club** (Tucson; ☎ **800/325-7832** or 520/544-5000): The craggy ramparts of Pusch Ridge rising to the east and some of the best sunsets in the state are two of the outstanding features of this resort. Add to that three golf courses, several good restaurants, riding stables, and plenty of other exercise facilities, and you have the makings of a thoroughly enjoyable resort stay. See chapter 10.

## 18 The Best Moderately Priced Hotels

- **San Carlos Hotel** (Phoenix; ☎ **800/528-5446** or 602/253-4121): Arizona doesn't have many historic hotels, and downtown Phoenix doesn't have many hotels period. So this restored Phoenix hotel is a welcome choice for anyone looking for character, economical rates, and a downtown location. See chapter 5.

- **Hotel Vendome** (Prescott; ☎ **800/252-7466** or 520/776-0900): Some of the rooms in this renovated 1917 boarding house still have claw-foot tubs, but otherwise they're fairly modern. This small historic hotel is only a couple of blocks off Courthouse Plaza. See chapter 6.

- **Sky Ranch Lodge** (Sedona; ☎ **520/282-6400**): Accommodations in Sedona tend to be pricey, but at this motel you get your money's worth in the form of spectacular mesa-top views of the red rocks and the city far below. See chapter 6.

- **Bright Angel Lodge** (Grand Canyon Village; ☎ **303/297-2757**): Located right on the rim of the Grand Canyon, this hotel offers a wide variety of room types and a wide range of rates. If you can get a reservation here, you'll get to experience the best hotel deal in the national park. See chapter 7.

- **Cameron Trading Post** (Cameron; ☎ **800/338-7385** or 520/679-2231): It's tough finding accommodations anywhere near the Grand Canyon during the summer, so if you're turned away at the park and don't mind a bit of a drive, this former trading post makes a good choice. See chapter 7.
- **Goulding's Lodge** (Monument Valley; ☎ **801/727-3231**): Anyone planning on staying the night near Monument Valley should try to get a reservation here first. From your balcony, you'll be able to see the buttes and mesas of the valley. See chapter 8.
- **Best Western Ghost Ranch Lodge** (Tucson; ☎ **800/456-7565** or 520/791-7565): This older motel isn't in a very attractive neighborhood, but a sign designed by Georgia O'Keeffe, a superb cactus garden, and a guest-ranch feel make this a good economical choice in Tucson. See chapter 10.
- **The Lodge on the Desert** (Tucson; ☎ **800/456-5634** or 520/325-3366): Sort of a poor-man's version of the Arizona Inn, this classic old desert lodge has adobe buildings, old gardens, and a sense of being removed from the modern Tucson that now surrounds it. See chapter 10.
- **Hacienda del Sol Guest Ranch Resort** (Tucson; ☎ **800/728-6514** or 520/299-1501): Set in the foothills near the prestigious Westin La Paloma, this moderately priced lodge is under new management but has a long history. At times it has been a guest ranch and a private school, and today it captures the feeling of old Arizona. See chapter 10.
- **High Desert Inn** (Bisbee; ☎ **800/281-0510** or 520/432-1442): This small hotel is Bisbee's most luxurious lodging and is housed in the former Cochise County Jail (ca. 1901). On the first floor is an excellent little restaurant. See chapter 11.

## 19  The Best Historic Inns & Hotels

- **Hassayampa Inn** (Prescott; ☎ **800/322-1927** or 520/778-9434): Built as a luxury hotel in 1927, the Hassayampa is Prescott's premier historic inn and sits only a block off Courthouse Plaza. Many of the rooms, which vary considerably in size, have original furnishings, and one is said to be haunted. See chapter 6.
- **El Tovar** (Grand Canyon Village; ☎ **303/297-2757**): This classic mountain lodge stands in Grand Canyon Village only feet from the south rim of the Grand Canyon. Although the rooms sport incongruous American colonial furniture, the lodge immerses guests in local atmosphere. See chapter 7.
- **Grand Canyon Lodge** (Grand Canyon North Rim; ☎ **303/297-2757**): This, the Grand Canyon's other grand lodge, sits right on the north rim of the canyon. Rooms are primarily in cabins, which aren't quite as impressive as the main lodge building, but guests tend to spend a lot of time sitting on the lodge's two viewing terraces or in the sunroom. See chapter 7.
- **Arizona Inn** (Tucson; ☎ **800/933-1093** or 520/325-1541): This small resort near downtown Tucson dates from 1930 and is built in the Southwest pueblo style with lush, fragrant gardens. Many rooms have original furniture that was built by disabled World War I veterans. See chapter 10.
- **Gadsden Hotel** (Douglas; ☎ **520/364-4481**): Though it isn't the most comfortable of the state's historic hotels, the Gadsden in Douglas still wears an early 19th-century air. The Grand Lobby is unique in the state and features a large Tiffany stained-glass window. See chapter 11.

## 20  The Best B&Bs

- **Inn at the Citadel** (Scottsdale; ☎ **800/927-8367** or 602/585-6133): Located north of downtown Scottsdale, this modern inn features rooms full of European antiques (most of which are for sale) and is equipped with large, luxurious bathrooms. Designer touches place this inn solidly ahead of the vast majority of B&Bs. See chapter 5.
- **La Estancia** (Phoenix; ☎ **602/808-9924**): While most people vacationing in the Phoenix area seem to want the whole resort experience, if you happen to prefer B&Bs, this one is your best bet. Rooms are luxurious and the 2-acre grounds include citrus groves and a pool. See chapter 5.
- **Rocamadour** (Prescott; ☎ **520/771-1933**): Set amid the rounded boulders of the Granite Dells just north of Prescott, this inn combines a spectacular setting with French antiques and very luxurious accommodations. You won't find a more memorable setting anywhere in the state. See chapter 6.
- **Briar Patch Inn** (Sedona; ☎ **520/282-2342**): Oak Creek Canyon, near Sedona, where this collection of cottages is located, is an oasis in the desert. Few experiences are more restorative than breakfast on the shady banks of the creek. See chapter 6.
- **The Inn on Oak Creek** (Sedona; ☎ **800/499-7896** or 520/282-7896): Built right out over Sedona's Oak Creek with shade trees all around and the Tlaquepaque shopping plaza only a block away, this inn offers a wide array of luxurious and interestingly decorated rooms, most of which have creek or red-rock views. See chapter 6.
- **Saddle Rock Ranch** (Sedona; ☎ **520/282-7640**): With some of the best views in Sedona, this stone-and-adobe home dates from 1926 and has its own little swimming pool. Of the three available rooms, the little cottage, with its peeled-log bed and flagstone floors, has the most Western character. See chapter 6.
- **El Presidio Bed & Breakfast Inn** (Tucson; ☎ **800/349-6151** or 520/623-6151): Located in the El Presidio historic district in downtown Tucson, this is one of the only 19th-century adobe homes in the state that operates as a B&B. Victorian architectural details have, however, hidden the adobe styling quite effectively. See chapter 10.
- **Casa Tierra** (Tucson; ☎ **520/578-3058**): This modern adobe home is located near Saguaro National Park west of downtown Tucson and is an ideal choice for anyone who really wants to feel as if they're staying in the desert. See chapter 10.
- **Red Setter Bed & Breakfast Inn** (Greer; ☎ **520/735-7441**): This large, new log home in the quaint mountain village of Greer is one of Arizona's most enjoyable and romantic B&Bs. It's set on the bank of the Little Colorado River in the shade of large ponderosa pine trees. The inn is also a great place for ski vacations. See chapter 9.
- **Paisley Corner Bed & Breakfast** (Eagar; ☎ **520/333-4665**): Although this inn is not nearly as luxurious as others on this list, it is noteworthy for its authenticity of interior design. Victorian antiques fill the house, and even the kitchen is completely vintage. There's even a vintage soda fountain in one of the parlors. See chapter 9.

# 21  The Best Restaurants

- **Vincent Guerithault on Camelback** (Phoenix; ☎ 602/224-0225): The bold flavors of the Southwest are the focus of this ever-popular Phoenix restaurant where presentation is every bit as important as taste. Even if you aren't a fan of chiles, you'll find plenty of unusual flavor combinations to tempt your palate. See chapter 5.
- **Christopher's** (Phoenix; ☎ 602/957-3214): With his skillful renditions of traditional French fare and flavorful new American dishes, Phoenix's chef Christopher Gross has kept his clientele loyal for many years now. See chapter 5.
- **Such Is Life** (Phoenix; ☎ 602/955-7822): This elegant little Mexican restaurant serves the sort of meals you might expect to find in a luxurious Mexico City restaurant. Don't look for any standard Mexican fare covered in melted cheese here— Phoenix's Such Is Life has higher standards. See chapter 5.
- **Marquesa** (Scottsdale; ☎ 602/585-4848): Located amid the Moorish architecture of the Scottsdale Princess resort, this Spanish restaurant specializes in Catalonian dishes. To dine here is to be totally immersed in a Mediterranean experience. See chapter 5.
- **Mary Elaine's** (Scottsdale; ☎ 602/423-2530): Located in Scottsdale's posh Phoenician resort, Mary Elaine's is where the elite dine in the Valley of the Sun. The menu focuses primarily on modern French flavors, though the chef doesn't limit himself. See chapter 5.
- **Heartline Cafe** (Sedona; ☎ 520/282-0785): Combining the zesty flavors of the Southwest with the best of the rest of the world, Sedona's Heartline Cafe frequently comes up with surefire winners guaranteed to please jaded palates. See chapter 6.
- **El Tovar Dining Room** (Grand Canyon Village; ☎ 520/638-2631): It would be hard to match the setting, a historic mountain lodge on the rim of the Grand Canyon, but this restaurant does its best. The menu features a mix of continental and Southwestern flavors, though those dishes showing a regional flavor are the better choices. See chapter 7.
- **Cafe Poca Cosa** (Tucson; ☎ 520/622-6400): It's small, it's hip, and it's very reasonably priced. Located in the Clarion Santa Rita Hotel & Suites, the Cafe Poca Cosa serves some of the most creative and complex Mexican food since *Like Water for Chocolate*. See chapter 10.
- **Janos** (Tucson; ☎ 520/884-9426): Housed in an old adobe building in the El Presidio historic district of Tucson, this popular restaurant serves a combination of regional and Southwestern dishes. See chapter 10.
- **The Tack Room** (Tucson; ☎ 520/722-2800): Superb service, creative Southwestern dishes, and an authentic Arizona atmosphere make Tucson's Tack Room one of the finest restaurants in the West. Though the steaks are the traditional favorite here, other dishes are well worth consideration. See chapter 10.

# 2 Getting to Know Arizona

**D**espite the searing summer temperatures of the deserts that cover much of the state, people have been lured to Arizona for generations. In the 16th century, the Spanish came looking for gold—but settled instead for saving souls. In the 19th century, cattle ranchers came despite frightful tales of spiny cactus forests and found that a few corners of the state were covered with lush grasslands. At the same time, sidetracked forty-niners were scouring the hills for gold (and found more than the Spanish did). However, boom-towns—both cattle and mining—soon went bust. Despite occasional big strikes (such as the silver strike at Tombstone), it would be the early 20th century before mining finally proved itself, but the mother lode was not gold or silver, but rather copper, which Arizona has in such abundance that it's called the Copper State.

In the 1920s and 1930s, Arizona struck a new vein of gold. The railroads made travel to Arizona easy, and the word of the mild winter climate spread to colder corners of the nation. Among the first "vacationers" were people suffering from tuberculosis. These "lungers," as they were known, rested and recuperated in the dry desert air. It didn't take long for the perfectly healthy to realize that they, too, could enjoy winter in Arizona, and wintering in the desert soon became fashionable with wealthy northerners.

Today it's still the golden sun that lures people to Arizona. Scottsdale, Phoenix, Tucson, and Sedona together are home to some of the most luxurious and expensive resorts in the world. The state has also seen a massive influx of retirees, many of whom have found the few pockets of Arizona where the climate is absolutely perfect—not too hot, not too cold, and plenty of sunshine.

But it's the Grand Canyon that attracts most visitors to Arizona. Though not the deepest or the widest canyon on earth, the Grand Canyon is without a doubt the most spectacular. However, it's only one of the natural wonders of Arizona—the largest natural travertine bridge in the world, the largest meteorite crater, the spectacular red-rock country of Sedona, and sandstone buttes of Monument Valley are just a few of the state's other natural spectacles.

The human hand has also left its mark on Arizona. More than 1,000 years ago, the Anasazi, Sinagua, and Hohokam tribes built villages on mesas, in valleys, and in the steep cliff walls of deep canyons. In more recent years, much larger structures have risen in canyons across the state. The Hoover and Glen Canyon dams on the

Colorado River are among the largest dams in the country and have created the nation's largest and most spectacular reservoirs, although at the expense of the rich riparian areas that once filled the now flooded desert canyons. Today these reservoirs are among the states most popular destinations, especially with Arizonans who flock to the water with an amazing variety of high-powered watercraft.

As compelling as its sunshine, resorts, and reservoirs are the tall tales of Arizona's fascinating history. This is the Wild West, the land of cowboys and Indians, of prospectors and ghost towns, coyotes and rattlesnakes. Scratch the glossy surface of modern, urbanized Arizona and you'll strike real gold—the story of the American West.

# 1  The Natural Environment

Though the very mention of Arizona may cause some people to turn the air conditioner on full blast, this state is much more than a searing landscape of cactus and creosote bush. From the baking shores of the lower Colorado River to the snow-capped heights of the San Francisco Peaks, Arizona encompasses virtually every climatic zone. Cactus flowers bloom in the spring, and in summer mountain wildflowers have their turn. In autumn the aspens color the White Mountains golden, and in winter snows blanket the higher elevations from the north rim of the Grand Canyon almost to the Mexican border.

But it's the Sonoran Desert, with its massive saguaro cacti, that most people associate with Arizona. The Sonoran Desert surrounds Phoenix and Tucson and is among the most biologically diverse deserts on the planet, in part because it's one of the wettest. Rain falls in the winter as well as during the late-summer monsoon season when clamorous thunderstorms send flash floods surging down arroyos. Before the coming of dams and deep wells, many rivers and streams flowed year-round and nurtured a huge variety of plants and animals. Today only a few rivers and creeks still flow unaltered through the desert. These include Sonoita Creek and the San Pedro, Verde, and Hassayampa rivers. The green riparian areas along these watercourses serve as magnets for wildlife and harbor rare birds as well as fish species that are unique to Arizona.

The Sonoran Desert's most conspicuous natural inhabitant is the saguaro cactus, which can stand 40 feet tall and weigh several tons. Massive and many-armed, these are the cacti of comic strips and Hollywood westerns. But there are also many other lesser-known species of cactus, such as the organ pipe cactus (closely related to the saguaro), the barrel cactus, and various species of prickly pears and chollas, all of which have adapted to this harsh environment by storing water in their stems, growing without leaves, and both protecting and shading themselves with spines. Despite spiny defenses, cactus is still relied upon by many desert animals for food and protection. Bats sip the nectar from saguaro flowers (and in the process, act as pollinators). Javelinas, similar to wild pigs and also known as collared peccaries, chow down on the prickly pear fruit—spines and all. Gila woodpeckers nest in holes in saguaro trunks, while cactus wrens build their nests in the branches of the cholla cactus.

## Impressions

*Do nothing to mar its grandeur . . . keep it for your children, your children's children, all who come after you, as the one great sight which every American should see.*
        —Pres. Theodore Roosevelt, after visiting the Grand Canyon in 1903

## Arizona: Hollywood Backlot

Spectacular landscapes, rugged deserts, ghost towns, and cowboy ethos have made Arizona the location for hundreds of films. From obscure B westerns starring long-forgotten singing cowboys to the seminal works of John Ford, Arizona has provided the backdrop to stories of life in the Wild West. This state has become so much associated with the Old West that Europeans, Asians, and Australians come from halfway around the world to walk where John Wayne once swaggered and where Clint Eastwood cultivated his outlaw image.

Arizona's landscape is so varied that over the years it has managed to double for Texas, Kansas, Mexico, and even New York, foreign planets, and a post-apocalyptic earth. It has played the past, the present, and the future. Production companies working on movies, television shows, and commercials have traveled to every corner of the state to find just the right setting for their productions.

In Tucson, in 1939, a movie set was built for the filming of the movie *Arizona*, and when the filming was over, the set was left to be used in other productions. Today this mock-Western town is known as Old Tucson Studios, and though much of it was destroyed by a fire in early 1995, it has since been rebuilt and is still used for film and video productions. Movies that have been filmed here include *Tombstone*; John Wayne's *Rio Lobo, Rio Bravo,* and *El Dorado;* Clint Eastwood's *The Outlaw Josey Wales;* Kirk Douglas's *Gunfight at the O.K. Corral;* and Paul Newman's *The Life and Times of Judge Roy Bean.* Old Tucson also doubled as Mankato on the television series *Little House on the Prairie.* Today the studios are not only used for filming but are a major tourist attraction in their own right, sort of a Wild West amusement park without the rides.

Though John Ford was not the first to film at Monument Valley, he made this otherworldly landscape a trademark of his filmmaking, using the valley as the backdrop for such films as *Stagecoach, She Wore a Yellow Ribbon, My Darling Clementine, Rio Grande,* and *The Searchers.* Other Westerns filmed here have included *How the West Was Won, The Legend of the Lone Ranger,* and *Mackenna's Gold.* The valley has also shown up in such non-Western films as *Back to the Future III, 2001: A Space Odyssey, Thelma and Louise,* and *Forrest Gump.* The red rocks of Sedona have also attracted many filmmakers over the years. *Broken Arrow, 3:10 to Yuma, The Cowboy and the Redhead, The Riders of the Purple Sage,* and *The Call of the Canyon* were all filmed in Sedona and the nearby Oak Creek Canyon.

Patagonia, in southeastern Arizona, is another town that has served as a backdrop for quite a few films, including *Oklahoma, Red River, McClintock, Broken Lance, David and Bathsheba,* and *A Star Is Born,* and television programs including *Little House on the Prairie, The Young Riders,* and *Red Badge of Courage.*

Among the films shot more recently in Arizona have been *Wyatt Earp, Geronimo, Red Rock West,* and *Maverick.*

Just as cacti have adapted to the desert, so, too, have the animals that live here. Many desert animals spend the sweltering days in burrows and only venture out in the cool of the night. Under cover of darkness, rattlesnakes and great horned owls hunt kangaroo rats, coyotes howl, and javelinas root about for anything edible. Gila lizards, among the only poisonous lizards in the world, drag their ungainly bodies though the dust, while tarantulas tiptoe silently in search of unwary insects.

Outside the desert regions there is great diversity as well. In the southern part of the state, solitary mountains and small mountain ranges rise abruptly from the desert floor, creating refuges for plants and animals that require cooler climates. It is these so-called mountain or sky islands that harbor the greatest varieties of bird species in the continental United States. Birds from both warm and cold climates find homes in such oases as Ramsey, Madera, and Cave Creek canyons.

Although rugged mountain ranges crisscross the state, only a few rise to such heights that they support actual forests. Among these are the Santa Catalinas outside Tucson, the White Mountains along the state's eastern border, and the San Francisco Peaks north of Flagstaff. However, it's atop the Mogollon Rim and the Kaibab Plateau that these ponderosa pine forests cover the greatest areas. The Mogollon Rim is a 2,000-foot-high escarpment that stretches from central Arizona all the way into New Mexico. The ponderosa pine forest here is the largest in the world and is dotted with lakes well known for their fishing. The Mogollon Rim area is also home to large herds of elk. At over 8,000 feet in elevation, the Kaibab Plateau is much higher than the Mogollon Rim, and it is through this plateau that the Grand Canyon cuts.

This then is the natural environment of Arizona, a land of extremes where summer temperatures in the Sonoran Desert top 120° Fahrenheit while snow still lies atop the San Francisco Peaks. Life here has adapted to these extremes in fascinating ways that are still being deciphered by biologists throughout the state.

# 2  The Regions in Brief

**The Valley of the Sun**   This name refers to the sprawling metropolitan Phoenix area, which covers more than 400 square miles and includes more than 20 cities and communities surrounded by several distinct mountain ranges. It's the economic and population center of modern Arizona.

**The Sonoran Desert**   Extending from Sonora, Mexico, in the south to central Arizona in the north, the Sonoran Desert is surprisingly green and characterized by the massive saguaro cactus. It's in the Sonoran Desert that most of Arizona's cities are found.

**The Four Corners**   The point where Arizona, Utah, Colorado, and New Mexico come together is the only place in the United States where four states share a common boundary. The Four Corners region of Arizona is almost entirely Hopi and Navajo reservation land. This high-plateau region of spectacular canyons and towering mesas and buttes includes Canyon de Chelly, the Painted Desert, the Petrified Forest, and Monument Valley.

**The White Mountains**   Located in eastern Arizona, the White Mountains are laced with trout streams, covered by a huge pine forest, and home to far more wildlife than people. Arizona's largest and most popular ski area is located here on the Apache Reservation near the town of McNary. Cooler temperatures make this region a very popular summer-vacation destination.

**Arizona's West Coast**   Though Arizona is a landlocked state, its western region is referred to as the West Coast because of the hundreds of miles of lakeshore that were created by the damming of the Colorado River. The low-lying stretches of the Colorado River are the hottest places in Arizona.

**Canyon Country**   From the Grand Canyon in the north to Oak Creek Canyon in the south, the rugged north-central part of the state alternates high, forested mountains with deep canyons. The 2,000-foot-high Mogollon Rim cuts through this region.

**The Arizona Strip**    Located north of the Grand Canyon and bordering on southern Utah, this is one of the most remote and untraveled sections of Arizona. The Grand Canyon acts as a natural boundary between this region and the rest of the state.

**Southeastern Arizona**    Mile-high elevations give this region one of the most temperate climates in the world. Tucson is at the northern edge of this region (and not so temperate), but otherwise there are few towns of any size. Mountain "islands" that rise out of the desert are home to more than 200 species of birds, and the wide grassy valleys make this a ranching region.

## 3  Arizona Today

Combining aspects of Indian, Hispanic, and European cultures, Arizona is one of the most culturally diverse states in the country. Here the Old West and the "New West" coexist. While the wealthy residents of Scottsdale raise Arabian horses as investments, the Navajos of the Four Corners region still raise sheep for sustenance and wool, herding their flocks from the backs of hard-working horses. Vacationers on Lake Powell water-ski through flooded canyons while cowboys in the southeast corner of the state still ride the range mending fences and rounding up cattle.

Although Arizonans are today more likely to drive Hondas and Toyotas than ride pintos and appaloosas, western wear is still the preferred fashion of rich and poor alike. Cowboy boots, cowboy hats, blue jeans, and bola ties are acceptable attire at almost any function in Arizona. Horses are still used on ranches around the state, but most are kept simply for recreational or investment purposes. In Scottsdale, one of the nation's centers of Arabian horse breeding, horse auctions attract a well-heeled (read lizard-skin boots) crowd, and horses sell for tens of thousands of dollars. Even the state's dude ranches, which now call themselves "guest ranches," have changed their images and many are as likely to offer tennis and swimming as horseback riding.

A long legacy of movies being filmed here has further blurred the line between the real West and the Hollywood West. More city slickers wander the streets of the Old Tucson movie set and videotape shoot-outs at the O.K. Corral than ever saddle up a palomino or ride herd on a cattle drive. Even dinner has been raised to a cowboy entertainment form at Arizona's many Wild West steakhouses, where families are entertained by cowboy bands, staged gunfights, hayrides, and sing-alongs, all in the name of reliving the glory days of "cowboys and Indians."

For Arizona's Indians, those were days of hardship and misery, and today the state's many tribes continue to strive for the sort of economic well-being enjoyed by the state's non-native population. However, traditional ways are still alive, though tribes must struggle to preserve their own unique cultures—their languages, religious beliefs and ceremonies, livelihoods, and architecture.

Arizona is home to the largest Indian reservation in the country—the Navajo nation—as well as nearly two dozen other smaller reservations. As elsewhere in the United States, poverty and alcoholism are major problems on Arizona reservations. However, several of the state's tribes have, through their arts and crafts, managed to both preserve some of their traditional culture and share it with nonnatives. Among these tribes are the Navajo, known for their rugs and silver jewelry; the Hopi, known for their pottery and kachinas; the Zuñi, known for their inlaid stone jewelry; and the Tohono O'odham, known for their baskets.

Lately, however, many nonnatives have been visiting reservations—not out of an interest in learning about another culture, but to gamble. Throughout the state, casinos have opened on reservation land, and despite the controversies surrounding such

## ❓ Did You Know?

- Arizona has more mountainous regions (19,280 square miles) than Switzerland, and more forestland (19,902,000 acres) than Minnesota.
- Arizona sided with the South during the American Civil War.
- Arizona was the last territory in the continental United States to become a state.
- The Four Corners, in the northeast corner of Arizona, adjoins Utah, Colorado, and New Mexico, the only spot where four states come together.
- The Grand Canyon is one of the seven natural wonders of the world.
- Some rocks in the Grand Canyon are more than two billion years old.
- The Hopi village of Oraibi is one of the two oldest continuously inhabited settlements in the United States (Acoma, New Mexico is the other).
- Wyatt Earp, Ike Clanton, and the McLaury brothers really did have a shoot-out at the O.K. Corral in Tombstone.
- Arizona has the highest per capita boat ownership of any state.
- The Spanish were in Arizona a quarter century before St. Augustine, Florida, was founded and 70 years before the British founded Jamestown, Virginia.
- The bola tie is the official state neckwear of Arizona.
- Arizonan Lorna Lockwood was the first woman chief justice of a state supreme court.
- Arizonan Sandra Day O'Connor was the first woman appointed to the United States Supreme Court.

enterprises, many native peoples are finally seeing some income on their once-impoverished reservations.

Many of the people who visit these new casinos are senior citizens, who are among the fastest-growing segment of Arizona's population. The mild winter climate in Arizona has attracted tens of thousands of retirees to the state over the past few decades. Many of these winter residents, known as snowbirds, park their RVs outside such warm spots as Yuma and Quartzsite. Others, however, have come to stay and have settled in such retirement communities as Sun City and Green Valley.

This graying of the population, combined with strong ranching and mining industries, has made Arizona one of the most conservative of states. Though by today's standards Barry Goldwater could almost be considered a liberal, his conservative politics were so much a part of the Arizona mind-set that the state kept him in the Senate for 30 years.

This conservative legacy continues to the present. Recent years have been characterized by numerous political controversies. When Arizona, under Gov. Evan Mecham, chose not to recognize the Martin Luther King, Jr., holiday, the state was branded racist and lost millions of dollars in potential income from sporting events (including the Super Bowl) and conventions that chose not to come to Arizona in protest. The state finally acquiesced to public opinion and agreed to observe the holiday, which is perhaps one reason why Phoenix finally was able to host the Super Bowl in 1996.

The controversial Governor Mecham was convicted in 1988 of illegally loaning state funds to his automobile dealership and of trying to block an investigation into charges that an aide made a death threat against a grand jury witness. (Mecham, by the way, was succeeded by Rose Mofford, the state's first woman governor.)

Within 3 years controversy again threw Arizona into the national limelight as Charles Keating was convicted of defrauding Lincoln Savings and Loan customers of $250 million. At least some of the money went into the ostentatious Phoenician resort in Scottsdale and a smaller sister hotel, the Crescent, in Phoenix.

In 1995 the state legislature angered environmentalists the world over by voting to exempt itself from both federal law and an international agreement to ban the manufacture of Freon, which is used in air-conditioning and may be partly responsible for the thinning of the ozone layer.

And that's only one of the environmental battles that have recently been fought in Arizona. Though many people think of the desert as a wasteland in need of transformation, others see it as a fragile ecosystem that has been endangered by the encroachment of civilization. Although saguaro cacti throughout the state are protected by law, the deserts they grow in are not. In Tucson, environmentalists have for several years been fighting (with little success) to stop the suburban sprawl that's pushing farther and farther into saguaro country.

Way up at the north end of the state, remote Grand Canyon National Park is suffering from its own popularity. With more than 5 million visitors a year, the park now sees summer traffic jams and parking problems that have made a visit to the park an exercise in patience. Plans are currently under way to try to save the park from being loved to death.

In early 1996, a couple of events altered the long-time status quo of the park. The shutdown of the federal government meant that Grand Canyon National Park was closed to the public, which proved such a blow to the Arizona economy that the state tried to bring in the National Guard to run the park. Unfortunately, the feds vetoed this idea and the park gates remained locked until Congress and the White House arrived at compromises to continue funding the government.

The second unusual event in the Canyon was an experiment: an attempt to duplicate the traditional spring floods that the Colorado River used to experience before the construction of the Glen Canyon Dam. The goal of the experiment was to try to duplicate the sort of seasonal deposition of sand and silt that used to occur along the riverbanks before the construction of the dam. The experiment was successful and it is likely that this seasonal artificial flooding will become a part of river policy within the park.

Mount Graham, one of the highest peaks in southern Arizona, has also been immersed in controversy for several years as the University of Arizona has constructed an astronomical observatory atop the peak in forestland that is the only home of the 400 remaining Mount Graham red squirrels. In spring of 1996, a forest fire on the flanks of Mount Graham emphasized the precariousness of the squirrels' existence in an area where a single fire could feasibly wipe out an entire mammal species.

Efforts at preserving the state's environment make it clear that Arizonans value the outdoors, but a ski boat in every driveway doesn't mean that the arts are ignored. Although it hasn't been too many years since evening entertainment in Arizona meant dance-hall girls or a harmonica by the campfire, Phoenix and Tucson have become centers for both the visual and the performing arts. The two cities share both an opera company and a ballet company, and the Valley of the Sun is also home to a number of symphony orchestras and theater companies.

Even in small cities, local arts centers and festivals attract performers of national renown: Sedona stages jazz and classical music festivals, and Grand Canyon Village, on the south rim of the Grand Canyon, hosts an annual chamber music festival.

Small towns around the state are also supporting the arts. Whole communities such as Jerome, Tubac, and Bisbee, all nearly ghost towns at one time, have been reborn as arts communities. Where miners and outlaws once walked, artists now offer their creations for sale.

In Arizona today, the New West and the Old West are coming to grips with each other. Hopi perform their ages-old dances atop their mesas, urban cowboys and cowgirls line dance in nightclubs around the state, grizzled wranglers lead vacationing Germans on horseback rides across open range, and ranchers find that they have something in common with environmentalists—saving Arizona's ranch lands.

# 4  History 101

Arizona is the site of North America's oldest cultures and one of the two longest continuously inhabited settlements in the United States (the Hopi village of Oraibi). Over the past 5 centuries this land has been Native American territory and part of New Spain, Mexico, and the United States. Early explorers and settlers saw little profit in the desert wasteland, but time proved them wrong: mineral resources, cattle grazing, and particularly cotton (after dams began providing irrigation water) all became important income sources. In this century, the economy has moved from the three Cs (copper, cattle, and cotton) to a service industries–based economy, with tourism one of its major resources.

**EARLY HISTORY**   More than 11,000 years ago Paleo-Indians known as the Clovis people lived in southeastern Arizona, where stone tools and arrowheads have been found as evidence of their presence. A mammoth-kill site has also been discovered and has proved to be an important source of information about these people, some of the earliest inhabitants of North America.

Few records exist of the next 9,000 years of Arizona's history, but by about A.D. 200, wandering bands of hunter-gatherers began living in Canyon de Chelly in the north. These people would come to be known as the Anasazi, a Navajo word that means "the ancient ones." The earliest Anasazi period, from A.D. 200 to 700, is called the Basketmaker period because of the numbers of baskets that have been found in Anasazi ruins from this time. During this period the Anasazi gave up hunting and gathering and took up agriculture, growing corn, beans, squash, and cotton on the canyon floors in northeastern Arizona.

During the Pueblo period, between 700 and 1300, the Anasazi began building multistory pueblos (villages) and cliff dwellings. It's unknown why the Anasazi began living in niches and caves high on

## Dateline

- **9700 B.C.** Paleo-Indians (the Clovis people) in southeastern Arizona are among the earliest recorded inhabitants in North America.
- **A.D. 200** The Anasazi people move into Canyon de Chelly.
- **450** Hohokam peoples farm the Salt and Gila river valleys, eventually building 600 miles of irrigation canals.
- **650** The Sinagua cultivate land northeast of present-day Flagstaff.
- **1100s** Hopi tribes build Oraibi village, the oldest continuously occupied village in the United States; the Anasazi build cliff dwellings in Canyon de Chelly; the Sinagua build Wupatki.
- **1250** The Sinagua abandon Wupatki and other pueblos.
- **1300** The Anasazi abandon cliff dwellings in Canyon de Chelly and Tsegi Canyon.
- **1350** The Hohokam build Casa Grande in the Gila River valley.
- **1400s** The Navajo peoples migrate south from Canada to northeastern Arizona.
- **1450** The Hohokam abandon lowland desert villages; the Sinagua abandon Verde Valley villages.
- **1539** Marcos de Niza ventures into present-day Arizona from Mexico (New Spain) in search of the Seven Cities of Cibola.

*continues*

- **1540s** Francisco Vésquez de Coronado leads an expedition to Arizona in search of gold.
- **1691** Jesuit Fr. Eusebio Kino begins converting Native Americans.
- **1751** The mission of Tumacacori and the presidio of Tubac are established, the first European settlement in Arizona.
- **1776** A Spanish garrison is posted in Tucson to protect the mission of San Xavier del Bac.
- **1821** Mexico gains independence from Spain and takes control of Arizona.
- **1848** Most of present-day Arizona ceded to the United States following the Mexican-American War.
- **1853** In the Gadsden Purchase, the United States acquires the remainder of Arizona from Mexico.
- **1862** Arizona becomes the Confederate Territory of Arizona but is reclaimed by the Union later that same year.
- **1863** Arizona becomes a U.S. territory.
- **1886** Geronimo surrenders to the U.S. Army.
- **1911** Theodore Roosevelt Dam, on the Salt River, enables irrigation and development of the desert.
- **1912** Arizona becomes the 48th state.
- **1919** Grand Canyon National Park established.
- **1936** Hoover Dam completed.
- **1948** Arizona Indians receive the right to vote.
- **1963** U.S. Supreme Court upholds Arizona's claim to Colorado River water.
- **1974** Construction begins on the Central Azizona Project aqueducts.

*continues*

the cliff walls of the canyons. It may have been to conserve farmland as their population grew and required larger harvests, or for protection from flash floods or attacks by hostile neighbors. Whatever the reason, the Anasazi cliff dwellings were all abandoned by 1300. It's also unknown why the villages were abandoned, but a study of tree rings indicates that the region experienced a severe drought between 1276 and 1299, which suggests that the Anasazi left in search of more fertile farmland. Keet Seel and Betatakin, at Navajo National Monument, and the many ruins in Canyon de Chelly, are Arizona's best-preserved Anasazi ruins.

During the Anasazi Basketmaker period, another culture was beginning to develop in the fertile plateau northeast of present-day Flagstaff and southward into the Verde River valley. The Sinagua, a Spanish name that means "without water," built their stone pueblos primarily on hills and mesas such as those at Tuzigoot near Clarkdale and Wupatki near Flagstaff. They also built cliff dwellings at such places as Walnut Canyon and Montezuma Castle. By the mid-13th century, Wupatki had been abandoned by the Sinagua, and by the early 15th century they had also abandoned Walnut Canyon and the lower Verde Valley region.

By A.D. 450 the Hohokam culture, from whom the Sinagua learned irrigation, had begun to farm the Gila and Salt river valleys between Phoenix and Casa Grande. Over a period of 1,000 years, they constructed a 600-mile network of irrigation canals, some of which can still be seen today. Because the Hohokam built their homes of earth, few Hohokam ruins remain. However, one building, the Casa Grande ruin, has been well preserved, and throughout the desert the Hohokam left petroglyphs (rock carvings) as a lasting reminder that they once dwelt in this region. By the 1450s, the tribe had abandoned its villages and disappeared without a sign, hence the name Hohokam, a Tohono O'odham word meaning "all used up" or "the people who have gone." Archaeologists believe that the irrigation of desert soil for hundreds of years had left a thick crust of alkali on the surface, and this made farming no longer possible.

**HISPANIC HERITAGE**    The first Europeans to visit the region may have been a motley crew of shipwrecked Spaniards among whom was a black man named Estévan de Dorantes. This unfortunate group spent 8 years wandering from a beach in Florida to a Spanish village in Mexico. These wanderers arrived back in Spanish territory with a fantastic story of seven cities filled with goldsmiths, where doorways were encrusted with jewels. No one is sure whether they actually passed through Arizona, but their story convinced the viceroy of New Spain (Mexico) to send a small expedition, led by Fr. Marcos de Niza and Estévan de Dorantes. Father de Niza's report of finding the fabled Seven Cities of Cibola also inspired Don Francisco Vésquez de Coronado to set off in search of wealth. However, instead of fabulously wealthy cities, Coronado found only pueblos of stone and mud. A subordinate expedition led by Garcia Lopez de Cérdenas stumbled upon the Grand Canyon, while another group of Coronado's men, led by Don Pedro de Tovar, visited the Hopi mesas.

In the 150 years that followed, only a handful of Spaniards visited Arizona. In the 1580s and 1600s, Antonio de Espejo and Juan de Oñate explored northern and central Arizona and found indications that there were mineral riches in the region. In the 1670s, the Franciscans founded several missions among the Hopi pueblos, but the Pueblo Revolt of 1680 obliterated this small Spanish presence.

In 1687 Fr. Eusebio Francisco Kino, a German-educated Italian Jesuit, began establishing missions in the Sonoran Desert region of northern New Spain. In 1691, he visited the Pima village of Tumacacori. Father Kino taught the inhabitants European farming techniques, planted fruit trees, and gave the natives cattle, sheep, and goats to raise. However, it was not until 1751, in response to a Pima rebellion, that the permanent mission of Tumacacori and the presidio (military post) of Tubac were built. Together these two Spanish outposts became the first European settlements in Arizona.

- **1975** Raul Castro becomes the first Hispanic governor of Arizona.
- **1981** Arizona judge Sandra Day O'Connor becomes the first woman appointed to the U.S. Supreme Court.
- **1985** The Central Arizona Project begins delivering water to Phoenix.
- **1988** Gov. Evan Mecham removed from office.
- **1991** A California jury finds Charles Keating guilty of defrauding Arizona investors who had deposited funds with Lincoln Savings and Loan.
- **1992** A Tucson jury awards $3 billion in damages to investors who were defrauded in the failed Lincoln Savings and Loan.
- **1995** The Arizona state legislature refuses to ban the manufacture and sale of Freon.
- **1996** After the state finally recognizes the Martin Luther King, Jr., holiday, Super Bowl XXX is played in Tempe's Sun Devil Stadium.
- **1997** Gov. Fife Symington is indicted on 23 felony counts ranging from bank fraud to extortion (and then announces that he will run for a third term as governor).

In 1775, a group of settlers led by Juan Bautista de Anza set out from Tubac to find an overland route to California, and in 1776 this group founded the city of San Francisco. That same year the Tubac presidio was moved to Tucson. Father Kino had visited the Tucson area in 1692 and in 1700 had laid out the foundations for the first church at the mission of San Xavier del Bac. However, construction of the present church, known as the White Dove of the Desert, probably did not begin until 1783.

In 1821, Mexico won its independence from Spain, and Tucson, with only 65 inhabitants, became part of Mexico. Mexico at that time extended all the way to northern California, but in 1848 most of this land, except for a small section of southern Arizona that included Tucson, became U.S. territory in the wake of the Mexican-American War. Five years later, in 1853, Mexico sold the remainder of southern Arizona to the United States in a transaction known as the Gadsden Purchase.

**INDIAN CONFLICTS**　At the time that the Spanish arrived in Arizona, the tribes living in the southern lowland deserts were peaceful farmers, while in the mountains of the east lived the Apache, a hunting-and-gathering tribe that frequently raided neighboring tribes. In the north, the Navajo, relatively recent immigrants to the region, fought over land with the neighboring Hopi (who were also fighting amongst themselves) and Ute.

Coronado's expedition through Arizona and into New Mexico and Kansas was to seek gold. To that end he attacked one pueblo, killed the inhabitants of another, and forced still others to abandon their villages. Spanish-Indian relations were never to improve, and the Spanish were forced to occupy their new lands with a strong military presence. Around 1600, 300 Spanish settlers moved into the Four Corners region, which at the time supported a large population of Navajo. The Spanish raided Navajo villages to take slaves, and angry Navajo responded by stealing Spanish horses and cattle.

For several decades in the mid-1600s, missionaries were tolerated in the Hopi pueblos, but the Pueblo tribes revolted in 1680, killing the missionaries and destroying the missions. Encroachment by farmers and miners moving into the Santa Cruz Valley in the south caused the Pima people to stage a similar uprising in 1751, attacking and burning the mission at Tubac. This revolt led to the establishment of the presidio at Tubac that same year. When the military garrison moved to Tucson, Tubac was quickly abandoned because of frequent raids by Apaches. In 1781, the Yuman tribe, whose land at the confluence of the Colorado and Gila rivers had become a Spanish settlement, staged a similar uprising that wiped out the settlement at Yuma.

By the time Arizona became part of the United States, it was the Navajo and the Apache who were proving most resistant to white settlers. In 1864 the U.S. Army, under the leadership of Col. Kit Carson, forced the Navajo to surrender by destroying their winter food supplies, and then shipped them to an internment camp in New Mexico. Within 5 years they were returned to their land, though they were now forced to live on a reservation.

The Apache resisted white settlement 20 years longer than the Navajo. Skillful guerrilla fighters, the Apache were able to attack settlers, forts, and towns despite the presence of U.S. Army troops sent to protect the white settlers. Geronimo and Cochise were the leaders of the last resistant bands of rebellious Apache. Cochise eventually died in his Chiricahua Mountains homeland and Geronimo was finally forced to surrender in 1886. Geronimo and many of his followers were subsequently relocated to Florida by the U.S. government. Open conflicts between whites and Indians finally came to an end.

**TERRITORIAL DAYS**   In 1846 the United States went to war with Mexico, which at the time extended all the way to northern California and included parts of Colorado, Wyoming, and New Mexico. When the war ended, the United States claimed almost all the land extending from Texas to northern California. This newly acquired land, called the New Mexico Territory, had its capital at Santa Fe. The land south of the Gila River, which included Tucson, was still part of Mexico, but when surveys determined that this land was the best route for a railroad from southern Mississippi to southern California, the U.S. government negotiated the Gadsden Purchase. In 1853 this land purchase established the current Arizona-Mexico border.

When the California Gold Rush began in 1849, many hopeful miners crossed Arizona en route to the goldfields, and some stayed to seek mineral riches in Arizona. Despite the ever-increasing numbers of settlers, the U.S. Congress refused to create a separate Arizona Territory. When the Civil War broke out, Arizonans, angered by Congress's inaction on their request to become a separate territory, sided with the Confederacy; in 1862 Arizona was proclaimed the Confederate Territory of Arizona.

## Impressions

*If the world were searched over, I suppose there could not be found so degraded a set of villains as then formed the principal society of Tucson.*

—J. Ross Browne, a visitor to Tucson in 1863

*O yes, I have heard of that country—it is just like hell. All it lacks is water and good society.*

—A 19th-century senator from Ohio

Although Union troops easily defeated the Confederate troops who had occupied Tucson, this dissension convinced Congress, in 1863, to create the Arizona Territory.

The capital of the new territory was temporarily established at Fort Whipple near Prescott, but later the same year the capital was moved to Prescott, and in 1867 to Tucson. Ten years later Prescott again became the capital, which it remained for another 12 years before the seat of government moved finally to Phoenix, which is today the Arizona state capital.

During this period mining flourished, and though small amounts of gold and silver were discovered, copper became the source of Arizona's economic wealth. With each mineral strike a new mining town would boom, and when the ore ran out the town would be abandoned. These towns were infamous for their gambling halls, bordellos, saloons, and shoot-outs in the street. Tombstone and Bisbee became the largest towns in the state, and were known as the wildest towns between New Orleans and San Francisco.

In 1867 farmers in the newly founded town of Phoenix began irrigating their fields using canals that had been dug centuries earlier by the Hohokam. In the 1870s ranching became another important source of revenue in the territory, particularly in the southeastern and northwestern parts of the state. In the 1880s the railroads finally arrived, and life in Arizona began to change drastically. Suddenly the mineral resources and cattle of the region were accessible to the East.

**STATEHOOD & THE 20TH CENTURY**   By the turn of the 20th century, Arizonans were trying to convince Congress to make the territory a state. Congress balked at the requests, but finally, in 1910, allowed the territorial government to draw up a state constitution. Territorial legislators were progressive thinkers and the draft of Arizona's state constitution included clauses for the recall of elected officials. Pres. William Howard Taft vetoed the bill that would have made Arizona a state because he opposed the recall of judges. Arizona politicians removed the controversial clause, and, on February 14, 1912, Arizona became the 48th state. One of the new state legislature's first acts was to reinstate the clause providing for the recall of judges.

Much of Washington's opposition to Arizona's statehood had been based on the belief that Arizona could never support economic development. This belief was changed in 1911 by one of the most important events in Arizona history—the completion of the Roosevelt Dam (later to be renamed the Theodore Roosevelt Dam) on the Salt River. The dam provided irrigation water to the Valley of the Sun and tamed the violent floods of the river. The introduction of water to the heart of Arizona's vast desert enabled large-scale agriculture and industry. Over the next decades more dams were built throughout Arizona. Completed in 1936, the Hoover Dam on the Colorado River became the largest concrete dam in the western hemisphere and formed the largest man-made reservoir in North America. Arizona's dams would eventually provide not only water and electricity but recreational areas.

Despite labor problems, copper mining increased throughout the 1920s and 1930s, and with the onset of World War II the mines boomed as military munitions manufacturing increased demand for copper. However, within a few years after the war, many mines were shut down. Arizona is still littered with old mining ghost towns that boomed and then went bust. A few towns, such as Jerome, Bisbee, and Chloride, managed to hang on after the mines shut down and were eventually rediscovered by artists, writers, and retirees. Bisbee and Jerome have now become artists' colonies and major tourist attractions.

World War II also created demand for beef, leather, and cotton (which became the state's most important crop). Clear desert skies were ideal for training pilots, and several military bases were established in the state. Phoenix's population doubled during the war years, and after the war many veterans returned with their families. However, it would take the invention of air-conditioning to truly open up the desert to major population growth.

During the postwar years, Arizona attracted a number of large manufacturing industries and slowly moved away from its agricultural economic base. Today, electronics manufacturing, aerospace engineering, and other high-tech industries provide employment for thousands of Arizonans. The largest segment of the economy, however, is now in the service industries, with tourism playing a crucial role.

Even by the 1920s, Arizona had become a winter destination for the wealthy, and the Grand Canyon, declared a national park in 1919, lured more and more visitors every year. The clear dry air attracted people suffering from allergies and lung ailments, and Arizona became known as a healthful place. Guest ranches of the 1930s eventually gave way to the resorts of the 1990s. Today Scottsdale and Phoenix together boast the greatest concentration of resorts in the United States. In addition, tens of thousands of retirees from as far north as Canada make Arizona their winter home and play a crucial role in Arizona's economy.

Continued population growth throughout the 20th century created an ever greater demand for water. However, despite the damming of virtually all of Arizona's rivers, the state still suffered from insufficient water supplies in the south-central population centers of Phoenix and Tucson. It would take the construction of the controversial and expensive Central Arizona Project (CAP) aqueduct to carry water from the Colorado River over mountains and deserts and deliver it where it was wanted. Construction on the CAP began in 1974, and in 1985 water from the project finally began irrigating fields near Phoenix. In 1992, the CAP finally reached Tucson. However, with the populations of Phoenix, Tucson, and Las Vegas skyrocketing, the future of Colorado River water usage may again become a question for hot debate.

By the 1960s, Arizona had become an urban state with all the problems confronting cities around the nation. The once-healthful air of Phoenix now rivals that of Los Angeles for the thickness of its smog. Allergy sufferers are plagued by pollen from the nondesert plants that have been planted to make this desert region look more lush and inviting. Resistance to construction of interstate freeways in the Phoenix area caused that city to become one of the most congested in the nation, and today major highway construction projects are only slowly beginning to relieve the congestion. In the early 1980s, as industry fled from the Rustbelt to the Sunbelt, Arizona experienced an economic boom that by the end of the decade had turned to a bust. Today, however, the state's economy is once again growing. High-tech companies continue to locate within the state, and the continued influx of both retirees and Californians fleeing earthquakes and urban problems is giving the state new energy and new ideas. The signing of the North American Free Trade Agreement (NAFTA) also gave the state an economic shot in the arm, and companies have been taking full advantage of the increased trade with Mexico, the state's southern neighbor.

## 5 Southwestern Cuisine

In the past decade regional cuisines have become all the rage with chefs across the United States. Southwestern cuisine, whose hallmarks are the spices of Mexico (especially chile peppers), the unusual fruit-and-meat pairings of nouvelle cuisine, and flame-broiling over mesquite, has won popularity across the country. The blue-corn industry has also been thriving as creative chefs in Arizona, New Mexico, and around the country try their hand at concocting new dishes with this colorful carbohydrate. Ingredients both familiar and foreign have found their way into this regional cuisine, much to the delight of daring diners.

Southwestern cuisine has become so much a part of the dining scene in Arizona that even in small-town restaurants you'll probably encounter dishes such as mesquite-grilled breast of chicken served with a fresh-fruit salsa. In the cities, meanwhile, chefs are still dreaming up new creations—say, pistachio-crusted breast of duckling with fig-and-orange chutney. Pacific salmon might be served with smoked yellow-pepper sauce and roasted black-bean and corn relish, while roast squab might be served with twice-cooked bacon and chipotle pepper and cider sauce. Other dishes might include marinated ahi with avocado-papaya salsa and cilantro-scallion aioli, or Southwestern bouillabaisse with grilled nopal cactus. Even desserts get the desert treatment as shown in such outlandish, though tasty, concoctions as chile-chocolate cake and raspberry-jalapeño ice cream.

With all those chile peppers, Southwestern just isn't for everyone, and unfortunately, many of the restaurants that once served dishes such as those mentioned above are now joining a trend toward milder, more subtle flavors. And while you can find Southwestern flavors in a wide range of eating establishments, for the most part, it's still the realm of expensive gourmet restaurants.

Arizona also offers some of the best Mexican food in the country. (A few years back, the mayor of Tucson even declared that the city was the Mexican restaurant capital of the universe!) One specialty that you're likely to encounter at Arizona's Mexican restaurants, especially in Tucson, is *carne seca*, which is air-dried beef that's shredded and added to various sauces. It has a very distinctive texture and shouldn't be missed.

## 6 A Look at Local Arts & Crafts

Though Santa Fe has claimed the spotlight in recent years, Arizona, too, is a mecca for artists. The Cowboy Artists of America, an organization of artists dedicated to capturing the lives and landscapes of the Old West, was formed in a tavern in Sedona in 1965 by Joe Beeler, George Phippen, Bob McLeod, Charlie Dye, John Hampton, and a few other local artists. Working primarily in oils and bronze, members of this organization depicted the lives of cowboys and Native Americans in their art, and today their work is sought after by collectors throughout the country.

As more and more artists and craftspeople headed for Arizona, the towns in which they congregated came to be known as artists' colonies, and galleries sprang up to serve a growing number of visitors. Although Sedona is probably the best known of these artists' communities, others include the former mining towns of Jerome and Bisbee, and Tubac, the first Spanish settlement in Arizona. All three have numerous galleries and crafts shops. However, it is upscale Scottsdale that has the state's highest concentration of art galleries.

Red-rock canyons, pensive Native Americans, hardworking cowboys, desert wildflowers, majestic mesas, and stately saguaros have been the themes of this century's representational artists of Arizona. Although contemporary abstract art can be found in museums and galleries, the style pioneered by Frederic Remington and Charles M. Russell in the early 20th century still dominates the Arizona art scene. Remington, Russell, and those who followed in their footsteps romanticized the West, imbuing their depictions of cowboys, Indians, settlers, and soldiers with mythic proportions that would be taken up by Hollywood.

Further back, even before the first Spanish explorers arrived in Arizona, the ancient Anasazi were creating an artistic legacy in their intricately woven baskets, painted pottery, and cryptic petroglyphs and pictographs. In recent years both contemporary Native American and non-native artists have been drawing on Anasazi designs for their works. Today's Hopi, Navajo, and Zuñi artisans have become well known for their jewelry, which is made of silver and semiprecious stones, primarily turquoise. The Hopi now carve images of their traditional kachinas for distribution in the marketplace, and the Navajo continue to weave traditional patterns in their rugs. The Zuñi, noted for their skill in carving stone, have focused on their traditional animal fetishes. However, since the founding of the Santa Fe Indian School in 1932, and later the Institute of American Indian Art, Indian artists have also ventured into the realm of painting. Hopi artist Fred Kabotie and his son, Michael Kabotie, are among the best-known Native American painters.

Collectors, and those with a casual interest in Southwestern art, will find local arts and crafts available in every corner of the state. From exclusive Scottsdale galleries to roadside stands on the Navajo reservation, Arizona arts and crafts are ubiquitous. The best places to look for Southwestern and cowboy (or Western) art are in Scottsdale, Tucson, Sedona, Tubac, and Jerome. Native American crafts can be found in these same towns, but it's somewhat more rewarding to visit trading posts and reservation galleries.

The best known of these are the Hubbell Trading Post in Ganado and the Cameron Trading Post in Cameron, but there are trading posts all over the state and almost all offer excellent selection and quality. Keep in mind that no matter where you shop for Native American arts and crafts, you'll find that prices are high.

The Indian tribes of Arizona tend to have one or two specialty crafts that they produce with consummate skill. Many of these crafts were disappearing when the first traders came to the reservations a century ago. Today most of the crafts are alive and well, but primarily as sale items. Prices are high because of the many hours that go into producing these items—what you're buying is handmade by a method that goes back for generations.

If you're looking for bargains, you'll be interested to know that museum gift shops do not charge sales tax. You can also avoid paying sales tax if you live outside Arizona and have your purchase shipped directly to your home. On a high-ticket item such as a Navajo rug, you could save quite a bit. Also keep in mind that it's a good idea to make your jewelry purchases from reputable stores rather than from roadside stalls, of which there are many in the Four Corners region of the state. Many of these stalls sell cheap imitation jewelry.

Following are brief discussions of individual native crafts (see also "A Native American Crafts Primer" in chapter 8).

**NAVAJO RUGS**   Rugs have been made only since traders came to the Navajo reservation. Before that the Navajo had woven only blankets. Women are the weavers in the Navajo tribe, and this skill is passed down from mother to daughter. A single rug only a few feet square takes hundreds of hours to make, much of the time spent in preparing the wool, dyeing it, and setting up the primitive loom. The best rugs are those made of hand-spun wool from local Navajo sheep and goats. Vegetal dyes, which generally produce very muted colors, are considered superior to chemical dyes, but are of course more time-consuming to prepare. When shopping for a rug, check the fineness of the weave and the amount of detail in the design. Finer weave and detail mean higher prices because of the additional time required to produce such a rug. Be prepared to spend $1,000 or more for even a small Navajo rug; even at this price the women who make the rugs are making less than minimum wage for their labor. At the Hubbell Trading Post in Ganado, you can see Navajo women weaving rugs.

**HOPI KACHINAS**   Kachinas, the colorful and bizarre figurines of the Hopi people, are representations of the spirits of animals, ancestors, places, and other things. First carved from cottonwood root or other wood, kachinas are then colorfully painted and decorated with feathers, leather capes, and bits of yarn. The finished figure is meant to closely resemble the costume and mask worn by kachina dancers during the annual religious ceremonies held in Hopi villages (styles of kachinas vary from village to village). Traditionally, kachinas have been given to young Hopi girls to help them learn about the different kachina spirits. Today, however, many carvers are creating kachinas specifically for sale. Among the more popular kachinas are the humorous *tsuku* or clown kachinas, which are often painted with bold black and white stripes. A detailed kachina will cost several hundred dollars.

**ZUÑI FETISHES**   The Zuñi have long been known for their stone-carving skills, which are best demonstrated in their small carved animal fetishes. A fetish is an object in which a spirit dwells, and such objects have always been important to the Zuñi people. Carved from various types of stone, including turquoise and jet, Zuñi fetishes traditionally depict eagles, bears, wolves, mountain lions, horses, and goats, each of which is associated with a particular compass direction. Often fetishes are decorated with turquoise and coral beads, feathers, and miniature arrowheads, all of which are tied to the body of the fetish with gut. Bear fetishes often feature inlaid heartlines (arrow-shaped lines running from the mouth down the side to the center of the body).

Before buying a fetish, it's a good idea to look at enough of them so that you can see the difference between one that's crudely carved and one that exhibits fine detail. Fetish prices start as low as $30, but most are at least $100.

**TOHONO O'ODHAM BASKETS**   Although virtually all the Arizona tribes produce some sort of basketry, the Tohono O'odham tribe, which has its reservation near Tucson, has come to be known for its baskets. Most Tohono O'odham baskets are made using the coil method. Bear grass is used as the center of the coil, which is then stitched together with bleached yucca and the dark outer covering of the devil's claw seedpod. The Tohono O'odham also make miniature baskets from horsehair. These baskets require all the skill of full-size baskets but are often no more than 2 inches across. One of the most common Tohono O'odham designs shows a human figure in the middle of a maze. This figure is I'itoi (Elder Brother), and the maze represents the route to his home in the Baboquivari Mountains. Simple small baskets can be purchased for less than $50, but a finely woven basket with a complex design may cost several hundred dollars.

**JEWELRY**   The Navajo, Hopi, and Zuñi all make jewelry, and each tribe has its own distinctive style. The Navajo are well known for heavy silver jewelry that's made primarily by sand casting. The squash-blossom necklace, which is based on an old Spanish symbol, actually features pomegranate blossoms rather than squash blossoms, but was adapted to Navajo tastes. The Navajo tend to place the emphasis on fine silver work accented by turquoise stones.

The Zuñi, on the other hand, use silver primarily as a setting for their stone carvings. Using turquoise, jet, coral, other semiprecious stones, and seashells, the Zuñi create colorful inlaid images. Another style of Zuñi jewelry features tiny pieces of cut and polished turquoise individually set in delicate grid and starburst patterns.

The Hopi are known for their overlay silver work, which uses two sheets of silver fused together. The upper sheet of silver has a design cut into it with a tiny saw, while the lower sheet is treated to produce a contrasting black background to the upper layer. In recent years Hopi jewelry has featured ancient Anasazi pottery designs.

Prices for jewelry vary widely depending on the amount of detail, the amount of silver, and the number of stones.

**POTTERY**    Although the tribes of New Mexico are much better known for their pottery, Arizona tribes such as the Hopi, Navajo, and Tohono O'odham also make pottery. For years Navajo pottery was crudely made and not very attractive, but in recent years Navajo potters have begun experimenting with new and ancient designs and have begun to produce appealing pottery for sale.

Hopi pottery is almost all made in the village of Hotevilla on First Mesa. It's an orange color and is sometimes incised or decorated with geometric designs in black.

Tohono O'odham pottery is very simple and not as well known as their basketry.

Pottery prices vary considerably, but generally are not nearly as high here as they are in the New Mexico pueblos.

## 7  Desert Architecture From Pueblos to Frank Lloyd Wright

Centuries before the first Europeans arrived in Arizona, the Anasazi people were building elaborate villages, which have come to be known by their Spanish name: pueblos. Many, but not all, of the Anasazi pueblos were built high on cliff walls in the rugged canyon lands of northern Arizona. Constructed of cut stones mortared together and roofed with logs and earth, the pueblo dwellings had thick walls that provided insulation from heat and cold. Pueblo architecture was characterized by small rooms with no windows, and it is believed that the buildings' flat roofs provided places to do chores. Some rooms were used for living, while others served as grain-storage rooms.

Earlier, the Anasazi developed a type of shelter known as a pit house, which was partially dug into the ground. Eventually these flat-roofed stone houses were adapted to apartment-style construction techniques when they moved up into the canyon walls. The pit-house style of architecture was retained in the form of the *kiva*, a round ceremonial room that's still used by the Hopi, Arizona's contemporary pueblo dwellers.

The Sinagua, a culture that developed at the same time as the Anasazi, built similar stone pueblos, but most Sinagua pueblos were on hills rather than in the canyons. At the Wupatki ruins, near Flagstaff, there are two unusual stone structures that were built by the Sinagua. One is a ball court similar in many ways to the ball courts of ancient Mexican and Central American cultures. The other unusual building is a low-walled round structure that may have been an amphitheater or large kiva.

Many Hopis still live in pueblos similar to those built by the Sinagua and Anasazi, with stone-walled rooms and round kivas that have ladders sticking through the roof (entrance to a kiva is prohibited to non-Hopis). The *hogan*, the traditional home of the Navajo people, displays a very different type of architecture. Usually built with six sides, hogans are constructed of logs and earth and resemble ancient dwellings of central Asia.

When the Spanish arrived in Arizona, they turned to sun-baked adobe bricks as their primary construction material. Because adobe walls must be made very thick, they provide excellent insulation. Very few adobe homes have survived from territorial days because, when not maintained, adobe quickly decays. The best place to see adobe homes is in Tucson, where several have been preserved in that city's downtown historic districts. However, when the railroads arrived in Arizona, many owners modified their adobe homes by adding slanted roofs, Victorian porches, and even siding. In the Barrio Histórico district of Tucson, town-house architecture characteristic of Sonora, Mexico, has been preserved. These buildings have no front yards but instead have walls right at the sidewalk. This style of architecture was common during the Mexican and early territorial periods of Arizona history.

With only the two mission churches of San Xavier del Bac and Tumacacori, the Spanish did not leave as great an ecclesiastical architectural legacy in Arizona as they did elsewhere in the New World. However, mission-revival architecture has been popular for much of this century. A somewhat idealized concept of the style—with stucco walls, arches, and courtyards—has come to epitomize the ideal of Arizona living.

In the mid-20th century, architect Frank Lloyd Wright established his winter home and school, called Taliesin West, north of Scottsdale, and eventually designed several buildings around the Phoenix area. The architect of the Biltmore Hotel, one of the state's oldest resorts, relied on Wright for assistance in designing the hotel, and the hand of Wright is evident throughout. One of Wright's students, an Italian architect named Paolo Soleri, decided to settle in Arizona and has for many years pursued his dream of building an environmentally sensitive, ideal city in the desert north of Phoenix. He calls this city Arcosanti and has partially financed its construction by selling wind-bells at his Cosanti foundry in Paradise Valley. Arcosanti, the Cosanti foundry, and Taliesin West are all open to the public.

# 8 Recommended Books

**GENERAL**  Few places on earth have inspired as much writing as Arizona's Grand Canyon. John Wesley Powell's *Down the Colorado: Diary of the First Trip Down the Grand Canyon* (E. P. Dutton, 1969), which was first published in 1869, and David Lavendar's *River Runners of the Grand Canyon* (University of Arizona, 1985), an illustrated history of river exploration, provide the explorers' and adventurers' view of the canyon. *The Grand Canyon: Early Impressions* (Pruett, 1989), edited by Paul Schullery, is a collection of first impressions by famous writers including John Muir and Zane Grey. *The Man Who Walked Through Time* (Random House, 1972), by Colin Fletcher, is a narrative of one man's hike through the rugged inner canyon. Even Barry Goldwater, a rather accomplished writer, had his say on the Grand Canyon in his book *Delightful Journey: Down the Green and Colorado Rivers* (Arizona Historical Foundation, 1970). In *Grand Canyon* (Morrow, 1968), Joseph W. Krutch, a brilliant observer of nature, distills his observations of the canyon into expressive prose.

Water rights and human impact on the deserts of the Southwest have raised many controversies this century, none more heated than those centering around the Colorado River. *Cadillac Desert: The American West and Its Disappearing Water* (Penguin, 1993), by Marc Reisner, focuses on the West's insatiable need for water, while *A River No More: The Colorado River and the West* (Knopf, 1981), by Philip L. Fradkin, addresses the fate of just the one river.

The famous Lost Dutchman Mine has inspired at least two books: *Fool's Gold* (Golden West, 1983), by Robert Sihorsky, and *The Treasure of the Superstitions* (Norton, 1973), by Gary Jennings.

*Arizona, A Bicentennial History* (Norton, 1976), by Lawrence Clark Powell, provides a thorough history of the state. *Arizona Memories* (University of Arizona, 1984), edited by Anne H. Morgan and Rennard Strickland, is an engaging collection of historical recollections by cowboys, miners, an Apache scout, a frontier doctor, a soldier's wife, and many other Arizonans. In *Home Is the Desert* (University of Arizona, 1984), Ann Woodin addresses the mental and spiritual development that her family experienced when they moved to the desert outside Tucson. In his book *The Desert Year* (Viking, 1963), naturalist Joseph W. Krutch combines his observations of Arizona's deserts with his own personal philosophical observations. Another book well worth searching out is *Cactus Country* (Time-Life Books, 1973), which is full of beautiful photos of the Sonoran Desert, but is more notable for its text by Edward Abbey, who was one of the desert's most outspoken and controversial supporters. Abbey is well known as a brilliant, though cynical, observer of the desert, and captures its many moods in *Desert Solitaire* (McGraw-Hill, 1968), a nonfiction work based on his time spent in southern Utah's Arches National Monument.

*Southwestern Indian Arts and Crafts, Southwestern Indian Ceremonials,* and *Southwestern Indian Tribes* (all KC Publications) is a trio of softcover books illustrated with color photos by Southwest Native American authority Tom Bahti, and provides an accessible source of information on several aspects of Southwest tribal life. Other books on Arizona's indigenous tribes include *The Navajo* (Harvard University Press, 1974), by Clyde Kluckhohn and Dorothea Leighton; *The People Called Apache* (Prentice-Hall, 1974), by Thomas E. Mails; and *Anasazi: Ancient People of the Rock* (Crown, 1974), with text by Donald G. Pike and photos by David Muench.

**FICTION** Arizona's rugged landscape, colorful history, and rich Native American culture have long served as backdrops for fiction writers. Tony Hillerman is perhaps the best-known contemporary author whose books rely on Arizona settings. Hillerman's murder mysteries are almost all set on the Navajo Reservation in the Four Corners area, and include many references to actual locations that can be seen by visitors to the area. Among Hillerman's Navajo mysteries are *Sacred Clowns, Coyote Waits, Thief of Time, The Blessing Way, Listening Woman,* and *The Ghostway*.

Barbara Kingsolver, a Tucson resident, biologist, and social activist, usually sets her novels either partly or entirely in Arizona. *The Bean Trees, Pigs in Heaven,* and *Animal Dreams* are peopled by Anglo, Indian, and Hispanic characters and their traditions, allowing for a quirky and humorous narrative with social and political overtones that allow insight into the cultural mélange of Arizona. *High Tide in Tucson* (HarperPerennial, 1996), Kingsolver's latest book is not a work of fiction but rather a collection of essays, many of which focus on her life in Tucson.

Edward Abbey's *The Monkey Wrench Gang* and *Hayduke Lives!* are tales of an unlikely gang of "eco-terrorists" determined to preserve the wildernesses of the Southwest. The former book helped inspire the founding of the radical Earth First! movement.

*Laughing Boy* (Buccaneer Books, 1981), by Oliver LaFarge, is a somewhat ideal-ized narrative of Navajo life that won the Pulitzer Prize in 1929. Many novels of pio-neer life in Arizona have been made into popular films. These include *Foxfire* (Houghton, 1950), by Anya Seton, the story of a young woman from the East who moves to Arizona to marry a part-Apache mining engineer, and Henry Will's *Mackenna's Gold* (Random House, 1963), a story of the search for a lost mine in the Arizona mountains.

Zane Grey spent many years living in north-central Arizona and based many of his Western novels on life in this region of the state. Among his books are *Riders of the Purple Sage, West of the Pecos, The Vanishing American, Call of the Canyon, The Arizona Clan,* and *To the Last Man.*

**TRAVEL**   *Arizona Highways* is a monthly magazine published by the Arizona De-partment of Transportation. The magazine has been known for decades for its out-standing photographs and stories on history and attractions.

If you're particularly interested in Native American art and crafts, you may want to search out a copy of *Trading Post Guidebook* (Northland Publishing, 1995) by Patrick Eddington and Susan Makov, which is an invaluable guide to trading posts, artists' studios, galleries, and museums of the Four Corners region.

# 3 Planning a Trip to Arizona

**W**hether you're headed to Arizona to raft the Grand Canyon or play golf in Phoenix, you'll find all the advance-planning answers you need at your fingertips in this chapter—everything from when to go to how to get there.

## 1 Visitor Information & Money

### VISITOR INFORMATION

If you have more questions than we can answer in this book, there are a number of places that may have the answers for you. For state-wide travel information, contact the **Arizona Office of Tourism,** 2702 N. Third St., Suite 4015, Phoenix, AZ 85004 (☎ **800/ 842-8257** or 602/230-7733; fax 602/240-5475). Also keep in mind that every city and town in Arizona has either a tourism office or a chamber of commerce that can provide you with information. See the individual chapters for addresses of these sources.

If you're a member of the **American Automobile Association (AAA),** remember that you can get a map and guidebook covering Arizona and New Mexico. You can also request the club's free *Southwestern CampBook,* which includes campgrounds in Arizona, Utah, Colorado, and New Mexico by calling your local AAA chapter.

### WWW.ARIZONA.COM

Although Yahoo (**http://www.yahoo.com/Recreation/Travel**), Excite (**http://www.excite.com/**), Lycos (**http://www.lycos.com/**), Infoseek (**http://www.infoseek.com/**), and the other major Internet indexing sites all have travel subcategories, one of the best hotlists for travel and destination-specific information in general is Excite's "City.net" (**http://www.city.net/countries/united_states/arizona/**).

The official site for the Arizona Office of Tourism is "ArizonaGuide" (**http://www.arizonaguide.com/**), which, along with plenty of information on the state, also includes links to official city Web sites throughout Arizona. The best one-stop shopping for information on parks, outdoor activities, and the flora and fauna of Arizona is GORP (**http://www.gorp.com/gorp/location/az/ az.htm#attraction**). The Grand Canyon's official site (**http:// www.thecanyon.com/**) includes a trip planner, maps, and just about anything you ever wanted to know about America's most famous national park.

## MONEY

What will a vacation in Arizona cost? That depends on your comfort needs. If you drive an RV or carry a tent, you can get by very inexpensively and find a place to stay almost anywhere in the state. If you don't mind staying in motels that date from the Great Depression and can sleep on a sagging mattress, you can stay for less money in Arizona than almost anyplace else in the United States (under $30 a night for a double). On the other hand, you can easily spend several hundred dollars a day on a room at one of the state's world-class resorts. If you're looking to stay in clean, modern motels at interstate highway off-ramps, expect to pay $45 to $65 a night for a double room in most places.

It's never a problem to find an ATM machine when you're on the road and access your bank account from home. Throughout the state, the Star, Cirrus, Plus, Global Access, Discover Novus, and American Express networks are widely available, so you can get cash as you travel. If you should have trouble finding one, you can call ☎ **800/424-7787** for Cirrus locations or ☎ **800/843-7587** for Plus locations.

But some people still prefer the security of traveler's checks, which are accepted at hotels, motels, restaurants, and most stores. Call American Express (☎ **800/221-7282**) for more information.

## 2 When to Go

Arizona is a year-round destination, though people head to different parts of the state at different times of year. In Phoenix, Tucson, and other parts of the desert, the high season runs from October to mid-May, with the highest hotel rates in effect during January and February. However, up at the Grand Canyon the busy season is during the summer; that's when hotel rates are the highest and crowds are the largest.

The all-around best times to visit are in spring and autumn, when temperatures are cool in the mountains and warm in the desert, but without extremes (although you shouldn't be surprised to get a bit of snow as late as Memorial Day in the mountains and thunderstorms in the desert in August and September). These are also good times to save money, because summer rates are in effect at the desert resorts and the crowds aren't as dense at the Grand Canyon. This time period sometimes also coincides with the spring wildflower season, which begins in mid-spring and extends until April and May, when the tops of saguaro cacti become covered with waxy white blooms.

If for some reason you happen to be visiting the desert in August, be prepared for sudden thunderstorms. These storms often cause flash floods that make many roads in the state briefly impassable. Road signs warning motorists not to enter low areas when flooded are meant to be taken very seriously.

## CLIMATE

The first thing you should know is that the desert can be cold as well as hot. Although winter is the prime tourist season in Phoenix and Tucson, night temperatures can be below freezing, and days can even be too cold for sunning or swimming. However, on the whole, winters in Arizona are positively delightful.

In the winter, sun seekers flock to the deserts, where temperatures average in the high 60s by day. In the summer, when desert temperatures are topping 110°F, the mountains of eastern and northern Arizona are pleasantly warm with daytime averages in the low 80s. Yuma is one of the desert communities where winter temperatures are the highest in the state, and Prescott and Sierra Vista, in the 4,000- to 6,000-foot elevation range, are two cities that claim to have among the best climates in the world—not too cold, not too hot.

The accompanying climate charts will give you an idea of the state's climatic diversity.

### Phoenix's Average Temperatures (°F) & Days of Rain

|  | Jan | Feb | Mar | Apr | May | June | July | Aug | Sept | Oct | Nov | Dec |
|---|---|---|---|---|---|---|---|---|---|---|---|---|
| Avg. High | 65 | 69 | 75 | 84 | 93 | 102 | 105 | 102 | 98 | 88 | 75 | 66 |
| Avg. Low | 38 | 41 | 45 | 52 | 60 | 68 | 78 | 76 | 69 | 57 | 45 | 39 |
| Days of Rain | 4 | 4 | 3 | 2 | 1 | 1 | 4 | 5 | 3 | 3 | 2 | 4 |

### Flagstaff's Average Temperatures (°F) & Days of Rain

|  | Jan | Feb | Mar | Apr | May | June | July | Aug | Sept | Oct | Nov | Dec |
|---|---|---|---|---|---|---|---|---|---|---|---|---|
| Avg. High | 41 | 44 | 48 | 57 | 67 | 76 | 81 | 78 | 74 | 63 | 51 | 43 |
| Avg. Low | 14 | 17 | 20 | 27 | 34 | 40 | 50 | 49 | 41 | 31 | 22 | 16 |
| Days of Rain | 7 | 6 | 8 | 6 | 3 | 3 | 12 | 11 | 6 | 5 | 5 | 6 |

## ARIZONA CALENDAR OF EVENTS

January

- **Fiesta Bowl Football Classic,** Sun Devil Stadium, Tempe. College football classic. For information, call ☎ 602/350-0900. January 1 or 2.
- **Phoenix Open Golf Tournament,** Phoenix. Prestigious PGA golf tournament at the Tournament Players Club. Phone ☎ 602/870-0163 for details. Mid- to late January.
- **Wings Over Willcox,** Willcox. Birding tours, workshops, and of course watching the sandill cranes at the Willcox sewage recycling ponds. Call ☎ 520/384-2272 for details. Third weekend in January.
- **Parada del Sol Parade and Rodeo,** Scottsdale. The state's longest horse-drawn parade, plus a street dance and rodeo. For more information, call ☎ 800/877-1117 or 602/990-3179. Late January.

February

- **Indian Arts Benefit Fair,** Old Town Artisans, Tucson. Craft sales and entertainment. For more information, phone ☎ 520/623-6024. Early February.
- **Tubac Festival of the Arts,** Tubac. Exhibits by North American artists and craftspeople. For more information, call ☎ 520/398-3269. Early February.
- **Arizona Renaissance Festival,** Apache Junction. This 16th-century English country fair has costumed participants and includes tournament jousting. Phone ☎ 602/463-2700 for details. Weekends from early February to March.
- **Flagstaff Winterfest.** Sled-dog races, sleigh rides, music and dance performances. For details, call ☎ 800/842-7293 or 520/774-4505. Early to mid-February.
- **Tucson Gem and Mineral Show.** This huge show at the Tucson Convention Center offers seminars, museum displays from around the world, and dealers selling just about any kind of rock you can imagine. For details, call ☎ 520/322-5773. Mid-February.
- **Tucson Chrysler Classic.** A major stop on the golf tour, held at the Omni Tucson National Golf Resort and Spa. Call ☎ 800/882-7660 for information. Mid- to late February.
- **O'odham Tash,** Casa Grande. Tohono O'odham tribal festival featuring rodeos, crafts shows, and dance performances. For details, call ☎ 520/836-4723. Mid-February.
- **All-Arabian Horse Show,** Scottsdale's Westworld. A celebration of the Arabian horse. For additional information, call ☎ 602/951-1180. Mid-February.

- **Tucson Rodeo Parade,** Tucson Rodeo Grounds. The world's largest non-motorized parade. Phone ☎ **520/741-2233** for information. Late February.
- **La Fiesta de los Vaqueros,** Tucson. Cowboy festival and rodeo at the Tucson Rodeo Grounds. Call ☎ **520/741-2233** for details. Late February.

March

- **Territorial Days,** Tombstone. Tombstone's birthday celebration. For more information, call ☎ **800/457-3423.** First weekend in March.
- **Heard Museum Guild Indian Fair,** Phoenix. Showcase of Native American arts and heritage, with more than 200 artists displaying their work. Call ☎ **602/252-8840** for details. First weekend in March.
- **Wa:k Pow Wow,** Tucson. Tohono O'odham celebration at Mission San Xavier del Bac featuring many Southwestern Native American groups. Call ☎ **520/294-5727** for more information. Early March.
- **Scottsdale Arts Festival,** Scottsdale Mall. This visual and performing arts festival has free concerts, an art show, and children's events. For more information, phone ☎ **602/994-ARTS.** Second weekend in March.
- **Chandler Ostrich Festival,** Chandler. Live country and big-band music, Irish and Hispanic entertainment, and, of course, ostrich races. For more details, call ☎ **602/963-4571.** Early to mid-March.
- **Phoenix Jaycee's Rodeo of Rodeos,** Arizona State Fairgrounds. One of the biggest and most popular indoor rodeos in the world. Call ☎ **602/263-8671** for more information. Mid-March.
- **Yaqui Easter Lenten Ceremony,** Tucson. Religious ceremonies at Old Pasqua Village blending Christian and Yaqui Native American beliefs. For further information, phone ☎ **520/791-4609.** Holy Week.
- **Spring Festival of the Arts,** Tempe. This large arts and entertainment festival features local and traveling artists and artisans along Mill Avenue. For details, phone ☎ **602/967-4877.** Late March to early April.

April

- **The Tradition,** Phoenix. This Senior PGA tournament at Cochise Course at Desert Mountain hosts the big names. Call ☎ **602/595-4070** for more information. Early April.
- **Tucson International Mariachi Conference.** Mariachi bands from all over the world come to compete. Call ☎ **520/884-9920,** ext. 243, for more information. Mid- to late April.
- **CIGNA Healthcare Celebrity Tennis Classic,** Tucson. One of the largest celebrity tennis events in the United States, held at the Randolph Tennis Center. Phone ☎ **520/623-6165** for more information. Mid- to late April.
- **Waila Festival,** Tucson. A Tohono O'odham festival at the Arizona Historical Society, featuring "chicken scratch" music, a kind of polka. Call ☎ **520/628-5774** for more information. Late April.
- **Maricopa County Fair,** Phoenix. The Arizona State Fairgrounds host a midway, agricultural and livestock exhibits, and entertainment. For details, phone ☎ **602/252-0717.** Late April.
- **La Vuelta de Bisbee,** Bisbee. A bicycle race among top cyclists around the hills of this historic mining town. Phone ☎ **520/432-5421** for information. Late April.

May

- **Cinco de Mayo,** Tucson, Phoenix, and other cities. Celebration of the Mexican victory over the French in a famous 1862 battle, complete with food, music, and dancing. Call ☎ **602/262-5025** for details on the festivities in Phoenix; call

☎ **520/623-8344** for more information on the celebration in Tucson's Kennedy Park. Around May 5.

- **Hopi Tu-Tootsvolla,** Uptown Sedona. The celebration features food prepared by Hopi elders and a rare opportunity to see the Hopi dances. Phone ☎ **520/282-6428** for details. Mid-May.
- **Phippen Western Art Show and Sale,** Prescott. This is the premier Western art sale. For more information, call ☎ **520/778-1385.** Memorial Day weekend.
- **Wyatt Earp Days,** Tombstone. Gunfight reenactments in memory of the shoot-out at the O.K. Corral. Call ☎ **800/457-3423** for further details. Memorial Day weekend.
- **A Celebration of Native American Art,** Flagstaff. Native American market, dances, and art exhibition at the Museum of Northern Arizona. For details, phone ☎ **520/774-5213.** May to September.
- **Sedona Chamber Music Festival,** Sedona. Chamber music is performed by companies from around the world at various venues. Phone ☎ **520/526-2256** for details. Late May to early June.

## June

- **Route 66 Festival,** Flagstaff. This carnival, car show, and more, centers around the theme of historic Route 66. For additional information, call ☎ **800/842-7293** or 520/774-9541. Early June.
- **Summerset Suite,** Tucson. Open-air jazz concerts. For details, call the Tucson Jazz Society at ☎ **520/743-3399.** Saturdays in June.

## July

- **Independence Day.** In Phoenix, the fireworks display is near the state capitol, accompanied by entertainment. For information, call ☎ **602/495-5490.** In Tucson, there are fireworks at the convention center downtown. Call ☎ **520/791-2601** for information. July 4.
- **Prescott Frontier Days,** Prescott. This is the oldest rodeo in the United States. Phone ☎ **800/266-7534** or 520/445-3103 for details. First week of July.
- **Annual Hopi Artists Exhibition,** Flagstaff. Exhibition and sale at the Museum of Northern Arizona. Call ☎ **520/774-5211** for more details. First weekend in July.
- **Annual Navajo Artists Exhibition,** Flagstaff. Exhibition and sale at the Museum of Northern Arizona. For details, call ☎ **520/774-5211.** Last weekend in July or first weekend in August.
- **Flagstaff Festival of the Arts,** Flagstaff. Multiday festival featuring musical performances including a Broadway musical, pops concert, and a performance for children. For more information, call ☎ **800/266-7740** or 520/774-7750. Late July to early August.

## August

- **Cowboy Poets,** Prescott. Not just traditional and contemporary poetry, but yodeling and storytelling that centers around the cowboy lifestyle. For more information, call ☎ **520/445-3122.** Mid-August.
- **Payson Rodeo,** Payson. The second of Arizona's rodeos claiming to be the world's oldest. For details, call ☎ **800/672-9766** or 520/474-4515. Mid-August.
- **La Fiesta de San Agustín,** Tucson. Celebration at the Arizona Historical Society to honor the patron saint of Tucson. For more information, phone ☎ **520/628-5774.** Late August.

## September

- **Navajo Nation Fair,** Window Rock. A rodeo, dances, a parade, and food. Call ☎ **520/871-6702** for more information. Early September.

- **Mexican Independence Day.** In Phoenix, this is celebrated as the **Fiesta Patrias,** at the Civic Plaza. For details, call ☎ **602/255-0980.** Tucson's celebration, with folkloric dances and food, is held in Kennedy Park. For more information, phone ☎ **520/623-8344.** Mid-September.
- **Scottsdale Center for the Arts Annual Gala.** Jazz, ballet, music, art exhibits, and special events. Phone ☎ **602/994-ARTS** for further information. Late September.
- **Jazz on the Rocks,** Sedona. Open-air jazz festival. For details, call ☎ **602/282-1985.** Late September.
- **State Championship Old Time Fiddler's Contest,** Payson. Fiddlers from around Arizona try their best to out-fiddle each other, along with clogging and buck dancing. For details, call ☎ **520/474-3398.** Late September.

October

- **Coors Rodeo Showdown,** Phoenix. Top rodeo stars compete in this world finals rodeo at the America West Arena. For details, call ☎ **602/379-7800.** Early to mid-October.
- **Sedona Arts Festival,** Sedona. One of the best arts festivals in the state. For additional information, phone ☎ **800/288-7336** or 520/204-9456. Mid-October.
- **Tucson Heritage Experience Festival (THE).** A celebration in El Presidio Park of Tucson's ethnic diversity. Phone ☎ **520/888-8816** for details. Mid-October.
- **Tucson Blues Festival.** Local, regional, and national blues masters perform in Reid Park. Call ☎ **520/791-4079** for more details. Mid-October.
- **Arizona State Fair,** Phoenix. This shindig at the Arizona State Fairgrounds features rodeos, top-name entertainment, and ethnic food. Phone ☎ **602/252-6771** for more information. Mid- to late October.
- **Fiesta de los Chiles,** Tucson. Lots of hot chiles, crafts, and music at the Botanical Gardens. For more information, call ☎ **520/326-9686.** Mid- to late October.
- **Annual Cowboy Artists of America Exhibition,** Phoenix. The Phoenix Art Museum hosts the most prestigious and best-known Western art show in the region. For details, call ☎ **602/257-1222.** Late October to late November.
- **Desert Botanical Garden Landscape Plant Sale,** Phoenix. The Desert Botanical Garden puts on a display and sells a variety of desert plants during blooming season. Call ☎ **602/941-1225** for information. Late October (and late March).
- **Helldorado Days,** Tombstone. Fashion show of 1880s clothing, tribal dancers, and street entertainment. Call ☎ **800/457-3423** for details. Mid-October.

November

- **Hot Air Balloon Race and Thunderbird Balloon Classic,** Scottsdale. More than 100 hot-air balloons fill the Arizona sky. Call ☎ **602/978-7208** for details. Early November.
- **Western Music Festival,** Tucson. Concerts and workshops by Western music performers. Phone ☎ **520/825-6621** for details. Mid-November.
- **Indian Arts Show and Benefit,** Tucson. Handcrafts and entertainment at Old Town Artisans. For more information, phone ☎ **520/623-6024.** Mid- to late November.

December

- **Fall Festival of the Arts,** Tempe. Hundreds of artists and artisans, featuring free entertainment and plenty of food, set up along Mill Avenue. For additional information, call ☎ **602/967-4877.** Early December.
- **Luminária Nights,** Tucson. A glowing display of holiday lights at the Botanical Gardens. For details, call ☎ **520/326-9686.** Early December.
- **Fourth Avenue Street Fair,** Tucson. Outdoor arts-and-crafts festival. Phone ☎ **520/624-5004** for more information. Mid-December.

- **Fiesta de Guadalupe,** Tucson. Celebration of Mexico's patron saint. For further information, call ☎ **520/299-9192.** Early December.
- **Fiesta Bowl Events,** Phoenix area. All manner of sports competitions, parades, and cultural events. Phone ☎ **602/350-0900** for more information. All month.
- **Festival of Lights,** Sedona. Thousands of *luminarias* are lit at dusk at the Tlaquepaque Arts and Crafts Village. For details, call ☎ **800/288-7336** or 520/282-4838. Mid-December.
- **Las Posadas,** Tucson. A tradition from Mexico in which children reenact Joseph and Mary's search for an inn; occurs at the Carillo School and half-a-dozen churches. Phone ☎ **520/617-6600** for details. Mid-December.

# 3  The Active Vacation Planner

Arizona is known the world over for active, adventure-oriented vacations for the sole reason that the state is home to the Grand Canyon—the most widely known white-water-rafting spot in the world. For others, Arizona is synonymous with winter golf and tennis. Whichever category of active vacationer you fall into, you'll find information below to help you arrange your trip to Arizona.

**BIKING**    With its wide range of climates, Arizona offers good biking somewhere in the state every month of the year. In the winter there's good road biking around Phoenix and Tucson, while from spring through fall, the southeastern corner of the state offers some good routes. Also in the summer, the White Mountains in the eastern part of the state and Kaibab National Forest between Flagstaff and Grand Canyon National Park offer good mountain biking. There is also excellent mountain biking at several Phoenix parks, and Tucson is one of the most bicycle-friendly cities in the country. **Backroads,** 801 Cedar St., Berkeley, CA 94710-1800 (☎ **800/462-2848** or 510/527-1555), offers a 5-day, inn-to-inn mountain-bike trip through the red-rock country of central Arizona.

Mountain-bike trips are also offered by **Arizona Offroad Adventures,** P.O. Box 3339, Tucson, AZ 85722 (☎ **800/689-BIKE** or 520/882-6567), which does 2- to 5-day trips with both camping and hotels for accommodations. Experience levels vary from beginner to extreme. This company also does half-day and full-day trips.

**BIRD WATCHING**    Arizona is a birder's bonanza. Down in the southeastern corner of the state, many species found primarily south of the border reach the northern limits of their territories. Combine this with several mountains that rise up like islands from out of the desert and provide an appropriate habitat for hundreds of species and you have some of the best bird watching in the country. Birding hot spots include Ramsey Canyon Preserve (known for its many species of hummingbirds), Cave Creek Canyon (nesting site for elegant trogons), Patagonia-Sonoita Creek Sanctuary (home to 22 species of flycatchers, kingbirds, and phoebes, as well as Montezuma quails), Madera Canyon (another "mountain island" that attracts many of the same species seen at Ramsey Canyon and Sonoita Creek), Buenos Aires National Wildlife Refuge (home to masked bobwhite quail and gray hawks), and the sewage ponds outside the town of Willcox (known for its avocets and sandhill cranes).

**FISHING**    The fishing scene in Arizona is as diverse as the landscape. Large and small lakes around the state offer excellent fishing for warm-water game fish such as largemouth, smallmouth, and striped bass, while up on the Mogollon Rim and in the White Mountains there is good trout fishing. There's also good trout fishing in the Grand Canyon, and the more easily accessible sections of the free-running Colorado River between Glen Canyon Dam and Lees Ferry.

Fishing licenses for nonresidents are available for 1 day, 5 days, 4 months, and 1 year. There are also various special stamps and licenses that may apply. Nonresident fishing-license prices range from $8 for a 1-day license to $18.50 for a 5-day license. Also keep in mind that if you're heading for an Indian reservation, you'll have to get a special permit for that reservation. For more information, contact the **Arizona Game and Fish Department,** 2221 W. Greenway Rd., Phoenix, AZ 85023-4312 (☎ **602/942-3000**).

**GOLF**   For many of Arizona's winter visitors, golf is the main reason to visit the state. The state's hundreds of golf courses range from easy public courses to PGA championship links that have challenged the best.

In Phoenix and Tucson, greens fees, like room rates, are seasonal. In the popular winter months, fees at resort courses range from $90 to $150 for 18 holes, though this usually includes a mandatory golf-cart rental. In the summer months fees often drop to less than half this amount. Almost all resorts also offer special golf packages as well.

For information on some of the state's top courses, see "Hot Links," the special golf feature in this chapter.

For more information on golfing in Arizona, contact the **Arizona Golf Association,** 7226 N. 16th St., Suite 200, Phoenix, AZ 85020 (☎ **800/458-8484** or 602/944-3035), which publishes a directory ($10) listing all the courses in the state. You can also contact *Golf Arizona,* 15704 Cholla Dr., Fountain Hills, AZ 85268 (☎ **800/942-5444**), which publishes a guide to where to play golf in Arizona.

**HIKING/BACKPACKING**   Despite its reputation as a desert state, a large percentage of Arizona is forestland, and within these forests are wilderness areas and countless miles of hiking trails. In northern Arizona, there are good day hikes in Grand Canyon National Park, in the San Francisco Peaks north of Flagstaff, outside Page (near Lake Powell), and in Navajo National Monument. In the Phoenix area, popular day hikes include the trails up Camelback Mountain and Squaw Peak and the many trails in South Mountain Park. In the Tucson area, there are good hikes on Mount Lemmon and in Saguaro National Park, Sabino Canyon, and Catalina State Park. In the southern part of the state, there are good day hikes in Chiricahua National Monument, Coronado National Forest, in the Nature Conservancy's Ramsey Canyon Preserve and Patagonia-Sonoita Creek Sanctuary, in Cochise Stronghold, and in Organ Pipe National Monument. See the individual chapters for details on these areas.

Among the state's two most popular overnight backpack trips are the hike down to Phantom Ranch and the hike into Havasu Canyon, a side canyon of the Grand Canyon. Another popular multiday backpack trip is through Paria Canyon, beginning in Utah and ending in Arizona at Lees Ferry. There are also backpacking opportunities in the San Francisco Peaks north of Flagstaff and in the White Mountains of eastern Arizona.

Guided backpack trips of various durations and levels of difficulty are offered by the **Grand Canyon Field Institute,** P.O. Box 399, Grand Canyon, AZ 86023 (☎ **520/638-2485**). **Backroads,** 801 Cedar St., Berkeley, CA 94710-1800 (☎ **800/462-2848** or 510/527-1555), better known for its bike trips, also offers a 6-day walking/hiking trip in Arizona.

**HORSEBACK RIDING/WESTERN ADVENTURES**   All over Arizona there are stables where you can saddle up for short rides. Among the more scenic spots for riding are the Grand Canyon, Monument Valley Navajo Tribal Park, Canyon de Chelly National Monument, the red-rock country around Sedona, Phoenix's South

Mountain Park, at the foot of the Superstition Mountains east of Phoenix, and at the foot of the Santa Catalina Mountains outside Tucson. See the individual chapters for listings of riding stables; see below for information on overnight guided horseback rides.

Ranch vacations are also immensely popular in the state, and Arizona boasts many outstanding guest ranches accommodating visitors of all riding abilities. For more information you can contact the **Arizona Dude Ranch Association,** Box 603, Cortaro, AZ 85652 or contact the **Arizona Office of Tourism,** 2702 N. Third St., Suite 4015, Phoenix, AZ 85004 (☎ **800/842-8257** or 602/230-7733; fax 602/240-5475) for brochures. We chose our favorites in chapter 1, "The Best of Arizona."

Among the most popular guided adventures in Arizona are the mule rides down into the Grand Canyon. These trips vary in length from 1 to 3 days; for more information, contact **Grand Canyon National Park Lodges,** Reservations Department, P.O. Box 699, Grand Canyon, AZ 86023 (☎ **520/638-2631**). If you want to go on a mule trip within 4 days, this is the number to call for a reservation. If you want to make reservations farther in advance, call ☎ **303/297-2757.**

It's also possible to do overnight horseback rides and cattle drives. For more information, contact **Don Donnelly Stables,** 6010 S. Kings Ranch Rd., Gold Canyon, AZ 85219 (☎ **800/346-4403** or 602/982-7822), which does overnight horseback trips in Monument Valley, the White Mountains, and the Superstition Mountains among other places; **Arizona Trail Tours,** P.O. Box 1218, Patagonia, AZ 85624 (☎ **520/394-2701**), which offers a 4-day trip through Coronado National Forest in southern Arizona; or **Rocky Mt. Cattle Moo-vers,** 8100 W. Tangerine Rd., Marana, AZ 85653 (☎ **800/826-9666** or 520/682-2088), which does day-long cattle drives and offers overnight accommodations in teepees.

**HOT-AIR BALLOONING**   For much of the year the desert provides the perfect environment for hot-air ballooning—cool, still air and wide-open spaces. Consequently, there are dozens of hot-air–balloon companies operating across the state. Most are found in the Phoenix and Tucson areas, but several others operate near Sedona, which is by far the most picturesque spot in the state for a balloon ride. See the individual chapters for specific information.

**HOUSEBOATING**   With the Colorado River turned into a long string of lakes, houseboat vacations are a natural in Arizona. Though this doesn't have to be an active vacation, fishing, hiking, and swimming are usually part of a houseboat vacation. Rentals are available on Lake Powell, Lake Mead, Lake Mohave, and Lake Havasu. However, the canyon lands scenery of Lake Powell makes it the hands-down best spot for a houseboat vacation—reserve well in advance for a summer trip. No prior experience (or license) is necessary, and plenty of hands-on instruction is provided before you leave the marina. See chapters 7 and 12 for more information on houseboat rentals.

**RAFTING**   The desert doesn't support a lot of roaring rivers, but with the white water in the Grand Canyon you don't need too many other choices. Day-long white-water-rafting trips are available on the upper Salt River and more leisurely inner-tube floats are popular on the lower Salt River. Plenty of waterproof sunscreen is a must for either of these trips. See below and in chapter 7 for further discussion on rafting and lists of rafting companies.

**ROCK CLIMBING**   With views down to Tucson far below, the climbs on Mount Lemmon are among the most popular in the state. Another climbing hot spot is to be found just outside Prescott, where huge granite boulders provide plenty of great climbs. Though hot, the Superstition Mountains also offer some climbing

## The Arizona Trail

While it sounds as though it could have been a movie starring John Wayne, the Arizona Trail is actually an ambitious plan to build a border-to-border trail across the state of Arizona from Utah to Mexico. The trail, which will link together many existing trails, will be open to nonmotorized travel only. Hikers, mountain bikers, horseback riders, and cross-country skiers will all be able to enjoy various sections of the trail, which will at times cross through designated wilderness areas (closed to mountain bikes).

Connecting alpine meadows and desert arroyos, free-flowing rivers and man-made reservoirs, ponderosa pine forests and stands of saguaros, the 750-mile-long trail will cross through the seven life zones and many landscapes that comprise Arizona. As it meanders across the state, the trail will take in some of the most spectacular scenery in the Southwest, including the Grand Canyon, the San Francisco Peaks, the Mogollon Rim, and the Santa Catalina Mountains.

For more information, contact the **Arizona Trail Association,** P.O. Box 36736, Phoenix, AZ 85067 (☎ **602/252-4794;** fax 602/952-1447; Web site: http://www.primenet.com/?aztrail).

opportunities, as do many of the state's other remote and rugged desert mountain ranges. To learn more about rock-climbing spots in Arizona or to find some partners for a climb, contact the **Arizona Mountaineering Club** (☎ **602/817-0271**).

If you're interested in learning some rock-climbing techniques or want to do some guided mountaineering or canyon exploring, contact **Ascend Guide Services,** 1911 W. Cheryl Dr., Phoenix, AZ 85021 (☎ **800/2-ASCEND** or 602/861-2513); **Venture Up,** 2415 E. Indian School Rd., Phoenix, AZ 85016 (☎ **602/955-9100**); or **Wilderness Adventures,** P.O. Box 63282, Phoenix, AZ 85082 (☎ **800/462-5788** or 602/949-2774).

**SKIING**   Although Arizona is better known as a desert state, it does have plenty of mountains and even a few ski areas. The two biggest and most popular ski areas are **Arizona Snowbowl** (☎ **800/828-7285** or 520/779-1951) outside Flagstaff and **Sunrise Park** (☎ **800/772-SNOW** or 520/735-7600) on the Apache reservation outside the town of McNary in the White Mountains. Snowbowl is the more popular because of the ease of the drive from Phoenix and its proximity to good lodging and dining options in Flagstaff. When it's a good snow year, Tucsonans head up to **Mount Lemmon Ski Valley** (☎ **520/576-1400**), the southernmost ski area in the United States. Snows here aren't as reliable as they are farther north. One last ski hill, the **Williams Ski Area** (☎ **520/635-9330**), is located just outside Williams. Although Arizona Snowbowl has more vertical feet of skiing, Sunrise offers almost twice as many runs and the same snow conditions. All of these ski areas offer ski rentals and lessons.

Cross-country skiers will find plenty of snow-covered forest roads to ski around Flagstaff (there's a Nordic center at Arizona Snowbowl), at the South Rim of the Grand Canyon, in the White Mountains around Greer and Alpine, outside Payson on the Mogollon Rim, and on Mount Lemmon outside Flagstaff.

However, the state's premier cross-country ski area is the **North Rim of the Grand Canyon,** which during the winter months is accessible only on skis or by snow van. Aside from snow camping, the only way to see this area in winter is to stay at the

## Hot Links

You don't have to be a hotshot golfer to get all heated up over the prospect of a few rounds of golf in Arizona. Combine near-perfect golf weather with great views, and some very unique challenges, and you've got all the makings of a great game. Phoenix and Tucson are well known as winter golf destinations, but the state also offers golf throughout the year at higher-altitude courses in such places as Prescott, Flagstaff, and the White Mountains.

State legislation aimed at conserving water now limits golf courses in Arizona to no more than 90 acres of irrigated land, far less than is found on most traditional golf courses. This legislation has not only conserved both water and the desert—it's given the state some of the most distinctive and difficult courses in the country. These desert or "target" courses are characterized by minimal fairways surrounded by natural desert landscapes. You might find yourself teeing off over the tops of cacti and searching for your ball amid boulders and mesquite (actual encounters with rattlesnakes are few). If your ball comes to lie in the desert, you can play the ball where it lies or drop the ball within two club lengths of the nearest point of grass, but no nearer the hole, with a one-stroke penalty.

Keep in mind that resort courses are not cheap. For most of the year, greens fees, which include golf-cart rentals, range from around $90 to $130 or more. Greens fees at semiprivate clubs are often about the same as at resort courses. Public courses, on the other hand, offer very reasonable greens fees of as low as $20 for 18 holes, with golf-cart rental costing extra (around $16).

You may not think so at first, but summer is really a good time to visit many of Arizona's golf resorts. Why? No, they don't have air-conditioned golf carts or indoor courses. It's because in summer greens fees can be less than half what they are in winter. How does $28 for a round on the famous Gold Course at The Wigwam Resort sound? Plus, most resorts charge next to nothing for rooms in the summer (and those rooms *do* have air-conditioning).

With more golf courses per capita than any other state—more than 250 in all—Arizona is a golfer's paradise. Now the only problem is choosing where you'd like to play.

The Phoenix/Scottsdale area, known as the Valley of the Sun, has the greatest concentration of golf courses in the state. Whether you're looking to play one of the area's challenging top-rated resort courses or an economical-but-fun municipal course, you'll find plenty of choices.

For spectacular scenery at a resort course, it's just plain impossible to beat **The Boulders** (☎ **800/553-1717**), located north of Scottsdale in the town of Carefree. Elevated tee boxes beside giant balanced boulders are enough to distract anyone's concentration. Way over on the east side of the valley in Apache Junction, the **Gold Canyon Golf Club** (☎ **602/982-9090**) has what have been rated as three of the best holes in the state (the 11th, 12th, and 13th). Jumping over to Litchfield Park, on the far west side of the valley, you'll find the **Wigwam Golf and Country Club** (☎ **602/935-9414**) and its three 18-hole courses; the Gold Course here is legendary. Other noteworthy resort courses in the area include the

**North Rim Nordic Center at Kaibab Lodge,** Canyoneers Inc., P.O. Box 2997, Flagstaff, AZ 86003 (☎ **800/525-0924** or 520/526-0924). The nordic center is located just outside the national park. In addition to miles of trails and guide trips,

links at **The Phoenician** (☎ 800/888-8234), mixing traditional and desert-style holes. This course has recently undergone expansion. The **Hyatt Regency Scottsdale Resort at Gainey Ranch** (☎ 602/951-0022) offers three decidedly different nine-hole courses (the Dunes, the Arroyo, and the Lakes courses), each with its own set of challenges.

The area's favorite public course is the **Papago Golf Course** (☎ 602/275-8428), which has a killer 17th hole. The semiprivate **Troon North Golf Club** (☎ 602/585-5300), however, a course that seems only barely carved out of raw desert, garners the most local accolades. If you want to swing where the pros do, beg, borrow, or steal a tee time on the Stadium Course at the **Tournament Players Club of Scottsdale** (☎ 602/585-3600). The **Superstition Springs Golf Club** (☎ 602/962-GOLF) is another popular course and also a PGA Tour qualifying site.

With nearly 40 courses, Tucson has been giving the Valley of the Sun some golf competition in recent years. Among the city's resort courses, the Mountain Course at the **Ventana Canyon Golf and Racquet Club** (☎ 520/577-1400) is legendary and has been ranked among Arizona's top 10 by *Golf Digest.* A spectacular 107-yard par-3 hole here is the most talked-about hole in the city. If you want to play where the pros play, book a room at the **Omni Tucson National Golf Resort and Spa** (☎ 520/575-7540), home of the Tucson Chrysler Classic. The eighth hole at the Sunrise Course of the **Sheraton El Conquistador Resort and Country Club** (☎ 520/544-1800) has been rated the toughest par 3 in Tucson.

Of Tucson's public courses, **Randolph North** (☎ 520/325-2811) gets the nod for best municipal course and is the site of an annual LPGA tournament. The **Silverbell Municipal Course** (☎ 520/743-7284 or 520/791-4336) boasts a bear of a par-5 17th hole. The **Starr Pass Golf Club** (☎ 520/670-0400) has been garnering a lot of praise the past few years and in the past co-hosted the Northern Telecom Open; the 15th hole is the signature hole here and plays through a narrow pass once used by stagecoaches.

Courses worth trying in other parts of the state include the 18-hole course at **Rancho de los Caballeros** (☎ 602/684-5484), a luxury ranch resort outside Wickenburg. *Golf Digest* has rated its course one of Arizona's top 10. For concentration-taxing scenery, there are few courses to compare with the **Sedona Golf Resort** (☎ 520/284-9355), which is surrounded by red-rock cliffs; try this course at sunset. In mile-high Prescott, the **Antelope Hills Golf Club** (☎ 800/972-6818 or 520/776-7888) offers two 18-hole courses that provide a respite from the summer heat in the lowlands. Even higher and cooler in summer, the **Alpine Country Club** (☎ 520/339-4944) offers golfing among the pine trees of the White Mountains. South of Tucson near Nogales, the **Rio Rico Resort and Country Club** (☎ 800/288-4746) offers a challenging back nine as well as cooler temperatures and lower greens fees than you'll find in Tucson.

*One last tip:* If your ball should happen to land in the coils of a rattlesnake, consider it lost and take your penalty. Rattlesnakes make lousy tees.

the lodge offers an overnight yurt trip. Rates start at $295 for a 2-night package that includes all meals, lodging, transportation from Jacob Lake, guided tours, and ski lessons.

**TENNIS** Resorts all over Arizona have tennis courts; after golf, this is the most popular winter sport in the desert. Many resorts require you to wear traditional tennis attire and don't include court time in the room rates. Although there may be better courts in the state, none can match the views you'll have from the courts at Enchantment Resort outside Sedona. Just don't let the scenery ruin your game.

**WHITE-WATER RAFTING** Rafting the Grand Canyon is the dream of nearly every white-water enthusiast. For a discussion and list of companies that run trips down the canyon, see chapter 7. For 1- and 2-day trips on the Colorado below the Grand Canyon, contact **Hualapai River Runners,** P.O. Box 246, Peach Springs, AZ 86434 (☎ **800/622-4409** or 520/769-2210). For a half- or full-day float on the Colorado above the Grand Canyon, contact **Wilderness River Adventures,** P.O. Box 717, Page, AZ 86040 (☎ **800/992-8022** or 520/645-3279), which runs its trips from the Glen Canyon Dam to Lees Ferry. **Sun Country Rafting** (☎ **800/ 2-PADDLE** or 602/493-9011); **Far Flung Adventures** (☎ **800/359-2627** or 602/ 425-7272); and **Desert Voyagers** (☎ **800/222-RAFT** or 602/998-RAFT) all run trips of varying lengths down the Upper Salt River (conditions permitting).

# 4 Educational & Volunteer Vacations

A number of opportunities exist in Arizona for those wishing to combine a vacation with an educational or volunteer experience.

If you'd like to turn a trip to the Grand Canyon into an educational vacation, contact the **Grand Canyon Field Institute,** P.O. Box 399, Grand Canyon, AZ 86023 (☎ **520/638-2485**), which offers a variety of programs from rim-based day hikes to backpacking to indoor classes. Programs are offered from early spring to late fall and include photography classes, programs on Native American history and culture, hands-on archaeology programs, birding trips, and plenty of guided hikes and backpacking trips.

The **Nature Conservancy,** 300 E. University Blvd., Suite 230, Tucson, AZ 85705 (☎ **520/622-3861**), is a nonprofit organization dedicated to the global preservation of natural diversity. It does this by identifying and purchasing land that is home to rare plants, animals, and natural communities. The organization has several preserves in Arizona, seven of which are open to the public for hiking, bird-watching, and nature study and to which they operate educational field trips of 1 to 4 days. Trips are listed in the Conservancy's Arizona chapter newsletter; information about overnight accommodations, trips, and membership ($25 annually) is also available by phone.

If you enjoy the wilderness and want to get more involved in preserving it, consider a Sierra Club Service Trip. These trips are for the purpose of building, restoring, and maintaining hiking trails in wilderness areas. It's a lot of work, but it's also a lot of fun. For more information on Sierra Club trips, contact the **Sierra Club Outing Department,** 85 Second St., Second Floor, San Francisco, CA 94105 (☎ **415/977-5630**). The Sierra Club also offers hiking, camping, and other sorts of adventure trips to various destinations in Arizona.

Another sort of service trip is being offered by the National Park Service. It accepts volunteers to pick up garbage left by thoughtless visitors to Glen Canyon National Recreation Area. In exchange for picking up trash, you'll get to spend 5 days on a houseboat called the *Trash Tracker,* cruising the gorgeous canyon lands scenery of Lake Powell. Volunteers must be at least 18 years old, and must provide their own food, sleeping bag, and transportation to the marina. For more information, contact **Glen Canyon National Recreation Area,** P.O. Box 1507, Page, AZ 86040 (☎ **520/ 608-6206**).

## Impressions

*From the hygienic point of view, whiskey and cold lead are mentioned as the leading diseases at Tombstone.*

—A Tombstone visitor in the 1880s

If you'd like to lend a hand at an archaeological dig, contact the **White Mountain Archaeological Center and Raven Site Ruin,** H.C. 30, Box 30, St. Johns, AZ 85936 (☎ **520/333-5857**), which is located near Springerville on the edge of the White Mountains.

Older travelers who want to learn something from their trip to Arizona or who simply prefer the company of like-minded older travelers should look into programs by **Elderhostel,** 75 Federal St., Boston, MA 02110-1941 (☎ **617/426-7788**). Elderhostel offers educational programs throughout the United States and in 50 other countries. To participate in an Elderhostel program, either you or your spouse must be at least 55 years old.

# 5  Health & Insurance

**STAYING HEALTHY**   If you've never been to the desert before, you should be sure to prepare yourself for this harsh environment. No matter what time of year it is, the desert sun is strong and bright. Use sunscreen when you're outdoors— particularly if you're up in the mountains, where the altitude makes sunburn more likely. The bright sun also makes sunglasses a necessity.

Even if you don't feel hot in the desert, the dry air still steals moisture from your body, so drink plenty of fluids. You may want to use a body lotion as well. The desert air dries out skin quickly.

It's not only the sun that makes the desert a harsh environment. There are poisonous creatures out there too, but with a little common sense and some precautions you can avoid them. Rattlesnakes are very common in the desert, but your chances of meeting one are slight (except during the mating season in April and May) because they tend not to come out in the heat of the day. However, never stick your hand into holes among the rocks in the desert, and look to see where you're going to step before putting your foot down.

Arizona also has a large poisonous lizard called the Gila monster. These black-and-orange lizards are far less common than rattlesnakes, and your chances of meeting one are slight.

Although the tarantula has developed a nasty reputation, the tiny black widow is more likely to cause illness. Scorpions are another insect danger of the desert. Be extra careful whenever turning over rocks or logs that might harbor either black widows or scorpions.

**INSURANCE**   Before going out and spending money on various sorts of travel insurance, check your existing policies to see if they'll cover you while you're traveling. Make sure your health insurance will cover you when you're away from home. Most credit and charge cards offer automatic flight insurance when you purchase an airline ticket with that card. These policies insure against death or dismemberment in the case of an airplane crash. Also, check your cards to see if any of them pick up the loss-damage waiver (LDW) when you rent a car. The LDW can run as much as $15 a day and can add 50% or more to the cost of renting a car. Check your automobile insurance policy too; it might cover the LDW as well. If you own a home or have renter's insurance, see if that policy covers off-premises theft and loss wherever it occurs. If you're traveling on a tour or have prepaid a large chunk of your travel expenses, you might want to ask your travel agent about trip-cancellation insurance.

If, after checking all your existing insurance policies, you decide that you need additional insurance, a good travel agent can give you information on a variety of different options. **Travelex,** P.O. Box 9408, Garden City, NY 11530-9408 (☎ **800/ 228-9792**), offers several different types of travel insurance policies for 1 day to 6 months. These policies include medical, baggage, trip-cancellation or interruption insurance, and flight insurance against death or dismemberment.

# 6 Tips for Travelers with Special Needs

**FOR TRAVELERS WITH DISABILITIES**   When making airline reservations, always mention your disability. Airline policies differ regarding wheelchairs and seeing-eye dogs. Most hotels now offer wheelchair-accessible accommodations, and some of the larger and more expensive resorts also offer TDD telephones and other amenities for the hearing and sight impaired.

If you plan to visit many of Arizona's national parks or monuments, you can avail yourself of the **Golden Access Passport.** This lifetime pass is issued free to any U.S. citizen or permanent resident who has been medically certified as disabled or blind. The pass permits free entry into national parks and monuments.

Rick Crowder of the **Travelin' Talk Network,** P.O. Box 3534, Clarksville, TN 37043-3534 (☎ **615/552-6670** Monday through Friday between noon and 5pm central time), organizes a network for disabled travelers. A directory listing people and organizations around the world who are networked to provide the disabled traveler with firsthand information about a chosen destination is available for $35.

**FOR GAY MEN & LESBIANS**   To get in touch with the Phoenix gay community, you can contact the **Gay and Lesbian Community Center,** 3136 N. Third Ave. (☎ **602/265-7283**). At the community center and at gay bars around Phoenix, you can pick up various community publications, including *Echo* and *Women's Center, Inc.* **Wingspan,** Tucson's lesbian, gay, and bisexual community center, is at 422 N. Fourth Ave. (☎ **520/624-1779**). *Observer* (☎ **520/622-7176**) is a local Tucson gay newspaper available at Wingspan and Antigone Bookstore a few doors down.

**FOR SENIORS**   When making airline reservations, always mention that you're a senior citizen—many airlines offer discounts. You should also carry some sort of photo ID card (driver's license, passport, etc.) to avail yourself of senior-citizen discounts on attractions, hotels, motels, and public transportation, as well as one of the best deals in Arizona for senior citizens: the **Golden Age Passport,** which is available for $10 to U.S. citizens and permanent residents age 62 and older. This federal government pass allows lifetime entrance privileges. You can apply in person for this passport at a national park, national forest, or other location where it's honored, and you must show reasonable proof of age.

If you aren't a member of the **American Association of Retired Persons (AARP),** 601 E. St. NW, Washington, DC 20077-1214 (☎ **800/424-3410**), you should consider joining. This association provides discounts at many lodgings and attractions throughout Arizona, although you can sometimes get a similar discount simply by showing your ID.

If you'd like to do a bit of studying on vacation, consider **Elderhostel** (see "Educational & Volunteer Vacations," earlier in this chapter).

Phoenix and the Valley of the Sun have long been popular with retirees. Over the years entire cities (such as Sun City) have developed for senior citizens. *Arizona*

*Senior World Newspaper* (☎ 602/438-1566) is a monthly newspaper with information relevant to senior citizens. You can find it in supermarkets and convenience stores.

## 7 Getting There

### BY PLANE

Arizona is served by many airlines flying to both Phoenix and Tucson from around the United States. Dozens of car-rental companies are located both at Sky Harbor International Airport in Phoenix and at Tucson International Airport.

Phoenix and Tucson are both served by the following airlines: **Aero México** (☎ 800/237-6639), **America West** (☎ 800/235-9292), **American** (☎ 800/433-7300), **Continental** (☎ 800/525-0280), **Delta** (☎ 800/221-1212), **Northwest** (☎ 800/225-2525), **Southwest** (☎ 800/435-9792), and **United** (☎ 800/241-6522). The following airlines serve Phoenix but not Tucson: **Alaska Airlines** (☎ 800/426-0333), **TWA** (☎ 800/221-2000), and **US Airways** (☎ 800/428-4322).

If you're searching for a great deal, you may be able to fly for less than the standard fare by contacting a **ticket broker** (also known as a bucket shop). These companies advertise in the Sunday travel sections of major city newspapers with small ads listing numerous destinations and ticket prices. You won't always be able to get the low price they advertise, but you're likely to save a bit of money off the regular fare. Call a few and compare prices, making sure you find out about all the taxes and surcharges that may not be included in the initial fare quote. In general, the more restrictions there are attached to an airfare, the lower it will be. However, when an airline runs a special deal, you won't always do better at the ticket brokers.

For last-minute bookings, contact **A Better Airfare** (☎ 800/FLY-ASAP or 800/454-7700), which can often get you tickets at significantly less than full fare.

### BY CAR

The distance to Phoenix from Los Angeles is approximately 369 miles; from San Francisco, 778 miles; from Albuquerque, 455 miles; from Salt Lake City, 660 miles; from Las Vegas, 287 miles; and from Santa Fe, 516 miles.

If you're planning to travel through northern Arizona anytime in the winter, carry chains.

### BY TRAIN

Flagstaff and Phoenix have **Amtrak** (☎ 800/872-7245 in the United States and Canada for information and reservations) service from Los Angeles to the west and Albuquerque, Santa Fe, Kansas City, and Chicago to the east aboard the *Southwest Chief.* The *Sunset Limited* connects Miami, New Orleans, Houston, San Antonio, El Paso, and Los Angeles with Tucson and Phoenix. The train stops in Flagstaff or Tucson, and passengers must take a shuttle bus to Phoenix. At press time, the fare from Los Angeles to Phoenix was $92 to $124 one way and $108 to $234 round trip. This trip, including shuttle bus, takes between 11 and 12 hours. Lower fares are possible depending on availability; that is, earlier bookings mean better discounts.

### PACKAGE TOURS

If you prefer to let someone else do all your travel preparations, then a package tour might be for you—whether you just want to lie by the pool at a resort for a week or see the whole state in 2 weeks. The best way to find out about package tours to Arizona is to visit a travel agent, who will likely have several booklets about different tours and airfare/hotel-room packages being offered by different airlines.

**Gray Line of Phoenix,** P.O. Box 21126, Phoenix, AZ 85036 (☎ **800/732-0327** or 602/495-9100), offers Arizona excursions lasting from 1 to 5 days. Tours include the Grand Canyon by way of Sedona and Oak Creek Canyon; and a canyon-lands tour that includes the Grand Canyon and Lake Powell, with stops in Utah and at Las Vegas.

**Maupintour,** 1515 St. Andrews Dr., Lawrence, KS 66047 (☎ **800/255-4266** or 913/843-1211), one of the largest tour operators in the world, offers several Arizona itineraries that cover the Grand Canyon, the Four Corners region, Phoenix, and Scottsdale.

Smaller companies offering similar tours include **Open Road Tours** (☎ **800/766-7117** or 602/997-6474) and **Silver Coach Tours** (☎ **800/607-3466** or 602/439-0337).

**SPECIALTY TOURS**    If you have an interest in the Native American cultures of Arizona, you may want to consider doing a tour with **Discovery Passages,** 1161 Elk Trail, Box 630, Prescott, AZ 86303 (☎ **520/717-0519**), which offers tours that visit the Hopi, Navajo, Apache, Tohono O'odham, Hualapai, Yavapai, and Havasupai. **Crossing Worlds,** P.O. Box 171, Young, AZ 85554 (☎ **800/350-2693** or 520/462-3356 in Young or 520/282-7148 in Sedona), a small company operating out of the remote town of Young, also offers 1-day and multiday tours throughout the Four Corners region. Tours go to the Hopi mesas, as well as back-country ruins on the Navajo Reservation to view cliff dwellings and rock art.

**Canyon Calling Tours,** 215 Disney Lane, Sedona, AZ 86336 (☎ **800/664-8922** or 520/282-0916), offers week-long tours of the Four Corners region for women only. These tours visit Canyon de Chelly, Lake Powell, the Grand Canyon, and even Havasu Canyon. The price for this tour is $1,495 per person.

If you'd like to add a tour into Mexico to your Arizona visit, contact **Ajo Stage Line,** 1041 Solana Rd., Ajo, AZ 85321 (☎ **800/942-1981** or 520/387-6467). Owner Will Nelson leads 1-day and multiday trips to the Gulf of California at Puerto Peñasco, to 17th-century missions in northern Mexico, and to the rugged El Pinacate region of the Sonoran Desert. Prices range from $60 to $395.

# 8  Getting Around

## BY CAR

Remember that this is a big state, and distances are large. For driving distances between cities in Arizona, see the "Arizona Driving Times & Distances" map in this chapter.

Because Phoenix and Tucson are major resort destinations, they both have dozens of **car-rental agencies.** Prices at rental agencies elsewhere in the state tend to be higher, so if at all possible, try to rent your car in either Phoenix or Tucson. Major rental-car companies with offices in Arizona include **Alamo** (☎ 800/327-9633), **Avis** (☎ 800/331-1212), **Budget** (☎ 800/527-0700), **Dollar** (☎ 800/800-4000), **Enterprise** (☎ 800/325-8007), **Hertz** (☎ 800/654-3131), **National** (☎ 800/227-7368), and **Thrifty** (☎ 800/367-2277).

Rates for rental cars vary considerably between companies and with the model you wish to rent, the dates you rent, and your pickup and drop-off points. If you call the same company three times and ask about renting the same model car, you may get three different quotes, depending on the company's current availability of vehicles. It pays to start shopping early and ask lots of questions—rental agents don't always volunteer information about how to save, so you have to experiment with all the

# Arizona Driving Times & Distances

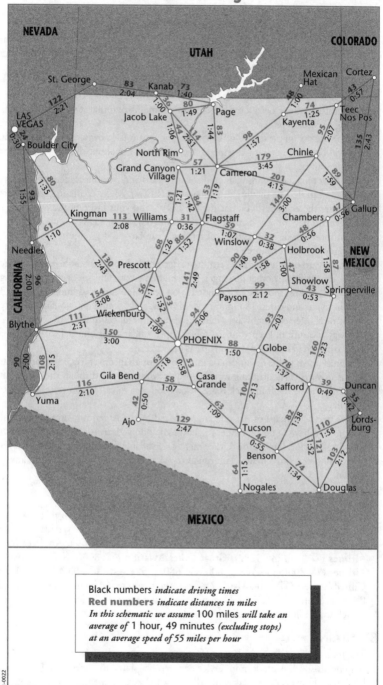

Black numbers *indicate driving times*
Red numbers *indicate distances in miles*
*In this schematic we assume* 100 miles *will take an average of* 1 hour, 49 minutes *(excluding stops) at an average speed of 55 miles per hour*

parameters. At press time, Budget was charging $160 per week or $34 per day for a compact car with unlimited mileage in Phoenix.

If you're a member of a frequent-flyer program, check to see which rental-car companies participate in the program. Also, when making a reservation be sure to mention any discount you might be eligible for, such as corporate, military, or AAA, and any specials offered. Beware of coupons offering discounts on rental-car rates—often these discount the highest rates only. It's always cheaper to rent by the week, so even if you don't need a car for 7 days, you might find that it's still cheaper than renting for 4 days only.

The state tax on car rentals is 9.55%, so if you want to know what your total rental cost will be before making a reservation, be sure to ask about the tax and the loss-damage waiver.

*One last tip:* Check with your credit/charge-card and auto-insurance companies to see if you can decline the loss-damage waiver (LDW). Many credit and charge cards now cover the charges if you decline the LDW, and your insurance may already be sufficient to pay for any damage you do to the rental car. LDW insurance can add $15 or more per day to the price of renting a car, so you'll save quite a bit if you're renting for a week or more.

A right turn on a red light is permitted after a complete stop. Seat belts are required for the driver and any other passenger, and children 4 years and younger, or who weigh 40 pounds or less, must be in a children's car seat. General speed limits are 25 to 35 mph in towns and cities, 15 mph in school zones, and 55 mph on two-lane highways, except rural interstate highways where the speed limit ranges from 65 to 75 mph.

Always be sure to keep your gas tank topped off. It's not unusual for it to be 60 miles between gas stations in many parts of Arizona.

A breakdown in the desert can be more than just an inconvenience—it can be dangerous. Always carry drinking water with you while driving through the desert, and if you plan to head off on back roads, it's a good idea to carry extra water for the car as well.

The best road maps of Arizona are produced by the American Automobile Association (you have to be a member to get these) and by *Arizona Highways* (☎ **800/543-5432**), a local magazine. Other maps are available from tourist information offices in Phoenix and Tucson. You can also pick up state road maps at almost any gas station.

## BY PLANE

Arizona is a big state (the sixth largest), so if your time is short, you might want to consider flying between cities. Several small commuter airlines offer service within the state. These include **Air Nevada Airlines** (☎ 800/634-6377), **America West Airlines** (☎ 800/235-9292), **Great Lakes Aviation** (☎ 800/274-0662), **Scenic Airlines** (☎ 800/535-4448 or 800/634-6801), **Skywest** (☎ 800/453-9417), and **United Express** (☎ 800/241-6522). Cities and towns served by these airlines include Phoenix, Scottsdale, Tucson, Flagstaff, the Grand Canyon, Sedona, Showlow, Fort Huachuca, Bullhead City, Lake Havasu City, Yuma, and Page.

## BY TRAIN

The train is not really a viable way of getting around much of Arizona because there is no north-south Amtrak train service between Flagstaff and Phoenix or Tucson and Phoenix. However, Amtrak will sell you a ticket to Phoenix, which includes a shuttlebus ride from Flagstaff or Tucson. There's also an excursion train that runs from Williams (30 miles west of Flagstaff) to Grand Canyon Village at the South Rim of the Grand Canyon (see chapter 7 for details).

## FAST FACTS: Arizona

**American Express**   There are offices or representatives in Phoenix, Tucson, Green Valley, Flagstaff, Sun City, and Scottsdale. For more information, call American Express at ☎ **800/528-4800.**

**Banks and ATM Networks**   ATMs in Arizona generally use the following systems: Star, Cirrus, Plus, Global Access, Discover Novus, and American Express.

**Bed-and-Breakfasts**   **Mi Casa-Su Casa,** P.O. Box 950, Tempe, AZ 85280-0950 (☎ **800/456-0682** or 602/990-0682), is a reservation service that can book accommodations at more than 65 homes in the Valley of the Sun (as well as elsewhere in the state). Rates range from $50 to $200 for a double room, depending on the location and luxury of the home. The **Arizona Association of Bed and Breakfast Inns,** P.O. Box 7186, Phoenix, AZ 85011 (☎ **800/284-2589**), is another organization representing B&Bs across the state. Contact it for a list of members. **Bed and Breakfast Inn Arizona,** 13802 N. Scottsdale Rd., Suite 104–87, Scottsdale, AZ 85254 (☎ **800/266-STAY** or 602/368-9250; Web site http://bnbreservations.com), represents B&Bs all over the state and charges between $80 and $300 for a double in the high season.

**Business Hours**   The following are general open hours; specific establishments may vary. **Banks:** Monday through Friday from 9am to 5pm (some are also open on Saturday from 9am to noon). **Stores:** Monday through Saturday from 10am to 6pm and on Sunday from noon to 5pm (malls usually stay open until 9pm Monday through Saturday). **Bars:** Although they generally open around 11am, bars in Arizona are legally allowed to be open Monday through Saturday from 6am to 1am and on Sunday from 10am to 1am.

**Camera/Film**   Because the sun is almost always shining in Arizona, you can use a slower film—that is, one with a lower ASA number. This will give you sharper pictures. If your camera accepts different filters, and especially if you plan to travel in the higher altitudes of the northern part of the state, you'd do well to invest in a polarizer, which reduces contrast, deepens colors, and eliminates glare. Also, be sure to protect your camera and film from heat. Never leave your camera or film in a car parked in the sun—temperatures inside the car can climb to more than 130°F, which is plenty hot enough to damage sensitive film.

**Car Rentals**   See "Getting Around," earlier in this chapter.

**Climate**   See "When to Go," earlier in this chapter.

**Driving Rules**   See "Getting Around," earlier in this chapter.

**Emergencies**   Throughout Arizona, ☎ **911** is the number to call in case of a fire, police, or medical emergency.

**Fruits, Vegetables, and Live Plants**   Because Arizona is one of the main citrus-growing states in the United States, there are restrictions on what fruits, vegetables, and live plants can be brought into the state. These restrictions are designed to protect local crops from imported insects and plant diseases and apply primarily to citrus fruits, but other plant matter may also be confiscated. If you'd like to find out more about restrictions, phone ☎ **602/255-4933.**

**Information**    See "Visitor Information" in section 1 of this chapter, and individual city chapters and sections for local information offices.

**Legal Aid**    If you're in need of legal aid, first look in the white pages of the local telephone book under "Legal Aid." You may also want to contact the Travelers Aid Society, which may also be found in the white pages. In Phoenix, the phone number for Community Legal Services is ☎ 602/258-3434. In Tucson, the number for Southern Arizona Legal Aid is ☎ 800/248-6789 or 520/623-9465, and for Travelers Aid of Tucson it's ☎ 520/622-8900.

**Liquor Laws**    The legal age for buying or consuming alcoholic beverages is 21. You cannot purchase any alcoholic drinks from 1 to 6am Monday through Saturday and from 1 to 10am on Sunday.

**Pets**    Many hotels and motels in Arizona accept pets, though there is sometimes a small fee charged to allow the pet to stay in your room. Others don't allow pets at all, especially bed-and-breakfast inns. If you plan to travel with a pet, it's always best to check when making hotel reservations. At Grand Canyon Village, there's a kennel where you can board your pet while you hike down into the canyon.

**Police**    In most places in Arizona, phone ☎ 911. A few small towns have not adopted this emergency phone number, so if 911 doesn't work, dial 0 (zero) for the operator and state the type of emergency.

**Safety**    When driving long distances, always carry plenty of drinking water, and if you're heading off onto dirt roads, extra water for your car's radiator is also a good idea. When hiking or walking in the desert, keep an eye out for rattlesnakes; these poisonous snakes are not normally aggressive unless provoked, so give them a wide berth and they'll leave you alone. Black widow spiders and scorpions are also desert denizens that can be dangerous, though the better-known tarantula is actually much less of a threat. If you go turning over rocks or logs, you're likely to encounter one of Arizona's poisonous residents.

**Taxes**    There's a state sales tax of 5% (local communities levy additional taxes), a car-rental tax ranging from 5% in Tucson to 9.55% in Phoenix, and hotel room taxes ranging from around 6% to around 14%.

**Time Zone**    Arizona is in the mountain time zone. However, the state does *not* observe daylight saving time, and so time differences between Arizona and the rest of the country vary with the time of year. From the last Sunday in October until the first Sunday in April, Arizona is 1 hour later than the West Coast and 2 hours earlier than the East Coast. The rest of the year Arizona is on the same time as the West Coast and is 3 hours earlier than the East Coast. There is an exception, however—the Navajo Reservation observes daylight saving time. However, the Hopi Reservation, which is completely surrounded by the Navajo Reservation, does not.

**Weather**    For current weather information, call ☎ 602/265-5550.

# For Foreign Visitors 4

The American West is well known and well loved in many countries. Arizona's images are familiar from Western novels, movies, television shows, and advertisements. And of course, the Grand Canyon is one of the wonders of the world. However, despite Arizona's being the Wild West, there will likely be typically American situations that you'll encounter in Arizona, and this chapter should help you prepare for your trip.

## 1 Preparing for Your Trip

### ENTRY REQUIREMENTS

**DOCUMENT REGULATIONS**    Canadian citizens may enter the United States without visas; they need only proof of residence.

British subjects and citizens of New Zealand, Japan, and most Western European countries traveling on valid passports may not need a visa for less than 90 days of holiday or business travel to the United States, providing that they hold a round-trip or return ticket and enter the country on an airline or cruise line participating in the visa-waiver program.

(Note that citizens of these visa-exempt countries who first enter the United States may then visit Mexico, Canada, Bermuda, and/or the Caribbean islands and then reenter the United States, by any mode of transportation, without needing a visa. Further information is available from any U.S. embassy or consulate.)

Citizens of countries other than those stipulated above, including citizens of Australia, must have two documents: (1) a valid passport, with an expiration date at least 6 months later than the scheduled end of the visit to the United States; and (2) a tourist visa, available without charge from the nearest U.S. consulate.

To obtain a visa, the traveler must submit a completed application form (either in person or by mail) with a 1 1/2-inch-square photo and demonstrate binding ties to a residence abroad.

Usually you can obtain a visa at once or within 24 hours, but it may take longer during the summer rush from June to August. If you cannot go in person, contact the nearest U.S. embassy or consulate for directions on applying by mail. Your travel agent or airline office may also be able to provide you with visa applications and instructions. The U.S. consulate or embassy that issues your visa will determine whether you will be issued a multiple- or single-entry visa and any restrictions regarding the length of your stay.

**MEDICAL REQUIREMENTS**   No inoculations are needed to enter the United States unless you're coming from, or have stopped over in, areas known to be suffering from epidemics, especially of cholera or yellow fever.

If you have a disease requiring treatment with medications containing narcotics or drugs requiring a syringe, carry a valid signed prescription from your physician to allay any suspicions that you're smuggling drugs.

**CUSTOMS REQUIREMENTS**   Every adult visitor may bring in free of duty: 1 liter of wine or hard liquor; 200 cigarettes *or* 100 cigars (but no cigars from Cuba) *or* 3 pounds of smoking tobacco; and $100 worth of gifts. These exemptions are offered to travelers who spend at least 72 hours in the United States and who have not claimed them within the preceding 6 months. It's altogether forbidden to bring into the country foodstuffs (particularly cheese, fruit, cooked meats, and canned goods) and plants (vegetables, seeds, tropical plants, and so on). Foreign tourists may bring in or take out up to $10,000 in U.S. or foreign currency with no formalities; larger sums must be declared to Customs on entering or leaving the country.

## INSURANCE

There is no national health-care system in the United States. Because the cost of medical care is extremely high, we strongly advise every traveler to secure health insurance coverage before setting out. You may want to take out a comprehensive travel policy that covers (for a relatively low premium) sickness or injury costs (medical, surgical, and hospital); loss or theft of your baggage; trip-cancellation costs; guarantee of bail in case you are arrested; and costs associated with accident, repatriation, or death.

Packages such as "Europe Assistance Worldwide Services" in Europe are sold by automobile clubs and travel agencies at attractive rates. **Travel Assistance International** (TAI; ☎ **800/821-2828** or 202/331-1609) is the agent for Europ Assistance Worldwide Services, so holders of this company's policies can contact TAI for assistance while in the United States.

Canadians should check with their provincial health scheme offices or call **HealthCanada** (☎ **613/957-3025**) to find out the extent of their coverage and what documentation and receipts they must take home in case they are treated in the United States.

## MONEY

**CURRENCY & EXCHANGE**   The U.S. monetary system has a decimal base: one American **dollar** ($1) = 100 **cents** (100¢).

Dollar bills commonly come in $1 ("a buck"), $5, $10, $20, $50, and $100 denominations (the last two are not welcome when paying for small purchases and are not accepted in taxis). There are also $2 bills (seldom encountered).

There are six denominations of coins: 1¢ (one cent, or a "penny"), 5¢ (five cents, or a "nickel"), 10¢ (ten cents, or a "dime"), 25¢ (twenty-five cents, or a "quarter"), 50¢ (fifty cents, or a "half dollar"), and the rare $1 piece.

The foreign-exchange bureaus so common in Europe are rare even at airports in the United States, and nonexistent outside major cities. Try to avoid having to change foreign money, or traveler's checks not denominated in U.S. dollars, at a small-town bank, or even a branch bank in a big city. In fact, leave any currency other than U.S. dollars at home—it may prove more nuisance to you than it's worth.

**CREDIT & CHARGE CARDS** The method of payment most widely used is credit and charge cards: Visa (BarclayCard in Britain), MasterCard (EuroCard in Europe, Access in Britain, Chargex in Canada), American Express, Diners Club, Discover, and Carte Blanche. You can save yourself trouble by using plastic rather than cash or traveler's checks in most hotels, motels, restaurants, and retail stores (most food and liquor stores now accept credit/charge cards). You must have a credit or charge card to rent a car. It can also be used as proof of identity (it often carries more weight than a passport) or as a cash card, enabling you to draw money from banks and automated-teller machines (ATMs) that accept it.

**TRAVELER'S CHECKS** Traveler's checks *denominated in U.S. dollars* are readily accepted at most hotels, motels, restaurants, and large stores, but may not be accepted at small stores or for small purchases. The best place to change traveler's checks is at a bank. Do not bring traveler's checks denominated in other currencies.

## SAFETY

**GENERAL** While tourist areas are generally safe, crime is on the increase everywhere, and U.S. urban areas tend to be less safe than those in Europe or Japan. Visitors should always stay alert. This is particularly true in large U.S. cities. Avoid deserted areas, especially at night. Don't go into any city park at night unless there is an event that attracts crowds. Generally speaking, you can feel safe in areas where there are many people and many open establishments.

Remember also that hotels are open to the public, and in a large hotel, security may not be able to screen everyone entering. Always lock your room door—don't assume that once inside your hotel you are automatically safe and no longer need be aware of your surroundings.

You may wish to contact the tourist information bureau in Phoenix or Tucson, or the Arizona state tourism office, before you arrive. They may be able to provide you with safety information. Contact information for those offices are: **Phoenix and Valley of the Sun Convention and Visitors Bureau,** One Arizona Center, 400 E. Van Buren St., Suite 600, Phoenix, AZ 85004-2290 (☎ **602/254-6500**); **Metropolitan Tucson Convention and Visitors Bureau,** 130 S. Scott Ave., Tucson, AZ 85701 (☎ **800/638-8350** or 520/624-1817); or the **Arizona Office of Tourism,** 2702 N. Third St., Suite 4015, Phoenix, AZ 85004 (☎ **800/842-8257** or 602/230-7733; fax 602/240-5475).

**DRIVING** Safety while driving is particularly important. Question your rental agency about personal safety, or ask for a brochure of traveler safety tips when you pick up your car. Obtain from the agency written directions, or a map with the route marked in red, to show you how to get to your destination. If possible, arrive and depart during daylight hours.

Recently more and more crime has involved cars and drivers. If you drive off a highway into a doubtful neighborhood, leave the area as quickly as possible. If you have an accident, even on the highway, stay in your car with the doors locked until you assess the situation or until the police arrive. If you are bumped from behind on the street or are involved in a minor accident with no injuries, and the situation appears to be suspicious, motion to the other driver to follow you to the nearest police precinct, gas station, or open store. *Never* get out of your car in such situations.

If you see someone on the road who indicates a need for help, *don't stop.* Take note of the location, drive on to a well-lit area, and telephone the police by dialing 911.

Park in well-lit, well-traveled areas if possible. Always keep your car doors locked, whether the vehicle is attended or unattended. Look around you before you get out of your car, and never leave any packages or valuables in sight. If someone attempts to rob you or steal your car, do *not* try to resist the thief/carjacker—report the incident to the police department immediately.

Also, make sure that you have enough gasoline in your tank to reach your intended destination, so that you're not forced to look for a service station in an unfamiliar and possibly unsafe neighborhood—especially at night.

## 2   Getting to the U.S.

Travelers from overseas can take advantage of the **APEX (advance-purchase excursion)** fares offered by the major U.S. and European carriers. Aside from these, attractive values are offered by Virgin Atlantic Airways (☎ **01/293-74-77-47** in the United Kingdom) from London to New York/Newark, where you can easily connect with a domestic flight heading to Arizona.

Airlines with direct or connecting service from London to Phoenix (along with their phone numbers in Great Britain) include **American** (☎ 0181/572-5555), **British Airways** (☎ 0345/345-757), **Continental** (☎ 012/9377-6464 in London), **Delta** (☎ 0800/414-767), **Northwest** (☎ 0990/56-1000), **TWA** (☎ 01293/439-0707), and **United** (☎ 0181/990-9900 in London, or 0800/888-555 outside London). All of these airlines except British Airways and TWA also fly into Tucson.

From Canada there are flights to Phoenix from Toronto on **American, Delta, Northwest, United,** and **US Airways,** and from Vancouver on **Alaska Airlines** (☎ 800/426-0333), **United** (☎ 800/241-6522), and **America West** (☎ 800/235-9292). There are flights to Tucson from Toronto on **American, Continental,** and **Delta,** and from Vancouver on **America West, Delta,** and **Reno Air.**

From New Zealand and Australia, there are flights to Los Angeles on **Qantas** (☎ 131211 in Australia) and **Air New Zealand** (☎ 0800/737-000 in Auckland, or 3/379-5200 in Christchurch). Continue on to Phoenix or Tucson on a regional airline such as **America West** or **Southwest.** If you're heading to the Grand Canyon, it's easier to take a flight from Los Angeles to Las Vegas.

The visitor arriving by air, no matter what the port of entry, should cultivate patience before setting foot on U.S. soil. Getting through Immigration control may take as long as 2 hours on some days, especially summer weekends. Add the time it takes to clear Customs and you'll see that you should make very generous allowance for delay in planning connections between international and domestic flights—an average of 2 to 3 hours at least.

In contrast, travelers arriving by car or by rail from Canada will find border-crossing formalities streamlined practically to the vanishing point. And air travelers from Canada, Bermuda, and some places in the Caribbean can sometimes go through Customs and Immigration at the point of departure, which is much quicker.

## 3   Getting Around the U.S.

For information specific to travel to and around Arizona, see "Getting There" and "Getting Around" in chapter 3.

**BY PLANE**   Some large airlines (for example, **American, Delta, Northwest, TWA,** and **United**) offer travelers on their transatlantic and transpacific flights special discount tickets under the name **Visit USA,** allowing travel between any U.S. destinations at minimum rates. These tickets are not on sale in the United States—they must be purchased before you leave home. This system is the best, easiest, and fastest way to see the United States at low cost. You should obtain information well in advance from your travel agent or the office of the airline concerned, since the conditions attached to these discount tickets can be changed without advance notice.

**BY CAR**  The United States is a car culture through and through. Driving is the most cost-effective, convenient, and comfortable way to travel through the West. The Interstate highway system connects cities and towns all over the country, and in addition to these high-speed, limited-access roadways, there's an extensive network of federal, state, and local highways and roads. Driving will give you a lot of flexibility in making, and altering, your itinerary and allowing you to see some off-the-beaten-path destinations that cannot be reached easily by public transportation. You'll also gain easy access to inexpensive motels at Interstate highway off-ramps.

**BY TRAIN**  Long-distance trains in the United States are operated by **Amtrak** (☎ 800/872-7245), the national rail passenger corporation. International visitors can buy a **USA Railpass,** good for 15 or 30 days of unlimited nationwide travel on Amtrak. The pass is available through many foreign travel agents and at any staffed Amtrak station in the U.S. The price at press time for a 15-day peak-period pass was $375, and for a 15-day off-peak-period pass $260; a 30-day peak-period pass cost $480, and a 30-day off-peak-period pass was $350. (With a foreign passport, you can also buy passes at major Amtrak offices in the United States, including locations in San Francisco, Los Angeles, Chicago, New York, Miami, Boston, and Washington, D.C.) Reservations are generally required and should be made for each part of your trip as early as possible. Amtrak also offers an **Air/Rail Travel Plan** that allows you to travel both by train and plane; for information call ☎ **800/321-8684.**

Visitors should be aware of the limitations of long-distance rail travel in the United States. Service is rarely up to European standards: delays are common, routes are limited and often infrequently served, and fares are rarely significantly lower than discount airfares. Thus, cross-country train travel should be approached with caution. See "Getting Around" in chapter 3 for specific information on Amtrak service in Arizona.

**BY BUS**  One of the cheapest ways to travel in the United States is by bus. **Greyhound** (☎ 800/231-2222), the nationwide bus line, offers an **Ameripass** for unlimited travel. At press time, a 7-day pass was $179, a 15-day pass was $289, a 30-day pass was $399, and a 60-day pass was $599. Bus travel in the United States can be both slow and uncomfortable, so this option is not for everyone.

## FAST FACTS: For the Foreign Traveler

**Accommodations**  It's always a good idea to make hotel reservations as soon as you know the dates of your travel. To make a reservation, you'll usually need to leave a deposit of 1 night's payment, which can be charged to your credit card and applied to your total bill when you check out. Some of the major hotels listed in this book maintain overseas reservation networks and can be booked either directly or through travel agents.

Phoenix, Scottsdale, and Tucson are particularly busy during winter, and hotels book up in advance. The Grand Canyon is busy all year. If you want to stay at one of the lodges in Grand Canyon National Park, you should reserve at least a year in advance. Also, because distances in Arizona are so great (it might be 60 miles or more to the next town), it's crucial to have a room reservation before heading off to remote yet very popular sections of the state such as the Four Corners region. If you don't have a reservation, it's best to look for a room in the midafternoon. If you wait until later in the evening you run the risk that all the hotels will be full.

In the United States, major downtown hotels, which cater primarily to business travelers, commonly offer weekend discounts of as much as 50% to entice vacationers to fill up the empty hotel rooms. However, resorts and hotels near tourist attractions tend to have higher rates on weekends.

Hotel room rates in most of Arizona tend to go up in winter when there's a greater demand. If you want to save money and don't mind the heat, consider visiting in another season. The really unbearable temperatures usually don't hit until mid-May and are over by the end of September.

**Automobile Organizations**    Auto clubs will supply maps, suggested routes, guidebooks, accident and bail-bond insurance, and emergency road service. The major auto club in the United States, with 955 offices nationwide, is the **American Automobile Association (AAA).** Members of some foreign auto clubs have reciprocal arrangements with the AAA and enjoy its services at no charge. If you belong to an auto club in your home country, inquire about AAA reciprocity before you leave. If your driver's license isn't in English, check with your foreign auto club to see if they can provide you with an **International Driving Permit** validating your foreign license in the United States. You may be able to join the AAA even if you're not a member of a reciprocal club. To inquire, call ☎ **800/AAA-HELP.** In addition, some automobile rental agencies now provide these services, so you should inquire about their availability when you rent your car.

**Automobile Rentals**    To rent a car you need a major credit or charge card and a valid driver's license. Sometimes a passport or an international driver's license is also required if your driver's license is in a language other than English. You usually need to be at least 25 years of age, although some companies do rent to younger people (they may add a daily surcharge). Be sure to return your car with the same amount of gasoline you started out with, as rental companies charge excessive prices for gas. Keep in mind that a separate motorcycle driver's license is required in most states. See "Getting Around" in chapter 3 for specifics on auto rental in Arizona.

**Business Hours**    The following are general open hours; specific establishments may vary. **Banks:** Monday through Friday from 9am to 5pm (some are also open on Saturday from 9am to noon); there's usually 24-hour access to ATMs at most banks and other outlets. **Stores:** Monday through Saturday from 10am to 6pm and on Sunday from noon to 5pm (malls usually stay open until 9pm Monday through Saturday). **Bars:** Although they generally open around 11am, bars in Arizona are legally allowed to be open Monday through Saturday from 6am to 1am and on Sunday from 10am to 1am.

**Climate**    See "When to Go," in chapter 3.

**Currency**    See "Preparing for Your Trip," earlier in this chapter.

**Currency Exchange**    You'll find currency-exchange services in major airports with international service (there's a Thomas Cook office (☎ **800/287-7362**) that offers this service at Sky Harbor Airport in Phoenix, but not at Tucson International Airport). Elsewhere, they may be quite difficult to come by. In Arizona, you can call the following banks to exchange money for you: **In Phoenix,** Norwest Bank, 3300 N. Central Ave. (☎ **602/248-1251**); or Bank of America, 101 N. First Ave. (☎ **602/594-2891**). **In Tucson,** call Bank One of Arizona, 201 N. Central Ave. (☎ **520/792-7200** or 520/221-1414).

**Drinking Laws**    The legal drinking age in Arizona—and most other states in the country—is 21. The penalties for driving under the influence of alcohol are stiff.

**Electricity**   The United States uses 110–120 volts, 60 cycles, compared to 220–240 volts, 50 cycles, as in most of Europe. In addition to a 110-volt transformer, small appliances of non-American manufacture, such as hair dryers or shavers, will require a plug adapter with two flat, parallel pins.

**Embassies and Consulates**   All embassies are located in Washington, D.C.; some consulates are located in major cities, and most nations have a mission to the United Nations in New York City.

Listed here are the embassies and consulates of the major English-speaking countries—Australia, Canada, Ireland, New Zealand, and the United Kingdom. If you're from another country, you can get the telephone number of your embassy by calling "information" in Washington, D.C. (☎ **202/555-1212**).

The embassy of **Australia** is at 1601 Massachusetts Ave. NW, Washington, DC 20036-2273 (☎ **202/797-3000**). There is no consulate in Arizona; the nearest is at Century Plaza Towers, 19th Floor, 2049 Century Park East, Los Angeles, CA 90067 (☎ **310/229-4800**). Other Australian consulates are in Honolulu, New York, and San Francisco.

The embassy of **Canada** is at 501 Pennsylvania Ave. NW, Washington, DC 20001 (☎ **202/682-1740**). There is no consulate in Arizona; the nearest is at 550 S. Hope St., 9th Floor, Los Angeles, CA 90071 (☎ **213/346-2700**). Other Canadian consulates are in Atlanta, Boston, Buffalo (N.Y.), Chicago, Detroit, Miami, Minneapolis, New York, and Seattle.

The embassy of the **Republic of Ireland** is at 2234 Massachusetts Ave. NW, Washington, DC 20008 (☎ **202/462-3939**). There is no consulate in Arizona; the nearest is at 44 Montgomery St., Suite 3830, San Francisco, CA 94104 (☎ **415/392-4214**). Other Irish consulates are in Boston, Chicago, and New York.

The embassy of **New Zealand** is at 37 Observatory Circle NW, Washington, DC 20008 (☎ **202/328-4800**). There is no consulate in Arizona; the nearest is in Los Angeles at 12400 Wilshire Blvd., Suite 1150, Los Angeles, CA 90025 (☎ **310/207-1605**). There is also another consulate in New York.

The embassy of the **United Kingdom** is at 3100 Massachusetts Ave. NW, Washington, DC 20008 (☎ **202/462-1340**). There is no consulate in Arizona; the nearest is in Los Angeles at 11766 Wilshire Blvd., Suite 400, Los Angeles, CA 90025 (☎ **310/477-3322**). Other British consulates are in Atlanta, Chicago, Houston, Miami, and New York.

**Emergencies**   Call ☎ **911** to report a fire, call the police, or get an ambulance. This is a toll-free call (no coins are required at a public telephone).

If you encounter problems, check the local telephone directory to find an office of the **Traveler's Aid Society,** a nationwide nonprofit social-service organization geared to helping travelers in difficult straits. Their services might include reuniting families separated while traveling, providing food and/or shelter to people stranded without cash, or even emotional counseling. If you're in trouble, seek them out.

**Gasoline (Petrol)**   One U.S. gallon equals 3.8 liters, while 1.2 U.S. gallons equals 1 imperial gallon. You'll notice there are several grades (and price levels) of gasoline available at most gas stations. And you'll also notice that their names change from company to company. The unleaded ones with the highest octane rating are the most expensive (most rental cars take the least expensive "regular" unleaded); leaded gas is the least expensive, but only older cars can take this anymore, so check if you're not sure. And often the price is lower if you pay in cash instead of by credit or charge card. Also, many gas stations now offer lower-priced self-service gas pumps—in fact, some gas stations, particularly at night, are all self-service.

**Holidays** On the following legal national holidays, banks, government offices, post offices, and many stores, restaurants, and museums are closed: January 1 (New Year's Day), third Monday in January (Martin Luther King, Jr., Day), third Monday in February (Presidents' Day/Washington's Birthday), last Monday in May (Memorial Day), July 4 (Independence Day), first Monday in September (Labor Day), second Monday in October (Columbus Day), November 11 (Veterans Day/Armistice Day), third Thursday in November (Thanksgiving Day), and December 25 (Christmas). The Tuesday following the first Monday in November is Election Day, and is a legal holiday in presidential-election years (2000 is an election year).

**Legal Aid** Foreign visitors probably never become involved with the American legal system. If, however, you are pulled up for a minor infraction (for example, of the highway code, such as speeding), never attempt to pay the fine directly to the police officer; you may wind up arrested on the much more serious charge of attempted bribery. Pay fines by mail, or directly into the hands of the clerk of the court. If you're accused of a more serious offense, it's wise to say and do nothing before consulting a lawyer. Under U.S. law, an arrested person is allowed one telephone call to a party of his or her choice. Call your embassy or consulate.

**Mail** Generally to be found at intersections, **mailboxes** are blue; they carry an eagle logo and the label "U.S. Postal Service." If your mail is addressed to a U.S. destination, don't forget to add the five-digit **postal code,** or ZIP (zone improvement plan) code, after the two-letter abbreviation of the state to which the mail is addressed (AZ for Arizona, CA for California, NY for New York, and so on).

Domestic **postage rates** are 20¢ for a postcard and 32¢ for a letter. To Canada, airmail postcards cost 40¢ and letters cost 46¢ for the first half ounce; postcards to other countries, with the exception of Mexico, cost 50¢, and letters cost 60¢ for the first half ounce.

**Medical Emergencies** To call an ambulance, dial ☎ **911** from any phone. No coins are needed.

**Newspapers/Magazines** National newspapers include *The New York Times, USA Today,* and the *Wall Street Journal.* National news weeklies include *Newsweek, Time,* and *U.S. News & World Report.* In large cities most newsstands offer a small selection of the most popular foreign periodicals and newspapers, such as *The Economist, Le Monde,* and *Der Spiegel.* For information on local publications, see the "Fast Facts" sections for Phoenix and Tucson.

**Post** See "Mail," above.

**Safety** See "Safety" in "Preparing for Your Trip," earlier in this chapter.

**Taxes** In the United States there is no VAT (value-added tax) or other indirect tax at a national level. Every state, and each county and city in it, is allowed to levy its own local tax on purchases (including hotel and restaurant checks, airline tickets, and so on) and services. Taxes are already included in the price of certain services, such as public transportation, cab fares, telephone calls, and gasoline. The amount of sales tax varies from about 4% to 12%, depending on the state and city, so when you're making major purchases, such as photographic equipment, clothing, or stereo components, it can be a significant part of the cost.

In Arizona, the state sales tax is 5%, but communities can add local sales tax on top of this. There's also a car-rental tax of 5% in Tucson and 9.55% in Phoenix, and hotel-room taxes range from around 6% to 14% (travelers on a budget should keep this hotel tax in mind when making accommodations choices).

**Telephone, Telegraph, Telex, and Fax**    The telephone system in the United States is run by private corporations, so rates, especially for long-distance service and operator-assisted calls, can vary widely—even on calls made from public telephones. Local calls in the United States usually cost 25¢ (they're 25¢ throughout Arizona).

Generally, hotel surcharges on long-distance and local calls are astronomical. You're usually better off by calling collect, using a telephone charge card, or using a **public pay telephone,** which you'll find clearly marked in most public buildings and private establishments as well as on the street. Outside metropolitan areas, public telephones are more difficult to find. Stores and gas stations are your best bet.

Most **long-distance and international calls** can be dialed directly from any phone (stock up on quarters if you're calling from a pay phone or use a telephone charge card). For calls to Canada and other parts of the United States, dial 1 followed by the area code and the seven-digit number. For international calls, dial 011 followed by the country code (Australia, 61; Republic of Ireland, 353; New Zealand, 64; United Kingdom, 44), then the city code (for example, 171 or 181 for London, 21 for Birmingham) and the telephone number of the person you wish to call.

Note that all calls to area code 800 are toll free. However, calls to numbers in area codes 700 and 900 (chat lines, bulletin boards, "dating" services, etc.) can be very expensive—usually a charge of 95¢ to $3 or more per minute, and they sometimes have minimum charges that can run as high as $15 or more.

For **reversed-charge or collect calls,** and for **person-to-person calls,** dial 0 (zero, *not* the letter "O") followed by the area code and number you want; an operator will then come on the line, and you should specify that you are calling collect, or person-to-person, or both. If your operator-assisted call is international, ask for the overseas operator.

For **local directory assistance** ("information"), dial ☎ 1/555-1212; for **long-distance information,** dial 1, then the appropriate area code and 555-1212.

Like the telephone system, **telegraph** and **telex** services are provided by private corporations like ITT, MCI, and, above all, Western Union, the most important. You can bring your telegram in to the nearest Western Union office (there are hundreds across the country) or dictate it over the phone (a toll-free call, ☎ **800/ 325-6000**). You can also telegraph money (using a major credit or charge card), or have it telegraphed to you, very quickly over the Western Union system. (Note, however, that this service can be very expensive—the service charge can run as high as 10% to 25% of the amount sent.)

Many hotels have **fax** machines available for guest use (be sure to ask about the charge to use it), and many hotel rooms are even wired for guests' fax machines. Almost all shops that make photocopies offer fax service as well.

**Telephone Directory**    There are two kinds of telephone directories. The general directory is the so-called *White Pages,* in which private and business subscribers are listed in alphabetical order. The inside front cover lists the emergency number for police, fire, and ambulance, and other vital numbers (like the poison-control center, crime-victims hotline, and so on). The first few pages are devoted to community-service numbers, as well as a guide to long-distance and international calling, complete with country codes and area codes.

The second directory, printed on yellow paper (hence its name, *Yellow Pages*), lists all local services, businesses, and industries by type of activity, with an index at the back. The listings cover not only such obvious items as automobile repairs by make of car, or drugstores (pharmacies) often by geographical location, but also restaurants by type of cuisine and geographical location, bookstores by special subject and/or language, places of worship by religious denomination, and other information that the tourist might otherwise not readily find. The *Yellow Pages* also include city plans or detailed area maps, often showing postal ZIP codes and public transportation routes.

**Time**   The United States is divided into six time zones. From east to west these are eastern standard time (EST), central standard time (CST), mountain standard time (MST), Pacific standard time (PST), Alaska standard time (AST), and Hawaii standard time (HST). Always keep the changing time zones in mind if you are traveling (or even telephoning) long distances in the United States. For example, noon in New York City (EST) is 11am in Chicago (CST), 10am in Phoenix (MST), 9am in Los Angeles (PST), 8am in Anchorage (AST), and 7am in Honolulu (HST).

Arizona is in the mountain time zone, but it does *not* observe daylight saving time (summertime). Consequently, from the first Sunday in April until the last Sunday in October, there is no time difference between Arizona and California and other states on the West Coast. However, there is a 2-hour difference to Chicago, and 3 hours to New York.

**Tipping**   This is part of the American way of life, on the principle that you must expect to pay for any service you get (many service personnel receive little direct salary and must depend on tips for their income). Here are some rules of thumb:

In **hotels,** tip bellhops $1 per piece and tip the chamber staff $1 per day. Tip the doorman or concierge only if he or she has provided you with some specific service (for example, calling a cab for you or obtaining difficult-to-get theater tickets).

In **restaurants, bars, and nightclubs,** tip the service staff 15% of the check, tip bartenders 10% to 15%, tip checkroom attendants $1 per garment, and tip valet-parking attendants $1 per vehicle. Tip the doorman only if he has provided you with some specific service (such as calling a cab for you). Tipping is not expected in cafeterias and fast-food restaurants.

Tip **cab drivers** 15% of the fare.

As for **other service personnel,** tip redcaps at airports or railroad stations $1 per piece and tip hairdressers and barbers 15% to 20%.

Tipping ushers in cinemas, movies, and theaters and gas-station attendants is not expected.

**Toilets**   Foreign visitors often complain that public toilets (or "rest rooms") are hard to find in most U.S. cities. True, there are none on the streets, but the visitor can usually find one in a bar, restaurant, hotel, museum, department store, or service station—and it will probably be clean (although service-station rest rooms sometimes leave much to be desired). Note, however, that a growing number of restaurants and bars display a notice like REST ROOMS ARE FOR THE USE OF PATRONS ONLY. You can ignore this sign, or better yet, avoid arguments by paying for a cup of coffee or soft drink. The cleanliness of toilets at railroad stations and bus depots may be more open to question. Some public places are equipped with pay toilets, which require you to insert one or more coins into a slot on the door before it will open. In rest rooms with attendants, leaving at least a 25¢ tip is customary.

# Phoenix 5

Like the phoenix of ancient mythology, Arizona's capital city of Phoenix rose from its own ashes—in this case, the ruins of an ancient Indian village. The name Phoenix, given to the city by an early settler from Britain, has repeatedly proven apt. Rising from the dust of the desert, this city has become one of the largest metropolitan areas in the country.

Though the city has had its economic ups and downs, the Phoenix metropolitan area, often referred to as the Valley of the Sun, is currently booming. The Camelback Corridor that leads through north-central Phoenix has become the corporate heartland of the city and shiny glass office towers keep pushing up toward the desert sky. This burgeoning stretch of road has also become a corridor of upscale restaurants and shopping plazas, anchored by the Biltmore Fashion Park, the city's temple of high-end consumerism. Today Phoenicians are flocking to this area both for work and play.

Even downtown Phoenix, long abandoned as simply a place to work, is taking on a radically new look of late. Two new museums—the Phoenix Museum of History and the Arizona Science Center—have been built adjacent to historic Heritage Square, and the Phoenix Museum of Art has undergone a major renovation and expansion. However, the biggest project in downtown Phoenix is the construction of the new Bank One Ballpark, a covered baseball stadium with a retractable roof that will be home to the Arizona Diamondbacks baseball team starting in 1998. Together these downtown developments are calculated to attract people back into inner-city Phoenix from the suburbs, where population growth and economic development has centered for many years now.

Throughout the metropolitan area the population is growing at such a rapid pace that an alarm has been raised: Slow the pace before we become another Los Angeles!

Why the phenomenal growth? In large part it's due to the climate. More than 300 days of sunshine a year is a powerful attraction. Sure, summers are hot, but the mountains, and cooler air, are only 2 hours away. However, it's in the winter that the Valley of the Sun truly shines. When most of the country is frozen solid, the valley is sunny and warm. This great winter climate has helped make this area the resort capital of the United States. However, with stiff competition from resorts in the Caribbean, Cancun, and Hawaii, Valley of the Sun resorts are beginning to undergo makeovers aimed at attracting

# Phoenix at a Glance

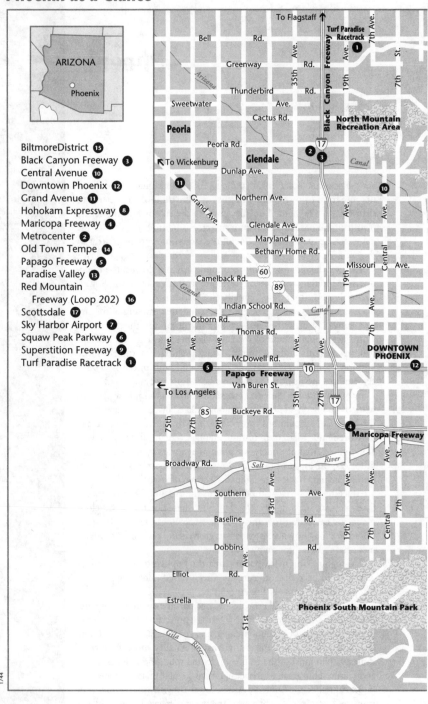

ARIZONA

Phoenix

To Flagstaff

Turf Paradise Racetrack **1**

Bell        Rd.
7th Ave.
Greenway        Rd.
35th   Ave.
19th   Ave.
7th   St.
Thunderbird        Rd.
Sweetwater        Ave.
Cactus Rd.

**Peoria**        North Mountain Recreation Area

Peoria Rd.
**17**
To Wickenburg        **Glendale**        **2** **3**        Canal
Dunlap Ave.
**11**        **10**
Northern Ave.
Grand Ave.        Ave.        Ave.
Glendale Ave.
Maryland Ave.
Bethany Home Rd.
**60**
Grand        Camelback Rd.        Missouri   Ave.
**89**        19th        Central
Indian School Rd.        Canal
Osborn Rd.        Ave.
Thomas Rd.        7th
Ave.   Ave.   Ave.        Ave.        **DOWNTOWN PHOENIX**
McDowell Rd.
**5**        **Papago  Freeway**        **10**        **12**
To Los Angeles        Van Buren St.
**85**        Buckeye Rd.        35th   27th        **17**
75th   67th   59th
**4**
**Maricopa Freeway**
Broadway Rd.        Salt        River        Ave.   Ave.        St.
Southern        Ave.
43rd        7th
Baseline        Rd.        19th   7th   Central
Dobbins        Rd.
Elliot        Rd.
Estrella        Dr.        **Phoenix South Mountain Park**
51st
Gila   River

**Black Canyon Freeway**

70

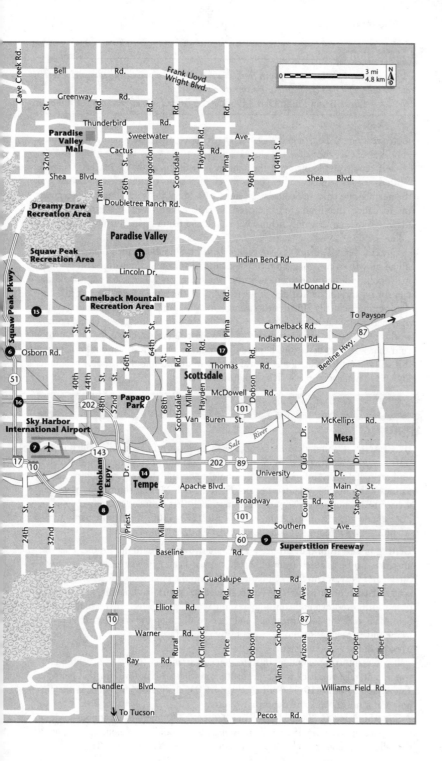

**Impressions**

*As the mythical phoenix rose reborn from its ashes, so shall a great civilization rise here on the ashes of a past civilization. I name thee Phoenix.*
— "Lord" Bryan Philip Darrel Duppa, the British settler who named Phoenix

more vacationers. To that end bigger and better pool areas have been making splashes at resorts all over the valley.

Golf, tennis, and lounging by the pool are only the tip of the iceberg (so to speak). With the cooler winter weather comes the cultural season, and between Phoenix and the neighboring cities of Scottsdale, Tempe, and Mesa, there's an impressive array of music, dance, and theater to be enjoyed. Scottsdale is also well known as a center of the visual arts, ranking only behind New York and Santa Fe in the number of its art galleries.

Over the years, Phoenix has enjoyed the benefits and suffered the problems of rapid urban growth. It has gone from tiny agricultural village to sprawling cosmopolitan metropolis in little more than a century. Along the way it has lost its past amid urban sprawl and unchecked development, while at the same time it has forged a city that's quintessentially 20th-century American. Shopping malls, the gathering places of America, are raised to an art form in Phoenix. Luxurious resorts create fantasy worlds of waterfalls and swimming pools. Wide boulevards stretch for miles across land that was once desert but has been made green through irrigation. Perhaps it's this willingness to create a new world on top of an old one that attracts people to Phoenix. Then again, maybe it's all that sunshine.

# 1  Orientation

## ARRIVING

**BY PLANE**   Centrally located 3 miles from downtown Phoenix, **Sky Harbor Airport** has three terminals—two, three, and four—and in these three terminals you'll find car-rental desks, information desks, hotel-reservation centers with direct lines to various valley hotels, and a food court. There's a free 24-hour shuttle bus operating every 5 to 10 minutes between the three terminals (less frequently during the night). For general airport information, call ☎ **602/273-3300;** for airport paging, call ☎ **602/273-3456;** for lost and found, call ☎ **602/273-3307.**

**Getting to and from the Airport**   There are two entrances to the airport. The west entrance can be accessed from either the Squaw Peak Parkway (Ariz. 51) or 24th Street, and the east entrance can be accessed from the Hohokam Expressway, which is an extension of 44th Street. If you're headed to downtown Phoenix, leave by way of the 24th Street exit and continue west on Washington Street. If you're headed to Scottsdale, take the 24th Street exit and then go north on the Squaw Peak Parkway to the Indian School Road or Lincoln Drive exit and then drive east. For Tempe or Mesa, take the 44th Street exit.

If you want to come and go in style, you can arrange to have a stretch limo pick you up and take you back to the airport (or anywhere else in town for that matter). **Transtyle** (☎ **800/410-5479** or 602/948-6131), charges $86.50 between the airport and most Phoenix and Scottsdale resorts.

**SuperShuttle** (☎ **800/331-3565** or 602/244-9000) offers 24-hour door-to-door van service between Sky Harbor Airport and resorts, hotels, and homes throughout the valley. If you are going to a private residence, fares average about $10 to $12 to the downtown and Tempe area ($5 for each additional person), and about $10 to $20 per person to the Scottsdale and northern area of the city. When heading back to the airport for a departure, call ☎ **602/244-9000.**

Taxis can also be found waiting outside all three airport terminals, or you can call **Yellow Cab** (☎ **602/252-5252**) or **Checker Cab** (☎ **602/257-1818**).

Valley Metro provides **public bus service** throughout the valley with the Red Line (R) operating between the airport and downtown Phoenix, Tempe, and Mesa. Note that the Red Line operates only Monday through Friday between 3:30am and 9:45pm. You can pick up a copy of *The Bus Book*, a guide and route map for the Valley Metro bus system, at either of the two downtown tourist information centers or at the Downtown Bus Terminal at the corner of First and Washington streets.

**BY CAR**   Phoenix is connected to Los Angeles and Tucson by I-10 and to Flagstaff via I-17. If you're headed to Scottsdale, the easiest route is to take the Squaw Peak Freeway north to Highland Avenue, continue a block north to Camelback Road, and then head east to Scottsdale Road. A new alternative is U.S. 101, which heads north toward Scottsdale from Tempe and is slowly being extended northward. The Superstition Freeway (U.S. 60) leads to Tempe, Mesa, and Chandler.

**BY TRAIN**   There is no passenger rail service to Phoenix. However, Amtrak's *Southwest Chief* connects Phoenix (via a bus connection from Flagstaff) with Los Angeles to the west and Albuquerque, Santa Fe, Kansas City, and Chicago to the east. Amtrak's *Sunset Limited* connects Phoenix (via a bus connection from Tucson) with New Orleans, Houston, San Antonio, El Paso, and Los Angeles. Amtrak connector buses arrive and depart from the old Phoenix **Amtrak railroad terminal,** 401 W. Harrison St. (☎ **800/872-7245** or 602/253-0121).

**BY BUS**   Greyhound connects Phoenix to the rest of the United States with its extensive bus system. The **Greyhound terminal** is at 2115 E. Buckeye Rd. (☎ **800/ 231-2222** or 602/271-7426).

## VISITOR INFORMATION

You'll find a **tourist information desk** in the baggage claim area of all three terminals at Sky Harbor Airport.

The **Phoenix and Valley of the Sun Convention and Visitors Bureau,** One Arizona Center, 400 E. Van Buren St., Suite 600, Phoenix, AZ 85004-2290 (☎ **602/ 254-6500**), also operates a visitors bureau at the northwest corner of Adams Street and Second Street in the same block as the Hyatt Regency and directly across the street from Civic Plaza.

The **Information Hotline** (☎ **602/252-5588**) has recorded information about current events in Phoenix.

## CITY LAYOUT

**MAIN ARTERIES & STREETS**   Over the past decade, the Phoenix area has seen the construction of numerous new freeways, and the construction is continuing. It won't be too many years now before it will be possible to reach Scottsdale by freeway rather than having to deal with stoplights and local traffic. U.S. 101, which currently exists only in two unconnected sections (one in Tempe and the other in Glendale and Peoria on the east side of the valley) will eventually form a loop around the east, north, and west sides of the city, providing freeway access to Scottsdale from I-17 on the north side of Phoenix and U.S. 60 in Tempe.

**I-17 (Black Canyon Freeway),** which connects Phoenix with Flagstaff, is the city's main north-south artery. This freeway curves to the east just south of downtown (where it is renamed the **Maricopa Freeway**), and then ends at I-10 just southwest of the airport. West of the airport, I-10 is known as the **Papago Freeway.** However, at the I-10–I-17 interchange, I-10 changes names to become the Maricopa Freeway as it continues east and then south across the valley.

Northwest of the airport, **Ariz. 202 (Red Mountain Freeway),** heads east from I-10 and passes along the north side of Tempe to connect with U.S. 101 and provide access to downtown Tempe and Arizona State University. On the east side of the airport, **Ariz. 143 (Hohokam Expressway)** connects Ariz. 202 with I-10.

At the interchange of I-10 and Ariz. 202, northwest of Sky Harbor Airport, **Ariz. 51 (Squaw Peak Freeway)** heads north through the center of Phoenix and is the best north-south route in the city.

Just south of the airport, **U.S. 60 (Superstition Freeway)** heads east to Tempe, Chandler, Mesa, and Gilbert. **U.S. 101** leads north from U.S. 60 toward Scottsdale. For now it only leads as far north as Thomas Road. However by the time you visit, it should have been extended farther north toward Scottsdale and if so will provide the best route from the airport to the Scottsdale resorts.

Secondary highways in the valley include the **Beeline Highway (Ariz. 87),** which starts out as Country Club Drive in Mesa and leads to Payson, and **Grand Avenue (U.S. 60 and U.S. 89),** which starts downtown and leads to Sun City and Wickenburg.

Phoenix and the surrounding cities of Mesa, Tempe, Scottsdale, and Chandler, and even those cities farther out in the valley, are laid out in a grid pattern with major avenues and roads about every mile. For traveling east to west across Phoenix, your best choices are Camelback Road, Indian School Road, and McDowell Road. For traveling north and south, 44th Street, 24th Street, and Central Avenue are good choices. Hayden Road is a north-south alternative to Scottsdale Road, which gets jammed at rush hours.

**FINDING AN ADDRESS    Central Avenue,** which runs north to south through downtown Phoenix, is the starting point for all east and west street numbering. **Washington Street** is the starting point for north and south numbering. North-to-south numbered *streets* are to be found on the east side of the city, while north-to-south numbered *avenues* will be found on the west. For the most part, street numbers change by 100 with each block. Odd-numbered addresses are on the south and east sides of streets, while even-numbered addresses are on north and west sides of streets.

For example, if you're looking for 4454 East Camelback Rd., you'll find it 44 blocks east of Central Avenue between 44th and 45th streets on the north side of the street. If you're looking for 2905 North 35th Ave., you'll find it 35 blocks west of Central Avenue and 29 blocks north of Washington Street on the east side of the street. Just for general reference, Camelback marks the 5,000 block north.

**STREET MAPS**    The street maps handed out by rental-car companies are almost useless for finding anything in Phoenix, so, as soon as you can, stop in at a minimart and buy a Phoenix map. Unfortunately, you'll probably also have to buy a separate Scottsdale map. You can also get a simple map at either the airport tourist information desks or at the downtown visitors' information center.

## NEIGHBORHOODS IN BRIEF

Because of urban sprawl, Phoenix has yielded its importance to the Valley of the Sun, an area encompassing Phoenix and its metropolitan area of more than 20 cities. Consequently, neighborhoods, per se, have lost much of their significance as outlying cities have taken on regional importance. However, this said, there are some neighborhoods worth noting.

**Downtown Phoenix**   Roughly bordered by Thomas Road on the north, Buckeye Road on the south, 19th Avenue on the west, and Seventh Street on the east, downtown is primarily a business, financial, and government district, where both the city hall and state capitol are located. However, in the past few years, downtown Phoenix has been rising from the ashes of neglect and positioning itself as the valley's prime sports, entertainment, and museum district. By the 1998 baseball season, the Arizona Diamondbacks should be playing big-league baseball in the **Bank-One Ballpark,** while the Phoenix Suns have already been burning up the basketball court at **America West Arena** for a few years now. Not surprisingly, several sports bars and a brewpub have opened in the area in recent years. In 1996, the historic **Orpheum Theatre** reopened after a complete renovation, and at press time, the Arizona Center shopping and entertainment plaza was in the process of getting a new multiplex movie theater. The **Phoenix Symphony Hall** and **Herberger Theater Center** are also both downtown and have for years served as the area's cultural anchors. Downtown museums that have been built in the past few years include the **Phoenix Museum of History** and the **Arizona Science Center,** both of which are located in Heritage and Science Park. Other attractions in the downtown area include **Heritage Square** (historic homes), **the Arizona State Capitol Museum,** and the **Arizona Mining & Mineral Museum.** On the northern edge of downtown are the **Heard Museum,** the **Phoenix Central Library** (an architectural gem), and the **Phoenix Art Museum,** which completed an extensive remodeling and expansion in 1996.

**Biltmore District**   The Biltmore District, also known as the **Camelback Corridor,** centers along Camelback Road between 24th Street and 44th Street and is Phoenix's upscale shopping, residential, and business district. The area is characterized by modern office buildings and is anchored by the Biltmore Hotel and Biltmore Fashion Park shopping mall. It's here you'll find such cultural icons as Planet Hollywood and the Hard Rock Cafe.

**Scottsdale**   A separate city of more than 175,000 people, Scottsdale extends from Tempe in the south to Carefree in the north, a distance of more than 20 miles. **"Resort Row"** is the name given to Scottsdale Road between Indian School Road and Shea Boulevard. Along this section of road are more than a dozen major resorts. **Old Scottsdale** capitalizes on its cowboy heritage and has become the valley's main shopping district, with boutiques, jewelers, Native American crafts stores, souvenir shops, and numerous restaurants.

**Tempe**   Tempe is the home of Arizona State University and has all the trappings of a university town. Nightclubs and bars abound here. The center of activity, both day and night, is **Mill Avenue,** which has dozens of unusual shops along a stretch of about 4 blocks. This is one of the few areas in the valley where locals actually walk the streets and hang out at sidewalk cafes (Old Town Scottsdale often has people on its streets, but few are locals).

**Paradise Valley**   If Scottsdale is Phoenix's Beverly Hills, then Paradise Valley is its Bel-Air. The most exclusive neighborhood in the valley is almost entirely residential, but you won't see too many of the more lavish homes because they're set on large tracts of land.

**Mesa**   This eastern suburb of Phoenix has in recent years become something of a high-tech area. Large shopping malls, several inexpensive motels, and a museum attract both locals and visitors to Mesa.

**Glendale**   Located west of Phoenix proper, Glendale has numerous historic buildings in its downtown and has become the antiques capital of the valley.

**Carefree and Cave Creek**   Located about 20 miles north of Scottsdale, these two communities represent the Old West and the New West. Carefree is a planned community and is home to the prestigious Boulders resort and El Pedregal shopping center. Cave Creek plays up its Western heritage in its architecture and preponderance of bars, steakhouses, and shops selling Western crafts and other gifts.

## 2 Getting Around

### BY CAR

Phoenix and the surrounding cities that together make up the Valley of the Sun sprawl over 420 square miles, so if you want to make the best use of your time, it's essential to have a car. Outside downtown Phoenix, there's almost always plenty of free parking around wherever you go.

**RENTALS**   All the major rental-car companies have offices in Phoenix, with desks inside the airline terminals at Sky Harbor Airport, and because this is a major tourist destination, there are often excellent rates. The best rates are those reserved at least a week in advance, but car-rental companies change rates frequently as demand goes up and down. If you book far enough in advance, you might get a compact car for less than $150 per week. See also chapter 3, "Planning a Trip to Arizona," for general tips on car rentals.

All the major rental-car companies have offices in Phoenix. Among them are the following: **Alamo,** 2246 E. Washington St. (☎ **800/327-9633** or 602/244-0897); **Avis,** Sky Harbor Airport (☎ **800/331-1212,** 800/831-2847, or 602/273-3222); **Budget,** Sky Harbor Airport (☎ **800/227-3678** or 602/267-1717) and several other locations; **Dollar,** Sky Harbor Airport (☎ **800/800-4000** or 602/267-0995); **Hertz,** Sky Harbor Airport (☎ **800/654-3131** or 602/267-8822) and many other locations around the area; **National,** Sky Harbor Airport (☎ **800/227-7368** or 602/ 275-4771); and **Thrifty,** 4114 E. Washington St. (☎ **800/367-2277** or 602/ 244-0311).

If you'd like a bit more style while you cruise from resort to golf course to nightclub to wherever, how about a Corvette? **Rent-a-Vette,** 1207 N. Scottsdale Rd., Tempe (☎ **602/941-3001**), can put you behind the wheel of a car that will get you a bit more respect from valet parking attendants at area restaurants. A Corvette will run you $129 to $269 a day. Rent-a-Vette also rents Porsches, Mercedes, Mustang GTs, and BMWs with rates topping out at $299 a day for a Porsche. At the opposite end of the alternative car-rental spectrum is **Scottsdale Jeep Rentals,** 7515 E. Butherus Dr., Scottsdale (☎ **602/951-2191**), which rents Jeep Wranglers for around $130 for 1 day (rates go down the more days you rent).

### BY PUBLIC TRANSPORTATION

Unfortunately **Valley Metro** (☎ **602/253-5000**), the Phoenix public bus system, is not very useful to tourists. It's primarily meant for use by commuters, and most routes stop running before 9pm at night. There's no bus service on Sunday, and some buses don't run on Saturday either. But if you decide you want to take the bus, pick up a copy of *The Bus Book* at one of the tourist information desks in the airport (where it's sometimes available), at either downtown tourist office, or at the Downtown Bus Terminal at the corner of First and Washington streets. There are both local and express buses. Local bus fare is $1.25 and express bus fare is $1.75. A 10-ride ticket book, all-day passes, and monthly passes are available.

Of more value to visitors is the **Downtown Area Shuttle (DASH),** which provides bus service for 30¢ a ride within the downtown area. These purple buses with orange racing stripes operate Monday through Friday between 6:30am and 5:30pm. The buses stop at regular bus stops every 6 to 12 minutes. Attractions along the bus's route include the state capitol, the tourist information center, the Arizona Science Center, Heritage Square, America West Arena, and the Arizona Center shopping mall. In Tempe, **FLASH** (Free Local Area Shuttle) buses provides a similar service on a loop around Arizona State University. The route includes Mill Avenue and Sun Devil Stadium, and as the name implies, these buses are free.

In Scottsdale, you can ride **Ollie the Trolley** (☎ **602/970-8130**) buses between many area resorts and shopping areas. An all-day pass is $4.

## BY TAXI

Because distances in Phoenix are so large, the price of an average taxi ride can be quite high. However, if you haven't got your own wheels and the bus isn't running because it's late at night or the weekend, you don't have any choice but to call a cab. **Yellow Cab** (☎ **602/252-5252**) charges $3 for the first mile and $1.50 per mile after that. **Scottsdale Cab** (☎ **602/994-1616**) charges $2 per mile with a $5 minimum.

## FAST FACTS: Phoenix

**American Express**    There are American Express offices at 2508 E. Camelback Rd. (☎ **602/468-1199**), open Monday through Saturday from 10am to 6pm; and at 6900 E. Camelback Rd., Scottsdale (☎ **602/949-7000**), open Monday through Friday from 10am to 6pm and Saturday from 10:30am to 3:30pm.

**Airport**    See "Orientation," earlier in this chapter.

**Baby-Sitters**    If your hotel can't recommend or provide a sitter, contact **Golden Grandmas** (☎ **602/843-4533**) or the **Granny Company** (☎ **602/264-5454**).

**Car Rentals**    See "Getting Around," earlier in this chapter.

**Climate**    See "When to Go," in chapter 3.

**Dentist**    Call the **Central Arizona Dental Society** at  ☎ **602/881-7237** or 602/957-4864 for a referral.

**Doctor**    Call the **Maricopa County Medical Society** (☎ **602/252-2844**) for doctor referrals.

**Emergencies**    For police, fire, or medical emergency, phone ☎ **911.**

**Eyeglass Repair**    The **Nationwide Vision Center** has more than 10 locations around the valley, including 933 E. University Dr., Tempe (☎ **602/966-4992**); 5130 N. 19th Ave. (☎ **602/242-5293**); and 4615 E. Thomas Rd. (☎ **602/952-8667**).

**Hospitals**    The **Good Samaritan Regional Medical Center,** 1111 E. McDowell Rd. (☎ **602/239-2000**), and the **Desert Samaritan Medical Center,** 1400 S. Dobson Rd., Mesa (☎ **602/835-3000**), are two of the largest hospitals in the valley.

**Hotlines**    The **Information Hotline** (☎ **602/252-5588**) provides recorded tourist information on Phoenix and the Valley of the Sun. **Pressline** (☎ **602/271-5656**) provides access to daily news, the correct time, and other topics.

**Information**    See "Visitor Information" in "Orientation," earlier in this chapter.

**Lost Property**    If you lose something in the airport, call ☎ **602/273-3307;** on a bus, call ☎ **602/261-8549.**

**Maps**    See "City Layout" in "Orientation," earlier in this chapter.

**Newspapers/Magazines**    *The Arizona Republic* is Phoenix's daily newspaper. The Friday paper has special sections with schedules of the upcoming week's movie, music, and cultural performances. *New Times* is a free weekly news and arts journal with comprehensive listings of cultural events, film, and rock-music club and concert schedules. The best place to find *New Times* is at Circle K convenience stores all over the valley. An extensive selection of newspapers and magazines can be found at **Mill Avenue News,** 1 E. Sixth St., Tempe (☎ **602/921-1612**).

**Pharmacies**    Call ☎ **800/WALGREENS** for the Walgreens pharmacy that's nearest you; some are open 24 hours a day.

**Photographic Needs/Camera Repairs**    **Photomark,** 1916 W. Baseline Rd., Mesa (☎ **602/897-2522**); 2202 E. McDowell Rd. (☎ **602/244-1133**); 204 E. University Dr., Tempe (☎ **602/894-8337**); or 5719 W. Northern Ave., Glendale (☎ **602/934-4441**), can supply camera needs or repairs.

**Police**    For police emergencies, phone ☎ **911.**

**Post Office**    The **Phoenix General Mail Facility** (main post office) is at 4949 E. Van Buren St. (☎ **602/407-2049**).

**Safety**    Don't leave valuables in view in your car, especially when parking in downtown Phoenix. Put anything of value in the trunk or under the seat if you're driving a hatchback. Take extra precautions after dark in the south-central Phoenix area and downtown. Angry freeway drivers here in Phoenix have been known to pull guns, so it's a good idea to be polite when driving. Aggressive drivers should be given plenty of room.

   Many hotels now provide in-room safes, for which there's a daily charge. Others will be glad to store your valuables in a safety-deposit box at the front office.

**Taxes**    State sales tax is 5% (plus variable local taxes). Hotel room taxes vary by city and range from 7.525% to 10.725%. The car-rental tax at the Phoenix airport (or anywhere else in Phoenix proper) is 14.05%. In Scottsdale, you'll pay 12.15% on a car rental.

**Taxis**    See "Getting Around," earlier in this chapter.

**Television**    Valley of the Sun stations are channels 3 (Warner Bros. Television), 5 (CBS), 8 (PBS), 10 (Fox), 12 (NBC), 15 (ABC), and 45 (United Paramount Network).

**Transit Information**    For **Phoenix Transit System** public bus information, call ☎ **602/253-5000.**

**Weather**    The phone number for weather information is ☎ **602/271-5656, ext. 1010.**

# 3  Accommodations

Because the Phoenix area has long been popular as a winter refuge from cold and snow, it now has the greatest concentration of resorts in the continental United States. Sunshine and spring training conspire to make February through April the busiest time of year in the valley, so if you're planning to visit at this time, make your reservations as many months in advance as possible. During the winter, the Phoenix metro area also has some of the highest room rates in the country. Sure, the city has plenty of moderately priced motels, but even these places tend to jack up their prices in winter ($90 for a Super 8!). Because the budget motels are still the cheapest rooms around, they tend to fill up fast, especially on winter weekends.

With the exception of valet parking services and parking garages at downtown convention hotels, parking is free at the majority of Phoenix hotels. If there is a parking charge, we have noted it. You'll find that almost all hotels now have no-smoking and wheelchair-accessible rooms.

Also, keep in mind that most resorts offer a variety of weekend, golf, and tennis packages, as well as special off-season discounts and corporate rates (which you can often get just by asking). We've given only the official "rack rates," or walk-in rates, below. But it always pays to ask if there's any kind of special discount or package available. Don't forget your AAA or AARP discounts if you are members of those organizations.

Other ways to save money on accommodations in Phoenix? Consider traveling during the shoulder seasons of late spring and late summer. Temperatures are not at their midsummer peak nor are room rates at their midwinter peaks. (And if you can stand the heat of summer, you can often save more than 50% on room rates.) If you'll be traveling with children, always ask whether your child will be able to stay for free in your room, and whether there's a limit to the number of children who can stay for free.

Request a room with a view of the mountains whenever possible. You can overlook a swimming pool anywhere, but some of the main selling points of Phoenix and Scottsdale hotels are the views of Mummy Mountain, Camelback Mountain, and Squaw Peak.

**BED-AND-BREAKFAST INNS**   While most people dreaming of an Arizona winter vacation have visions of luxury resorts dancing in their heads, there are also plenty of bed-and-breakfast inns around the valley. **Mi Casa-Su Casa,** P.O. Box 950, Tempe, AZ 85280-0950 (☎ **800/456-0682** or 602/990-0682), is a reservation service that can book accommodations at more than 65 homes in the Valley of the Sun (as well as elsewhere in the state). Rates range from $50 to $200 for a double room, depending on the location and luxury of the home. **Bed and Breakfast Inn Arizona,** 13802 N. Scottsdale Rd., Suite 104–87, Scottsdale, AZ 85254 (☎ **800/266-STAY** or 602/368-9250; Web site http://bnbreservations.com), represents B&Bs all over the state and charges between $80 and $300 for a double in the high season. **Arizona Trails Bed & Breakfast Reservation Service,** P.O. Box 18998, Fountain Hills, AZ 85269-8998 (☎ **888/799-4284** or 602/837-4284; fax 602/816-4224; Web site: www.arizonatrails.com), was, at press time, representing nearly 50 B&Bs across the state with everything from two-room homestays to inns with more than a dozen rooms. The **Arizona Association of Bed and Breakfast Inns,** P.O. Box 7186, Phoenix, AZ 85011 (☎ **800/284-2589**), is another organization representing B&Bs across the state, though it has only a couple of local members.

**PRICE CATEGORIES**   Because it is such a popular winter resort destination, The Valley of the Sun is one of the more expensive places in the United States for a vacation. If you've been thinking of saving money by skipping the Caribbean or Hawaii this year, think again. When a standard room at a top resort goes for well over $250 and a Super 8 Motel charges close to $100, price categories become very subjective. Consequently, we have categorized accommodations based on their relative cost when compared with other Valley of the Sun accommodations.

In the following listings, price categories are based on the rate for a double room (with tax included) in high season (most resorts and hotels charge the same for a single or double room) and are as follows: "Very Expensive," more than $250 per night; "Expensive," $150 to $250 per night; "Moderate," $80 to $149 per night; and "Inexpensive," under $80 per night. Keep in mind, however, that these are what

# Phoenix Accommodations

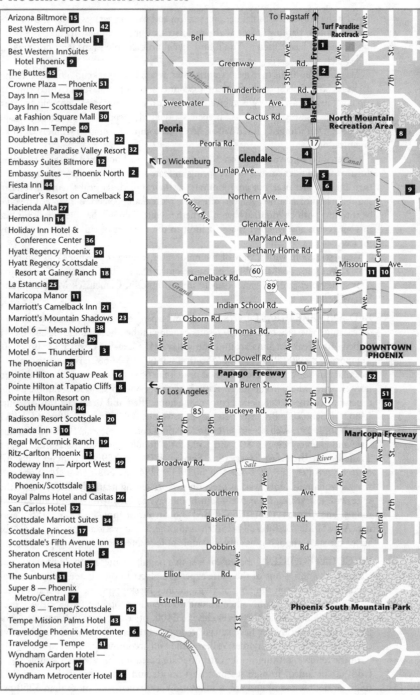

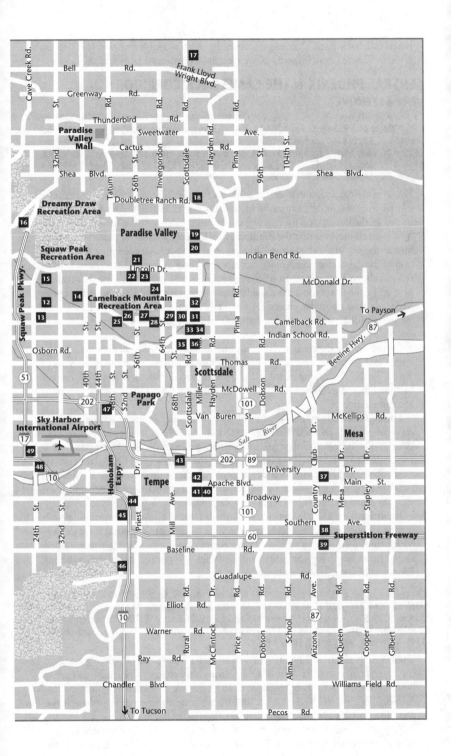

hotels call "rack rates." Various discounts are often available that will reduce these rates, so be sure to ask if there are any specials or discounted rates available.

# CENTRAL PHOENIX & THE CAMELBACK CORRIDOR
## VERY EXPENSIVE

✪ **Arizona Biltmore Resort & Spa.** 24th St. and Missouri Ave., Phoenix, AZ 85016. ☎ **800/950-0086** or 602/955-6600. Fax 602/954-2548. 600 rms, including 50 suites. A/C TV TEL. Mid-Sept to Dec $220–$340 double, from $420 suite; Jan 1 to early May $330–$475 double, from $605 suite; early May to mid-June $230–$350 double, from 430 suite; mid-June to early Sept, $130–$195 double, from $310 suite; early Sept to Dec 31 $235–$355 double, from $435 suite. AE, CB, DC, DISC, EURO, JCB, MC, V.

For tasteful elegance, superb service, prime location (near the foot of Squaw Peak and not far from Biltmore Fashion Park), and historic character (Frank Lloyd Wright helped in the design), no other resort in the valley can touch the Arizona Biltmore. What this all means is that the Biltmore is *the* Phoenix address for those who can afford to stay anywhere they want. Although wealthy vacationers comprise a good portion of the guests here, conference facilities also bring in corporate travelers, and the inn has always been the resort of choice for celebs and politicos. While the two superb golf courses are the main draw for many guests, the children's activities center has made this a popular choice for families as well. In the summer of 1997, the Biltmore added a state-of-the-art, full-service health spa to its already wide range of amenities.

Of the several different styles of accommodations, the "resort rooms" are the largest and most comfortable and have balconies or patios. Some also offer views of Squaw Peak. The rooms in the main building are the smallest and have neither balconies nor patios. The villa suites are the Biltmore's most spacious and luxurious accommodations.

**Dining/Entertainment:** Wright's offers a moderately informal setting (no jackets required) and serves excellent new American cuisine amid the handiwork of F. L. Wright. The Biltmore Grill serves meals with a touch of the Southwest both in flavors and decor. There's a quiet lobby bar, and the Cabana Club Restaurant and Bar serves drinks and light meals beside the pool. Afternoon tea is served in the lobby.

**Services:** Concierge, 24-hour room service, limousine, massages, valet/laundry service, car-rental service, baby-sitting.

**Facilities:** Two 18-hole golf courses, 18-hole putting course, five swimming pools (including one with a water slide and one with rental cabanas around it for that extra touch of luxury), two whirlpool spas, eight lighted tennis courts, fitness center, sauna, steam room, jogging paths, rental bicycles, lawn games, board games, beauty salon, business center, several shops.

✪ **Hermosa Inn.** 5532 N. Palo Cristi Rd., Paradise Valley, AZ 85253. ☎ **800/241-1210** or 602/955-8614. Fax 602/955-8299. 17 rms, 18 suites. A/C TV TEL. Jan 1 to early May $235–$300 double, $395–$575 suite; early May to mid-June $150–$205 double, $310–$425 suite; mid-June to mid-Sept $120–$175 double, $275–$395 suite; mid-Sept to Dec 31 $185–$235 double, $345–$475 suite. AE, CB, DC, DISC, MC, V.

Once a guest ranch, this luxurious boutique hotel is now one of the only hotels in the Phoenix area to offer a bit of Old Arizona atmosphere. Originally built as the home of Western artist Lon Megargee in 1930, the inn is situated in a quiet residential neighborhood and is set on more than 6 acres of neatly landscaped gardens. If you don't like the crowds of big resorts, but do enjoy the luxury, this is the spot for you.

Rooms here vary from cozy to spacious and are all individually decorated in tastefully contemporary Western and Southwestern decor that would look at home on the pages of any interior-design magazine. The largest suites incorporate a mixture of contemporary and antique Southwestern furnishings and accent pieces; these have more Southwestern flavor than any other rooms in the area.

**Dining/Entertainment:** Lon's, the hotel's dining room, is named for former owner and cowboy artist Lon Megargee and is located in the original adobe home. Excellent new American and Southwestern cuisine is served in the rustic, upscale setting.

**Services:** Concierge.

**Facilities:** Situated around the grounds are a small outdoor pool, a couple of whirlpools (one in a shady garden setting), and three tennis courts.

✪ **Royal Palms Hotel and Casitas.** 5200 E. Camelback Rd., Phoenix, AZ 85018. ☎ **800/ 672-6011** or 602/840-3610. Fax 602/840-6927. 116 rms and suites. A/C TV TEL. Nov–Apr $300–$2,800 double; May–Oct $175–$2,000 double. Rates include full breakfast. AE, CB, DC, DISC, MC, V.

The Royal Palms, located midway between Scottsdale and Biltmore Fashion Park and not far from The Phoenician, has been a fixture on the Phoenix resort scene for 50 years, and in spring of 1997, the resort reopened after a total and very thorough renovation. Although the resort opened too late for us to have a look at it, because it is under the same ownership as the nearby Hermosa Inn (our favorite area boutique hotel), we are confident that this resort will be a winner. The main building, once the winter home of Cunard Steamship executive Delos Cooke, is filled with European antiques that once belonged to Cooke, and the gardens are filled with exotic plants added by his wife Florence. Antique water fountains, some as much as 450 years old, and lush walled gardens give the property the feel of a Mediterranean monastery cloister, a tranquil retreat from life's stresses.

The interior design of the 19 casitas and other areas of the resort were handled by members of the American Society of Interior Designers (ASID) as part of an ASID Designer's Showhouse benefit for the Phoenix Symphony Guild. Consequently, each of these rooms is unique.

**Dining/Entertainment:** In keeping with the resort's architectural styling, T. Cook's, the resort's main dining room, serves Mediterranean cuisine. There's a nice view of Camelback Mountain from the restaurant. Adjacent to the swimming pool, you'll find the Cabana Grill.

**Services:** Concierge, room service, valet/laundry service, business services.

**Facilities:** Swimming pool complete with cabanas, tennis court, exercise room. Although the resort does not have its own golf course, the staff can arrange tee times at area courses.

## EXPENSIVE

**Embassy Suites Biltmore.** 2630 E. Camelback Rd., Phoenix, AZ 85016. ☎ **800/EMBASSY** or 602/955-3992. Fax 602/955-6479. 232 suites. A/C TV TEL. Jan 1–May 24 $199–$235 double; May 25–Sept 8 $119–$139 double; Sept 9–Dec 31 $179–$199 double. Rates include full breakfast. AE, CB, DC, DISC, EURO, MC, V.

Located across the parking lot from the Biltmore Fashion Park (Phoenix's most upscale shopping center), this atrium hotel makes a great base if you want to be within walking distance of such places as Planet Hollywood, the Hard Rock Cafe, and half a dozen other good restaurants. Public areas of the hotel received a modern Southwestern makeover in 1996 and now the huge atrium is filled with interesting tile work (including colorful lizards) and other artistic touches, as well as tropical greenery, waterfalls, and ponds filled with koi (Japanese carp). The curved wall of glass that forms the atrium looks out on a fairly large oval pool.

The rooms, all suites, are a bit of a let down after passing through the atrium greenhouse, but they're certainly large enough to spread out in. Every suite has a microwave, refrigerator, wet bar, coffeemaker, two TVs, two dual-line phones, iron and ironing board, and hair dryer.

**Dining/Entertainment:** Within its desert oasis setting, the hotel's atrium houses the breakfast area, a romantic lounge with huge banquettes shaded by palm trees. Just off the atrium is a steakhouse with a surprisingly contemporary decor (lots of halogen lights).

**Services:** Concierge, room service, valet/laundry.

**Facilities:** Large outdoor pool, whirlpool, fitness room. Preferred tee times are available nearby at the Arizona Biltmore's two golf courses.

✪ **La Estancia.** 4979 E. Camelback Rd., Phoenix, AZ 85018. ☎ **602/808-9924.** Fax 602/808-9925. 5 rms. A/C. $165–$195 double. AE, DISC, MC, V.

Perhaps because the area is so closely associated with resorts, Phoenix has never been much of a B&B town. However, there is now a very tasteful option for anyone seeking a luxurious bed-and-breakfast inn along the Camelback Corridor. Built in 1930 and situated on 2 acres of lawns and citrus groves, this Monterey Revival–style home is located almost across the road from the famed Phoenician about midway between Old Town Scottsdale and the Biltmore Fashion Park shopping plaza. Among the five guest rooms (all of which have whirlpool tubs), you can choose from different themes, including Southwestern, garden, and country. However, for only slightly more than the other rooms, you can opt for the Mountain View Room, which has a balcony with a view of Camelback Mountain. Breakfasts, which are usually served in the sunroom or on the patio, usually include some sort of citrus dish made with fruit from the inn's trees, and there is often fresh-squeezed lemonade available. In the afternoons, wine and cheese are set out. There is also a small swimming pool here, although it gets a lot of noise from Camelback Road traffic.

✪ **The Ritz-Carlton Phoenix.** 2401 E. Camelback Rd., Phoenix, AZ 85016. ☎ **800/241-3333** or 602/468-0700. Fax 602/468-9883. 281 rms, 14 suites. A/C MINIBAR TV TEL. Late Sept to mid-June $225–$300 double, $350–$1,500 suite; mid-June to early Sept $140–$175 double, $225–$1,500 suite. AE, CB, DC, DISC, EURO, JCB, MC, V. Valet parking $9.50.

Located directly across the street from the Biltmore Fashion Park shopping center in the heart of the Camelback Corridor business and shopping district, the Ritz-Carlton is the city's finest nonresort hotel and is known for providing impeccable service. The public areas are filled with European antiques, and though this decor may seem a bit out of place in Phoenix, it's still utterly sophisticated. In the guest rooms, all of which were partially redecorated in 1996, you'll find reproductions of antique furniture and marble bathrooms with ornate fixtures. For additional pampering, opt for the Club Level (breakfast and other snacks and drinks included in the rates). Although there's no golf course here, the Arizona Biltmore's courses are quite close.

**Dining/Entertainment:** In Bistro 24, a casual and lively French bistro atmosphere prevails, with a menu to match. The elegant lobby lounge serves afternoon tea as well as cocktails, while in The Club, fine cigars and premium spirits are the order of the day. There's also a bar and grill by the pool.

**Services:** Concierge, 24-hour room service, valet/laundry service, baby-sitting, car-rental desk, massages, complimentary golf shuttle.

**Facilities:** Small outdoor pool (with bar and grill), tennis court, fitness center, saunas.

> ### ⊕ Family-Friendly Hotels
>
> **Hyatt Regency Scottsdale Resort at Gainey Ranch** *(see p. 86)* Not only is there a totally awesome water playground complete with sand beach and water slide, but the Kamp Hyatt Kachina program provides supervised structured activities.
>
> **The Phoenician** *(see p. 88)* Kids absolutely love the water slide here; it's the fastest resort slide in the valley. Kids and parents both appreciate the Funicians Club, a supervised activities program for children ages 5 to 12. Kids get to play games, make crafts, and burn up lots of excess energy. A putting green and croquet court offer further diversions.
>
> **Doubletree La Posada Resort** *(see p. 89)* If you're a kid, it's hard to imagine a cooler pool than the one here. It's got a two-story waterfall, a swim-through cave, and bug (artificial boulders) all around. There are also horseshoe pits, a volleyball court, and a pitch-and-putt green.
>
> **The Pointe Hilton at Squaw Peak** *(see p. 93)* A water slide, tubing river, waterfall, water volleyball, a miniature golf course, a video games room, and a kids' program together guarantee that your kids will be exhausted by the end of the day. This is *the* best resort in the valley for families.

## MODERATE

In addition to the listings below, there are also a couple of moderately priced chain motels in the central Phoenix and Camelback Corridor areas worth recommending. These are the **Best Western InnSuites Hotel Phoenix,** 1615 E. Northern Ave. at 16th Street (☎ **602/997-6285**), charging $99 to $122 double; and the **Ramada Inn 3,** 502 W. Camelback Rd. (☎ **602/264-9290**), charging $97 double. Rates are for the high season; for toll-free phone numbers, see the appendix.

**Hacienda Alta.** 5750 E. Camelback Rd., Phoenix, AZ 85018. ☎ and fax **602/945-8525.** 2 rms. TV. $90 double. Rates include full breakfast. No credit cards.

Located adjacent to The Phoenician, yet very much in its own separate world surrounded by a desert landscape, this home offers a very convenient location, reasonable rates, and a chance to feel away from it all in the middle of the city. This is a very casual and eclectic sort of place, so don't expect the fussiness of most other B&Bs. Owners Margaret and Ed Newhall make this a fun place to call home for a few days. The inn is housed in a 1920s territorial-style adobe home, and in the old gardens you'll find orange and grapefruit trees, which often provide juice for breakfast.

**Maricopa Manor.** 15 W. Pasadena Ave. (P.O. Box 7186), Phoenix, AZ 85011-7186. ☎ **800/ 292-6403** or 602/274-6302. Fax 602/266-3904. 6 suites. A/C TV TEL. Sept–May $129–$189 double; June–Aug $89–$139 double. Rates include continental breakfast. AE, DISC, MC, V.

Centrally located between downtown Phoenix and Scottsdale and particularly popular with business travelers, this elegant B&B is just a block off busy Camelback Road. However, the orange trees, palms, and large yard all lend an air of the country. The inn's main home was built in 1928 and is designed to resemble a Spanish manor house. All the guest rooms are large suites, two of which are located in a separate guest house. One suite has a sunroom and kitchen, while another has two separate sleeping areas. Breakfast is delivered to your door each morning in a basket and can be eaten in the room or at one of the tables in the garden. The inn has a pool and hot tub, and guests also have access to a nearby health club.

# SCOTTSDALE
## VERY EXPENSIVE

**Gardiner's Resort on Camelback.** 5700 E. McDonald Dr., Phoenix, AZ 85253. ☎ **800/ 245-2051** or 602/948-2100. Fax 602/483-3386. 100 rms and suites. Late Dec to mid-May $255 double, $355–$605 suite; mid-May to mid-Sept $105 double, $205–$305 suite; mid-Sept to late Dec $205 double, $305–$505 suite. Tennis packages available. AE, MC, V.

If tennis is your game, you'll definitely want to consider making this resort your address in Phoenix. Located on the north slope of Camelback Mountain, Gardiner's Resort has a long history of helping tennis players improve their games. The resort is small and its gated entry gives the feel of a private country club. There are plenty of courts, and with eight pools, there are plenty of places to cool off as well.

Guest rooms are individually decorated condos, and some have large balconies or sunrooms. All rooms have computer jacks, coffeemakers, and hair dryers. The resort also has houses for rent, and some of these have their own private pool or tennis court. Fresh-squeezed orange juice and the newspaper at your doorstep each morning is a nice touch.

**Dining/Entertainment:** There's a great view of Mummy Mountain from the bar and dining room, where the menu includes a very tempting mix of new American and continental dishes.

**Services:** Room service, valet/laundry service, tennis lessons, cooking classes, children's programs, baby-sitting.

**Facilities:** 21 tennis courts, eight pools, whirlpools, sauna, fitness center, business center, and full-service health spa offering various massages and body treatments.

✪ **Hyatt Regency Scottsdale Resort at Gainey Ranch.** 7500 E. Doubletree Ranch Rd., Scottsdale, AZ 85258. ☎ **800/233-1234** or 602/991-3388. Fax 602/483-5550. 493 rms, 7 casitas, 25 suites. A/C MINIBAR TV TEL. Jan 1–late May $315–$445 double; $1,080–$1,925 casita; $495–$2,400 suite. Late May–early Sept $155–$290 double; $800–$1,800 casita; $225–$1,200 suite. Early Sept–Dec 31 $300–$405 double; $1,050–$2,055 casita; $405–$1,950 suite. AE, DC, DISC, MC, V.

From the ranks of tall palms to the gridwork of wooden awnings shading the windows, this luxurious resort is designed to take the breath away. Future archaeologists excavating this site would certainly be convinced that it was once a temple. And what did they worship here? Water, of course. Surrounded by a lake, gardens, fountains, and fishponds, a 2½-acre water playground is the resort's focal point. This extravagant complex of 10 swimming pools includes a water slide, a sand beach, water-volleyball pool, waterfalls, and a whirlpool spa. As if this weren't enough, the resort also offers 27 holes of outstanding golf, 8 tennis courts, and trails for jogging and cycling.

The grounds are planted with hundreds of tall palm trees that frame the gorgeous views of the distant McDowell Mountains. Original works of art throughout the resort add visual interest close at hand. The guest rooms are everything you'd expect in this price range, with robes, hair dryers, scales, and marble-top tables.

**Dining/Entertainment:** The Golden Swan, serving excellent Southwestern cuisine, includes a popular terrace dining area with a duck's-eye view out over a fish pond. See "Dining" below for more information. The Squash Blossom provides a casual atmosphere and also serves Southwestern cuisine. Ristorante Sandolo is an Italian cafe that offers after-dinner gondola rides. A lobby bar features live music nightly. There are also two bars (one with karaoke music) and a grill near the pool.

**Services:** Concierge, 24-hour room service, valet parking, valet/laundry service, children's programs, gondola rides, in-room massages.

**Facilities:** Twenty-seven holes make this one of the major resorts luring golfers to Phoenix. The course is noteworthy for its water hazards and for utilizing its valley-floor location. In addition to the pool area, you'll find eight lighted tennis courts, a croquet court, jogging and bicycling trails, and a health spa with exercise equipment, aerobics classes, and sauna.

✪ **Inn at the Citadel.** 8700 E. Pinnacle Peak Rd., Scottsdale, AZ 85255. ☎ **800/927-8367** or 602/585-6133. Fax 602/585-3436. 11 suites. A/C TV TEL. Jan–May $295–$335 double; June–Aug $125–$175 double; Sept–early Jan $155–$175 double. Rates include continental breakfast. AE, DC, DISC, MC, V.

Although frequented primarily by people building homes in the area, this luxurious and tasteful little inn, located 20 minutes north of downtown Scottsdale in an up-scale shopping and business complex, is a great choice if you aren't into the resort scene. Antiques and original works of art give the rooms a unique atmosphere, and some of the antique furnishings, which tend toward Spanish colonial pieces, are even for sale. Some suites have fireplaces while others have small balconies. Many also have good views of the surrounding desert and mountains. The bathrooms, which are huge, are done in marble and have lace shower curtains; other guest room amenities include safes, terry robes, coffeemakers, and hair dryers. In the same building that houses the inn, you'll find several exclusive shops, a beauty salon, and a shady court-yard with a beautiful little pond.

✪ **Marriott's Camelback Inn.** 5402 E. Lincoln Dr., Scottsdale, AZ 85253. ☎ **800/4-CAMEL** or 602/948-1700. Fax 602/951-8469. 457 rms, 28 suites. A/C MINIBAR TV TEL. Early Jan to May $225–$379 double, $385–$2,000 suite; June–Aug $89–$119 double, $180–$750 suite; Sept–Dec $235–$279 double, $285–$1,050 suite. AE, CB, DC, DISC, JCB, MC, V.

Opened in 1936, the Camelback Inn was the first Marriott resort and is today one of the grande dames of the Phoenix hotel scene, and as one of the oldest and most traditionally Southwestern of the area's many resorts, it attracts a well-heeled and conservative crowd. Set at the foot of Mummy Mountain and overlooking Camel-back Mountain, the Camelback Inn offers a tranquil setting only 5 minutes from downtown Scottsdale. Although the resort's two 18-hole golf courses are the main attraction for most guests here, the spa is among the finest in the state and would be a reason to visit in its own right. In early 1997, however, a new pool complex sure to appeal to families, was added to the resort's many recreational offerings.

The guest rooms are decorated with contemporary Southwestern furnishings and art, and all have balconies or patios. The bathrooms are well lit and come with hair dryers, a large basket of toiletries, and a shaving mirror.

**Dining/Entertainment:** The Chaparral, serving continental fare, is one of the best restaurants in the valley. The Navajo Room is a more casual place. Light snacks are available at Hoppin' Jack's or the Oasis Lounge, and you'll find healthy meals at Sprouts (in the spa). Golfers can dine at the Camelback Golf Club. For a quiet drink, there's the Chaparral Lounge, and for espresso and pastries, there's the Kokopelli Cafe.

**Services:** Concierge, room service, baby-sitting, valet/laundry service, car-rental desk.

**Facilities:** Two outstanding 18-hole golf courses, a pitch-and-putt course, six ten-nis courts, three pools, three whirlpools, a playground, basketball and volleyball courts, and a hiking trail. The renowned full-service health spa offers numerous body, skin, and beauty treatments, a lap pool, aerobics room and classes, saunas, steam rooms, whirlpools, and a lot of exercise equipment.

✪ **The Phoenician.** 6000 E. Camelback Rd., Scottsdale, AZ 85251. ☎ **800/888-8234** or 602/941-8200. Fax 602/947-4311. 567 rms, 73 suites. A/C MINIBAR TV TEL. Jan 1–mid-June $370–$505 double, $1,000–$1,650 suite; mid-June–early Sept $180–$310 double, $475–$1,100 suite; early Sept–Dec 31 $355–$405 double, $1,075–$1,725 suite. AE, CB, DC, DISC, EURO, JCB, MC, V. Valet parking $10.

Situated on 250 acres at the foot of Camelback Mountain, the Phoenician is this city's most ostentatious resort, with a shimmering expanse of polished marble and sparkling crystal for a lobby. While some people find the formality of the resort a bit out of place in casual Arizona, others revel in the rarefied atmosphere. With uniformed employees waiting around every corner, service is second to none, and there's no denying that the pool complex is one of the finest in the state and a fabulous place to while away a day. The Center for Well Being, the resort's noted spa, offers all the pampering anyone could ever need, and there are 27 challenging holes of golf.

The guest rooms here are as elaborate as the public areas and include sunken bathtubs for two, Berber carpets, muted color schemes, three phones, computer jacks, large patios, two closets, terry robes, bathroom scales, hair dryers, and wall safes. And this is just the *standard* room. For the added cache of a boutique hotel within the main resort, opt for a room or suite in the Canyon Building, which has its own private pool complete with rental cabanas.

**Dining/Entertainment:** Mary Elaine's, featuring modern French cuisine, offers elegant dining and great views. In the Terrace Dining Room, the atmosphere is slightly less formal and Italian dishes are served. Windows on the Green features Southwestern cuisine and a view of the golf course. For quick snacks, there are the poolside Oasis and Canyon Bar & Grill, as well as the Café & Ice Cream Parlor. The Lobby Tea Court serves afternoon tea, while the Thirsty Camel, with its view of the valley, is the resort's most popular place for a drink, especially after sunset when the city's lights sparkle on the horizon.

**Services:** Concierge, 24-hour room service, valet/laundry service, baby-sitting, children's programs.

**Facilities:** The beautiful setting of the 27-hole golf course, right at the foot of Camelback Mountain, makes The Phoenician one of the more attractive resort courses in Scottsdale. The Center for Well Being is a superb spa that includes a fitness center, saunas, steam rooms, whirlpools, aerobics room, beauty salon, and barbershop, as well as a wide variety of body and beauty treatments. Other facilities include seven pools (including one lined with opalescent tiles and one with a water slide), a putting green, 12 tennis courts (11 lighted), a whirlpool, lawn games, a volleyball court, rental bikes, jogging trails, and a shopping arcade. A car-rental desk and business center are also available.

✪ **Scottsdale Princess.** 7575 E. Princess Dr., Scottsdale, AZ 85255. ☎ **800/344-4758** or 602/585-4848. Fax 602/585-0091. 507 rms, 144 suites. A/C MINIBAR TV TEL. Jan 1 to late May $320–$440 double, $490–$2,500 suite; late May to early Sept $145–$185 double, $215–$1,250 suite; early Sept to Dec 31 $260–$330 double, $380–$2,000 suite. AE, CB, DC, DISC, EURO, JCB, MC, V.

With its royal palms, tiled fountains, waterfalls, and classical art and antiques, the Princess is a modern rendition of a Moorish palace and offers a truly exotic atmosphere unmatched by any other valley resort. Located a 20-minute drive north of downtown Scottsdale, this resort will delight anyone in search of a romantic hideaway. It's also home to the Phoenix Open golf tournament, as well as a professional tennis tournament, which means the two golf courses here are superb and the courts are top-notch. For those not tempted by golf or tennis, there's a full-service spa and fitness center.

The guest rooms all have distinct living and work areas, wet bars, refrigerators, and private balconies. The decor is elegant Southwestern, and the bathrooms, roomy enough for even the most fastidious guest, include two sinks, a separate shower and tub, a vanity, and a telephone. For more space or if you're traveling with the family, there's a wide variety of suites available.

**Dining/Entertainment:** The Marquesa is a highly acclaimed, and high-priced, Spanish restaurant. Equally highly praised locally is La Hacienda, a gourmet Mexican restaurant with strolling mariachis. See "Dining" below for more information. More casual dining is available at restaurants in the main building, in the golf clubhouse, and by the pool. Lounge options include a quiet spot and a rowdy saloon with country dance music.

**Services:** Concierge, 24-hour room service, valet/laundry service, baby-sitting, health and beauty treatments, shopping shuttle.

**Facilities:** In addition to the two noted 18-hole golf courses, there are seven tennis courts (six lighted); three pools; whirlpools; racquetball, squash, and basketball courts; a fitness trail; a complete spa and fitness center; boutiques; tennis and golf pro shops; and a business center. There's even a fishing pond here (which kids love).

## EXPENSIVE

✪ **Doubletree La Posada Resort.** 4949 E. Lincoln Dr., Scottsdale, AZ 85253. ☎ **800/733-5466** or 602/952-0420. Fax 602/852-0151. 264 rms, 11 suites. A/C TV TEL. Mid-Jan to May $225–$245 double, $375–$550 suite; June to mid-Sept $139–$159 double, $225–$425 suite; mid-Sept to mid-Jan $205–$225 double, $275–$500 suite. AE, CB, DC, DISC, ER, JCB, MC, V.

If you prefer to spend your time by the pool rather than on the fairway, you'll love La Posada. The pool covers half an acre and features its own two-story waterfall that cascades over artificial boulders. Connecting the two halves of the pool is a swim-through grotto with its own bar/cafe. Of course, the resort also offers other diversions such as tennis and racquetball courts and a pitch-and-putt green.

Mission-revival architecture prevails here, though the interior of the lobby is more Vegas glitz than Spanish colonial. The guest rooms are larger than average and feature Southwestern-style furnishings. The bathrooms have two sinks, plenty of counter space, and tile floors.

**Dining/Entertainment:** The Garden Terrace restaurant has a nice view of Camelback Mountain and features continental cuisine with many Southwestern touches. The adjacent lounge is a large, flashy place with occasional live music.

**Services:** Concierge, room service, laundry/valet service.

**Facilities:** In addition to facilities mentioned above, there are four whirlpools, sauna, volleyball court, horseshoe pits, pro shop, beauty salon, and car-rental desk.

✪ **Doubletree Paradise Valley Resort.** 5401 N. Scottsdale Rd., Scottsdale, AZ 85250. ☎ **800/222-TREE** or 602/947-5400. Fax 602/946-1524. 387 rms, 17 suites. A/C MINIBAR TV TEL. Jan–May $139–$230 double, $230–$2,000 suite; May to early Sept $59–$95 double, $230–$480 suite; early Sept to Dec $139–$209 double, $230–$2,000 suite. AE, CB, DC, DISC, MC, V.

This lushly landscaped resort gives a bow to the pioneering architectural style of Frank Lloyd Wright, and for this reason stands out from many other comparable Scottsdale resorts. Built around several courtyards containing swimming pools, bubbling fountains, palm trees, and desert gardens, the resort has much the look and feel of

Hyatt's nearby Gainey Ranch mega-resort, but on a less grandiose scale. Mature palm trees lend a sort of Moorish feel to the grounds and cast fanciful shadows in the gardens.

At press time, a complete renovation of guest rooms was scheduled, so you can expect very comfortable new accommodations if you visit this year.

**Dining/Entertainment:** Off to one side of the lobby is a skylit dining room serving Southwestern dishes. A lobby lounge serves drinks and light meals to the accompaniment of live music many evenings. There's also a patio bar adjacent to the main pool.

**Services:** Concierge, room service, valet/laundry service, baby-sitting.

**Facilities:** The two outdoor pools, which have small waterfalls, are set in attractive, palm-shaded courtyards. There are also two lighted tennis courts, a fitness center, two racquetball courts, saunas, steam room, whirlpools, a beauty salon, a business center, a gift shop, and a car-rental desk.

**Holiday Inn Hotel & Conference Center.** 7353 E. Indian School Rd., Scottsdale, AZ 85251. ☎ **800/695-6995** or 602/994-9203. Fax 602/941-2567. 206 rms, 6 suites. A/C TV TEL. Late Dec to late Apr $150 double, $260–$360 suite; late Apr to early June $120 double, $160–$230 suite; early June to late Aug $90 double, $130–$180 suite; late Aug to late Dec $120 double, $190–$260 suite. AE, CB, DC, DISC, MC, V.

If you're in town to shop or attend a performance at the Scottsdale Center for the Arts (rather than to play golf or lounge by the pool), this Holiday Inn is well worth considering. The low-rise hotel is located on the beautifully landscaped Scottsdale Civic Center Mall (a park, not a shopping center) and is adjacent to the Scottsdale Center for the Arts and the popular Fifth Avenue Shops. The best rooms are those opening onto the mall.

**Dining/Entertainment:** Bola's Grill features regional dishes and patio dining overlooking the park. There's also a lively lounge adjacent to the restaurant.

**Services:** Room service, shopping shuttle, bicycle rentals.

**Facilities:** Small outdoor pool, tennis court, whirlpool.

**Marriott's Mountain Shadows Resort and Golf Club.** 5641 E. Lincoln Dr., Scottsdale, AZ 85253. ☎ **800/228-9290** or 602/948-7111. Fax 602/951-5430. 336 rms, 19 suites. A/C MINIBAR TV TEL. Jan–May $194–$249 double, $360–$650 suite; June–Aug $94–$119 double, $180–$285 suite; Sept–Dec $199–$224 double, $320–$600 suite. AE, CB, DC, DISC, MC, V.

Located across the road from the Camelback Inn, Mountain Shadows offers better views of Camelback Mountain but an entirely different ambience. Mountain Shadows was built in the late 1950s and its architecture is dated; still, the property is well maintained and appeals to families and younger travelers looking for a more informal atmosphere than is found at the Camelback Inn. An 18-hole resort course on the premises keeps most guests happy, but for the more serious golfer, there is access to the Camelback Inn's two outstanding courses. Guests here can also use the Camelback Inn's spa facilities.

Standard rooms are large and have high ceilings, wet bars, king-size beds, and balconies. The rooms around the main pool can be a bit noisy; avoid these if you want peace and quiet. Those rooms in the Palm section offer the best views of the mountain. Some suites include whirlpool tubs, brass beds, and private patios.

**Dining/Entertainment:** Shell's Oyster Bar & Seafood Restaurant offers both indoor and terrace dining. Family dining can be had at the moderately priced Cactus Flower Cafe. There's casual dining at the Country Club Dining Room, and coffee and pastries at the Kachina Cafe.

**Services:** Concierge, room service, valet/laundry service, car-rental desk, baby-sitting, guided mountain hikes.

**Facilities:** Three 18-hole golf courses, eight lighted tennis courts, three pools, two whirlpools, saunas, fitness center (and access to the Camelback Inn's noted spa), volleyball court, beauty salon, pro shop.

**Radisson Resort Scottsdale.** 7171 N. Scottsdale Rd., Scottsdale, AZ 85253-3696. ☎ **800/333-3333** or 602/991-3800. Fax 602/948-1381. 318 rms, 35 suites. A/C TV TEL. Mid-Jan to late May $210–$225 double, $325–$1,500 suite; late May to mid-Sept $89–$99 double, $165–$1,500 suite; mid-Sept to early Jan $189–$199 double, $270–$1,500 suite. AE, CB, DC, DISC, ER, JCB, MC, V.

Not nearly as lavishly appointed as the area's top resorts, this well-maintained resort opts for a formal and traditional atmosphere that seems to appeal to an older clientele, many of whom come to play tennis on the resort's 21 tennis courts and two 18-hole golf courses. The pool area, set in a flower-filled courtyard, has plenty of space for lounging. If you don't need glitz and snob appeal, this place offers a good value for Scottsdale. Many rooms include marble-top tables, comfortable chairs, private patios, and marble bathrooms with two sinks. The bilevel suites feature kitchenettes, sleeping lofts, second-floor decks, and two bathrooms. The golf-course rooms are our favorites simply because of the views of the McDowell Mountains.

**Dining/Entertainment:** Andre's, a conservative French provincial dining room, serves continental fare. Markers Lounge has pool tables and a lively atmosphere at night. During the day the Cabaña Bar serves drinks and light meals to swimmers and sunbathers. You'll find the resort's patisserie (an appreciated bit of convenience) tucked into a corner of the lobby.

**Services:** Concierge, 24-hour room service, valet/laundry service, car-rental desk, massages and other body and skin treatments, tennis lessons.

**Facilities:** In addition to golf and tennis facilities, you'll find a pro shop, three pools, whirlpool, volleyball court, and a health club.

**Regal McCormick Ranch.** 7401 N. Scottsdale Rd., Scottsdale, AZ 85253-3548. ☎ **800/243-1332** or 602/948-5050. Fax 602/991-5572. 125 rms, 3 suites, 51 condominium villas. A/C MINIBAR TV TEL. Jan 1–May 31 $175–$259 double, $250–$350 suite, from $275 villa; June 1 to mid-Sept $109–$189 double, $150 suite, from $175 villa; mid-Sept to Dec 31 $185–$265 double, $275 suite, from $275 villa. AE, CB, DC, DISC, MC, V.

If you like the heat but not the desert, this resort, with its lakefront setting, is a good bet. Surrounded by green lawns and a golf course (and with bellmen wearing knickers and argyle socks), Regal McCormick Ranch does what it can to make you think you're not in the desert, and because it's smaller than many resorts in the area, it has a more personal feel. The focal point is, of course, the lake, where you can rent small sailboats if you like. More traditional resort activities are available at the two 18-hole golf courses and on the four tennis courts. The guest rooms all have their own private balcony or patio, and more than half the rooms overlook the lake. If you're here with your family, consider the spacious villas.

**Dining/Entertainment:** The Piñon Grill features bold Southwestern decor and a menu to match and is one of the better Southwestern restaurants in the valley. Diamondbacks Bar and Grill continues the Southwestern theme.

**Services:** Concierge, room service, valet/laundry service, tennis lessons and clinics, golf-course shuttle.

**Facilities:** Two 18-hole golf courses, four lighted tennis courts, pool, whirlpool, boat rentals, walking and jogging paths, tennis pro shop.

**Scottsdale Marriott Suites.** 7325 E. Third Ave., Scottsdale, AZ 85251. ☎ **800/228-9290** or 602/945-1550. Fax 602/945-2005. 251 suites. A/C TV TEL. Jan–May $184–$209 double; June–Sept $89–$184 double; Sept–Jan $175–$209 double. Rates include continental breakfast. AE, CB, DC, DISC, EURO, JCB, MC, V.

Although this seems to be primarily a business hotel, it also makes an excellent base if shopping is your raison d'être. The hotel is located only 2 blocks from the famous Fifth Avenue Shops, and Scottsdale Fashion Square is only slightly farther. All the rooms here are suites and have two telephones and two TVs, as well as computer jacks, refrigerators, wet bars, coffeemakers, and irons and ironing boards. In the marble bathrooms you'll find a hair dryer and separate showers and tubs. This all adds up to spaciousness and luxury that even non-business travelers will appreciate.

**Dining/Entertainment:** Allie's American Grille is a casual restaurant serving moderately priced meals.

**Services:** Concierge, room service, valet/laundry service.

**Facilities:** Outdoor pool, whirlpool, exercise room, saunas, car-rental desk, business center.

✪ **The Sunburst.** 4925 N. Scottsdale Rd., Scottsdale, AZ 85251. ☎ **800/528-7867** or 602/945-7666. Fax 602/946-4056. 206 rms, 4 suites. A/C MINIBAR TV TEL. Jan 1 to mid-May $195–$250 double, $325–$525 suite; mid-May to early Sept $90–$125 double, $175–$325 suite; early Sept to Dec 31 $155–$190 double, $265–$450 suite. AE, CB, DC, DISC, JCB, MC, V.

An exceptional location in the heart of the Scottsdale shopping district is the prime appeal of this recently renovated and upgraded resort. A new Southwestern character dominates the interior design here. The focal point of the lobby is a massive sandstone fireplace, and all around are lounging chairs that evoke the Southwest in their styling. Loud piped-in music, however, precludes doing any business or peaceful lounging in the lobby. The resort's courtyard is lushly planted and features a small lagoon-style pool complete with sand beach, short water slide, and flame-topped columnar waterfalls. An artificial stream, waterfalls, and fake sandstone ruins all add up to a fantasy island landscape that is among the most fun in town (though on a much smaller scale than some other area pool complexes).

Guest rooms are decorated in new "Old West" styling, and they've been done well. They're comfortable and have a sense of place about them. French doors open onto patios.

**Dining/Entertainment:** The same new Southwestern styling seen in the lobby prevails in the restaurant as well. The menu here features a mix of Mediterranean and Southwestern flavors. In addition, there's a lobby bar.

**Services:** Concierge, room service, valet/laundry service.

**Facilities:** A whirlpool and fitness room add to the recreational facilities here. Although there is no golf course, tee times can be arranged at nearby courses.

## MODERATE/INEXPENSIVE

In addition to the hotel listed below, Scottsdale does have a few inexpensive and moderately priced chain motel options, although during the winter season prices are a bit higher than you might expect. The rates given here are for the high season; see the appendix for toll-free telephone numbers. Try the **Days Inn—Scottsdale Resort at Fashion Square Mall,** 4710 N. Scottsdale Rd. (☎ **602/947-5411**), charging $79 to $127 double; **Motel 6—Scottsdale,** 6848 E. Camelback Rd. (☎ **602/946-2280**), charging $53 double; and **Rodeway Inn—Phoenix/Scottsdale,** 7110 E. Indian School Rd. (☎ **602/946-3456**), charging $133 to $150 double.

**Scottsdale's Fifth Avenue Inn.** 6935 Fifth Ave., Scottsdale, AZ 85251. ☎ **800/528-7396** (outside Arizona) or 602/994-9461. Fax 602/947-1695 attn 5th. 92 rms. A/C TV TEL. Jan 15–Apr 30 $87–$92 double; May 1–Sept 30 $45–$50 double; Oct 1–Jan 15 $57–$62 double. Rates include continental breakfast. AE, CB, DC, DISC, MC, V.

For convenience and price, this motel can't be beat (at least not in Scottsdale). Located at the west end of the Fifth Avenue shopping district, this motel is within walking distance of some of the best shopping and dining in Scottsdale. The guest rooms are large and have held up well since their last renovation. The three-story building is arranged around a central courtyard where you'll find the pool and a whirlpool.

# NORTH PHOENIX
## VERY EXPENSIVE

✪ **The Pointe Hilton at Squaw Peak.** 7677 N. 16th St., Phoenix, AZ 85020-9832. ☎ **800/ 876-4683** or 602/997-2626. Fax 602/997-2391. 564 suites, studios, and casitas. A/C MINIBAR TV TEL. Jan 1 to late May $229–$400 suite, studio, or casita; late May to late Sept $99–$179 suite, studio, or casita; late Sept to Dec 31 $165–$250 suite, studio, or casita. AE, CB, DC, DISC, EURO, JCB, MC, V.

Located at the foot of Squaw Peak, this is a lushly landscaped family- and convention-oriented resort in north Phoenix, and in recent years the resort has made a splash with its impressive aquatic playground, which features a tubing "river," water slide, waterfall, sports pool, and lagoon pool. The resort is done in the Spanish villa style so common throughout the Southwest and California. All the guest rooms here are suites, studios, or two-story casitas furnished in a mixture of Spanish colonial style and contemporary furnishings.

**Dining/Entertainment:** Aunt Chilada's Mexican restaurant is a fun place housed in an old adobe building that was built in 1880. Hole-in-the-Wall, the resort's Western-theme restaurant, is housed in a building that dates from the 1930s. Lantana Grill is the resort's upscale dining room and serves contemporary American and Southwestern dishes.

**Services:** Concierge, room service, valet/laundry service, rental-car desk, complimentary afternoon cocktails, baby-sitting, children's programs.

**Facilities:** The Hole-in-the-Wall River Ranch aquatic playground is the resort's star attraction. However, there are also four other swimming pools, as well as whirlpool spas scattered around the property. An 18-hole golf course (4 miles away), four tennis courts, jogging trails, rental bikes, shops, and a business center round out the adult facilities, while an 18-hole putting course, game room, and activity center are popular with kids. The Tocasierra Spa offers massages and other body treatments and includes a beauty salon and a fitness center (with racquetball courts, aerobics classes, free weights, exercise machines, a lap pool, sauna, steam room, and exercise instructors).

**The Pointe Hilton at Tapatio Cliffs.** 11111 N. Seventh St., Phoenix, AZ 85020. ☎ **800/ 876-4683** or 602/866-7500. Fax 602/993-0276. 584 suites. A/C MINIBAR TV TEL. Jan 1 to late May $229–$400 suite; late May to late Sept $99–$179 suite; late Sept to Dec 31 $165–$250 suite. AE, CB, DC, DISC, EURO, JCB, MC, V.

Situated on the shoulder of North Mountain (on the north side of Phoenix of course), Tapatio Cliffs offers the steepest and lushest grounds of the three Pointe resorts (get your heart and your brakes checked before staying here). The Falls is this resort's entry into the valley's bigger-and-splashier pool competition. More adult-oriented than the aquatic playground at the Pointe Hilton at Squaw Peak, the Falls includes two lagoon pools connected by a 138-foot water slide and impressive 40-foot-high cascades that tumble over real and artificial boulders and through terraced pools. Poolside rental cabanas provide an extra dash of luxury for those who can afford it. Unfortunately, the landscaping will need a few years to mature here at The Falls. If you're a hiker, you'll enjoy the easy access to desert trails in the adjacent North Mountain Recreation Area. If you're not a hiker, you can avail yourself of the resort's golf course, which has been rated one of the best in the state. A small spa here offers massages and a variety of body and beauty treatments. As at other Pointe resorts, all rooms here are spacious suites. Furnishings reflect the Southwest, and some have high ceilings. Corner rooms, with their extra windows, are particularly bright.

**Dining/Entertainment:** The hilltop Different Pointe of View offers stupendous views from both lounge and dining room. The menu is international, and the wine cellar is extensive (see "Dining," below). For Wild West dining, there's the Waterin' Hole in an old house with sawdust on the floor and steaks on the grill. Marble floors and mahogany paneling give Pointe in Tyme a classic clublike atmosphere. For light poolside meals, there's La Cantina.

**Services:** Concierge, room service, complimentary afternoon cocktails, massages, rental-car desk, free shuttle between Pointe Hilton properties, horseback riding, babysitting.

**Facilities:** In addition to the facilities mentioned above, there are 11 lighted tennis courts, six other swimming pools, whirlpool spas, a fitness center, steam room, sauna, game room, rental bikes, gift shop, tennis shop, golf shop, and business center.

## EXPENSIVE

✪ **Embassy Suites—Phoenix North.** 2577 W. Greenway Rd., Phoenix, AZ 85023-4222. ☎ **800/362-2779** or 602/375-1777. Fax 602/375-4012. 314 suites. A/C TV TEL. Sept 16–May 15 $190 double; May 16–Sept 15 $140 double. Rates include full breakfast. AE, CB, DC, DISC, MC, V.

This resortlike hotel in north Phoenix, though right off I-17, is well away from the rest of the valley's resorts (and good restaurants), but if you happen to have relatives in Sun City or are planning a trip north to Sedona or the Grand Canyon, it makes a good choice. The lobby of this Mission-style, all-suite hotel has the feel of a Spanish church interior, but instead of a cloister off the lobby, there is a garden courtyard with a huge swimming pool and lots of palm trees. The guest rooms feature motel-grade furnishings, but there are two TVs in every suite, as well as wet bars, refrigerators, coffeemakers, safes, irons and ironing boards, and computer jacks. The bathrooms are small, but they do have hair dryers.

**Dining/Entertainment:** The restaurant in the lobby is a casual place with moderately priced meals. Also in the lobby is a piano lounge, and beside the pool, there's the Cabana Bar. Complimentary cocktails are served each evening.

**Services:** Room service, valet/laundry service.

**Facilities:** In addition to the large pool, there are two tennis courts, an exercise room, whirlpool, sauna, sand volleyball court, and two racquetball courts.

**Sheraton Crescent Hotel.** 2620 W. Dunlap Ave., Phoenix, AZ 85021. ☎ **800/423-4126** or 602/943-8200. Fax 602/371-2856. 342 rms, 12 suites. A/C TV TEL. Jan 1 to late May $139–$244 double, $230–$550 suite; late May to early Sept $71–$144 double, $230–$550 suite; early Sept to Dec 31 $129–$229 double, $230–$550 suite. AE, CB, DC, DISC, EURO, JCB, MC, V.

Located in the north-central high-tech business district and across I-17 from the Metrocenter mall, this business hotel is a sister property to The Phoenician and displays much the same decorative style, albeit on a more subdued level. Although located away from downtown and the Camelback Corridor business districts, this is still one of the city's better choices for business travelers, especially for those who like to exercise when they aren't working. Marble abounds in the lobby and also shows up in guest room bathrooms. Guest rooms are designed with business travelers in mind, and offer plenty of space, comfort, and convenience, with dual-line phones, irons and ironing boards, and hair dryers. The king rooms with balconies are my favorites.

**Dining/Entertainment:** Charlie's Grill is a big, casual restaurant combining tropical decor with a regional American menu. The adjacent lounge is small and subdued.

**Services:** Concierge, room service, valet/laundry service.

**Facilities:** In the summer of 1997, a 166-foot-long waterslide was slated to be added to the recreational facilities here, which should make this hotel a bit more appealing to families. The hotel's small main pool is in a lush garden setting. Other facilities include a large fitness center, whirlpool spa, sauna, two tennis courts, two squash courts, volleyball and basketball courts.

**Wyndham Metrocenter Hotel.** 10220 N. Metro Pkwy. E., Phoenix, AZ 85051. ☎ **800/ 996-3426** or 602/997-5900. Fax 602/997-1034. 284 rms, 18 suites. A/C TV TEL. Jan 1 to late May $159–$218 double, $189–$279 suite; late May to mid-Sept $84–$128 double, $114–$179 suite; mid-Sept to Dec 31 $139–$218 double, $169–$279 suite. AE, CB, DC, DISC, MC, V.

This business hotel benefits from its location in the heart of Phoenix's north-central business district, adjacent to the largest shopping mall in Arizona. The guest rooms, though refurnished just a couple of years ago, aren't always in top shape, but their unusual styling gives them character. Hair dryers, coffeemakers, and dual-line phones are definite pluses. There's also a concierge floor.

**Dining/Entertainment:** Copper Creek Bar and Grill offers both indoor and patio dining at reasonable prices and a bar area with lots of polished brass and varnished oak.

**Services:** Room service, airport shuttle, valet/laundry service, car-rental desk.

**Facilities:** Olympic-size swimming pool, whirlpool spa, tennis court, exercise room, and sauna.

## MODERATE/INEXPENSIVE

Among the better moderately priced chain motels in north Phoenix are the **Travelodge Phoenix Metrocenter I-17,** 8617 N. Black Canyon Hwy. (☎ **602/ 995-9500**), charging $69 to $99 double; and the **Best Western Bell Motel,** 17211 N. Black Canyon Hwy. (☎ **602/993-8300**), charging $70 to $85 double. Rates are for the high season; for toll-free phone numbers, see the appendix.

Among the better budget chain motels in the north Phoenix area are the **Motel 6—Thunderbird,** 2735 W. Sweetwater Ave. (☎ **602/942-5030**), charging $48 double; and **Super 8—Phoenix Metro/Central,** 4021 N. 27th Ave. (☎ **602/248- 8880**), charging $50 to $55 double. Rates are for the high season; for toll-free phone numbers, see the appendix.

# DOWNTOWN PHOENIX & THE AIRPORT AREA
## EXPENSIVE

**Crowne Plaza—Phoenix.** 111 N. Central Ave., Phoenix, AZ 85004. ☎ **800/359-7253**, 800/ 227-6963, or 602/257-1525. Fax 602/254-7926. 532 rms, 70 suites. A/C MINIBAR TV TEL. Oct– Apr $169–$179 double, $189–$458 suite; May–Sept $59–$79 double, $79–$358 suite. AE, CB, DC, DISC, MC, V. Valet parking $8.

This business and convention hotel is currently your best choice in downtown. A Mediterranean villa theme has been adopted throughout the public areas with slate flooring and walls painted to resemble cracked stucco. Guest rooms continue the Mediterranean feel and are designed with the business traveler in mind. Dual-line phones with modem ports, hair dryers, safes, irons and ironing boards, and coffeemakers all add up to a high level of convenience.

**Dining/Entertainment:** Marston's is the hotel's main dining room and has a contemporary atmosphere. However, the Adams Bar & Grill has more character.

**Services:** Room service, massages, airport shuttle ($4 per person), valet/laundry service, car-rental desk.

**Facilities:** Fitness room, swimming pool, whirlpool spa, jogging track, beauty salon and barbershop, gift shop.

**Hyatt Regency Phoenix at Civic Plaza.** 122 N. Second St., Phoenix, AZ 85004. ☎ **800/ 233-1234** or 602/252-1234. Fax 602/254-9472. 712 rms, 45 suites. A/C TV TEL. Mid-Sept to May $205–$230 double, $750–$1,000 suite; June to mid-Sept $145–$175 double, $750–$1,000 suite. AE, CB, DC, DISC, MC, V. Valet parking $8; self-parking $6.

Located directly across the street from the Phoenix Civic Plaza, this high-rise Hyatt is almost always packed with conventioneers and consequently does not offer the sort of seasonal price breaks of other area hotels. Whether packed or empty, the hotel always seems understaffed, so don't expect top-notch service if you're stuck here on a convention. The rooms are fairly standard, though comfortably furnished. Ask for a room above the eighth floor to take advantage of the views from the glass elevators.

**Dining/Entertainment:** The Compass Room is Arizona's only rotating rooftop restaurant and serves Southwestern dishes. The food is usually decent and the views are fascinating. There's also the more casual and inexpensive Theater Terrace Café in the hotel's atrium.

**Services:** Concierge, room service, valet/laundry service, car-rental desk.

**Facilities:** Small outdoor pool, exercise room, whirlpool, tennis courts, several gift shops.

## MODERATE

Among the better moderately priced chain motels in the downtown Phoenix and airport area are the **Best Western Airport Inn,** 2425 S. 24th St. (☎ **602/273-7251**), charging $90 to $99 double; and **Rodeway Inn Airport West,** 1202 S. 24th St. (☎ **602/244-2211**), charging $69 to $109 double. Rates are for the high season; for toll-free phone numbers, see the appendix.

✪ **San Carlos Hotel.** 202 N. Central Ave., Phoenix, AZ 85004. ☎ **800/528-5446** or 602/ 253-4121. Fax 602/253-6668. 115 rms, 11 suites. A/C TV TEL. Jan–May $109 double, $179 suite; June–Aug $79 double, $129 suite; Sept–Dec $89–$99 double, $149–$159 suite. AE, CB, DC, DISC, MC, V. Valet parking $10; self-parking $6.

Built in 1928 and listed on the National Register of Historic Places, the San Carlos is a small European-style hotel that provides that touch of elegance and charm missing from the other standardized high-rise hotels downtown. You're close to shopping, the Phoenix Convention Center, sightseeing, and theaters, which makes this a good choice for both vacationers and conventioneers. Crystal chandeliers, a travertine check-in desk, and comfortable couches give the small lobby sophistication. The rooms, though smaller than today's standard hotel room, feature wingback chairs, ceiling fans, and coffeemakers. At press time, this hotel was scheduled for a complete renovation, which should be done by early 1998.

Nick's on Central, with its sunken dining room just off the lobby, serves good Italian and Greek meals, while an Irish pub and a cafe add up to plenty of other dining and drinking options. The hotel also features valet/laundry service, complimentary coffee, a rooftop pool, and an exercise room.

**Wyndham Garden Hotel—Phoenix Airport.** 427 N. 44th St., Phoenix, AZ 85008. ☎ **800/ WYNDHAM** or 602/220-4400. Fax 602/231-8703. 210 rms, 24 suites. A/C TV TEL. Sept–May $129–$169 double, $139–$179 suite; May–Sept $94 double, $104 suite. AE, CB, DC, DISC, MC, V.

Located only a mile from the east exit from the airport, this is a comfortable, modern, and conveniently located hotel if you are in town for just a day or two or are getting in late. The "king" rooms are particularly well designed, each with a comfortable chair, a work desk, and a bureau that separates the sleeping area from the sitting/working area. Other room amenities include hair dryers, coffeemakers, and two telephones.

**Dining/Entertainment:** There's a clublike lounge to one side of the lobby, and an inexpensive casual restaurant as well.

**Services:** Complimentary airport shuttle, room service, valet/laundry service.

**Facilities:** The outdoor pool is surrounded by an attractive patio with desert-style landscaping, but jet noises will prevent you from doing much relaxing out here.

# TEMPE, MESA & SOUTH PHOENIX
## VERY EXPENSIVE

○ **The Buttes.** 2000 Westcourt Way, Tempe, AZ 85282. ☎ **800/843-1986** or 602/225-9000. Fax 602/438-8622. 343 rms, 9 suites. A/C MINIBAR TV TEL. Jan 1 to late May $255–$315 double, $475–$1,500 suite; late May to early Sept $145–$205 double, $375–$1,500 suite; early Sept to Dec 31 $230–$290 double; $475–$1,500 suite. AE, CB, DC, DISC, JCB, MC, V.

Located only 3 miles from Sky Harbor Airport, this spectacular resort makes the utmost of its craggy hilltop location, and although some people complain that the freeway in the foreground ruins the view, I disagree. From its circular restaurant to its free-form swimming pool and desert landscaping, every inch of this resort is calculated to take your breath away. The moment you step into the flagstone-floored lobby, you can't help but gawk. Behind the reception desk is a cactus garden through which flows a stream that cascades over a precipice into a fish pond in the restaurant on the lower level. The desert landscaping gives the resort grounds the feel of a botanic garden, and the rocky setting firmly plants this resort in the desert (if you want lush, try somewhere else).

The guest rooms have shutters instead of curtains on the windows, and many have good views across the valley (marred slightly by the adjacent freeway). TV cabinets and minibars are discreetly hidden inside the walls beneath the picture windows. Unfortunately for fans of long soaks, most bathrooms have only $3/4$-size tubs.

**Dining/Entertainment:** The Top of the Rock restaurant snags the best view around, and sunset dinners are always packed (see "Dining," below). An informal dining room, complete with waterfall and fish pond, is located below the lobby. There are bars below Top of the Rock (with only a limited view), in the lobby, and by the pool.

**Services:** Concierge, 24-hour room service, valet/laundry service, complimentary airport shuttle, car-rental desk.

**Facilities:** Two free-form pools with waterfalls and a connecting swim-through canal (with a glass wall) are the best reason to stay here, but among the four whirlpools tucked into the rocks is the most romantic whirlpool in the valley. Four tennis courts and a fitness center round out the facilities.

**The Pointe Hilton Resort on South Mountain.** 7777 S. Pointe Pkwy., Phoenix, AZ 85044. ☎ **800/876-4683** or 602/438-9000. Fax 602/431-6535. 638 suites. A/C MINIBAR TV TEL. Jan 1 to late May $229–$400 double; late May to late Sept $99–$179 double; late Sept to Dec 31 $165–$250 double. AE, CB, DC, DISC, EURO, JCB, MC, V.

Located on the flanks of South Mountain (just outside the Tempe city limits), this Pointe Hilton resort is surrounded by a 16,000-acre nature preserve, though the resort's manicured grounds keep nature at a distance. Inside, the lobby with its high ceiling, sweeping stairs, and crystal chandeliers, is calculated to impress, and the grandiose scale is meant to accommodate conventions rather than make individual travelers feel at home. If you're an active type, however, you'll find enough to keep you busy here for days. Golfers get great views, urban cowboys can ride right into South Mountain Park, and the fitness center is among the biggest and best I've ever seen at a resort.

All the guest rooms are suites and feature contemporary Southwestern furnishings; even the smallest are quite roomy. Mountainside suites offer the best views of the golf course and South Mountain.

**Dining/Entertainment:** Another Pointe in Tyme features a mahogany-paneled interior and continental cuisine, with live jazz in the evenings. Rustler's Rooste is a popular Western-theme restaurant featuring cowboy bands, rattlesnake appetizers, and a slide from the lounge to the dining room (loads of fun). See "Dining," below. Aunt Chilada's serves Mexican food, and Sports Club Dining provides light and healthy meals.

**Services:** Concierge, room service, valet/laundry service, massages, rental-car desk, complimentary afternoon cocktails, baby-sitting.

**Facilities:** 18-hole golf course, 10 lighted tennis courts, five racquetball courts, seven swimming pools, two volleyball courts, riding stables, beauty salon, gift shop, pro shop. The large health club offers aerobics classes, fitness equipment, free weights, and a lap pool.

## EXPENSIVE

**Sheraton Mesa Hotel.** 200 N. Centennial Way, Mesa, AZ 85201. ☎ **800/456-6372** or 602/898-8300. Fax 602/964-9279. 273 rms, 5 suites. A/C MINIBAR TV TEL. Jan 1 to late Apr $135–$165 double; late Apr to early Sept $85–$105 double; early Sept to Dec 31 $99–$119 double. Suites $185–$310 year-round. AE, CB, DC, DISC, MC, V.

Located in the heart of downtown Mesa and convenient to the convention center, amphitheater, and area businesses, this high-rise convention hotel offers great views of the valley from its upper floors. The guest rooms are comfortable in a corporate sort of way but don't offer much local flavor. They do, however, have computer jacks. If there is a concert scheduled at the amphitheater, you could get a view from your room. You'll also have no trouble hearing the music, so if you want peace and quiet, make sure your visit doesn't coincide with a rock concert.

**Dining/Entertainment:** The hotel's main dining room is a warehouselike space serving unremarkable fare. There's also a large Mexican theme bar that's popular with concert crowds.

**Services:** Concierge, room service, valet/laundry service, airport shuttle (no charge but gratuities accepted).

**Facilities:** Small outdoor pool, whirlpool, small fitness room, business center.

**Tempe Mission Palms Hotel.** 60 E. Fifth St., Tempe, AZ 85281. ☎ **800/547-8705** or 602/894-1400. Fax 602/968-7677. 303 rms, 6 suites. A/C TV TEL. Jan–May $199–$239 double, $395 suite; June–Aug $119–$139 double, $249 suite; Sept–Dec $169–$189 double, $339 suite. AE, CB, DC, DISC, EURO, MC, V.

College students and their families and anyone else who wants to be close to Tempe's nightlife will find this an ideal, though overpriced, location. Situated right in the heart of the Mill Avenue shopping, restaurant, and nightlife district, this hotel sports a hip contemporary style. The courtyard poolside patio, with its turquoise and purple lounge chairs, is a great place to hang out on a hot day. The guest rooms feature comfortable furnishings with a Southwest look. All the rooms also have computer jacks.

**Dining/Entertainment:** The restaurant serves Southwestern meals at reasonable prices, and in the aptly named Monster Bar, a large alligator sculpture hangs from the ceiling.

**Services:** Room service, complimentary airport shuttle, valet/laundry service, baby-sitting.

**Facilities:** Medium-size outdoor pool, two lighted tennis courts, fitness center (plus access to nearby health club), whirlpool, sauna, business center.

## MODERATE/INEXPENSIVE

Apache Boulevard in Tempe becomes Main Street in Mesa and along this stretch of road there are numerous old motels charging some of the lowest rates in the valley. However, these motels are very hit-or-miss. If you're used to staying at nonchain motels, you might want to cruise this strip and check out a few places. Otherwise, try the chain motels mentioned below (which tend to charge $20 to $40 more per night than nonchain motels).

Chain motel options in the Tempe area include the **Days Inn—Tempe,** 1221 E. Apache Blvd. (☎ **602/968-7793**), charging $75 to $89 double; **Super 8—Tempe/ Scottsdale,** 1020 E. Apache Blvd. (☎ **602/967-8891**), charging $77 to $87 double; and **Travelodge—Tempe,** 1005 E. Apache Blvd. (☎ **602/968-7871**), charging $65 to $82 double. See the appendix for toll-free phone numbers.

Chain motel options in the Mesa area include the **Days Inn—Mesa,** 333 W. Juanita Ave. (☎ **602/844-8900**), charging $70 to $101 double; **Motel 6—Mesa North,** 336 W. Hampton Ave. (☎ **602/844-8899**), charging $46 double; and **Super 8—Mesa,** 6733 E. Main St. (☎ **602/981-6181**), charging $72 to $78 double. See the appendix for toll-free numbers.

✪ **Fiesta Inn.** 2100 S. Priest Dr., Tempe, AZ 85282. ☎ **800/528-6481** or 602/967-1441. Fax 602/967-0224. 270 rms, 4 suites. A/C TV TEL. Jan 1–May 31 $132–$159 double, $225–$275 suite; June 1–Sept 30 $77–$82 double, $100–$135 suite; Oct 1–Dec 31 $113–$133 double, $150–$195 suite. AE, CB, DC, DISC, MC, V.

Reasonable rates, extensive recreational facilities (three tennis courts, putting green, driving range, pool, health club with sauna and whirlpool, and jogging trails), and a location close to ASU and Tempe's Mill Avenue make this older, casual resort hotel one of the best deals in the valley. You're also only a few minutes from the airport. The grounds are lush, with lots of mature trees providing plenty of shade. OK, so it isn't as fancy as the resorts in Scottsdale, but who can argue with the rates? Guest rooms are large and all have refrigerators, coffeemakers, and hair dryers. Local phone calls are free. The restaurant serves reliable American fare, and the lounge features a copper bar and a big-screen TV. Services include concierge, room service, complimentary airport shuttle, complimentary morning paper, and valet/laundry.

## OUTLYING VALLEY OF THE SUN RESORTS

✪ **The Boulders.** 34631 N. Tom Darlington Dr. (P.O. Box 2090), Carefree, AZ 85377. ☎ **800/553-1717** or 602/488-9009. Fax 602/488-4118. 160 casitas. A/C MINIBAR TV TEL. Late Dec to late May $395–$700 double; late May to mid-Sept $175–$375 double; mid-Sept to early Dec $395–$575 double; early Dec to late Dec $225–$350 double. AE, CB, DC, MC, V.

Set amid a jumble of giant rocks 45 minutes north of Scottsdale, The Boulders epitomizes the Southwest aesthetic and is the state's premier golf resort. Adobe buildings blend unobtrusively into the desert, as do the two noted golf courses, which feature the most breathtaking tee boxes in Arizona. If you can tear yourself away from the greens, you can relax around either of two pools, play tennis (no boulders on the courts), or take advantage of the facilities and treatments at a renowned full-service spa. The distance from Scottsdale is this resort's only real shortcoming, so if you want to stay here, plan on staying put for at least a few days.

The lobby is an organic adobe structure with tree-trunk pillars, a flagstone floor, and a collection of Native American artifacts on display. The guest rooms continue the adobe styling with stucco walls, beehive fireplaces, and beamed ceilings. The bathrooms are large and luxuriously appointed with tubs for two, separate showers, double sinks, and hair dryers. The rooms vary in size, with the smallest being a bit cramped (what with all the attractive furnishings). The best views are from second-floor rooms.

**Dining/Entertainment:** The Latilla Room, the resort's premier restaurant, serves innovative American cuisine; jackets are required for men at dinner. The Palo Verde Room, a less formal spot serving regional dishes, features a tile-front exhibition kitchen. At the country club is a dining room that emphasizes grilled meats and seafood. A fourth restaurant, serving Mexican food, is in the resort's upscale El Pedregal shopping plaza. A comfortable lounge features live jazz in the evenings.

**Services:** Concierge, room service, valet/laundry service, airport shuttle, babysitting, children's programs.

**Facilities:** Two 18-hole golf courses, six tennis courts, two pools, jogging and hiking trails, a pro shop, rental bikes. There's also a full-service spa as well as a fitness center with a lap pool, sauna, and exercise machines.

**Carefree Inn.** 37220 Mule Train Rd. (P.O. Box 3500), Carefree, AZ 85377-3500. ☎ **800/637-7200** or 602/488-5300. Fax 602/488-5779. 138 rms, 50 suites and casitas. A/C TV TEL. Jan 1 to mid-June $165–$215 double, $255–$295 suite, $285–$710 casita; mid-June to mid-Sept $85–$95 double, $135–$150 suite, $145–$360 casita; mid-Sept to Dec 31 $135–$175 double, $195–$205 suite, $195–$510 casita. AE, CB, DC, DISC, MC, V.

Located well off the mainstream of the resort scene, yet close to the exclusive Boulders resort, the Carefree Inn dates back to 1963. However, it was closed for 9 years until its renovation and reopening in late 1996. Today the inn is capitalizing on its proximity to as-yet-undeveloped desert and the lack of streetlights in the surrounding retirement community of Carefree. The lack of lights means the night skies out here are among the finest you'll gaze up at from any resort in the state. The surrounding desert can be explored both on guided hikes and mountain-bike rides offered by the resort. These unusual options right out the resort door give this resort a welcome eco-tourism slant that sets it apart from other valley resorts. The north valley location also makes this a slightly better choice if you plan on doing day trips to Sedona or the Grand Canyon.

There's a wide variety of room styles, which range from very large standard rooms to house-size casita suites (my favorite is the Saguaro Casita, which has a huge saguaro cactus growing through the patio roof ). Surprisingly the casita king-size rooms are actually smaller than standard rooms. If tennis is your game, opt for a room or suite in the tennis villas. Decor is Southwestern modern and rooms come with hair dryers, coffeemakers, and irons and ironing boards.

**Dining/Entertainment:** The resort has a single fairly casual dining room with a terrace dining area overlooking the main pool and cactus garden. The menu is American eclectic with enough variety to please most people. There's also an adjacent bar.

**Services:** Concierge, room service, valet/laundry service, tennis lessons, guided hikes and mountain-bike rides.

**Facilities:** The main pool is a modest free-form affair, and there is a second smaller pool by the tennis villas. The full-service spa, which includes an extensive fitness room, offers a wide range of body and beauty treatments, and prices are among the lowest in the valley. At the Carefree Tennis & Bike Ranch, where there are five lighted tennis courts, you can also rent mountain bikes and electric bikes.

**Gold Canyon Ranch.** 6100 S. Kings Ranch Rd., Gold Canyon, AZ 85219. ☎ **800/624-6445** or 602/982-9090. Fax 602/983-9554. 57 rms. A/C TV TEL. Late Dec to mid-May $150–$230 double; mid-May to Sept $105–$155 double; Oct–late Dec $145–$205 double. AE, DC, DISC, MC, V.

Although Gold Canyon Ranch is way out on the east side of the valley near Apache Junction, it's popular with golfers who come to play some of the most scenic holes in the state. The Superstition Mountains are the backdrop for the resort's two 18-hole courses, and even nongolfers will appreciate the scenery. The small outdoor pool here is meant for cooling off after a round of golf, not as a place to lounge away the day. You can also soothe your aches in a whirlpool or play some tennis on the two lighted courts. The guest rooms here are large and are housed in pueblo-influenced buildings painted a bright white that fairly jumps out of the surrounding brown desert landscape. Some rooms have fireplaces while others have whirlpools and all have hair dryers and coffeemakers. The resort has been undergoing extensive remodeling and expansion over the past couple of years, with the emphasis on remodeling the golf courses and adding more rooms. If you haven't been here in a while, you'll definitely need to pay a visit soon.

**Dining/Entertainment:** If you don't like chiles or the vibrant flavors of Southwestern cuisine, your choices can be very limited here. Although the regional cuisine in the dining room here is quite good, it can be rather spicy. A fair number of people end up eating in the bar and grill, which serves basic burgers and sandwiches.

**Services:** Room service, baby-sitting.

**Facilities:** Two gorgeous 18-hole golf courses, pool, whirlpool, two lighted tennis courts, horseback riding, rental bikes, access to nearby health club.

**The Wigwam.** 300 Indian School Rd., Litchfield Park, AZ 85340. ☎ **800/327-0396** or 602/935-3811. Fax 602/935-3737. 331 rms, 70 suites. A/C MINIBAR TV TEL. Jan–May $296–$356 double, $356–$446 suite; May–Sept $126–$166 double, $166–$206 suite; Sept–Jan $230–$280 double, $280–$380 suite. AE, DC, DISC, MC, V.

Located 20 minutes west of downtown Phoenix and twice that far from Scottsdale, this resort opened its doors to the public in 1929 and remains one of the nation's premier golf resorts. Three challenging golf courses and superb service are the reasons most people choose this resort, which, though elegant, is set amid flat lands that lack the stunning desert scenery of the Scottsdale area.

Most of the guest rooms are in small pueblo-style buildings and are surrounded by green lawns and colorful gardens. All the rooms have contemporary Southwestern furniture and offer plenty of space. Some rooms have fireplaces, but the most popular rooms are those along the golf course.

**Dining/Entertainment:** The resort's Terrace Dining Room serves continental cuisine indoors or on the terrace beside the pool and is popular for dining and dancing (ballroom of course) in the evening. The equally elegant Arizona Kitchen serves acclaimed Southwestern cuisine and features an exhibition grill. Golfers have their own conveniently located restaurant in the clubhouse. Afternoon tea and evening cocktails are served in a lobby lounge, and sports fans can retreat to the Arizona Bar to catch the games on big-screen TVs.

**Services:** Concierge, room service, valet/laundry service, massages, golf lessons, tennis lessons, holiday and summer children's programs.

**Facilities:** Three golf courses, putting green, nine tennis courts, two pools, bicycles, volleyball, croquet, trap and skeet shooting range, exercise room, sauna, pro shop.

# 4 Dining

Just as the Valley of the Sun boasts some terrific resorts, so, too, is it full of excellent restaurants. Scottsdale and the Biltmore District are home to most, but not all. If you can afford only one expensive meal while you're here, I'd suggest having it at one of the resort restaurants that offers a view of the city lights. Other meals not to be missed are the cowboy dinners served amid Wild West decor at such places as Pinnacle Peak and Rustler's Rooste.

# PHOENIX
## EXPENSIVE

**The Bistro.** In the Biltmore Financial Center, 2398 E. Camelback Rd. (at 24th St.). ☎ **602/ 957-3214.** Reservations recommended. Main courses $7–$17 at lunch, $19–$26 at dinner. AE, CB, DC, MC, V. Mon–Fri 11am–3pm, daily 5–10pm. FRENCH/INTERNATIONAL.

The meals here are created in the same kitchen that prepares the pricey dishes for Christopher's, the adjacent restaurant. Some of the same dishes, such as Christopher's tender alder-smoked salmon, are also available at The Bistro (and nearly a requirement of dining here).

So what's the difference other than price? Well, noise level for one. This is a bistro, with marble floors and cherrywood paneling, and the customers tend to be business types and well-to-do-families who most certainly do not converse in hushed tones.

The main courses are frequently straightforward and paired with sauces designed to bring out the flavor of the dish, such as grilled prime beef with pepper sauce or mahimahi with dijon mustard sauce. Desserts run the gamut from soufflés to a banana split to a delicately latticed tower of chocolate. More than 70 wines are available by the glass.

✪ **Christopher's.** In the Biltmore Financial Center, 2398 E. Camelback Rd. (at 24th St.). ☎ **602/957-3214.** Reservations highly recommended. Main courses $32; menu prestige $85 ($125 with wines). AE, CB, DC, DISC, MC, V. Tues–Sun 6–9pm. FRENCH/NOUVELLE AMERICAN.

Plush burgundy carpeting and brocade-upholstered chairs set a tone of traditional elegance at Christopher's, which is located in a modern office building. The dining room is small with only a handful of tables. Conversation tends to be hushed, and the clientele sports top-of-the-line suits and multicarat diamonds.

Chef Christopher Gross calls his creations contemporary French cuisine, and his versions of traditional dishes (such as venison with roasted artichokes in a huckleberry, cognac, and red wine sauce) are truly memorable. His wife, sommelier Paola Gross, has assembled what may be the best wine collection in Phoenix. The house smoked salmon and Christopher's own foie gras are both signature appetizers. The menu changes regularly. For those who crave the full treatment whatever the cost, there's a *menu dégustation* with five courses and wines from around the world. If the prices here are beyond your means, don't despair. Christopher's also operates The Bistro (see above), where prices are a bit more down to earth.

✪ **Lon's.** At the Hermosa Inn, 5532 N. Palo Cristi Rd. ☎ **602/955-7878.** Reservations recommended late in the week. Main courses $7.50–$12 at lunch, $17–$24 at dinner. AE, MC, V. Mon–Fri 11:30am–2pm and 6–10pm, Sat 5:30–10pm, Sun 10am–2pm (brunch) and 6–9pm. SOUTHWESTERN.

What we like most about this place is the setting. It's one of the most "Arizonan" places in the Phoenix area—a Mexican-style hacienda with tile roof and gardens all around. The hacienda once belonged to Lon Megargee, a cowboy artist whose paintings decorate the interior of the restaurant. We found that the food here holds its own with other Southwestern cuisine served in the area. At midday this place is popular with both retirees and the power-lunching set. We began with rosemary-infused sourdough rolls, and a large platter of fried sweet potatoes and onion rings, which were delicious—salty-sweet and crispy. It seemed as though everyone else had the same idea. Grilled pineapple chicken on focaccia bread was so juicy that the bread fell apart. Dinner entrees include wood-grilled filet mignon with horseradish mashed potatoes and lamb with a shallot-basil couscous and wild mushroom ragout.

**Roxsand.** 2594 E. Camelback Rd. ☎ **602/381-0444.** Reservations recommended. Main courses $8.50–$12 at lunch, $20–$30 at dinner. AE, DC, MC, V. Mon–Thurs 11am–4pm and 5–10pm, Fri–Sat 11am–4pm and 5–10:30pm, Sun noon–4pm and 5–9:30pm. NEW AMERICAN.

Located on the second floor of the exclusive Biltmore Fashion Park shopping mall, Roxsand serves fusion cuisine, a creative combination of international influences. We attempted to choose among Moroccan b'stilla (braised chicken in phyllo with roasted eggplant puree), African spicy shrimp salad, and rice tamales with curried lamb and Thai peanut sauce. And those were just the appetizers. Perhaps because of the diversity of the menu, some of the dishes can be hit or miss. Sauces sometimes lack complexity, but we can recommend the air-dried duck with pistachio onion marmalade, buckwheat crêpes, and three sauces: Szechuan black-bean sauce, evil jungle prince sauce, and plum sauce. After dinner, get some exercise and walk to the dessert case to select a dessert, which will be served to you on a dinner plate adorned with additional cookies and perhaps a dollop of sorbet. Service can be on the pretentious side.

✪ **Vincent Guerithault on Camelback.** 3930 E. Camelback Rd. ☎ **602/224-0225.** Reservations highly recommended. Main courses $6–$10 at lunch, $14.50–$23 at dinner. AE, DC, MC, V. Mon–Fri 11:30am–2:30pm and 6–10:30pm, Sat 5–10:30pm, Sun 6–10:30pm. Closed on Sun from after Mother's Day to mid-Oct. SOUTHWESTERN.

Vincent Guerithault has long been a local restaurant celebrity, and his restaurant has an intimate, unpretentious French country atmosphere. Despite the continental decor, the cuisine is solidly Southwestern, with chiles appearing in numerous guises. For a starter, it's hard to beat the aggressive flavors of a smoked salmon quesadilla with dill and horseradish cream. Moving on to the main course, grilled meats and seafood are the specialty here and might come accompanied by an ancho chile and honey glaze or by habañero pasta. The extensive wine list is equally divided between Californian and French wines. There's a valet parking attendant at the door, and the number of luxury cars here should tip you off that this is one of Phoenix's top restaurants. At lunch the menu is basically the same as at dinner (only with smaller portions), and since nearly all items are under $10, it's a great opportunity to taste the food here if you're on a budget.

## MODERATE

✪ **Altos.** 5029 N. 44th St. (at the NE corner of 44th St. and Camelback). ☎ **602/808-0890.** Reservations recommended. Main courses $7–$11 at lunch, $13–$22 at dinner. AE, DC, MC, V. Mon–Thurs 11:30am–2pm and 5:30–10pm, Fri 11:30am–2pm and 5:30–11pm, Sat 5:30–11pm, Sun 5:30–9pm. SPANISH.

This is a cool, out-of-the-way place to enjoy some tapas (appetizers) and a glass of fruit-filled sangria from the large jar on the bar, but the entrees are also quite good. Located in the back of a shopping plaza, Altos is a little difficult to find, but it's worth searching out. We enjoyed dipping bread in a thick, bread-based sauce with lots of garlic, black pepper, and parsley, which was very savory and delicious. Other dusky flavors from Spain included a tapas of artichoke hearts stuffed with serano ham and Spanish goat cheese, dipped in saffron batter and fried. As you might imagine, it burst with flavor. Paella with seafood, chicken basque sausage, and saffron rice is a complex melding of flavors, while some dishes are more straightforward, such as the *pinchos* (kebabs). A dish of flan, bread pudding, or crème brûlée rounds out the experience.

**Arizona Café & Grill.** 3113 E. Lincoln Dr. ☎ **602/957-0777.** Reservations recommended on weekends. Main courses $8–$20. AE, DC, DISC, MC, V. Mon–Thurs 11am–9:30pm, Fri–Sat 11am–10pm, Sun 11am–9pm. SOUTHWESTERN.

# Phoenix Dining

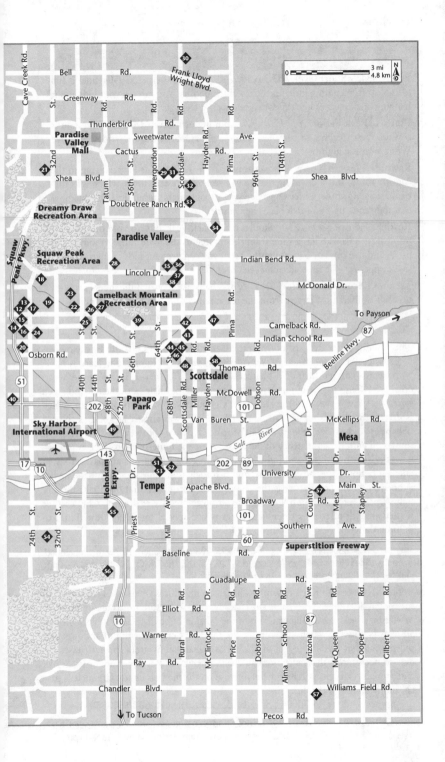

---

### 🎠 Family-Friendly Restaurants

**Ed Debevic's Short Orders Deluxe** *(see p. 121)*   This classic 1950s diner is full of cool stuff, including little jukeboxes in the booths. You can tell your kids about hanging out in places like this when you were a teenager.

**Pinnacle Peak Patio** *(see p. 120)*   Way out in north Scottsdale, this restaurant is a Wild West steakhouse complete with cowboys, shoot-outs, hayrides, and live Western music nightly.

**Rawhide Western Town & Steakhouse** *(see p. 120)*   Kids love dancing to the country music and pretending they're in a real old Western town, which isn't difficult, since Rawhide, with its big wide street, looks pretty authentic. Did you know that they cook up 50 *tons* of beans here annually?

**Rustler's Rooste** *(see p. 121)*   Similar to Pinnacle Peak, but closer to the city center, Rustler's Rooste has a slide from the lounge to the main dining room, a big patio, and live cowboy bands nightly. See if you can get your kids to try the rattlesnake appetizer—it tastes like chicken.

**Trenino's Scottsdale Station** *(see p. 118)*   Kids like to watch the model train set here which takes up a large part of the restaurant and makes lots of fun noises.

---

This restaurant, located just north of the Camelback Corridor, is run by the owners of Christopher's restaurant and is a casual Southwestern eatery. The place is huge, with booths covered in Indian blankets, and in a far corner, a TV plays old Westerns. Salsa seems to be ubiquitous in the Southwest, but here both the red and green salsas were tasty. We tried the restaurant's popular yellow bell-pepper soup, which is drizzled with red-pepper sauce, and thought it was almost as good as the red bell-pepper soup we've had at Christopher's Bistro. However, we were most impressed with the consistency of the crust on the mesquite-smoked chicken pizza— it was crispy, but fluffy and light as well. Other menu options are pasta, roasted chicken (a house specialty), burgers, and fish such as salmon and ahi tuna. The bar is noisy and very popular, as is the covered outdoor terrace that overlooks the city lights (make a reservation if you want to sit on the terrace at dinner). Check to see if they are still offering a three-course early-bird special for $9.95 from 11am to 6:30pm daily.

**Bobby McGee's.** 8501 N. 27th Ave. ☎ **602/995-5982.** Reservations highly recommended. Main courses $8–$26; early dinner (5–6pm) $5–$10. AE, DC, DISC, MC, V. Sun–Thurs 5–10pm, Fri–Sat 5–11pm (lounge stays open until 1am). AMERICAN.

Bobby McGee's isn't just a restaurant, it's an event. This is where local families head for special occasions. The restaurant is always full, so be sure to make a reservation or you may be in for a long wait. From the outside Bobby McGee's looks a bit like an old, dilapidated warehouse, but on the inside it's crammed full of antiques and old photos that give it the feel of a Wild West saloon. Waiters and waitresses are dressed in costumes that range from antebellum gowns to Boy Scout uniforms. Steaks and prime rib are the specialties here, but also on the menu is lighter fare such as pastas and fresh fish of the day.

Another branch is at 7000 E. Shea Blvd., Scottsdale ( ☎ **602/998-5591**).

✪ **Che Bella.** 2420 E. Camelback Rd. ☎ **602/956-5705.** Reservations recommended. Main courses $10–$20. AE, DC, DISC, MC. V. Mon–Thurs 11am–10pm, Fri–Sat 11am–11pm, Sun 11am–9pm. TUSCAN.

What drew me into this restaurant were the desserts on display—tiramisu, torta di ricotta, and panna cotta al caramello. Like a romantic Italian poem, they won my heart, and the antipasti platters—containing artichoke hearts, salami and ham, grilled red peppers, hearts of palm, marinated mushrooms, radicchio, and oven-dried tomatoes—looked as inviting as a Renaissance painting. But there are other things to eat, too, at this spacious high-tech restaurant in Biltmore Fashion Park, like *gnocchi di patate,* a tender, rich dish of potato dumplings in a marscarpone creme sauce with deep fried basil leaves, and *risotto ai frutti de mare,* risotto rice crammed full of crab claws, big shrimp, and tender scallops. There are several fish choices, such as prosciutto-wrapped sea bass; and frogs' legs, chicken, veal, and sausage make appearances in various Tuscan-style treatments. In spite of the delicious entrees, people sometimes come here solely for dessert.

✪ **Eddie's Grill.** 4747 N. Seventh St. ☎ **602/241-1188.** Reservations recommended. Main courses $8–$13 at lunch, $15–$25 at dinner. AE, DISC, MC, V. Mon–Thurs 11:30am–2:30pm and 5–11pm, Fri 11:30am–2:30pm and 5pm–midnight, Sat 5pm–midnight, Sun 4–9pm. NEW AMERICAN.

Chef Eddie Matney is passionate about his cooking. I must agree that I share his enthusiasm for his bacon, tomato, and basil-flavored meatloaf, or his sesame seared ahi tuna served with spinach, artichokes, and feta cheese. The combination plate looked like a party and was filled with spicy, piquant, tongue-tingling stuff, such as crusted sea scallops with Cajun dill wasabe sauce, and awesome seared portobello mushrooms in a black-bean dressing with red-pepper coulis. And yes, the fresh rosemary bread is outstanding. Seating choices are nearly as diverse as the menu—a high-tech bistro upstairs, a more formal wine-cellar atmosphere downstairs, and a patio with a pond and gazebo/bar outside. We sat on the patio and were entertained by our very friendly waiter and a leatherback turtle sunning himself on a rock.

**The Fish Market.** 1720 E. Camelback Rd. ☎ **602/277-3474.** Reservations recommended. Main courses $7–$28 downstairs, $9–$39 upstairs. AE, DISC, MC, V. Downstairs, Mon–Thurs 11am–9:30pm, Fri–Sat 11am–10pm, Sun noon–9:30pm. Upstairs, Sun–Thurs 5–9:30pm, Fri–Sat 5–10pm. SEAFOOD.

The Fish Market is divided into two restaurants: the large and casual downstairs dining room and the smaller, tonier, and slightly more expensive Top of the Market upstairs. If you feel more comfortable in jeans than in a suit and tie, stay downstairs. The Fish Market offers seafood from around the world, including fish caught by the restaurant's own boats. In the tin-ceilinged and tile-floored oyster bar, you can start your evening with some Puget Sound oysters. Mesquite charcoal-broiling is the specialty downstairs, though there are a few grilled or fried dishes as well. Upstairs you'll find delicious seafood pastas and a greater variety of preparation styles.

**Havana Café.** 4225 E. Camelback Rd. ☎ **602/952-1991.** No reservations taken, but call ahead for a large party. Main courses $4.50–$12 at lunch, $8–$23 at dinner. AE, CB, DC, DISC, MC, V. Mon–Sat 11:30am–10pm, Sun 4–9pm. CUBAN/SPANISH/LATIN AMERICAN.

At this cozy, windowless restaurant in the Camelback Court, Cuban music played and we began our repast with some appetizers of *tostones* (twice-fried green plantains with a black-bean dip), and then moved on to a Cuban tamale with ground corn and pork. There are so many appetizers on the menu that this is a good place to come just for them. Chicken marinated with lime, orange, and garlic was good, but didn't compare to the other dishes. Other choices include different Latin-inspired preparations of meat, poultry, fish, and a few unique vegetarian dishes. Save room for a key lime tart, which is refreshingly piquant. The best accompaniment to a meal is a pitcher of sangria. Waiters wear tuxedo shirts and black tie, but you can dress up or down as you wish.

**Mr. Sushi Japanese Restaurant.** 8041 N. Black Canyon Hwy., Suite 112 (at the corner of Northern Ave.). ☎ **602/864-9202.** Reservations accepted for parties of 6 or more. Sushi $1.50–$8; main courses $8.50–$20. AE, MC, V. Tues–Thurs 11:30am–2pm and 5–9:30pm, Fri 11:30am–2pm and 5–10pm, Sat 5–10pm, Sun 5–9pm. JAPANESE.

This little neighborhood sushi place is tucked into a nondescript office complex away from the tourist track, but it's worth searching out. The sushi chefs don't speak much English, but they can whip up some outrageous concoctions—the best of which aren't even on the menu. Of course, there are also plenty of cooked dishes for those who haven't developed a taste for sea urchin, raw quail eggs, or thinly sliced octopus. Prices are quite moderate if you stick to the cooked dishes, but your bill can escalate if you start ordering off the sushi menu.

**Oyster Grill.** 455 N. Third St. (downtown in the Arizona Center). ☎ **602/252-6767.** Reservations recommended. Main courses $6–$14 at lunch, $8–$25 at dinner. AE, DISC, MC, V. Mon–Sat 11am–10pm, Sun noon–9pm. SEAFOOD.

Coming in from the noon heat of downtown Phoenix, the cool sea-green walls here made us forget for a while that we were in the desert, as did the profusion of seafood offerings. We began with both fried oysters and raw oysters on the half shell—there's usually a choice of three or four different types. If you like your seafood steamed, there are clams, cockles, and six different types of mussels. Swordfish, salmon, trout, or whatever fish is fresh that day comes grilled over an alderwood fire. You'll also find a dozen or so different types of pizza and pasta, some with seafood, some without, and an assortment of seafood-infused soups and salads.

**Richardson's.** 1582 E. Bethany Home Rd. ☎ **602/265-5886** or 602/230-8718. Reservations accepted only for parties of 4 or more. Main courses $8–$15. AE, CB, DC, MC, V. Mon–Fri 11am–midnight, Sat–Sun 10am–midnight. NEW MEXICAN.

Tucked into an older corner shopping center with far too few parking spaces, Richardson's is almost invisible amid the glaring lights and flashing neon of this otherwise unmemorable neighborhood. However, if you enjoy creative and spicy cooking at good prices, you'll be glad you found this place. Downstairs a bar and a dozen or so booths and tables are usually crowded and noisy, so you might want to ask for a table upstairs where it's quieter. If you're in the mood for a light meal, try the Southwestern skewers—chicken, beef, shrimp, and sausage grilled over pecan wood. A more substantial appetite may be assuaged by a New Mexican platter containing a tamale, a chile relleno, a burrito, rice and beans, and green chile. The pecan-wood pizza oven is always fired up to cook an extensive list of delicious pizzas, and for dessert, prickly pear–syrup flan is as creamy as a good crème brûlée. Richardson's serves Southwestern-style breakfasts daily until 4pm.

**Sam's Cafe.** In the Arizona Center, 455 N. Third St. ☎ **602/252-3545.** Reservations recommended. Main courses $7–$20. AE, DC, DISC, MC, V. Mon–Thurs 11am–10pm, Fri–Sat 11am–11pm, Sun 11am–9pm. SOUTHWESTERN.

Sam's Cafe, one of only a handful of decent downtown restaurants, serves food that's every bit as imaginative, but not nearly as expensive, as that served at other (often-overrated) Southwestern restaurants in Phoenix. Breadsticks served with picante-flavored cream cheese, grilled tuna tacos, and penne pasta in a spicy peanut sauce with black beans and goat cheese all have a nice balance of flavors and are not too spicy—but spicy enough. Salads and dipping sauces are complex and interesting. The downtown Sam's has a large patio that stays packed with the lunchtime, after-work, and convention crowd and overlooks a fountain and palm garden.

Other Sam's restaurants are located in the Biltmore Fashion Park at 2566 E. Camelback Rd. (☎ **602/954-7100**) and in Scottsdale at N. Scottsdale Road and Shea Boulevard (☎ **602/368-2800**).

**San Carlos Bay Seafood Restaurant.** 1901 E. McDowell Rd., just west of the Squaw Peak Parkway (Ariz. 51). ☎ **602/340-0892.** Reservations recommended on weekends. Main courses $10–$21. No credit cards. Daily 10am–9pm. MEXICAN.

If you've ever spent time in a Mexican beach town, you probably have fond memories of great fish dinners. But unfortunately you rarely get great Mexican seafood dishes north of the border. This basic little place remedies that problem. From whole fried fish to octopus in garlic to shrimp stew, San Carlos Bay does seafood and it does it right. This restaurant is very popular with the local Hispanic population (you'll probably be the only outsider here), so you might want to practice your Spanish before making a foray to Bahía San Carlos.

**The Stockyards Restaurant.** 5001 E. Washington St. ☎ **602/273-7378.** Reservations recommended. Main courses $6–$15 at lunch, $14–$35 at dinner. AE, CB, DC, DISC, MC, V. Mon–Fri 11am–2pm and 5–10:15pm, Sat 5–10:15pm, Sun 4:30–9:15pm. STEAK/SEAFOOD.

Once surrounded by 200 acres of feedlots and frequented almost exclusively by cattlemen in town to sell a few thousand head of cattle, this steakhouse knows its business. Today it attracts the Arizona gentry, who come to enjoy perfectly cooked steaks and cowboy beans amid a traditional 1889 decor. There are several dining rooms, two of which have muraled walls.

✪ **Such Is Life.** 3602 N. 24th St. ☎ **602/955-7822.** Reservations recommended. Main courses $7–$23. AE, DC, DISC, MC, V. Mon–Fri 11:30am–2:30pm and 5:30–9pm, Sat 5:30–9pm. MEXICAN.

If you're tired of unidentifiable Mexican food smothered in melted cheese and sour cream, then you're a candidate for Such Is Life. This is simply the best Mexican food in Phoenix. The three salsas alone are enough to justify a visit: Each has its own distinctive flavor and none is too hot. There are daily specials, but we suggest trying one of the Mexican casseroles known as *guisados*. The mole poblano guisado was made with one of the best mole sauces we've ever had. Fresh juices and creamy flan cheesecake, with a wonderful liquor-infused caramel sauce, also excel. There's also a second location at 7000 E. Shea Blvd., Scottsdale (☎ **602/948-1753**), which opens for dinner at 5pm.

**T-Bone Steakhouse.** 10037 S. 19th Ave. ☎ **602/276-0945.** Reservations recommended for 8 or more. Main courses $9–$21. AE, DC, MC, V. Sun–Thurs 5–10pm, Fri–Sat 5–11pm. STEAK.

With some of the best steaks in Phoenix and a great view north across the valley from the skyscrapers of Phoenix to Camelback and Squaw Peak, the T-Bone Steakhouse is hard to beat. Though there are checkered tablecloths, sawdust on the floor, and a barbecue grill out front, this place is more a locals' hangout than a tourist attraction. The menu is basic and includes only four types of steak and chicken. To reach the restaurant, head south on 19th Avenue until it seems to dead-end, hang a right for about 100 feet, and then turn left and continue on 19th Avenue for 1.5 miles.

## INEXPENSIVE

**Big Wong.** 616 W. Indian School Rd. ☎ **602/277-2870.** Reservations accepted for parties of 4 or more. Main courses $5–$16. MC, V. Mon–Fri 11am–2:30pm and 5–9:30pm, Sat 5–10pm, Sun 5–9:30pm. CANTONESE/MANDARIN/HUNANESE.

What you won't find here is standard watered-down Chinese food; instead you'll get memorable dishes like garlic-imbued yu-choi greens on a ginger-studded sizzling plate with oysters and green onions. Two menus, one more Americanized and the other more tailored to an authentic Chinese dining experience, offer sizzling dishes, hot pots, and soups. You'll find unusual dishes for adventurous palates (shark-fin soup, sea cucumber and duck feet hot pot, jellyfish). The small room is always busy, and you might have to wait for a table. If you take along a crowd, you'll get a chance to sample an abundance of these interesting dishes.

✪ **The Farm at South Mountain.** 6106 S. 32nd St. ☎ **602/276-6360.** Sandwiches and salads $6–$7. No credit cards. Winter Tues–Sat 8am–5pm; summer Tues–Sat 8am–2pm. Take Exit 151A off I-10 and go south on 32nd St. SANDWICHES & SALADS.

If being in the desert has you dreaming of shady trees and green grass, you'll enjoy this little oasis reminiscent of a New England orchard or Midwestern farm. A rustic outbuilding surrounded by potted flowers has been converted to a stand-in-line restaurant where you can order a real turkey sandwich with cranberry relish on wholegrain bread or have a choice of fresh salads such as haricots verts with organic spinach, red potatoes, black olives, and feta cheese with a lemon vinaigrette dressing. Breakfast choices are baked goods such as muffins and scones, teas, and juices. The grassy lawn is ideal for a picnic on a blanket under the pecan trees.

**Filiberto's.** 10802 N. 32nd St. ☎ **602/971-7015.** Tacos, burritos, and combination plates $2–$6. No credit cards. Daily 24 hours. FAST FOOD/MEXICAN.

We're always on the lookout for the city's best fish taco, and Filiberto's manages to turn out a delectable one: stuffed with batter-fried fish, drizzled with a good tartar sauce, and accented by crunchy chopped cabbage. We enjoyed these little goodies while sitting on the outside patio on a warm spring night, with Phoenix traffic rushing by. The Mexican soup here, called *caldo Tlalpeño* , is a filling bowl of vegetables, shredded chicken, and smoky jalepeño chiles that is both flavorful and fiery.

Here are several other locations; call for additional locations throughout the Valley of the Sun: 4014 N. 43rd Ave., Phoenix (☎ **602/352-0697**); 2240 W. Indian School Rd., Phoenix (☎ **602/277-4334**); 3433 W. Camelback Rd., Phoenix (☎ **602/973-3390**); 1270 E. Apache Blvd., Tempe (☎ **602/966-5091**).

**Garcia's Mexican Restaurant.** 4420 E. Camelback Rd. ☎ **602/952-8031.** Reservations recommended on weekends. Main courses $6–$13. AE, DISC, MC, V. Sun–Thurs 11am–10pm, Fri–Sat 11am–11pm. MEXICAN/SONORAN.

For more than 40 years, Garcia's has been serving Mexican food in Phoenix, where the lively atmosphere, large portions, and low prices attract a family-oriented crowd. Located next to a tennis complex on busy Camelback Road, this Garcia's looks like a corporate-style hacienda from the outside. Inside, you're transported to a Mexican colonial home with a sunken courtyard. We'll give you a couple of tips on the menu—try the *espinaca con queso,* a concoction of spinach, jalapeños, cheese, and onions served with tortilla chips. After that fresh start, skip to the house specialties or try one of the traditional Sonoran combination dinners. Happy hour here is from 3 to 8pm. Try a coconut, melon, or peach margarita, along with the free buffet, which lasts from 3 to 7pm.

Other branches of this popular restaurant are at 3301 W. Peoria Ave. (☎ **602/ 866-1850**); 1940 E. University Ave., Mesa (☎ **602/844-0023**); 2394 N. Alma School Rd., Chandler (☎ **602/963-0067**); and 17037 N. 59th Ave., Glendale (☎ **602/843-3296**).

**The Great Wall.** 5055 N. 35th Ave. ☎ **602/973-1112.** Reservations not accepted. Main courses $6–$12. MC, V. Mon–Thurs 11am–11pm, Fri 11am–1am, Sat 10am–midnight, Sun 10am–11pm (dim sum, daily 11am–3pm). CHINESE.

Located south of Bethany Home Road at the corner of Camelback and 35th Avenue, the Great Wall is just about large enough to double as a hangar for Boeing 747s, and on weekend afternoons it seems as though Phoenix's entire Chinese community packs in here to savor the best dim sum in Phoenix. We particularly like the broccoli, which wasn't on the cart the last time we went, so we ordered it from a waiter. Consider coming after 1:30pm for dim sum, when the crowds begin to thin out.

**Pho Bang Restaurant.** 1702 W. Camelback Rd. ☎ **602/433-9440.** Main courses $4.25–$13. MC, V. Daily 10am–10pm. VIETNAMESE.

Sure, the names are unpronounceable and the decor leaves a lot to be desired, but after you've had your first taste of the summer rolls, you'll know you've come to the right place. The hot-and-sour fish soup is a real winner, as is the marinated shrimp and beef that's cooked at your table. If you're daring, try some pickled lemonade or dried longan in syrup. Lunch specials are offered Monday through Friday from 10am–2pm. This restaurant is located in a Vietnamese and Thai shopping center that contains several other southeast Asian businesses.

✪ **Pizzeria Bianco.** 4709 N. 20th St., in the Town & Country Shopping Center. ☎ **602/381-1779.** Reservations accepted for 6 or more. Pizzas $8–$11. MC, V. Tues–Fri 11:30am–2pm and 5:30–10pm, Sat 5:30–10pm, Sun 5:30–9pm. ITALIAN.

This place is tiny and always crowded, mainly because the wood-burning oven turns out such deliciously rustic, chewy-crusted pizzas. The options are simplified and pretty much traditional, with such choices as a red onion, Parmesan, rosemary, and crushed-pistachio pizza. Pizzeria Bianco makes their own fresh mozzarella cheese, which can be ordered as an appetizer or on a pizza. We also liked the roasted vegetables and the salad with fennel, radicchio, parsley, and orange, drizzled with olive oil.

**Texaz Grill.** 6003 N. 16th St. ☎ **602/248-STAR.** Reservations taken for 6 or more. Main courses $3.50–$6 at lunch, $7–$15 at dinner. AE, MC, V. Mon–Thurs 11am–10pm, Fri 11am–11pm, Sat noon–11pm, Sun 4–10pm. STEAK.

Outside the heat is blazing; inside, there's a twangy Texas favorite playing on the jukebox, and it's cool and dim, with a well-mannered chaos of stuffed armadillos, license plates, and other Texan memorabilia adorning every surface. The folks here are friendly, even if you aren't a Texan, and will be pleased to dish you up the house special: chicken-fried steak with mashed potatoes and gravy.

**Tucchetti.** 2135 E. Camelback Rd. ☎ **602/957-0222.** Reservations recommended. Main courses $8–$14. AE, DISC, MC, V. Mon–Thurs 11:15am–10pm, Fri 11:15am–11pm, Sat noon–11pm, Sun 4:30–9pm. SOUTHERN ITALIAN.

Located in the parking lot of the Town and Country Shopping Center and looking like a Hollywood rendition of an old Mexican cantina, Tucchetti is one of Phoenix's most popular Italian restaurants. The food here is your basic no-frills, no-fancy-ingredients, southern Italian fare, and no one goes away hungry. The salad bar is excellent.

**Vintage Market.** 24th St. and Camelback Rd. (Biltmore Fashion Park). ☎ **602/955-4444.** Reservations not necessary. Salads/sandwiches $5–$6. AE, DC, MC, V. Mon–Wed 10am–8pm, Thurs–Sat 10am–10pm, Sun 11am–6pm. UPSCALE DELI.

You certainly can't complain about the cost of a light meal at this small gourmet market/deli—it's not likely that you could get the equivalent of a grilled vegetable tart with red-pepper coulis or a Southwest grilled-chicken sandwich anywhere else in this neighborhood for a similar price. Plus, there's a wine bar where you can choose from a couple of dozen wines by the glass, some of them local. And, last time we stopped by, a classical guitarist was strumming outside. Such a deal.

# SCOTTSDALE

Several of the restaurants mentioned above also have locations in Scottsdale. Those restaurants are **Bobby McGee's, Sam's Cafe,** and **Such Is Life.** See "Dining" in Phoenix, above, for details.

## EXPENSIVE

**The Chaparral.** At Marriott's Camelback Inn, 5402 E. Lincoln Dr. ☎ **602/948-1700** or 602/948-6644. Reservations highly recommended. Main courses $19–$28. AE, CB, DC, DISC, MC, V. Daily 5–10pm. CONTINENTAL.

The Camelback Inn was built in 1936, and ever since its opening it has been known as the home of some of the valley's finest restaurants. The Chaparral is possibly the most consistently reliable continental restaurant in the valley. The decor is Southwestern, with a view of Camelback Mountain through the curving glass wall and a carved silhouette of the mountain on the back of each chair. Tableside cooking is one of the specialties of the house and for many diners is an essential part of any meal here. The menu features a balanced mixture of exquisitely prepared old standards and nouvelle offerings displaying the chef's creative flair. For a bit of culinary showmanship, try the wilted-spinach salad, which is prepared and flamed at your table. Traditionalists will enjoy filet mignon Diane, which is also prepared tableside, while gourmets with a more adventurous palate will most likely find themselves tempted by ever-changing specialties.

Call for summer hours. This is a five-star dining experience, so be sure to dress the part.

**El Chorro Lodge.** 5550 E. Lincoln Dr. ☎ **602/948-5170.** Reservations recommended. Full dinner $14.50–$44. AE, CB, DC, DISC, MC, V. Mon–Fri 11am–3pm and 5:30–11pm, Sat 9–11am and 5:30–11pm, Sun 9am–3pm (brunch) and 5:30–11pm. CONTINENTAL.

Built in 1934 as a school for girls and converted to a lodge and restaurant 3 years later, El Chorro Lodge is a valley landmark set on its own 22 acres of desert. At night spotlights shine on the palo verdes and cacti, and the restaurant takes on a timeless tranquillity, even if the interior is a little dowdy. The adobe building houses several dining rooms, but on a chilly night the patio, with its crackling fireplace, is the place to sit. Both decor and menu offerings are traditional and popular with old-timers and families, with such classic dishes as chateaubriand and rack of lamb. In addition to the favorites, there are several dishes that are low in salt and fat. El Chorro's sticky buns are legendary, so save room.

✪ **Golden Swan.** At the Hyatt Regency Scottsdale Resort at Gainey Ranch, 7500 E. Doubletree Ranch Rd. ☎ **602/991-3388.** Reservations recommended. Main courses $19–$33. AE, DC, DISC, MC, V. Daily 6–10pm, Sun brunch 9:30am–2:30pm. REGIONAL AMERICAN.

Located within the Hyatt Regency Resort at Gainey Ranch, the cuisine and atmosphere here combine to make a great special dinner. Dramatically spotlit royal palms, geometric architecture, and the sound of fountains and waterfalls set the tone, while the food is just as pleasurable, beautifully presented with plenty of attention to details. We began with an olive oil fondue, a concoction of basil, tomatoes, and olives in olive oil, which arrived with olive bread. Each of our entrees had more than one focus with several distinctive flavors, each subtly bold. Achiote swordfish with a crab-and-shrimp-stuffed pasilla chile had just the right fire and smoky grilled flavor. Ahi tuna was seared, but rare on the inside, with a wasabi aioli on a bed of round-cut vegetables, accompanied by a wonton stuffed with crab and crunchy vegetable pearls, a flavorful melt-in-your-mouthful. Chocolate mousse cake with fresh berries soaked in zinfandel sauce accented by bright green crushed pistachios had a very smooth texture. After dinner, the open-air lounge at the resort is a romantic place to have a drink and listen to live music.

✪ **La Hacienda.** At the Scottsdale Princess resort, 7575 E. Princess Dr. (about 12 miles north of downtown Scottsdale). ☎ **602/585-4848.** Reservations recommended. Main courses $18–$26. AE, DC, DISC, MC, V. Daily 6–10pm. GOURMET MEXICAN.

This is not your local neighborhood Mexican restaurant, but an upscale, glamorous-but-rustic rendition of an early 1900s Mexican ranch house replete with stone tiled floor, Mexican glassware and crockery, and a beehive fireplace. It may seem like an oxymoron, but there really is such a thing as gourmet Mexican cuisine, and this is where you get it. Offerings include such dishes as smoked pork tenderloin with a three-chile sauce and charcoal-broiled lamb chops in a pumpkin-seed crust, sauced with roasted tomatoes and mint. Grilled shrimp and baked sea bass are simpler dishes but just as delicious, as are the desserts such as orange flan and fried bananas with ice cream.

**Mancuso's.** At the Borgata, 6166 N. Scottsdale Rd. ☎ **602/948-9988.** Reservations recommended. Pastas $15–$18; main dishes $17–$26. AE, CB, DC, DISC, MC, V. Sun–Thurs 5–10pm, Fri–Sat 5–10:30pm. ITALIAN/FRENCH/CONTINENTAL.

The Borgata is built in the style of a medieval European village with ramparts, towers, stone walls, and narrow, uneven alleyways leading through the complex. When you reach your castle banquet hall for a repast of gourmet Italian cuisine, a pianist will be playing soft jazz (alas, no Gregorian chants) amid a soaring ceiling, stone walls, arched windows, and huge roof beams and walls of mirrors (which make the restaurant seem far larger than it really is). If you lack the means to start your meal with the beluga caviar, perhaps *carpaccio di manzo*—sliced raw beef with mustard sauce and capers—will do. Although there's an extensive selection of main courses, including an entire page of veal dishes, we find it difficult to get past the pasta offerings: Mancuso's serves no fewer than a dozen different types in 16 different preparations. If you want something other than pasta, there are dozens of meat and seafood dishes. The professional service will have you feeling like royalty by the time you finish your dessert and coffee.

✪ **Marquesa.** At the Scottsdale Princess resort, 7575 E. Princess Dr. (about 12 miles north of downtown Scottsdale). ☎ **602/585-4848.** Reservations recommended. Main courses $26–$34; champagne brunch $35. AE, DC, DISC, MC, V. Daily 6–10pm, Sun brunch 10:30am–2:30pm. SPANISH/CATALONIAN.

Located at the Scottsdale Princess, a resort designed with Moorish influences in mind, the Marquesa is a romantic dining splurge. High-backed chairs, chandeliers, muted lighting, and large classical Spanish paintings create an ambience reminiscent of an 18th-century Spanish villa. The cuisine, however, is Catalonian with a contemporary interpretation by chef Reed Groban. Crabmeat and fontina cheese in baked sweet red peppers with garlic aioli and lobster and leek-filled pasta with cognac sauce are robustly flavored starters, and paella with lobster, chicken, pork, shellfish, chistora, and saffron rice is the restaurant's signature dish. Some dishes are prepared to be especially low in fat and sodium but not the desserts, which are displayed on carts that flank the entryway. Crème fraîche flan with a black-walnut crust is just one such tempting work of art definitely to be considered. There's a separate tapas bar outside the main dining area, and brunch, one of the best in the valley, is served Sunday on the outdoor patio in a Spanish marketplace setting.

❖ **Mary Elaine's.** At The Phoenician, 6000 E. Camelback Rd., Scottsdale. ☎ **602/423-2530.** Reservations highly recommended. Jacket required for men. Main courses $32–$39; 5-course seasonal tasting menu $105 ($45 additional with wine). AE, CB, DC, DISC, EURO, JCB, MC, V. Sun–Fri 6–10pm, Sat 6–11pm. MODERN FRENCH.

Located on the top floor of The Phoenician's main building, Mary Elaine's is one of the finest hotel restaurants in the valley and boasts one of the city's best views as well. The restaurant is the height of Phoenician elegance and sophistication, with original artwork on the walls and soft jazz performed live in the lounge. The tables are set with fine German crystal, Reed and Barton silver, and a custom-pattern china by Mikasa. Patios with fire pits provide a more relaxing setting for those who'd like to enjoy the Arizona evening outdoors.

Executive chef Alessandro Stratta focuses on the flavors of the modern French kitchen but also makes forays into other cuisines, with such recent offerings as foie gras sauté with oven-roasted nectarines and 100-year-old balsamic vinegar; mesquite-grilled squab with butternut squash, endives, and caramelized orange; and herb-crusted rack of lamb with roasted peppers and tapenade. For the health-conscious, some dishes are particularly low in sodium, fat, and cholesterol. The extensive wine list has won several awards.

**Windows on the Green.** At The Phoenician, 6000 E. Camelback Rd., Scottsdale. ☎ **602/ 423-2530.** Reservations recommended. Shirts with collars required for men. Main courses $23–$35; lunch/brunch $15–$25. AE, CB, DC, DISC, EURO, JCB, MC, V. Mon–Sat 11am–3pm and 6–10pm, Sun 10am–3pm (brunch) and 6–10pm. SOUTHWESTERN.

Slightly more casual than The Phoenician's premier restaurant, Mary Elaine's, but no less elegant, Windows on the Green has a sweeping view of the resort's golf course. Chef Robert McGrath combines ingredients of the region, such as jicama, nopales (cactus), and cilantro, with meats (sometimes including wild game), fowl, fish, and vegetables to produce a menu that runs the gamut from mild to very spicy. A sampling of the menu includes cracked crab with avocado, grilled pork tenderloin with green chile gnocchi, and chile-cured Arizona grown ostrich. The wine list is chosen to complement these regional flavors. Lunch and Sunday brunch provide an opportunity to sample the kitchen's creations at reduced prices.

## MODERATE

**Café Patou.** 7000 E. Shea Blvd., Scottsdale. ☎ **602/951-6868.** Reservations recommended on weekends. Main courses $15–$25, pastas $13–$21. AE, DISC, MC, V. Mon–Fri 11:30am– 2:30pm and 5:30–11pm or later, Sat–Sun 5:30pm–midnight. FRENCH/ITALIAN.

Playful murals here illustrate Parisian street scenes, and although it's indoors, the restaurant feels like a sidewalk cafe. A casual and fun atmosphere prevails, with an emphasis on French and Mediterranean cuisines. A potato, walnut, and roquefort crêpe and an authentic salad niçoise made me feel as though I was back in Paris eating at cafes again. Flatbreads, pizza-like creations topped with a few simple ingredients such as olives, anchovies, and cheeses, and gnocchi Romana—baked semolina dumplings with parmesan, tomato, and basil—are both hearty dishes with robust flavors that are quite satisfying. Café Patou has a full bar with many wine and beer selections from around the world. And don't forget the chocolate mousse.

❖ **Café Terra Cotta.** At the Borgata, 6166 N. Scottsdale Rd., Suite 100. ☎ **602/948-8100.** Reservations recommended for dinner. Main courses $11–$22. AE, CB, DC, MC, V. Sun–Thurs 11am–10pm, Fri–Sat 11am–11pm. SOUTHWESTERN/INTERNATIONAL.

Café Terra Cotta started out in Tucson, where it has been a perennial favorite, so it should come as no surprise that Phoenix has beaten a path to the door of this casually sophisticated and low-key restaurant. The menu is long and includes wood-oven pizzas, sandwiches, and smaller meals as well as full-size main courses. Imaginative combinations are the rule here, so you'll want to take your time with the menu before ordering. Just for example, roll this one over your imaginary taste buds: grilled chicken breast with achiote-sherry glaze on mole verde with garlic-chipotle whipped potatoes.

**Chez Georges Bistro/Bar.** In the Scottsdale Promenade, 7000 E. Shea Blvd., Scottsdale. ☎ **602/991-9484.** Reservations recommended, especially on weekends. Main courses $12–$18. AE, DC, MC, V. Mon–Sat 5–10pm. FRENCH/ITALIAN.

Sandwiched between two other restaurants in a shopping mall, Chez Georges doesn't quite get away from feeling like a space in a mall, but there are pleasing touches of white linen tablecloths and a cloud-painted ceiling. The menu is simple, offering such dishes as mussels with white wine, garlic, and parsley; filet mignon with peppercorn sauce; or veal marsala with mushrooms. Nightly specials may include the likes of New Zealand rack of lamb, and prices are quite reasonable.

✪ **Franco's Trattoria.** 8120 N. Hayden Rd., Scottsdale. ☎ **602/948-6655.** Reservations recommended. Pastas $13–20, main courses $15–$25. AE, MC, V. Mon–Thurs 5–10pm, Fri–Sat 5–10:30pm. Closed Sun–Mon in summer; also closed from early July to early Aug. TUSCAN ITALIAN.

Franco's hasn't been at this location long, but the owner has had plenty of previous experience; he's from New York, where he's had several other restaurants. Located in a newer area of Scottsdale, the photographs of old Italy and operatic music make a fitting background for authentic Tuscan cuisine. The *insalata capricciosa,* a salad of fennel, goat cheese, sun-dried tomatoes, beans, arugula, radicchio, and red onion, fairly bursts with flavor, as do the risotto dishes with either porcini mushrooms or seafood. And if you opt for any of the veal dishes, you can't go wrong. If you're here for a romantic dinner, there's no better way to top it off than with a chocolate hazelnut truffle tart, bittersweet chocolate with a Frangelico pastry cream and hazelnut caramel.

**Jean Claude's Petit Cafe.** 7340 E. Shoeman Lane. ☎ **602/947-5288.** Reservations recommended. Main courses $6–$13 at lunch, $15–$22 at dinner. AE, CB, DC, MC, V. Mon–Fri 11:30am–2pm and 6–9:30pm, Sat 6–9:30pm. FRENCH.

It's small and quiet, and those who know about it prefer to keep it a secret. Shoeman Lane runs parallel to Camelback Road east of Scottsdale Road, and you'll find the restaurant a few blocks east of the latter. There are several small dining rooms, the nicest of which overlook the lighted fountain in the courtyard. Other than this little fountain, there's nothing in the simple decor to distract you from the well-prepared French food. All the favorites of the French kitchen are here—escargots bourguignonne, pâté, brie with apples and pears—but for an hors d'oeuvre, you can't miss with the steamed mussels in a cream sauce, liberally sprinkled with fennel seeds. For a main dish, try the fragrant rack of lamb with fresh mint sauce or poached trout stuffed with seafood mousse in a lobster sauce. The desserts are as tempting as the rest of the menu; crème caramel à l'orange is our favorite choice.

**L'Ecole.** At the Scottsdale Culinary Institute, 8100 E. Camelback Rd. (near Hayden Rd.). ☎ **602/990-7639.** Reservations recommended. 3 courses $6.25–$10 at lunch; $15–$38 at dinner. DISC, MC, V. Mon–Fri 11:30am–1pm and 6:30–8:30pm. CONTINENTAL/ INTERNATIONAL.

This culinary opportunity is a well-kept local secret—there aren't many places where you can get a three-course meal for under $20. The cooking and serving is all done by students, and the decor is somewhat sedate and elegant. For an appetizer, you might try the maytag bleu-cheese salad; for an entree chicken breast stuffed with prosciutto, shrimp, and basil leaves is nice, followed by cherries jubilee flamed tableside with house-made ice cream. There is a respectable selection of wines and liquors to accompany the meal, as well as a reasonably priced wine selection of the week.

**Malee's on Main.** 7131 E. Main St. ☎ **602/947-6042.** Reservations recommended for dinner. Main courses $9–$19. AE, DC, MC, V. Mon–Wed 11:30am–2:30pm and 5–9:30pm, Thurs–Fri 11:30am–2:30pm and 5–10pm, Sat noon–2:30pm and 5–10pm, Sun 5–9pm. THAI.

The casual comfort of soft Southwest colors and the delicious aroma of Thai food is an enticing combination at downtown Scottsdale's Malee's. One of our barometers of good Thai cooking is pad thai noodles, which here were saucy and tangy. Among the dishes at Malee's is Panang curry, with your choice of beef, chicken, shrimp, duck, or tofu in a sauce of spicy red kaffir lime-based curry with coconut cream. (Unfortunately, on our visit, there wasn't a sprig of cilantro in any dish.) Those who like spicy food can order dishes "Thai hot," somewhere on the other side of very hot. The outside patio and streetside seating are quiet in the evenings when downtown shuts down.

**Pepin.** 7363 Scottsdale Mall. ☎ **602/990-9026.** Reservations recommended. Main courses $11–$25. AE, CB, DC, DISC, MC, V. Tues–Sat 11:30am–11pm, Sun 3–11pm. Happy hour, Tues–Fri 4:30–6:30pm. SPANISH.

Located on the Scottsdale Mall, this elegant little Spanish restaurant offers such a wide selection of tapas that you can easily have dinner without ever glancing at the main-course list. However, if you should limit your tapas consumption, there are several different styles of paella and a zarzuela de marisco, most of which are seafood extravaganzas. Thursday through Saturday evenings there are live flamenco performances, and from 10pm on Friday and Saturday there's Latin salsa dancing.

**Rancho Pinot Grill.** 6208 N. Scottsdale Rd. (south of Lincoln Dr.). ☎ **602/468-9463.** Reservations recommended. Main courses $16–$22. MC, V. Tues–Sat 5:30–10pm. Closed Aug. NEW AMERICAN.

Rancho Pinot combines Southwestern decor with an airy setting at the back of a shopping mall that's adjacent to the Borgata. The menu is short and changes regularly, which keeps fashionable Scottsdalites coming back for more. On a recent visit we tried a salad of shaved fennel, red onion, orange, and parsley with lemon and Parmesan, and an entree of Chilean sea bass with red and golden beet vinaigrette and potato–olive oil puree. Although the flavors are not as exciting and punchy as the Southwestern fare here used to be, the food is well prepared and the staff is friendly and treats you like a regular even if it's your first visit.

**Razz's Restaurant and Bar.** 10321 N. Scottsdale Rd., Scottsdale. ☎ **602/905-1308.** Reservations recommended. Main courses $15–$23. MC, V. Tues–Sat 5–10pm. INTERNATIONAL.

Razz Kamnitzer, a native Venezuelan, is one in a line of seven chefs in his family. No wonder his new restaurant is such a hit. Located in a non-descript shopping mall on the southeast corner of Shea Boulevard and Scottsdale Road, the restaurant is chic but not stuffy, crowded, and lively. Razz has been on the Phoenix restaurant scene for some years and is known for his cuisine, which includes edible flowers, herbs, and exotic vegetable and fruits. On a recent night, the menu included such wide-ranging dishes as twice-roasted duck breast with lingonberry-orange sauce; an Indonesian-style noodle dish with chicken, shrimp, and fried plantains; and pork tenderloin crusted with almonds and Parmesan and served with a mango risotto.

**6th Avenue Bistro.** 7150 E. Sixth Ave. ☎ **602/947-6022.** Reservations recommended. Main courses $17–$19. AE, MC, V. Mon 5–10pm, Tues–Fri 11:30am–2pm and 5–10pm, Sat 5–10pm, Sun 5–9pm (shorter hours in July). CLASSIC FRENCH.

Who says French has to be fussy? This little bistro less than a block off Scottsdale Road is as casual as a French restaurant gets. Stucco walls and a concrete floor are the antithesis of Scottsdale chic, though lace curtains soften the interior a bit. The draw here is a simple menu of reliable dishes at very reasonable prices. A bit of country pâté, tenderloin of pork with port-wine sauce, a hearty Beaujolais, all topped off with mousse au chocolat and you have a perfect French dinner. Lunch here is a great deal.

**Sushi on Shea.** In the Scottsdale Promenade, 7000 E. Shea Blvd., Scottsdale. ☎ **602/483-7799.** Reservations not accepted. Main courses $6–$12 at lunch, $11–$17 at dinner. AE, DISC, MC, V. Mon–Sat 11:30am–2:30pm and 5:30–10pm, Sun 5:30–10pm. JAPANESE.

This small restaurant and sushi bar is usually quite busy (expect to wait a bit), but there are comfortable chairs outside for that very purpose. Inside at the sushi bar, the chefs intently prepare beautiful arrangements of sushi and sashimi of yellowtail, crab, quail egg, tuna, and just about any other kind you can imagine. Of course you can also get crispy and succulent shrimp tempura, salmon teriyaki, and other cooked dishes. Prices for lunch and dinner are fairly reasonable for this type of restaurant, but when you start ordering sushi, it begins to add up (but some experiences are worth it).

## INEXPENSIVE

**Carlsbad Tavern.** 3313 N. Hayden Rd., Scottsdale. ☎ **602/970-8164.** Reservations recommended. Main courses $5–$15. AE, DISC, MC, V. Mon–Sat 11am–10pm, Sun 4–10pm; limited menu available until 1am. NEW MEXICAN.

Carlsbad Tavern features the fiery tastes of New Mexican cuisine in a funky ambience featuring photographs and bats (a humorous reference to Carlsbad Caverns). And, a meal won't cost an arm and a leg. On the menu you'll find traditional New Mexican dishes, such as lamb pierna, braised and wood-grilled lamb, and carne adovada, simmered in a fiery red chile sauce. Nouvelle Southwestern specialties include a flashy chipotle pasta filled with smoked duck and topped with creamy brie sauce, and shrimp marinated in tequila and glazed with orange-cilantro pesto. Cool off your taste buds with a margarita made with fresh-squeezed juice or a prickly-pear ale. This place is popular with workers in the food-service industry who can still get a bite to eat after other area restaurants close up.

**✪ El Guapo's Taco Shop & Salsa Bar.** 3015 N. Scottsdale Rd., Scottsdale ☎ **602/423-8385.** Main dishes $2–$7.50. No credit cards. Mon–Sat 10:30am–8pm. MEXICAN.

El Guapo means "handsome," which certainly couldn't refer to this little hole-in-the-wall taco shop, but might be referring to Danny, the proprietor—he *is* El Guapo. The tacos—among them grilled mahimahi, carne asada, or marinated pork—are prepared without the standard lettuce and tomatoes so that you can build your own by liberally dousing your order with salsa and vegetable toppings from the salsa cart. It takes two or three tacos to make a meal, so you can try a few different types. El Guapo has homemade-style cheese crisps, burritos, and nachos, too. Try the armadillo eggs—jalapeño peppers stuffed with cheese and deep-fried. There are only half a dozen tables here, and the salsa bar takes up a good part of the shop.

**Oregano's Pizza Bistro.** 3622 N. Scottsdale Rd. (south of Indian School Rd.). ☎ **602/970-1860.** Reservations not accepted. Main courses $6–$17. AE, DISC, MC, V. Mon–Thurs 11am–10pm, Fri–Sat 11am–11pm, Sun noon–10pm. PIZZA/PASTA.

The originator of Oregano's has created a restaurant based on the memory of his father's recipes and fondness for entertaining at home. The prices are very reasonable, and both the thin-crust pizzas—spread with barbecue chicken and feta cheese (and, by the way, too much for one person)—and the Chicago stuffed pizza are all the good things pizza should be. But pizza isn't all they have here—there's artichoke lasagna with a cream and a marinara sauce, barbecue wings, a variety of salads, and even a pizza cookie for dessert. This place is enormously popular with the young Scottsdale set, so if you want to get a table quickly you may have to sit inside rather than on the outdoor patio.

**Trenino's Scottsdale Station.** 6910 E. Shea Blvd., Scottsdale. ☎ **602/905-5200.** Reservations not accepted. Main courses $4.25–$14, kid's menu $3.95. AE, DISC, MC, V. Mon–Fri 4–10pm, Sat–Sun 11am–10pm. PIZZA/PASTA/CHICKEN.

Kids like to watch the model train set here which takes up a large part of the restaurant and makes lots of fun noises, and they'll be distracted by the blinking railroad signals and other train-theme paraphernalia. Other things to do include coloring on the menu, or slurping down a kiddie cocktail such as a strawberry colada topped with coconut flakes and whipped cream. Adults will enjoy the beer-battered zucchini, Chicago-style pizza, and chicken picatta.

# TEMPE/MESA/CHANDLER
## MODERATE

♻ **House of Tricks.** 114 E. Seventh St., Tempe. ☎ **602/968-1114.** Reservations recommended. Main courses $11–$16. AE, CB, DC, DISC, MC, V. Mon–Thurs 11am–9pm, Fri–Sat 11am–10pm. NEW AMERICAN.

Because this restaurant is housed in a Craftsman bungalow surrounded by a garden of shady trees, it has a completely different feeling from the main drag of Mill Avenue, located only 2 blocks away. This is where Arizona State University students take their parents when they come to visit, but it is also a nice spot for a romantic evening. There are only a few tables inside the tiny dining room, which has a cozy fireplace, and slightly more outside on the grape arbor–covered patio where there's also a shady bar. The menu changes regularly and consists of a single page of tempting salads, appetizers, and main dishes. Besides a garlic-inspired Caesar salad, what stood out on our last visit was grilled chicken with fresh sorrel pasta and lemon-sage butter sauce. A warm scallop salad with pancetta (bacon), artichokes, and an orange-ginger vinaigrette made for a flavorful and unusual appetizer.

**Monti's La Casa Vieja.** 3 W. First St. (at the corner of Mill Ave.), Tempe. ☎ **602/967-7594.** Reservations recommended for dinner. Main courses $6.25–$22. AE, CB, DC, DISC, MC, V. Sun–Thurs 11am–10pm, Fri–Sat 11am–midnight. AMERICAN.

If you're tired of the glitz and glamour of the Valley of the Sun and are looking for Old Arizona, head down to Tempe to Monti's La Casa Vieja. The adobe building was constructed in 1873 (*casa vieja* means "old house" in Spanish) on the site of the Salt River ferry in the days when the Salt River flowed year-round and Tempe was nothing more than a ferry crossing. Today local families who have been in Phoenix for generations know Monti's well and rely on the restaurant for solid meals and low prices. You can get a filet mignon for under $10—or even less when it's the Monday-night special. The dining rooms are dark and filled with memorabilia of the Old West.

## INEXPENSIVE

**In Season Deli.** 414 S. Mill Ave., Tempe. ☎ **602/966-0334.** Salads/soups/pastas $2.50–$6. Credit cards not accepted. Mon–Fri 10:30am–3pm, Sat 11am–3pm. NATURAL FOODS DELI.

# In case you want to see the world.

At American Express, we're here to make your journey a smooth one. So we have over 1,700 travel service locations in over 120 countries ready to help. What else would you expect from the world's largest travel agency?

do more ®

**Travel**

http://www.americanexpress.com/travel

# In case you want to be welcomed there.

We're here to see that you're always welcomed at establishments everywhere. That's why millions of people carry the American Express® Card – for peace of mind, confidence, and security, around the world or just around the corner.

do more ®

Cards

# In case you're running low.

We're here to help with more than 118,000 Express Cash locations around the world. In order to enroll, just call American Express before you start your vacation.

do more

**Express Cash**

# And just in case.

We're here with American Express® Travelers Cheques and Cheques *for Two*® They're the safest way to carry money on your vacation and the surest way to get a refund, practically anywhere, anytime.

Another way we help you…

do more ®

**Travelers Cheques**

Located in a shaded courtyard in downtown Tempe (just behind Changing Hands Bookstore), this is a nice place to get a quick, healthful lunch off the beaten path. I tried the blue-corn tamale with a salad sampler, and a lovely large glass of honey raspberry tea. Each day of the week there's a list of special salads, soups, and what have you. They do take-out, too.

**Guedo's Taco Shop.** 108 W. Broadway Rd., Mesa. ☎ **602/461-3660.** Main courses $1.50–$5. No credit cards. Tues–Sat 11am–6pm. MEXICAN.

The freshness of the ingredients and the authenticity of the recipes have made this place the best little taco house in Phoenix, well worth a drive out to Mesa or Chandler. There are no sides of tasteless rice or beans, so be sure to order at least two tacos, three if you're hungry. Wash it all down with fresh horchata, a creamy drink made from rice and spices.

A second Guedo's is at 71 E. Chandler Blvd., Chandler (☎ **602/899-7841**), open the same days but until 9pm.

## A NEARBY RESTAURANT

**The Arizona Kitchen.** At the Wigwam Resort, W. Indian School Rd., Litchfield Park. ☎ **602/935-3811.** Reservations highly recommended. Main courses $13–$30. AE, CB, DC, DISC, MC, V. Summer Tues–Sat 6–10pm; Winter daily 6–10pm. SOUTHWESTERN.

It's a long way out to Litchfield Park and the Wigwam Resort, but if you have succumbed to the spicy flavors of Southwestern cuisine and want to taste some of the best, you may want to make the drive. In The Arizona Kitchen, the Wigwam's Southwestern ambience takes the guise of a blue-and-white-tiled exhibition kitchen in a dining room paved with bricks and filled with Spanish colonial-style furnishings. Here you'll find true regional offerings. Don't miss the opportunity to sample the traditional mainstay of the Hopi diet, piki bread. This paper-thin cornmeal bread is served with various creative fillings. Lobster and shrimp pasta tacos with piñon sauce are another specialty. Innovative pizzas are an inexpensive dinner choice and are made with a stone-ground cornmeal crust. However, once you encounter such pricier main dishes as quinoa-and-wild-rice-stuffed pheasant glazed with mint, coconut, and jalpeños, you may forget your budget.

## DINING WITH A VIEW

**Different Pointe of View.** At the Pointe Hilton Resort at Tapatio Cliffs, 11111 N. Seventh St. ☎ **602/863-0912.** Reservations highly recommended. Main courses $22–$34. AE, CB, DC, DISC, MC, V. Mon–Thurs 5:30–9:30pm, Fri–Sat 5:30–10pm (lounge open later), Sun 10am–1:30pm (brunch) and 5:30–9:30pm. AMERICAN REGIONAL.

The lounge at Different Pointe of View faces north and the restaurant faces south, and both have curving walls of glass that let in sweeping vistas of the city, mountains, and desert. Come early and enjoy both views. The building is built right into the top of the mountain (the road to the restaurant is incredibly steep, so we advise leaving your car at the bottom of the hill and taking the free shuttle up to the front door). The restaurant sports a Southwestern flavor in its decor.

Regional American cuisine is featured and presents imaginative twists on old favorites: Lobster is wrapped in paper-thin bread and served with roasted garlic sauce as an appetizer, while seared sea bass shows up with a creamed artichoke sauce as an entree. However, despite the excellent food, award-winning wine list, and live jazz Tuesday through Saturday, it's still the view that's the star of the show here.

✪ **Top of the Rock.** At The Buttes, 2000 Westcourt Way, Tempe. ☎ **602/225-9000.** Reservations recommended. Main courses $16–$27 at dinner; Sun brunch $28 for adult, $14 child. AE, CB, DC, DISC, MC, V. Mon–Thurs 5–10pm, Fri–Sat 5–11pm, Sun 10am–2pm (brunch) and 5–10pm. NEW AMERICAN/SOUTHWESTERN.

All the best views in Phoenix are from resorts and their restaurants, so if you want to dine with a view of the valley, you're going to have to pay the price. Luckily, quality accompanies the high prices here at the Top of the Rock in The Buttes resort. And in addition to the stunning and romantic setting of the resort, you can enjoy some very creative cuisine. Appetizers such as lobster layered with wonton and Boursin cheese with white-wine chervil sauce and Dungeness crab cakes with smoked chile cream and roasted corn are real standouts. Sauces on the entree menu offer a good range of mellow as well as bold flavors, so even those who aren't chile fanatics can enjoy a dinner here. The ambience is a little on the formal side, so dress up for this dining experience.

## COWBOY STEAKHOUSES

Though Arizona doesn't claim to have invented the steakhouse or cow towns, the state certainly has cornered the market on combining the two. Wild West–theme restaurants abound here in the Phoenix area. These family restaurants generally provide big portions of grilled steaks and barbecued ribs, outdoor and "saloon" dining, live country music, and various sorts of entertainment, including stagecoach rides and shoot-outs in the street.

**Pinnacle Peak Patio.** 10426 E. Jomax Rd., Phoenix. ☎ **602/585-1599.** Reservations recommended on weekends. Main courses $5.50–$23. AE, MC, V. Mon–Thurs 4–10pm, Fri–Sat 4–11pm, Sun noon–10pm. Take Scottsdale Rd. north to Pinnacle Peak Rd., turn right, and continue to Pima Rd., where you turn left; at this point just follow the signs. STEAK.

Businessmen beware! Wear a tie into this restaurant and you'll have it cut off and hung from the rafters. The casual dress code is strictly enforced at this Wild West restaurant about 20 minutes north of downtown Scottsdale up in the hills overlooking the valley.

A meal at the Pinnacle Peak Patio is more an event than an opportunity to satisfy your hunger. Though you can indulge in mesquite-broiled steaks (they even have a 2-pound porterhouse monster) with all the traditional trimmings, the real draw here is all the free Wild West entertainment—gunfights, cowboy bands, two-stepping, and cookouts.

✪ **Rawhide Western Town & Steakhouse.** 23023 N. Scottsdale Rd. (4 miles north of Bell Rd.), Scottsdale. ☎ **602/502-5600.** Reservations accepted for parties of 9 or more. Main courses $12–$26. AE, DISC, MC, V. June–Sept daily 5–10pm; Oct–May Mon–Thurs 5–10pm, Fri–Sun 11am–10pm. STEAKS.

At Rawhide, one of our favorite valley restaurants, there's plenty of entertainment, including country-music bands, shoot-outs, stagecoach rides, a petting zoo, and a resident magician. Kids love dancing to the country music and pretending they're in a real old Western town, which isn't difficult, since Rawhide, with its big wide street, looks pretty authentic. Along with mesquite-broiled steaks, including not only beef but buffalo and elk, you'll find a few barbecue items and fruit pie à la mode. They get a lot of visitors here, as evidenced by the fact that they cook up about 200,000 pounds of steak and 50 tons of beans annually.

**Rockin' R Ranch.** 6136 E. Baseline Rd., Mesa. ☎ **602/832-1539.** Reservations recommended. Main courses $12–$22. MC, V. Days and hours vary with season, call ahead. STEAKS.

This cowboy steakhouse includes two different venues, one a steakhouse and the other a cowboy dinner theater. Both dish out big juicy steaks with all the fixins. If you opt for the Chuckwagon Dinner Theater, you'll be entertained with gunfights, wagon rides, and live cowboy music. You enter this place through an artificial cave that kids will love.

✪ **Rustler's Rooste.** At the Pointe Hilton on South Mountain, 7777 S. Pointe Hwy., Phoenix. ☎ **602/431-6474.** Reservations recommended. Main courses $9–$22. AE, CB, DC, DISC, MC, V. Sun–Thurs 5–10pm, Fri–Sat 5–11pm. STEAKS.

This location doesn't exactly seem like cowboy country. However, up at the top of the hill you'll find a fun Western-theme restaurant where you can slide from the bar down to the main dining room. The view north across Phoenix is entertainment enough for most people, but there are also Western bands playing for those who like to kick up their heels. If you've ever been bitten by a snake, you can exact your revenge here by ordering the rattlesnake appetizer. Follow that (if you've got the appetite of a hardworking cowpoke) with the enormous cowboy "stuff" platter consisting of, among other things, broiled sirloin, barbecued pork ribs, cowboy beans, beer-batter shrimp, barbecued chicken, and swordfish kebabs.

## NOSTALGIA DINING

You may want to know that Phoenix has a **Hard Rock Cafe,** 2621 E. Camelback Rd. (☎ **602/956-3669**), and a **Planet Hollywood,** 2402 E. Camelback Rd. (☎ **602/954-7827**). These international chains hardly need introduction anymore. The memorabilia is the thing, not the food. The two restaurants are almost opposite each other, with Planet Hollywood claiming the more trendy location in Biltmore Fashion Park. And while these two restaurants are not the same as those mentioned below, they have a common theme in that they strike a chord in people's hearts by conjuring up images of the past.

**Ed Debevic's Short Orders Deluxe.** 2102 E. Highland Ave. ☎ **602/956-2760.** Reservations not accepted. Sandwiches and blue-plate specials $3–$7. AE, MC, V. Sun–Thurs 11am–9pm, Fri–Sat 11am–10pm. AMERICAN.

Hidden away behind the Smitty's supermarket in the Town and Country Shopping Center, Ed's is a classic 1950s diner right down to the little jukeboxes in the booths. Not only do they make their own burgers, chili, and bread, but they serve the best malteds in Phoenix. The sign in the front window that reads "Waitresses wanted— people skills not necessary" should give you a clue that service here is unique. This place stays busy, and the waitresses are overworked (though they do break into song now and again), so don't be surprised if your waitress sits down in the booth with you to wait for your order. That's just the kind of place Ed runs, and as Ed says, "If you don't like the way I do things—buy me out."

**5 & Diner.** 5220 N. 16th St. ☎ **602/264-5220.** Sandwiches/plates $4.50–$8. AE, MC, V. Daily 24 hours. AMERICAN.

If it's 2am and you just have to have a big burger and a side of fries after a night of dancing, head for the 24-hour 5 & Diner. You can't miss it; it's the classic streamlined diner that looks as if it just materialized from New Jersey.

There's two other locations in Phoenix at 7541 W. Bell Rd. (☎ **602/979-3073**) and 12802 N. Tatum Blvd. (☎ **602/996-0033**) and one in Scottsdale at Scottsdale Pavillions, 9069 E. Indian Bend Rd. (☎ **602/949-1957**).

✪ **MacAlpine's Nostalgic Soda Fountain & Coffee Shoppe.** 2303 N. Seventh St. ☎ **602/ 252-7282.** Sandwiches/specials $2.50–$5. AE, MC, V. Mon–Thurs 6:30am–9pm, Fri–Sat 6:30am–midnight, Sun 10am–6pm. AMERICAN.

This very authentic place hasn't changed much since its beginnings in 1928— actually, it's the oldest operating soda fountain in the Southwest. The atmosphere is laid back, helped along by a jukebox that plays favorite oldies. They'll be glad to fix you up a breakfast egg on a bagel, or a big hamburger or tuna-fish sandwich on good bread. To wash it down, order a malted, chocolate phosphate, or vanilla coke. For the full experience, there's a shop next door that is crammed full of antiques.

## CAFES & COFFEEHOUSES

At Central Avenue and Camelback Road in the Uptown Plaza, the **Orbit Café** (☎ 602/265-2354) is a big trendy space with large colorful artwork, food, and live music. Call for the schedule. **Coffee Plantation** has several locations, but two of the largest are at the corner of Sixth Street and Mill Avenue in Tempe (☎ 602/ 829-7878), one of the happening places in Tempe; and at Biltmore Fashion Park, East Camelback Road and 24th Street (☎ 602/553-0203). Or for an equally good cup that's less expensive and presented with more personal service, try **European Espresso,** a coffee cart on the corner of East Sixth Street and Mill Avenue in Tempe. **Dos Baristas,** at the Town and Country Shopping Center, 4743 N. 20th St. (☎ 602/957-2236), has good days and bad days when it comes to serving java. **Jamaican Blue,** tucked into a small mall at 4017 N. Scottsdale Rd., Scottsdale (☎ 602/947-2160), has live performances in the evening. **The Willow House,** 149 W. McDowell Rd. (☎ 602/252-0272), is unusual in that it isn't located in a mall, but in an off-the-tourist-track neighborhood in a 1920s house with a bohemian atmosphere.

## AFTERNOON TEA

A full tea is served in the cool Frank Lloyd Wright–inspired lobby of the **Arizona Biltmore,** 24th Street and Missouri Avenue (☎ 602/955-6600), between 3 and 4:30pm Monday through Saturday. Reservations are required. **The Ritz-Carlton Phoenix,** 2401 E. Camelback Rd. (☎ 602/468-0700), serves a quintessential high tea from 1:30 to 3pm Monday through Saturday in the lobby lounge. Between 3 and 5pm every afternoon, a full tea including wonderful scones with Devonshire cream is served in the lobby at **The Phoenician,** 6000 E. Camelback Rd., Scottsdale (☎ 602/423-2530). The setting looks out over the manicured lawns and palm trees of the resort. Reservations are recommended for the latter two.

## BRUNCH/BREAKFAST

Most of Phoenix's best **Sunday brunches** are to be had at the major hotels. Among the finest are the Marquesa at the Scottsdale Princess, the Golden Swan at the Hyatt Regency Scottsdale Resort at Gainey Ranch, (see "Dining," earlier in this chapter, for more information). Wright's at the Arizona Biltmore Resort & Spa, and the Terrace Dining Room at The Phoenician (see "Accommodations," earlier in this chapter, for more information).

In the fall, Eddie's Grill serves a Sunday brunch buffet within the environs of the fascinating **Desert Botanical Garden** (☎ 602/941-8818). Call for specific weeks. The cost is $16.95 for adults, $9.95 for children, but the price does not include admission to the gardens.

The best continental breakfast I can think of is at **Pierre's Pastry Café,** 7119 E. Shea Blvd., Scottsdale (☎ 602/443-2510), where the croissants and brioche have a luxurious, buttery texture (desserts here are also irresistible).

For fruit smoothies and muffins and things of a healthful nature, we like **Reay's Ranch Market Natural Foods,** with several locations, two of which are at 3933 E. Camelback Rd. (☎ 602/954-0584) and 9689 N. Hayden Rd., Scottsdale (☎ 602/ 596-9496). Almost three dozen different kinds of bagels, plus large, inexpensive delicatessen-style breakfasts can be had at **Chompie's,** 3202 E. Greenway Rd. (☎ 602/971-8010) and 9301 E. Shea Blvd. (☎ 602/860-0475). **Bagels N' Bialys,** 6990 E. Shea Blvd., Scottsdale (☎ 602/991-3034), also does a good bagel.

If you're looking for a Southwestern-style breakfast, try **Richardson's,** 1582 E. Bethany Home Rd. (☎ **602/265-5886** or 602/230-8718). See Richardson's under "Dining" for more information.

## 5  Seeing the Sights

### DISCOVERING THE DESERT & ITS NATIVE CULTURES

✪ **Heard Museum.** 22 E. Monte Vista Rd. ☎ **602/252-8840.** Admission $6 adults, $5 seniors and students, $3 children 4–12; free for everyone Wed 5–8pm. Mon–Tues and Thurs–Sat 9:30am–5pm, Wed 9:30am–8pm, Sun noon–5pm. Closed some holidays. Bus: O.

One of the nation's finest museums dealing exclusively with Native American cultures, the Heard Museum makes a very informative first stop before heading out to discover the indigenous cultures of Arizona. At press time, the museum had just started construction on a new addition.

"Native Peoples of the Southwest" is an extensive exhibit that examines the culture of each of the major tribes of the region. Included in the exhibit are a Navajo hogan, an Apache wickiup, and a Hopi corn-grinding display. A large kachina doll gallery will give you an idea of the number of different kachina spirits that populate the Hopi and Zuñi religions. *Our Voices, Our Land* is an audiovisual presentation in which Indians express their thoughts on their heritage.

"Old Ways, New Ways" is an unusual interactive exhibit that's aimed at children, but is also interesting to adults. You can join a drumming group on a video, duplicate a Northwest tribal design, or set up a miniature tepee. On many weekends there are performances by Native American singers and dancers, and throughout the week artists demonstrate their work. Guided tours of the museum are offered daily.

The biggest event of the year is the **Guild Indian Fair and Market,** which is held on the first weekend in March and includes performances of traditional dances as well as arts and crafts demonstrations and sales.

The museum also operates the **Heard Museum North** satellite gallery in El Pedregal Festival Marketplace, 34505 N. Scottsdale Rd. (☎ **602/488-9817**), adjacent to The Boulders resort and the town of Carefree. This fairly large gallery features changing exhibits and is open Monday through Saturday from 10am to 5:30pm and Sunday from noon to 5pm. Admission is $2 for adults and $1 for children ages 5 to 12.

**Desert Botanical Garden.** In Papago Park, 1201 N. Galvin Pkwy. ☎ **602/941-1225** or 602/ 481-8134 (24-hour activities hotline). Admission $7 adults, $6 senior citizens, $1 children 5–12, free for children 4 and under. Oct–Apr daily 8am–8pm; May–Sept daily 7am–10pm. Closed Dec 25. Bus: 3.

Located adjacent to the Phoenix Zoo and devoted exclusively to cacti and other desert plants, the Desert Botanical Garden has on display more than 20,000 plants from all over the world. One fascinating section of the garden is the "Plants and People of the Sonoran Desert" trail. This trail explains the science of ethnobotany through interactive displays that demonstrate how the inhabitants of the Sonoran Desert once used wild and cultivated plants. You can practice grinding corn and pounding mesquite beans, or make a yucca-fiber brush. The **Center for Desert Living** features demonstration gardens and the Desert House, an energy- and water-conservation research house. If you come late in the day, you can stay until after dark and see night-blooming flowers and dramatically lit cacti. A restaurant on the grounds is under the same management as the popular Eddie's Grill (see "Dining" in this chapter). The Sunday brunch is particularly popular (make reservations). Frequent Sunday concerts turn a visit to the garden into a special event.

# Phoenix Attractions

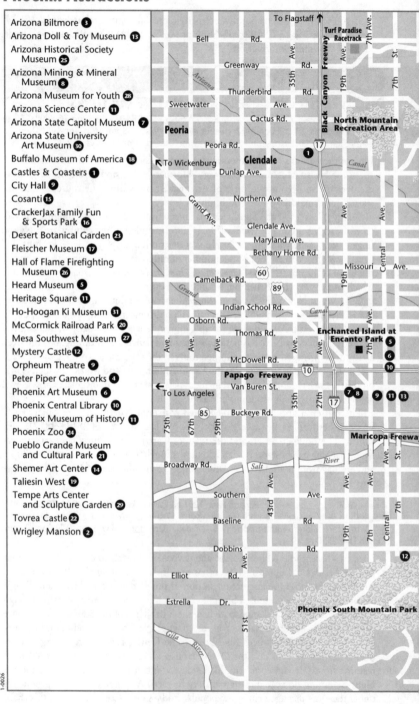

1-0026

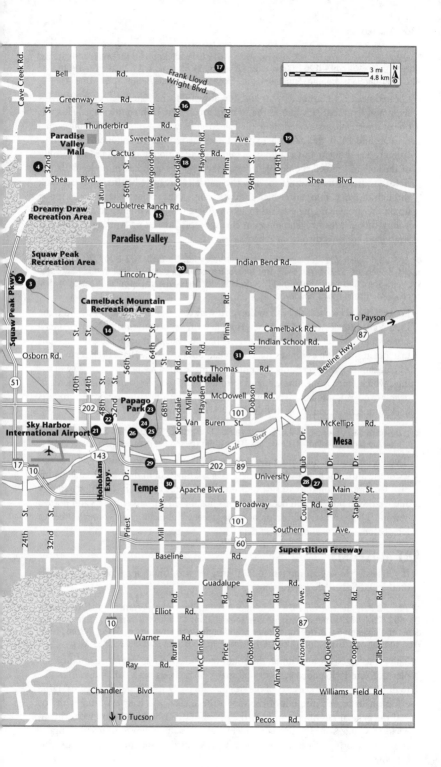

**Pueblo Grande Museum & Cultural Park.** 4619 E. Washington St. (between 44th St. and 48th St.). ☎ **602/495-0901.** Admission $2 adults, $1.50 seniors, $1 children 6–17; free on Sun. Mon–Sat 9am–4:45pm, Sun 1–4:45pm. Closed major holidays. Bus: Yellow Line (Y).

Located near Sky Harbor Airport and downtown Phoenix, the Pueblo Grande Museum and Cultural Park houses the ruins of an ancient Hohokam village. This was one of several villages located along the Salt River between A.D. 300 and 1400. Sometime around 1450, this and other villages were mysteriously abandoned. One speculation is that drought and a buildup of salts from irrigation water reduced the fertility of the soil and forced the people to leave their homes and seek more fertile lands. Before touring the grounds to view the partially excavated ruins, you can walk through the small museum, which exhibits many of the artifacts that have been dug up on the site. Changing exhibits focus on different aspects of ancient and contemporary Indian cultures. The museum also sponsors interesting workshops, demonstrations, and tours throughout the year.

**Deer Valley Rock Art Center.** 3711 W. Deer Valley Rd. ☎ **602/582-8007.** Admission $3 adults, $2 seniors, $1 children 6–12, free for children 5 and under. Late Sept to mid-May Tues–Sat 9am–5pm, Sun noon–5pm; mid-May to late Sept Tues–Fri 8am–2pm, Sat 9am–5pm, Sun noon–5pm. Closed major holidays.

Located in the Hedgepeth Hills in the northwest corner of the Valley of the Sun, the Deer Valley Rock Art Center preserves an amazing concentration of Native American petroglyphs, some of which date from 10,000 years. Although these petroglyphs may not at first seem as impressive as more famous images that have been reproduced ad nauseam in recent years, the sheer numbers make this a fascinating spot. The drawings, which range from simple spirals to much more complex renderings of herds of deer, are on volcanic boulders along a ¼-mile trail. An interpretive center provides background information on this site and on rock art in general.

**Ho-Hoogam Ki Museum.** 10000 E. Osborn Rd., Scottsdale. ☎ **602/874-8190.** Admission $1. Oct–May Mon–Fri 10am–4:30pm, Sat 10am–2pm (closed Sat in other months).

If you're interested in learning more about the Native American history of the Valley of the Sun, you might want to visit this small museum in the Pima-Maricopa Indian Community on the east side of Scottsdale. There are exhibits on Pima basketry and Maricopa pottery, and occasionally it's possible to see basketmakers and potters at work. There are also exhibits on how the ancient Hohokam people farmed this area long before the arrival of white settlers.

## ART MUSEUMS

If you're developing an interest in local arts, see also "Shopping," below, for details on the Old Scottsdale gallery scene.

✪ **Phoenix Art Museum.** 1625 N. Central Ave. (at the northeast corner of McDowell Rd.). ☎ **602/257-1222.** Free admission; special exhibitions $5 adults, $4 senior citizens, $2 students and children 6–12, free for children 5 and under; free for everyone Thurs 5–9pm. Tues–Wed and Sat–Sun 10am–5pm, Thurs–Fri 10am–9pm. Closed major holidays. Bus: O.

This is the largest art museum in the Southwest and a renovation and expansion completed in late 1996 added acres of wall space. With all its space, the museum is able to display many huge canvases of the size that are rarely seen in most museums. Little exhibit halls tucked into out-of-the-way corners, dead-end hallways hung with art, and the general rambling nature of the museum's two buildings (connected by an enclosed stainless-steel pedestrian bridge) make this a museum to be given plenty of time for exploring. It's easy to completely miss entire exhibit areas if you're the linear type.

Housed within this modest labyrinth, you'll find a very respectable collection that spans the major artistic movements from the Renaissance to the present. The collection of modern and contemporary art is particularly good, with works by Diego Rivera, Frida Kahlo, Pablo Picasso, Karel Appel, Mark Rothko, Willem de Kooning, Alexander Calder, Henry Moore, Georgia O'Keeffe, Henri Rousseau, and Auguste Rodin.

The large first-floor gallery is used for special exhibits including major touring retrospectives. The Thorne Miniature Collection is one of the museum's most popular exhibits and consists of tiny rooms on a scale of 1 inch to 1 foot. The rooms are exquisitely detailed, right down to the leaded-glass windows of an English lodge kitchen. Other exhibits include decorative arts, historic fashions, Asian art, Spanish colonial furnishings and religious art, and of course, a Western American exhibit featuring works by members of the Cowboy Artists of America.

One-hour tours of the museum are offered Tuesday through Sunday. On the first Friday of each month there are evening jazz concerts (admission charged). There's also an excellent cafe here (as at the Desert Botanical Gardens, under the same management as Eddie's Grill).

✪ **Arizona State University Art Museum.** In the Nelson Fine Arts Center, 10th St. and Mill Ave., Tempe. ☎ **602/965-2787.** Free admission. Tues 10am–9pm, Wed–Sat 10am–5pm, Sun 1–5pm. Closed major holidays. Bus: Red or Yellow Line (R or Y).

Though it isn't very large, the Arizona State University Art Museum is memorable for its innovative architecture and excellent temporary exhibitions. The building, stark and angular, captures the colors of sunset on desert mountains with its purplish gray stucco facade and pyramidal shape. The museum entrance is down a flight of stairs that lead to a cool underground garden area. Inside are galleries for crafts, prints, contemporary art, Latin American art, a temporary exhibition gallery, and two outdoor sculpture courts. The museum's collection of American art includes works by Georgia O'Keeffe, Edward Hopper, and Frederic Remington.

**Fleischer Museum.** At Perimeter Center, 17207 N. Perimeter Dr., Scottsdale. ☎ **602/585-3108.** Free admission. Daily 10am–4pm. Closed major holidays.

This was the country's first museum dedicated to the California school of American Impressionism, which drew extensively on French Impressionist styles and holds a quiet place in American art history. There is also an exhibit of Russian Impressionist paintings.

You'll find this small museum in a business park off Pima Road near the intersection with Frank Lloyd Wright Boulevard, which is an extension of Bell Road.

**Shemer Art Center.** 5005 E. Camelback Rd. ☎ **602/262-4727.** Free admission. Tues 10am–9pm, Wed–Fri 10am–5pm, Sat 9am–1pm. Bus: 50.

Housed in a historic Santa Fe mission–style home built in the 1920s, the Shemer Art Center stages changing exhibits of traditional and contemporary art. The center also offers classes, concerts, sales, and lectures.

**Tempe Arts Center & Sculpture Garden.** Tempe Beach Park, Mill Ave. and First St., Tempe. ☎ **602/968-0888.** Admission $2 adults, $1 students, free for children 11 and under; free for everyone Sun. Tues–Sun 10am–5pm. Bus: Red Line (R).

Though this arts center is tiny, it often stages very interesting exhibits of contemporary art and crafts by living artists. Outside the gallery, in an area that was once a public swimming pool, is a small sculpture garden with contemporary pieces by local, regional, and national artists. There's also a small gift shop full of one-of-a-kind crafts and art.

## ❓ Did You Know?

- The Phoenix metropolitan area has almost 150 golf courses and more than 1,000 tennis courts.
- Phoenix is the seventh-largest metropolitan area in the United States.
- The Valley of the Sun hosts the spring-training camps of seven major-league baseball teams: the Oakland A's, San Francisco Giants, Chicago Cubs, Milwaukee Brewers, Seattle Mariners, California Angels, and San Diego Padres.
- Each year Phoenix enjoys sunshine during 86% of all daylight hours, for a total of 300 to 315 sunny days.
- The tallest water fountain in the world (560 feet) is in the community of Fountain Hills east of Scottsdale.

## HISTORIC LANDMARKS & HISTORY MUSEUMS

**Phoenix Museum of History.** 105 N. Fifth St. ☎ **602/253-2734.** Admission $5 adults, $3.50 seniors, $2.50 children 6–11, free for children under 6. Mon–Sat 10am–5pm, Sun noon–5pm. Closed major holidays. Bus: Red or Yellow Line (R or Y).

Located adjacent to Heritage Square in downtown Phoenix, this relatively new museum is one of the anchors of the city's downtown revitalization plan. It presents an interesting look at the history of a city that, to the casual visitor, might not seem to *have* any history. Interactive exhibits get visitors involved in the displays, while unusual aspects of the city's history make this place much more interesting than your average local history museum. Aroma barrels offer a sniff of how Phoenix once smelled. A beer-bottle sidewalk shows how one saloonkeeper solved the problem of muddy streets—a problem that once plagued the city. Yet another exhibit shows how "lungers" (tuberculosis sufferers) inadvertently helped originate the tourism industry in Arizona.

**Arizona Historical Society Museum—Marley Center.** In Papago Park, 1300 N. College Ave. (just off Curry Rd.), Tempe. ☎ **602/929-0292.** Free admission. Mon–Sat 10am–4pm, Sun noon–4pm. Bus: Red Line (R).

This museum, at the new headquarters for the Arizona Historical Society, focuses its modern, well-designed exhibits on the history of central Arizona during the 20th century. The primary focus is on the lives and works of the people who helped shaped this region of the state. One of the more interesting exhibits features life-size statues of everyday people from Arizona's past (a Mexican miner, a Chinese laborer, and so on). Quotes relate their individual stories and props reveal what items they might have traveled with during their days in the desert.

**Heritage Square.** 115 N. Sixth St., at Monroe. ☎ **602/262-5029** or 602/262-5071. Rosson House tours, $3 adults, $2 senior citizens, $1 children 6–12, free for children 5 and under. Wed–Sat 10am–3:30pm, Sun noon–3:30pm (call for summer hours). Bus: Red or Yellow Line (R or Y).

Though the city of Phoenix was founded as recently as 1870, much of its history has been obliterated. Heritage Square is a collection of some of the few remaining houses in Phoenix that date from the last century and the original Phoenix townsite. All the buildings here are listed on the National Register of Historic Places, and most display Victorian architectural styles popular just before the turn of the century. Today the buildings house museums, restaurants, and gift shops. The Eastlake Victorian Rosson House is furnished with period antiques and is open for tours. The Silva House, a neoclassical revival-style home, houses historical exhibits on

**Frommer's Favorite Phoenix Experiences**

**Hiking up Camelback Mountain or Squaw Peak.** Hiking up to the top of these two mountains very early in the morning is a tradition among the city's more active residents. Both are steep climbs, but the views from up top are superb. Bring water!

**Having Dinner with a View.** There's something bewitching about gazing down at the twinkling lights of the city while enjoying a delicious meal at one of Phoenix's restaurants with a view.

**Lounging by the Pool.** Nothing is more relaxing than lounging by one of the spectacular pools and gazing up at the desert mountains from a world-class Valley of the Sun resort.

**Tubing down the Salt River.** The best way to see the desert is from an inner tube as you float downriver. A few companies provide inner tubes and shuttles.

**Taking the Scottsdale Art Walk.** Thursday evenings from October to May both dilettantes and connoisseurs turn out to visit the nearly 60 art galleries in downtown Scottsdale, many of which provide complimentary refreshments and have artists on hand.

**Attending a Spring Training Baseball Game.** Get a head start on all your fellow baseball fans by going to a spring-training game while you're in Phoenix.

**Mountain Biking in South Mountain or Papago Park.** The trails of these two desert parks are ideal for mountain biking, and whether you're a novice making your first foray into the dirt or a budding downhill racer, you'll find miles of riding that are just your speed.

**A Day at a Health Spa.** While we sometimes think we might be type-A personalities, that doesn't mean we can't find time to fit a day at a spa into our schedules. When it comes to stress relief, there's nothing like a massage, a healthy meal, and lounging around doing nothing.

turn-of-the-century life in the Valley of the Sun. In the Stevens-Haustgen House, you'll find a combination shop and museum focusing on Native American crafts and history. The Arizona Doll and Toy Museum can be found in a 1912 schoolhouse. The Burgess Carriage House contains a gift shop and ticket window for the Rosson House tours. The Teeter House, an 1899 bungalow, is a tea room. An 1897 mule barn houses the Carriage House Cafe. The old Baird Machine Shop contains Pizzeria Bianco, and the Thomas House is a bakery.

✪ **Arizona State Capitol Museum.** 1700 W. Washington St. ☎ **602/542-4581.** Free admission. Mon–Fri 8am–5pm. Closed state holidays. Bus: Yellow Line (Y).

In the years before Arizona became a state, the territorial capital moved from Prescott to Tucson, then back to Prescott, and finally settled in Phoenix. In 1898 a stately territorial capitol building was erected with a copper roof to remind the local citizenry of the importance of that metal in the Arizona economy. A statue, *Winged Victory,* stands atop the polished copper. This building no longer serves as the actual state capitol, but has been restored to the way it appeared in 1912, the year Arizona became a state. Among the rooms on view are the senate and house chambers, as well as the governor's office. Excellent historical exhibits provide interesting perspectives on early Arizona events and lifestyles. There is also a USS *Arizona* exhibit here.

# SCIENCE & INDUSTRY MUSEUMS

**Arizona Science Center.** 600 E. Washington St. ☎ **602/716-2000.** Admission $6.50 adults, $4.50 senior citizens and children 4–12, free for children 3 and under. Daily 10am–5pm. Closed Thanksgiving and Christmas. Bus: Red Line (R), Yellow Line (Y), or O.

Aimed primarily at children but also a lot of fun for adults, the Arizona Science Center, a hands-on facility, moved to its new building in the spring of 1997. In this expanded facility you'll find state-of-the-art interactive exhibits covering such topics as "How We Live With the Sun," "Psychology: Understanding Ourselves, Understanding Each Other," and "Networking." However, it is not the topics so much as the individual displays that are what make this museum so much fun. There's a huge ant farm, a virtual reality game that puts you inside a video game, a massive truck tire weighing almost 4 tons, and a flight simulator. The ever-popular soap-bubble play area is housed on a terrace on the museum's roof, as is a star-gazing area. In addition to the many exhibits, the new facility includes a planetarium and large-screen theater, both of which carry additional charges.

**Mesa Southwest Museum.** 53 N. MacDonald St. (at the corner of First St.), Mesa. ☎ **602/644-2230.** Admission $4 adults, $3.50 senior citizens and students, $2 children 3–12, free for children 2 and under. Tues–Sat 10am–5pm, Sun 1–5pm. Closed major holidays. Bus: Red Line (R).

Located in downtown Mesa, this museum appeals mostly to children, but its exhibits on prehistoric indigenous cultures in the region will likely interest adults as well. Kids will love the fossils (including a complete mammoth skeleton) and animated dinosaurs, and they can even pan for gold. The mine and jail (this really *was* the old jail) displays are also a lot of fun for kids.

There are usually a couple of different temporary exhibits at any given time, and these may include displays of contemporary art or regional history.

The museum also operates the nearby **Sirrine House Historic Home Museum,** 160 N. Center St., which is filled with period antiques from the late 19th and early 20th centuries. This historic home is open Saturday from 10am to 5pm and Sunday from 1 to 5pm.

# A MUSEUM MISCELLANY

**Champlin Fighter Aircraft Museum.** 4636 Fighter Aces Dr., Mesa (at Falcon Field Airport off McKellips Rd.). ☎ **602/830-4540.** Admission $6.50 adults, $3 children 5–12, free for children under 5. Daily 10am–5pm. From U.S. 60, take the Greenfield exit and go north to McKellips Blvd.

This aeronautical museum is dedicated exclusively to fighter planes and the men who flew them. Aircraft from World Wars I and II, the Korean War, and the Vietnam War are on display, with a strong emphasis on the wood-and-fabric biplanes and triplanes of World War I. There are several Sopwiths and Fokkers. From World War II, there's a Spitfire, a Messerschnitt, and a Goodyear Corsair. Jet fighters from more recent battles include a MiG-15, a MiG-17, and an F4 Phantom. In addition to the restored fighter planes, there is memorabilia of famous fighter aces.

**Buffalo Museum of America.** 10261 N. Scottsdale Rd. (at the southeast corner of Shea Blvd.), Scottsdale. ☎ **602/951-1022.** Admission $3 adults, $2.50 senior citizens, $2 children 6–17, free for children 5 and under. Mon–Fri 9am–5pm. Closed major holidays. Bus: 72 or 106.

Scottsdale may not be the home where the buffalo roam, but it does have a fascination with the Old West, so it seems appropriate to find here a museum dedicated to these fabled behemoths of the plains. This small museum is the culmination of one man's infatuation with the American bison, which is commonly known as the buffalo. The museum houses stuffed buffaloes, bronze buffaloes, buffalo paintings, and all manner of buffalo memorabilia, including a rifle that once belonged to Buffalo Bill Cody.

**Hall of Flame Firefighting Museum.** In Papago Park, 6101 E. Van Buren St. ☎ **602/ 275-3473.** Admission $5 adults, $4 senior citizens, $3 children 6–17, free for children 5 and under. Mon–Sat 9am–5pm, Sun noon–4pm. Closed Jan 1, Thanksgiving, and Dec 25. Bus: 3.

The world's largest fire-fighting museum houses a fascinating collection of vintage fire trucks. The displays date from a 1725 English hand-pumper but also include several classic fire engines from this century. All are beautifully restored and, of course, fire-engine red (mostly). In all, there are more than 100 vehicles on display.

**Arizona Mining & Mineral Museum.** 1502 W. Washington St. ☎ **602/255-3791.** Free admission. Mon–Fri 8am–5pm, Sat 1–5pm. Closed state holidays. Bus: Yellow Line (Y).

It was the search for mineral wealth that attracted the first Spanish explorers to Arizona and over the years, gold, silver, and copper all had their time dominating the economy of the state. Today Arizona still extracts more nonfuel minerals than any other state. This small downtown museum is dedicated to this industry, but rather than playing up the historical or profit-making side of the industry, exhibits focus on the amazing variety and beauty of Arizona minerals. Azurite, chalcanthite, chalcoaluminate, malachite, chrysocolla—these are just some of the tongue-twisting names given to the richly colored and fascinatingly textured minerals that have come out of the state's countless mines. Even the names of mines themselves hint at how Arizonans have been romancing the stones for more than a century—Copper Queen, Sleeping Beauty, No-Name Creek, Lucky Boy, Bluebird.

## ARCHITECTURAL HIGHLIGHTS

In addition to the architectural landmarks listed below, there are a couple of other buildings of which Phoenix is justly proud.

The **Arizona Biltmore,** 24th Street and Missouri Avenue (☎ 602/955-6600), though not designed by Frank Lloyd Wright, shows the famed architect's hand in its distinctive cast-cement blocks and also displays sculptures, furniture, and stained glass designed by Wright. The best way to soak up the ambience of this exclusive resort (if you can't afford to stay here) is over dinner, a cocktail, or tea. If you'd like to spend the day by the pool, you can even rent a cabana.

**Tovrea Castle,** 5041 E. Van Buren St. (☎ 602/262-6412), another architectural confection of the Phoenix landscape, has been likened to a giant wedding cake and is currently under renovation. However, the castle is scheduled to open to the public some time in 1999. Call for information.

The most recent buildings to garner architectural praise in Phoenix are the **new City Hall** and restored **Orpheum Theatre,** which sit back to back on Third Avenue between Washington and Adams streets. The new City Hall is a bold contemporary construction as intriguing as the main library, while the Orpheum is a classically elegant historic building. Together the two create a clash of styles that typifies old and new Phoenix.

**Phoenix Central Library.** 1221 N. Central Ave. ☎ **602/262-4636.** Free admission. Mon– Wed 9am–9pm, Thurs–Sat 9am–6pm, Sun 1–5pm. Closed major holidays. Bus: Red Line (R) or O.

Opened in 1995, the Phoenix Central Library is the most daring piece of public architecture in the city. No fan of futurist art or science fiction should miss a visit. The entrance, with all its steel and glass and elevators rising above, makes you feel as though you've just stepped inside a gargantuan computer or 21st-century space station.

The five-story cube is partially clad in ribbed copper sheeting, enough copper in fact to produce roughly 17,500,000 pennies (it took a lot of overdue books to pay for that feature). The building's design makes use of the desert's plentiful sunshine to provide plenty of light for reading, but also incorporates computer-controlled louvers and shade sails to reduce heat and glare. The fifth floor reading room, which covers more than an acre and is the largest library reading room in the United States, is topped by a "floating" ceiling that is suspended from cables. Either you'll love it or you'll hate it, but don't miss it.

✪ **Taliesin West.** 12621 Frank Lloyd Wright Blvd. (at 114th St.), Scottsdale. ☎ **602/ 860-2700.** Basic tours, Oct 1–May 31 $12 adults, $9 seniors and students, $3 children 4–12, free for children 3 and under. June 1–Sept 30 $10 adults, $7 students and seniors, $3 children 4–12, free for children 3 and under. Oct 1–May 31 daily 10am–4pm; June 1–Sept 30 daily 8am– 3pm. Closed Easter, Thanksgiving, Christmas, New Year's Day, and occasional special events. From Scottsdale Rd., go east on Shea Blvd. to 114th St., then north 1 mile to the entrance road.

Architect Frank Lloyd Wright fell in love with the Arizona desert and in 1937 opened a winter camp here that served as his office and school. Today Taliesin West is the headquarters of the Frank Lloyd Wright Foundation and School of Architecture.

Tours explain the buildings of this campus and also include a general background introduction to Wright and his theories of architecture. Wright believed in using local materials in his designs, and this shows up at Taliesin West where local stone was used for building foundations. He developed a number of innovative methods for dealing with the extremes of the desert climate, such as sliding wall panels to let in varying amounts of air and light.

Architecture students, and anyone interested in the work of Wright, will enjoy browsing through the gift shop full of excellent books. Expanded basic tours called Insight Tours ($14 to $16 adults and $10 to $12 for seniors, students, and children), behind-the-scenes tours ($25 to $30 per person), and guided desert hikes ($14 per person) are also available at certain times of year and at specific times of day. Call ahead and check the schedule to be sure you can get the tour you want at the time you want.

**Wrigley Mansion.** 2501 E. Telawa Trail. ☎ **602/955-4079.** Tours $10.70. Tours held Tues– Fri 10:30am and 3pm. Bus: 24.

Situated on a hilltop overlooking the Arizona Biltmore, this classically elegant mansion was built by chewing-gum magnate William Wrigley, Jr., between 1929 and 1931 as a present for his wife, Ada. Built with Italianate styling, the many levels and red-tile roofs make it seem as though the mansion is an entire village. Today the mansion is a National Historic Landmark with the interior restored to its original elegance, and although the mansion is a private club, it is open for tours. The dining room is also open to the public (by reservation only) for Sunday brunch. After touring this sprawling residence, it's hard to believe that the mansion was only used for 1 or 2 months each year.

**Cosanti.** 6433 Doubletree Ranch Rd. (1 mile west of Scottsdale Rd.), Scottsdale. ☎ **602/ 948-6145.** Admission: $1 donation. Daily 9am–5pm. Closed major holidays.

This complex of cast-concrete structures served as a prototype and learning project for architect Paolo Soleri's much grander Arcosanti project currently under construction north of Phoenix (see chapter 6, "Central Arizona," for details). It's here at Cosanti that Soleri's famous bells are cast, and you can see the foundry in action on most weekday mornings.

**Mystery Castle.** 800 E. Mineral Rd. ☎ **602/268-1581.** Admission $4 adults, $3 senior citizens, $1.50 children 6–15. Tues–Sun 11am–4pm. Closed July–Sept.

Built for a daughter who longed for a castle more permanent than those built in sand at the beach, Mystery Castle is a work of folk-art architecture. Boyce Luther Gulley, who had come to Arizona in hopes of curing his tuberculosis, constructed the castle during the 1930s and early 1940s using stones from the property. The resulting 18-room fantasy has 13 fireplaces, a wedding chapel, parapets, and many other unusual touches. This castle is a must for fans of folk-art constructions.

## ZOOS & PARKS

Among the city's most popular parks are its natural areas and preserves. These include South Mountain Park, Papago Park, Phoenix Mountains Preserve (site of Squaw Peak), North Mountain Preserve, North Mountain Recreation Area, and Camelback Mountain-Echo Canyon Recreation Area. For more information on these parks, see "Hiking," "Bicycling," and "Horseback Riding" under "Outdoor Pursuits," later in this chapter.

**Phoenix Zoo.** In Papago Park, 455 N. Galvin Pkwy. ☎ **602/273-1341.** Admission $8.50 adults, $7.50 senior citizens, $4.25 children 3–12, free for children 2 and under. May 1–Labor Day daily 7am–4pm; Labor Day–Apr daily 9am–5pm. Closed Dec 25. Bus: 3.

"Wow! Look at all the turtles." That's almost always the first reaction when visitors approach this zoo on a bridge over a very primordial-looking pond. Home to more than 1,300 animals, the Phoenix Zoo is known for its mixed-species 4-acre African veldt exhibit and its baboon colony. The Southwestern animal exhibits are also of particular interest, but the resident giant Galápagos tortoises are my personal favorites here. All the animals in the zoo are kept in naturalistic enclosures and what with all the palm trees and tropical vegetation, it's easy to forget that this is the desert. In fact, in 1997 a rain-forest exhibit was added. For an additional charge, you can take a narrated tram tour of the grounds.

Kids will love the 11-acre children's zoo, where they can see baby animals and pet some of the more friendly residents.

**Wildlife World Zoo.** 16501 W. Northern Ave., Litchfield Park. ☎ **602/935-9453.** Admission $6.75 adults, $4 children 3–12, free for children under 3.

Unique animals are a specialty of this private zoo, where you'll see tiny mammals, mammals that fly, kangaroos and wallabies, white tigers and black panthers, and plenty of snakes and lizards. Several exhibits and shows let visitors get close to the animals. You'll find the zoo way out on the west side of the valley.

## ESPECIALLY FOR KIDS

In addition to the activities suggested below for children, they're also likely to enjoy the Arizona Science Center, the Mesa Southwest Museum, Mystery Castle, the Hall of Flame Firefighting Museum, the Phoenix Zoo, and the Wildlife World Zoo—all described in detail above.

**Arizona Doll & Toy Museum.** In Heritage Square, 602 E. Adams St. ☎ **602/253-9337.** Admission $2 adults, 50¢ children. Tues–Sat 10am–4pm, Sun noon–4pm. Closed Aug. Any downtown bus.

Located in the Stevens House on Heritage Square in downtown Phoenix, the Arizona Doll and Toy Museum is as interesting to adults as it is to kids. There's a 1912 schoolroom display in which the children are all antique dolls.

**Arizona Museum for Youth.** 35 N. Robson St. (between Main and First sts.), Mesa. ☎ **602/644-2467.** Admission $2, free for children under 2. Fall–spring Sun and Tues–Fri 1–5pm, Sat 10am–5pm; summer Tues–Fri 9am–5pm, Sat 10am–5pm, Sun 1–5pm. Closed for 2 weeks between exhibits.

Using both traditional displays and participatory activities, this museum allows children to explore the fine arts and their own creativity. The museum is housed in a refurbished grocery store, which has for past exhibits been transformed into a zoo, a farm, and a foreign country depending on the theme of the show. Exhibits are geared mainly to toddlers through 12-year-olds, but all ages can work together to make an object or experience the activities.

**McCormick Railroad Park.** 7301 E. Indian Bend Rd., Scottsdale. ☎ **602/994-2312.** Train and carousel rides $1. Hours vary with the season, call for schedule. Bus: 72.

If you or your kids happen to be enamored of trains, then you won't want to miss this Scottsdale park dedicated to railroading. Within the park are a $5/12$-scale model railroad that takes visitors around the park, restored cars and engines, two old railway depots, and a 1929 carousel. In the spring and summer months there are concerts in the park. You'll find the park on the corner of Scottsdale Road.

**Castles & Coasters.** 9445 N. Metro Pkwy. E. ☎ **602/997-7575.** Ride and game prices vary (all-day passes available). Summer Sun–Thurs 10am–10 or 11pm, Fri–Sat 10am–midnight. Fall–spring Fri–Sun 10am–10 or 11pm. Bus: Red Line (R) or 27.

Located adjacent to Metrocenter, Arizona's largest shopping mall, this amusement park boasts a very impressive roller coaster and plenty of tamer rides as well. There are also four 18-hole miniature-golf courses and a huge pavilion full of video games.

**CrackerJax Family Fun & Sports Park.** 16001 N. Scottsdale Rd. ($1/4$ mile south of Bell Rd.), Scottsdale. ☎ **602/998-2800.** Activity prices vary. Daily (hours change seasonally, call ahead). Bus: 72.

Three miniature-golf courses are the main attraction here, but you'll also find a driving range (bilevel), batting cages, go-cart tracks, sand volleyball courts, and a video-game arcade.

**Enchanted Island at Encanto Park.** 1202 W. Encanto Blvd. ☎ **602/254-2020.** Activity prices vary. Daily (hours change seasonally, call ahead). Bus: 8.

This amusement park is geared toward younger kids and is set on an island in Encanto Park, one of Phoenix's more popular urban parks. There are train rides, kiddie roller coasters, bumper boats, a vintage carousel, a pirate ship, paddle boats, and a video-game arcade.

**Peter Piper Gameworks.** 10620 N. 32nd St. ☎ **602/404-2200.** Activity prices vary. Sun–Thurs 10am–10pm, Fri–Sat 10am–midnight (shorter hours in winter). Bus: Blue Line (B), 500, or 502.

This indoor fun park is aimed at kids 12 and under and features bumper boats, bumper cars, a small roller coaster, a trilevel maze, a moon walk, and a video-game arcade.

# 6 Organized Tours

The Valley of the Sun is a sprawling, often congested, place, and if you are unfamiliar with the area, you may be surprised at how great the distances are here. If map reading and urban navigation are not your strong points, you may want to consider taking a guided tour. There are numerous companies offering tours of both the Valley of the Sun and the rest of Arizona. However, tours of the valley tend to include only brief stops at highlights.

**Gray Line of Phoenix** (☎ **800/732-0327** or 602/495-9100) is one of the largest tour companies in the valley. They offer a 3-hour tour of Phoenix and the Valley of the Sun for $27 per adult. The tour points out such local landmarks as the state capitol, downtown Phoenix, Barry Goldwater's home, the Wrigley Mansion, and Camelback Mountain. There's also a stop in Scottsdale for lunch and shopping.

If photography is your interest and you'd like a few tips on camera techniques while you see the state, contact **Ancient Trails Tours** (☎ **602/953-1296**), which offers tours around the valley and to such scenic locations as Sedona, the Apache Trail, and Tucson. Half-day tours are $58 and full-day tours are $88 (four-person minimum).

Far more fun are desert Jeep tours. These are offered by a dozen or more companies around the valley. Most hotels and resorts have particular companies that they work with, so if you want to do a Jeep tour, try contacting the concierge at your hotel. Alternatively, you can contact one of the following companies. Most companies will pick you up at your hotel, take you off through the desert, give you lots of information on this corner of the West, and maybe even let you try shooting a six-gun while you're out in the desert. Tour prices are around $60 to $80 for a four-hour tour. Reliable companies to try include **Arizona Awareness Desert Jeep Tours** (☎ **602/947-7852**); **Arizona Bound Tours** (☎ **602/994-0580**); **Carefree Jeep Adventures** (☎ **800/294-JEEP** or 602/488-0023); **Desert Mountain Jeep Tours** (☎ **602/860-1777**); **Desert Storm Hummer Tours** (☎ **602/922-0020**); and **Wild West Jeep Tours** (☎ **602/941-8355**).

Some Jeep tour companies also offer the chance to do some gold panning. If this prospect interests you, contact **Arizona Awareness Desert Jeep Tours** (☎ **602/947-7852**), which also does ghost-town excursions, or **Arrowhead Desert Tours** (☎ **800/514-9063** or 602/942-3361). Expect to pay $60 or $65 per person.

To get an even more up close and personal look at the desert, you can go out on an ATV (all-terrain vehicle) with **Good Time ATV Tours** (☎ **602/956-6598**) or **Water Trix ATV Tours** (☎ **602/649-1418**), both of which charge $80 for a 4-hour tour.

If you're short on time but still want to at least see the Grand Canyon (or Lake Powell or the red rocks of Sedona), you can book an air tour in a small plane with **Scenic Airlines** (☎ **800/445-8738** or 602/991-8252) or **Westwind Aviation** (☎ **800/244-0866** or 602/991-5557). Expect to pay around $200 for a scenic flight to the Grand Canyon and back. If you'd like a glimpse of the Valley of the Sun from the air, consider a helicopter tour. These are offered by **Papillon Helicopters** (☎ **800/528-2418** or 602/967-6150) and **Southwest Jet Aviation** (☎ **602/991-7076**). Tours start around $80 per person. Expect to pay double that amount for a flight out over the Superstition Mountains.

How about a cruise? Yes, that's right, a cruise in the middle of the desert. The *Desert Princess* (☎ **602/230-7600**) does sightseeing, breakfast, lunch, and dinner cruises on Lake Pleasant, a reservoir 45 minutes northwest of Phoenix. Cruise prices range from $10 to $66. The sightseeing cruises are the least expensive and are generally only offered from May through October on the first Friday of each month and on selected summer holidays. To reach the marina on Lake Pleasant, take the Carefree Highway exit off I-17 and go west to Ariz. 74 and follow signs to Pleasant Harbor Marina on Lake Pleasant.

# 7 Outdoor Pursuits

**BALLOONING**   The still morning air of the Valley of the Sun is perfect for hot-air ballooning and, not surprisingly, there are quite a few companies offering balloon rides around Phoenix. Companies to try include **A Aerozona Adventure** (☎ **888/991-4260** or 602/991-4260), **Adventures Out West** (☎ **800/755-0935** or 602/

996-6100), **Sky Climber Balloon Adventures** (☎ **800/854-1798** or 602/483-8208), and the **Unicorn Balloon Company** (☎ **800/HOT-AIR8** or 602/991-3666). Expect to pay anywhere from $100 to $135 for a balloon ride, which makes this one of the cheapest places in the country to do a hot-air balloon flight.

**BICYCLING**  Though the Valley of the Sun is a sprawling place, it's mostly flat, which makes bicycling a breeze as long as it isn't windy or in the heat of summer. **Wheels 'n Gear,** 7607 E. McDowell Rd., Scottsdale (☎ **602/945-2881**), rents mountain bikes for between $15 and $40 per day and has off-road trail maps available. Among the best mountain-biking spots in the city are South Mountain Park (use the entrance off 48th Street), Papago Park (at Van Buren Street and Galvin Parkway), and North Mountain Recreation Area (off Seventh Street between Dunlap Avenue and Thunderbird Road).

If you'd rather have someone show you some of the desert's best mountain biking, contact **Arizona Bicycle/Desert Biking Adventures** (☎ **602/320-4602**), which leads 2-, 3-, and 4-hour mountain-bike tours through the desert (and specializes in downhill rides). Tour prices range from $50 for a 2-hour tour to $82 for a 4-hour tour. For a guided bike ride around parts of Scottsdale, Tempe, and Phoenix's Papago Park, contact **Arizona Scenic Biking** (☎ **602/905-2453**), which charges $50 to $55 for its half-day ride.

**FISHING**  There are six large lakes in the mountains northeast of Phoenix, and all offer good fishing. You'll need a fishing license from the Arizona Game and Fish Commission. These licenses are generally available wherever fishing gear is sold. Lake Pleasant, northwest of Phoenix, is another popular fishing hole.

**GOLF**  With more than 140 courses in the Valley of the Sun, golf is just about the most popular sport in Phoenix and one of the main reasons people flock here during the winter months. Sunshine, spectacular views, and coyotes, quail, and doves for company make playing a round of golf in the valley a truly memorable experience.

However, despite the number of courses, it can still be difficult to get a tee time on any of the more famous and popular courses. If you are staying at a resort with a golf course, be sure to make your tee-time reservations at the same time you make your room reservations. If you aren't staying at a resort, you may still be able to play around on a resort course if you can get a tee time. Try one of the tee-time reservation services below.

The only thing harder than getting a winter tee time in the Valley of the Sun is facing the bill at the end of your 18 holes. Greens fees at most public and resort courses range from around $90 to $125, with the top courses at the most expensive resorts often charging around $150. Municipal courses, on the other hand, charge less than $30.

You can get more information on Valley of the Sun golf courses from the **Phoenix and Valley of the Sun Convention and Visitors Bureau,** One Arizona Center, 400 E. Van Buren St., Suite 600, Phoenix, AZ 85004 (☎ **602/254-6500**). You can also pick up a copy of the *Phoenix and Valley of the Sun Golf Guide* at the Visitors Bureau, golf courses, and many hotels and resorts.

To assure that you get to play those courses you've been dreaming about, it's a good idea to make reservations well in advance. Many companies around the valley will save you the hassle of booking tee times by making reservations for you. Some of these companies include **Resort Tee Times** (☎ **800/GO-TRY-18** or 602/962-GOLF), **Golf Express** (☎ **800/878-8580** or 602/404-GOLF), or **Par-Tee-Time Golf** (☎ **800/827-2223** or 602/230-7223), or, for last-minute bookings, try **Stand-By Golf** (☎ **602/905-2665** or 888/303-2665).

The valley's many resort courses are, of course, the favored fairways of valley visitors. For spectacular scenery, the two Jay Morrish–designed 18-hole courses at **The Boulders,** 34631 N. Tom Darlington Dr., Carefree (☎ **800/553-1717**), just can't be beat. Given the option, play the South Course, and watch out as you approach the tee box on the seventh hole—it's a real heart stopper.

Jumping over to Litchfield Park, on the far west side of the valley, you'll find **The Wigwam Golf and Country Club,** 300 Indian School Rd. (☎ **602/935-9414**), and, count 'em, three championship 18-hole courses. The Gold Course here is legendary, but even the Blue and Red courses are worth playing. These are traditional courses, for purists who want vast expanses of green instead of cactus and boulders.

Way over on the east side of the valley at the foot of the Superstition Mountains, the **Gold Canyon Golf Club,** 6100 S. Kings Ranch Rd., Apache Junction (☎ **602/982-9090**), has what have been rated as three of the best holes in the state (the 11th, 12th, and 13th). This resort has been in the process of adding and renovating its golf course and by the time this book is out there should be two 18-hole courses here. Well worth the drive.

If you want to swing where the pros do, beg, borrow, or steal a tee time on the Tom Weiskopf and Jay Morrish–designed Stadium Course at the **Tournament Players Club of Scottsdale,** 17020 N. Hayden Rd. (☎ **602/585-3600**). The 18th hole here has standing room for 40,000 spectators, but hopefully there won't be that many (or any TV cameras) around the day you pull a double bogey on this hole. The TPC's second 18, the Desert Course, is actually a municipal course thanks to an agreement with land-owner, the Bureau of Land Management.

At the **Gainey Ranch Golf Club,** at the Hyatt Regency Scottsdale Resort at Gainey Ranch, 7600 E. Gainey Club Dr. (☎ **602/951-0022**), you'll find three decidedly different nine-hole courses (the Dunes, the Arroyo, and the Lakes courses), each with its own set of challenges.

If a traditional course that has challenged presidents and celebrities alike interests you, then try to get a tee time at one of the two 18-hole courses at the **Arizona Biltmore Country Club,** 24th Street and Missouri Avenue (☎ **602/955-9655**). The two courses here are more relaxing than challenging, good courses to play if you're not yet up to par. There's also a championship 18-hole putting course here at the Arizona Biltmore.

The two courses at the **Camelback Golf Club,** 7847 N. Mockingbird Lane (☎ **602/596-7050**), offer distinctly different experiences. The Padre Course has lots of dog legs and well-bunkered greens, while the Indian Bend course is a links-style course with great mountain views and lots of water hazards.

In 1996, **The Phoenician Golf Club,** 6000 E. Camelback Rd. (☎ **800/888-8234**), added another 9 holes for a total of 27 that mix traditional and desert styles.

Of the valley's many public and semiprivate golf courses, it is the two 18-hole courses at **Troon North Golf Club,** 10320 E. Dynamite Blvd., Scottsdale (☎ **602/585-5300**), that seem just barely carved out of raw desert and garner the most local accolades. However, the Pete Dye–designed **ASU-Karsten Golf Course,** 1125 E. Rio Salado Pkwy., Tempe (☎ **602/921-8070**), part of Arizona State University, is also highly praised and is a very challenging training ground for top collegiate golfers. If you haven't yet gotten your handicap down, but want to try a desert-style course, then head to **Tatum Ranch Golf Club,** 29888 N. Tatum Ranch Dr., Cave Creek (☎ **602/962-GOLF**), which is regarded as a forgiving course with a desert sensibility.

Of the municipal courses in Phoenix, **Papago Municipal Golf Course,** 5595 E. Moreland St. (☎ **602/275-8428**), at the foot of the red sandstone Papago Buttes, offers fine views and economical rates and has a killer 17th hole. **Encanto Municipal Golf Course,** 2775 N. 15th Ave. (☎ **602/253-3963**), is equally inexpensive for a round of golf.

**HIKING**  Several mountains around Phoenix, including Camelback Mountain and Squaw Peak, have been set aside as parks and nature preserves, and these natural areas are among the city's most popular hiking spots. The city's largest nature preserve, **Phoenix South Mountain Park,** said to be the largest city park in the world, contains miles of nature, hiking, mountain-biking, and horseback-riding trails. The views of Phoenix from here are spectacular, especially at sunset. To reach the park, simply drive south on Central Avenue or 48th Street.

Perhaps the single most popular hiking trail in the city is the trail to the top of **Camelback Mountain,** which is near the boundary between Phoenix and Scottsdale. This is the highest mountain in Phoenix, and the 1.2-mile trail to the summit is very steep. Don't attempt this one in the heat of the day, and take at least a quart of water with you. The reward for your effort is the city's finest view. To reach the trailhead for Camelback Mountain, drive up 44th Street until it becomes McDonald Drive, then turn right on East Echo Canyon Drive and continue up the hill until the road ends at a large parking lot.

**Squaw Peak** in the Phoenix Mountains Preserve offers a slightly less strenuous hike and views that are almost as spectacular as those from Camelback Mountain. Squaw Peak is reached from Squaw Peak Drive off Lincoln Drive between 22nd Street and 23rd Street.

For much less vigorous hiking, try the **North Mountain Recreation Area** in North Mountain Preserve. This natural area, which is located on either side of Seventh Street between Dunlap Avenue and Thunderbird Road, has more flat hiking than Camelback Mountain or Squaw Peak.

Farther afield there are numerous hiking opportunities in the Superstition Mountains to the east and the McDowell Mountains to the north.

**HORSEBACK RIDING**  Even in the urban confines of the Phoenix metro area people like to play at cowboying, and if you get the urge to saddle up, there are plenty of places around the valley to rent a horse. On the south side of the city, try **Ponderosa Stables,** 10215 S. Central Ave. (☎ **602/268-1261**), or **South Mountain Stables,** 10005 S. Central Ave. (☎ **602/276-8131**), both of which lead rides into South Mountain Park and charge $14 to $15 per hour. In the Scottsdale area, try **Trail Horse Adventures** at WestWorld of Scottsdale, 16601 N. Pima Rd., Scottsdale (☎ **602/502-9534**), which leads rides into the foothills of the McDowell Mountains and charges $20 for a 1-hour ride and $35 for a 2-hour ride (longer rides are also available). Also in Scottsdale is **McDonald's Ranch,** 26540 N. Scottsdale Rd. (☎ **602/585-0239**), which charges $20 for a 1-hour ride and $30 for a 2-hour ride (1-hour free ride on your birthday). There are also several riding stables out near the Superstition Mountains on the east side of the valley. See the "The Apache Trail" in the "Side Trips from Phoenix" section of this chapter for details. Keep in mind that most stables require reservations.

**IN-LINE SKATING**  In the Scottsdale area, you can rent in-line skates at **Scottsdale Bladez,** 10155 E. Via Linda (☎ **602/391-1139**), for $4 per hour, including all protective equipment. You can also rent equipment at **Wheels 'n Gear,** 7607 E. McDowell Rd. (☎ **602/945-2881**), which is in the Plaza Del Rio Shopping Center and charges $5 for 2 hours, $6 for 4 hours, and $10 for 24 hours.

The folks at these shops can point you toward nearby spots that are good for skating (or call the hotline listed below). One of the best places to skate is the **Indian**

**Bend Wash greenbelt,** a 9-mile multiuse path. It runs parallel to Hayden Road in Scottsdale from McKellips Road to 92nd Street and Shea Boulevard, and can be accessed at Hayden and Indian School Road.

For more information on the Phoenix skate scene, call the **Valley Inline Hotline** (☎ **602/831-2166**), which is operated by Orbital FX, an in-line skate school that can give you some lessons while you're in town.

**PERFORMANCE DRIVING**   Want to learn how to drive like a grand-prix racer? At the **Bob Bondurant School of High Performance Driving** (☎ **800/842-7223** or 602/961-0143) you can do just that. For nearly 3 decades this school has been training drivers in how to handle cars the way the pros do. Courses from 1 to 4 days are available with rates set at $765 per day. To take one of these courses, you generally need to make reservations 3 months in advance.

**ROCK CLIMBING**   Wanna get high? How about doing some guided rock climbing? You can take a beginning lesson or have a knowledgeable guide take you to some challenging walls. Contact **Ascend Guide Services** (☎ **800/2-ASCEND** or 602/ 968-6100) or **Wilderness Adventures** (☎ **800/462-5788** or 602/949-2774) to arrange a trip or lesson. Both of these companies also offer guided hikes.

**SKYDIVING**   If you're feeling really adventurous and daring and are game for a truly different experience, how about taking the great leap of faith and doing some skydiving? **Parachutes Over Phoenix Desert Skydiving Center** (☎ **800/441-5867** or 602/271-0440), which operates out of the Buckeye Airport 20 miles west of Phoenix, offers tandem free-fall or static-line jumps. Prices are $125 for the former and $110 for the latter.

**SOARING**   The thermals that form above the mountains in the Phoenix area are ideal for sailplane (glider) soaring. On the south side of the valley, **Arizona Soaring** (☎ **800/861-2318** or 602/821-2903), on Ariz. 238, 6$\frac{1}{2}$ miles west of Maricopa, offers sailplane rides as well as instruction. A basic 20-minute flight is $50, and for $85 you can take an aerobatic flight with loops, rolls, and inverted flying. On the north side of the valley, there's **Turf Soaring School,** 8700 W. Carefree Hwy., Peoria (☎ **602/439-3621**), which charges $65 for a basic flight and $95 for an aerobatic flight.

**TENNIS**   Tennis is second only to golf in popularity in the Phoenix area. Most major hotels have a few tennis courts, and there are several tennis resorts around the valley. Other places to play include the **City Center Tennis Courts,** 121 E. Adams St. (at the top of the Hyatt Regency Parking Garage), Phoenix (☎ **602/256-4120**); **Scottsdale Ranch Park,** 10400 E. Via Linda, Scottsdale (☎ **602/994-7774**); **Encanto Park,** 15th Avenue and Encanto Boulevard (☎ **602/261-8443**); the **Phoenix Tennis Center,** 6330 N. 21st Ave. (☎ **602/249-3712**); and **Mountain View Tennis Center,** 1104 E. Grovers Ave. (☎ **602/788-6088**).

**WATER PARKS**   At **Waterworld Safari Water Park,** 4243 W. Pinnacle Peak Rd., Glendale (☎ **602/581-1947**), you can free-fall 6$\frac{1}{2}$ stories down the Avalanche speed water slide or catch a gnarly wave in the wave pool. Other water slides offer tamer times. **Mesa Golfland-Sunsplash,** 155 W. Hampton, Mesa (☎ **602/834-8318**), has a wave pool and a tunnel called "the Black Hole." **Big Surf,** 1500 N. McClintock Rd. (☎ **602/947-7873**), has a wave pool, underground tube slides, and more.

All three of these parks charge $13.50 for adults and $11.25 for children 4 to 11 ($9 per person after 4pm at Waterworld and Sunsplash and after 3pm at Big Surf). All three parks are open Memorial Day to Labor Day, Monday through Saturday from 10am to 9pm (Big Surf until 6pm only) and Sunday from 11am to 7pm.

**WHITE-WATER RAFTING & TUBING ON THE SALT RIVER**   The desert may not seem like the place for white-water rafting, but up in the mountains to the northeast of Phoenix, the Upper Salt River still flows wild and free and offers some exciting rafting. **Sun Country Rafting** (☎ **800/272-3353** or 602/493-9011) runs full-day, overnight, and multiday trips (conditions permitting) down the Upper Salt River. Prices range from $85 to $645. **Desert Voyagers** (☎ **800/222-RAFT** or 602/998-RAFT) also runs trips down the Salt. The Upper Salt River run is dependent on snow melt, and the season usually lasts from March to May. Both of these rafting companies also offer trips on the Gila River.

Tamer river trips can be had from **Salt River Recreation** (☎ **602/984-3305**), which has its headquarters 20 miles northeast of Phoenix on the Bush Highway at the intersection of Usery Pass Road in the Tonto National Forest. For $8.25 they'll rent you a large inner tube and shuttle you by bus upriver for the float down. The inner-tubing season runs from mid-April through mid-September.

# 8  Spectator Sports

Phoenix has gone nuts over pro sports. With the addition of the NHL's Phoenix Coyotes in the 1996–1997 season and the Arizona Diamondbacks baseball team in 1998, Phoenix becomes one of only 10 U.S. cities with all four of the major sports teams (baseball, basketball, football, and hockey). Add to this baseball's spring training, a second ice hockey team, professional women's basketball, three major golf tournaments, the annual Fiesta Bowl college football classic, and ASU football, basketball, and baseball, and you have enough action to keep even the most rabid sports fans happily cheering on a local team no matter what month of the year. However, the all-around best month to visit is probably March when you could feasibly catch spring baseball training, the Suns, the Coyotes, the Mercury, and ASU basketball and baseball, as well as the Franklin Templeton Tennis Classic, The Tradition, and the Standard Register PING LPGA Tournament.

Call **Dillard's Box Office** (☎ **800/638-4253** or 602/503-5555) or **Ticketmaster** (☎ **602/784-4444**) for tickets to most of the events below. For tickets to sold-out events, try **Danny's Tickets Unlimited** (☎ **800/289-8497** or 602/840-2340) or **Ticket Exchange** (☎ **800/800-9811** or 602/254-4444) or check in the Friday edition of *The Arizona Republic* in the Weekend section.

**AUTO RACING**   At the **Firebird International Raceway Park,** at 20000 Maricopa Rd. (at Exit 162A off I-10), Chandler (☎ **602/268-0200**), you can see NHRA races and amateur drag racing. At the **Phoenix International Raceway,** 7602 115th Avenue (at Baseline Road), Avondale (☎ **602/252-2227**), there is NASCAR and Indy car racing on the world's fastest 1-mile oval. Tickets are available at Dillard's Box Office outlets (☎ **800/638-4253** or 602/503-5555).

**BASEBALL**   Starting in 1998, with the completion of the new Bank One Ballpark, Phoenix will no longer have to content itself with spring-training games and minor league ball. The 1998 baseball season should see the **Arizona Diamondbacks** (☎ **602/514-8400**), which will be coached by former New York Yankees manager Buck Showalter, take to the field as the newest team in the National League West. Bank One Ballpark, located in downtown Phoenix is a state of the art stadium with a retractable roof that will allow for comfortable play during Phoenix's blistering summer temperatures and will also allow the field to have natural grass. Tickets will range from $1 to $50 and there is even going to be a swimming pool (available for rent) out in the right field stands.

For decades, however, it has been spring training that has given Phoenix its annual shot of baseball, and don't think that the Cactus League's spring-training exhibition games will be any less popular just because the Diamondbacks are in town. Spring-training games may rank second only to golf in popularity with winter visitors to the valley. Seven major league baseball teams have spring-training camps in various cities around the valley during March and April. These teams include the **San Francisco Giants** (Scottsdale Stadium, 7408 E. Osborn Rd., Scottsdale), **Oakland A's** (Phoenix Municipal Stadium, 5999 E. Van Buren St., Phoenix), **Anaheim Angels** (Tempe Diablo Stadium, 2200 W. Alameda Dr., Tempe), **Chicago Cubs** (Hohokam Park Stadium, 1235 N. Center St., Mesa), **San Diego Padres** (Peoria Sports Complex, 16101 N. 83rd Ave., Peoria), **Seattle Mariners** (Peoria Sports Complex, 16101 N. 83rd Ave., Peoria), and **Milwaukee Brewers** (Compadre Stadium, 4001 S. Alma School Rd., Chandler). Get a schedule from the convention and visitors bureau, a Dillard's Box Office outlet, or check the *Arizona Republic* while you're in town. Tickets ($3 to $16) are sold through either Ticketmaster (☎ 602/784-4444) or Dillard's Box Office outlets (☎ 800/638-4253 or 602/503-5555). Games often sell out, especially on weekends, so be sure to order tickets in advance if you're a serious fan and don't want to miss a game.

In addition, the **Phoenix Firebirds,** a farm team for the San Francisco Giants, play AAA Pacific Coast League professional ball at Scottsdale Stadium, 7408 E. Osborn Rd. (☎ 602/275-0500). Tickets cost $4 to $8 and can be purchased at Scottsdale Stadium or Dillard's Box Office locations.

For those who just can't get enough baseball, there is also the **Arizona Fall Baseball League** (☎ 602/496-6700) with games from October to December. The six teams in this league are comprised of the top rookies from throughout the major leagues. Games are held at the same stadiums used for spring training.

**BASKETBALL** The NBA's **Phoenix Suns** play at the America West Arena, 201 E. Jefferson St. (☎ 602/379-7867 or 602/379-7800). Tickets are $11 to $80 and are available at the America West Arena box office and through Dillard's Box Office outlets (☎ 800/638-4253 or 602/503-5555). Suns tickets are hard to come by. If you want good seats, you really have to buy your tickets on the day they go on sale in mid-September. If you forgot to plan ahead, try contacting the box office the day before or the day of a game to see if tickets have been returned.

As this book went to press, Phoenix was scheduled to get a Women's Basketball Association (WBA) team beginning in the 1997–1998 season. The **Phoenix Mercury** (☎ 602/379-7800) will play at the America West Arena.

**FOOTBALL** The **Arizona Cardinals** (☎ 800/999-1402 or 602/379-0102) play at Arizona State University's Sun Devil Stadium, which is also home to the Fiesta Bowl Football Classic and was the site of Super Bowl XXX. Tickets are $20 to $50. Except for a few specific games each season, it is generally possible to get Cardinals tickets.

While the Cardinals get to use Sun Devil Stadium, this field really belongs to Arizona State University's **Sun Devils** (☎ 602/965-2381). Tickets for Sun Devils' games are also available through Dillards Box Office outlets (☎ 800/638-4253 or 602/503-5555).

**GOLF TOURNAMENTS** It's not surprising that with more than 140 golf courses and ideal golfing weather throughout the winter and spring, the Valley of the Sun is host to three major PGA tournaments each year. Tickets for all three tournaments are available through Dillards Box Office outlets (☎ 800/638-4253 or 602/503-5555).

The **Phoenix Open Golf Tournament** (☎ 602/870-0163) in January is the largest. Held at the Tournament Players Club (TPC) of Scottsdale, this tournament attracts more spectators than any other golf tournament in the world (nearly 450,000 each year). The 18th hole of the TPC has standing room for 40,000. Tickets usually go on sale in July or August with prices starting around $20.

Each March, the **Standard Register PING LPGA Tournament** (☎ 602/495-4653) lures the top 100 women golfers from around the world. The tournament, held each year at the Moon Valley Country Club, is a fundraiser to provide care for cancer patients at Samaritan hospitals. Daily ticket prices range from around $10 to $15 and weekly tickets are around $75.

**The Tradition** (☎ 602/595-4070), a Senior PGA Tour event held each April at the Desert Mountain golf course, has a loyal following of fans who would rather watch the likes of Jack Nicklaus and Arnold Palmer than see Tiger Woods win yet another tournament. Only weekly tickets ($100 to $200) are sold, and these usually go on sale beginning in mid-November.

**HOCKEY**　I just can't seem to get into the idea of ice hockey in the desert, but there are enough hockey fans (refugees from colder climes?) here in the valley to support not one, but two professional hockey teams. The 1996–1997 season saw the addition of the NHL's **Phoenix Coyotes** (☎ 602/379-7800) to the Phoenix ice-hockey scene. The Coyotes play at America West Arena, 201 E. Jefferson St. (lucky for the Suns they don't have to play on ice). Tickets range from $8.75 to $200 (up against the glass). The IHL's **Phoenix Roadrunners** play at Veterans' Memorial Coliseum, 1826 W. McDowell Rd. (☎ 602/340-0001). Call Ticketmaster (☎ 602/784-4444) for tickets, which range from $10 to $17.

**HORSE/GREYHOUND RACING**　The **Phoenix Greyhound Park,** 3801 E. Washington St. (☎ 602/273-7181), is one of the nation's premier greyhound tracks. The large, fully enclosed, and air-conditioned facility offers seating in various grandstands, lounges, and restaurants. There's racing nightly throughout the year, and tickets are $1.50 to $3. Parking is $1 to $2.

Out in Apache Junction, you'll find the **Apache Greyhound Park** (☎ 602/244-2729 or 602/982-2371) on Apache Trail at Delaware Drive. Races are held from October or November through early April and there is no admission charge. To reach the racetrack, take the Signal Butte exit off the Superstition Freeway (U.S. 60), drive north to Apache Trail and then turn east.

**Turf Paradise,** 1501 W. Bell Rd. (☎ 602/942-1101), is Phoenix's horse-racing track. The season runs from September to May, with post time at 12:30pm Friday through Tuesday. Admission ranges from $1 to $5. Parking runs $1 to $3.

**TENNIS TOURNAMENTS**　Each March, top international men's tennis players compete at the **Franklin Templeton Tennis Classic** (☎ 602/922-0222), which is held at the Scottsdale Princess Resort in Scottsdale. This tournament has twice been won by Andre Agassi, who, however, was eliminated fairly early during the 1997 tournament.

## 9 Day Spas

Ever since the first "lungers" showed up in the Phoenix area hoping to cure their tuberculosis, the desert has been a magnet for those looking to get healthy. In the first half of this century, health spas were all the rage in Phoenix, and with the health-and-fitness trend continuing to gather steam, it comes as no surprise that health spas are rapidly regaining popularity in the Valley of the Sun.

In the past few years, several of the area's top resorts have added new full-service health spas or expanded existing ones to cater to guest's increasing requests for such services as massages, body wraps, mud masks, and salt glows.

If you can't afford to stay at a top resort and avail yourself of the resort's spa, you may still be able to indulge yourself. Most of the valley's resorts open the doors of their spas to the public, and, for the cost of a body treatment or massage, you can spend the day at the spa, taking classes, working out in a fitness room, lounging by the pool, and otherwise living the life of the rich and famous. Barring this indulgence, you can slip into a day spa, of which there are many scattered around the valley, and take a stress-reduction break the way other people take a latte break.

For our money, a day at **The Spa at Camelback Inn,** 5402 E. Lincoln Dr., Scottsdale (☎ **800/922-2635** or 602/596-7020), is a better deal. Here you can use all the facilities, which include a lap pool, for nothing more than the cost of a single 1-hour treatment, which will cost you a minimum of $85. However, there are also multiple-treatment packages ranging from $129 to $182.

The **Centre for Well Being,** at The Phoenician, 6000 E. Camelback Rd., Scottsdale (☎ **800/888-8234** or 602/423-2452), is the valley's most prestigious day spa, the place to head if you want to be pampered with the rich and famous. For anywhere from $110 to $185 you can spend the day at the spa receiving several treatments and utilizing the spa's many facilities.

If you want a truly spectacular setting for your day at the spa (and it happens to be June, July, or August), head north to Carefree and the **Sonoran Spa at The Boulders,** 34631 N. Tom Darlington Dr. (☎ **800/553-1717** or 602/488-9009, ext. 158). Here individual treatments cost $95 across the board, and a day-at-the-spa package will run you $165 to $265. Included with any treatment is use of the extensive facilities and lap pool. Other months of the year, this spa is not open to the public.

Also here in Carefree, you'll find **The Spa at Carefree Inn,** 37220 Mule Train Rd. (☎ **800/637-7200** or 602/488-1029), which is one of the valley's most economical day spas. Massages and body treatments range from $70 to $75 for 1 hour.

At press time, the famed **Arizona Biltmore** was in the process of adding a large, full-service health spa. If a historic setting and convenient location appeal to you, give them a call.

Nonresort day spas are also to be found around the valley. The **Elizabeth Arden Red Door Salon,** 2472 E. Camelback Rd. (☎ **602/553-8800**), which bears the name of one of Arizona's health spa pioneers, is conveniently located in Biltmore Fashion Park. In old town Scottsdale, you'll find **Spa du Soleil,** 7040 E. Third Ave., Scottsdale (☎ **602/994-5400**), and **Candela,** 6939 E. Main St. (☎ **602/949-0100**). This latter day spa even offers cosmetic laser therapy!

# 10  Shopping

For the most part, shopping in the valley means malls. They're everywhere and they're air-conditioned, which, we're sure you'll agree, makes shopping in the desert far more enjoyable than in 110° heat.

Scottsdale and the Biltmore District of Phoenix are the valley's main upscale shopping areas. Old Scottsdale (one of the few outdoor shopping areas) plays host to hundreds of boutiques, galleries, jewelry stores, and Native American crafts stores. The Western atmosphere of Old Scottsdale is partly real and partly a figment of the local merchants' imaginations, but nevertheless it's the single most popular tourist shopping area in the valley. It also happens to be the heart of the valley's art market, with dozens of art galleries along Main Street.

# Ten Fun Ways to Blow $100 (More or Less) in the Valley of the Sun

With greens fees for 18 holes of golf as high as $150, it is obvious that the Valley of the Sun is not exactly a cheap place for a vacation. Still, if you've budgeted plenty of money for your vacation or simply want to splurge on a memorable experience, there are quite a few great ways to blow a hundred bucks while in town. Here are some of our favorites.

1. **Spend a day at Camelback Spa.** It's not often you can blow a hundred bucks and come away feeling good about it, but for between $80 and $120, you can spend the day at this luxurious spa getting pampered and de-stressed.

2. **Rent a Vette.** For $129 a day, you can rent a new Corvette from Rent-a-Vette for the day and head out for a high-speed spin in the desert or just cruise around Scottsdale looking like you belong.

3. **Hire a stretch limo for a couple of hours.** For $110 you can rent a six-passenger stretch limo from Transtyle for 2 hours. Just ride around or maybe have the limo take you to a resort for a cocktail.

4. **Play a round of golf on an Arizona legend.** If you can get a tee time, $100 will get you on the Gold Course at the Wigwam Resort out west in Litchfield Park. This is one of the oldest and most famous courses in the valley.

5. **Rent a cabana at the Arizona Biltmore.** Maybe you decided to stay at The Phoenician this year, but still miss the classic old-money ambience at the Arizona Biltmore or maybe you've got a Motel 6 vacation budget and Arizona Biltmore tastes. Well, for as little as $92 you can rent a poolside cabana here and lounge in the lap of luxury for the day. More luxurious cabanas are also available, but they'll cost you.

6. **Take a hot-air balloon ride.** There is no better way to see the desert than drifting above it at dawn in a hot-air balloon, and there's just about no cheaper way in the country to take to the air than in the oldest form of flying machine. For $100 to $135 you can get airborne.

7. **Take a hummer of a back-roads tour.** Why ride in a Jeep when you can ride in a Hummer, the ultimate off-road vehicle? Desert Storm Hummer Tours will give you a ride to remember and you'll get an up close and personal look at the Arizona desert.

8. **Order the seasonal tasting menu at Mary Elaine's.** If you've never had a $100 dinner, maybe now is the time to indulge. How else will you ever be able to call yourself a true gourmand? This five-course dinner will set you back $105 (not including tax, tip, wine or cost of proper dining attire).

9. **Spend an evening at Harrah's Phoenix Ak-Chin Casino.** No longer is it necessary to risk your life and your bank account by driving to Laughlin or Las Vegas, now it's possible to blow your hard-earned cash without ever leaving the Valley of the Sun.

10. **Go on a C-note shopping spree at Biltmore Fashion Park.** I know $100 isn't going to buy much at this boutique-filled upscale shopping plaza, but the fun of it can be trying to find the best $100 buy in the mall. Now there's a challenge to keep a shopaholic busy for the afternoon.

Shopping hours are usually Monday through Saturday from 10am to 6pm and on Sunday from noon to 5pm, and malls usually stay open until 9pm Monday through Saturday.

## ANTIQUES

Glendale is antique central for the valley, with the highest concentration of shops in downtown Glendale. In this area, you'll find more than three dozen antiques stores specializing in everything from automobilia to 1950s kitsch to vintage sports equipment.

**The Antique Gallery/Central Antiques.** In Uptown Plaza, Central Ave. and Camelback Rd. ☎ **602/241-1174** or 602/241-1636.

These two antique malls house about 130 antiques dealers in two stores and offer a wide variety of collectibles and antiques. This is one of the more upscale antiques malls in the area and includes a lot of furniture.

**Antique Trove.** 2020 N. Scottsdale Rd., Scottsdale. ☎ **602/947-6074.**

This is one of the biggest antiques malls in the valley and, though it isn't as clean and modern as The Antique Gallery, it has a larger selection. If you make only one antiques mall stop, make it here. Within a block of this antiques mall, there are also three others.

**Arizona West Galleries.** 7149 E. Main St., Scottsdale. ☎ **602/994-3752.**

Nowhere else in Scottsdale will you find such an amazing collection of cowboy collectibles and Western antiques. There are antique saddles and chaps, old rifles and six-shooters, sheriff's badges, spurs, and the like.

**Bishop Gallery for Art & Antiques.** 7164 Main St., Scottsdale. ☎ **602/949-9062.**

This cramped shop is wonderfully eclectic, featuring everything from Asian antiques to unusual original art. Definitely worth a browse through.

✪ **Bo's Funky Stuff.** 5605 W. Glendale Ave., Glendale. ☎ **602/842-0220.**

Billing itself the "wildest shop north of the border," Bo's is a repository of midcentury modern collectibles, including Beatles memorabilia, 1950s furniture, neon signs, old advertisements, bakelite jewelry, Western collectibles, and generally odd and unusual stuff. Note that this store doesn't open until 11am.

## ART

The galleries mentioned below are all within walking distance of each other in **Old Scottsdale.** The streets of Old Scottsdale seem to be divided by the style of art available. On Main Street, you'll find primarily cowboy art, both traditional and contemporary. On North Marshall Way, you'll find much more imaginative and daring contemporary art. For a more extensive listing of galleries and exhibitions in the area, pick up a copy of the *Valley of the Sun Gallery Guide*, available at art galleries.

**Art One.** 4120 N. Marshall Way, Scottsdale. ☎ **602/946-5076.**

If you want to see the possible directions that area artists will be heading in the next few years, stop in at this Marshall Way gallery that specializes in works by art students and other area cutting-edge artists. The works here can be surprisingly good.

**Feathers Gallery.** 7100 E. Main St., Scottsdale. ☎ **602/423-8119.**

Here you'll find Native American and Southwest art, including ceramics, colorful paintings, bronzes, home furnishings, and unusual sculptures. They also sell old Native American baskets and pottery.

✪ **Joanne Rapp Gallery.** 4222 N. Marshall Way, Scottsdale. ☎ **602/949-1262.**

Along with its companion gallery, the Hand and the Spirit, these are currently two of my favorite places to visit in downtown Scottsdale. Work displayed is at the cutting edge of new crafts, using new materials or traditional materials in innovative ways; even the jaded art viewer will be impressed. Between the two galleries is a sculpture courtyard.

✪ **Lisa Sette Gallery.** 4142 N. Marshall Way, Scottsdale. ☎ **602/990-7342.**

If you aren't a fan of cowboy or Native American art, you may think that Phoenix has little serious art to offer. Think again, then stop by Lisa Sette. Among other artists, Lisa Sette represents premier glass artist William Morris. International, national, and local artists share wall space here, with a wide mix of media represented.

**Meyer Gallery.** 7173 E. Main St. ☎ **602/947-6372.**

This gallery is most notable for its selection of original paintings from 1930s and 1940s pulp Western magazines. Steely-eyed cowboys with blazin' six guns are the quintessential image of pre-television Westerns, and today they make for interesting artwork with a nostalgic twist.

**Overland Gallery.** 7155 Main St., Scottsdale. ☎ **602/947-1934.**

Traditional Western paintings and a collection of Russian Impressionist paintings form the backbone of this gallery's fine collection. These are museum-quality works (prices sometimes approach $100,000) and are definitely worth a look.

## BOOKS

**Changing Hands Bookstore.** 414 Mill Ave., Tempe. ☎ **602/966-0203.**

Located in the heart of Mill Avenue, adjacent to Arizona State University, this bookstore satisfies cravings for an intellectual collegiate atmosphere. It's not big—only three small floors—but there are books both new and used on all kinds of topics and easy chairs in which to relax.

**T.A. Swinford, Bookseller.** 7134 Main St., Scottsdale. ☎ **602/946-0022.**

Rare and out-of-print books about the American West are the specialty of this bookshop in Old Scottsdale. Whether you're looking for *The Cegiha Language* (1890), *Triggernometry, A Gallery of Gunfighters* (1934), or *Range Murder: How the Red-Sash Gang Dry-Gulched Deputy United States Marshal George Wellman* (1955), you'll find it here.

## A CHOCOLATERIE

**Chocolaterie Bernard C.** In Hilton Village, 6137 N. Scottsdale Rd. ☎ **602/483-3139.**

If you have *ever* had a genuine Belgian praline (chocolate, not one of those puffy cookies), then you will not want to leave Scottsdale without paying a visit to this chocolate shop. If you have *never* had a Belgian chocolate, you won't want to miss this shop either. The exquisite chocolate confections here will make you forget all about Godiva.

## CRAFTS

✪ **Mind's Eye Gallery.** 4200 N. Marshall Way, Scottsdale. ☎ **602/941-2494.**

You'll find the finest contemporary crafts from around the nation at this Scottsdale gallery. There's an emphasis on American craftspeople in the collection of jewelry, ceramics, wood, clothing, paper, and glass. The wildly imaginative kaleidoscopes are fascinating and the contemporary grandfather clocks are timelessly beautiful.

## FASHION

See also "Western Wear," below.

## Women's Wear

In addition to the shops mentioned below, there are also many excellent shops in malls all over the city. Favorite spots for upscale fashions include Biltmore Fashion Park, The Borgata of Scottsdale, El Pedregal Festival Marketplace, and Scottsdale Fashion Square. See "Malls/Shopping Centers," below for details on these malls and shopping plazas.

**Activo.** In The Borgata, 6166 N. Scottsdale Rd., Suite 203. ☎ **602/991-2104.**

Scottsdale casual wear and resort wear are the focus on the racks in this boutique. Last season colorful tropical-print separates filled the store. You'll also find men's resort wear here. A second store is in Scottsdale Fashion Square (☎ **602/946-7456**).

**Carol Dolighan.** At The Borgata, 6166 N. Scottsdale Rd., Scottsdale. ☎ **602/922-0616.**

The hand-painted, handwoven, and handmade dresses, skirts, and blouses here abound in rich colors. Each is unique. There's another Carol Dolighan store in El Pedregal Festival Marketplace, 34505 N. Scottsdale Rd. (☎ **602/488-4505**) in Carefree.

**Everything But Water.** In Scottsdale Fashion Square, 7014 E. Camelback Rd., Scottsdale. ☎ **602/941-4623.**

If by some bizarre twist of fate you have arrived in the Valley of the Sun sans swimsuit, stop by this shop where you can choose from among 1,000 or more bathing suits.

**✪ The Hand & the Spirit.** 4200 N. Marshall Way, Scottsdale. ☎ **602/949-1262.**

You'll find gorgeous, high-end accessories and garments done up in hand-designed fabrics. Trunk shows are given of editions and one-of-a-kind pieces. See the listing for this store in "Jewelry," below.

**Paris Paris.** In Biltmore Fashion Park, 2438 E. Camelback Rd. ☎ **602/955-9666.**

Up-to-the-minute fashion separates are pulled together on the racks of this upscale boutique so you can visualize the effect before heading to the dressing room. There's very pricey lingerie in the loft and men's fashions in the basement.

**Uh Oh.** In Hilton Village, 6137 N. Scottsdale Rd., Scottsdale. ☎ **602/991-1618.**

Simple, tasteful, and oh so elegant fashions, footwear, jewelry, and accessories. That sums up what you'll find in this Scottsdale boutique. The Southwestern contemporary styling makes this a great place to pick up something to be seen in while you're here in the Valley of the Sun.

**The White House.** In The Borgata, 6166 N. Scottsdale Rd. ☎ **602/922-7161.**

A stunning display of white fashions dazzles the eye and makes you feel cool just looking at it. At first glance it seems all the dresses, separates, and lingerie in this store are white, but on closer inspection, you'll find a few other neutral colors. Prices are very reasonable.

## Men's Wear

**The Clotherie Ltd.** In Biltmore Fashion Park, 2552 E. Camelback Rd. ☎ **602/956-8600.**

The address alone should tip you off that the fashions here don't come cheap. Executive styles with a European slant predominate.

## Children's Wear

**The Children's Collection.** 7001 N. Scottsdale Rd., Suite 185, Scottsdale. ☎ **602/998-1401.**

If you happen to be staying at a Scottsdale resort, then you'll probably be able to afford to buy your grandkids some of the outfits in this store. If you're staying at the Motel 6, don't even think about coming here. Linen separates, velvet T-shirts, and the like fill the racks.

**Lil'People.** At the Arizona Center, Third and Van Buren sts. in downtown Phoenix. ☎ **602/252-2241.**

"Oh, isn't that cute!" Exclamations like that keep this shop doing a brisk business in gifts for the little ones. Cute and bright cotton playwear for children newborn to 6 years old are the mainstays here.

**The Moushka Bambino Co.** 8700 E. Pinnacle Peak Rd., Scottsdale. ☎ **602/585-4300.**

If you like to have only the best for the baby in your life, drive out to this upscale children's fashion boutique. The clothing is primarily for the under-5 set and includes lace and crocheted dresses and darling hats. Many pieces are from France. (It's in the same location as Hollywood Cowboy; see "Western Wear," below.)

## GIFTS/SOUVENIRS

One of the best places to shop for souvenirs is the Arizona Center mall in downtown Phoenix. See "Malls/Shopping Centers," below for details.

**Arizona Highways Gift Shop.** In Arizona Center, 455 N. Third St. ☎ **602/257-0381.**

If you're familiar with the magazine *Arizona Highways,* then you'll know what to expect from this store—beautiful photographs everywhere and interesting Arizona-theme gifts.

✪ **Arizona State University Art Museum Store.** In the Arizona State University Art Museum, Nelson Fine Arts Center, 10th St. and Mill Ave., Tempe. ☎ **602/965-2787.**

A selection of not-too-expensive and pretty good stuff in the way of Mexican folk art, pottery, children's toys, jewelry, books, T-shirts, and greeting cards can be found here.

✪ **Bischoff's Shades of the West.** 7247 Main St., Scottsdale. ☎ **602/945-3289.**

One-stop shopping for all things Southwestern is the name of the game in this sprawling store. From T-shirts to regional foodstuffs, Shades of the West has it all. It's got a good selection of wrought-iron cabinet hardware that can give your kitchen a Western look, and there are imported Turkish rugs and Mexican crafts that all fit in with a Southwest interior decor.

**Heard Museum Gift Shop.** In the Heard Museum, 22 E. Monte Vista Rd. ☎ **800/252-8344** or 602/252-8344.

As museum stores go, this place is pretty big, and there's no better place to buy Native American arts and crafts. The museum sells only the best, with prices to prove it, but because the store doesn't charge sales tax, you'll save a bit of money.

**Phoenix Art Museum Store.** In the Phoenix Art Museum, 1625 N. Central Ave. (at the northeast corner of McDowell Rd.). ☎ **602/257-2182.**

Crafts, greeting cards, unique photo frames and other decorative items, and a wide selection of art-related books make up a large portion of the choices available here.

**The UNICEF Shop.** At the Town and Country Shopping Center, 4741 N. 20th St. ☎ **602/956-0781.**

If you're looking for unusual gifts and crafts from around the world, take a look in this interesting little shop. They've got a lot of pieces you won't find anywhere else, and the profits go to UNICEF.

## GOLF & TEAM LOGO SHOPS

**Arizona Sports Corner.** 144 E. Washington St. ☎ **602/716-9506.**

Located not far from America West Arena and right next door to Majerle's Sports Grill, this shop sells all manor of logo gear for the many Phoenix sports teams.

✪ **In Celebration of Golf.** 7001 N. Scottsdale Rd., Suite 172, Scottsdale. ☎ **602/951-4444.**

Sort of a supermarket for golfers (with a touch of Disneyland thrown in), this amazing store sells everything from clubs and golf shoes to golf art and golf antiques. There are even unique golf cars on display in case you want to take to the greens in a custom car. A golf simulation room allows you to test out new clubs and get in a bit of video golfing at the same time. An old clubmaker's workbench, complete with talking mannequin, makes a visit to this shop educational as well as a lot of fun.

**Phoenix Suns' Team Shop.** America West Arena, 201 E. Jefferson St. ☎ **602/514-8321.**

If you're a fan of the Suns, you can stock up on hats, shirts, and all kinds of other stuff emblazoned with the Suns' logo.

## JEWELRY

**Chief Dodge Indian Jewelry Store.** 1332 N. Scottsdale Rd., Scottsdale. ☎ **602/970-1133.**

You can watch Indian craftspeople create beautiful silver jewelry, sand paintings, rugs, and other crafts right in the store, and then peruse the cases searching for a kachina, bowl, or basket to take home.

**Gilbert Ortega's Indian Arts.** 7155 E. Fifth Ave. ☎ **602/941-9281.**

You'll find cases and cases of Indian jewelry at Gilbert Ortega shops. Some of the many other branches are located at 7237 E. Main St., Scottsdale (☎ **602/481-0788**); 7252 E. First Ave., Scottsdale (☎ **602/945-1819**); at Koshari I in The Borgata, 6166 N. Scottsdale Rd., Scottsdale (☎ **602/998-9699**); and at the Hyatt Regency Hotel, 122 N. Second St., Phoenix (☎ **602/265-9923**).

✪ **The Hand & the Spirit.** 4200 N. Marshall Way, Scottsdale. ☎ **602/949-1262.**

Each piece of jewelry here is an individual work of art—ornate, contemporary, one-of-a-kind pieces that share a talismanlike quality. The work of many different jewelry artists are displayed, and unique and stylish artist-created garments take up the rest of the shop/gallery.

✪ **Heard Museum Gift Shop.** In the Heard Museum, 22 E. Monte Vista Rd. ☎ **800/ 252-8344** or 602/252-8344.

The Heard Museum has an awesome collection of very aesthetic, extremely well crafted, and very expensive Native American jewelry. However, you'll save a bit of money here; the store doesn't charge sales tax.

**Jewelry by Gauthier.** 4164 N. Marshall Way, Scottsdale. ☎ **602/941-1707.**

This store sells the designs of the phenomenally talented jewelry designer Scott Gauthier. Very stylish, modern designs using precious stones make every piece of jewelry in this shop a miniature work of art. This is the only place you'll see Gauthier's work for sale in the United States.

**Molina Fine Jewelers.** 3134 E. Camelback Rd. ☎ **602/955-2055** or 800/257-2695.

If you're in the market for famous-name jewelry or a watch, then make an appointment to visit Molina. This shop specializes in Hermès, Tiffany, Cartier, and the like. They even offer complimentary limousine service to serious buyers.

## MALLS/SHOPPING CENTERS

**Arizona Center.** Van Buren St. between Third and Fifth sts. ☎ **602/949-4353.**

Revitalizing downtown Phoenix, this mall houses several nightclubs and restaurants as well as shops and a food court. The gardens and fountains are a peaceful oasis amid downtown's asphalt. This is a great place to shop for Arizona souvenirs (check out the Arizona Highways Gift Shop).

**Biltmore Fashion Park.** E. Camelback Rd. and 24th St. ☎ **602/955-8400.**

Since this is a "fashion park" and not just a shopping mall, it comes as no surprise that the shops bear the names of international designers and exclusive boutiques. Saks Fifth Avenue anchors the mall, with the likes of Polo by Ralph Lauren, Gucci, Laura Ashley, and Williams-Sonoma filling the smaller stores. Limousine service from certain hotels and valet parking are both available. This is *the* place to be seen if shopping is your obsession and you keep your wallet full of platinum cards.

✪ **The Borgata of Scottsdale.** 6166 N. Scottsdale Rd. ☎ **602/998-1822.**

Designed to resemble a medieval Italian village complete with turrets, stone walls, and ramparts, The Borgata is far and away the most architecturally interesting shopping mall in the valley. There are about 50 upscale boutiques, art galleries, and restaurants, including Dos Cabezas, a store with fun and colorful designs in women's clothing and home furnishings. Another of our favorite stores here is The White House, which sells only white (and off-white) clothing and accessories.

✪ **El Pedregal Festival Marketplace.** Scottsdale Rd. and Carefree Hwy. ☎ **602/488-1072.**

Located adjacent to the spectacular Boulders Resort north of downtown Scottsdale, El Pedregal is the most self-consciously Southwestern shopping center in the valley. It's worth the long drive out here just to see the neo–Santa Fe architecture and colorful accents. The shops offer high-end merchandise, fashions, and art. Among our favorites are Imagine Gallery and Conrad Leather Boutique, which carry upscale Southwestern fashions. The Heard Museum also has a branch here.

**Hilton Village.** Scottsdale Rd. between Lincoln and McDonald drives. ☎ **602/998-1822.**

This upscale shopping plaza in the heart of Scottsdale's resort row is worth a stop between rounds of golf and visits to Old Scottsdale galleries. Fashions and home furnishings are the strengths here. However, our favorite shop is Chocolaterie Bernard, which sells superb Belgian-style chocolates.

**Metrocenter.** 9617 Metro Pkwy. W. ☎ **602/997-2641** or 602/678-0017.

This is one of the largest shopping centers in the Southwest, with more than 200 specialty shops, five major department stores (Dillard's, Macy's, Robinsons-May, JCPenney, and Sears), and about 40 eating establishments.

**Scottsdale Fashion Square.** 7000 E. Camelback Rd. (at Scottsdale Rd.), Scottsdale. ☎ **602/941-2140.**

Scottsdale has long been the valley's shopping mecca, and for years this huge mall was the reason why. It houses three major department stores—Dillard's, Neiman Marcus, and Robinsons-May—and smaller stores such as the Nature Company and a Godiva Chocolatier. This is *the* hang-out for wealthy teenage mallrats.

**Town & Country.** 20th St. and Camelback Rd. ☎ **602/955-6850.**

This open-air shopping plaza is a sort of Western anchor for the Camelback Corridor, currently the shopping, business, dining, and nightlife center for Phoenix. Town & Country offers a much more affordable alternative to the nearby Biltmore

Fashion Park. You'll find high fashion as well as bargains, kitsch gifts, the UNICEF Shop, a Bookstar discount bookstore, and many other small shops.

## NATIVE AMERICAN ARTS & CRAFTS

**Grey Wolf.** 7239 E. First Ave., Scottsdale. ☎ **602/423-0004.**

You'll find the valley's largest selection of Indian artifacts—everything from shields to war bonnets—plus hand-crafted kachina dolls, sterling silver jewelry, music, rugs, and pottery. There are Northwest and Plains Indians artifacts here as well.

**✪ John C. Hill.** 6962 E. First Ave., Scottsdale. ☎ **602/946-2910.**

This store is for collectors and has one of the finest selections of Navajo rugs in the valley, including quite a few older ones. There are also kachinas, superb Navajo and Zuñi silver-and-turquoise jewelry, baskets, and pottery. They sell only the highest quality here, so you can familiarize yourself with what the best looks like.

**Old Territorial Shop.** 7220 E. Main St., Scottsdale. ☎ **602/945-5432.**

This is the oldest arts-and-crafts store on Main Street, and there's good value and a lot of selection here—jewelry, sand paintings, concha belts, kachinas, fetishes, pottery, and Navajo rugs.

## OUTLET MALLS

**Arizona Factory Shops.** 4520 W. Honda Bow Rd. ☎ **602/465-9500.** Take Exit 229 (Desert Hills Rd.) off I-17.

If your idea of a great afternoon is searching out deals at factory outlet stores, then you'll be in heaven at this large outlet mall. Among the stores here are Saks Off Fifth, Ann Taylor, Bugle Boy, Geoffrey Beene, and Levi's. It's a 30-minute drive from downtown Phoenix and is a popular stop for northbound travelers.

**Wigwam Outlet Stores.** 1400 N. Litchfield Rd. ☎ **602/935-9733.** Take Exit 128 off I-10.

If you're headed west from Phoenix and need a shopping break, you'll likely find some good deals at this outlet mall near the famous Wigwam resort. Bass, Bugle Boy, Harry & David, Mikasa, and Levi's are just some of the many stores.

## SWAP MEETS

**American Park 'n' Swap.** 3801 E. Washington St. ☎ **602/273-1258.**

This is Phoenix's oldest and largest swap meet and takes place weekends in the parking lot of the Phoenix Greyhound Park. Come early for the best selection and to beat the heat. Good selection of Arizona T-shirts.

**Swapmart.** 5115 N. 27th Ave. ☎ **602/246-9600.**

If it's the middle of summer, or Friday or Saturday, and you still want to hit a swap meet (flea market), try this 3-acre indoor market. You'll find plenty of Southwestern crafts at prices lower than in the gift shops around town.

## WESTERN WEAR

**Az-Tex Hat Company.** 3903 N. Scottsdale Rd., Scottsdale. ☎ **602/481-9900** or 800/972-2116.

If you're looking to bring home a cowboy hat from your trip to Arizona, this is a good place to pick one up. A second store is at 15044 N. Cave Creek Rd., Phoenix (☎ **602/971-9090**).

**Frontier Boot Corral.** 641 E. Van Buren. ☎ **602/258-2830.**

Say you're in Phoenix for a convention, you're staying downtown, and you suddenly decide to go line dancing. No problem. Jog on over to the almost-deserted Phoenix

Mercado shopping plaza and you'll be scootin' yer boots in no time. There's a second store inside the Hyatt Regency, 122 N. Second St. (☎ **602/440-3159**).

**☻Heritage Hats.** 13602 N. Cave Creek Rd. ☎ **602/867-3323.**

If it ain't for your head, they ain't got it. A huge selection of hats in countless styles makes this the best place in the valley to shop for a cowboy hat. They've got all the styles you've seen on your favorite country music stars. Prices range from $15 to $400, and custom hats can be ordered.

**Hollywood Cowboy.** 8700 E. Pinnacle Peak Rd., Scottsdale. ☎ **602/585-4300.**

If I wanted to treat myself to a buckskin jacket with oodles of fringe (and costing about that many dollars), I'd head out to this very small boutique with a choice selection of high-end cowgirl and cowboy leather trappings.

**Out West.** In El Pedregal Festival Marketplace, 34505 N. Scottsdale Rd. ☎ **602/488-0180** or 888/454-WEST.

If the revival of 1950s-style Wild West styles has hit your nostalgia button, then you'll want to hightail it up to this eclectic shop. All things Western are available and the fashions are both beautiful and lots of fun, though fancy and pricey. They've even got home furnishings. In-store TVs play B Westerns.

**Saba's Western Stores.** 7254 Main St., Scottsdale. ☎ **602/949-7404.**

Since 1927 this store has been outfitting Scottsdale's cowboys and cowgirls, visiting dude ranchers, and anyone else who wants to adopt the look of the Wild West. Call for other locations around Phoenix.

**☻Sheplers Western Wear.** 9201 N. 29th Ave. ☎ **602/870-8085.**

This just may be the largest Western-wear store in the valley, sort of a department store of cowboy duds. If you can't find it here, it just ain't available in these parts. Another location is at 8979 E. Indian Bend Rd., Scottsdale (☎ **602/948-1933**).

**Stockman's Cowboy & Southwestern Wear.** 23587 N. Scottsdale Rd. (at the corner of Pinnacle Peak Rd.), Scottsdale. ☎ **602/585-6142.**

This is one of the oldest Western-wear businesses in the valley, though the store is now housed in a modern shopping plaza. You'll find swirly skirts for cowboy dancing, denim jackets, suede coats, and flashy cowboy shirts. Prices are reasonable and quality is high.

## 11 Phoenix After Dark

The best place to look for nightlife listings is in the *Phoenix New Times*, a weekly newspaper that tends to have the most comprehensive listings of what's going on. This is also the publication to check for club listings and schedules of rock concerts at various concert halls. *The Arizona Republic* is another good place to look for entertainment listings, though you won't find as many club listings as in the *New Times*. The Weekend section, which appears on Friday, and the Arts Plus section, which appears on Sunday, have listings of upcoming events and performances. Other publications to check for abbreviated listings are *Key to the Valley* and *Where—Phoenix/Scottsdale*, which are free and can usually be found at hotels and resorts.

Tickets to many concerts, theater performances, and sporting events are available through **Ticketmaster** (☎ **602/784-4444**), which has outlets at Blockbuster Records, Tower Records, and Robinsons-May department stores. Tickets are also available at all **Dillards** department store box offices (☎ **800/638-4253** or 602/503-5555).

# THE CLUB & MUSIC SCENE

The Valley of the Sun has a very diverse club and music scene that's spread out across the length and breadth of the valley. However, there are a few concentrations of clubs and bars.

As I'm sure you know if you're a denizen of any urban club scene, nightclubs come and go like clockwork. If you're interested in being seen in the club of the moment, check the *New Times* for ads of clubs that play your kind of music. Many dance clubs in the Phoenix area are only open on weekends, so be sure to check what night the doors will be open. Bars and clubs are allowed to serve alcohol until 1am.

With at least three sports bars, as many other bars, a massive multiplex movie theater, and half a dozen restaurants, downtown Phoenix's **Arizona Center** is a veritable entertainment Mecca. Within a few blocks of this mega-entertainment complex are Phoenix Symphony Hall, the Herberger Theater Center, and Majerle's Sports Grill. With all this going on, downtown Phoenix has become a magnet for barhoppers. However, much of the action revolves around games and concerts at the America West Arena. When the Bank One Ballpark opens and the Arizona Diamondbacks finally take to the field, you can bet that downtown bars will really be packed on game nights. Convention attendees and the after-show crowds leaving the Herberger Theater Center and Phoenix Symphony Hall further add to the crowds filling downtown bars.

Another place to wander around until you hear your favorite type of music is **Mill Avenue** in Tempe. Because Tempe is a college town, there are plenty of clubs and bars on this short stretch of road.

In **Scottsdale**, you'll find an eclectic array of clubs in the neighborhoods surrounding the corner of Camelback Road and Scottsdale Road. On Stetson Drive, behind the ill-fated and out-of-business Scottsdale Galleria shopping mall, you'll find three clubs within a block of each other.

## FOLK & COUNTRY

**Handlebar-J.** 7116 E. Becker Lane, Scottsdale. ☎ **602/948-0110.** No cover Sun–Thurs, $3 Fri–Sat.

We're not saying that this Scottsdale landmark is a genuine cowboy bar, but cowpokes do make this one of their stops when they come in from the ranch. You'll hear live git-down two-steppin' music and can even get free dance lessons on Wednesday and Thursday.

**The Rockin' Horse.** 7316 E. Stetson Dr., Scottsdale. ☎ **602/949-0992.** Cover varies from free to $5.

Located in the heart of Scottsdale, the Rockin' Horse is an ever-popular bar that has diverged from its solid country roots to showcase an eclectic blend of country, blues, jazz, swing, and world music.

**Toolie's Country Saloon & Dance Hall.** 4231 W. Thomas Rd. (at SE 43rd Ave.). ☎ **602/ 272-3100.** Cover varies from free to $6.

Once a Safeway supermarket, Toolie's is now the best country-and-western bar in the valley (and some say in the whole country). A false-front cow-town facade beckons enthusiasts of all ages to come on in and git down. Nationally known acts make this their Phoenix stop, and when the famous aren't on stage, Toolie's books the best of the local C&W bands.

## ROCK/R&B

**Anderson's Fifth Estate.** 6820 Fifth Ave., Scottsdale. ☎ **602/994-4168.** Cover varies from free to $4.

Phoenix has a thriving scene for alternative music, and this is where a lot of it gets played. Most nights there's a DJ spinning the dance music, but there are also occasional live shows. Wednesdays are currently trash disco night.

**Balboa Café.** 404 S. Mill Ave., Tempe. ☎ **602/966-1300.** No cover.

Located in downtown Tempe, Balboa's is a restaurant with a college bar atmosphere serving pizza and sandwiches. Local bands play nightly, but it's really the drink specials that draw in the crowds.

✪ **Electric Ballroom.** 1216 E. Apache Blvd. ☎ **602/894-0707.**

This massive temple to rock is the hot club these days for alternative acts from around the country. Lots of neon, acres of parking, two stages, and ticket sales through Ticketmaster all add up to a rock club the likes of which you'd need to travel all the way to Hollywood to find.

**Gibson's.** 410 S. Mill Ave., Tempe. ☎ **602/967-1234.** Cover $3–$12.

Overlooking the Hayden Square Amphitheatre in the heart of Tempe's Mill Avenue college hangout district, Gibson's is a glossy club that stays packed. Step through the door and you almost trip onto the dance floor. High above you is the stage and higher still is a huge video screen. Local bands alternate with touring groups that are just starting to get national attention.

**Long Wong's.** 701 S. Mill Ave. ☎ **602/966-3147.** Cover varies from free to $3.

This scruffy club is tiny and stays packed most nights with college students who come to hear the best of the local rock bands and nosh on great Buffalo wings.

**Tribeca.** 1420 N. Scottsdale Rd. (SW corner of Scottsdale Rd. and McDowell). ☎ **602/423-8499.** Cover $4 on weekends.

This dark discotheque has lots of dance-floor lighting and plays modern rock, hip-hop, salsa/merengue, and retro music. Every night is a different style of music, and weekends there's an after-hours scene here until 4am.

## BLUES

**The Blue Note.** 8708 E. McDowell Rd., Scottsdale. ☎ **602/946-6227.**

If you're looking to hear some blues not far from the resorts of Scottsdale, check out this club. There's live music 7 nights a week.

**Char's Has the Blues.** 4631 N. Seventh Ave. ☎ **602/230-0205.** Cover $3 weekends.

Yes, indeed, Char's does have those mean-and-dirty, lowdown blues, and if you want them too, this is where you head in Phoenix. All the best blues brothers and sisters from around the city and around the country make the scene here to the enjoyment of hard-drinkin' crowds.

**The Rhythm Room.** 1019 E. Indian School Rd. ☎ **602/265-4842.** Cover varies from free to $15.

This blues club books quite a few national acts as well as the best of the local scene, and has a dance floor if you want to move to the beat.

## JAZZ

Call the **Jazz in AZ Hotline** (☎ **602/254-4545**) for a schedule of jazz performances all over the state.

**All That Jazz Restaurant & Jazz Club.** 333 E. Jefferson St. ☎ **602/256-1437.** Cover $5 whenever there's a major act performing, charged only if you're not having dinner.

All That Jazz is a supper club serving up Southern food and live jazz that runs the gamut from traditional to contemporary, with an emphasis on contemporary. Occasionally there are open jam nights.

**Orbit Cafe & Jazz Club.** In Uptown Plaza, Central Ave. and Camelback Rd. ☎ **602/265-2354.**

What started out as just a coffeehouse has now grown into a restaurant and jazz club. The music actually includes jazz, blues, and Motown, so if you're looking for strictly jazz, you might want to check the schedule. Big and trendy, this space has a very urban feel to it.

✪ **Timothy's.** 6335 N. 16th St. ☎ **602/277-7634.** No cover.

For an elegant evening of dining and listening to lively jazz, Timothy's is hard to beat. The restaurant and lounge both attract a well-off crowd. There's live jazz nightly performed by either the house band or touring combos.

## COMEDY & CABARET

**The Tempe Improv.** 930 E. University Dr., Tempe. ☎ **602/921-9877.** Cover $12–$15; dinner main courses $6–$14.

With the best of the national comedy circuit harassing the crowds and rattling off one-liners, the Improv is the valley's most popular comedy club. Weekend lines are long, but your reward is a chance to see the same folks that appear on TV stand-up comedy shows. Dinner is served and reservations are advised.

**Yesterday's.** 9035 N. Eighth St. ☎ **602/861-9080.** No cover; $15 minimum.

Singing waiters and waitresses perform Broadway show tunes and other songs from the 1920s to the 1990s, while host David Lindsay plays Hammond organ and makes comic observations on life in Phoenix. Meals range from $14 to $18, and reservations are required. In the winter you should book at least a week in advance. Closed on Monday.

## DANCE CLUBS/DISCOS

**Bobby McGee's.** 8501 N. 27th Ave. ☎ **602/995-5982.** Cover $4 Wed and Fri–Sun after 9pm.

A wacky family restaurant with costumed waitresses may not seem like the place for a hot singles bar, but nevertheless, the bar in back is known throughout the valley for luring a young and attractive crowd. There's a strict dress code to keep out questionable types, so be sure to dress up a bit (no torn jeans or open-toed shoes, etc.). A second Bobby McGee's, at 7000 E. Shea Blvd., Scottsdale ( ☎ **602/998-5591**), also does everything from male reviews to a variety show to live blues and jazz.

**Club Rio.** 430 N. Scottsdale Rd., Tempe. ☎ **602/894-0533.** Cover $4–$5.

This cavernous club has a dance floor big enough for football practice. From barely legal ASU students to the Porsche-and-pony set from Scottsdale, everyone agrees that Club Rio is *the* place to dance to the latest Top 40, alternative, and R&B. Plenty of live shows, too. Closed Tuesday.

**Jetz & Stixx.** 7077 E. Camelback Rd., Scottsdale. ☎ **602/970-6001.** Cover varies from free to $7.

Located across from the Scottsdale Fashion Square mall, Jetz is currently one of Phoenix's hottest singles' scenes. Deep tans, blond hair, and hard bodies are the order of the day. Both live bands and DJs provide the music. Stixx is Jetz's upscale pool hall. This club is popular with celebrities and Phoenix Suns basketball players. Closed Sunday and Monday.

**Studebakers.** 1290 N. Scottsdale Rd., Tempe. ☎ **602/829-8617.** Cover varies from free to $3.

With an old Studebaker coupe parked in the middle of the club, this spot leaves no question as to the sort of music that's played. Disc jockeys play music from the 1950s to 1970s. On Tuesday nights there are West Coast swing lessons, and Wednesdays are ballroom dancing night (very popular with the over-50 crowd). There are free happy-hour buffets Wednesday through Friday night.

**The Works.** 7223 E. Second St., Scottsdale. ☎ **602/946-4141.** Cover $3–$10.

This cavernous industrial-looking building is decidedly out of place in Old Scottsdale, but that doesn't prevent it from being one of the most popular dance clubs in the valley. Thursday through Sunday the club pounds to the beat of the latest in trance and hip-hop vibes. There are several different areas in the club, each with a different ambience. Impressive lights shows.

# THE BAR, LOUNGE & PUB SCENE
## BARS

**AZ88.** 7353 Scottsdale Mall, Scottsdale. ☎ **602/994-5576.**

Located across the park from the Scottsdale Center for the Arts, this sophisticated bar has a cool ambience that's right for a martini before or after a performance.

**Buzz.** Southeast corner of Scottsdale Rd. and Shea Blvd. ☎ **602/991-FUNN.**

In Scottsdale, folks like to think big. The resorts are big, the houses are big, the cars are big, the restaurants are big, and even the bars are big. Fresh on the scene as we prepared this book, Buzz was hoping to become *the* place in Scottsdale for the new cigar-and-martini crowd. Buzz boasts five different theme areas under one roof, plus a patio on top of that same roof.

**Durants.** 2611 N. Central Ave. ☎ **602/264-5967.**

For more than 40 years this has been *the* place for downtown money merchants to stop on their way back to their rooms with a view. While serving up steaks is the main business here, the bar sees plenty of action as well.

**Giligin's.** 4251 N. Winfield St. ☎ **602/874-2264.**

Located just east of Scottsdale Road between Fourth and Fifth avenues, this self-proclaimed "sand bar & scrimp [sic] hut" is a wild escape from the glitz of Scottsdale. Jumbo tiki cocktails and martinis are served up side by side with fried catfish and shrimp amid a shrimp-shack atmosphere. Have a few tiki cocktails and it's easy to imagine you hear the crash of the surf. Aloha.

**Moondoggie's Toorist Trap and Beach Bar.** In Arizona Center, 455 N. Third St. ☎ **602/253-5200.**

This is the latest watering hole to take up residence in the popular Arizona Center shopping plaza in downtown Phoenix. Sporting a beach theme, it bills itself as a retro dance club and should prove to be a popular addition to the downtown bar scene.

**Phoenix Live! at Arizona Center.** 455 N. Third St. ☎ **602/252-2112** or 602/252-2502.

With three different clubs and a restaurant side by side in a modern shopping mall, this sprawling bar complex is the fulcrum of downtown after-hours activity and offers Phoenix barhoppers a chance to do all their hopping under one roof. Included here are Ltl Ditty's, a piano bar; Decades, a dance club playing '70s, '80s, and '90s music; and America's Original Sports Bar.

**Chez Nous Cocktail Lounge.** 675 W. Indian School Rd. ☎ **602/266-7372.**

OK, so it's in a crummy neighborhood and it looks crummy from the outside. Hey, if you're a fan of the lounge scene, this is the place, the genuine artifact. In business for more than 30 years, Chez Nous was serving martinis long before most of its current patrons were ever born.

## LOUNGES

**Another Pointe in Tyme.** In the Pointe Hilton on South Mountain, 7777 S. Pointe Pkwy. ☎ **602/431-6472.**

If you feel most comfortable when surrounded by walls of mahogany and sitting on brocade or velvet, or if a little light jazz or piano music is your idea of the perfect music to drink by, then you'll be content at Another Pointe in Tyme.

✪ **Arizona Biltmore Lobby Lounge.** 24th St. and Missouri Ave. ☎ **602/955-6600.**

Even if you can't afford the lap of luxury, at least you can pull up a comfortable chair here at the Arizona Biltmore Lounge. Sink into a seat next to the one you love and watch the sunset test its color palate on Camelback Mountain. Alternatively you can slide into a seat near the piano and let the waves of mellow jazz wash over you. For the mere cost of a drink, you can have a Biltmore experience.

✪ **Hyatt Regency Scottsdale at Gainey Ranch Lobby Bar.** 7500 E. Doubletree Ranch Rd., Scottsdale. ☎ **602/991-3388.**

The open-air lounge just below the main lobby of this posh Scottsdale resort sets a romantic stage for nightly live music. Wood fires burn in patio firepits, and royal palms are dramatically uplit. The terraced gardens offer plenty of dark spots for a bit of romance, and off in the distance the pools glow an ethereal turquoise color. Last season classical guitarist Estéban was packing in the crowds. Check to see if he's in residence again this year.

## PUBS

**Bandersnatch Brew Pub.** 125 E. Fifth St., Tempe. ☎ **602/966-4438.**

With good house brews and a big patio in back, Bandersnatch is a favorite of those unusual ASU students who prefer quality to quantity when it's beer-drinking time. There's live folk or Irish music here at least 1 night each week.

✪ **Coyote Springs Brewing Company.** In the Town and Country Shopping Plaza, 4883 N. 20th St. ☎ **602/468-0403.**

This brewpub is a casual, friendly place, and on any given night it has the valley's largest selection of hand-crafted beers and ales on tap (the best, too). There's also live music, mostly blues and R&B, on weekends. A second pub is located in downtown Phoenix at 122 E. Washington St. (☎ **602/256-6645**). This latter pub has a sports theme in keeping with its location near the America West Arena and new Bank One Ballpark.

**Hops! Bistro & Brewery.** 7000 E. Camelback Rd., Scottsdale. ☎ **602/945-4677.**

Take a down-home idea—brewing your own beer—and mix it up with a bit of Scottsdale chic (by way of San Diego) and you get Hops!, an upscale brewpub that includes a patio with live acoustic music, a bar, a separate sports-bar area, and a dining room that serves creative contemporary American cuisine.

There are other branches at the Biltmore Fashion Park, at 2584 E. Camelback Rd. (☎ **602/468-0500**), and 8668 E. Shea Blvd., Scottsdale (☎ **602/998-7777**).

**Murphy's Irish Pub.** 1810 E. Apache Blvd., Tempe. ☎ **602/894-0103.**

If nothing else will do for you but to tip a pint of Guinness amid surroundings that would do Dublin proud, then check out this pub near the ASU campus.

**Timber Wolf.** 740 E. Apache Blvd., Tempe. ☎ **602/517-9383.**

While this is not a brewpub, it does have an astounding 400-plus brews from all over the world, and more than 100 of these are on tap! You can't miss this place as you drive east from Mill Avenue on Apache Boulevard. It's the huge log cabin that looks as if it's pining for some snow.

## COCKTAILS WITH A VIEW

The Valley of the Sun has more than its fair share of spectacular views. Unfortunately, most of them are from expensive restaurants. Fortunately, however, all these restaurants have lounges where, for the price of a drink (and perhaps valet parking), you can sit back and ogle a crimson sunset and the purple mountains' majesty.

Your choices include **Different Pointe of View** at the Pointe Hilton at Tapatio Cliffs, **Rustler's Rooste** at the Pointe Hilton on South Mountain, and **Top of the Rock** at The Buttes. All these restaurants can be found in the restaurant section of this chapter. One other choice is **The Thirsty Camel** at The Phoenician resort. You may never drink in more ostentatious surroundings than here at Charles Keating's Xanadu.

## SPORTS BARS

**America's Original Sports Bar.** 455 N. Third St. ☎ **602/252-2112** or 602/252-2502.

Located in the Arizona Center, this huge sports bar (nearly an acre) is a sort of fun center for grown-ups. There's a huge back deck, 60 TVs, 10 giant-screen TVs, a sand volleyball court, and a small video-games arcade. There's even a Phoenix Sports Hall of Fame.

**Majerle's Sports Grill.** 24 N. Second St. ☎ **602/253-9004.**

If you're a Phoenix Suns fan, you won't want to miss this sports bar only a couple of blocks from the America West Arena where the Suns play. Suns memorabilia covers the walls, and the players often drop in.

✪ **Max's.** 6727 N. 47th Ave., Glendale. ☎ **602/937-1671.**

These days it seems that sports bars are as common as knee injuries on the football field. Most are little more than a bar with a big-screen TV, but Max's is the real thing. In fact, it's a sports museum, restaurant, dinner theater, and off-track betting parlor all wrapped up in one. Yes, after perusing the glass cases full of football helmets and other sports memorabilia, you can sit down to some prime ribs and a cold glass of beer, and wager on the horses or greyhounds.

## GAY & LESBIAN BARS

✪ **Ain't Nobody's Business.** 3031 E. Indian School Rd. ☎ **602/224-9977.**

This bar, with a DJ and dartboards, located in a shopping plaza, is the city's most popular lesbian bar. Sometimes there's live music by local musicians. Weekends the dance floor is usually packed.

**Charlie's.** 727 W. Camelback Rd. ☎ **602/265-0224.**

This nondescript bar just a dozen or so blocks off I-17 is a good bet if you're staying in the Camelback corridor area. Country music dominates the airwaves here, and the boys like to do the urban cowboy thing.

**Metro.** 4201 E. Thomas Rd. ☎ **602/224-9457.**

Whatever your idea of the perfect gay bar, you'll probably like what you find at this large and varied club. There's a dance floor packed with hot, sweaty bodies on weekends, a separate lounge for the rough-trade crowd, and even a patio where you can get away from the heat and noise inside.

**Nu Towne Saloon.** 5002 E. Van Buren St. ☎ **602/267-9959.**

A big red truck parked inside this bar acts as a visual focal point, but the real draws are the food-and-drink specials every Sunday. After 20 years of popularity it's obvious that the friendly, funky atmosphere here works.

**307 Lounge.** 222 E. Roosevelt St. ☎ **602/252-0001.**

Drag shows and talent contests keep this gay bar lively Tuesday through Sunday and make it one of the most fun scenes in the valley.

# THE PERFORMING ARTS

The performing-arts scene in the Valley of the Sun grows more robust with each passing year. Major performing-arts venues are scattered across the valley, so no matter where you happen to be staying, you're likely to find performances being held somewhere nearby. However, downtown Phoenix claims the valley's greatest concentration of performance halls, including Phoenix Symphony Hall, the Orpheum Theatre, and the Herberger Theater Center. However, there are also large performance halls in Scottsdale, Mesa, Tempe, Chandler, and Sun City.

Calling these venues home are the valley's major performance companies—the Phoenix Symphony, Scottsdale Symphony Orchestra, Mesa Symphony, the Arizona Opera Company, Ballet Arizona, Center Dance Ensemble, Actors Theatre Company, and Arizona Theatre Company. Adding to the performances held by these companies are the wide variety of touring companies that make stops in the valley throughout the year. These national and international acts give the valley just the diversity of performers you would expect to find in a city of this size.

While you'll find box office phone numbers listed below, you can also purchase most performing-arts tickets through **Dillard's Box Office** outlets (☎ **800/ 638-4253** or 602/503-5555), which can be found in Dillard's department stores around the city. For tickets to sold-out shows in the Valley Broadway Series at Gammage Auditorium, try Ticket Exchange (☎ **800/800-9811** or 602/254-4444), which charges a premium for its tickets.

## MAJOR PERFORMING-ARTS CENTERS

Phoenix's premier performance venue is the **Phoenix Symphony Hall,** 225 E. Adams St. (☎ **800/AT-CIVIC,** 602/262-7272, or 602/495-1999), which is home to the Phoenix Symphony and the Arizona Opera Company and also hosts other classical music performances, touring Broadway shows, and various other concerts and theatrical productions. The box office is at the entrance to the Phoenix Convention Center, Lobby 2, Plaza South, and is open Monday through Friday from 9:30am to 5pm.

With the reopening of the renovated **Orpheum Theatre,** Adams Street and Second Avenue (☎ **602/262-7272**), in 1996, Phoenix saw the culmination of a long-time dream. This historic Spanish colonial baroque theater was built in 1929 and at the time was considered the most luxurious theater west of the Mississippi. Today its ornately carved sandstone facade stands in striking contrast to the glass-and-steel City Hall building with which the theater shares a common wall (step inside the lobby of City Hall to see the exposed brick wall of the theater). Today, the Orpheum is once again the most elegant performance hall in the valley, and if you have time for only one show while in town, I'd try to make it here.

In Scottsdale, the **Scottsdale Center for the Arts,** 7380 E. Second St., Scottsdale (☎ **602/994-2787**), on the Scottsdale Mall, hosts a wide variety of performances and series ranging from alternative dance to classical music. It may be the wealth of the local population, but for whatever reason, this center seems to get the best of the touring performers who come through the valley. The box office and galleries are open Monday through Saturday from 10am to 5pm (to 8pm on Thursday) and on Sunday from noon to 5pm. Ticket prices range from $7 to $36.

The Frank Lloyd Wright–designed **Grady Gammage Memorial Auditorium,** at Mill Avenue and Apache Boulevard on the Arizona State University campus in Tempe (☎ **602/965-3434**), is at once massive and graceful. This 3,000-seat hall hosts everything from barbershop quartets to touring Broadway shows. The box office is open Monday through Friday from 10am to 6pm and on Saturday from 10am to 4pm.

Several other halls around the valley also schedule interesting performances throughout the year. The **Kerr Cultural Center,** 6110 N. Scottsdale Rd. (☎ **602/ 965-5377**), offers up an eclectic season that includes music from around the world. The **Chandler Center for the Arts,** 250 N. Arizona Ave., Chandler (☎ **602/ 786-2680**), books a few name entertainers each year and fills out its season with a variety of other acts. The **Sundome Center for the Performing Arts,** 19403 R. H. Johnson Blvd., Sun City West (☎ **602/975-1900**), seats more than 7,000 people and stages shows that will appeal to the many retirees who call Sun City home. The **Tempe Performing Arts Center,** 132 E. Sixth St., Tempe (☎ **602/350-8101**), is small but manages to book a good range of performances and also stages shows by a resident children's theater company.

## OUTDOOR VENUES

With all that sunshine, it should come as no surprise that Phoenicians like to go to performances under the stars.

The city's top outdoor venue is the **Blockbuster Desert Sky Pavilion** (☎ **602/ 254-7200**), located half a mile north of I-10 between 79th Avenue and 83rd Avenue. This 20,000-seat amphitheater is open year-round and hosts everything from Broadway musicals to rock concerts; tickets run $20 to $55.

The **Scottsdale Center for the Arts** (☎ **602/994-2787**) heads outdoors for many of its summer concerts, which are held in the Scottsdale Amphitheater on the Scottsdale Mall.

The **Mesa Amphitheater,** at the corner of University Drive and Center Road in Mesa (☎ **602/644-2567**), is a much smaller amphitheater that holds rock concerts throughout the summer and occasionally other months of the year as well; tickets run from roughly $10 to $35.

In Tempe, the small **Hayden Square Amphitheatre,** at Fourth Street and Mill Avenue (☎ **602/967-1234**), schedules rock concerts throughout the year.

Outdoor concerts are also held at various parks and plazas around the valley during the warmer months of the year. Check local papers for listings of such events.

Two perennial favorites of valley residents take place in particularly attractive surroundings. The Music in the Garden concerts at the **Desert Botanical Garden,** 1201 N. Galvin Pkwy. (☎ 602/941-1225), in Papago Park, are held on different days of the week depending on the season of the year, with Sunday brunch concerts in spring particularly popular. The season always includes an eclectic array of musical styles. Tickets are $13 and include admission to the gardens. Sunday brunch is an additional $15. Way up in Carefree, the **El Pedregal Festival Marketplace** (☎ 602/488-1072) stages concerts Thursday evenings from 7 to 9:30pm (jazz, blues, country, and rock concerts) from April through September (tickets $5 to $10).

## OTHER VENUES

When big-name music stars come to town, they often perform at the **America West Arena,** 201 E. Jefferson St. (☎ 602/379-7800), which is known locally as the Purple Palace. This arena is also home to the Phoenix Suns, NHL's new Phoenix Coyotes hockey team, the Arizona Rattlers arena football team, and many other sporting and entertainment events.

One venue that defies categorization but that often holds interesting events is **Westworld of Scottsdale,** 16601 N. Pima Rd., Scottsdale (☎ 800/488-4887 or 602/483-8800). This sprawling complex provides an amazing variety of entertainment and sporting events. There are rodeos, polo matches, and an Arabian horse show, but there are also country music concerts, hot-air balloon races, a steakhouse, horse rentals, and horseback-riding instruction. Ticket prices vary with the event.

## CLASSICAL MUSIC, OPERA & DANCE

The **Phoenix Symphony** (☎ 800/776-9080 or 602/495-1999), the Southwest's leading symphony orchestra, performs at the Phoenix Symphony Hall (tickets run $13 to $41), while the **Scottsdale Symphony Orchestra** (☎ 602/945-8071 or 602/994-2787) performs at the Scottsdale Center for the Arts (tickets go for $12 to $15). The **Mesa Symphony** (☎ 602/897-2121) stages a limited number of concerts each season at the Chandler Center for the Arts (tickets range from $12 to $22).

Opera buffs may want to see what the **Arizona Opera Company** (☎ 602/266-7464) has scheduled. This company stages up to five operas, both familiar and more obscure, each year and splits its time between Phoenix and Tucson (tickets cost $14 to $56). Performances are held in Phoenix Symphony Hall.

**Ballet Arizona** (☎ 602/381-1096) performs at the Phoenix Symphony Hall and the Herberger Theater Center and stages both classical and contemporary ballets (tickets run $17 to $41). The **Center Dance Ensemble** (☎ 602/482-6410), the city's contemporary dance ensemble, stages performances at the Herberger Theater Center (tickets go for $7 to $15). **Southwest Dance** (☎ 602/482-6410) brings to Phoenix acclaimed dance companies from around the world, with performances staged at various area venues (tickets range from about $9 to $36).

## THEATER

In the past few years, Phoenix has been expanding the range of its theater productions. With nearly a dozen professional companies and the same number of nonprofessional companies taking to the boards throughout the year, there is almost always some play being staged somewhere in the valley. So, if you're a fan of live theater, check around. You're likely to find something to pique your interest. For a listing of all the companies operating in the Phoenix metro area and their current schedules, contact the **Arizona Theatre Alliance,** P.O. Box 7436, Chandler, AZ 85246.

The city's main hall for live theater is the **Herberger Theater Center,** 222 E. Monroe St. (☎ **602/252-8497**), which is located downtown and vaguely resembles a Spanish colonial church. Its two Broadway-style theaters together host more than 600 performances each year, including productions by the **Actors Theatre of Phoenix (ATP)** (☎ **602/253-6701**) and the **Arizona Theatre Company (ATC)** (☎ **602/256-6995** or 602/252-8497). ATP has, in the past decade, become one of Phoenix's premier acting companies. Plays tend to be smaller, lesser-known works, with musicals, dramas, and comedies equally represented; tickets go for $25 to $28. ATC splits its performances between Phoenix and Tucson and tends toward big productions and well-known works. Founded in 1967, the ATC has grown into a major force in the Arizona thespian scene; tickets run $19 to $37. Also staging performances at the Herberger is the **Arizona Jewish Theatre Co.** (☎ **602/252-8497**), which, of course, stages plays by Jewish playwrights and with Jewish themes. Tickets range from $19.25 to $21.25.

The **Phoenix Theatre,** 100 E. McDowell Rd. (☎ **602/258-1974** or 602/254-2151), has been around for more than 70 years and stages a wide variety of productions on three different stages; tickets are $7 to $25. If your interest lies in Broadway plays, see what the **Valley Broadway Series** (☎ **602/965-3434**) has scheduled; their focus is mostly on comedies and musicals. This series is held at the Gammage Auditorium in Tempe; tickets cost $35 to $65. The **Theater League** (☎ **602/262-7272**) is another series that brings in Broadway musicals. Performances are held in the Orpheum Theatre and Phoenix Symphony Hall, and tickets cost $26.50 to $32.50. In Old Scottsdale, check the schedule at the **New Scottsdale Playhouse,** 7219 E. Main St. (☎ **602/503-5555** or 602/675-8811), which is affiliated with Theater League. Tickets here range from $15 to $21.

## CHILDREN'S THEATER COMPANIES

If you're looking for a show to take the kids to while you're in town, there are a number of possibilities. **Childsplay** (☎ **602/350-8101**) performs at the Herberger Theater Center with a mix of children's classics and lesser known works. The **Great Arizona Puppet Theater,** 32 W. Latham St. (☎ **602/262-2050**), stages more than a dozen puppet productions each year and hosts touring companies as well. If you're staying at a Scottsdale resort and are looking for some way to entertain the kids for a few hours, see what **Greasepaint Scottsdale Youtheatre** (☎ **602/990-7646**) has scheduled at Stagebrush Theatre, 7020 E. Second St., Scottsdale. Other area children's theater companies include **Mesa Youtheatre,** Mesa Arts Center, 155 N. Center St., Mesa (☎ **602/644-2242**); **Phoenix Theatre's Cookie Company,** Phoenix Theatre's Little Theatre, Central Avenue and McDowell Road (☎ **602/254-2151**); and **Valley Youth Theatre,** Tower Plaza Shopping Center, 38th Street and Thomas Road (☎ **602/267-3880**).

## FAMILY ENTERTAINMENT

If your tastes run to country music, you may want to consider a night at the **Red River Opry,** 730 N. Mill Ave., Tempe (☎ **602/829-OPRY**). This theater just across the Salt River from ASU presents Western variety shows similar to those in Branson, Missouri. There are also frequent pop, rock, jazz, and country music concerts; tickets are $15.50 to $32.

# FILM

**Cine Capri.** Camelback Rd. and 24th St. ☎ **602/956-4200**. Before 6pm, $4.50; after 6pm, $6.50.

This aging movie palace may not give you the choices of a multiplex theater, but no other theater in Phoenix can offer the sort of grandiose atmosphere and awesome size. Well worth an evening. At press time fans of this theater were fighting to save it from being torn down to make way for developers.

**IMAX Theatre Scottsdale.** Fifth Ave. and Civic Center Blvd. ☎ **602/945-4629.** Tickets $7–$9.75 adults, $6–$8.50 seniors, $5–$7.50 children 12 and under.

The massive IMAX screen puts you in the midst of the action. There are usually two different films showing here on any given day.

## CASINOS

**Fort McDowell Casino.** On Fort McDowell Rd. off Ariz. 87, 2 miles east of Shea Blvd., Fountain Hills. ☎ **800/THE-FORT.**

Phoenicians, once among the mainstay clientele of casinos in Nevada, now need not even leave the valley to throw their hard-earned dollars at the slot and video-poker machines. This casino's open 24 hours a day, and there's even free transportation from Phoenix.

**Harrah's Phoenix Ak-Chin Casino.** 15406 Maricopa Rd., Maricopa. ☎ **800/HARRAHS.**

Located 25 miles south of Phoenix and just south of the town of Maricopa, this glitzy casino on the Ak-Chin Indian Reservation brings Las Vegas–caliber gambling to the Phoenix area. Lots of slot machines, video poker, a card room, keno, and bingo. To reach the casino, take Exit 164 (Queen Creek Road) off I-10, turn right and drive 17 miles to Maricopa.

# 12  Side Trips from Phoenix

## THE APACHE TRAIL

There isn't a whole lot of desert or history left in Phoenix, but only an hour's drive to the east you'll find quite a bit of both. The Apache Trail, a winding, partially gravel road that snakes its way around the north side of the Superstition Mountains, offers some of the most scenic desert driving in central Arizona. Along the way there are ghost towns and legends, saguaros and century plants, ancient ruins and artificial lakes.

This tour includes a lot of driving on narrow, winding gravel road, and if you'd rather leave the driving to someone else, you can take a tour of this area with **Apache Trail Tours** (☎ 602/982-7661), which offers four-wheel-drive tours of different lengths ($50 to $115 per person), as well as hiking trips ($10 per person per hour) into the Superstition Mountains.

To start this drive, head east on U.S. 60 to the town of Apache Junction and then head north on Ariz. 88. North of Apache Junction 3¹/₂ miles, you'll come to **Goldfield Ghost Town** (☎ 602/983-0333), a reconstructed 1890s gold-mining town. Though it's a bit of a tourist trap—gift shops, an ice-cream parlor, and the like— it's also home to the **Superstition Mountain/Lost Dutchman Museum** (☎ 602/983-4888) with interesting exhibits about the history of the area. Of particular note is the exhibit on the Lost Dutchman gold mine, perhaps the most famous mine in the country despite the fact that its location is unknown. Admission to the museum is $3 for adults, $2.50 for seniors, and $1 for children. **Goldfield Ghost Town and Mine Tours** (☎ 602/983-0333) provides guided tours of the gold mine beneath the town ($4 for adults, $2 for children). They also operate the only narrow-gauge railroad train in the state of Arizona, which circles the town (rides are $4 for adults, $2 for children). More adult entertainment can be found in the form of the **Mammoth Steakhouse & Saloon** (☎ 602/983-6402), which has live country music Friday through Sunday nights.

Not far from Goldfield is **Lost Dutchman State Park** (☎ 602/982-4485), where you can hike into the rugged Superstition Mountains and see what the region's gold seekers have been up against. Park admission is $3 per vehicle, and there is a campground that charges $8 per site.

If you're game to see the Superstitions from horseback, contact **Superstition Riding Stables,** 2151 N. Warner Rd., Apache Junction (☎ 602/982-6353), which offers rides ranging in length from 1 to 4 hours ($17 to $50) or longer. They also arrange riding lessons, overnight pack trips, picnics, and hayrides. You can also try **OK Corral Horse Rentals** (☎ 602/982-4040), which is close to Goldfield ghost town and charges $17 for a 1-hour ride.

You can also get a bird's-eye-view on a helicopter tour with **Heliservices** (☎ 602/830-9410), which operates out of Goldfield Ghost Town. Fares range from $39 for a 12-minute flight to $105 for a 36-minute flight.

Continuing northeast, you'll next come to **Canyon Lake,** the first of three reservoirs on the Salt River. The three lakes provide much of Phoenix's drinking water, without which the city would never have been able to grow as large as it is today. Here at Canyon Lake you can go for a swim or take a cruise on the *Dolly* steamboat (☎ 602/827-9144). A 90-minute cruise on this reproduction paddlewheeler costs $13 for adults and $8 for children 6 to 12. You can also rent powerboats at the Canyon Lake Marina. If you're hungry, you can grab a bite at the Lakeside Restaurant, which overlooks the marina. However, for a taste of the Old West, hold out for **Tortilla Flat** (☎ 602/984-1776), an old stagecoach stop that has a restaurant, saloon, and general store, all of which are papered with more than $50,000 worth of dollar bills and business cards left by travelers who have stopped here. The prickly pear ice cream served here is worth a try (guaranteed no spines).

A few miles past Tortilla Flat, the pavement ends and the truly spectacular desert scenery begins. Among the rocky ridges, arroyos, and canyons of this stretch of road, you'll see saguaro cacti and century plants (a type of agave that sends up a 15-foot-tall flower stalk once, after years or even decades of slow growth, and then dies). Next you'll come to **Apache Lake,** which is in a deep canyon flanked by colorful cliffs and rugged rock formations. This lake also has a marina, as well as a campground, motel, restaurant, and general store.

Shortly before reaching pavement again you'll come to the **Theodore Roosevelt Dam.** This dam, which forms Roosevelt Lake, is the largest masonry dam in the world and was built in 1911. A recent renovation has given it a facelift and increased the holding capacity of Roosevelt Lake.

Continuing on Ariz. 88, you'll next come to ✪ **Tonto National Monument** (☎ 520/467-2241), which preserves the southernmost cliff dwellings in Arizona. These pueblos were built between 1100 and 1400 by the Salado people, and are some of the few remaining traces of the Salado people who once cultivated lands now flooded by Roosevelt Lake. The lower ruins are half a mile up a steep trail from the visitor center, and the upper ruins are a 3-mile round-trip hike from the visitor center. The latter ruins are only open on Saturday and Sunday November through April by reservation. The park is open daily from 8am to 5pm, and the admission is $4 per car.

Continuing on Ariz. 88 will bring you to the copper-mining town of **Globe.** The mines here are open pits, and though you can't see the mines themselves, the tailings (remains of rock removed from the copper ore) can be seen piled high all around

## The Lost Dutchman of the Superstitions

The Superstition Mountains rise up to the east of Phoenix, dark and ominous, jagged and hot. Cacti bristle across the mountains' flanks, and water is almost nonexistent. Yet for more than a century, gold-crazed prospectors have been scouring these forbidding mountains for a gold mine that may not even exist. The power of a legend is strong, and few legends are as well documented as the legend of the Lost Dutchman gold mine.

The year was 1870 when two German miners, Jacob Waltz and Jacob Weiser, set off into the Arizona wilderness east of Phoenix in hopes of striking it rich. When these two "Dutchmen" (an appellation derived from the German word *Deutsch*) next returned to civilization, they carried with them pouches filled with gold nuggets. Though unsavory prospectors tried to track them to their mother lode in hopes of claim jumping, none was successful. Through visits to saloons and brothels, the two Jacobs remained tight-lipped about their mine's whereabouts.

Jacob Weiser eventually disappeared from the scene amid speculation that his partner did him in so as to keep all the gold to himself. Waltz eventually gave up prospecting in the Superstitions in 1889 at the age of 80. On his deathbed in 1891, he gave detailed directions to a Phoenix woman he had befriended. She and her foster son and the foster son's father and brother spent the next 40 years searching fruitlessly for Waltz's Lost Dutchman mine. Waltz's dying directions just weren't good enough to lead the searchers through these rugged, uncharted mountains.

Clues to the mine's location abound, and hopeful prospectors and treasure hunters have followed every possible lead in their quest for the mine. However, gold fever has led more than a few to their deaths in this harsh wilderness. While skeptics say that there's no proof there ever was a Lost Dutchman mine, others see in the mine's continued elusiveness hope that they might one day be the prospector to find this fabled mother lode.

the town. In Globe, be sure to visit ✪ **Besh-Ba-Gowah Archaeological Park** (☎ 520/425-0320), which is on the eastern outskirts of town (open daily from 9am to 5pm; admission $2). This Salado Indian pueblo site has been partially reconstructed, and several rooms are set up to reflect the way they might have looked when they were first occupied about 700 years ago. These are among the most fascinating ruins in the state. To reach Besh-Ba-Gowah, head out of Globe on South Broad Street to Jesse Hayes Road.

From Globe, head west on U.S. 60. On the west side of Superior, you'll come to **Boyce Thompson Southwestern Arboretum** (☎ 520/689-2811), which is dedicated to researching and propagating desert plants and instilling in the public an appreciation for desert plants (open daily from 8am to 5pm; admission $4 adults and $2 children 5 to 12, free for children 4 and under). This was the nation's first botanical garden established in the desert, and the cactus gardens here are quite impressive. The setting in Queen Creek and Anett canyons is quite dramatic with cliffs for a backdrop and a stream running through the gardens. As you hike the miles of nature trails, watch for the two bizarre boojum trees. If you live in the Southwest, you can learn a lot here about landscaping in the desert.

The home that Colonel William Boyce Thompson built when he established his arboretum here is now open to the public with guided tours conducted several days a week. Known as **Picketpost House** (☎ 520/689-2845), this 26-room castle of a home is now filled with 200 antique porcelain dolls and antiques from around the world. The mansion overlooks Boyce Thompson Arboretum, and a tour is a pleasant addition to a stop to visit the gardens.

If it's not too late and you didn't go riding in the morning, you can finish your day with a horseback ride at **Don Donnelly Stables,** 6010 S. Kings Ranch Rd. (☎ 602/982-7822), in the community of Gold Canyon. A 2-hour sunset ride costs $32 per person. These stables also do overnight rides, cookouts, and hayrides.

If after a long day on the road you're looking for a good place to eat, stop in at **Gold Canyon Ranch** (☎ 602/982-9090), which has a good, though expensive, dining room serving creative Southwestern cuisine. There's also a bar and grill serving basic burgers and sandwiches.

You can also finish this trip with an evening at the **Barleen Family Country Music Dinner Theatre,** 2275 Old West Hwy., Apache Junction (☎ 602/982-7991), which serves up Branson-style country music and comedy for the whole family. Dinner and show are $15.50 for adults and $9.50 for kids ages 4 to 12.

On weekends in February and March, you might want to skip this entire tour and instead spend the day at the **Arizona Renaissance Festival** (☎ 602/463-2700), which is held east of Gold Canyon Ranch. During the festival, knights and ladies replace the cowboys and Indians one would expect to see here in the desert. Tickets are $11 to $12 for adults, $10 for senior citizens, and $4 to $5 for children ages 5 to 12.

## CAVE CREEK & THE OLD WEST

A drive north from Phoenix can give you glimpses into how the pioneers once lived—and how Hollywood always imagined Western towns should look.

Head north out of Phoenix on I-17 for about 20 miles and take the Pioneer Road exit. Here you'll find the **Pioneer Arizona Living History Museum,** 3901 W. Pioneer Rd. (☎ 602/465-1052). This museum includes more than 20 original and reconstructed buildings, and inside (or near) these buildings you'll find costumed interpreters practicing traditional frontier activities. Among the buildings here are a carpentry shop, a blacksmith shop, a miner's cabin, a stagecoach station, a one-room schoolhouse, an opera house, a church, farmhouses, and a Victorian mansion. Each November over Veterans Day weekend, there are Civil War battle reenactments and a gathering of modern-day mountain men here. Mountain men also gather here in mid-February. Special events ranging from murder-mystery dinners to ice-cream socials are also held here. The museum is open October through May, Wednesday through Sunday from 9am to 5pm. Admission is $5.75 for adults, $5.25 for senior citizens and students, and $4 for children 4 to 12, free for children 4 and under. Wear sturdy shoes.

Heading back south on I-17, take Exit 223 and head east to the funky community of **Cave Creek** and its more polished neighbor, Carefree. Cave Creek, founded as a mining camp in the 1870s, clings to its Wild West image. To learn more about the history of this area, stop in at the **Cave Creek Museum,** at the corner of Skyline Drive and Basin Road (☎ 602/488-2764).

Cave Creek is home to several Western steakhouses, saloons, and shops selling Western and Native American crafts and antiques. At **Crazy Ed's Satisfied Frog Saloon,** 6245 E. Cave Creek Rd. (☎ 602/488-3317), you can sample Cave Creek chili beer, each bottle of which has a chili pepper in it.

**Carefree** is a much more subdued place, a planned community established in the 1950s and popular with retirees. Ho and Hum roads and Easy Street are just a couple of local street names that reflect the sedate nature of the town, which is home to the exclusive Boulders resort. Boasting one of the most spectacular settings of any resort in Arizona, The Boulders also has a couple of excellent restaurants.

On Easy Street, in what passes for downtown in Carefree, you'll find one of the world's largest sundials. The dial is 90 feet across, and the gnomon (the part that casts the shadow) is 35 feet tall. From the gnomon hangs a colored-glass star and in the middle of the dial, there's a pool of water and a fountain. This elaborate timepiece shows the correct time on vernal and autumnal equinoxes, but on other days of the year, you have to consult a chart next to the sundial to figure out what time to set your watch to.

In downtown Carefree, you'll also find a sort of reproduction Spanish village shopping area, and just south of town, adjacent to The Boulders resort, you'll find the upscale El Pedregal Festival Marketplace shopping center, where there are lots of interesting shops, art galleries, and a few restaurants.

## FLORENCE & CASA GRANDE

Driving southeast from Phoenix on I-10 for about 60 miles will bring you to the Florence and Casa Grande area, where you can learn about Indian cultures both past and present and view the greatest concentration of historic buildings in Arizona.

At Exit 175 (Casa Blanca Road), you'll find the **Gila River Arts and Crafts Center** (☎ 520/963-3981), which is located on the Gila River Indian Reservation. The center has a museum with historical photos and artifacts, including beautiful Pima baskets. In the adjacent Heritage Park are replicas of several different types of Indian villages including Tohono O'odham, Maricopa, and Apache. During the winter months, there are frequent dance performances here at the center. The biggest performances are the weekend after Thanksgiving and the third weekend in March. The center is open daily from 8am to 5pm, and admission is free.

To reach Florence, continue south on I-10 to Exit 185 (Ariz. 387) and head east. Before reaching Florence, near the town of Coolidge, you'll come to ✪ **Casa Grande Ruins National Monument** (☎ 520/723-3172). In Spanish, the name means "Big House," and that's exactly what you'll find. In this instance, the big house is an earth-walled ruin that was built 650 years ago by the Hohokam people. Although it's still not known what purpose this unusual structure served, the building provides a glimpse of a style of ancient architecture rarely seen. Instead of using adobe bricks or stones, the people who built this structure used layers of hard-packed soil that have survived the ravages of the weather. The Hohokam people who once occupied this site began farming the valleys of the Gila and Salt rivers about 1,500 years ago, and eventually built an extensive network of irrigation canals for watering their fields. By the middle of the 15th century, however, the Hohokam had abandoned both their canals and their villages and disappeared without a trace. The monument is open daily from 8am to 5pm (closed December 25), and admission is $2 for adults.

Continuing east, you'll soon come to the farming community of **Florence.** Though at first glance this town may seem like any other small town, closer inspection turns up more than 150 buildings on the National Register of Historic Places. The majority of these buildings are constructed of adobe and were originally built in the Sonoran style, a style that was influenced by Spanish architectural ideas. Most buildings were altered over the years and now display aspects of various architectural styles popular during territorial days in Arizona.

Before touring the town, stop in at the **Pinal County Historical Society Museum** on South Main Street to learn more about the history of the area. It's open April to November Wednesday to Sunday from noon to 4pm; December to March

Wednesday to Saturday 11am to 4pm and Sunday noon to 4pm (closed from mid-July through August). Admission is by donation.

At the corner of Main Street and Ruggles Street, you'll find the **McFarland State Historic Park** (☎ **520/868-5216**), which is housed in a former Pinal County Courthouse that was built in 1878. It's open Thursday to Monday from 8am to 5pm; admission is $2 adults, $1 children ages 12 to 17. The current county courthouse, built in 1891, rises above the center of town and displays an unusual combination of different architectural styles.

To find out more about the buildings of Florence, stop in at the **Pinal County Visitors Center,** at Butte Avenue and Florence Street (☎ **520/868-4331**), or the **Florence Visitors Center,** 291 N. Bailey St. (☎ **800/437-9433** or 520/868-9433), which is housed in a historic 1889 grocery store in the center of town. Each year on the first Saturday in February there's a tour of historic buildings. Contact the chamber of commerce for more information.

If you're hungry and it's time for lunch, try **Murphy's Soup and Salad,** 310 N. Main St. (☎ **520/868-0027**), at the corner of Eighth Street in Florence, a simple eatery in a historic building downtown. The restaurant takes its name from the movie *Murphy's Romance,* which starred James Garner and Sally Field and was filmed here in Florence. Murphy's is only open Monday through Friday from 11am to 2 or 3pm.

If you're interested in shopping deals, there are a couple of **factory-outlet shopping malls** in the town of Casa Grande at Exits 194 and 198 off I-10. These are only a short distance out of your way to the south if you are headed back to Phoenix.

If you are continuing south toward Tucson from Florence, I suggest taking the scenic **Pinal Pioneer Parkway** (Ariz. 79), which was the old highway between Phoenix and Tucson. Along the way you'll see signs identifying desert plants and a memorial to silent-film star Tom Mix, who died in a car crash here in October 1940.

Alternatively, if you're heading to Tucson by way of I-10, and it isn't too hot out, consider a stop at **Picacho Peak State Park** (☎ **520/466-3183**), which is 20 miles south of Casa Grande at Exit 219. Picacho Peak, a wizard's cap of rock rising 1,500 feet above the desert, is a visual landmark for miles around. Hiking trails lead around the lower slopes of the peak and up to the summit, and these trails are especially popular in spring, when the wildflowers bloom (the park is well known as one of the best places in Arizona to see wildflowers, in fact). In addition to its natural beauty, Picacho Peak was the site of the only Civil War battle to take place in Arizona.

# Central Arizona  6

Encompassing the Mogollon Rim, the fertile Verde River valley, Oak Creek Canyon, the red rocks of Sedona, the pine-forested mountains around Prescott, and the desert in the Wickenburg area, central Arizona packs an amazing amount of variety within its boundaries and has played an important role in Arizona history for more than 1,500 years.

Ancient Hohokam and Sinagua peoples, as well as early settlers, were drawn to the fertile valley of the Verde River. Though these tribes had disappeared by the time the first white settlers arrived in the area in the 1860s, hostile Apache and Yavapai tribes inhabited the area. It was in order to protect these settlers that the U.S. Army established Fort Verde in 1871.

When Arizona became a U.S. territory in 1863, Prescott, due to its central location, was chosen as its capital. Though the town would later lose that title to Tucson and then to Phoenix, it was the most important city in Arizona for part of the late 19th century. Wealthy merchants and legislators rapidly transformed this pioneer outpost into a beautiful town filled with stately Victorian homes surrounding an imposing county courthouse.

Settlers were lured to this region not only by fertile land, but by the mineral wealth that lay hidden in the ground. Miners founded a number of communities in central Arizona, among them Jerome. When the mines shut down, Jerome was almost completely abandoned, but artists and craftspeople have now moved in to reclaim and revitalize the old mining town.

Artists also found their way to Sedona, but only after the movie industry had hit upon its red-rock country as a striking backdrop for exciting Westerns. Situated at the mouth of Oak Creek Canyon, one of Arizona's major recreational areas, Sedona now attracts artists, retirees, and New Agers (who come to visit Sedona's mystical vortexes).

Once called the dude ranch capital of the world, Wickenburg clings to its Western roots and has restored much of its downtown to its 1880s appearance. There are even a few dude ranches—now called guest ranches—still in business.

## 1  Wickenburg

53 miles NW of Phoenix; 61 miles S of Prescott; 128 miles SE of Kingman

Once the "Dude Ranch Capital of the World," Wickenburg attracted celebrities and families from all over the country. Those were the days when the West had only just stopped being wild and being able to spend the winter in Arizona was both a blessing and an adventure. Today, though the area has only a handful of dude (or guest) ranches still in business, Wickenburg clings to its Wild West image. A chance to ride the range (and maybe play some golf or tennis) is the area's main attraction, and the dude ranches that remain range from rustic to luxurious.

Wickenburg lies at the northern edge of the Sonoran Desert on the banks of the Hassayampa River, one of the last clear, free-flowing rivers in the Arizona desert. The town was founded in 1863 by Prussian gold prospector Henry Wickenburg, who discovered what would eventually become the most profitable gold and silver mine in Arizona: The Vulture Mine. Today the abandoned mine and surrounding ghost town can be toured.

When the dude ranches flourished back in the 1920s and 1930s, Wickenburg realized that visitors wanted a taste of the Wild West, so the town gave the tenderfoots what they wanted—trail rides, hayrides, cookouts, the works. To play up its Western heritage, Wickenburg has now preserved one of its downtown streets much as it may have looked in 1900. If you've come to Arizona searching for the West the way it used to be, Wickenburg is a good place to look.

### ESSENTIALS

**GETTING THERE**    From Phoenix, take U.S. 60, which heads northwest and becomes Ariz. 93/U.S. 89. U.S. 89 also comes down from Prescott in the north, while U.S. 60 comes in from I-10 in western Arizona. U.S. 93 comes down from I-40 in northwestern Arizona. **Airport Express of Wickenburg** (☎ 888/684-TOMS or 520/684-0925) offers a shuttle from the Phoenix Sky Harbor Airport to Wickenburg for $65 per person (they request 24 hours' notice).

**VISITOR INFORMATION**    For more information about Wickenburg, contact the **Wickenburg Chamber of Commerce,** 216 N. Frontier St., Wickenburg, AZ 85390 (☎ 800/942-5242 or 520/684-5479; fax 520/684-5470).

**SPECIAL EVENTS    Gold Rush Days,** held each year on the second full weekend in February, is the biggest festival of the year in Wickenburg. Events include gold panning, a rodeo, and shoot-outs in the streets. Each year on the first weekend in December, Wickenburg holds its annual **Cowboy Poetry Gathering,** with lots of poetry and music.

### WHAT TO SEE & DO

A **stroll around the old section of downtown Wickenburg** provides a glimpse of the Old West. Most of the buildings here were built between 1890 and the 1920s, although a few are older.

The old **Santa Fe train station** is now the Wickenburg Chamber of Commerce, which should be your first stop in town. They'll give you a map that tells a bit about the history of the town's older buildings. The brick **post office** building, almost across the street from the train station, once had a ride-up window providing service to people on horseback. **Frontier Street** is preserved as it looked in the early 1900s. The covered sidewalks and false fronts are characteristic of old Western architecture, which often disguised older adobe buildings. The oldest building in town is the **Etter**

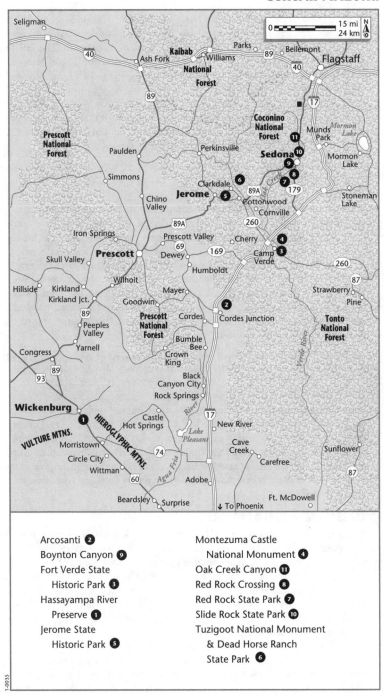

# Central Arizona

Arcosanti ②

Boynton Canyon ⑨

Fort Verde State
   Historic Park ③

Hassayampa River
   Preserve ①

Jerome State
   Historic Park ⑤

Montezuma Castle
   National Monument ④

Oak Creek Canyon ⑪

Red Rock Crossing ⑧

Red Rock State Park ⑦

Slide Rock State Park ⑩

Tuzigoot National Monument
   & Dead Horse Ranch
   State Park ⑥

**General Store,** adjacent to the Gold Nugget Restaurant. The old adobe-walled store was built in 1864 and has long since been disguised with a false wooden front.

Two of the town's most unusual attractions aren't buildings at all. The **Jail Tree,** behind the Circle K store at the corner of Wickenburg Way and Tegner Street, is an old mesquite tree that served as the local hoosegow. Outlaws were simply chained to the tree. Their families would often come to visit and have a picnic in the shade of the tree. The second, equally curious, town attraction is the **Wishing Well,** which stands beside the bridge over the Hassayampa. Legend has it that anyone who drinks from the Hassayampa River will never tell the truth again, and so drinking water was always drawn from this well. How it became a wishing well is unclear.

**Desert Caballeros Western Museum.** 21 N. Frontier St. ☎ **520/684-2272.** Admission $5 adults, $4 senior citizens, $1 children 6–16; free for children under 6. Mon–Sat 10am–5pm, Sun noon–4pm.

Wickenburg thrives on its Western heritage, and inside this museum you'll find Western art depicting life on the range in the days of "cowboys and Indians." Though it's not too large, the museum manages to convey a great deal about the history of this part of Arizona. There's an excellent display of colorful minerals and a small collection of Indian artifacts. Branding and barbed-wire exhibits cover the ranching history of the area. On the main floor, dioramas depict important scenes from the history of the Wickenburg region. Downstairs, a 1900 street scene from a Western town is re-created, complete with general store. There are also regularly scheduled special exhibits and an art collection containing work by Remington, Russell, and members of the Cowboy Artists of America.

**Robson's Arizona Mining World.** Ariz. 71, 26 miles west of Wickenburg. ☎ **520/685-2609.** Admission $4 adults, free for children 10 and under. Mon–Fri 10am–4pm, Sat–Sun 8am–dark. Closed May 1–Oct 1. Head west out of Wickenburg on U.S. 60 and, after 22 miles, turn north on Ariz. 71.

Boasting the world's largest collection of antique mining equipment, this museum is a must for anyone who is fascinated by Arizona's rich mining history. Located on the site of an old mining camp, the museum consists of 26 buildings filled with antiques. More like a ghost town than a museum, Robson's buildings contain displays pertaining to life in a mining camp. In addition to touring the museum, you can pan for gold or hike to see Native American petroglyphs. A hotel and restaurant are also on the premises.

## ✪ Hassayampa River Preserve

At one time the Arizona desert was laced with rivers that flowed for most, if not all, of the year. In the past 100 years these rivers, and the riparian (waterside) habitats they once supported, have disappeared at an alarming rate because of the damming of rivers and lowering water tables. Riparian areas support trees and plants that require more water than is usually available in the desert, and this lush growth provides food and shelter for hundreds of species of birds, mammals, and reptiles. Thus, the rapidly disappearing riparian areas of the state play an ever more important role in supporting wild plants and animals in the desert.

The Nature Conservancy, a nonprofit organization dedicated to purchasing and preserving threatened and endangered habitats, owns and manages the Hassayampa River Preserve, accessed 3 miles south of Wickenburg on U.S. 60. (☎ **520/684-2772**). Nature trails lead along the river beneath cottonwoods and willows and past the spring-fed Palm Lake. More than 230 species of birds have been spotted within the preserve.

Naturalist-guided walks are offered; call the preserve for the current schedule. Though the guided walks are free, reservations are required. Admission to the preserve is free, but there's a suggested donation of $5. From October 1st to mid-May, hours are Wednesday to Sunday from 8am to 5pm; from mid-May to September, it's Wednesday to Sunday from 6am to noon.

## OUTDOOR PURSUITS

Even if you aren't staying at a guest ranch, you can go horseback riding in the Wickenburg area. **No Fences on Moonlight Mesa** (☎ 520/684-3308) is run by Dianna Tangen, who offers guided horseback rides of varying lengths. Rides cost $20 per person, and a half day of riding costs $50.

Jeep tours of the area are available through **Wickenburg Desert Tours,** 295 E. Wickenburg Way (☎ 800/596-5337 or 520/684-0438). Tour prices are $50 for adults, $25 for children ages 5 to 12.

If you want to play a round of golf, try **Los Caballeros Golf Club,** 1551 S. Vulture Mine Rd. (☎ **520/684-2704**).

If you'd like to look like a cowboy, stop in at **Double D Western World,** 955 Wickenburg Way (☎ 520/684-7987), for some discount Western duds.

If you'd rather do some hiking, there are a couple of interesting options. You can climb **Vulture Peak,** southwest of town, or hike through a box canyon formed by the Hassayampa River. Stop by the chamber of commerce information center for directions and maps.

# WHERE TO STAY
## GUEST RANCHES
**Flying E Ranch.** 2801 W. Wickenburg Way, Dept. E, Wickenburg, AZ 85390. ☎ **520/ 684-2690.** Fax 520/684-5304. 19 rms. A/C TV. $190–$250 double. 2- to 4-night minimum stay. Rates include all meals. No credit cards. Closed May–Oct. Drive 4 miles west of town on U.S. 60.

Of the handful of guest ranches still operating in Wickenburg, this is the only real working cattle ranch, and there are 20,000 high, wide, and handsome acres for you and the cattle to roam. Family owned since 1952, this ranch attracts plenty of repeat business, with families finding it a particularly appealing and down-home kind of place. The main lodge features a spacious lounge where guests like to gather by the fireplace. The guest rooms vary in size, but all have Western-style furnishings. There are either twin or king-size beds in the rooms.

**Dining/Entertainment:** Three family-style meals are served in the wood-paneled dining room, but there's no bar, so you'll need to bring your own liquor. There are also breakfast cookouts, lunch rides, and evening chuck-wagon dinners.

**Services:** Hayrides, guest rodeos, square dances in the barn.

**Facilities:** Small outdoor pool, whirlpool, sauna, exercise room, tennis court, shuffleboard, table tennis, horseshoes, horseback riding (not included in room rates; approximately $20 to $30 per day).

**Kay El Bar Guest Ranch.** Rincon Rd. (off U.S. 93; P.O. Box 2480), Wickenburg, AZ 85358. ☎ **800/684-7583** or 520/684-7593. 8 rms, 1 cottage. $225 double; $240 cottage. Rates include all meals. MC, V. Closed May 1 to mid-Oct.

This is the smallest and oldest of the Wickenburg guest ranches, and its old adobe buildings, built between 1914 and 1925, are listed in the National Register of Historic Places. However, at press time, the ranch was in the process of being sold and its future was uncertain. If it is still operating as a guest ranch, you'll find, in the main lodge, a rustic lounge where a piano provides music for sing-alongs and a stone fireplace provides warmth in winter. Though the ranch has only 60 acres, it abuts thousands of acres of public lands where guests can ride or hike. The guest rooms in the adobe main lodge are much smaller but have original Western-style furnishings. From the moment you arrive, you'll feel at home on the range here.

**Dining/Entertainment:** A tile floor and beehive fireplace in the dining room provide an authentic Southwestern feel. The meals vary from Chinese to prime rib, and are served in heaping portions. There's also a fully stocked bar.

**Services:** Horseback riding (included in rates).

**Facilities:** Small outdoor pool.

**✪ Merv Griffin's Wickenburg Inn Dude Ranch and Tennis Club.** P.O. Box P, Wickenburg, AZ 85358. ☎ **800/942-5362** or 520/684-7811. Fax 520/684-2981. 9 lodge rms, 55 casitas. A/C TV TEL. Feb–Apr $260 double, $295–$340 studio or 1-bedroom casita, $490 2-bedroom casita; May–Sept $210 double, $240–$280 studio or 1-bedroom casita, $430 2-bedroom casita; Oct–Jan $260 double, $295–$340 studio or 1-bedroom casita, $490 2-bedroom casita. Rates include all meals and horseback riding. MC, V.

Located 8 miles north of Wickenburg and calling itself a dude ranch and tennis club, the Wickenburg Inn caters both to those who want to become trail hands and those who want to perfect their backhand. Wranglers provide riding instruction, while tennis pros give private lessons and group clinics. Unlimited tennis privileges and daily horseback rides are included in room rates. The ranch also places an emphasis on natural history with its nature center and educational programs for kids. Since being purchased by Merv Griffin's company a few years ago, this guest ranch has undergone extensive renovations and expansion, including the addition of a new pool area (that includes a kids' pool with a sand beach). Ten two-bedroom casitas were also added to further cater to families.

Casitas are cottages built to resemble old Spanish colonial adobes, with red-tile roofs and porches made from rough-hewn logs. Inside are kitchenettes with tile counters, fireplaces, high-beamed ceilings, and wet bars. Deluxe suites have sundecks, and studios have similar styling to suites. Lodge rooms have rough-hewn wood walls and furniture plus a deck or balcony.

**Dining/Entertainment:** Meals are a combination of Southwestern and continental fare, and a couple of nights each week there are campfire cookouts in the desert.

**Services:** Horseback riding and lessons, tennis lessons, holiday children's programs, baby-sitting, guided nature hikes.

**Facilities:** Outdoor pool, whirlpool, nine tennis courts, self-service laundry, volleyball court, playground, arts-and-crafts center, nature center, jogging trail.

**✪ Rancho de los Caballeros.** 1551 S. Vulture Mine Rd. (off U.S. 60 west of town), Wickenburg, AZ 85390. ☎ **520/684-5484.** Fax 520/684-2267. 77 rms, inc. 12 suites. A/C TV TEL. Oct–Jan $266–$314 double, $399 suite; Feb–May $306–$386 double, $499 suite. Rates include all meals. 14% gratuity added to all bills. No credit cards. Closed mid-May to Oct.

Located on 20,000 acres 2 miles west of Wickenburg, Rancho de los Caballeros is part of an exclusive country club–resort community. Peace and quiet are the keynotes of a stay at this ranch, where most stays focus on golfing and horseback riding. The lobby, classically Southwestern, has sandstone floors, brick walls, open ceiling beams, a large copper fireplace, and a painting by Frederic Remington. The guest rooms have either tile floors or carpeting and rustic Spanish colonial furnishings. Exposed-beam ceilings and Indian rugs complete the Southwestern motif. Some rooms have their own fireplaces. The 12 luxury suites are definitely the best rooms on the ranch.

**Dining/Entertainment:** The dining room features traditional Southwestern furnishings, and the dinner menu includes a choice of five main dishes. Proper attire is required in the dining room. At lunch there's a poolside buffet.

**Services:** Laundry service, in-room massages (extra charge), children's programs, baby-sitting.

**Facilities:** Small outdoor pool, four tennis courts, 18-hole golf course ($75 greens fee and cart), pro shop, horseback riding ($28 to $45 per ride), trap and skeet shooting ($25 per round).

## A BED & BREAKFAST

**Sombrero Ranch Bed & Breakfast.** 31910 W. Bralliar Rd. (1 mile outside of town off U.S. 89), Wickenburg, AZ 85390. ☎ **520/684-0222.** 5 rms. $75 double. MC, V.

If you aren't up for doing the dude ranch thing but want to spend some time out Wickenburg way, consider this comfortable B&B. Set atop a steep hill on 47 acres of desert land, the lodge has a commanding view of the town and its surroundings. The lodge itself dates from 1937 and was built in mission revival style. Rooms are simply furnished, though spacious. For relaxing, there is a swimming pool in the garden.

## A MOTEL

**Best Western Rancho Grande.** 293 E. Wickenburg Way, Wickenburg, AZ 85390. ☎ **800/ 854-7235** or 520/684-5445. Fax 520/684-7380. 80 rms, 6 suites. A/C TV TEL. $59–$100 double or suite. AE, CB, DC, DISC, MC, V.

Located right in the heart of downtown Wickenburg, this Best Western is built in Spanish colonial style, with tile roofs, stucco walls, arched colonnades, and tile murals on the walls. There's a wide range of room types and prices. At the higher end you get a larger room, a larger bathroom (with a phone), large towels, and a coffeemaker. The suites are housed in 120- and 150-year-old buildings, one of which is an old adobe. However, remodeling has updated these buildings completely. The motel's restaurant and lounge are across the street. The hotel also offers an outdoor pool, a whirlpool, and a tennis court.

## WHERE TO DINE

**Charley's Steakhouse.** 1187 W. Wickenburg Way. ☎ **520/684-2413.** Reservations recommended. Complete dinners $10–$17. DISC, MC, V. Tues–Sun 5–9pm. Closed in summer. STEAKS.

Out on the west side of town is Wickenburg's favorite steakhouse. Though the building looks quite modern from the outside, the interior is done in rustic pine paneling, and collectors' whiskey bottles are lined up all over the dining room. Dinners of steak, chicken, or seafood come with salad, baked potato, cowboy beans, rolls and butter, tea, and dessert—so bring a hearty appetite. For small people, there's a children's menu.

**Griff's at the Wickenburg Inn.** U.S. 89 (Prescott Hwy.). ☎ **520/684-7811.** Reservations recommended. Dinner $9–$22; lunch $7–$9; breakfast $8. AE, DC, DISC, MC, V. Daily 7–10am and noon–2:30pm; Sun–Mon and Wed–Fri 6–8:30pm, Tues and Sat 5:30–10pm (cookout). AMERICAN/CONTINENTAL.

The Wickenburg Inn is north of town in a picturesque setting of rolling desert hills. Its dining room, open to the public with advance reservations, has the feeling of an old-fashioned Southwestern lodge. Stone and raw wood give it a rugged feeling, but creature comforts are not overlooked. Main-course choices include steaks, seafood, chicken, pasta, and various Southwestern specialties. Cookouts are offered on Tuesday and Saturday nights.

**House Berlin.** 169 E. Wickenburg Way. ☎ **520/684-5044.** Main courses $9–$14. MC, V. Tues–Sun 11:30am–2:30pm and 5–9pm. GERMAN/CONTINENTAL.

For some strange reason, Germans seem to love the desert, so it shouldn't really come as a surprise that good German food is available in Wickenburg. The restaurant is small and casual and serves a mix of German and other continental dishes. Because of bad visibility when exiting from the restaurant's parking lot, it's a good idea to park on the street here.

**Rancho de los Caballeros.** 1551 S. Vulture Mine Rd. ☎ **520/684-5484.** Reservations required. Jackets required for men. Lunch $11–$14, complete dinner $23. No credit cards. Mon–Sat 12:30–1:30pm. Sun noon–2pm (buffet lunch), daily 6:30–8:30pm. Closed mid-May to Sept 30. CONTINENTAL/SOUTHWESTERN.

Wickenburg's most exclusive guest ranch also opens its excellent restaurant to the public. The menu changes daily. However, you always have a choice of two soups, two salads, five main courses, and six or seven desserts. The regular menu entrees tend toward the familiar such as roast pork loin, pasta primavera, and fried oysters. However, if none of these dishes appeals to you, there are slightly more expensive alternatives such as marlin with kiwi-mango salsa. Men are required to wear a jacket, and women must also dress appropriately.

## EN ROUTE TO PRESCOTT

Between Wickenburg and Prescott, U.S. 89 climbs up out of the desert at the town of **Yarnell,** which lies at the top of a steep stretch of road. The landscape around Yarnell is a jumble of weather-worn granite boulders that give the town a unique appearance. There are several little craft and antiques shops here in Yarnell that are worth a stop, but the town's main claim to fame is that it's the site of **St. Joseph's Shrine** (☎ 520/427-3534), which is known for its carved stone stations of the cross.

If you happen to be hungry, don't miss the **Buzzard's Roost Cafe** (☎ 520/427-6500), which is right on U.S. 89 toward the north end of town. Mesquite-smoked barbecue is the specialty here.

## 2 Prescott

100 miles N of Phoenix; 60 miles SW of Sedona; 87 miles SW of Flagstaff

In 1863 the Walker party discovered gold in the mountains of central Arizona, and soon miners were flocking to the area to seek their own fortunes. A year later, in 1864, Arizona became a U.S. territory and the new town of Prescott, located right in the center of Arizona, was made the territorial capital. Prescott later lost its statewide influence when the capital moved to Phoenix, but because of the importance of ranching and mining in central Arizona, Prescott continued to be a very important regional town.

A stately courthouse on a tree-shaded square in the middle of town, a well-preserved historic downtown business district, and quite a few old Victorian homes give Prescott a timeless American hometown atmosphere. Several small museums, a couple of historic hotels, and the nearby Prescott National Forest assure that visitors with a diverse range of interests spend time here.

In summer, when Phoenix is baking, Prescott is generally 20° cooler, which makes this a popular weekend getaway for Phoenicians. Prescott is also gaining importance as a retirement community, as retirees (primarily from California) rediscover Arizona's once-bustling territorial capital.

## ESSENTIALS

**GETTING THERE** Prescott is at the junction of U.S. 89, U.S. 89A, and Ariz. 69. If you're coming from Phoenix, take the Cordes Junction exit (Exit 262) from I-17.

If you're coming from Flagstaff, the most direct route is to take I-17 to Ariz. 169 to Ariz. 69. From Sedona, just take U.S. 89A all the way.

There is regularly scheduled service between Prescott's Ernest A. Love Airport, on U.S. 89, and the Phoenix Sky Harbor Airport on **America West** airlines (☎ **800/ 235-9292** for schedule information).

Shuttle "U" provides shuttle service between Prescott and the Phoenix Sky Harbor Airport. The fare is $21 one way and $37 round-trip. Phone ☎ **520/772-6114** or 800/304-6114 (out of the Prescott area) for schedule information.

**ORIENTATION**    U.S. 89 comes into Prescott on the northeast side of town, where it joins with Ariz. 69 coming in from the east. The main street into town is **Gurley Street,** which forms the north side of the Courthouse Plaza. **Montezuma Street,** also known as Whiskey Row, forms the west side of the plaza. If you continue south on Montezuma Street, you'll be on U.S. 89 heading toward Wickenburg.

**VISITOR INFORMATION**    For more information on Prescott, contact the **Prescott Chamber of Commerce,** 117 W. Goodwin St. (P.O. Box 1147), Prescott, AZ 86302 (☎ **800/266-7534** or 520/445-2000). The visitor information center here is open in the summer Monday through Saturday from 8am to 5pm and on Sunday from 10am to 4pm; winter hours are Monday through Friday from 9am to 5pm, Saturday from 9am to 4pm, and on Sunday from 10am to 2pm.

**GETTING AROUND**    If you need to rent a car, contact **Alamo** (☎ **800/ 327-9633**), **Budget** (☎ **800/527-0700** or 520/778-3806), or **Enterprise Rent-A-Car** (☎ **800/325-8007** or 520/778-6506). If you need a taxi, call **Ace City Cab** (☎ **520/445-1616**).

**SPECIAL EVENTS**    The World's Oldest Rodeo is held each year in early July as part of the city's **Prescott Frontier Days** celebration. Also included in this celebration is a Western art show, a golf tournament, a carnival, and a parade. **Territorial Days,** held in early to mid-June, is another big annual festival with special art exhibits, performances, tournaments, races, and lots of food and free entertainment.

## EXPLORING THE TOWN

A walk around the **Courthouse Plaza** should be your first introduction to Prescott. The stately old courthouse in the middle of the tree-shaded plaza sets the tone for the whole town. The building, far too large for a small regional town such as this, dates from the days when Prescott was the capital of the Arizona Territory.

Surrounding the courthouse and extending north for a block is Prescott's **historic business district.** Stroll around admiring the brick buildings and you'll get an idea that Prescott was once a very important place. Duck into an old saloon or the lobby of one of the town's two historic hotels and you'll understand that the town was also part of the Wild West. After you've gotten a taste of Prescott, there are several museums, listed below, you might like to visit.

If you'd like to learn more about the history of Prescott, contact **Prescott Historical Tours,** 815 Bertrand Ave. (☎ **520/445-4567**), which charges $7 for an informative tour of the city. Call for a reservation.

**Sharlot Hall Museum.** 415 W. Gurley St. ☎ **520/445-3122.** Admission by suggested donation, $4 adult, $3 senior citizens, $5 family. Mar–Oct Mon–Sat 10am–5pm, Sun 1–5pm; Nov–Feb Mon–Sat 10am–4pm, Sun 1–5pm.

In 1882, at the age of 12, Sharlot Hall traveled to the Arizona territory with her parents. From an early age she was fascinated by frontier life. As an adult, she became a writer and historian and began collecting artifacts from Arizona's pioneer days.

From 1909 to 1911 she was the territorial historian, an official government position. In 1928 she opened this museum in Prescott's **Old Governor's Mansion,** a log home that had been built in 1864. Eventually, through the donations of others and the activities of the local historical society, the museum grew into the present complex of historic buildings and gardens.

In addition to the Old Governor's Mansion, which is furnished much as it might have been when it was built, there are several other interesting buildings that can be toured. The **John C. Frémont House** was built in 1875 for the fifth territorial governor. Its traditional wood-frame construction shows how quickly Prescott grew from a remote logging and mining camp into a civilized little town. The 1877 **William Bashford House** reflects the Victorian architecture that was popular throughout the country around the turn of the century. The **Sharlot Hall Building** was built of stone and pine logs in 1934 and now houses museum exhibits on prehistoric and historic Native American artifacts and the history of Prescott. Other buildings of interest include a blacksmith's shop, a schoolhouse, a gazebo, a ranch house built by Sharlot Hall, and an old windmill.

The museum's rose garden honors famous women of Arizona. Every year in early summer, artisans, craftspeople, and costumed exhibitors participate in the **Folk Arts Fair.**

**Phippen Museum of Western Art.** 4701 U.S. 89N. ☎ **520/778-1385.** Admission $3 adults, $2 senior citizens, $1 students. Mon and Wed–Sat 10am–4pm, Sun 1–4pm.

Located on a hill a few miles north of town, the Phippen Museum of Western Art is named after the first president of the prestigious Cowboy Artists of America. The museum exhibits works by both established Western artists and newcomers.

Each year on Memorial Day weekend the museum sponsors the **Phippen Western Art Show.** In the museum store, more than 100 Arizona artists are represented.

**The Smoki Museum.** 147 N. Arizona St. ☎ **520/445-1230** or 520/778-7554. Admission $2. May–Oct Mon–Tues and Thurs–Sat 10am–4pm, Sun 1–4pm. Closed Nov–Apr.

This interesting little museum, which houses a collection of Native American artifacts in a historic stone building, is named for the fictitious Smoki tribe. The tribe was actually dreamed up in 1921 by a group of non-Indians who wanted to inject some new life into Prescott's July 4th celebrations. Despite its phony origins, the museum contains genuine artifacts from many different tribes.

✪ **The Bead Museum.** 140 S. Montezuma St. ☎ **520/445-2431.** Free admission. Mon–Sat 9:30am–4:30pm, Sun by appointment.

This small museum in downtown Prescott is one of the only museums in the country dedicated to beads and body ornamentation. There are cases full of unusual beads from around the world, and half the museum is a bead shop selling many interesting beads.

## SHOPPING

Downtown Prescott, especially along the historic **Whiskey Row** section of Montezuma Street, has numerous interesting shops selling Indian arts and crafts, antiques, and gifts. There are also a few art galleries. One of the most interesting shopping areas here is the brick-paved alley beneath the Hotel St. Michael. You'll find stores selling imports and exclusive fashions. Another Whiskey Row shop worthy of note is the **Arts Prescott Gallery,** 134 S. Montezuma St. (☎ 520/776-7717), a collective of local artists showcasing their locally made crafts.

Prescott makes a lot of superlative claims, including the fact that it's the "Antiques Capital of Arizona." Whether or not this is true, there are plenty of antiques stores downtown. Most of the shops are concentrated along Cortez Street in the block north of Gurley Street and the courthouse.

## ENJOYING THE OUTDOORS

Prescott's most readily recognizable natural landmark is **Thumb Butte,** a rocky outcropping that towers over the forest just west of town. If you'd like to go hiking on Thumb Butte, head west out of town on Gurley Street, which becomes Thumb Butte Road. Where the pavement ends, there is a parking and picnic area and a trailhead for the trail that leads up the butte. The trail itself is very steep, but paved much of the way. The view from the saddle near the top of the butte is superb. The very summit of the butte is a popular rock climbing spot. An alternative return trail makes a loop hike possible.

A few miles north of town is an unusual and very scenic area known as the **Granite Dells.** Here, jumbled hills of rounded granite suddenly jut up from the landscape, creating a maze of huge boulders and smooth rock. Set in this strange geological feature is an artificial lake that makes the scene even more picturesque. This is a great place to go for a walk or to shoot some photos. The best access to the Granite Dells area is at Watson Lake Park just a few miles north of Prescott on Ariz. 89.

Prescott is situated on the edge of a wide expanse of high plains with the pine forests of **Prescott National Forest** at its back. There are hiking trails, several lakes, and campgrounds within the national forest. For maps and information, stop by the Prescott National Forest Office, 344 S. Cortez St. (☎ 520/771-4700).

**Rafter 6 Outdoor Adventures,** P.O. Box 2787, Prescott, AZ 86302 (☎ 520/771-0840), offers overnight cowboy campouts by horseback to the Upper Verde River. On the way they stop at an Indian ruin.

**Granite Mountain Stables** (☎ 520/771-9551), 7 miles north of downtown Prescott, offers trail rides, sunset steak rides, and hayrides. Rates start at $28 for a 1¹/₂ hour ride.

Ready for something a bit more adventurous? How about hang gliding? The **Arizona Hang Gliding Center,** 150 S. Ariz. 69, Suite L, Dewey, AZ 86327 (☎ 800/757-2442 or 520/772-4114), offers tandem flights, either foot-launched or by towplane launch. Prices range from $95 to $250.

Reasonably priced golfing is available at the **Antelope Hills Golf Course,** 19 Clubhouse Dr. (☎ 800/972-6818 in Arizona, or 520/776-7888).

Prescott bills itself as the "Softball Capital of the World," and on summer weekends it's hard to argue with this claim. At parks all over town, teams from around the world play **championship softball.**

## WHERE TO STAY

### EXPENSIVE

✪ **Hassayampa Inn.** 122 E. Gurley St., Prescott, AZ 86301. ☎ 800/322-1927 or 520/778-9434. 58 rms, 10 suites. A/C TV TEL. Apr–Oct $109–$129 double; $150–$175 suite. Nov–Mar $99–$119 double; $140–$160 suite. Rates include full breakfast. AE, CB, DC, DISC, MC, V.

Listed on the National Register of Historic Places, the Hassayampa Inn was built as a luxury hotel in 1927 and evokes the time when Prescott was the bustling capital of the Arizona Territory. In the lobby, stenciled exposed ceiling beams, wrought-iron chandeliers, and arched doorways all reflect a Southwestern heritage, and there are even two pianos, one of which guests may play.

All the guest rooms are a bit different, and feature either original furnishings or antiques. One room here is even said to be haunted, and any hotel employee will be happy to tell you the story of the ill-fated honeymooners whose ghosts are said to reside here.

**Dining/Entertainment:** The Peacock Room (see "Where to Dine," below) exudes the same classic elegance as the rest of the hotel. A small lounge with art nouveau styling provides a quiet place to have a drink in the evening.

**Services:** Room service, laundry service, access to nearby health club.

**Facilities:** Business center.

**Prescott Resort, Conference Center and Casino.** 1500 Hwy. 69, Prescott, AZ 86301. ☎ **800/967-4637** or 520/776-1666. Fax 520/776-8544. 80 rms, 80 suites. A/C TV TEL. $118–$140 double; $148–$170 suite. AE, CB, DC, DISC, MC, V.

This is Prescott's only full-service resort hotel, and with its small casino, it is aiming to siphon off some of the business that once went to Laughlin or Las Vegas. Built high on a hill overlooking the city and the surrounding valley and mountains, the resort mixes urban sophistication and Western chic. Red recessed lights and modern furnishings are offset by a baby grand piano, and Western art is on display throughout. The guest rooms are spacious and comfortable, and each room has its own balcony overlooking the valley.

**Dining/Entertainment:** The Thumb Butte Room, serving American dishes, offers a stunning panorama to accompany the fine meals. For a drink and conversation, there's a lobby lounge. The 24-hour casino is the resort's biggest draw for many guests.

**Services:** Room service, valet/laundry service.

**Facilities:** Outdoor pool, tennis courts, racquetball courts, exercise room, art gallery, beauty salon.

## MODERATE

**Hotel Vendome—Clarion Carriage House Inn.** 230 S. Cortez St., Prescott, AZ 86303. ☎ **800/252-7466** or 520/776-0900. Fax 520/771-0395. 17 rms, 4 suites. TV TEL. $69–$99 double; $125–$159 suite. Rates include continental breakfast. AE, DC, DISC, MC, V.

Built in 1917 as a lodging house, this restored two-story brick building is only 2 blocks from the action of Whiskey Row but far enough away from the noise that you'll get a good night's sleep. The guest rooms are outfitted with new furnishings, but some still have original claw-foot tubs in the bathrooms. Others have modern oval tubs, and all have built-in water filters, air filters, and overhead fans. Of course, this hotel has its own resident ghost as well. Not quite as luxurious as the Hassayampa, yet not as basic as the St. Michael, this hotel offers a good middle-price choice for anyone who wants to stay in a historic hotel.

**Mount Vernon Inn.** 204 N. Mount Vernon Ave., Prescott, AZ 86301. ☎ **520/778-0886.** 4 rms, 3 cottages. TEL. $90–$120 double. Rates include full breakfast. DISC, MC, V.

Built in 1900 by a local bootlegger, this B&B is located on one of the most attractive tree-lined streets in Prescott. The location is quiet, yet convenient to the bustle of downtown. The rooms vary from the comfortable ones of the main house to spacious cottages—one of which was the tack house and one of which was the carriage house. The cottages have full kitchens; consequently breakfast is not included in cottage rates.

**Prescott Country Inn.** 503 S. Montezuma St. (U.S. 89), Prescott, AZ 86303. ☎ **520/445-7991.** 12 rms. TV TEL. $89–$129 double. Rates include continental breakfast. AE, DISC, MC, V.

If you've traveled any sections of old highway in Arizona, you've seen the motor courts that sprang up in the 1930s and 1940s to cater to travelers heading to California. Before being totally renovated, the Prescott Country Inn was just such a motel. Today it's a surprisingly comfortable place to stay. Despite the name, this bed-and-breakfast inn is located only a few blocks from Courthouse Plaza. All the rooms here feature country decor and have their own kitchenettes. Some also have small gas fireplaces. This inn also operates two more suites on the other side of town.

**Prescott Pines Inn.** 901 White Spar Rd. (U.S. 89), Prescott, AZ 86303. ☎ **520/445-7270.** 13 rms. TV TEL. $65–$219 double. MC, V.

As the name implies, this inn is located amid the pines in the mountains to the south of downtown Prescott. The main house is a 1902 Victorian homestead, and the country Victorian theme is maintained throughout the several cottages that comprise this inn. However, all the rooms here have modern furnishings. Numerous porches and verandas and a garden patio invite guests to sit back and relax in the cool shade of the pines. An A-frame chalet sleeping up to four couples is available for large families and groups. It comes with its own deck, a wood stove, and a kitchen. A full breakfast is available for $5 per person.

✪ **Rocamadour Bed & Breakfast for (Rock) Lovers.** 3386 N. Hwy. 89, Prescott, AZ 86301. ☎ **520/771-1933.** 4 rms. A/C TV TEL. $85–$125 double (discounts for stays of 2 or more nights). Rates include full breakfast.

The Granite Dells, just north of Prescott, are the area's most amazing feature, but until recently there was no place to stay amid these giant weathered boulders. Now, at this inn named for a town in France, you can enjoy luxurious surroundings in the midst of this fantastic landscape. Owners Mike and Twila Coffey honed their innkeeping skills as owners of a 40-room château. Pieces of antique furniture from the château can now be found throughout this inn; however, the most elegant pieces can be found in the Chambre Trucy, which also has an amazing underlit whirlpool tub. For those who want to be truly in the midst of the rocks, there is a cottage built into the boulders. This cottage also has a huge whirlpool tub on its deck. Everywhere you turn at this inn there are thoughtful details that make a stay here extremely comfortable. The unique setting, engaging innkeepers, and luxurious touches make this one of the state's must-stay inns.

**Willow Tree Manor.** 306 S. Marina St., Prescott, AZ 86303. ☎ **520/771-9310.** 2 rms (both with shared bath), 1 suite. $95 double; $130 suite. Rates include full breakfast. MC, V.

Located only a couple of blocks from Courthouse Plaza and surrounded by neatly manicured gardens, the Willow Tree Manor is a 1902 Victorian home filled with beautiful and unusual antiques. By far the most appealing of the rooms here is the suite, which includes a turret room with a king-size bed and a private balcony. Breakfast is served with a view of the gardens. If the inn seems strangely familiar to you, that may be because it was used in the filming of the Steve McQueen film *Junior Bonner.*

## INEXPENSIVE

In addition to the following hotel, Prescott has several budget chain motels. See the appendix for toll-free phone numbers. Try the **Super 8 Motel,** 1105 E. Sheldon St. (☎ 520/776-1282), charging $47 to $58 double; and **Motel 6,** 1111 E. Sheldon St. (☎ 520/776-0160), charging $43 to $46 double.

✪ **Hotel St. Michael.** 205 W. Gurley St., Prescott, AZ 86301. ☎ **800/678-3757** or 520/776-1999. Fax 520/776-7318. 72 rms, 3 suites. A/C TV TEL. $36–$62 double; $62–$72 suite. Rates include continental breakfast. AE, MC, V.

Located right on Whiskey Row, this restored hotel offers a historic setting at budget prices. The Hotel St. Michael even has its own resident ghost and features the oldest elevator in Prescott. All rooms are different, and some have only bathtubs (no showers) in their bathrooms. Among the St. Michael's past guests have been Teddy Roosevelt and Barry Goldwater. The casual Café St. Michael, where the complimentary breakfast is served, has brick walls and a pressed-tin ceiling and overlooks Courthouse Square.

## CAMPGROUNDS

In the immediate vicinity of Prescott, there are eight National Forest Service campgrounds. Of these, the Lynx Lake and Granite Basin campgrounds are the most popular, but those south of town are also pleasant and are very convenient to town. Contact the **Prescott National Forest,** 344 S. Cortez St., Prescott, AZ 86303 (☎ 520/771-4700), for more information. For reservations, call **National Forest Recreation Reservations** (☎ 800/280-2267). However, my personal favorite campground in the area is at **Watson Lake County Park,** which is set near a lake in the beautiful Granite Dells area north of town.

## WHERE TO DINE

In addition to the restaurants mentioned below, we enjoy the historic ambience at the **Café St. Michael** for espresso and dessert. It's located at 205 W. Gurley St. (☎ 520/776-1999), across from the courthouse.

### MODERATE

**Murphy's.** 201 N. Cortez St. (a block from Courthouse Plaza). ☎ **520/445-4044.** Reservations recommended for parties of 5 or more. Main courses $12–$18; Sun brunch $5–$14. AE, DISC, MC, V. Mon–Thurs 11am–3pm and 4:30–10pm, Fri–Sat 11am–3pm and 4:30–11pm, Sun 11am–3pm (brunch) and 4:30–10pm. AMERICAN.

"All goods guaranteed to be first class." That was the motto of the store that once occupied this location, and it's now the motto of this popular and traditional restaurant. Murphy's is housed in the oldest mercantile building in the Southwest. The building, which is on the National Register of Historic Places, was built in 1890, and many of the shop's original shelves can be seen in the restaurant's lounge area. Sparkling leaded-glass doors usher diners into a high-ceilinged room with fans turning slowly overhead. In keeping with the historical nature of the building, antiques are on display throughout the restaurant. Mesquite-broiled prime rib is the specialty of the house, and steaks and seafood cooked over the same fire are equally tasty. There's also a daily fresh menu.

✪ **The Palace.** 120 S. Montezuma St. ☎ **520/541-1996.** Reservations suggested on weekends. Main courses $5–$9 at lunch, $10–$17 at dinner. AE, MC, V. Daily 11:15am–2:30pm and 5–9pm. SOUTHWEST/STEAK.

The Palace is the oldest frontier bar in Arizona and just recently was beautifully renovated and returned to the way it might have looked around the turn-of-the-century. This grand hall tends to be noisy and bustling, and is a good place for people-watching. The menu caters to city tastes and includes such choices as a tasty appetizer of grilled tiger prawns wrapped in basil and prosciutto ham, Cajun Caesar salad, and generous portions of steak, pork chops, or meatloaf. The bar area in front is an alternative to waiting for a table, but it may be smoky.

**The Peacock Room.** In the Hassayampa Inn, 122 E. Gurley St. ☎ **520/778-9434.** Reservations recommended. Main courses $13–$20. AE, DC, DISC, MC, V. Mon–Fri 6:30am–2pm and 5–9pm; Sat–Sun 7am–1pm and 5–9pm. CONTINENTAL.

Located in the elegant Hassayampa Inn just off Courthouse Plaza, the Peacock Room evokes a period when Prescott played an important role as the capital of the Arizona Territory. High ceilings, frosted-glass windows, tiny bistro lamps, and spacious

# Now that you know your way around, let's move on to something simple.

**1 800 CALL ATT**®

**For card and collect calls.**

1 800 CALL ATT is the only number you need to know when you're away from home. Dial it from any phone, anywhere* and your calls will always go through to AT&T.
*Available in U.S. and Canada. © 1997 AT&T

**AT&T**

tapestry-upholstered booths give the restaurant a grand and elegant old style. The menu is long and features a lot of variety calculated to keep hotel guests and other diners happy, but the emphasis is definitely on traditional fare such as pasta primavera, lamb chops, and chicken scaloppini. However, you'll also find such less familiar dishes as chicken crêpes Normande, scallops Vera Cruz, and duck au poivre. The wine list is extensive, and the dessert tray always has a few irresistible treats on it. A Sunset Menu is served from 5 to 6pm and is a deal at $12.95.

✪ **Siena Restaurant.** 111 Grove Ave. ☎ **520/771-1285.** Reservations recommended. Main courses $6.50–$12 at lunch, $14–$21 at dinner. AE, DC, DISC, MC, V. Thurs–Sun 11am–2pm, Thurs–Sat 5–9pm. Also open Tues–Wed 11am–2pm and 5–9pm during the summer months. NEW AMERICAN/NEW ITALIAN.

Siena, located in a renovated Victorian cottage several blocks away from Courthouse Plaza, has a great atmosphere and the food to match. The colorful interior is filled with original artworks and out front there is a small patio. What has made the restaurant's reputation are probably first and foremost the fabulous breads (which are available to go as well as for accompanying meals) and dishes such as puffy crayfish and potato fritters, shrimp-and-asparagus pizza with feta cheese, and lamb chops in Mediterranean herbs. The sandwiches at lunch (on that great bread) are not to be missed.

## INEXPENSIVE

**Gurley St. Grill.** 230 W. Gurley St. ☎ **520/445-3388.** Reservations only for parties of 5 or more. Main courses $6–$14. AE, DISC, MC, V. Sun–Thurs 11am–11pm; Fri–Sat 11am–midnight. ITALIAN/AMERICAN.

Run by the same people who operate Murphy's, the Gurley Street Grill is located a block off Courthouse Plaza. Brick walls, ceiling fans, and beveled glass reflect the building's historic heritage. You'll see lots of families here who come for the pastas, pizzas, steaks, burgers, and rotisserie chicken. At lunch, the Sonoran black-bean turkey chili is a good bet, while at dinner, the roast chicken with asiago cheese and pasta is not only delicious but plentiful. The restaurant's bar has many microbrews on tap and attracts a lively, professional crowd.

**Kendall's Famous Burgers & Ice Cream.** 113 S. Cortez St. ☎ **520/778-3658.** Burgers $4–$6. No credit cards. Mon–Sat 11am–8pm, Sun 11am–6pm. BURGERS.

"Do I have to eat all this?" asked a customer once when we were here. "Either that or use it for art," answered the server at the counter. Ask anyone in town where to get the best burger in Prescott and you'll be sent to Kendall's on Courthouse Plaza. This bright and noisy luncheonette serves juicy burgers with a choice of 14 condiments. A basket of fries is a mandatory accompaniment.

**Prescott Brewing Company.** 130 W. Gurley St. ☎ **520/771-2795.** Main courses $5.25–$9. AE, DISC, MC, V. Sun–Thurs 11am–midnight, Fri–Sat 11am–1am. AMERICAN/PUB FOOD.

Popular primarily with a younger crowd, this brewpub keeps a good selection of its own beers and ales on tap, but is just as popular for its cheap and filling meals. Fajita fondue is a specialty here, and of course there are such traditionals as fish and chips, bangers and mash, and even a vegetarian pot pie. There are also several interesting salads and other vegetarian dishes. And what better accompaniment to a good wheat beer than a slice of rich, heavy chocolate ale cake.

## PRESCOTT AFTER DARK

Back in the days when Prescott was the territorial capital and a booming mining town, it supported dozens of rowdy saloons, most of which were concentrated along

Montezuma Street on the west side of Courthouse Plaza. This section of town was known as **Whiskey Row,** and legend has it that there was a tunnel from the courthouse to one of the saloons so lawmakers wouldn't have to be seen ducking into the saloons during regular business hours. On July 14, 1900, a fire consumed most of Whiskey Row, including 25 saloons and bawdy houses. However, concerned cowboys and miners managed to drag the tremendously heavy bar of the Palace Saloon across the street before it was damaged by the fire. (The saloon continued to do business in its new open-air location.)

Today Whiskey Row is no longer the sort of place where respectable women shouldn't be seen, although it does still have a few noisy saloons with genuine Wild West flavor. The **Prescott Brewing Company,** 130 W. Gurley St. (☎ 520/771-2795), across from the Courthouse, is today's answer to the saloons of yore, brewing and serving its own microbrews. Good pub fare is also served. Another place for a drink and some pub food, albeit smaller and quieter, is **The County Seat Bar,** 214 S. Montezuma St. (☎ 520/778-9570), half a block from the Courthouse.

The **Prescott Fine Arts Association,** 208 N. Marina St. (☎ 520/445-3286), sponsors plays, music performances, children's theater, and art exhibits (tickets $3 to $9). The association's main building is a former church that was built in 1899 and is on the National Register of Historic Places.

The **Yavapai College Performance Hall,** 1100 E. Sheldon St. (☎ 520/776-2033), schedules a wide variety of performances throughout the year. Check with the performance hall or the chamber of commerce for a schedule of upcoming events. The Phoenix Symphony Orchestra does several performances annually in Prescott; for information on the schedule, contact the **Yavapai Symphony Association** (☎ 520/776-4255).

## EN ROUTE TO OR FROM PHOENIX: INNOVATIVE ARCHITECTURE & FRESH PRODUCE

If you have an interest in innovative architecture, you may want to continue another 25 miles south from Camp Verde on I-17 to Cordes Junction and Italian architect Paolo Soleri's vision of the future. **Arcosanti** (☎ 520/632-7135) is the slow realization of Soleri's dream of a city that merges architecture and ecology.

Soleri, who came to Arizona to study with Frank Lloyd Wright at Taliesin West, envisions a compact, energy-efficient city that disturbs the natural landscape as little as possible—and that's just what's rising out of the Arizona desert here at Arcosanti. The organic design of this city built of cast concrete will fascinate both students of architecture and those with only a passing interest in the discipline. Arcosanti has been built primarily with the help of students and volunteers who come and live here for various lengths of time.

To help finance the construction, Soleri designs and sells **wind bells** that are cast in bronze or made of ceramic. These distinctive bells are available at the gift shop here.

If you'd like to stay overnight, there are basic accommodations available by reservation, but you must arrive before 5pm. You'll also find a bakery and cafe on the premises. Arcosanti is open daily from 9am to 5pm, and **tours** are held hourly from 10am to 4pm ($5 suggested donation).

If you crave a taste of the country life, stop by **Young's Farm** (☎ 520/632-7272), a country store at the intersection of Ariz. 69 and 169 between I-17 and Prescott. This country farm stand in the middle of the desert sells a wide variety of produce as well as gourmet and unusual foods. Last time we stopped by, the store was pushing its super-hot habañero-pepper pretzel nuggets, just one sample of which left my mouth on fire for at least 30 minutes! Here at Young's Farm, you'll also find a restaurant, nursery, and seasonal festivals (such as hayrides on the Fourth of July and a pumpkin festival in October).

## 3 Jerome & Vicinity

35 miles NE of Prescott, 28 miles W of Sedona, 130 miles N of Phoenix

Clinging to the slopes of Cleopatra Hill high on Mingus Mountain, Jerome beckons to the traveler today just as it once did to miners. The town's fortunes were made and lost on copper from several mines that operated between 1882 and 1950. Over the years Jerome experienced an economic roller-coaster ride as the price of copper rose and fell, and when it was finally no longer profitable to mine the ore, the last mining company shut down its operations and almost everyone left town.

By the early 1960s Jerome looked as if it was on its way to becoming just another ghost town. But just then artists discovered the phenomenal views and dirt-cheap rents to be had here. Before long the town was being called an artists' colony and tourists were beginning to visit to see, and buy, the artwork that was being created.

Today Jerome is far from a ghost town, and on summer weekends the streets are packed with visitors shopping at galleries and crafts shops. The same remote and rugged setting that once made it difficult and expensive to mine copper here has now become one of the town's main attractions.

Jerome is divided into two sections by an elevation of 1,500 vertical feet, with the upper part of town 2,000 feet above the Verde Valley. On a clear day (of which there are quite a few), the view from up here is stupendous—it's possible to see for more than 50 miles, with the red rocks of Sedona, the Mogollon Rim, and the San Francisco Peaks all visible in the distance.

Because Jerome is built on a 30° slope, streets through town switchback from one level of houses to the next. Old brick and wood-frame buildings built into the side of the mountain have windows gazing out into the distance. Narrow streets, alleys, and stairways connect the different levels of town. Jerome is so steep that in the 1920s a dynamite blast loosened the town jail from its foundations and the building slid 225 feet down the hill to its present location.

In recent years the artists who have moved into town have begun to restore and renovate the old houses. Residences, studios, shops, and galleries all stand side by side looking (externally, anyway) much as they did when Jerome was an active mining town. The entire town has been designated a National Historic Landmark.

## ESSENTIALS

**GETTING THERE**   Jerome is on Ariz. 89A roughly halfway between Sedona and Prescott. Coming from Phoenix, take Ariz. 279 from Camp Verde.

**VISITOR INFORMATION**   For information on Jerome, contact the **Jerome Chamber of Commerce,** 50 Main Ave. (P.O. Drawer K), Jerome, AZ 86331 (☎ **520/634-2900**). There is also a trailer in town where visitor information is available.

## SHOPPING & EXPLORING THE TOWN

Simply wandering the streets, soaking up the atmosphere, and shopping are the main pastimes in Jerome. The shops offer an eclectic blend of urban art, chic jewelry, one-of-a-kind handmade fashions, and unusual imports and gifts. **Sky Fire,** 140 Main St. (☎ **520/634-8081**), has a fascinating collection of Southwestern gifts and furnishings and Central American imports. The **Raku Gallery,** at 250 Hull Ave., both upstairs and down, (☎ 520/639-0239), is a place to see and buy interesting art by many artists. The view is fabulous! The **Jerome Gallery,** 240 Hull Ave. (☎ 520/634-7033), has good quality raku ware and ceramics.

Many of the old storefronts in downtown Jerome have now become **artists' studios.** You can watch the artists at work and then have a look at some of the completed pieces being offered for sale.

If you're interested in learning more about the town's mining history there's the **Jerome State Historic Park,** off U.S. 89A on Douglas Road in the lower section of town (☎ 520/634-5381). Located in a mansion that was built in 1916 as a home for mine owner "Rawhide Jimmy" Douglas and as a hotel for visiting mining executives, the Jerome State Historic Park contains both exhibits on mining and a few of the mansion's original furnishings. Built on a hill above Douglas's Little Daisy Mine, the mansion overlooks Jerome and, dizzyingly far below, the Verde Valley. Constructed of adobe bricks made on the site, the mansion contained a wine cellar, billiard room, marble shower, steam heat, and a central vacuum system. The mansion's library has been restored as a period room, while other rooms contain exhibits on copper mining and the history of Jerome. Various types of colorful ores are on display, along with the tools that were once used to extract the ore from the mountain. Admission is $2.50 for adults, $1 for children 7 to 13, and free for children 6 and under. It's open daily from 8am to 5pm, except Christmas Day.

## WHERE TO STAY

**Ghost City Inn.** 541 N. Main St. (P.O. Box 382), Jerome, AZ 86331. ☎ **888/63-GHOST** or 520/63-GHOST. 5 rms (1 with bath). TV. $75–$95 double. Rates include full breakfast. AE, DISC, MC, V.

With its long verandas on both floors, this restored old house is hard to miss as you drive into Jerome from Clarkdale. Most of the rooms here have great views across the Verde River Valley and all are furnished with antiques.

**The Inn at Jerome.** 309 Main St. (P.O. Box 901), Jerome, AZ 86331. ☎ **800/634-5094** or 520/634-5094. 8 rms, 2 with bath. TV. $55–$85 double. AE, DISC, MC, V.

This B&B has similar styling to the Ghost City Inn, with antiques in most rooms. One room has a rustic log bed so tall that you have to climb up into it. Other rooms have equally attractive beds, including a wrought-iron bed, a spool bed, and a sleigh bed. All the rooms have terry robes, ceiling fans, and evaporative coolers (almost as good as air-conditioning). Reception is at the restaurant downstairs. Note that breakfast is not included in the room rate.

**Jerome Grand Hotel.** 200 Hill St. (P.O. Box 757), Jerome, AZ 86331. ☎ **520/634-8200.** Fax 520/639-0299. 20 rms. $55–$85 double. AE, DISC, MC, V.

Although not quite as grand as the name implies, this hotel, the largest in town, is housed in Jerome's former hospital which was built in 1926. The views are certainly grand, as this is just about the highest building in town. The rooms, however, lack the sort of vintage character one would hope for in such an establishment

**✪ The Surgeon's House.** P.O. Box 988, Jerome, AZ 86331. ☎ **800/639-1452** or 520/639-1452. 2 rms (with shared bath), 2 suites. $85–$95 double; $125 suite. Rates include full breakfast. AE, MC, V.

Built in 1917 as the home of Jerome's resident surgeon, this Mediterranean-style home has a jaw-dropping view of the Verde Valley and is surrounded by beautiful gardens. The suite in the old chauffeur's quarters is definitely the room to request.

Located in a separate cottage across the inn's garden, this room has a wall of glass opposite the bed so you can soak in the view from under the covers. Rather unconventional in design, this room has an old tub in one corner and a wall of glass blocks around the toilet. The two rooms in the main house are much more traditional and are filled with antiques that conjure up Jerome's heyday. The inn is on a narrow side lane toward the top of town.

## WHERE TO DINE

**Flatiron Café.** In the Flatiron Building, at the corner of Main St. and Hull Ave. ☎ **520/ 634-2733.** Breakfast and sandwiches $1.50–$7. No credit cards. Daily 7:30am–5pm. BREAKFAST/LIGHT MEALS.

The tiny Flatiron Café serves breakfast and light food such as black-bean hummus, sandwiches, fresh juices, and coffee drinks. It looks as though you could hardly squeeze in here, but there's more seating across the street.

**House of Joy.** Hull Ave. ☎ **520/634-5339.** Reservations required. 4-course meal $22. No credit cards. Sat 3–9pm, Sun 3–8pm. CONTINENTAL.

If you know exactly when you'll be in town, and it happens to be a Saturday or Sunday, you might want to reserve for dinner at the House of Joy. This excellent continental restaurant is housed in a building that was once a bordello, and the interior decor is reminiscent of its colorful history, albeit with dozens of costumed teddy bears all over the dining room. Reservations are an absolute necessity and must be made several weeks in advance because there are only seven tables in the restaurant.

**Jerome Market Deli-Café.** 515 Main St. ☎ **520/634-5165.** Breakfast/sandwiches $3–$7. No credit cards. Daily 11am–6pm, sometimes later in summer. DELI/VEGETARIAN.

This laid-back deli is a meeting point for Jerome's many counter-cultural types and serves homey delights such as frittata made with eggs from free-range chickens, veggie burgers, garlicky grilled eggplant sandwiches, salads of wild greens, and warm apple pie with cheddar cheese. Much more a locals' hangout than other Jerome eateries.

**Wedge on the Edge.** Near the corner of Main St. and Hull Ave. ☎ **520/634-5554.** Pizzas $7.50–$20. No credit cards. Tues–Sun 11am–7pm, sometimes later on Fri–Sat. PIZZA/BAKERY.

You'll find all sorts hanging out here, and Zen philosophy in the bathroom as well. Pizzas are good, and luckily they also sell by the slice in the case of a hunger emergency. Once we bought a pie here and took it out to eat at a viewpoint overlooking the valley. I definitely believe that the awesome view enhanced the pizza's flavor.

## 4 The Verde Valley

Camp Verde: 30 miles S of Sedona; 95 miles N of Phoenix; 20 miles E of Jerome

For thousands of years people have been drawn to the Verde Valley (Green Valley), which was named by the Spanish because it is so lush compared to the surrounding desert. With its headwaters in the Juniper Mountains of the Prescott National Forest, the Verde River flows down through a rugged canyon before meandering slowly across the wide Verde Valley plains. Today these plains are among Arizona's richest agricultural and ranching regions, but long before the first white explorers entered the Verde Valley, the Sinagua were living by the river and irrigating their fields with its waters. Sinagua ruins can still be seen at Tuzigoot and Montezuma national monuments. Later, when white settlers and the area's Yavapai and Apache tribes clashed, the U.S. Army established Fort Verde to protect settlers.

# ESSENTIALS

**GETTING THERE**  Camp Verde is just off I-17 at the junction with Ariz. 260. This latter highway leads northwest through the Verde Valley for 12 miles to Cottonwood.

**VISITOR INFORMATION**  For more information on the Camp Verde area, contact the **Camp Verde Chamber of Commerce,** 435 S. Main St. (P.O. Box 1665), Camp Verde, AZ 86322 (☎ **520/567-9294**).

# EXPLORING THE VERDE VALLEY

When the town of Jerome was busily mining copper, a railway was built to link the booming town with the territorial capital at nearby Prescott. Because of the rugged mountains between Jerome and Prescott, the railroad was forced to take a longer but less difficult route north along the Verde River before turning back south toward Prescott. Today you ride these same tracks aboard the **Verde Canyon Railroad,** 300 N. Broadway, Clarkdale (☎ **800/293-7245** or 520/639-0010). The fare is $34.95 for adults, $30.95 for seniors, $19.95 for children 12 and under (a first-class ticket is $52.95). Call for the schedule and reservations. The route through the Verde River Canyon traverses unspoiled desert that's inaccessible by car and is part of the Prescott National Forest. The views of the rocky canyon walls are quite dramatic, and if you look closely, you can even see traces of ancient Sinagua cliff dwellings in the canyon.

**Dead Horse Ranch State Park** (☎ **520/634-5283**), set on the banks of the Verde River, offers picnicking, fishing, and camping.

Just outside Clarkdale, on the road to Jerome, you'll find **Arizona Botanical Gardens,** 1601 U.S. 89A (☎ **520/634-2166**), which specializes in desert plants. If you live in the state, this is a good place to buy plants for your garden, and even if you don't live here, it's still interesting for avid gardeners.

Six miles away from Jerome, Cottonwood isn't nearly as atmospheric. It does have a few blocks of historic buildings that are slowly filling up with interesting shops that seem to be spillovers from the old hippie days in Jerome. **Old Town Cottonwood's Main Street,** one side of which has a covered sidewalk, contains several shops, galleries, and cafes and is a pleasant place to stroll.

## SPECTACULAR INDIAN DWELLINGS—TUZIGOOT & MONTEZUMA CASTLE NATIONAL MONUMENTS

**TUZIGOOT NATIONAL MONUMENT**  (☎ **520/634-5564**), located just outside Clarkdale off U.S. 89A, preserves a **Sinagua ruin** that perches atop a hill overlooking the Verde River and was inhabited between 1125 and 1400. The Sinagua people, whose name is Spanish for "without water," were contemporaries of the better-known Anasazi, who lived in the canyon lands of northeastern Arizona. The Sinagua were traditionally dry-land farmers relying entirely on rainfall to water their crops. When the Hohokam, who had been living in the Verde Valley since A.D. 600, moved on to more fertile land around 1100, the Sinagua moved in. Their buildings progressed from individual homes called pit houses to communal pueblos. Here at Tuzigoot they built atop a hill, but in other areas they built into the cliffs, just as the Anasazi were doing at that same time.

An interpretive trail leads through the ruins, explaining different aspects of Sinaguan life, and inside the visitor center is a small **museum** displaying many of the artifacts unearthed here. Desert plants, many of which were utilized by the Sinagua, are also identified along the trail.

Monument admission is $2 for adults, free for children 16 and under. Hours in summer are daily from 8am to 7pm; in winter, daily from 8am to 5pm.

**MONTEZUMA CASTLE NATIONAL MONUMENT**   Exit 289 off I-17, is neither castle nor Aztec dwelling—as the name with its reference to the Aztec ruler Moctezuma, traditionally Montezuma, implies. Rather, the Sinagua cliff dwelling, among the best preserved in Arizona, consists of two impressive stone pueblos. The more intriguing of the two is set in a shallow cave 100 feet up in a cliff overlooking Beaver Creek. Construction on this five-story, 20-room village began sometime in the early 12th century. Because Montezuma Castle has been protected from the elements by the overhanging roof of the cave in which it was built, the original adobe mud that was used to plaster over the stone walls of the dwelling is still intact. Another structure, containing 45 rooms on a total of six levels, stands at the base of the cliff. This latter dwelling is not nearly as well preserved as the cliff dwelling because it has been subjected to rains and floods over the years.

For some as-yet-unknown reason these buildings were abandoned by the Sinagua people, who disappeared without a trace in the early 14th century. In the visitor center are **artifacts** that have been unearthed at the ruins.

Deserts are supposed to be dry places where water is scarce, so **Montezuma Well** comes as quite a surprise. Located 11 miles north of Montezuma Castle, Montezuma Well is another prehistoric site. Occupied by both the Hohokam and Sinagua at different times in the past, this desert oasis measures 368 feet across and 65 feet deep. The rock of this area is porous limestone, which is often laced with caverns and underground streams. Montezuma Well resulted when a cavern in the limestone rock collapsed to form a sinkhole. Springs that still flow today soon filled the sinkhole, and eventually local tribes discovered this reliable source of year-round water. The water was used for irrigation by both the Hohokam and Sinagua, and their irrigation channels can still be seen. An excavated **Hohokam pithouse,** built around 1100, and **Sinagua houses and pueblos** stand around the sinkhole.

Admission to Montezuma Castle is $2 for adults, free for children 16 and under; there's no charge to see Montezuma Well. In summer, hours are daily from 8am to 7pm; winter, daily 8am to 5pm. For more information, call ☎ **520/567-3322.**

## FORT VERDE STATE HISTORIC PARK

Just south of Montezuma Castle and Montezuma's Well, in the town of Camp Verde, you'll find **Fort Verde State Historic Park** (☎ **520/567-3275**). Established in 1871, Fort Verde was the third military post in the Verde Valley and was occupied until 1891, by which time tensions with the Indian population had subsided and made the fort unnecessary. The military had first come to the Verde Valley in 1865 at the request of settlers who wanted protection from the local Tonto Apache and Yavapai. The tribes, traditionally hunters and gatherers, had been forced to raid the settlers' fields for food after their normal economy was disrupted by the sudden influx of whites and Mexicans into the area. Between 1873 and 1875 most of the Indians in the area were rounded up and forced to live on various reservations. An uprising in 1882 led to the last clash between local tribes and Fort Verde's soldiers.

Today the state park, which covers 10 acres, preserves three officers' quarters, an administration building, and some ruins. The buildings that have been fully restored house exhibits on the history of the fort and what life was like here in the 19th century. With their white lattices and picket fences, gables, and shake-shingle roofs, the buildings of Fort Verde suggest that life at this remote post was not so bad, at least for officers.

### MORE TO SEE & DO IN CAMP VERDE

There are **costumed reenactments** here on the third Saturday in May and the second Saturday in October.

Admission is $2 for adults, $1 for children 7 to 13, free for children 6 and under. Hours are daily 8am to 5pm.

If you have an interest in 19th-century reenactments or antique cowboy and military gear, stop in at **Kicking Mule Outfitters,** 545 S. Main St., Camp Verde (☎ **520/567-2501**). This store specializes in making reproduction Western leather holsters, gun belts, saddles, and the like. They also sell Western antiques and rent equipment to movie companies.

For a completely different sort of entertainment in Camp Verde, drop by the **Cliff Castle Casino,** 353 Middle Verde Rd. (☎ **520/567-6121**), at exit 289 off of I-17.

## WHERE TO STAY

**Best Western Cliff Castle Lodge & Casino.** P.O. Box 3430, Camp Verde, AZ 86322. ☎ **800/528-1234** or 520/567-6611. Fax 520/567-9455. 82 rms. A/C TV TEL. $58–$99 double. AE, CB, DC, DISC, MC, V.

Although most people staying at this motel just off I-17 at Exit 289 are here to do a little gambling in the adjacent casino, the motel also makes a good base for exploring the Verde Valley. Rooms are standard motel rooms, and there is a pool in summer and a whirlpool year-round.

## WHERE TO DINE

**Blazin' M Ranch Chuckwagon Suppers.** Off 10th St., Cottonwood. ☎ **800/WEST643** or 520/634-0334. Reservations recommended. $14.95 adults, $7.95 children age 8 and under. MC, V. Wed–Sat 5:30–9pm. Closed Jan and Aug. AMERICAN.

Located adjacent to the Dead Horse State Park, the Blazin' M Ranch is more a slice of the Old West than just a place to have dinner. The chuckwagon suppers here include not only a belly-fillin' heap of food, but also a Western variety show. Lots of fun for kids.

**Gas Works Mexican Restaurant.** 1033 N. Main St., Cottonwood. ☎ **520/634-7426.** Meals $2–$8. MC, V. Sun–Fri 9am–5pm. MEXICAN.

If you happen to be hungry and can't hold out for Jerome (or couldn't handle the crowds up at the top of the hill), check out this eclectic hole in the wall in old town Cottonwood. Not only can you get good burritos, but you can also shop for mid-century collectibles and check out the very spendy hand-embroidered denim jackets.

## 5 Sedona & Oak Creek Canyon

106 miles S of the Grand Canyon; 116 miles N of Phoenix; 56 miles NE of Prescott

Though the first settlers didn't arrive in this area until 1877 and the town wasn't incorporated until 1987, Sedona has become one of the most popular destinations in Arizona. People are drawn by the spectacular beauty of the surrounding red-rock cliffs, mesas, and buttes and a mild year-round climate.

How Sedona got its name is one of those legends of the Wild West. It's a simple story of convenience and influence. It seems the postal service didn't like either of the names that had been suggested for the new town at the mouth of Oak Creek Canyon (both were too long to fit on a postal cancellation stamp). So, at the suggestion of his brother, early pioneer and first postmaster Carl Schnebly named the town after his wife, Sedona (a name that fits very nicely on a cancellation stamp).

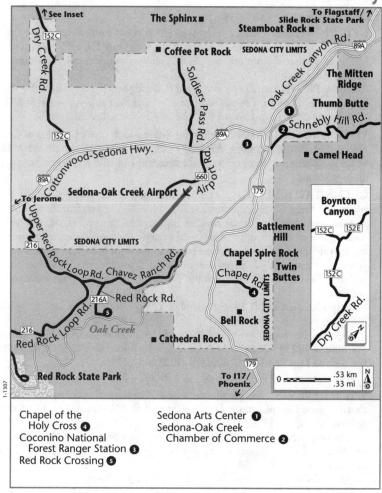

# Sedona & Vicinity

Chapel of the
Holy Cross ❹
Coconino National
Forest Ranger Station ❸
Red Rock Crossing ❺

Sedona Arts Center ❶
Sedona-Oak Creek
Chamber of Commerce ❷

Hollywood producers were among the first to discover the beauty of Sedona. Next came artists, lured by the red-rock landscapes and desert light. More recently the spectacular views and mild climate were discovered by retirees, and when a New Age channeler discovered the "Sedona vortexes," a whole new group descended on the town.

This unusual history has created an ideal destination for lovers of the arts as well as lovers of nature. However, an unfortunate side effect of Sedona's popularity has been unchecked suburban sprawl, which detracts from the beauty of the red rocks. During much of the year, expect traffic jams and parking problems.

The waters of Oak Creek Canyon that first lured settlers, and native peoples before them, still lure visitors to Sedona. Two of Arizona's finest swimming holes are located on Oak Creek, only a few miles from Sedona; one of them, Slide Rock, has been made into a state park.

Sedona is also a good base for exploring much of central Arizona. Several ancient Indian ruins, including an impressive cliff dwelling, are within easy driving distance.

# ESSENTIALS

**GETTING THERE**   Sedona is on Ariz. 179 at the mouth of scenic Oak Creek Canyon. From Phoenix, take I-17 to Ariz. 179 north. From Flagstaff, head south on I-17 until you see the turnoff for U.S. 89A and Sedona. U.S. 89A also connects Sedona with Prescott.

**Sedona Phoenix Shuttle** operates several trips daily between the Phoenix Sky Harbor Airport and Sedona. The one-way fare is $35 and the round-trip fare is $60. Call ☎ **800/448-7988** in Arizona (or 520/282-2066) for schedule information.

**VISITOR INFORMATION**   Contact the **Sedona–Oak Creek Chamber of Commerce,** P.O. Box 478, Sedona, AZ 86339 (☎ **800/288-7336** or 520/282-7722), which also operates a visitor center on the corner of U.S. 89A and Forest Road near uptown Sedona.

**GETTING AROUND**   Gas can be quite a bit more expensive in Sedona than elsewhere in the region, so gas up elsewhere if possible. Also be prepared for slow traffic on roads around Sedona; drivers are often distracted by the red-rock views. Whether traveling in a car or on foot you'll also need to cultivate patience when trying to cross major roads in town. Traffic in Sedona is some of the worst in the state. You may hear or see references to the "Y" while you're in Sedona. The term refers to the intersection of Ariz. 179 and U.S. 89A between the Tlaquepaque shopping plaza and uptown Sedona.

**Budget Rent-a-Car** (☎ **800/527-0700** or 520/282-4602) is located at the Sedona Airport.

Jeeps can be rented for around $80 to $110 a day at **Canyon Jeep Rentals** (☎ **800/224-2229** or 520/282-6061), **Desert Jeep Rentals** (☎ **520/284-1099**), and **Sedona Jeep Rentals** (☎ **800/879-JEEP** or 520/282-2227).

For a taxi, call **Bob's Sedona Taxi** (☎ **520/282-1234**).

**SPECIAL EVENTS**   You can find out what will be happening during your visit by contacting the **City of Sedona Department of Arts & Culture,** P.O. Box 30002, Sedona, AZ 86339 (☎ **520/204-7120**).

Each year in May, Hopi artists gather for the **Hopi Show** (☎ **520/282-6428**), which takes place in uptown Sedona and includes Hopi art, dances, food, and cultural exhibits.

One of the year's big events is the **Sedona Chamber Music Festival,** held each year in late May though early June; contact the Sedona Chamber Music Society, P.O. Box 153, Sedona, AZ 86339-0153 (☎ **520/526-2256** or 520/204-2415), for details.

The **Jazz on the Rocks Benefit Festival** is held each year on the fourth Saturday in September in an outdoor amphitheater with a superb view of the red rocks. For more information contact Sedona Jazz on the Rocks, P.O. Box 889, Sedona, AZ 86339 (☎ **520/282-1985**).

In mid-December each year Sedona celebrates the **Festival of Lights** at Tlaquepaque (☎ **520/282-4838**) by the lighting of thousands of luminárias (paper bags partially filled with sand and containing a single candle each) beginning at sunset.

# EXPLORING RED ROCK COUNTRY

Rugged cliffs, needlelike pinnacles, and isolated buttes rise up from the green forest floor at the mouth of Oak Creek Canyon in Sedona. Layers of different-colored stone deposited during various prehistoric ages form bands through the cliffs above, the most prominent of these bands being the layer of red sandstone called the Schnebly Hill Formation. Because this rosy sandstone predominates around Sedona, the region

## Vortex Power

In recent years Sedona has become one of the world's centers for the New Age movement; large numbers of people come to experience the "power vortexes" of the surrounding red-rock country. You'll see local bulletin boards and publications advertising such diverse New Age services as past-life regressions, crystal healing, astrology readings, reiki, axiatonal therapy, electromagnetic field balancing, soul retrieval, channeling, aromatherapy, myofacial release, and holographickinesiology.

According to believers, a vortex is a site where the earth's unseen lines of power intersect to form a particularly powerful energy field. Page Bryant, a member of the New Age movement, determined through channeling that there were four vortexes around Sedona. Scientists may scoff, but Sedona's vortexes have become so well known that the chamber of commerce visitor center has several handouts to explain them and guide you to them. (Many of the most spectacular geological features of the Sedona landscape also happen to be vortexes.)

The four main vortexes include Bell Rock, Cathedral Rock, Airport Mesa, and Boynton Canyon. **Bell Rock** and **Airport Mesa** are both said to contain masculine or electric energy that boosts emotional, spiritual, and physical energy. **Cathedral Rock** is said to contain feminine or magnetic energy, good for facilitating relaxation. The **Boynton Canyon** vortex is considered an electromagnetic energy site, which means it has a balance of both masculine and feminine energy.

If you're not familiar with vortexes and want to learn more about the ones here in Sedona, consider a vortex tour. These are offered by several companies around town including **Earth Wisdom Tours** (☎ 520/282-4714), **Dorian Tours** (☎ 800/728-4562 or 520/282-4562), and **Sedona Nature Excursions** (☎ 520/282-6735). All offer vortex tours that combine aspects of Native American and New Age beliefs. Tours last about 3 hours and cost about $50 to $55 per person.

You can also stock up on books, crystals, and other spiritual supplies at such stores as **Crystal Magic,** 2978 W. Hwy. 89A (☎ 520/282-1622); or **The Eye of the Vortex Book Center,** 1405 W. Hwy. 89A (☎ 520/282-5614).

---

has come to be known as the red-rock country. Each evening at sunset the red rocks put on a light show that's reason enough for visiting Sedona.

Days can be spent exploring the red-rock country in any of half a dozen different modes of transport. There are Jeep tours, hot-air-balloon flights, horseback rides, mountain-bike trails, hiking trails, and scenic drives suitable for standard cars. (See the following sections, "Organized Tours" and "Sports & Outdoor Pursuits.")

For a relatively easy and yet spectacular red-rock viewing, head south out of Sedona on Ariz. 179, turn left after you cross the bridge over Oak Creek, and head up the unpaved **Schnebly Hill Road.** The road climbs up into the hills above town; every turn yielding a new and breathtaking view. The road eventually climbs to the top of the Mogollon Rim. At the rim is the Schnebly Hill overlook, offering the very best view in the area.

Just south of Sedona, on Ariz. 179, you'll see the aptly named **Bell Rock** on the east side of the road. There's a parking area at the foot of Bell Rock and trails leading up to the top. From Bell Rock, you can see **Cathedral Rock** to the west. This rock is the most photographed formation in Sedona. Adjacent to Bell Rock is **Courthouse Rock,** and not far from Bell Rock and visible from Chapel Road, are **Eagle Head Rock** (from the front door of the Chapel of the Holy Cross—see "Attractions in Town," below—look three-quarters of the way up the mountain to see the eagle's head), the **Twin Nuns** (two pinnacles standing side by side), and **Mother and Child Rock** to the left of the Twin Nuns.

If you head west out of Sedona on U.S. 89A and turn left onto Airport Road, you'll drive up onto **Airport Mesa,** which consists of three small hills commanding an unobstructed panorama of Sedona and the red rocks.

One of the most beautiful areas around Sedona is **Boynton Canyon.** To reach this spectacular canyon, drive west out of Sedona on U.S. 89A, turn right on Dry Creek Road, take a left at the T intersection, and at the next T intersection take a right. On the way to Boynton Canyon, look north from U.S. 89A and you'll see **Coffee Pot Rock,** which is also known as Rooster Rock, rising 1,800 feet above Sedona. Three pinnacles, known as the **Three Golden Chiefs** by the Yavapai tribe, stand beside Coffee Pot Rock. As you drive up Dry Creek Road, you'll see on your right **Capitol Butte,** which resembles the U.S. Capitol building. Just outside the gates of the Enchantment Resort is a parking area for the **Boynton Canyon trailhead.** From the parking area the trail leads 3 miles up into the canyon. The ancient Sinagua people once lived in Boynton Canyon, and the ruins of their homes can still be seen.

South of U.S. 89A and a bit west of the turnoff for Boynton Canyon is Upper Red Rock Loop Road, which leads to **Red Rock Crossing,** a National Forest Service recreation area that has become a must-see spot for almost everyone who visits Sedona these days. Its popularity stems from a beautiful photograph of Oak Creek, with Cathedral Rock in the background—an image that has been reproduced countless times in Sedona promotional literature and on postcards. Unfortunately, a flood a few years ago rearranged the creek so that it no longer looks just as it did when the photo was taken. Nevertheless, it is still an incredibly scenic spot. Hiking trails beginning here lead up to Cathedral Rock. Park admission is $3.

If you continue on Upper Red Rock Loop Road, it becomes gravel for a while before turning into Lower Red Rock Loop Road and reaching **Red Rock State Park** (☎ **520/282-6907**), which flanks Oak Creek. The views here take in many of the rocks listed above, and you have the additional bonus of being right on the creek (though no swimming or wading is allowed). The park admission is $5 per vehicle.

## OAK CREEK CANYON

The **Mogollon Rim** is a 2,000-foot escarpment cutting diagonally across central Arizona and on into New Mexico. At the top of the Mogollon Rim are the ponderosa pine forests of the high mountains, while at the bottom the lowland deserts begin. Among the canyons cutting down from the rim, Oak Creek Canyon is the best known.

U.S. 89A runs down through the canyon from Flagstaff to Sedona, winding its way down from the rim and paralleling Oak Creek. Along the way there are overlooks, parks, picnic areas, campgrounds, cabin resorts, and small inns.

If you have a choice of how first to view Oak Creek Canyon, come at it from the north. Your first stop after traveling south from Flagstaff will be the **Oak Creek Canyon overlook,** which provides a view far down the valley to Sedona and beyond. The overlook is at the edge of the Mogollon Rim, and the road suddenly drops in tight switchbacks just south of here. You may notice that one rim of the canyon is lower than the other. This is because Oak Creek Canyon is on a geologic fault line; one side of the canyon is moving in a different direction from the other.

Though the top of the Mogollon Rim is a ponderosa pine forest and the bottom is a desert, Oak Creek Canyon supports a forest of sycamores and other deciduous trees. In the autumn the canyon is ablaze with red and yellow leaves. **U.S. 89A** is perhaps the most beautiful road in Arizona, and there's no better time to drive it than between late September and mid-October, when the leaves are usually changing.

At the **Cave Spring Campground** there is a self-guided nature walk that describes the riparian environment of Oak Creek. (A riparian area is one along a body of water.) Different plants live in this moist environment, and the plants and water attract a wide variety of animals. Riparian habitats are especially crucial in deserts.

The most popular spot in all of Oak Creek Canyon is **Slide Rock State Park** (☎ 520/282-3034). Located 7 miles north of Sedona on the site of an old homestead, this park preserves a natural water slide. On hot summer days the park is jammed with people splashing in the water and sliding over the algae-covered sandstone bottom of Oak Creek. Sunbathing and fishing are other popular pastimes here. Admission is $5 per vehicle. There's another popular swimming area at **Grasshopper Point,** several miles closer to Sedona. Admission here is $3 per vehicle.

Within Oak Creek Canyon several hikes of different lengths are possible. By far the most popular is the 6-mile round-trip hike up the **West Fork of Oak Creek.** This is a classic canyon-country hike with steep canyon walls rising up from the creek. At some points the canyon is no more than 20 feet wide with walls rising up more than 200 feet. Stop by the Sedona–Oak Creek Chamber of Commerce to pick up a free map listing hikes in the area. The **Coconino National Forest ranger station** (☎ 520/282-4119) on Brewer Road, just west of the intersection of U.S. 89A and Ariz. 179, is also a good source of hiking information.

## ATTRACTIONS IN TOWN

Sedona's most notable architectural landmark is the **Chapel of the Holy Cross,** a small church built right into the red rock on the south side of town. If you're driving up from Phoenix, you can't miss the chapel. It sits high above the road just off Ariz. 179. With its very contemporary styling, the chapel is one of the most architecturally important modern churches in the country. Marguerite Brunswig Staude, a devout Catholic painter, sculptor, and designer, had the inspiration for the chapel in 1932, but it wasn't until 1957 that her dream was finally realized here in Sedona. The chapel's design is dominated by a simple cross forming the wall that faces the street. The cross and the chapel seem to grow directly from the rock. The stark beauty of the church allows the natural beauty of the red rock to speak for itself. The chapel is open daily from 9am to 5pm.

The **Sedona Arts Center,** U.S. 89A at Art Barn Road (☎ 520/282-3865 or 520/282-3809), near the north end of town, serves both as a gallery for artwork by local and regional artists and as a theater for plays and music performances. There are also art classes held here.

A new Sedona Cultural Park is also in the works out on the west side of town and, when completed, will contain an amphitheater and buildings for classes, workshops, and exhibitions, as well as nature trails and picnic areas. Contact the **Sedona–Oak Creek Chamber of Commerce** for details.

## ORGANIZED TOURS

The red-rock country surrounding Sedona is the city's greatest natural attraction, and there's no better way to explore the red-rock country than in a four-wheel-drive vehicle. For more than 30 years, **Pink Jeep Tours** (☎ 800/873-3662 or 520/282-5000) has been heading deep into the Coconino National Forest. They offer several different tours ranging in length from 1 1/2 hours ($30) to 4 hours ($65). You can travel the Sedona backcountry or simply visit the best views in the area.

**Sedona Red Rock Jeep Tours,** 270 N. U.S. 89A (P.O. Box 10305), Sedona, AZ 86339 (☎ **800/848-7728** or 520/282-6826), offers similar tours for $30 to $52. This latter company also does helicopter-Jeep tours and horseback rides.

If you're interested in getting an aerial view of the area, you have several options. **Arizona Helicopter Adventures** (☎ **800/282-5141** or 520/282-0904), and **Skydance Helicopters** (☎ **800/882-1651** or 520/282-1651) both offer short flights to different parts of this colorful region. Prices start around $36 for a 10-minute flight.

If you loved the romance of the film *The English Patient,* don't leave Sedona without going for a ride in a Waco open-cockpit biplane with **Red Rock Biplane Tours** (☎ **888/TOO-RIDE** or 520/204-5939). A 20-minute tour is about $59 per person.

If something a bit slower is more your speed, **Red Rock Balloon Adventures** (☎ **800/258-3754** or 520/284-0040) and **Northern Lights Balloon Expeditions** (☎ **800/230-6222** or 520/282-2274) offer peaceful hot-air-balloon rides over the canyons and sculpted buttes. Expect to pay around $135 for a 1 to 1 1/2 hour ride.

## SPORTS & OUTDOOR PURSUITS

Surprisingly, Sedona has not yet been ringed with golf courses. However, what few courses there are offer superb views to distract you from your game. The **Oak Creek Country Club,** 690 Bell Rock Blvd. (☎ **520/284-1660**), south of town off Ariz. 179, has stunning views from the course (greens fees $25 to $65). The **Sedona Golf Resort** (☎ **520/284-9355**), also located south of town on Ariz. 179, offers similar magnificent views of the red rocks (greens fees $75 Monday through Thursday, $85 Friday though Sunday).

**Kachina Stables,** Lower Red Rock Loop Road (☎ **520/282-7252**), offers guided horseback trail rides. Prices range from $25 for a 1-hour ride to $128 for an all-day ride (includes lunch). There are also breakfast, full-moon, lunch, sunset, personal quest rides, and 2- to 6-day pack trips. Lower Red Rock Loop Road is west of Sedona on U.S. 89A. **El Rojo Grande Ranch and Stables** (☎ **800/36-COWBOY** or 520/ 282-1898), also located in this same area west of Sedona, offers 1- and 1 1/2-hour trail rides ($22 and $32), as well as stagecoach rides ($18 adults, $12.50 children).

Sedona is rapidly becoming one of the mountain-biking Meccas of the Southwest. The red rock here is every bit as challenging and scenic as the famed slick-rock country of Moab, Utah, and much less crowded. Using Sedona as a base, mountain bikers can ride year-round by heading up to Flagstaff in summer and down into the desert lowlands in winter. You can rent a mountain bike from **Sedona Sports,** 245 U.S. 89A (☎ **520/282-6956**) or **Mountain Bike Heaven,** 1695 W. Hwy. 89A (☎ **520/282-1312**). Rates start around $5 per hour or $25 to $35 per day. **Sedona Bike & Bean Shop,** 376 Jordan Rd. in Uptown Sedona (☎ **520/282-3515**), also rents bikes, has a coffee bar, and does group rides. Either of these stores can sell you a map or guide to area rides.

If you want to take the family fishing, try the **Rainbow Trout Farm,** 4 miles north of Sedona on U.S. 89A (☎ **520/282-3379**).

The **tennis courts** at Poco Diablo Resort, on the south side of Sedona, are open to the public for $12 per hour. To make reservations, call the resort at ☎ **520/ 282-7333.**

## SHOPPING

Sedona is well known as an arts community, and it was here that the highly respected Cowboy Artists of America organization was founded in 1965. You'll see their works in some of the nearly 50 art galleries in town. Most of these galleries specialize in traditional Western, contemporary Southwestern, and Indian art. You'll find the greatest concentration of galleries and shops in the many shopping centers around town.

Unfortunately, many of Sedona's shops now specialize in cheap Southwestern gifts that have little to do with art, and it can be difficult weeding through the tacky gift shops to find the real art galleries. For a brochure listing art galleries in Sedona, contact the Sedona Gallery Association, P.O. Box 2038, Sedona, AZ 86339. (☎ 520/282-4037), or pick up the small magazine *Art Life,* available at the Sedona–Oak Creek Chamber of Commerce.

**Compass Rose.** Hillside Courtyard, 671 Ariz. 179. ☎ **520/282-7904.**

Oddly out of place, but certainly welcome on the overly souvenir-oriented Sedona shopping scene, this store sells old maps (up to $3,000), old prints, and Edward S. Curtis sepia-tone photos.

**Garland's Indian Jewelry.** At Indian Gardens, 4 miles north on U.S. 89A. ☎ **520/282-6632.**

A great location in the shade of Oak Creek Canyon and a phenomenal collection of concho belts, squash blossom necklaces, and bracelets make this a worthwhile distraction in this scenic canyon.

✪ **Garland's Navajo Rugs.** 411 Ariz. 179. ☎ **520/282-4070.**

With a very large collection of both contemporary and antique Navajo rugs (they claim it's the biggest in the world), Garland's is the premier Navajo rug shop in Sedona. It also carries a line of Native American baskets and pottery, Hopi kachina dolls, and Navajo sandpaintings.

**Hillside Courtyard.** 671 Ariz. 179. ☎ **520/282-4500.**

This is a shopping center dedicated to art galleries, retail shops, and a couple of restaurants. Carol Dolighan, carrying artistic women's fashions, and Exposures Gallery of the West, featuring Jack Acrey's large-format photographs of red-rock landscapes, are located here.

**Hoel's Indian Shop.** 9440 N. U.S. 89A. ☎ **520/282-3925.**

Located in Oak Creek Canyon, 10 miles north of Sedona past Hoel's Cabins in a private residence, this Native American arts-and-crafts gallery is one of the finest in the region and sells pieces of the highest quality almost exclusively to collectors. It's a good idea to call before coming out here to make sure that the store will be open.

**Sinagua Plaza.** 320 N. U.S. 89A. No phone.

Located in uptown Sedona, this shopping center includes shops such as Joe Wilcox Western Wear, galleries, and restaurants.

✪ **Son Silver West.** 1476 Ariz. 179 (outside Sedona on the south side). ☎ **520/282-3580.**

For those who love everything Southwestern, this shop is a treasure trove of all kinds of interesting stuff, from Native American and Hispanic arts and crafts to antique santo (saint) carvings and rifles, to big imported pots, chile strings, and garden art.

✪ **Tlaquepaque Arts & Crafts Village.** Ariz. 179 (at the bridge over Oak Creek on the south side of Sedona). ☎ **520/282-4838.**

This premier shopping center, with more than 40 stores and restaurants, is named after a famous arts-and-crafts neighborhood in the suburbs of Guadalajara, Mexico, and is designed to resemble an old Mexican village. The maze of narrow alleys, connecting courtyards, fountains, and even a chapel and a bell tower, are worth a visit even if you aren't in a buying mood. Occasionally you'll see artists working here in their combination gallery-studios.

**Touchstone.** 25 Schnebly Hill Rd. (at Ariz. 179). ☎ **520/282-2380.**

Western designers provide the drapey Sedona look for women in handwovens, hand-dyed silk, rayon, cotton, and linen, done up in dresses and matching separates. Colors and textures are beautiful.

# WHERE TO STAY
## VERY EXPENSIVE

✪ **Enchantment Resort.** Boynton Canyon, 525 Boynton Canyon Rd., Sedona, AZ 86336. ☎ **800/826-4180** or 520/282-2900. Fax 520/282-9249. 162 rms and suites. A/C TV TEL. $210–$275 double; $365–$425 one-bedroom suite; $535–$675 two-bedroom suite. AE, DISC, MC, V.

Located at the mouth of Boynton Canyon, this resort more than lives up to its name. The setting is breathtaking, the pueblo-style architecture of the hotel blends in with the canyon landscape, and at press time a new spa was being planned to further pamper guests of the resort. The individual casitas (little houses) of this resort can be booked as two-bedroom suites, as one-bedroom suites, or as single rooms. It's worth booking a suite just so you can enjoy a casita living room. These feature high, beamed ceilings, beehive fireplaces, and built-in shelves set with Native American crafts. The large patios provide dramatic views of the canyon, while skylights brighten the large bathrooms. Computer jacks, coffeemakers, and hair dryers are standard in all the rooms.

**Dining/Entertainment:** The resort's main restaurant (the Yavapai Dining Room; see "Where to Dine," below) and more casual bar and grill both offer terrace tables as well as indoor dining and drinking. Lunch on the terrace here is a meal not to be missed. At dinner the Yavapai Dining Room takes on a more formal atmosphere. The menu in both restaurants features innovative American cuisine.

**Services:** Concierge, room service, tennis lessons, guided hikes, complimentary morning juice and newspaper, local airport shuttle, in-room massages, children's program.

**Facilities:** Four pools, 12 tennis courts, croquet court, whirlpools, fitness center, hiking trails, six-hole golf course, putting green, spa (with aerobics classes, personal training, fitness programs, massages, facials, and aromatherapy).

✪ **Garland's Oak Creek Lodge.** P.O. Box 152, Sedona, AZ 86339. ☎ **520/282-3343.** 16 cabins. $165–$185 double. Rates include breakfast and dinner. MC, V. Closed mid-Nov to Mar 31 and Sun throughout the year.

Located in the heart of Oak Creek Canyon, this lodge may be the hardest place to get a reservation in the whole area. People have been coming here for so many years and like it so much that they make reservations a year in advance (last-minute cancellations do occur, so don't despair). What makes this lodge so special? Maybe it's that you have to drive *through* Oak Creek to get to your log cabin (don't worry, the water's shallow and the creek bottom is paved). Maybe it's the beautiful gardens overlooking the creek. Or maybe it's the atmosphere of an old-time summer getaway that gets people to slow down. Cabins have all been well maintained and are comfortable, yet rustic. The larger cabins have their own fireplaces.

**Dining/Entertainment:** Breakfast and dinner are included in the rates and are served in a rustic dining hall. However, the food is anything but. Organic fruits and vegetables grown on the property are frequently used, and each evening features a different entree accompanied by soup, salad, homemade breads, and dessert. Cocktails and wine are available.

**Services:** Baby-sitting.
**Facilities:** Tennis court.

**Junipine Resort.** 8351 N. Hwy. 89A, Sedona, AZ 86336. ☎ **800/742-PINE** or 520/282-3375. Fax 520/282-7402. 50 condos. TV TEL. $180–$220 one-bedroom condo; $210–$250 two-bedroom condo. AE, DC, DISC, MC, V.

If you're coming up this way with the family and are looking for a place in the cool depths of Oak Creek Canyon, consider this condominium resort. All the condos (here called creek houses) have loads of space (some with lofts), skylights, decks, stone fireplaces, decorative quilts on the walls, full kitchens, and contemporary styling. Some condos also have hot tubs. Best of all, the creek is right outside the door of most condos.

**Dining/Entertainment:** The resort's dining room serves a surprisingly sophisticated Southwestern and regional American menu at reasonable prices, so there's no need to drive all the way into Sedona for a good meal.

**Services:** Baby-sitting and in-room massages are available.

**Los Abrigados.** 160 Portal Lane, Sedona, AZ 86336. ☎ **800/521-3131** or 520/282-1777. Fax 520/282-2614. 172 suites, 1 house. A/C TV TEL. $210–$275 one-bedroom suite for 2; $395 two-bedroom suite for 2; $1,500 house. AE, CB, DC, DISC, MC, V.

If you were born to shop, this might be your idea of heaven; the famous Tlaquepaque shopping center is just across the parking lot from this mission-revival resort on the banks of Oak Creek. And though the resort attempts to be an architectural extension of the shopping center, it doesn't quite succeed.

The suites, though spacious, tend to be Spartanly furnished with a blend of Spanish colonial and contemporary pieces. Microwave ovens provide a bit of convenience, and in the bathrooms you'll find hair dryers and lighted shaving/makeup mirrors. Many of the suites also have fireplaces, whirlpool tubs, and views of the red rocks. The stone house is a historic building with two bedrooms and luxurious upgrades such as steam showers and a whirlpool tub.

**Dining/Entertainment:** With four restaurants, the resort tries to cater to all tastes. Southern Italian and burgers and ribs are the fare at two of the restaurants. The two formal dining rooms focus on steaks and continental fare. Lounge areas include a billiard-and-cigar room and a more lively space with nightly entertainment

**Services:** Concierge, room service, valet/laundry service, baby-sitting.
**Facilities:** Outdoor pool, three tennis courts, hair salon, sauna, whirlpools, health spa (with massages, facials, and other treatments).

## EXPENSIVE

**Apple Orchard Inn of Sedona.** 656 Jordan Rd., Sedona, AZ 86336. ☎ **800/663-6968** or 520/282-5328. Fax 520/204-0044. 7 rms. $120–$160 double. A/C TV TEL. Rates include full breakfast. MC, V.

Situated on a quiet back street in the uptown Sedona area, this inn backs up to parkland that gives it a country feel despite its proximity to shopping and restaurants. Guests often spot javelinas, coyotes, and deer right off the back porch. Built of red sandstone, the inn is owned by the former fire chief of Sedona, and all around are pieces of fire-fighting equipment. Rooms all feature Western themes from Victoriana (not nearly as frilly as most inns, just authentic feeling) to old mission (with Stickley furniture) to a room with the feel of an old barn. The views from the breakfast room and patio are enough to keep you lingering over breakfast right through to lunch.

✪ **Briar Patch Inn.** 3190 N. U.S. 89A, Sedona, AZ 86336. ☎ **520/282-2342.** Fax 520/282-2399. 16 cottages. $149–$295 double. Rates include full breakfast. MC, V.

Located 3 miles north of Sedona on the banks of Oak Creek, this inn's cottages are set amid beautiful shady grounds where birdsong and a babbling creek set the mood. The cottages date back to the 1930s but have all been very attractively renovated and updated (some with flagstone floors). A Western style predominates, and some rooms have a fireplace and kitchenette. Breakfast is often served on a terrace above the creek. All in all, the Briar Patch offers a delightful combination of solitude and sophistication, the quintessential romantic hideaway.

**Canyon Villa Bed & Breakfast Inn.** 125 Canyon Circle Dr., Sedona, AZ 86351. ☎ **800/ 453-1166** or 520/284-1226. Fax 520/284-2114. 11 rms. A/C TV TEL. $125–$205 double. MC, V.

Located in the Village of Oak Creek, 6 miles south of Sedona, this big bed-and-breakfast offers luxurious accommodations and spectacular views of the red rocks. All but one room have views, as do the swimming pool area, living room, and dining room. If you want to just hole up at the inn, you won't be missing the best of the area; it's right out your window. Guest rooms are varied, so there's one to appeal to almost anyone's fancy—Victorian, Santa Fe, country, rustic, Americana, wicker—but no matter what the decor, the furnishings are impeccable, and there are such amenities as terry robes, whirlpool tubs, and double sinks. All the rooms also have balconies or patios, and several also have fireplaces. Breakfasts are lavish affairs meant to be lingered over, and in the afternoons there is an elaborate spread of snacks.

✪ **The Graham Bed & Breakfast Inn & Adobe Village.** 150 Canyon Circle Dr., Sedona, AZ 86351. ☎ **800/228-1425** or 520/284-1425. Fax 520/284-0767. 3 rms, 3 suites, 4 casitas. A/C TV TEL. $129–$189 double; $149–$229 suite; $269–$369 casita. Rates include full breakfast. DISC, MC, V.

Located in the Village of Oak Creek, 6 miles south of Sedona, this inn lies almost at the foot of Bell Rock and features a variety of individually decorated rooms and suites. However, it is the new casitas that are the inn's most impressive rooms. In fact, these are the most impressive rooms in the Sedona area. From the outside, the four casitas, which are approached through a huge Spanish colonial–style gateway, look like an old adobe village arranged around courtyard gardens. However, inside each is very different. The Purple Lizard room comes the closest to matching the exterior design and opts for a sort of colorful Taos-style interior design (lots of purple, teal, and magenta) and includes lots of Southwestern art. The Wilderness is a log cabin inside and has a fireplace that can be seen from both the living room and the double whirlpool tub. The Lonesome Dove is a sort of upscale cowboy cabin complete with wide plank floors, a saddle, guitar, flagstone fireplace, pot-belly stove, and swinging saloon doors leading into the bathroom, which has a round hot tub in a "barrel." The Sunset Casita features a sort of Mediterranean modern aesthetic that includes an elaborate wrought-iron four-poster bed with eight pillows and brocade bedspread, fireplaces in both the bathroom (beside the double whirlpool tub) and the living room, and a wall of glass. In all the casitas, you'll arrive to the fragrance of fresh-baked bread in your own breadmaker and room-appropriate music playing on the CD player. In addition to the whirlpool tubs, there are showers that have cascades of water rather than the usual spray you might expect.

**The Inn on Oak Creek.** 556 Hwy. 179, Sedona, AZ 86336. ☎ **800/499-7896** or 520/ 282-7896. Fax 520/282-0696. 11 rms. A/C TV TEL. $140–$215 double. Rates include full breakfast. AE, DISC, MC, V.

Located right on Oak Creek and just around the corner from the Tlaquepaque shopping plaza, this luxurious modern inn offers the best of both worlds. A shady creekside setting lends it the air of a forest retreat, yet much of Sedona's shopping and many of its best restaurants are within walking distance. There is even a private little park on the bank of the creek. Guest rooms vary considerably in size, but all have interesting theme decors. Some of our personal favorites are the Garden Gate (with a picket fence headboard on the bed), Hollywood Out West (with old movie posters), the Rose Arbor (with creek views from both the tub and the bed), and the Angler's Retreat (with bentwood furniture, fly-fishing decor, and a fabulous view). Because the inn is built out over the creek, staying here is almost like staying on a cruise ship; you can look straight down into the water from your balcony. All the rooms come with VCRs and gas fireplaces, too.

**L'Auberge de Sedona.** 301 L'Auberge Lane (P.O. Box B), Sedona, AZ 86339. ☎ **800/ 272-6777** or 520/282-1661. Fax 520/282-2885. 98 rms, suites, and cottages. A/C TEL. Dec–Feb (excluding Christmas holiday) $150–$190 double, $210–$235 suite, $225–$335 cottage; Mar–Nov and Christmas holiday $170–$220 double, $230–$270 suite, $305–$385 cottage. AE, CB, DC, DISC, MC, V.

Located in the heart of uptown Sedona, this romantic getaway offers a variety of room types, all of which are done in an incongruous country French decor (the desert doesn't really conjure up images of France). With two restaurants and only a pool and whirlpool for activities, this resort definitely aims for the less active guest who prefers fine dining to working up a sweat.

If you want spectacular views and sunsets, opt for the Orchards rooms, which face the red rocks. Our personal favorites are the rooms with gas fireplaces. If you crave a creekside cottage set beneath shady sycamores, choose one of the cottages on the banks of Oak Creek. These are decorated in a frilly, country French style, with canopy beds and fireplaces but no TVs. If the atmosphere of a French hunting lodge appeals, try a lodge room, which will have a few rustic furnishings.

**Dining/Entertainment:** L'Auberge (see "Where to Dine," below) is one of Sedona's finest and most expensive restaurants. Pink linens and bone china set the tone for the five-course French dinners. A more casual restaurant in the Orchards section serves simpler meals.

**Services:** Concierge, room service, in-room massage, baby-sitting.

**Facilities:** Small outdoor pool, whirlpool, French boutique.

**The Lodge at Sedona.** 125 Kallof Place, Sedona, AZ 86336. ☎ **800/619-4467** or 520/ 204-1942. Fax 520/204-2128. 10 rms, 3 suites. A/C. $120–$160 double; $185–$225 suite. Rates include full breakfast. MC, V.

Located on the newer, west side of Sedona, this large B&B is surrounded by desert landscaping that includes rock gardens, waterfalls, and pine trees. The rooms are all individually decorated, and our personal favorites are the Lariat Room and the Master Suite (which is absolutely huge and has a stone fireplace). Upstairs rooms tend to be small and have showers only (instead of shower/tub combinations), so, if you can afford to spend a little more, opt for a downstairs room, several of which have their own whirlpool tubs. With 13 rooms and suites, this lodging may seem large for a bed-and-breakfast inn, but size doesn't limit the hospitality of the owners, who make all their guests feel very much at home.

**Poco Diablo.** 1752 S. Hwy. 179 (P.O. Box 1709), Sedona, AZ 86339. ☎ **800/528-4275** or 520/282-7333. Fax 520/282-9712. 149 rms, 3 suites. A/C TV TEL. Mid-Feb to mid-Nov $95–$245 double, $240–$360 suite; mid-Nov to mid-Feb $75–$245 double $240–$360 suite. AE, DC, DISC, MC, V.

This golf and tennis resort is located on the southern outskirts of Sedona, with Oak Creek running right through the 25-acre grounds, and the green fairways of the nine-hole golf course provide a striking contrast to the red rocks and blue skies. The small lobby exudes Arizona sophistication with mission-style furnishings, contemporary Southwestern art, and Native American baskets and pottery. Ask for one of the newly refurbished rooms, of which those with golf course or red-rock views are the best. These latter rooms have whirlpool tubs and fireplaces and are done in a neo-rustic Southwest decor. The views here are not as good as at other comparable properties in the area, but the staff is courteous and helpful. As the only golf resort in Sedona, Poco Diablo will appeal to golfers. The lower end rooms are quite economical, though the upper end rooms seem a bit overpriced.

**Dining/Entertainment:** The restaurant offers views of the golf course and red rocks and a menu that features Southwestern and continental dishes. The small dark lounge is basically a sports bar.

**Services:** Concierge, room service, valet/laundry service, in-room massages.

**Facilities:** Two small pools, three whirlpools, four tennis courts (two lighted), racquetball courts, nine-hole golf course.

✪ **Saddle Rock Ranch.** 255 Rock Ridge Dr., Sedona, AZ 86336. ☎ **520/282-7640.** Fax 520/282-6829. 3 rms. A/C. $125–$145 double. Rates include full breakfast. No credit cards.

The stunning views alone would make this one of Sedona's best lodging choices, but on top of the views, you get classic Western ranch styling (the house was built in 1926) in a home that once belonged to Barry Goldwater. Walls of stone and adobe, a flagstone floor in the living room, huge exposed beams, and plenty of windows to take in the scenery are enough to enchant guests even before they reach their rooms. And the rooms don't disappoint, either. In one you'll find Victorian elegance, in another an English canopy bed and stone fireplace. Dressing areas and private gardens add to the charm. The third room is a separate little Western cottage with a lodgepole-pine bed, flagstone floors, and beamed ceiling. The pool and whirlpool are surrounded by a flagstone terrace and enjoy one of the best red-rock views in town.

## MODERATE

**Best Western Arroyo Roble Hotel.** 400 N. Hwy. 89A (P.O. Box NN), Sedona, AZ 86336. ☎ **800/7-SEDONA,** 520/282-4001, or 602/252-4483 in Phoenix. Fax 520/282-4001. 53 rms, 7 suites, 1 cottage, 7 villas. A/C TV TEL. $85–$135 double; $135–$175 suite; $155–$195 cottage; $250–$300 villa. AE, CB, DC, DISC, MC, V.

This five-story hotel crowding up against U.S. 89A in uptown Sedona perches above Oak Creek with views of the red rocks and provides many of the amenities of a more expensive resort. All rooms come with king- or queen-size beds and a private balcony or patio. Surrounded by Oak Creek Canyon's shady sycamores, the villas are below the main hotel building and consist of two-bedroom condominiums with two fireplaces, $2^1/2$ bathrooms, two TVs, a stereo, a VCR, and two private patios or balconies. These latter accommodations are ideal for families, and the extensive athletic facilities are sure to keep the kids happy. The hotel doesn't have its own restaurant, but there are plenty within walking distance.

**Facilities:** An outdoor and an indoor/outdoor pool, whirlpools, two tennis courts, handball and racquetball courts, a billiard room, an exercise room, a steam room and sauna, and a video-games room.

**Matterhorn Motor Lodge.** 230 Apple Ave., Sedona, AZ 86336. ☎ **520/282-7176.** Fax 520/282-0727. 23 rms. A/C TV TEL. Mar–Nov $74–$94 double; Dec–Feb $49–$74 double. AE, MC, V.

Located in the heart of the uptown shopping district, the Matterhorn is convenient to restaurants and shopping, and all rooms have excellent views of the red-rock canyon walls. The motel has had a complete makeover in the past few years and now has an adobe-style exterior and modern furnishings in the guest rooms. In-room amenities include coffeemakers, hair dryers, and refrigerators. An outdoor pool and whirlpool provide recreation. Although the hotel overlooks busy U.S. 89A, if you lie in bed and keep your eyes on the rocks, you'll never notice the traffic below you.

**Rose Tree Inn.** 376 Cedar St., Sedona, AZ 86336. ☎ **888/282-2065** or 520/282-2065. 5 rms. TV. $85–$125 double. AE, MC, V.

This little inn is located only a block from Sedona's uptown shopping district and is tucked amid pretty gardens on a quiet street. The inn consists of an eclectic cluster of older buildings that have all been renovated. Four of the rooms have kitchenettes, which makes these good choices for families, or for a longer stay. All the rooms are furnished a little bit differently—one Victorian, one Southwestern, another with a gas fireplace. There's also a whirlpool here, and complimentary coffee and tea are available.

✪ **Sky Ranch Lodge.** Airport Rd. (P.O. Box 2579), Sedona, AZ 86339. ☎ **520/282-6400.** Fax 520/282-7682. 94 rms. A/C TV TEL. $75–$155 double. MC, V.

This motel is located atop Airport Mesa, which gives it the most stupendous view in town. From here you can see the entire red-rocks country, with Sedona filling the valley below. Of course, the rooms with the best views are also the most expensive ($100 to $155), but if you're willing to walk a few feet for your view, you can stay here for much less. The rooms are fairly standard motel style.

## INEXPENSIVE

**Sedona Motel.** P.O. Box 1450 (almost at the intersection of Ariz. 179 and U.S. 89A), Sedona, AZ 86339. ☎ **520/282-7187.** 16 rms. A/C TV TEL. $32–$95 double. AE, DISC, MC, V.

The Sedona Motel looks like any other older motel from the outside, but once you check in, you'll find a few surprises. First and foremost is the view across the parking lot. You can pay twice as much in Sedona and not have views this good. The windows are double-paned so the rooms stay cool and quiet. New carpets, wallpaper, and pine furniture, as well as contemporary bathroom fixtures, all add up to comfort and a good value.

## CAMPGROUNDS

Within the reaches of Oak Creek Canyon along U.S. 89A, there are four National Forest Service campgrounds. Of these Bootlegger Campground, 9 miles north of town, is the largest, though Manzanita Campground, 6 miles north of town, is the most pleasant. Other Oak Creek Canyon campgrounds include Pine Flat, 13 miles north of town, and Cave Springs, 12 miles north of town. For more information on area campgrounds stop by the **Coconino National Forest ranger station** (☎ **520/ 282-4119**) on Brewer Road, just west of the intersection of U.S. 89A and Ariz. 179.

## WHERE TO DINE

In addition to the restaurants described below, **The Atrium** (☎ 520/282-5060) at Tlaquepaque shopping center is a good place to stop for breakfast or lunch.

## VERY EXPENSIVE

**L'Auberge.** In L'Auberge de Sedona, 301 L'Auberge Lane. ☎ **520/282-1667.** Reservations recommended. Main courses $28–$36; fixed-price 6-course dinner $60. AE, CB, DISC, DC, MC, V. Mon–Sat 7:30–10:30am, Sun 7:30–10am; daily 11:30am–2pm and 5:30–9pm. FRENCH.

The name conjures up an image of a French country inn, and though this particular L'Auberge happens to lie in the red-rock country of central Arizona, it manages to live up to its name. Oak Creek and a terrace are just outside the windows, and sycamores shade the banks. Inside, all is country elegance in the fairly fussy French decor. The menu is changed daily, but you'll always have a choice of several hors d'oeuvres and main dishes. Among the main-course choices on a recent evening were salmon with Dungeness crab and lobster sauce and a filet mignon with wild mushrooms and black truffle sauce. For dessert there was an array of delicate pastries.

## EXPENSIVE

**René at Tlaquepaque.** Tlaquepaque, Ariz. 179. ☎ **520/282-9225.** Reservations highly recommended. Main courses $8–$11 at lunch, $17–$27 at dinner. AE, MC, V. Daily 11:30am–2:30pm; Mon–Thurs 5:30–8:30pm, Fri–Sat 5:30–9pm. CONTINENTAL/AMERICAN.

Located in Tlaquepaque, the city's upscale south-of-the-border-theme shopping center, René's is an elegant and traditional dining experience. This is a place for a special lunch or dinner in a refined atmosphere with lace curtains and paintings by Southwestern artists. We began with *escargots* with garlic butter and *salade* Walter, a flavorful blend of baby spinach and sautéed wild mushrooms. Next came a tender venison of antelope with whiskey juniper-berry sauce and potato-encrusted red snapper, which was both crispy and juicy. We finished off with a flambéed dessert and selections from the after-dinner drink cart, then settled back to enjoy a warm glow of well-being. Rack of Colorado lamb (served for two people), though expensive, is superb and is the house signature dish.

✪ **Yavapai Dining Room.** In the Enchantment Resort, 525 Boynton Canyon Rd. ☎ **520/204-6000.** Reservations highly recommended. Main courses $8–$12 at lunch, $17–$33 at dinner. AE, DISC, MC, V. Daily 7am–2:30pm and 5:30–9:30pm; brunch Sun 10:30am–2:30pm. SOUTHWESTERN.

If you crave a taste of the good life, make a reservation for dinner at the Enchantment Resort's dining room. Put on your best clothes and ensconce yourself in the realm of the rich and famous. It may be expensive, but where else can you dine inside a genuine power vortex?

The best time to come is at sunset, when the desert sun paints the red rocks in fiery hues, but if you can't make it for dinner, be sure to take in the view at lunch. The dinner menu changes regularly, but on a recent visit included a rose of smoked salmon with mesquite honey and thyme vinaigrette as an appetizer. The salads are made with the finest produce of the season, and even simple black-bean soup gets a special touch with applewood-smoked bacon and cumin-scented tortilla strips. Though you never know what you might find on the day's menu, you might try chef Kevin Maguire's seared tangerine pork tenderloin with an apricot chipotle glaze. The dessert tray is, of course, enchantingly decadent.

## MODERATE

✪ **Cowboy Club.** 241 N. U.S. 89A. ☎ **520/282-4200.** Reservations recommended. Main courses $8–$30. AE, MC, V. Daily 11am–9 or 10pm. SOUTHWESTERN.

With its big green booths, huge steer horns over the bar, and saddles and guns adorning the walls, this place looks like a glorified cowboy steakhouse, but when you see the menu, you'll know this is more than your average meat-and-potatoes place. This is big flavor country, where chicken, steak, venison, buffalo, fish, and shrimp dishes are served with sauces such as smoked-Gouda cream, cherry chili, or raspberry-plum barbecue. Salad dressing choices include black bean–orange with star anise, red pepper–papaya, and banana-garlic (sounds wierd—tastes great). Smaller and simpler sandwiches, burgers, and pasta are available, too. Desserts are a high culinary art form here; when we heard the descriptions, we just couldn't say no. Service is relaxed and friendly.

**Fournos Restaurant.** 3000 W. U.S. 89A. ☎ **520/282-3331.** Reservations highly recommended. Main courses $13–$15. No credit cards. Thurs–Sat seatings at 6 and 8pm, Sun (brunch), seating at noon. GREEK.

Pots and ladles hang from the kitchen ceiling in this tiny place where chef Demetrios cooks up a storm, preparing such dishes as Greek salads with homemade kalamata olives and shrimp flambéed in ouzo and baked with feta cheese. Greek music plays, and his engaging wife, Shirley, seats guests at tables. A lot of the people who come here know each other, and even if you don't, Shirley has a way of making everybody feel at home. The menu is written on a chalkboard and includes such specialties as Colorado lamb Cephalonian with herbs and potatoes, and baked fish Mykonos with a sauce of yogurt, onions, mayonnaise, and butter. Other specialties are rack of lamb and lamb Wellington, for a slightly higher price than the usual dinners. Greek pastry such as a flourless semolina-honey sponge cake comes with ice cream and fruit for a textural and decadent dessert.

✪ **The Heartline Cafe.** 1610 W. U.S. 89A. ☎ **520/282-0785.** Reservations recommended. Main courses $7–$12 at lunch, $11–$26 at dinner. AE, DISC, MC, V. Mon–Sat 11:30am–3pm; daily 5:30–9:30pm. SOUTHWESTERN/INTERNATIONAL.

The heartline, from Zuñi mythology, is a symbol of health and longevity, and also a symbol for the food here—healthful, and very creative. Service is good, and crusty bread appears on the table immediately (accompanied by unusual spreads such as one made from butternut squash). Creative Southwestern flavor combinations are the rule here with such dishes as duck with a cranberry-pear-walnut compote and grilled salmon marinated in tequila and lime and served with ancho-chile aioli showing up on a recent menu. Lunch fare leans toward tasty sandwiches and salads. A beautiful courtyard outside and a traditionally elegant interior are both places to savor a meal and enjoy a selection from the reasonably priced wine list, or desserts such as white-chocolate mousse, crème brûlée, or fruit berry tart with warm hazelnut sauce.

**Pietro's Italian Restaurant.** 2445 W. U.S. 89A. ☎ **520/282-2525.** Reservations recommended. Main courses $16–$23; pastas $14–$17. AE, CB, DC, MC, V. Spring–fall daily 5:30–9:30pm; winter daily 5–9pm. TUSCAN.

For excellent Italian meals in Sedona, it's almost impossible to beat Pietro's, which pushes the envelope of Italian creativity. Pietro's is located in a nondescript little building—you would never guess that it's one of the better places in town. You'll find appetizers such as calamari with smoked tomato-and-basil aioli and grilled eggplant rolled with goat cheese in a red-pepper sauce. For a pasta you might try fettuccine with duck confit, savoy cabbage, shiitake mushrooms, and figs in a port-wine sauce. Main courses are not quite as daring, but such dishes as boneless game hen with fresh rosemary, lemon, garlic, and olive oil are certainly tasty. A wide range of wines, including many rare Italian reds and American boutique wines are available by the glass. Between 5 and 6:30pm, less expensive southern Italian dinners, such as lasagne, are served.

**Sedona Swiss Restaurant & Cafe.** 350 Jordan Rd. ☎ **520/282-7959.** Reservations recommended. Main courses $12–$24. MC, V. Restaurant Mon–Sat 11am–2pm and 5:30–9:30pm. Pastry shop Mon–Sat 7:30am–6pm. SWISS/FRENCH.

Chef Robert Ackermann, this restaurant's founder and formerly the executive chef at the Swiss embassy in Washington, D.C., is the raison d'être for this authentically Swiss restaurant located in a quiet spot near old-town Sedona. You'll find classic Swiss and French fare such as *Rahmschnitzel* (sautéed pork scaloppini in a mushroom-cream sauce), rack of lamb Provençale, and the house specialty, *Galgenspiess*—beef tenderloin dramatically flambéed at your table. You can dine inside the cozy restaurant or outside on the patio. Visit the cafe and pastry shop for dessert and coffee that are truly a European experience.

---
**Readers Recommend**
---

**Judi's Restaurant & Lounge,** 40 Soldier Pass Rd. at La Pasada Plaza, U.S. 89A. ☎ **520/282-4449.** "What was special: 1. The outdoor garden with roses and tables was a romantic relief from the desert. 2. Good blend of traditional and adventure-some on menu, e.g.curried scallops with grapes. 3. Fresh homemade desserts—raspberry-jalapeño ice cream! 4. Five types of fresh bread to accompany meal. 5. Good wine selection and waitstaff."

—Carolyn G. Volan, Chandler, AZ

---

## INEXPENSIVE

**Dara Thai.** 34 Bell Rock Plaza, in the Village of Oak Creek. ☎ **520/284-9167.** Reservations recommended Thurs–Sun. Main courses $7–$13. MC, V. Tues–Sun 11am–9pm. THAI.

This is a little oasis for good Asian food in the Village of Oak Creek. *Pad Thai,* fried noodles with shrimp, chicken, bean sprouts, and topped with peanuts, was medium-spicy and well-flavored. Our appetizer, *Tod Mun,* patties of ground fish and curry paste, was juicy and spicy with *galangal,* a root spice, and cooled by a cucumber sauce. Although prices seemed a little on the high side for Thai food, they are probably in line with other prices in Sedona.

**The Hideaway Restaurant.** Country Square, Ariz. 179. ☎ **520/282-4204.** Reservations for 10 or more only. Main courses $5–$8 at lunch, $6.50–$10 at dinner. AE, DISC, MC, V. Summer daily 11am–10pm; winter daily 11am–9pm. ITALIAN/DELI.

Hidden away at the back of a shopping plaza near the "Y," this casual family restaurant is as popular with locals as it is with visitors. Pizzas, subs, spaghetti, and lasagne are the mainstays here, and though they're all as good as you'd expect, it's the views that really make a meal here a special event. From the shady porch there are views of the creek down below and the red rocks rising up across the canyon.

**Muse Literary Cafe.** In Artesania Plaza, 251 Ariz. 179. ☎ **520/282-3671.** Reservations recommended for dinner. Main courses $9–$16. AE, DISC, MC, V. Tues–Sun 11:45am–8pm. INTERNATIONAL.

Located at the "Y," this casual place is a combination New Age bookstore and cafe. There are views of the red rocks out the windows and live music in the evening. In other words. this is a totally mellow place to enjoy an economical sunset dinner, with a variety of choices from steaks to pastas. Well-done vegetables and niçoise olives in the salad are nice touches, and the breads, which include a tasty focaccia and cheese roll-up, are fabulous. A key lime tart, wonderfully tangy, lives up to its name. Until 5pm, Cuban sandwiches and other creative combinations of ingredients stuffed between two pieces of bread (mostly baguettes and focaccia) are served.

## SEDONA AFTER DARK

If you're searching for the best margarita in town, head for **El Rincon** (☎ **520/282-4648**), a Mexican restaurant in Tlaquepaque Village. For a more sophisticated ambience, try a resort hotel lounge. Without a doubt, the lounge and patio at the Enchantment Resort are the best choices for a sunset cocktail. (See above under "Where to Stay" for directions.)

Sedona now has its own microbrewery. **Oak Creek Brewing Co.,** 2050 Yavapai Dr. (☎ **520/204-1300**), makes amber and nut brown ales as well as seasonal brews and has a small tasting room and beer garden rather than a full-scale brewpub.

The **Sedona Arts Center,** U.S. 89A at Art Barn Road (☎ **520/282-3865** or 520/282-3809), has frequent performances of music and plays.

# 7

# The Grand Canyon & Northern Arizona

The Grand Canyon—the name is at once apt and inadequate. How can words sum up the grandeur of 2 billion years of the earth's history sliced open by the power of a single river? Once a barrier to explorers and settlers, today the Grand Canyon attracts visitors from all over the world who gaze awestruck into its seemingly infinite depths.

Yet other parts of northern Arizona also contain worthwhile, and less crowded, attractions. Only 60 miles south of the great yawning chasm stand the San Francisco Peaks, the tallest of which, Humphreys Peak, rises 12,643 feet above sea level. These peaks, sacred to the Hopi and Navajo, are ancient volcanoes. Smaller volcanoes in this region once made the land fertile enough to support an ancient Sinagua culture that has long since disappeared, leaving only the ruins of its ancient villages.

Amid northern Arizona's miles of windswept plains and ponderosa pine forests is the city of Flagstaff, which at 7,000 feet in elevation is one of the highest cities in the United States. It's also home to Northern Arizona University, whose students ensure that it's a lively town. Born of the railroads, Flagstaff has preserved its Western heritage in its restored downtown historic district.

In the name of progress and developing the desert, the great river canyons of Arizona have been dammed. Their sometimes quiet, sometimes angry waters have been turned into vast lakes. Among these is Lake Powell, created by the construction of the Glen Canyon Dam. The bitter fight to preserve Glen Canyon is a thing of the past, and today the lake is popular with boaters, anglers, and water-skiers. This lake, with its miles of water mirroring steep canyon walls hundreds of feet high, is one of northern Arizona's curious contrasts—a vast artificial reservoir in the middle of barren desert canyons.

## 1 Flagstaff

150 miles N of Phoenix; 32 miles E of Williams; 80 miles S of Grand Canyon Village

Due to its wide variety of accommodations and restaurants, Flagstaff is the best all-around staging point for explorations of the Grand Canyon and the rest of northern Arizona. Its university supports a lively cultural community, and the town is also home to one of the finest museums in Arizona: the Museum of Northern Arizona.

The San Francisco Peaks, just outside the city, are one of Arizona's winter playgrounds, with the Arizona Snowbowl attracting thousands of skiers to the slopes. In summer, sightseers ride the lift to the top of the mountain for the views, and hikers come to explore the miles of mountain trails. Hikers and photographers also enjoy exploring Sunset Crater National Monument, a colorful cinder cone created by a volcanic eruption hundreds of years ago.

Situated at 7,000 feet above sea level, Flagstaff is one of the highest cities in the country, and is the county seat of Coconino County, the second-largest county in the United States. The town has done much to preserve its pioneer heritage, but its history goes much farther back. Within a short drive of the city are ancient Sinagua cliff dwellings and the ruins of large pueblos that were built more than 700 years ago.

## ESSENTIALS

**GETTING THERE**   Flagstaff is on I-40, one of the main east-west interstates in the United States. I-17 also starts here and heads south to Phoenix. U.S. 89A connects Flagstaff to Sedona by way of Oak Creek Canyon. U.S. 180 connects Flagstaff with Grand Canyon Village, and U.S. 89 with Page.

Flagstaff's Pulliam Airport, which is located 3 miles south of town off I-17, is served by **America West Express** (☎ 800/235-9292) from Phoenix.

Flagstaff is also served by **Amtrak** (☎ 800/872-7245 or 520/774-8679 for schedule information) from Chicago and Los Angeles. The train station is at 1 E. Rte. 66.

**VISITOR INFORMATION**   The **Flagstaff Visitors' Center,** at 1 E. Rte. 66 (☎ 800/842-7293 or 520/774-9541), is open Monday through Saturday from 7am to 6pm and on Sunday from 7am to 5pm.

**GETTING AROUND**   Car rentals are available from **Avis** (☎ 800/331-1212 or 520/774-8421), **Budget** (☎ 800/527-0700 or 520/779-0306), **Enterprise** (☎ 800/325-8007 or 520/526-1377), **Hertz** (☎ 800/654-3131 or 520/774-4452), and **National** (☎ 800/227-7368 or 520/774-3321).

If you need a taxi, call **Friendly Cab** (☎ 520/774-4444).

**Pine Country Transit** (☎ 520/779-6624), provides public bus transit around the city; the fare is 75¢ for adults. In summer, **Flagstaff Trolleybuses** operate between many of Flagstaff's hotels, the downtown area, the university, and most of the city's museums. A day pass costs $6. Phone **Nava-Hopi Tours** (☎ 520/774-5003) for more information.

**ORIENTATION**   Downtown Flagstaff is located just north of I-40. Milton Road, which at its southern end becomes I-17 to Phoenix, leads past the Northern Arizona University on its way into downtown where it becomes Route 66. Santa Fe Avenue runs parallel to the railroad tracks. Downtown's main street is San Francisco Street, while Humphreys Street leads north out of town toward the San Francisco Peaks and the South Rim of the Grand Canyon.

**CURRENCY EXCHANGE**   Foreign currency can be exchanged at **Bank One,** which has offices at 100 W. Birch St. (☎ 520/779-7411) and 2520 N. Fourth St. (☎ 520/779-7351).

## ENJOYING THE OUTDOORS

Flagstaff is northern Arizona's center for outdoor activities. Chief among these is snow skiing at **Arizona Snowbowl** (☎ 520/779-1951 for information; or 520/779-4577 for a snow report, 602/957-0404 in Phoenix for a snow report) on the slopes of Mount Agassiz, from which you can see all the way to the North Rim of the Grand Canyon. There are four chair lifts, 32 runs, and 2,300 vertical feet of slopes. There

# The Grand Canyon & Northern Arizona

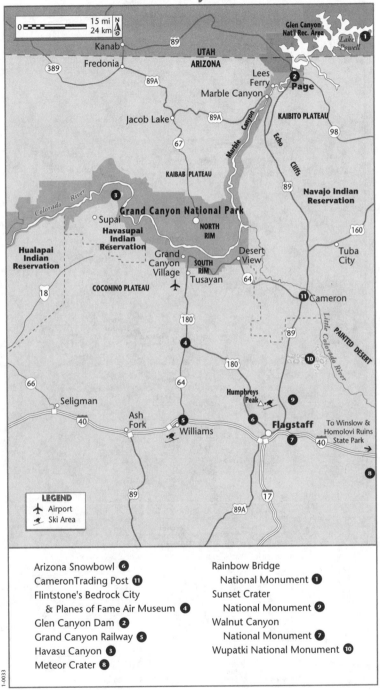

LEGEND
✈ Airport
🎿 Ski Area

Arizona Snowbowl ❻
CameronTrading Post ⓫
Flintstone's Bedrock City
  & Planes of Fame Air Museum ❹
Glen Canyon Dam ❷
Grand Canyon Railway ❺
Havasu Canyon ❸
Meteor Crater ❽

Rainbow Bridge
  National Monument ❶
Sunset Crater
  National Monument ❾
Walnut Canyon
  National Monument ❼
Wupatki National Monument ❿

1-0033

# Flagstaff

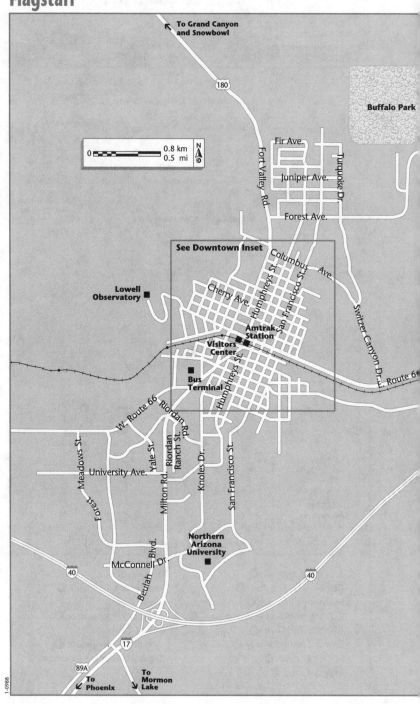

To Grand Canyon and Snowbowl

Buffalo Park

180

Fort Valley Rd.

Fir Ave.

Juniper Ave.

Turquoise Dr.

Forest Ave.

0    0.8 km
     0.5 mi
N

See Downtown Inset

Columbus Ave.

Lowell Observatory

Cherry Ave.

Humphreys St.

San Francisco St.

Switzer Canyon Dr. E

Amtrak Station

Visitors Center

Route 66

Bus Terminal

Humphreys St.

W. Route 66

Riordan Rd.

Meadows St.

Yale St.

Riordan Ranch St.

Knoles Dr.

San Francisco St.

Forest

University Ave.

Milton Rd.

40

Beulah Blvd.

McConnell Dr.

Northern Arizona University

40

17

89A

To Phoenix

To Mormon Lake

1-0988

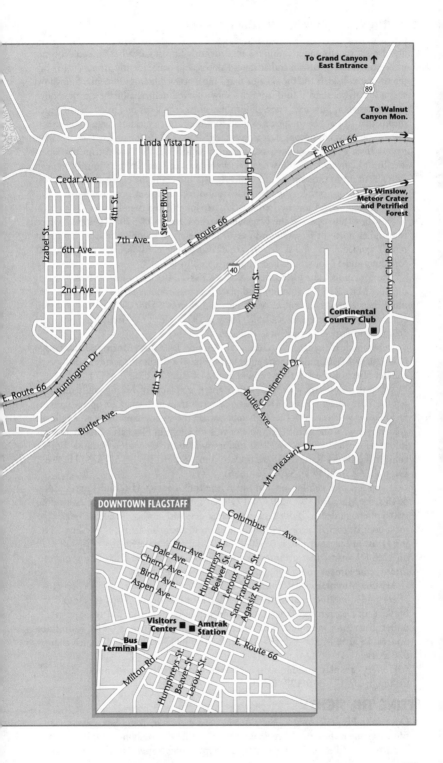

To Grand Canyon
East Entrance

89

To Walnut
Canyon Mon.

E. Route 66

Linda Vista Dr.

Cedar Ave.

4th St.

Fanning Dr.

To Winslow,
Meteor Crater
and Petrified
Forest

Izabel St.

Steves Blvd.

7th Ave.

E. Route 66

Country Club Rd.

6th Ave.

40

2nd Ave.

Elk Run St.

Continental
Country Club

Huntington Dr.

4th St.

Continental Dr.

E. Route 66

Butler Ave.

Butler Ave.

Mt. Pleasant Dr.

**DOWNTOWN FLAGSTAFF**

Columbus Ave.

Elm Ave.

Dale Ave.

Cherry Ave.

Birch Ave.

Aspen Ave.

Humphreys St.

Beaver St.

Leroux St.

San Francisco St.

Agassiz St.

Visitors
Center

Amtrak
Station

Bus
Terminal

E. Route 66

Milton Rd.

Humphreys St.

Beaver St.

Leroux St.

are also ski rentals and a children's ski program. This ski area has an excellent mix of beginner, intermediate, and advanced slopes, and consequently attracts many different types of skiers. As the ski area that's most accessible from Phoenix, Snowbowl sees a lot of weekend traffic from the snow-starved denizens of the desert. Snow, sometimes good powder, is not, unfortunately, as reliable as one might wish, which means that this is not the place to head for your winter vacation unless you're certain of the snow conditions. Lift tickets range from $19 for a half-day midweek pass to $31 for a weekend all-day pass. There's a shuttle bus ($4 round-trip) that operates from highway U.S. 180 whenever chains are required. In the summer you can ride a chair lift to the summit of Mount Agassiz and enjoy the expansive views across seemingly all of northern Arizona. The round-trip lift ticket price is $9 for adults, $6.50 for seniors, $5 for children 6 to 12, free for children 5 and under.

Snowbowl also operates the **Flagstaff Nordic Center** (☎ 520/779-1951), which is 16 miles north of Flagstaff and has 40 kilometers of groomed track. Equipment rentals, guided tours, and ski lessons are all available here. All-day trail passes are $12 for adults and $7 for seniors and children ages 8 to 12.

The **Mormon Lake Ski Center** (☎ 520/354-2240), 28 miles south of Flagstaff on Lake Mary Road, is another good place for cross-country skiing. This center has more than 21 miles of groomed ski trails and charges $5 for a 1-day trail pass. Ski rentals and lessons are also available. There are a couple of easy trails here, but most are in the intermediate to advanced range.

Snowmobile rentals are also available at Mormon Lake from **Mormon Lake Lodge** (☎ 520/774-0462). Rates start at $24 per hour. If a sleigh ride is more your speed, contact **Hitchin' Post Stables,** 4848 Lake Mary Rd. (☎ 520/774-1719).

When there's no snow on the ground, there are plenty of **hiking trails** throughout the San Francisco Peaks. Many national forest trails in the area are open to mountain bikes as well as hikers. Late September, when the aspens have turned to a brilliant golden yellow, is one of the best times of year for a hike in Flagstaff's mountains. For information on the many excellent hiking trails in the Coconino National Forest, contact the **Peaks Ranger District,** Coconino National Forest, 5075 N. Hwy. 89, Flagstaff, AZ 86004 (☎ 520/526-0866).

If you feel like saddlin' up and hittin' the trail, contact **Hitchin' Post Stables,** 4848 Lake Mary Rd. (☎ 520/774-1719 or 520/774-7131). This horseback-riding stable offers guided trail rides, sunset steak rides, and cowboy breakfast rides. The most popular trail ride goes into Walnut Canyon, site of ancient cliff dwellings. **Flying Heart at Flagstaff** (☎ 520/526-2788), located 3¹⁄₂ miles north of Flagstaff Mall on U.S. 89, leads rides up into the foothills of the San Francisco Peaks and out through the juniper and pinyon forests of the lower elevations.

**Arizona Mountain Bike Tours** (☎ 800/277-7985 in Arizona, or 520/779-4161) offers guided mountain-bike rides for all levels of experience. Trips are around the outskirts of Flagstaff or to the canyons and volcanoes of northern Arizona. If you'd rather just rent a mountain bike and head out on your own, stop by **Mountain Sports,** 1800 S. Milton Rd. (☎ 800/286-5156 or 520/779-5156), which charges $20 a day.

Golfers can play a round at the 18-hole **Elden Hills Golf Course,** 2380 N. Oakmont Dr. (☎ 520/527-7997).

## SEEING THE SIGHTS

Downtown Flagstaff along Santa Fe Avenue, San Francisco Street, Aspen Avenue, and Birch Avenue is the city's **historic district.** The old brick buildings of this neighborhood are now filled with interesting little shops selling Native American handcrafts, arts and crafts by local artisans, and various other Arizona souvenirs such as rocks, minerals, and crystals. This historic area is worth a walk through even if you aren't shopping.

## MUSEUMS, PARKS & CULTURAL ACTIVITIES

✪ **Museum of Northern Arizona.** 3101 N. Fort Valley Rd. (2 miles north of downtown Flagstaff on U.S. 180). ☎ **520/774-5213.** Admission $5 adults, $4 seniors, $3 students, $2 children 7–17. Daily 9am–5pm. Closed Jan 1, Thanksgiving, and Dec 25.

This small but surprisingly thorough museum is a good first stop to acquaint yourself with this region. Here you'll learn through state-of-the-art exhibits about the archaeology, ethnology, geology, biology, and fine arts of the region. The cornerstone exhibit of the museum is an exhibit that explores life on the Colorado Plateau from 15,000 B.C. to the present. Among the other displays are a life-size kiva ceremonial room and a small but interesting collection of kachinas. The large gift shop is full of contemporary Native American arts and crafts. Throughout the summer there are special exhibits focusing on Hopi, Navajo, and Zuñi arts and crafts. A recent expansion has given this museum much more exhibit space.

The museum building itself is made of native stone and incorporates into its design a courtyard featuring vegetation from the six life zones of northern Arizona. Outside the museum is a short self-guided nature trail that leads through a narrow canyon strewn with boulders.

**Lowell Observatory.** 1400 W. Mars Hill Rd. ☎ **520/774-2096.** Admission $3 adults, $1 children 5–17. Visitor center and exhibits Apr–Oct daily 9am–5pm; Nov–Mar daily noon–5pm. Evening telescope viewing is more frequent in summer than in winter.

Located atop aptly named Mars Hill is one of the oldest astronomical observatories in the Southwest. Founded in 1894 by Percival Lowell, the observatory has played important roles in contemporary astronomy. Among the work carried out here was Lowell's study of the planet Mars and his calculations that led him to predict the existence of the planet Pluto. It wasn't until 13 years after Lowell's death that Pluto was finally discovered, almost exactly where he had predicted it would be. Today this is still an important research facility, but most astronomical observations are now carried out at Anderson Mesa, which is 10 miles farther away from the lights of Flagstaff.

The facility consists of several observatories, a large new visitor center with numerous fun and educational exhibits, and outdoor displays. Keep in mind that the telescope domes are not heated, so if you come up to observe the stars on a wintry night, be sure to dress appropriately.

**Arizona Historical Society/Pioneer Museum.** 2340 N. Fort Valley Rd. ☎ **520/774-6272.** Admission $1 donation. Mon–Sat 9am–5pm. Closed Jan 1, Thanksgiving, and Dec 25.

This museum houses a historical collection from northern Arizona's pioneer days. The main museum building is a large stone structure that was built in 1908 as a hospital for the indigent. Among the exhibits are pieces of camera equipment used by Emery Kolb at his studio on the South Rim of the Grand Canyon. Many of Kolb's photos are also on display. Several small exhibit rooms cover various aspects of life in northern Arizona during the pioneer days and later. You'll see a doctor's office filled with frightening instruments, barbed wire and brands, dolls, saddles, and trapping and timber displays.

**Riordan Mansion State Park.** 1300 Riordan Ranch St. (off Milton Rd./U.S. 89A, just north of the junction of I-40 and I-17). ☎ **520/779-4395.** Admission $4 adults, $2.50 youths 7–13, free for children 6 and under. May–Sept daily 8am–5pm; Oct–Apr daily 11am–5pm. Guided tours on the hour. Closed Dec 25.

Built in 1904 for local timber barons Michael and Timothy Riordan, this 13,000-square-foot mansion is actually two houses connected by a large central hall. Each of the two Riordan brothers and his family occupied one half of the house and they had the rooflines constructed differently so that visitors could tell the two sides apart. The home is built in the Craftsmen style and though it looks like a log cabin, it's actually only faced with log slabs.

The Riordans played important roles in the early history of Flagstaff. They helped establish the first Roman Catholic church, the first library, the power company, and the phone company.

**The Arboretum at Flagstaff.** Woody Mountain Rd. ☎ **520/774-1441.** Admission May–Oct $3 adults ($1 other months), free for children 6 and under. May–Oct daily 9am–4pm; Mar 16–Apr and Nov–Dec 23 Mon–Fri 9am–4pm. Guided tours at 11am and 1pm. Closed Dec 24–Mar 15.

Covering 200 acres, this arboretum focuses on plants of the high desert, coniferous forests, and alpine tundra, all of which are environments found in the vicinity of Flagstaff. There are also a butterfly garden, an herb garden, a shade garden, and a passive solar greenhouse.

## ORGANIZED TOURS

**Gray Line/Nava-Hopi Tours** (☎ **800/892-8687** or 520/774-5003) operates several day-long tours of northern Arizona. These tours include excursions to the South Rim of the Grand Canyon; Lake Powell and Page (including a float trip on the Colorado River); Sedona and the Verde Valley; the Navajo Indian Reservation; the Hopi Indian Reservation; and the Petrified Forest, Painted Desert, and Meteor Crater. Other smaller companies offering similar tours include **Northern Arizona Scenic Tours** (☎ **520/773-7788**) and **Sun Tours** (☎ **800/483-4488** or 520/774-7400).

## JOINING AN ARCHAEOLOGICAL DIG

On the north side of Flagstaff on U.S. 89 there is a small archaeological site called Elden Pueblo. These Sinagua ruins are not much to look at, but if you'd like to help out with the excavation of the site, you can. Each summer, the **Elden Pueblo Archaeological Project,** P.O. Box 3496, Flagstaff, AZ 86003 (☎ **520/527-3475**), hosts several public days as well as field schools for members of the Arizona Archaeological Society (AAS). Field schools cost $65 per week plus the $20 AAS membership dues.

# WHERE TO STAY
## EXPENSIVE

✪ **The Inn at 410.** 410 N. Leroux St., Flagstaff, AZ 86001. ☎ **800/774-2008** or 520/774-0088. 9 rms. $110–$155 double. Rates include full breakfast. MC, V.

Located only 2 blocks from downtown Flagstaff, this restored 1907 bungalow provides convenience, pleasant surroundings, comfortable rooms, and delicious breakfasts. The rooms are all individually decorated (the cowboy and Santa Fe rooms are our personal favorites). The living room and dining room are very bright, and in addition, you'll find a large front porch with a swing and a patio dining area. Some of the rooms are in a new building to one side of the old house, and one of these rooms is wheelchair-accessible.

## MODERATE

**Arizona Mountain Inn.** 685 Lake Mary Rd., Flagstaff, AZ 86001. ☎ **520/774-8959.** 3 rms, 16 cabins. $90–$110 double; $75–$105 cabin. DISC, MC, V.

Located just a few minutes south of downtown Flagstaff, the Arizona Mountain Inn is a quiet mountain retreat set beneath shady pine trees. Though there are three bed-and-breakfast rooms in the main building, all the rest of the accommodations here are cabins that can sleep anywhere from 2 to 16 people. Many of the rustic cabins are A-frames or chalets and each is a little bit different from the others. The family-oriented inn has 13 acres surrounding it, and beyond this are miles of national forest. Facilities include volleyball and basketball courts, a playground, horseshoe pits, and a coin laundry.

✪ **Best Western Woodlands Plaza Hotel.** 1175 W. Route 66, Flagstaff, AZ 86001. ☎ **800/ 528-1234** or 520/773-8888. Fax 520/773-0597. 183 rms, 2 suites. A/C TV TEL. $59–$129 double; $75–$135 suite. AE, CB, DC, DISC, MC, V.

With its elegant marble-floored lobby, the Woodlands Plaza is easily the most up-scale and luxurious hotel in Flagstaff. A baby grand piano, crystal chandelier, traditional European furnishings, and contemporary sculpture all add to the unexpected luxury, as do intricately carved pieces of furniture and architectural details from different Asian countries. Traditional European styling, with Southwestern touches, is used in the guest-room decor.

One of the two restaurants here serves Japanese meals with tableside cooking and a sushi bar, while the other features traditional American fare with a few international and Southwestern dishes. The hotel also offers room service, an outdoor pool, two whirlpools, a sauna, steam room, and fitness center.

**Embassy Suites.** 706 S. Milton Rd., Flagstaff, AZ 86001. ☎ **800/EMBASSY** or 520/774-4333. Fax 520/774-0216. 119 suites. A/C TV TEL. $89–$139 double. Rates include full breakfast. AE, DC, DISC, ER, JCB, MC, V.

Conveniently located near both Northern Arizona University and downtown Flagstaff, this all-suite hotel is a good choice for families or business travelers. Breakfast is served in a bright, plant-filled room, and in the evening complimentary cocktails are served in a librarylike lounge. The guest rooms are all divided into sleeping rooms and living rooms, with wet bar, refrigerator, microwave oven, two TVs, and two phones. The hotel also has a pool, a whirlpool, and a small exercise room. Room service is available.

**Little America.** 2515 E. Butler Ave., Flagstaff, AZ 86003. ☎ **800/352-4386** or 520/ 779-2741. Fax 520/779-7983. 248 rms, 9 suites. A/C TV TEL. $65–$119 double; $135–$225 suite. AE, CB, DC, DISC, MC, V. Take Exit 198 off I-40.

At first it might seem as if Little Americas, of which there are several around the West, are little more than glorified truck stops, but on closer inspection you'll find that this one is an excellent economy hotel. It's a spread-out complex beneath the pines on the east side of Flagstaff. The rooms vary in size but all have small private balconies. The interior decor is dated but fun, with a French provincial theme throughout the guest rooms. The TVs are absolutely huge. Suites include one with a fireplace and one with a sauna.

There's a casual dining room that's open 24 hours a day, plus a more formal restaurant that serves continental dishes and features live piano music in the evenings. The hotel also offers room service, laundry/dry cleaning, courtesy van, a pool, health club passes, badminton, volleyball, croquet, and jogging/hiking trails. There's also a large gift shop just off the lobby.

## INEXPENSIVE

In addition to the hotel listed below, you'll also find many budget chain motels in Flagstaff. These include **Motel 6,** 2440 E. Lucky Lane (☎ **520/774-8756**), charging $36 to $48 for a double; **Motel 6,** 2745 S. Woodlands Village (☎ 520/779-3757), charging $38 to $56 for a double; and **Travelodge,** 2520 E. Lucky Lane (☎ 520/779-5121), charging $51 to $64 for a double.

✪ **Hotel Monte Vista.** 100 N. San Francisco St., Flagstaff, AZ 86001. ☎ **800/545-3068** or 520/779-6971. Fax 520/779-2904. 65 rms, 58 with bath; 5 suites. TV TEL. $25–$40 double without bath, $40–$90 double with bath; $85–$110 suite. Lower rates in winter. AE, MC, V.

Originally opened in 1927, the Hotel Monte Vista was renovated in the mid-1980s and today is a historic budget hotel with old-fashioned flair. In its heyday the Monte Vista is said to have hosted Clark Gable, John Wayne, Walter Brennan, Alan Ladd, Jane Russell, Spencer Tracy, Lee Marvin, Carole Lombard, and Gary Cooper. In the small, dark lobby (which is still a bit the worse for wear) are painted ceiling beams and Victorian furniture. Shops and a rather noisy bar take up most of the space on the ground floor. The rooms vary in size and many are furnished with oak furniture and ceiling fans. We like the corner rooms best because they have windows on two sides. You'll find a coffee shop and lounge on the first floor. The hotel also has a dormitory for hostelers, with beds going for $12 a night.

## A NEARBY LODGE

**Mormon Lake Lodge.** P.O. Box 38012, Mormon Lake, AZ 86038. ☎ **520/354-2227.** Fax 520/354-2356. 13 cabins. $45–$98 per cabin. 2-night minimum on summer weekends and holidays. AE, MC, V.

Located 30 miles southeast of Flagstaff on the shore of a wide, shallow lake that seems to be more meadow than lake these days, this lodge is an authentically rustic place that is popular in both summer and winter. In summer, the lodge is a favorite escape from the heat for desert dwellers, and in winter this is a base for cross-country skiers and snowmobilers. Cabins range from rustic log cabins (our favorites) to modern duplex cabins that unfortunately lack character. In the restaurant and saloon, which have a real Old West flavor, moose and buffalo heads hang from the walls.

# WHERE TO DINE

## MODERATE

**Black Bart's.** 2760 E. Butler Ave. (take Exit 198 off I-40). ☎ **520/779-3142.** Reservations recommended. Main courses $12–$24. AE, MC, V. Sun–Thurs 5–9pm, Fri–Sat 5–10pm (until 9pm in winter). STEAK/SEAFOOD.

Arizona is full of odd restaurants and Black Bart's must surely be classified as one of the most unusual. Part of an RV park and antique store, this warehouse-size restaurant serves gigantic steaks complete with cowboy beans, "leaves-and-weeds" salads, and sourdough biscuits. But the restaurant's other main draw is the entertainment, provided by a player piano and the service staff (local university students), who get up on stage and sing for your supper.

**Chez Marc Bistro.** 503 Humphreys St. ☎ **520/774-1343.** Reservations recommended. Main courses $13–$23. AE, DC, MC, V. Daily 11:30am–2:30pm and 5:30–9pm. FRENCH.

If it weren't for the busy street in front, this stone and half-timbered house could pass for a country inn. The renovated old house has a big front porch and inside are several small dining rooms, one of which has a cozy fireplace. Creative combinations are the rule here, though country French cooking is the main focus. The wine list is excellent. This is the most elegant restaurant in town.

**Cottage Place Restaurant.** 126 W. Cottage Ave. ☎ **520/774-8431.** Reservations recommended. Main courses $13–$22.50. AE, MC, V. Tues–Sun 5–9:30pm. CONTINENTAL.

Located in a rather run-down neighborhood between the railroad tracks and the university, Cottage Place is just what its name implies—a little cottage. There are only a few tables in each of the dining rooms, so dining here is an intimate and somewhat formal affair. We like the front rooms with their walls of windows, especially at sunset on a summer evening. Though the menu is primarily continental, there are French, Southwestern, and Middle Eastern influences as well. The house specialties are chateaubriand and rack of lamb (both served for two), and for vegetarians there are always several choices. There's a good wine list, and every evening there's a different selection of tempting desserts.

**Down Under.** In the Carriage House Antique Mall, 413 N. San Francisco St. ☎ **520/ 774-6677.** Reservations for parties of 6 or more only. Main courses $4–$8 at lunch, $10–$20 at dinner. AE, MC, V. Mon–Fri 11am–3pm; Tues–Sat 5:30–9pm. NEW ZEALAND/ INTERNATIONAL.

What exactly is New Zealand cuisine? That question draws many people into having a meal in this cozy restaurant in a historic carriage house built in 1910. Well, it's a bit like British food (meat pies, sausage rolls, potato-leek soup), but there is also, as you would expect, lots of lamb—lamb stew, grilled rack of lamb with minted lemon sauce, and a lamb-and-mushroom casserole. However, this is just the beginning. The chef also prepares the likes of pine nut–encrusted chicken breast with white wine and raisin sauce, fruit-stuffed pork tenderloin with port wine sauce, and several vegetarian dishes. For dessert you can have a traditional bread pudding, a Swiss pastry from the Swiss patisserie in Sedona, or New Zealand's light-and-fruity pavlova. Wines are fairly inexpensive.

**Kelly's Christmas Tree Restaurant.** 5200 E. Cortland Blvd. ☎ **520/526-0776.** Reservations recommended. Main courses $12–$20. AE, MC, V. Mon–Sat 11:30am–3pm and 5–10pm, Sun 4–9pm. AMERICAN.

This oddly named restaurant is located in a shopping center on the east side of town and has long been a Flagstaff favorite with diners who like to stick to familiar fare. A festive holiday atmosphere reigns year-round in the red, white, and green dining room, and the menu runs the gamut from fettuccine Alfredo to curried chicken to beef Stroganoff. There are daily seafood specials as well as such menu standards as sautéed scallops. Chicken and dumplings is, however, Kelly's most popular dish.

**✪ Marc's Cafe Americain Brasserie & Wine Bar.** 801 S. Milton Rd. ☎ **520/556-0093.** Reservations recommended. Main courses $8.50–$22. AE, DC, DISC, MC, V. Daily 11am–3pm and 5–10pm. FRENCH.

This spinoff from Chez Marc is a more casual brasserie style eatery in a strip mall along Milton Road. Surprisingly, Marc's manages to rise high above its location. Crêpes, pastas, and rotisseried meats are the specialties here, but you can also get bouillabaisse and a few other seafood dishes. An open kitchen in the middle of the restaurant provides a bit of entertainment. More than 30 wines are available by the glass.

**Sakura Restaurant.** In the Woodlands Plaza Hotel, 1175 W. Route 66. ☎ **520/773-9118.** Reservations recommended. Main courses $12–$20. AE, DC, DISC, MC, V. Mon–Sat 11:30am– 2pm and 5–10pm, Sun 5–10pm. JAPANESE.

Though major cities around the world have had teppanyaki Japanese restaurants in the form of Benihanas for years, this style of tableside cooking is still something of a novelty in Flagstaff. Dinner or lunch here is an event, with the chef's culinary floor show at a grill in front of your table. Steaks, grilled seafood, and chicken are the mainstays of the menu, but there's also crispy tempura, warming miso soup for cold winter nights, and, at the sushi bar, sushi made with fresh fish flown in from Los Angeles. Shoji screens give the dining room a Japanese atmosphere.

## INEXPENSIVE

✪ **Beaver Street Brewery.** 11 S. Beaver St. ☎ **520/779-0079.** Main courses $7–$9. AE, DISC, MC, V. Mon–Thurs 11:30am–10pm, Fri–Sat 11:30am–midnight, Sun 11:30am–9pm. BURGERS/PIZZA.

This big microbrewery and cafe located in a former supermarket on the south side of the railroad tracks in downtown Flagstaff serves up several good brews, but it also does great pizzas and burgers. The Beaver Street pizza, which is made with roasted garlic pesto, sun-dried tomatoes, fresh basil, and soft goat cheese is particularly tasty. There are also good salads, such as a Mongolian beef salad with sesame-ginger dressing, and even fondue. A pot-bellied stove surrounded by easy chairs and a selection of reading material makes this place feel homey.

**The Black Bean Burrito Bar & Salsa Co.** 12 E. Route 66. ☎ **520/779-9905.** Burritos $3–$6. No credit cards. Sun–Thurs 11am–9pm, Fri–Sat 11am–2am. WRAPS/INTERNATIONAL.

If you're looking for quick eats in downtown Flagstaff, this hole-in-the-wall on a little plaza off Route 66 between San Francisco and Leroux streets is a good bet. They've got a wide variety of filling wraps (meals rolled up in a tortilla), from Thai peanut steak to tropical chicken to eggplant parmesan. Plenty of vegetarian wraps, too. This is basically a take-out place.

**Café Espress.** 16 N. San Francisco St. ☎ **520/774-0541.** Dinner $6.50–$9. MC, V. Sun–Thurs 7am–10pm, Fri–Sat 7am–11pm. INTERNATIONAL/VEGETARIAN.

Grab a newspaper from the table by the door, sit down at one of the tables by the front window, and ensconce yourself in college life all over again. If you happen to be a student, this place will certainly be your favorite dining spot in Flagstaff. You can start the day with granola, move on to tempeh or turkey burgers for lunch, and then have spanakopita for dinner.

**Galaxy Diner.** 931 W. Route 66. ☎ **520/774-2466.** Meals $5–$8. AE, DC, DISC, MC, V. Sun–Thurs 6am–11pm, Fri–Sat 6am–midnight. BURGERS/SANDWICHES.

What would a Route 66 town be without its retro diner? In this case, the diner is covered with enough neon to have you thinking you made a wrong turn and ended up in Vegas. Drop a quarter in the jukebox, order up a "Big Boppin" burger, and sit back for a night of nostalgia. Don't forget the chocolate malted.

✪ **Macy's European Coffee House & Bakery.** 14 S. Beaver St. ☎ **520/774-2243.** Meals $4–$6. No credit cards. Sun–Wed 6am–8pm, Thurs–Sat 6am–10pm. COFFEE/BAKERY.

Good espresso and baked goodies draw people in here the first time, but there are also decent pasta dishes, soups, salads, and other old college-town standbys. There are plenty of vegetarian dishes and sandwiches as well. This is a great place to meet local students.

**Pasto Fun Italian Dining.** 19 E. Aspen St. ☎ **520/779-1937.** Reservations recommended. Main dishes $9–$14. MC, V. Sun–Thurs 5–9:30pm, Fri–Sat 5–10pm (later in summer). ITALIAN.

Operated by the same folks who run Café Espress, Pasto is a health-conscious Italian restaurant in downtown Flagstaff popular with the hip and young-at-heart. The sign outside says "Fun Italian Dining," which gives an indication of the flamboyant decor and casual atmosphere here. The menu includes a good assortment of pastas, of course, but there are also dishes such as eggplant parmigiana and artichoke orzo.

# FLAGSTAFF AFTER DARK

Check *Flagstaff Live!,* a free weekly arts-and-entertainment newspaper available at shops and restaurants downtown for events taking place during your visit. The university has many musical and theatrical groups that perform throughout most of the year, and several clubs around town book a variety of live music.

Each summer, the **Flagstaff Festival of the Arts,** P.O. Box 22402, Flagstaff, AZ 86002-2402 (☎ **800/266-7740** or 520/774-7750), brings to town a month's worth of music performances that are scheduled at venues around the city. Ticket prices range from $11 to $26 for individual events.

The rest of the year, the **Flagstaff Symphony Orchestra** (☎ **520/774-5107**) provides the city with a full season of classical music. Performances are held at Ardrey Auditorium on Knoles Drive on the campus of Northern Arizona University. Ticket prices range from $12 to $25.

The city's community theater group, **Theatrikos** (☎ **520/774-1662**), performs at the Flagstaff Playhouse, 11 W. Cherry St. Tickets are $9 to $12.

For a livelier scene, check out the **Museum Club,** 3404 E. Route 66 (☎ **520/526-9434**). Built in the early 1900s and often called the Zoo Club, this cavernous log saloon is filled with deer antlers, stuffed animals, and trophy heads. There's live music, predominantly country-and-western, with varying admission prices, and country swing dance lessons (call for times). Willie Nelson, John Lee Hooker, Dr. Hook, Asleep at the Wheel, and Mose Allison are some of the musicians who have appeared here in the past. If you call ☎ **520/774-4444,** you can sometimes get a complimentary ride to and from the Museum Club.

## SIDE TRIPS FROM FLAGSTAFF, EAST OF THE CITY

Heading east from Flagstaff for a day of exploring, you can visit two very different Indian ruin sites, one of the most fascinating natural attractions on earth, and a waterfall in the middle of the desert.

The remains of hundreds of 13th-century Sinagua cliff dwellings can be seen at **Walnut Canyon National Monument** (☎ **520/526-3367**) in a dry, wooded canyon 7 miles east of Flagstaff on Walnut Canyon Road (take Exit 204 off I-40). The undercut layers of limestone in this 400-foot-deep canyon proved ideal for building dwellings well protected both from the elements and from enemies. The Sinagua were the same people who built and then abandoned the stone pueblos found in Wupatki National Monument to the north of here. It's theorized that when the land to the north lost its fertility, the Sinagua began migrating southward, and settled for 150 years in Walnut Canyon.

A self-guided trail leads from the visitor center on the canyon rim down 185 feet to a section of the canyon wall where 25 cliff dwellings can be viewed and entered. Look closely and you can see handprints in the mud that was used to cement the dwellings' stone walls together. There's also a picnic area near the visitor center. Admission is $4 per car. The monument is open daily with hours varying with the season.

At the next exit east off I-40 (Exit 207), you can head north to **Grand Falls,** situated at the end of the packed-dirt Indian Route 70 on the Navajo Reservation. This waterfall on the Little Colorado River is little more than a trickle most of the year, but after a summer thunderstorm or during spring snowmelt season, muddy waters roar over the falls. The road in is generally passable to standard passenger cars when dry, but impassable when wet (don't even think about it). To reach Indian Route 70, take Exit 207 off I-40 and go north and then west on Indian Route 15. Indian Route 17 heads north in about 12 miles.

Continuing east to Exit 233 off I-40 (35 miles east of Flagstaff), you'll come to a 570-foot-deep **Meteor Crater** (☎ **520/289-2362**), one of the natural wonders of the world. This gaping hole in the barren desert landscape was created 49,000 years ago when a meteorite estimated to be about 100 feet in diameter slammed into the ground at 45,000 miles per hour. Standing on a platform on the crater rim it's difficult to imagine the instant devastation that occurred when this meteorite struck the earth. Billed as "this planet's most penetrating natural attraction," Meteor Crater is the best-preserved impact crater on earth. So closely does this crater resemble craters on the surface of the moon that in the 1960s, NASA used this area as a training site for Apollo program astronauts.

The crater is privately owned, and on the rim you'll find a small **museum,** part of which is dedicated to the exploration of space. An Apollo space capsule is also on display. The rest of the museum is devoted to astrogeology and includes a meteorite weighing nearly three-quarters of a ton.

Admission is $8 for adults, $7 for senior citizens, $2 for children 6 to 17, and free for children 5 and under. From May 15 to September 15, hours are daily from 6am to 6pm; from September 16 to May 14, hours are daily from 8am to 5pm.

On the windswept plains north of Winslow (1.3 miles north of I-40 at Exit 257), you'll find **Homolovi Ruins State Park** (☎ **520/289-4106** ), which preserves more than 300 ancient Anasazi archaeological sites, several of which have been partially excavated. Though these ruins are not nearly as impressive as those at Wupatki or Walnut Canyon, a visit here will give you a better understanding of the interrelationship of the many ancient pueblos of this region. Also in the park are numerous petroglyphs; ask directions at the visitor center. Admission is $3 per car, and hours are 8am to 5pm daily. There is also a campground here.

## NORTH OF THE CITY

North of Flagstaff off U.S. 89 you'll find a pair of national monuments that provide a fascinating look at both the natural and human history of this region.

Dotting the landscape northeast of Flagstaff in **Sunset Crater Volcano National Monument** (☎ **520/526-0502**) are more than 400 volcanic craters, of which Sunset Crater Volcano (18 miles north of Flagstaff off U.S. 89) is the youngest. Taking its name from the sunset colors of the cinders near its summit, Sunset Crater Volcano stands 1,000 feet tall and began forming in A.D. 1064. Over a period of 100 years the volcano erupted repeatedly, creating the red-and-yellow cinder cone we see today and eventually covering an area of 800 square miles with ash, lava, and cinders. There's a mile-long interpretative trail that passes through a desolate landscape of lava flows, cinders, and ash as it skirts the base of this volcano. In the visitor center you can learn more about the formation of Sunset Crater and about volcanoes in general.

Monument admission is $4 per car (which includes admission to Wupatki National Monument). Hours are daily from sunrise to sunset; the visitor center operates daily from 8am to 5pm (until 6pm in summer; closed December 25). Near the visitor center at the west entrance to the national monument is a small campground that's open from spring to fall.

The landscape northeast of Flagstaff is desolate and windswept, a sparsely populated region carpeted with volcanic ash deposited in the 11th century. It comes as quite a surprise, then, to learn that this area contains hundreds of prehistoric and historic habitation sites. The most impressive ruins are those left by the Sinagua (the name means "without water" in Spanish) people who inhabited this area from around A.D. 1100 until shortly after 1200. The Sinagua people built small villages of stone similar to the pueblos on the nearby Hopi reservation, and today the ruins of these ancient villages can still be seen, 36 miles north of Flagstaff off U.S. 89 at **Wupatki National Monument** (☎ 520/679-2365).

The largest of the prehistoric pueblos is the Wupatki ruin in the southeastern part of the monument. Here the Sinagua built a sprawling three-story pueblo containing nearly 100 rooms. They also constructed what is believed to be a ball court, which though quite different in design from the courts of the Aztec and Maya, leaves no doubt that a similar game was played. Another circular stone structure just below the main ruins may have been an amphitheater or dance plaza.

The most unusual feature of Wupatki, however, is a natural phenomenon: a blowhole, which may have been the reason this pueblo was constructed here. A network of small underground tunnels and chambers acts as a giant barometer, blowing air through the blowhole when the underground air is under greater pressure than the outside air. On hot days, cool air rushes out of the blowhole with amazing force.

Several other ruins within the national monument are easily accessible by car. These include Nalakihu, Citadel, and Lomaki, which are the closest to U.S. 89, and Wukoki, which is near Wupatki. Wukoki ruin is built atop a huge sandstone boulder and is particularly picturesque.

Admission to the national monument is $4 per car. Hours are daily from sunrise to sunset. The visitor center, which is located adjacent to the Wupatki ruins, is open daily from 8am to 5pm (until 6pm in summer; closed December 25). Inside the visitor center, you'll find interesting exhibits on the Sinagua and Anasazi people who once inhabited the region.

## 2 Williams

58 miles S of the Grand Canyon; 32 miles W of Flagstaff; 220 miles E of Las Vegas

Although it's almost 60 miles south of the Grand Canyon, Williams is still the nearest real town. Consequently it has dozens of motels catering to people who were unable to get a room at the park. However, Williams, founded in 1880 as a railroading and logging town, also has a bit of Western history to boast about. Old brick commercial buildings dating to the late 19th century line its main street while modest Victorian homes line the tree-shaded streets spreading south from the railroad tracks.

In recent years mid-20th-century history has taken center stage. Williams was the last town on historic Route 66 to be bypassed by I-40, and consequently, the town plays up its Route 66 heritage.

Named for famed mountain man Bill Williams, the town sits at the edge of a ponderosa pine forest atop the Mogollon Rim, and surrounding the town is the Kaibab National Forest. Within the forest and not far out of town are good fishing lakes, hiking and mountain-biking trails, and a small downhill ski area.

Williams is also where you'll find the Grand Canyon Railway depot. The excursion train that leaves from here provides not only a fun ride on the rails but is also an alternative to dealing with traffic congestion within the park. Of course, there are also the obligatory on-your-way-to-the-Grand-Canyon tourist traps nearby.

## ESSENTIALS

**GETTING THERE**   Williams is on I-40 just west of the junction with Ariz. 64, which leads north to the South Rim of the Grand Canyon.

The **Grand Canyon Railway,** Grand Canyon Railway Depot, Grand Canyon Boulevard (☎ 800/843-8724), operates vintage steam and diesel locomotives and 1920s coaches between Williams and Grand Canyon Village. Round-trip fares range from $49.50 to $114 for adults and $19.50 to $84 for children 3 to 16 (these fares do not include tax or $6 per person national park entrance fee). Although this is primarily a day-excursion train, it's possible to ride up one day and return on a different day—just let the reservationist know. If you opt to stay overnight, you'll want to be sure you have a reservation at one of the hotels right in Grand Canyon Village, otherwise, you'll end up having to take a shuttle bus or taxi out of the park to your hotel, which can be inconvenient and add quite a bit to your daily costs.

**Nava-Hopi Tours** (☎ 800/892-8687 or 520/774-5003) has bus service connecting Williams with the Grand Canyon ($18 round-trip), Flagstaff ($14 round-trip), and connections to Phoenix.

**VISITOR INFORMATION**    For more information on the Williams area, contact the **Williams–Grand Canyon Chamber of Commerce,** 200 W. Railroad Ave., Williams, AZ 86046-2556 (☎ 520/635-4061). The visitor center here is open Monday through Saturday from 8am to 5pm and Sunday from 8am to 4pm. There's a good selection of books on the Grand Canyon and Arizona (and no sales tax is charged).

**GETTING AROUND**    Car rentals are available from **Budget** (☎ 800/527-0700 or 520/635-4478) at the Grand Canyon Railway depot.

## WHAT TO SEE & DO: ROUTE 66 & BEYOND

These days, most people coming to Williams are here to board the Grand Canyon Railway (see "Getting There," above, for details).

Route 66 fans will want to drive Williams' main street, which not surprisingly is named **Route 66.** Along this stretch of the old highway, you can check out the town's vintage buildings, many of which now house shops selling Route 66 souvenirs. There are also lots of antiques stores selling collectibles from the heyday of Route 66.

Both east and west of town there are other stretches of the "Mother Road" that you can drive. East of town, take Exit 167 off I-40 and follow the graveled Old Trails Highway (the predecessor to Route 66). A paved section of Route 66 begins at Exit 171 on the north side of the interstate and extends for 7 miles to the site of the Parks General Store. From Parks, you can continue to Brannigan Park on a graveled section of Route 66.

West of Williams, take Exit 157 and go south. If you turn east at the T intersection, you will be on a gravel section of the old highway; if you turn west, you'll be on a paved section. Another stretch can be accessed at Exit 106. If you continue another 12 miles west and take Exit 139, you will be on the longest uninterrupted stretch of Route 66 left in the country. It stretches from here through the town of Seligman, which has several interesting buildings, and all the way to Kingman.

For information on hiking, mountain biking, and fishing in the area, stop by or contact the **Williams–Grand Canyon Chamber of Commerce,** 200 W. Railroad Ave. (☎ 520/635-4061), which has lots of trail maps for the adjacent national forest.

If you've got the kids along, you'll want to take them by the **Grand Canyon Deer Farm,** 100 Deer Farm Rd. (☎ 800/926-DEER or 520/635-4073), at Exit 171 off I-40. Here the kids can walk around in a herd of very friendly deer. June and July are when fawns are born, always a fun time to visit. The farm is open daily except Thanksgiving and Christmas; admission $5 adults, $4 seniors, $2.75 children 3 to 13.

During winters when there is sufficient snow on the ground, the **Williams Ski Area** (☎ 520/635-9330) offers downhill and cross-country skiing. The ski area has one poma lift and a rope tow, a dozen or so runs, and 650 vertical feet of skiing. The ski area is open Thursday through Monday, and lift tickets cost from $16 to $21 for a full day. To find the slopes head south on Fourth Street and continue for 1 1/2 miles.

In summer, horseback riding is an option. Contact **Mountain Ranch Stables** at the Quality Inn Mountain Ranch (☎ **520/635-2639** or 520/635-0706), which is located 6 miles east of Williams at Exit 171 off I-40, or **Stable in the Pines,** 1000 Circle Pine Rd. (☎ **520/635-4545** or 520/635-2626), which is 2 miles east of Williams at Exit 167 off I-40. Both stables charge $17 for a 1-hour ride and $32 for a 2-hour ride.

In Williams, you can also play a round of golf at the **Elephant Rocks Golf Course,** Country Club Road (☎ **520/635-4936**). Greens fees are a very reasonable $16 to $26 and golf carts are another $16.

# WHERE TO STAY
## EXPENSIVE

**Best Western Inn of Williams.** 2600 W. Route 66, Williams, AZ 86046. ☎ **800/528-1234** or 520/635-4400. Fax 520/635-4488. 79 rms. Late May to mid-Nov $119–$177 double; mid-Nov to late May $87–$109 double. Rates include full breakfast. AE, DC, DISC, MC, V.

Contemporary styling and a location in the pines at the west end of town make this modern motel a good bet for comfortable accommodations. Guest rooms even have a couple of features you only expect in deluxe accommodations—hair dryers and bathroom phones. Plus, you'll find a pool (albeit outdoors and with a very limited season) and a whirlpool tub. In addition to the breakfast, complimentary drinks are served in the evening.

✪ **Fray Marcos Hotel.** 235 N. Grand Canyon Blvd., Williams, AZ 86046. ☎ **800/843-8724** or 520/635-4010. Fax 520/773-1610. 89 rms. A/C TV TEL. Apr 1–Labor Day $119 double. Mar, Sept–Oct, and Thanksgiving and Christmas/New Year's holidays $99 double. Nov 1–Feb 28 $69 double. AE, DISC, MC, V.

Named for Fray (Father) Marcos de Niza who, some say, was the first European to set foot in what is today the state of Arizona, this hotel (the second to bear the adventuresome Franciscan's name) is affiliated with the Grand Canyon Railway. The railway, which runs vintage trains to the Grand Canyon, has its depot adjacent to the hotel, which makes this the ideal lodging choice if you are planning on riding the rails. The original Fray Marcos Hotel, built in 1908, now houses the Depot Cafe and a railroad museum.

The hotel combines modern comforts with the style of a classic Western railroad hotel. The high-ceilinged lobby features a large flagstone fireplace, lots of comfortable seating, and original paintings of the Grand Canyon. Guest rooms are very comfortable and feature Southwestern styling.

**Dining/Entertainment:** There is no restaurant here, but the lounge, which features a beautiful 100-year-old bar brought over from England, serves simple meals. There is also the adjacent Depot Cafe in the original hotel.

**Services:** Train reservations can be arranged.

**Facilities:** Gift shop, adjacent railroad museum, and display trains.

**Terry Ranch Bed & Breakfast.** 701 Quarterhorse St., Williams, AZ 86046. ☎ **800/210-5908** or 520/635-4171. 4 rms. May–Aug $90–$110 double; Sept–Dec $70–$90 double; Jan–Apr $60–$80 double. Rates include full breakfast. AE, DISC, MC, V.

This modern log inn on the edge of town looks as though it should be surrounded by a big cattle spread, but instead it's close to the train depot and the restaurants in downtown Williams. The guest rooms, which are furnished in Western country style, all have king beds and claw-foot tubs, as well as antiques, and are named for brides who lived at the Terry Ranch in Utah back in the 1800s. Unfortunately, the neighborhood around the inn is not nearly as attractive as the inn itself.

## MODERATE

**Canyon Country Inn.** 442 Route 66, Williams, AZ 86046. ☎ **800/643-1020** or 520/635-2349. 13 rms. TV TEL. $60–$95 double. Lower rates in winter. Rates include continental breakfast. DISC, MC, V.

This quaint country inn (right in town) is a cross between a motel and a bed-and-breakfast. Though it's not a historic building and is located in the middle of Williams's motel row, all rooms are individually furnished and feature crafts made by local women and plenty of teddy bears to keep guests company.

✪ **Quality Inn Mountain Ranch.** Rte. 1, Box 35 (at Exit 171 from I-40), Williams, AZ 86046. ☎ **800/228-5151** or 520/635-2693. 73 rms. A/C TV TEL. Mid-May to Oct and spring break week (late Mar) $85–$102 double; Nov to mid-May $65–$75 double. AE, DC, DISC, MC, V.

Located 6 miles east of town, this motel is surrounded by 26 acres of forest and meadow that give it a secluded feeling. This seclusion and the activities (horseback riding, a pool, whirlpool, sauna, two tennis courts, volleyball, basketball, and a putting green) available here make this the best choice in the Williams area. However, the rooms, though large and mostly with views of forest and mountains, are strictly motel issue. There's a restaurant on the premises, so you don't have to drive into town to eat.

**Ramada Inn Canyon Gateway.** 642 Route 66, Williams, AZ 86046. ☎ **800/462-9381** or 520/635-4431. Fax 520/635-2292. 96 rms. A/C TV TEL. June–Oct $89–$125 double; Nov–May $65–$85 double. AE, CB, DC, DISC, MC, V.

Located at the east end of town, this large motel is popular with tour groups. The rooms are medium size with large windows, some with mountain views. The large restaurant and lobby lounge are perhaps the best reasons to stay here. They provide a Western steakhouse atmosphere and in summer, there's sometimes live music in the lounge. The hotel also offers a pool and whirlpool and room service is available.

## INEXPENSIVE

In addition to the motels and B&Bs listed below, there are several budget chain motels in Williams. (Rates are for the summer high season; see the appendix for toll-free phone numbers.) There's the **Comfort Inn,** 911 Route 66 (☎ **520/635-4045**), charging $68 to $98 double; **Motel 6,** 831 Route 66 (☎ **520/635-9000**), charging $50 double; and **Super 8,** 2001 Route 66 (☎ **520/635-4700**), $50 to $60 double.

**The Johnstonian.** 321 W. Sheridan St., Williams, AZ 86046. ☎ **520/635-2178.** 4 rms (one with private bath). $55–$60 double with shared bath, $70 double with private bath. Rates include full breakfast. No credit cards.

Located only 2 blocks off historic Route 66, this quaint Victorian home, which dates from 1900, is set on a shady street and is filled with antique oak furniture. The three guest rooms that share a bath are on the second floor, while the room with private bath is on the first (and has a waterbed). This inn is conveniently located within walking distance of the train depot but is off the main drag, so it has a more tranquil, neighborhood atmosphere.

**Norris Motel.** 1001 Route 66 (P.O. Box 388), Williams, AZ 86046. ☎ **800/341-8000** or 520/635-2202. Fax 520/635-9202. 33 rms. A/C TV TEL. $34–$74 double. AE, DISC, MC, V.

Run by a British family, the Norris Motel may not look like anything special from the street, but the friendliness of the welcome will immediately let you know that this is not your ordinary motel. Most of the guest units have been remodeled and have a homey feel. Many rooms also have refrigerators. There's even a whirlpool bath to soak away your aches and pains in the evening, and at press time, there were plans to add a swimming pool.

✪ **The Red Garter Bed & Bakery.** 137 W. Railroad Ave., Williams, AZ 86046. ☎ **800/328-1484** or 520/635-1484. 4 rms. $65–$105 double. Rates include continental breakfast. Lower rates off-season. AE, DISC, MC, V.

The Wild West lives again at this restored 1897 bordello, but these days the only extras that come with the rooms are breakfasts in the bakery downstairs. Located across the street from the Grand Canyon Railway terminal at the top of a steep flight of stairs, this B&B sports high ceilings, new carpets, attractive wood trim, and reproduction period furnishings. A couple of rooms even have graffiti written by visitors in the early part of this century.

### CAMPGROUNDS

There are several campgrounds near Williams in the Kaibab National Forest. These include Cataract Lake (2 miles northwest of Williams on Cataract Lake Road), Dogtown Lake (8 miles south of Williams off Fourth Street/County Road 73), Kaibab Lake (4 miles northeast of Williams off Ariz. 64), and Whitehorse Lake (15 miles south of Williams off Fourth Street/County Road 73).

## WHERE TO DINE

**Rod's Steak House.** 301 E. Route 66. ☎ **520/635-2671.** Main courses $9–$25. MC, V. Summer daily 11:30am–10pm; winter Tues–Sun 11:30am–9:30pm. STEAKS/SEAFOOD.

If you're looking for a good dinner in Williams, just look for the red neon steer at the east end of town. This is the sign that beckons hungry canyon explorers to come on in and have a great steak. The menu is short and comes printed on a paper cutout of a steer, but what Rod's does have is always reliable. Prime rib au jus, the house specialty, comes in three different weights to fit your hunger.

## ON THE DRIVE FROM WILLIAMS TO THE GRAND CANYON: MEET THE FLINTSTONES

The **Flintstone's Bedrock City** (☎ 520/635-2600), at the junction of Ariz. 64 and U.S. 180, may be more interesting to your youngsters than the Grand Canyon itself. Sure it's tacky, but kids love all the Bedrock buildings and the "live" volcano.

At the same highway junction is an attraction calculated to appeal to the older set. The **Planes of Fame Air Museum** (☎ 520/635-1000) displays more than a dozen vintage planes including a 1928 Ford trimotor and several World War II and Korean War fighter planes. The museum is open daily; admission is $5 adults and $1.95 children 5 to 12.

## 3 The Grand Canyon South Rim

60 miles N of Williams; 80 miles NE of Flagstaff; 230 miles N of Phoenix; 340 miles N of Tucson

A strange hush clings to the edge of this mile-deep canyon. It's the hush of reverential awe. For the first-time visitor to the canyon, there's no better approach than from the south, across the barren windswept scrubland of the Colorado Plateau. You hardly notice the elevation gain and the change to pine and juniper forest. Suddenly, it's there. No preliminaries, no warnings. Stark, quiet, a maze of colors and cathedrals sculpted by nature.

A mile deep, 277 miles long, and 18 miles wide in places, the Grand Canyon is truly one of the great wonders of the world, and it comes as no surprise to learn that the cartographers who mapped the area sensed the spiritual beauty of the canyon. Their reverence is reflected in the names of its formations: Apollo Temple, Venus Temple, Thor Temple, Zoroaster Temple, Horus Temple, Buddha Temple, Vishnu Temple, Krishna Temple, Shiva Temple, Confucius Temple, the Tabernacle, Solomon Temple, Angels Gate.

Banded layers of sandstone, limestone, shale, and schist give the canyon its color, and the interplay of shadows and light from dawn to dusk creates an ever-changing palette of hues and textures. Written in these bands of stone are more than 2 *billion* years of history. Formed by the cutting action of the Colorado River as it flows through the Kaibab Plateau, the Grand Canyon is an open book exposing the secrets of the geologic history of this region. Geologists believe that it has taken between 3 and 6 million years for the Colorado River to carve the Grand Canyon, but the canyon's history extends much further back in time. Millions of years ago vast seas covered this region. Sediments carried by seawater were deposited and over millions of years turned into sedimentary limestone and sandstone. When the ancient seabed was thrust upward to form the Kaibab Plateau, the Colorado River began its work of cutting through the plateau. Today 21 sedimentary layers, the oldest of which is more than a billion years old, can be seen in the canyon. However, beneath all these layers, at the very bottom, is a stratum of rock so old that it has been metamorphosed, under great pressure and heat, from soft shale to a much harder stone called schist. Called Vishnu schist, this layer is the oldest rock in the Grand Canyon and dates from 2 billion years.

In the more recent past the Grand Canyon has been home to several Native American cultures, including the Anasazi, who are best known for their cliff dwellings in the Four Corners region. About 150 years after the Anasazi and Coconino peoples abandoned the canyon in the 13th century, another tribe, the Cerbat, moved into the area. The Hualapai and Havasupai tribes, descendants of the Cerbat people, still live in and near the Grand Canyon on the south side of the Colorado River. On the North Rim lived the Southern Paiute, and in the west the Navajo.

In 1540 Spanish explorer Garcia Lopez de Cárdenas became the first European to set eyes on the Grand Canyon. However, it would be another 329 years before the first expedition would travel through the entire canyon. John Wesley Powell, a one-armed Civil War veteran, was deemed crazy when he set off to navigate the Colorado River in wooden boats. His small band of men spent 98 days traveling 1,000 miles down the Green and Colorado rivers. Their expedition was not without mishap. When some boats were wrecked by the powerful rapids, part of the group abandoned the journey and set out on foot, never to be heard from again.

Today the Grand Canyon is the last major undammed section of the Colorado River, and the river, which once flowed reddish brown from the immense load of silt it carried, now flows cold and clear from the bottom of the upriver Glen Canyon Dam. By raft, by mule, on foot, in helicopters and small planes—five million people come to the canyon each year seeking one of nature's Meccas.

Such a massive number of visitors, as well as events outside the park, have impacted the park in recent years. The biggest impact is caused by the cars that enter the park during the busy months from spring to fall. Traffic jams have become a serious problem all along the South Rim, and the park is currently looking into ways to reduce this congestion. Some visitors also notice that the air in the canyon isn't always very clear. Yes, there is even smog in the Grand Canyon, smog that has been blamed on both Las Vegas and Los Angeles to the west and a coal-fired power plant to the east near Page. Scrubbers installed on the power plant should help the park's air quality. The Colorado River once flowed brown and muddy through the Grand Canyon, but with the construction of the Glen Canyon Dam in the 1960s, the river's silt load was eliminated and the natural processes that once supported a lush riparian area along the riverbanks within the canyon were halted. In early 1996, an experiment altering the flow rate coming out of Glen Canyon Dam attempted to duplicate the traditional spring flooding that once annually rearranged the banks of the river. The experiment seems to have been successful and may become a part of maintaining the river within the Canyon.

Today the Canyon is at a turning point. Though the land is protected, the Canyon is not exactly pristine or preserved as it was before the arrival of Europeans in this region. The National Park Service is taking some actions to help maintain the natural integrity of the park, but more needs to be done soon. However, despite crowding and smog and altered water flows, the Grand Canyon still more than lives up to its name and is one of the most amazing sights on earth.

## ESSENTIALS

**GETTING THERE** **By Car** In the past few years parking problems, traffic jams, and traffic congestion have become the norm at Grand Canyon Village during the popular summer months (and are becoming common in spring and fall as well). If at all possible, we suggest that you travel into the park by some means *other* than car. (Alternatives include taking the Grand Canyon Railway from Williams, flying into the Grand Canyon Airport and then taking the Tusayan-Grand Canyon Shuttle or a taxi, or taking the Nava-Hopi Tours bus service from either Williams or Flagstaff.) There are plenty of scenic overlooks, hiking trails, restaurants, and lodges in the village area, and a free shuttle operates along the West Rim Drive in summer.

If you do drive, be sure that you have plenty of gasoline in your car before setting out for the canyon; there are few service stations in this remote part of the state. The South Rim of the Grand Canyon is 60 miles north of Williams and I-40 on Ariz. 64 and U.S. 180. Flagstaff, the nearest city of any size, is 78 miles away. From Flagstaff it's possible to take U.S. 180 directly to the South Rim or U.S. 89 to Ariz. 64 and the east entrance to the park.

**By Plane** The Grand Canyon Airport is 6 miles south of Grand Canyon Village in Tusayan. It's served by **Air Nevada Airlines** (☎ 800/634-6377), which charges $159 round-trip; **Air Vegas** (☎ 800/255-7474, ext. 212, 520/638-0445, or 702/736-3599), which charges between $58 and $170 round-trip; **Eagle Airlines** (☎ 800/446-4584 or 520/638-0445), which charges $131 to $188.50 round-trip; and **Scenic Airlines** (☎ 800/634-6801 or 702/739-1900), which charges $199 round-trip. Other than these options, you'll have to fly into Flagstaff and then arrange another mode of transportation the rest of the way to the national park.

**By Train** The **Grand Canyon Railway** operates excursion trains between Williams and the South Rim of the Grand Canyon. See the "Williams" section of this chapter for details.

For long-distance connections, **Amtrak** (☎ 800/872-7245 or 520/774-8679) provides service to Flagstaff. From Flagstaff it's then possible to take a bus directly to Grand Canyon Village. Another option is to take a Greyhound bus to Williams and then take the Grand Canyon Railway excursion train from there to Grand Canyon Village.

**By Bus** Bus service between Phoenix, Flagstaff, Williams, and Grand Canyon Village is provided by **Nava-Hopi Tours** (☎ 800/892-8687 or 520/774-5003).

Round-trip fares are as follows: $69 between Phoenix and Grand Canyon Village; $25 between Flagstaff and Grand Canyon Village; and $18 between Williams and Grand Canyon Village.

**VISITOR INFORMATION**   You can get information on the Grand Canyon before leaving home by contacting the **Grand Canyon National Park,** P.O. Box 129, Grand Canyon, AZ 86023 (☎ **520/638-7888**). You can also check out the canyon on the web at www.thecanyon.com/nps.

Once there, you should stop by the **Grand Canyon National Park Visitor Center,** located on Village Loop Drive 6 miles north of the south entrance. Here you'll find an information desk, brochures, exhibits about the canyon, and a bookshop selling maps as well as books about the canyon. The center is open daily. *The Guide,* a small newspaper crammed full of useful information about the park, is available at all entrances.

**ORIENTATION**   Grand Canyon Village is built on the South Rim of the canyon and is roughly divided into two sections. At the east end of the village is the visitor center, Yavapai Lodge, Trailer Village, and Mather Campground. At the west end are El Tovar Hotel and Bright Angel, Kachina, Thunderbird, and Maswik lodges, as well as several restaurants, the train depot, and the trailhead for the Bright Angel Trail.

**GETTING AROUND**   As mentioned earlier, the Grand Canyon Village area can be extremely congested, especially during the summer months. If possible you may want to use one of the transportation options below to avoid the park's traffic jams and parking problems. Just to give you an idea, you can expect at least a 20- to 30-minute wait at the South Rim entrance gate. You can cut the waiting time here by acquiring a national park pass (Golden Eagle, Golden Age, or Golden Access) before arriving. With pass in hand, you can use the express lane for seasonal pass holders.

**By Bus**   The **Tusayan–Grand Canyon Shuttle** (☎ **520/638-0871** or 520/638-0821) operates between the Grand Canyon Airport in Tusayan, at the park's south entrance, and Grand Canyon Village, with stops in Tusayan at the Canyon Squire Inn, the IMAX Theater, and the Village Store and in Grand Canyon Village at Maswik Lodge and Yavapai Lodge (except in summer). A day pass is $7 and buses leave every 75 minutes between 8:30am and 6:30pm in summer (other months every hour but with trips starting at 9am and ending at 5pm).

Between April and September three free shuttles operate within the park—between the park's visitor center and village lodges, along West Rim Drive (which is closed to private vehicles during the summer), and out to Yaki Point and the South Kaibab Trailhead. Other months of the year, there is a hiker shuttle ($3 each way) from Grand Canyon Village to the South Kaibab trailhead. This shuttle is popular with hikers headed down to the bottom of the canyon for overnight trips and is a good way to avoid parking problems at the South Kaibab trailhead.

**Trans Canyon** (☎ **520/638-2820**) offers shuttle-bus service between the South Rim and the North Rim. The vans leave the South Rim at 1:30pm and arrive at the North Rim at 6:30pm. The return trip leaves the North Rim at 7am, arriving back at the South Rim at 11:30am. The fare is $60 per person one way, $100 per person round-trip.

**By Car   Budget Rent A Car** (☎ **800/527-0700** or 520/638-9360) maintains a desk in the main terminal of the Grand Canyon Airport at the south entrance to the park.

There are **service stations** at Grand Canyon Village, in Tusayan, and at Desert View near the east entrance (this station is seasonal). Be forewarned that gas in

Tusayan is usually much more expensive than it is at Grand Canyon Village, so you might want to wait and gas up inside the park. Gas is even less expensive in Williams and Cameron. Because of the long distances within the park and to towns outside the park, be sure that you have plenty of gas before setting out on a drive.

**By Taxi**    There is taxi service available to and from the airport, trailheads, and other destinations. Phone ☎ **520/638-2822.**

## FAST FACTS: The Grand Canyon

**Admission**    The admission to Grand Canyon National Park is $20 per car or $10 per person if you happen to be coming in on a bus, by taxi, or on foot. This admission pass is good for 7 days.

**Banks and ATM Networks**    There's an ATM at the Bank One at the shopping center near Yavapai Lodge. The bank is open Monday through Thursday from 10am to 3pm and on Friday from 10am to 3pm and 4 to 6pm as well.

**Bus Tours**    If you'd rather leave the driving to someone else and enjoy more of the scenery, you can opt for a bus or van tour of one or more sections of the park. The **Grand Canyon National Park Lodges** company (☎ **303/297-2757**) operates the Fred Harvey Transportation Company, which offers several trips ranging in length from 2 to 11 hours. Inside the park, tours visit the east rim and west rim, while beyond the park boundaries they raft through Glen Canyon and visit Monument Valley, Wupatki National Monument, Sunset Crater, and Walnut Canyon National Monument. Tours can be booked by calling the above phone number or by stopping at one of the transportation desks, which are located at the Visitors Center, and Bright Angel, Maswik, and Yavapai lodges. Prices range from $12 to $86 for adults and $6 to $50 for children.

**Climate**    The climate at the Grand Canyon is quite different from that of Phoenix, and between the rim and the canyon floor there's also a considerable difference. Because the South Rim is at 7,000 feet, it gets very cold in the winter. You can expect snow anytime between November and May and winter temperatures can be below 0°F at night, with daytime highs in the 20s or 30s. Summer temperatures at the rim range from highs in the 80s to lows in the 50s. The North Rim of the canyon is slightly higher and stays a bit cooler throughout the year, and is open to visitors only from May to October because the access road is not kept cleared of snow.

On the canyon floor temperatures are considerably higher. In summer the mercury can top 100°F with lows in the 70s, while in the winter temperatures are quite pleasant with highs in the 50s and lows in the 30s. July, August, and September are the wettest months because of frequent afternoon thunderstorms. April, May, and June are the driest months, though it might still rain or even snow. Down on the canyon floor there is much less rain year-round.

**Drugstores**    There's a pharmacy in Grand Canyon Village on Clinic Drive, which is off Center Road (the road that runs past the National Park Service ranger office). The drugstore is open Monday through Saturday. Call ☎ **520/638-2460** for information.

**Emergencies**    Dial ☎ **911;** from hotel or motel rooms, dial 9-911.

**Hospitals/Clinics**    The **Grand Canyon Clinic** (☎ **520/638-2551** or 520/638-2469) is located on Clinic Drive, which is off Center Road (the road that runs past the National Park Service ranger office). The clinic is open Monday through Friday from 8am to 5:30pm and on Saturday from 9am to noon. It also provides 24-hour emergency service.

**Laundry**    A coin-operated laundry is located near Mather Campground in the Camper Services building.

**Lost and Found**    Report lost items or turn in found items at the visitor center or Yavapai observation station. Call ☎ **520/638-7798** Tuesday through Friday between 8am and 5pm. For items lost or found at a hotel, restaurant, or lounge, call ☎ **520/638-2631**, ext. 6503.

**Newspapers/Magazines**    Current newspapers and magazines are available at souvenir stores and lodges in the village.

**Photographic Needs**    Film is available at all village curio shops.

**Police**    In an emergency, dial ☎ **911.** Ticketing speeders is one of the main occupations of the park's police force, so obey the posted speed limits.

**Post Office**    The post office is located in the shopping center near Yavapai Lodge.

**Safety**    The most important safety tip to remember is to be careful near the edge of the canyon. Footing can be unstable and may give way. Also be sure to keep your distance from wild animals, no matter how friendly they may appear. Don't hike alone, and keep in mind that the canyon rim is more than a mile above sea level (it's harder to breathe up here). Don't leave valuables in your car or tent.

# GRAND CANYON VILLAGE & VICINITY: YOUR FIRST LOOK

Grand Canyon Village is the main destination of the vast majority of the more than 5 million people who visit the Grand Canyon every year. Consequently it is the most crowded place in the park, but it also has the most overlooks and visitor services. Its many historic buildings, while nowhere near as impressive as the canyon itself, are worth visiting.

For most visitors that first glimpse of the canyon comes at **Mather Point,** which is the first canyon overlook you reach if you enter the park through the south entrance. Continuing west toward the village proper, you next come to **Yavapai Point,** which is a favorite spot for sunrise and sunset photos and is the site of the **Yavapai Observation Station.** This historic building houses a small museum and has excellent views through its large windows. Yavapai point is at the east end of a paved hiking trail that extends for almost 3 miles to the west side of Grand Canyon Village.

The next stop along Village Loop Drive is the **Visitor Center** (☎ **520/638-7888**), which is one of the busiest places in the park and is usually the hardest place to find a parking space. The Visitor Center is open daily and, in addition to providing answers to all your questions about the Grand Canyon, also contains exhibits on the canyon's natural history, history, and exploration. Throughout the day, slide and video programs are shown. There's also an excellent little bookstore here where you can find books on all aspects of the canyon. In the center's courtyard are several boats that have navigated the canyon over the years.

If you want to avoid parking headaches, try using the lot in front of the general store, which is up a side road across from the Visitor Center (near Yavapai Lodge). From this large parking area, a paved hiking trail leads to the historic section of the village in less than 1 1/2 miles and most of the route is along the rim.

In the historic district, in addition to numerous canyon viewpoints, you'll find the historic **El Tovar Hotel** and **Bright Angel Lodge,** both of which are worth brief visits.

# Grand Canyon Village

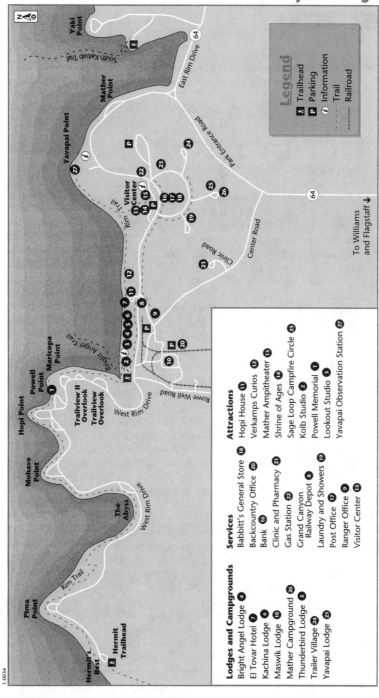

**Legend**

- 🏛 Trailhead
- 🅿 Parking
- ⓘ Information
- ----- Trail
- ++++ Railroad

Yaki Point

South Kaibab Trail

Mather Point

Yavapai Point

East Rim Drive

64

Park Entrance Road

Visitor Center

Rim Trail

Clinic Road

Center Road

To Williams and Flagstaff →

64

Maricopa Point

Powell Point

Hopi Point

Trailview II Overlook

Trailview Overlook

Bright Angel Trail

West Rim Drive

Rowe Well Road

Mohave Point

The Abyss

West Rim Drive

Pima Point

Rim Trail

Hermit's Rest

Hermit Trailhead

## Lodges and Campgrounds

Bright Angel Lodge ❹
El Tovar Hotel ❼
Kachina Lodge ❻
Maswik Lodge ❿
Mather Campground ㉖
Thunderbird Lodge ❺
Trailer Village ㉔
Yavapai Lodge ㉓

## Services

Babbitt's General Store ⓲
Backcountry Office ❿
Bank ⓰
Clinic and Pharmacy ㉑
Gas Station ㉒
Grand Canyon Railway Depot ❽
Laundry and Showers ⓳
Post Office ⓱
Ranger Office ❾
Visitor Center ⓯

## Attractions

Hopi House ⓫
Verkamps Curios ⓬
Mather Ampitheater ⓭
Shrine of Ages ⓮
Sage Loop Campfire Circle ㉕
Kolb Studio ❷
Powell Memorial ❶
Lookout Studio ❸
Yavapai Observation Station ㉗

231

## Impressions

*We are imprisoned three quarters of a mile in the depths of the earth and the great unknown river shrinks into insignificance as it dashes its angry waves against the walls and cliffs that rise to the world above.*
  —Maj. John Wesley Powell, on his successful trip through the Grand Canyon

Adjacent to El Tovar are two historic souvenir and curio shops. **Hopi House Gift Store and Art Gallery,** the first shop in the park, was built in 1905 to resemble a Hopi pueblo and to serve as a place for Hopi artisans to work and sell their crafts. Today it's full of Hopi and Navajo arts and crafts, including expensive kachinas, rugs, jewelry, and pottery. The second floor of the Hopi House is an art gallery. The nearby **Verkamps Curios** originally opened in a tent in 1898, but after John Verkamp went out of business, it was not reopened until 1905. Today it's the main place to look for souvenirs and crafts. Just inside the door is a 535-pound meteorite. Both shops are open daily; hours vary seasonally.

To the west of Bright Angel Lodge, two buildings cling precariously to the rim of the canyon. These are the **Lookout and Kolb studios,** and though they have very different early histories, both have been listed on the National Register of Historic Places.

**Lookout Studio,** built in 1914 from a design by Mary Jane Colter, was the Fred Harvey Company's answer to the Kolb brothers' studio. Photographs and books about the canyon were sold at the studio, which incorporates architectural styles of the Hopi and the Anasazi. The use of native limestone and an uneven roofline allows the studio to blend in with the canyon walls and gives it the look of an old ruin. Today the studio houses a souvenir store and two lookout points.

**Kolb Studio** is named for Ellsworth and Emory Kolb, two brothers who set up a photographic studio on the rim of the Grand Canyon in 1904. The construction of this studio generated one of the Grand Canyon's first controversies—over whether buildings should be allowed on the canyon rim. Because the Kolbs had friends in high places, their sprawling studio and movie theater remained. Emory Kolb lived here until his death in 1976, by which time the building had been listed as a historic building and could not legally be torn down. Today it serves as a bookstore, and the auditorium houses special exhibits. Both studios are open daily; hours vary seasonally.

## THE WEST RIM DRIVE

The West Rim Drive is an 8-mile-long road leading west from Grand Canyon Village to Hermits Rest. During the summer, this road is closed to private automobiles, but a free shuttle operates frequently and stops at most of the scenic overlooks. The rest of the year it's possible to drive this scenic road in your own car, stopping whenever and wherever you wish.

The first stops are **Trailview Overlook** and **Paiute Point.** From either of these points you have a view of Grand Canyon Village to the east with the Bright Angel Trail winding down into the canyon from the village. The trail leads 3,000 feet below the rim to the Tonto Plateau, site of Indian Gardens, where there is a campground in a grove of cottonwood trees.

The next stop on the West Rim Drive is **Maricopa Point.** Here you can see the remains of the Orphan Mine, which began operation in 1893. The mine went out of business because transporting the copper to a city where it could be sold was too expensive. Uranium was discovered here in 1954, but in 1966 the mine was shut

## Shooting the Canyon: Tips for Photographers

By the time most people leave the Grand Canyon they've shot several rolls of film. This is not at all surprising considering the beauty of this rugged landscape. But it's not always easy to capture the canyon's spirit on film. Here are some tips to help you bring back the best possible photos from your trip:

A polarizing filter is a great investment if you have the kind of camera that will accept lens filters. A polarizing filter will reduce haze, lessen the contrast between shadowy areas and light areas, and deepen the color of the sky.

The best times to photograph the canyon are at sunrise and sunset, when filtered and sharply angled sunlight paints the canyon walls in beautiful shades of lavender and pink. At these times the shadows are also at their most dramatic. To capture these ephemeral moments it's best to use a tripod and a long exposure. The worst time to photograph the canyon is at noon when there are almost no shadows, and thus little texture or contrast. The National Park Service includes a table with sunrise and sunset times in *The Guide*, the park's official visitor newspaper.

Something else to keep in mind is that the Grand Canyon is immense. A wide-angle lens may leave the canyon looking on paper like a distant plane of dirt. Try zooming in on narrower sections of the canyon to emphasize a single dramatic landscape element. If you're shooting with a wide-angle lens, try to include something in the foreground (people or a tree branch) to give the photo perspective and scale.

When shooting portraits against a sunrise or sunset, use a flash to illuminate your subjects; otherwise your camera meter may expose for the bright light in the background and leave your subjects in shadow.

down and the land became part of Grand Canyon National Park. If you look carefully at the bottom of the canyon you can see some of the black Vishnu schist, which is among the oldest exposed rock on earth.

The **Powell Memorial,** which is the next stop, is dedicated to John Wesley Powell, who, in 1869 with a party of nine men, became the first person to navigate the Colorado River through the Grand Canyon.

Next along the drive is **Hopi Point,** from which you can see a long section of the Colorado River. Because of the great distance, the river seems to be a tiny, quiet stream, but in actuality the section you see is more than 100 yards wide and races through Granite Rapids.

**Mohave Point** is the next stop. From here you can see (and sometimes hear) Hermit Rapids, another section of white water. As with almost all rapids in the canyon, these are formed at the mouth of a side canyon where boulders loosened by storms and carried by flooded streams are deposited in the Colorado River.

The next pull-off is at **The Abyss,** the appropriately named 3,000-foot drop-off created by the Great Mojave Wall. This vertiginous view is one of the most awe-inspiring in the park. The walls of The Abyss are red sandstone that's more resistant to erosion than the softer shale in the layer below. Other layers of erosion-resistant sandstone have formed the freestanding pillars that are visible from here, the largest of which is called the Monument.

From **Pima Point** it's possible to see the remains of Hermit Camp on the Tonto Plateau. Built by the Santa Fe Railroad, Hermit Camp was a popular tourist destination between 1911 and 1930 and provided cabins and tents. Today only foundations remain.

At the end of the West Rim Drive is **Hermit's Rest,** named for Louis Boucher, a prospector who came to the canyon in the 1890s and was known as the Hermit. The log-and-stone Hermit's Rest building, designed by Mary Jane Colter and built in 1914, is on the National Register of Historic Places.

## THE EAST RIM DRIVE

The East Rim Drive extends for 25 miles from Grand Canyon Village to Desert View. The first stop is **Yaki Point,** which is near the trailhead for the South Kaibab Trail leading to Phantom Ranch. The spectacular view from here encompasses a wide section of the central canyon. The large flat-topped butte to the northeast is Woman's Throne, one of the canyon's easily recognizable features.

The next stop, **Grandview Point,** affords a view of Horseshoe Mesa, another interesting feature of the canyon landscape. The mesa was the site of the Last Chance Copper Mine in the early 1890s. Later that same decade the Grandview Hotel was built and served canyon visitors until its close in 1908.

Next along the drive is **Moran Point,** from which you can see a bright red layer of shale in the canyon walls. This point is named for a 19th-century landscape painter named Thomas Moran.

The **Tusayan Museum** (open daily except December 25; admission free) is the next stop along the East Rim Drive. This small museum is dedicated to the Hopi tribe and ancient Anasazi people who inhabited this region 800 years ago and inside the museum are artfully displayed exhibits on various aspects of Anasazi life. Outside the museum is a short self-guided trail through the ruins of an Anasazi village. Free guided tours are available.

At **Lipan Point** you can see the Grand Canyon supergroup: several strata of rock that are tilted at an angle to the other layers of rock in the canyon. Their angle indicates that there was a period of geological mountain building prior to the deposition of layers of sandstone, limestone, and shale. The red, white, and black rocks of the supergroup are composed of sedimentary rock and layers of lava. From **Navajo Point,** the Colorado River and Escalante Butte are both visible.

**Desert View,** with its trading post, cafeteria, service station, and watchtower, is the end of this scenic drive. The road does continue east from here, but it soon leaves the park (outside the park, the Little Colorado River overlook is worth a stop). The views are breathtaking from anywhere at Desert View, but the best lookout is from atop the Desert View Watchtower (open daily, admission 25¢). Though the watchtower looks as though it had been built centuries ago, it's actually only 65 years old. Architect Mary Jane Colter, who is responsible for much of the park's historic architecture, designed the tower to resemble the prehistoric towers that dot the Southwestern landscape. Built as an observation tower and rest stop for tourists, the watchtower incorporates Native American designs and art. The curio shop on the ground floor is a replica of a kiva (sacred ceremonial chamber) and has lots of interesting souvenirs, Southwestern crafts, and books. The tower's second floor features artwork by Hopi artist Fred Kabotie. Covering the walls are pictographs incorporating traditional designs. On the walls and ceiling of the upper two floors are more traditional images, this time reproductions of petroglyphs from throughout the Southwest by Fred Geary. From the roof, which is the highest point on the South Rim (7,522 feet above sea level) it's possible to see the Painted Desert to the northeast, the San Francisco Peaks to the south, the Colorado River, and Marble Canyon to the north. Coin-operated binoculars provide close-up views of some of the noteworthy landmarks of this end of the canyon. On the roof are several black-mirror "reflectoscopes" that provide interesting darkened views of some of the most spectacular sections of the canyon. The gift shop offers a pamphlet describing the watchtower in detail.

# UNIQUE WAYS TO SEE THE CANYON
## INTERPRETIVE PROGRAMS

Numerous interpretive programs are scheduled throughout the year at various South Rim locations. There are ranger-led walks that explore various aspects of the canyon, geology talks, lectures on the cultural and natural resources of the canyon, nature hikes, trips to fossil beds, and stargazing gatherings. At Tusayan Ruin there are guided tours. Evening programs are held at Mather Amphitheater in the summer and at the Shrine of the Ages the rest of the year. Consult your copy of *The Guide* for information on times and meeting points.

## THE GRAND CANYON FIELD INSTITUTE

If you are the active type or you'd just like to turn your visit to the Grand Canyon into more of an educational experience, you may want to consider doing a trip with the **Grand Canyon Field Institute,** P.O. Box 399, Grand Canyon, AZ 86023 (☎ **520/638-2485**). Cosponsored by the Grand Canyon National Park and the Grand Canyon Association, the field institute schedules an amazing variety of guided, educational trips. Not only are there challenging backpacking trips through the canyon (some for women only), but there are also programs lasting anywhere from 1 day to 11 days. Subjects covered include wilderness studies, geology, natural history, human history, photography, and arts. What sort of things can you do on one of these trips? How about a 5-day hands-on archaeology program or maybe a rim-to-rim backpacking trip? Maybe you'd like to observe raptors on the South Rim or learn more about the wildflowers of the inner canyon.

## RIDING THE RAILS

In the early part of this century most visitors to the Grand Canyon came by train, and today it's once again possible to travel to the canyon along the steel rails. The **Grand Canyon Railway** (☎ **800/843-8724**), which runs from Williams to the South Rim of the Grand Canyon at Grand Canyon Village, uses turn-of-the-century steam engines (during the summer) and 1950s-vintage diesel engines (other months) to pull 1920s-vintage passenger cars and a 1954 dome coach car. Trains depart from the Williams Depot, which is housed in the renovated Fray Marcos Hotel. Built in 1908, the old hotel now houses a railroad museum, gift shop, and cafe (Grand Canyon Railway also operates a new Fray Marcos Hotel, which really is a hotel). At Grand Canyon Village, the trains use the 1910 log railway terminal in front of El Tovar Hotel.

Passengers have the choice of five classes of service, including coach, club (with a full bar), Coconino main (downstairs in the dome car), Coconino dome (upstairs with the dome windows), and chief car (a parlor car with plush couches and chairs). Actors posing as cowboys provide entertainment including music performances aboard the train. The round-trip takes 8 hours (including 3½ hours at the Canyon), and fares range from $49.50 to $114 for adults, and $19.50 to $84 for children 3 to 16 (these rates do not include tax or $6 per person national park admission).

Not only is this a fun trip that provides great scenery and a trip back in time, but by taking the train, you can avoid the traffic congestion and parking problems in Grand Canyon Village. When booking your train trip, you can also book a bus tour in the park, which will help you see more than you would see on foot. The railway also operates its own hotel, the Fray Marcos Hotel, in Williams and offers different room/train packages.

## A BIRD'S-EYE VIEW

Despite controversies over noise and safety (there have been a few crashes over the years), airplane and helicopter flights over the Grand Canyon remain one of the most popular ways to see these natural wonders. Several companies operating out of the Grand Canyon Airport in Tusayan offer air tours lasting from 30 minutes to about 2 hours.

Companies offering air tours by small plane include the following: **Air Grand Canyon** (☎ 800/247-4726 or 520/638-2686); **Airstar Airlines** (☎ 800/962-3869 or 520/638-2139); **Grand Canyon Airlines** (☎ 800/528-2413 or 520/638-2407); and **Windrock Aviation** (☎ 800/247-6259 or 520/638-9591). Rates (depending on company and length of flight) range from $65 to $130 for adults and from $50 to $100 for children.

Helicopter tours are available from **Airstar Airlines** (☎ 800/962-3869 or 520/ 638-2622); **Kenai Helicopters** (☎ 800/541-4537 or 520/638-2764); and **Papillon Grand Canyon Helicopters** (☎ 800/528-2418 or 520/638-2419). Rates range from around $90 to around $160.

## MULE RIDES

After having a look at the steep drop-offs and narrow path of the Bright Angel Trail, you might decide that this isn't exactly the place to trust your life to a mule. However, the trail guides will be quick to reassure you that they haven't lost a rider yet. Mule rides into the canyon are some of the most popular activities at Grand Canyon Village and have been since the turn of the century when the Bright Angel Trail was a toll road. Trips of various lengths and to different destinations are offered. The 1-day trip descends to Plateau Point, where there's a view of the Colorado River 1,320 feet below. This is a grueling trip requiring riders to spend 6 hours in the saddle. Those who want to spend a night down in the canyon can choose an overnight trip to Phantom Ranch, where there are cabins and dormitories available at the only lodge actually in the canyon. From mid-November to mid-March there's also a 3-day/2-night trip to Phantom Ranch. Mule trips range in price from $105.50 for a 1-day ride to Plateau Point to $265 for an overnight ride to Phantom Ranch to $372 for a 2-night ride to Phantom Ranch. Couples receive discounts on overnight rides.

There are a couple of rider qualifications that you should keep in mind before making a reservation. You must weigh less than 200 pounds fully dressed and stand no less than 4 feet 7 inches tall. Pregnant women are not allowed on mule trips.

Because these trail rides are very popular (especially in summer), make a reservation as soon as you know when you'll be visiting. For more information or to make a reservation, contact the **Grand Canyon National Park Lodges,** South Rim, Grand Canyon, AZ 86023 ☎ **303/297-2757.** Fax 303/297-3175. If you arrive without a reservation and decide that you'd like to go on a mule ride, stop by the Bright Angel Transportation Desk to get your name on the day's waiting list.

## ON HORSEBACK

Trail rides on the rim (but not into the canyon) are available from **Apache Stables,** P.O. Box 158, Grand Canyon, AZ 86023 (☎ 520/638-2891 or 520/638-2424), at the south entrance to the park. There are rides of various lengths; prices range from $25 for a 1-hour ride to $65 for a 4-hour ride. Wagon rides ($8.50) are also offered.

## Impressions

*Ours has been the first and will doubtless be the last party of whites to visit this profitless locality.*
— Lt. Joseph C. Ives, exploring the Colorado River by steamboat (1857–58)

# HIKING THE CANYON

There are no roads leading into the Grand Canyon, so if you want to visit the inner canyon you have to fly, float, ride a mule, or hike. The ever-changing views are as spectacular as those from the rim, and up close there are fossils, old mines, petroglyphs, wildflowers, and wildlife to see. Keep in mind, however, that no hike below the rim of the canyon is easy.

The Grand Canyon offers some of the most rugged and strenuous hiking anywhere in the United States, and for this reason anyone attempting even a short walk should be well prepared. Each year several people are injured or killed because they set out to hike the canyon without preparing properly. Most of these injuries and fatalities are suffered by day hikers who set out without sturdy footgear and without food or adequate amounts of water. Don't become another Grand Canyon statistic! Take precautions. Unless you have proper footgear and at least 1 quart of water, you won't even be allowed on the daily ranger-led nature walk along the South Kaibab Trail. Even a short 30-minute hike in the summer can dehydrate you, and a long hike into or out of the canyon in the heat can necessitate drinking more than a gallon of water. Remember while hiking that mules have the right of way; always stay to the inside of the trail when being passed by a mule train. Don't attempt to hike from the rim to the Colorado River and back in 1 day. Many people who have tried this have suffered injury or death.

## DAY HIKES

There are no loop-trail day hikes possible in the Grand Canyon, but the vastly different scenery in every direction makes a return trip on the same trail a totally new experience. The easiest day hikes are those along the rim. There's a 1 1/2-mile paved trail leading from the Yavapai Museum to the Powell Memorial. From the Powell Memorial the trail becomes dirt and continues another 8 miles to Hermits Rest, from which, in summer, you can take a free shuttle back to Grand Canyon Village.

Trails leading down into the canyon include the Bright Angel Trail, the South Kaibab Trail, Grandview Trail, and the Hermit Trail. If you plan to hike for more than 30 minutes, carry 2 quarts of water per person. If you're game to do it, hiking into the canyon even just a short distance before doubling back will allow you to escape the ever-present crowds.

The **Bright Angel Trail** starts just west of Bright Angel Lodge in Grand Canyon Village. It's the main route down to Phantom Ranch and is the most popular trail into the canyon. Day hikes on this trail include the trips to Indian Gardens or Plateau Point. Both of these trips are long and very strenuous. There are rest houses at 1 1/2 and 3 miles (during the summer they have water), which make good turn-around points for a 3-mile or 6-mile round-trip hike.

The **South Kaibab Trail** begins near Yaki Point east of Grand Canyon Village and is the alternative route to Phantom Ranch. This trail offers the best views of any of the day hikes in the canyon. From the trailhead it's a 3-mile round-trip to Cedar Ridge. The hike is very strenuous and there's no water available along the trail.

The **Grandview Trail** is a steep, unmaintained trail that should be attempted only by people with experience hiking in the desert. It's a very strenuous 6-mile round-trip hike to Horseshoe Mesa, and there's no water available along the trail. Allow at least 7 hours for this rugged hike.

The **Hermit Trail** begins near Hermits Rest and is also steep and unmaintained. Don't attempt this trail if you don't have some experience hiking in the desert. It's a 5-mile round-trip to Santa Maria Springs and a 6-mile round-trip to Dripping Springs. Water from these springs must be treated before it's safe to drink.

## BACKPACKING

There are many miles of trails deep in the canyon and several established campgrounds for backpackers. The best times of year to backpack in the canyon are spring and autumn. During the summer, temperatures at the bottom of the canyon are regularly over 100°F, while in the winter ice and snow at higher elevations make footing on trails precarious. Be sure to carry at least 2 quarts, and preferably 1 gallon, of water whenever backpacking in the canyon.

A **Backcountry Use Permit** is required of all hikers planning to overnight in the canyon unless you'll be staying at Phantom Ranch in one of the cabins or in the dormitory.

Because a limited number of hikers are allowed into the canyon on any given day, it's important to make reservations as soon as it is possible to do so. Reservations are taken in person, by mail, and by fax (but not by phone). Contact the **Backcountry Reservations Office,** Grand Canyon National Park, P.O. Box 129, Grand Canyon, AZ 86023 (☎ **520/638-7875** between 1 and 5pm for information; fax 520/638-2125). Holiday periods are the most popular. The office begins accepting reservations on the first of every month for the following 5 months. If you want to hike over the Labor Day weekend, be sure you make your reservation on May 1! If you show up without a reservation, go to the Backcountry Reservations Office (open daily from 8am to noon and from 1 to 5pm) and put your name on the waiting list. When applying for a permit you'll have to specify your exact itinerary and, once in the canyon, you must stick to this itinerary. As of 1997, there is a nonrefundable $20 backcountry permit fee and a $4 per person per night backcountry camping fee.

There are **campgrounds** at Indian Gardens, Bright Angel Campground (near Phantom Ranch), and at Cottonwood, but hikers are limited to 2 nights per trip at each of these campgrounds (except from November 15 to February 28 when 4 nights are allowed at each campground). Other nights can be spent camping at undesignated sites in certain regions of the park.

The *Backcountry Trip Planner* publication has information to help you plan your itinerary. It's available through the Backcountry Office.

If you are interested in guided backpacking trips, see the information on the Grand Canyon Field Institute above.

## RAFTING THE COLORADO RIVER

Rafting down the Colorado River as it roars and tumbles through the mile-deep gorge of the Grand Canyon is the adventure of a lifetime. Ever since John Wesley Powell ignored everyone who knew better and proved that it was possible to travel by boat down the tumultuous Colorado River, running the big river has become a passion and an obsession with adventurers. Today anyone, from grade schoolers to grandmothers, can join the elite group who have made the run. However, be prepared for some of the most furious white water in the world.

There are 17 companies offering trips through various sections of the canyon. You can spend as few as 3 days on the river or as many as 16. You can go down the river in a huge motorized rubber raft, in a paddled- or oar-powered raft, a kayak, or a wooden dory.

Most trips start from Lees Ferry near Page and Lake Powell. It's also possible to start or finish a trip at Phantom Ranch, hiking in or out from either the north or South Rim. The main rafting season is from April to October, but some companies operate year-round. Trip prices range from around $650 for a 3-day trip to around $2,500 for a 14-day trip. Rafting trips tend to book up well in advance and some companies begin taking reservations in April for the following year's trips.

The following companies are currently authorized to operate trips through the Grand Canyon: **Aramark-Wilderness River Adventures,** P.O. Box 717, Page, AZ 86040 (☎ **800/992-8022** or 520/645-3296); **Arizona Raft Adventures,** 4050-F E. Huntington Dr., Flagstaff, AZ 86004 (☎ **800/786-RAFT** or 520/526-8200); **Arizona River Runners,** P.O. Box 47788, Phoenix, AZ 85068-7788 (☎ **800/ 477-7238** or 602/867-4866); **Canyon Explorations,** P.O. Box 310, Flagstaff, AZ 86002 (☎ **800/654-0723** or 520/774-4559); **Canyoneers,** P.O. Box 2997, Flagstaff, AZ 86003 (☎ **800/525-0924** or 520/526-0924); **Colorado River and Trail Expeditions,** P.O. Box 57575, Salt Lake City, UT 84157-0575 (☎ **800/253-7328** or 801/261-1789); **Diamond River Adventures,** P.O. Box 1316, Page, AZ 86040 (☎ **800/343-3121** or 520/645-8866); **Expeditions,** 625 N. Beaver Rd. (Route 4, Box 755), Flagstaff, AZ 86001 (☎ **520/779-3769**); **Grand Canyon Expeditions Company,** P.O. Box O, Kanab, UT 84741 (☎ **800/544-2691** or 801/644-2691); **Hatch River Expeditions,** P.O. Box 1200, Vernal, UT 84078 (☎ **800/433-8966** or 801/789-3813); **High Desert Adventures,** P.O. Box 40, St. George, UT 84771-0040 (☎ **801/673-1200**); **Moki Mac River Expeditions,** P.O. Box 21242, Salt Lake City, UT 84121 (☎ **800/284-7280** or 801/268-6667); **OARS/Grand Canyon Dories,** P.O. Box 216, Altaville, CA 95221 (☎ **800/346-6277** or 209/736-0805); **Outdoors Unlimited,** 6900 Townsend Winona Rd., Flagstaff, AZ 86004 (☎ **800/637-7238** or 520/526-4546); **Tours West,** P.O. Box 333, Orem, UT 84059 (☎ **800/453-9107** or 801/225-0755); and **Western River Expeditions,** 7258 Racquet Club Dr., Salt Lake City, UT 84121 (☎ **800/453-7450** or 801/942-6669).

## TWO TAMER ALTERNATIVES

For those not addicted to adrenaline, there are two Colorado River rafting alternatives. **Wilderness River Adventures,** 50 S. Lake Powell Blvd. (P.O. Box 717), Page, AZ 86040 (☎ **800/528-6154** or 520/645-3279), operates half- and full-day smoothwater raft trips between the Glen Canyon Dam and Lees Ferry. They offer two half-day trips and one full-day trip daily mid-May to mid-September. Half-day trips cost $44 for adults and $37 for children; full-day trips cost $65 for adults and $57 for children. In spring and fall one half-day trip is offered daily. It's also possible to arrange this trip through the **Fred Harvey Transportation Co.,** P.O. Box 709, Grand Canyon, AZ 86023 (☎ **520/638-2631**), which will transport you between Grand Canyon Village and Page. This trip costs $86 for adults and $43 for children ages 2 to 11.

West of Grand Canyon Village, on the Hualapai Indian Reservation, **Hualapai River Runners,** P.O. Box 246, Peach Springs, AZ 86434 (☎ **800/622-4409** or 520/769-2210), operates 1- and 2-day river trips that include half the time in white water and half the time in smooth water. These trips can include accommodations the night before and the night after the trip. One-day trips are $221 without accommodations and $308 with accommodations; 2-day trips are $321 without accommodations and $408 with accommodations.

## VIRTUAL REALITY: THE GRAND CANYON ON THE BIG SCREEN

In addition to the IMAX Theatre, you'll find a collection of short Cinemascope films about the canyon being shown in the Galaxy Four Theatres, a bizarre building that consists of interconnected domes (it's the strangest sight in Tusayan).

✪ **Grand Canyon IMAX Theatre.** Ariz. 64/U.S. 180, Grand Canyon. ☎ **520/638-2203.** Admission $7.50 adults, $4.50 children 3–11. Mar–Oct daily 8:30am–8:30pm; Nov–Feb daily 10:30am–6:30pm.

Located in the village of Tusayan at the south entrance to the park, the Grand Canyon IMAX Theatre devotes its seven-story screen to a 34-minute film about the canyon. A reenactment of John Wesley Powell's first navigation of the Colorado River is the central focus of the film, but geology, ancient history, and cultural and natural history are also included. However, the star of the show is, of course, the heart-stopping IMAX cinematography. The huge screen that fills your field of vision and the amazing high definition of the film together create an astoundingly realistic image of the canyon.

## WHERE TO STAY

Keep in mind that the Grand Canyon is one of the most popular national parks in the country and hotel rooms within the park are in high demand. If you want to stay in the park, make your reservations as far in advance as possible. For rim cabins at the Bright Angel Lodge, it's often necessary to make a reservation a year in advance. Hotels outside the park are especially popular with tour groups, which during the busy summer months keep many hotels full.

Don't head up here in summer without a reservation and expect to find a room. If you do, you may wind up having to drive to Williams or Flagstaff to find a vacancy. However, if you do find yourself here without a room and suddenly decide you want to stay, you can check to see if there have been any cancellations for that day. You can also call Grand Canyon National Park Lodges (☎ **520/638-2631**) to check on same-day availability . Who knows, you might get lucky.

### INSIDE THE PARK

**Moderate**

✪ **El Tovar Hotel.** AmFac Parks & Resorts, 14001 E. Iliff Ave., Suite 600, Aurora, CO 80014. ☎ **303/297-2757.** Fax 303/297-3175. 65 rms, 10 suites. A/C TV TEL. $112–$169 double; $192–$277 suite. AE, DC, DISC, MC, V.

This is the park's premier lodge, and it first opened its doors in 1905. Built of local rock and Oregon pine by Hopi craftsmen, the El Tovar is a rustic yet luxurious mountain lodge that perches on the edge of the canyon with awe-inspiring views (but only from some rooms). The lobby, entered from a verandah set with rustic furniture, has a small fireplace, cathedral ceiling, and log walls from which moose, deer, and antelope heads hang.

The rooms are not, however, done in the same rustic style as the hotel's public rooms. A renovation a few years back added carpets and colonial-style furniture that would be more appropriate in Williamsburg, Virginia. The standard rooms are rather small, as are the bathrooms, which were added after the hotel was built. Deluxe rooms provide more leg room, and the suites, with their private terraces and stunning views, are extremely spacious.

**Dining/Entertainment:** The El Tovar Dining Room (see "Where to Dine," below) is the best restaurant in the village and serves excellent continental and Southwestern cuisine. Just off the lobby is a cocktail lounge with a view.

**Services:** Concierge, room service, tour desk.

**Thunderbird & Kachina Lodges.** AmFac Parks & Resorts, 14001 E. Iliff Ave., Suite 600, Aurora, CO 80014. ☎ **303/297-2757.** Fax 303/297-3175. 104 rms. A/C TV TEL. $98–$108 single or double. AE, DC, DISC, MC, V.

Although these two motel-style lodges date to the 1960s, they are the newest lodges on the canyon rim. Despite the use of native sandstone in their construction, the 1960s motel modern styling clashes with the traditional design of the adjacent historic lodges. However, if you want modern amenities and a fairly large room, these should be your in-park choice in this price range. Thunderbird Lodge registration is handled by Bright Angel Lodge, and Kachina Lodge registration is handled by El Tovar Hotel.

The rooms in both lodges have large windows, although you'll have to request a canyon-side room on the second floor if you want a view of something more than a parking lot or the crowds milling along the rim trail. The canyon-view rooms are only $10 more than those without views and are well worth the extra cost. The Thunderbird Lodge was recently renovated and is currently the better choice of these two lodges.

**Yavapai Lodge.** AmFac Parks & Resorts, 14001 E. Iliff Ave., Suite 600, Aurora, CO 80014. ☎ **303/297-2757.** Fax 303/297-3175. 348 rms. TV TEL. $83–$98 double. AE, DC, DISC, MC, V.

Located in several buildings at the east end of Grand Canyon Village, the Yavapai is the largest lodge in the park. The rooms in the Yavapai East section of the hotel are set under shady pines and are more attractive than the rooms in the Yavapai West section (well worth the $10 price difference). There are no canyon views here, which is why this lodge is less expensive than the Thunderbird and Kachina lodges. It's also a 1-mile hike to the main section of the village.

There's a cafeteria serving burgers, sandwiches, pizza, and salads at relatively economical prices. The lodge also has a tour desk.

### Inexpensive

✪ **Bright Angel Lodge & Cabins.** AmFac Parks & Resorts, 14001 E. Iliff Ave., Suite 600, Aurora, CO 80014. ☎ **303/297-2757.** Fax 303/297-3175. 34 rms (10 with sink only, 10 with sink and toilet, 14 with bath), 55 cabins. $40 double with sink only, $46 double with sink and toilet, $56 double with bath; $66–$222 cabin. AE, DC, DISC, MC, V.

Bright Angel Lodge began operation in 1896 as a collection of tents and cabins on the edge of the canyon, but the current lodge didn't open until 1935. With its flagstone floor, huge fireplace, log walls, and soaring ceiling, the lodge's lobby is the epitome of a rustic retreat (albeit a very crowded one).

This is the most affordable lodge in the park and offers the greatest variety of accommodations. In addition to rooms with shared bathrooms, there are also roomier cabins, including four rim cabins that have their own fireplaces. These rim cabins are the most popular and are usually booked a year in advance. The other rooms should be booked at least 6 months in advance. Most of the rooms and cabins feature rustic furnishings, but have been recently renovated. The Buckey Suite, the oldest structure on the canyon rim, is arguably the best room in the park, with a canyon view, fireplace, and a king-size bed.

The Bright Angel Coffee Shop (see "Where to Dine," below) serves all meals, while the Arizona Steak House (see "Where to Dine," below) is open for dinner only. For snacks, sandwiches, and ice cream, there's the Bright Angel Fountain. The lodge also has a tour desk and museum.

**Maswik Lodge.** AmFac Parks & Resorts, 14001 E. Iliff Ave., Suite 600, Aurora, CO 80014. ☎ **303/297-2757.** Fax 303/297-3175. 250 rms, 28 cabins. TV TEL. $59–$107 double. AE, DC, DISC, MC, V.

Set back a bit from the rim, the Maswik Lodge offers spacious rooms and rustic cabins. If you crave modern appointments, opt for one of the Maswik North rooms. More rugged types will prefer the less expensive old cabins, which aren't too attractive but are economically priced. The cabins have bathtubs but not showers in their bathrooms.

There's a large cafeteria (see "Where to Dine," below) and a sports lounge with a big-screen TV. There's also a tour desk here.

**Phantom Ranch.** AmFac Parks & Resorts, 14001 E. Iliff Ave., Suite 600, Aurora, CO 80014. ☎ **303/297-2757.** Fax 303/297-3175. Reconfirmations ☎ 520/638-3283 or 520/638-2631, ext. 6015. 11 cabins, 40 dorm beds. $58 double in the cabins; $21 dormitory bed. Mule trip overnights (with all meals and mule ride included) are $265 for 1 person and $472 for 2 people (2-night trips are available mid-Nov through Mar). AE, MC, V.

This is the only lodge at the bottom of the Grand Canyon and as such is very popular with both hikers and mule riders. Built in 1922, Phantom Ranch has a classic ranch atmosphere. The accommodations are in rustic stone-walled cabins or 10-bedded gender-segregated dormitories. Evaporative coolers keep both the cabins and the dorms cool in the summer. Make reservations as early as possible (up to a year in advance) and don't forget to reconfirm. It's also possible to get a room on the day of departure if there are any last-minute cancellations. To attempt this, you must be at the Bright Angel Lodge transportation desk before 6am (some people show up as early as 4am) on the day you wish to stay at Phantom Ranch.

**Dining/Entertainment:** Family-style meals must be reserved in advance. The menu consists of beef-and-vegetable stew or vegetarian dinner for $16.75, or steak for $26.75. Breakfasts ($11.75) are hearty and sack lunches ($5.50) are available. Between meals the dining hall becomes a canteen selling snacks, drinks, gifts, and necessities. After dinner the dining hall becomes a beer hall. Services here include a public phone and mule-back baggage transfer between Grand Canyon Village and Phantom Ranch ($46 each way).

## TUSAYAN (OUTSIDE THE SOUTH ENTRANCE)

If you can't get a reservation for a room in the park, this is the next closest place to stay. Unfortunately, this area can be very noisy because of the many helicopters and airplanes taking off from the airport and other places around town.

### Expensive

**Grand Canyon Suites.** P.O. Box 3251, Grand Canyon, AZ 86023. ☎ **888/538-5353** or 520/638-3100. Fax 520/638-2747. 32 suites. A/C TV TEL. $168–$208 double. AE, MC, V.

At press time, this was the newest lodging in Tusayan, and was also the most interesting. Each of the 32 suites is decorated in a different theme, and all have separate parlors and bedrooms. Some of the room themes of note include a Route 66 suite, Navajo and Hopi suites, a Wild Bill Hickock suite, and a Zane Grey suite. Although the prices here are high, the rooms have more character than most of the other accommodations in the area. Microwaves, coffeemakers, refrigerators, and VCRs are all standard. Unfortunately, there is no pool or whirlpool. This hotel is tucked in behind the Holiday Inn Express.

## Moderate

**Best Western Grand Canyon Squire Inn.** P.O. Box 130, Grand Canyon, AZ 86023-0130. ☎ **800/528-1234** or 520/638-2681. Fax 520/638-2782. 250 rms, 4 suites. A/C TV TEL. Mar to mid-Oct and Christmas week $99–$140 double, $195 suite; mid-Oct to Nov $65–$80 double, $195 suite. Dec–Mar (excluding Christmas week) $49–$65 double; $195 suite. AE, CB, DC, DISC, MC, V.

If you prefer playing tennis to riding a mule, this may be the place for you. The rooms are large and come with two double beds and comfortable easy chairs. One wall of each guest room is made of local stones and there are large windows that let in plenty of light.

The dining room here is the best restaurant in the area, and serves continental cuisine and regional American specialties at reasonable prices. Less expensive fare is available in the coffee shop. Before or after dinner you can sit by the fireplace in the lounge. The inn offers free airport shuttle service, a pool, two tennis courts, a whirlpool, sauna, bowling alley, pool room, video arcade, and tour desk. There's even a sort of cowboy museum in the lobby.

**Holiday Inn Express—Grand Canyon.** P.O. Box 3245, Grand Canyon, AZ 86023. ☎ **800/ HOLIDAY** or 520/638-3000. Fax 520/638-0123. 166 rms, 3 suites. A/C TV TEL. $55–$128 double, $99–$168 suite. Rates include continental breakfast. AE, DC, DISC, MC, V.

This is one of the newest lodgings in the area and has modern, well-designed, if a bit sterile and characterless, guest rooms. No pool or restaurant mean you'll likely be spending a lot of your time away from your room.

**Moqui Lodge.** AmFac Parks & Resorts, 14001 E. Iliff Ave., Aurora, CO 80014. ☎ **303/297-2757.** Fax 303/297-3175. 136 rms. TV TEL. $83–$98 double. Rates include full breakfast. AE, DC, DISC, MC, V. Closed Dec to mid-Feb.

Managed by the same company that operates all the lodges within the park, this motel is located just outside the south entrance to the park. With its tall A-frame construction, Moqui Lodge has the feel of a ski lodge at first, but unfortunately lacks the appropriate character. The best of accommodations here are standard motel-style rooms with large windows that for the most part look out onto wide expanses of parking lot, while the worst are cramped, poorly furnished, and overpriced. About the only thing this lodge has going for it is its proximity to the park entrance, its riding stables, and the fact that the shuttle bus stops here. Moderately priced Mexican and American meals are served in the dining room amid Spanish-colonial decor, and just off the main lobby is a dark lounge with a stone fireplace. There's also a tour desk here.

**Quality Inn Grand Canyon.** P.O. Box 520, Grand Canyon, AZ 86023. ☎ **800/221-5151** or 520/638-2673. Fax 520/638-9537. 176 rms, 56 suites. A/C TV TEL. $68–$140 double, $138–$198 suite. AE, CB, DC, DISC, MC, V.

This relatively luxurious hotel at the park's south entrance is built around two enclosed skylit courtyards, one of which houses a restaurant and the other a bar and whirlpool spa. There's also an outdoor whirlpool, as well as an outdoor pool. The rooms are large and comfortable, and have balconies or patios. Most also have minibars. For extra space, there are now suites with separate small living rooms, microwaves, refrigerators, and coffeemakers. The hotel is located next to the IMAX Theatre and is very popular with tour groups.

**Red Feather Lodge.** P.O. Box 1460, Grand Canyon, AZ 86023. ☎ **800/538-2345** or 520/ 638-2414. Fax 520/638-9216. 230 rms. A/C TV TEL. $69–$128 double. AE, DC, MC, V.

Try to get one of the newer rooms, of which there are 130. These are a bit more comfortable than the older rooms. However, no matter which type of room you get, you'll be able to avail yourself of an outdoor pool (seasonal) and whirlpool, as well as a fitness room. Kids will appreciate the game room. There is also a casual restaurant on the premises.

**Seven Mile Lodge.** P.O. Box 56, Grand Canyon, AZ 86023. ☎ **520/638-2291.** 20 rms. A/C TV TEL. $58–$80 double. AE, DISC, MC, V.

This small and nondescript little motel is consistently the least expensive lodging in Tusayan (aside from the campground). The rooms are simply furnished, but large enough to hold two queen beds.

## OTHER AREA ACCOMMODATIONS

✪ **Cameron Trading Post Motel.** P.O. Box 339, Cameron, AZ 86020. ☎ **800/338-7385** or 520/679-2231. Fax 520/679-2350. 62 rms, 4 suites. A/C TV TEL. $74–$84 double; $145–$175 suite. AE, DC, MC, V.

Located 54 miles north of Flagstaff on U.S. 89 at the junction with the road to the east entrance to the national park, this motel offers some of the most attractive rooms anywhere in the vicinity of the Grand Canyon. The motel is adjacent to the historic Cameron Trading Post and is built around the old trading post's terraced gardens, which are a shady oasis. The rooms are furnished with Southwestern-style pine furniture and are attractively decorated. Most of the rooms have balconies and some have views of the canyon of the Little Colorado River. There are two restaurants here as well as one of the best trading posts in the state.

**Grand Canyon Days Inn.** Valle, AZ 86046. ☎ **800/329-7466** or 520/635-9203. Fax 520/635-2345. 73 rms. A/C TV TEL. Apr–Oct $89–$94 double; Nov–Mar $49–$64 double. AE, DISC, MC, V.

Located 30 miles south of Grand Canyon Village, this motel is the next closest lodging to the south entrance after those at Tusayan. If you've got small children, this might be a good choice. Directly across the street is Bedrock City (a Flintstones theme park).

## CAMPGROUNDS

### Inside the Park

On the South Rim, there are two campgrounds and an RV park. **Mather Campground** is in Grand Canyon Village and has 350 campsites. For reservations, contact DESTINET, P.O. Box 85705, San Diego, CA 92186-5705 (☎ **800/365-2267**), which takes reservations beginning 5 months in advance of your intended reservation dates but only if you plan to visit between March 1 and December 1. Other times of year, no reservations are accepted. Reservations are a necessity if you want to be certain to get a campsite in the park. However, if you don't have a reservation, your next best bet is to arrive in the morning when campsites are being vacated. Campsites are $12 per night between September and May and $15 per night between June and August.

**Desert View Campground,** with 50 sites, is located 26 miles east of Grand Canyon Village and is only open from mid-May to mid-October. No reservations are accepted for this campground. Campsites are $10 per night.

The **Trailer Village RV park** is located in Grand Canyon Village. Reservations are made through the Grand Canyon National Park Lodges, 14001 E. Iliff Ave., Aurora, CO 80014 (☎ **303/297-2757**; fax 303/297-3175). There are 192 full hookup sites here. RV sites are $19 per night.

### Outside the Park

Getting a campsite inside the park is no easy feat, and if you get shut out, your next best choices lie within a few miles of the south entrance to the park. In Tusayan, you'll find **Grand Canyon Camper Village,** P.O. Box 490, Grand Canyon, AZ 86023-0490 (☎ **520/638-2887**), which is open year-round. This is primarily an RV park, but it also has a surprisingly attractive area for tent camping. The only drawback is that you're right in town, which I'm sure is hardly what you were dreaming of when you planned your trip to the Grand Canyon. Rates here are $23 for full hook-up RV sites, $21 for sites with water and electric, $19 for sites with electricity only, and $15 for tent sites. There are also teepees here that rent for $19 per night.

Three miles south of Tusayan you'll find the U.S. Forest Service's **Ten-X Campground.** The campground is open from May 1 to October 1 and campsites are $10.

You can also camp just about anywhere within the Kaibab National Forest, which borders Grand Canyon National Park, as long as you are more than a quarter mile away from Ariz. 64/U.S. 180. Several dirt roads lead into the forest from the highway, and though you won't find designated campsites or toilets along these roads, you will find spots where others have obviously camped before. This so-called dispersed camping is usually used by campers who have been unable to find sites in campgrounds. Anyone equipped for backpacking could also just hike in a ways from any forest road rather than camping right beside the road. One of the most popular roads for this sort of camping is just north of Tusayan on the west side of the highway leading to the south park entrance. For more information, contact the **Tusayan Ranger District,** Kaibab National Forest, P.O. Box 3088, Grand Canyon, AZ 86023 (☎ **520/638-2443**).

## WHERE TO DINE

In addition to the restaurants listed below, which are all within the park, you'll find several restaurants just outside the south entrance in Tusayan. The best of these is the **Coronado Dining Room** at the Best Western Grand Canyon Squire Inn. You'll also find a steakhouse and a pizza place, as well as familiar chains such as McDonald's, Taco Bell, Pizza Hut, and Subway.

### INSIDE THE PARK

#### Expensive

✪ **El Tovar Dining Room.** In the El Tovar Hotel. ☎ **520/638-2631,** ext. 6432. Reservations required at dinner. Main courses $15–$25. AE, DC, DISC, MC, V. Daily 6:30–11am, 11:30am–2pm, and 5–10pm. CONTINENTAL/SOUTHWESTERN.

Rough-hewn ceiling beams and log walls are a surprising contrast to the fine china, crystal, and linen table settings in the El Tovar Dining Room. World-class continental cuisine with touches of Southwestern flavor thrown in for good measure is the hallmark of the restaurant's excellent chef. Most of the ingredients used in the El Tovar's kitchen are flown in daily to assure freshness and quality. On a recent visit the dinner menu featured fennel-crusted soft-shell crabs with cilantro corn relish among the appetizers. For a main course you might try the likes of medallions of veal with apricots and red peppercorns in orange-muscat sauce. The view out the picture windows is one of the best in the world, and the service is excellent. Make reservations as soon as possible to get the dinner time you want.

#### Moderate

**Arizona Steak House.** In the Bright Angel Lodge. ☎ **520/638-2631.** Reservations not accepted. Dinner $12–$20. AE, DC, DISC, MC, V. Daily 5–10pm. STEAKS.

If you have a craving for a thick juicy steak or a crisp cool salad, a visit to this steakhouse is in order. The decor is contemporary Southwest with a desert palette of pastel colors. A wall of glass along one side of the restaurant assures everyone of a view of the canyon beyond. Since the restaurant is open only for dinner (although group tours dine here at lunch), you should get here as early as possible to enjoy the sunset view and to avoid a long wait for a table.

**Bright Angel Coffee Shop.** In the Bright Angel Lodge. ☎ **520/638-2631.** Reservations not accepted. Main dishes $6–$13. AE, DC, DISC, MC, V. Daily 6:30–10:45am and 11:15am–10pm. AMERICAN.

Muted desert tones, lodgepole pine beams and pillars, and wrought-iron chandeliers give this spacious and casual dining room a distinctive Southwestern feel. Waiters in black bola ties and vests are friendly and efficient. What's on the menu are Southwestern favorites such as enchiladas, tacos, and fajitas, and foods comforting to a hungry and tired hiker such as spaghetti and meatballs. Wines are available. If you put your name on the waiting list, the wait usually isn't very long.

### Inexpensive

If you're looking for a quick, inexpensive meal, there are plenty of options. In Grand Canyon Village, choices include **cafeterias** at the Yavapai and Maswik lodges and a **delicatessen** at Babbitt's General Store (across from the visitor center). **Hermits Rest Fountain** on the West Rim Drive is a snack bar. At Desert View (on the East Rim Drive) is the **Desert View Trading Post Cafeteria.** All of these places are open daily for all three meals, and all serve meals for $7 and under.

## THE GRAND CANYON AFTER DARK

Most people visiting the Grand Canyon aren't thinking about anything other than a campfire when they think of evening entertainment, but in fact there's quite a bit of nightlife for those who haven't been exhausted by a day of hiking or mule riding. The **Maswik Cafeteria** has a sports bar with big-screen TV, and there are lounges at **El Tovar Hotel** and **Bright Angel Lodge.** The lounge at **Moqui Lodge** is reputed to have the best margaritas in the area.

In addition, there are more traditional national park evening programs such as stargazing and lecture/slide shows on cultural and natural-history aspects of the Grand Canyon (see *The Guide* for information). Most of these programs are held in the Shrine of the Ages near the visitor center. In September there's the **Grand Canyon Chamber Music Festival** (☎ 520/638-9215).

## EN ROUTE TO OR FROM PAGE/LAKE POWELL OR FLAGSTAFF

The **Cameron Trading Post** (☎ 800/338-7385 or 520/679-2231), at the crossroads of Cameron where Ariz. 64 to Grand Canyon Village branches off U.S. 89, is the best trading post in the state and should not be missed. The original stone trading post, a historic building, now houses a gallery of old and antique Indian artifacts, clothing, and jewelry. This gallery offers museum-quality pieces and even if you don't have $10,000 or $15,000 to drop on an old rug or basket, you can still look around. The main trading post is a more modern building and is the largest trading post in northern Arizona. Don't miss the beautiful old terraced gardens in back of the original trading post.

## 4 Havasu Canyon

70 miles N of Ariz. 66; 155 miles NW of Flagstaff; 115 miles NE of Kingman

Imagine hiking for hours through a dusty brown landscape of rocks and cacti. The sun overhead is blistering and bright. The air is hot and dry. Rock walls rise up higher and higher as you continue your descent through a mazelike canyon. Eventually the narrow canyon opens up into a wide plain shaded by cottonwood trees, a sure sign of water, and within a few minutes you hear the sound of a babbling stream. The water, when you finally reach it, is cool and crystal clear, a pleasant surprise. Following the stream, you pass through a dusty Indian village of modern homes. Every yard seems to be a corral for horses, not surprising in a village 8 miles beyond the last road. You pass through the village, still following the stream. As the trail descends again, you spot the first waterfall.

The previously crystal-clear water is now brilliant turquoise blue at the foot of the waterfall. The sandstone walls look redder than before. No, you aren't having a heat-induced hallucination—the water really is turquoise, and it fills terraces of travertine to form deep pools of cool water at the base of three large waterfalls. Together these three waterfalls form what many claim is the most beautiful spot in the entire Grand Canyon.

This is Havasu Canyon, the canyon of the Havasupai tribe, whose name means "people of the blue-green waters." For centuries the Havasupai have called this idyllic desert oasis home.

## ESSENTIALS

**GETTING THERE    By Car**    It isn't possible to drive all the way to Supai village or Havasu Canyon. The nearest road ends 8 miles from Supai at Hualapai Hilltop. This is the trailhead for the trail into the canyon and is at the end of Indian Route 18, which runs north from Ariz. 66. The turnoff is 6 miles east of Peach Springs and 21 miles west of Seligman. Many Arizona maps show an unpaved road between U.S. 180 and Hualapai Hilltop, but this road is not maintained on a regular basis and is only passable to four-wheel-drive vehicles *when* it's clear of fallen logs.

**By Helicopter**    The easiest and fastest (and by far the most expensive) way to reach Havasu Canyon is by helicopter from the Grand Canyon Airport. Flights are operated by **Papillon Grand Canyon Helicopters** (☎ **800/528-2418** or 520/638-2419). The round-trip air-and-ground day excursion is $440 and the overnight excursion is $482.

There are also helicopters that carry Supai villagers back and forth between the village and Hualapai Hilltop. Occasionally it is possible for visitors to get rides on these helicopters, but don't count on it.

**By Horse**    The next-easiest way to get to Havasu Canyon is by horse. Both you and your luggage can ride from Hualapai Hilltop, the trailhead for Supai and Havasu Canyon. Pack and saddle horses can be rented from the **Havasupai Tourist Enterprise** (☎ **520/448-2121**), which is based in Supai. Round-trip rates are $110 from Hualapai Hilltop to the campground, $80 from Hualapai Hilltop to Supai village, and $80 from Supai village to the campground. One-way rates are also available—many people who hike in decide that it's worth the money to ride out, or at least have their backpack packed out. Be sure to confirm your horse reservation a day before driving to Hualapai Hilltop. Sometimes no horses are available and it's a long drive back to the nearest town.

**On Foot**    The cheapest, slowest, and most difficult way to reach Havasu Canyon is on foot. Start early to avoid the heat of the day. The hike is beautiful, but it's 10 miles to the campground. The steepest part of the trail is the first mile or so from Hualapai Hilltop. After this section it's relatively flat.

**FEES & RESERVATIONS**    There's a $15 per-person entry fee to Havasu Canyon from April to October, $12 the rest of the year. Everyone is required to register at the Tourist Office across from the sports field as you enter the village of Supai. Because it's a long walk in to the campground, be sure you have a confirmed reservation before setting out from Hualapai Hilltop. It's good to make reservations as far in advance as possible, especially for holiday weekends. The tourist enterprises at Supai operate on a cash-only basis, so be sure to bring enough.

## HIKING, SWIMMING & MORE

The waterfalls are the main attraction here and most people are content to sun themselves on the sand, go for dips in the cool waters, and gaze for hours at the turquoise waters.

When you tire of these pursuits, you can go for a hike up the small side canyon to the east of Havasu Falls. Another trail leads along the west rim of Havasu Canyon and can be reached by carefully climbing up a steep rocky area near the village cemetery. There's also a trail that leads all the way down to the Colorado River, though this is an overnight hike.

In Supai village is a small museum dedicated to the culture of the Havasupai people. Its exhibits and old photos will give you an idea of how little the lives of these people have changed over the years.

## OTHER AREA ACTIVITIES

In addition to visiting Havasu Canyon, you may want to tour the **Grand Canyon Caverns** (☎ 520/422-3223), which are located just outside Peach Springs. The caverns are accessed via a 210-foot elevator ride. Admission is $8.50 for adults and $5.75 for children.

Also in this area, you can raft down the Colorado River with **Hualapai River Runners,** P.O. Box 246, Peach Springs, AZ 86434 (☎ **800/622-4409** or 520/769-2210), which operates 1- and 2-day river trips that include half the time in white water and half the time in smooth water. These trips can include accommodations the night before and the night after the trip. One-day trips are $221 without accommodations and $308 with accommodations; 2-day trips are $321 without accommodations and $408 with accommodations.

## WHERE TO STAY & DINE
### IN HAVASU CANYON

**Havasu Campground.** Havasupai Tourist Enterprise, Supai, AZ 86435. ☎ **520/448-2121.** 400 sites. Apr–Oct $10 per person per night. Nov–Mar $9 per person per night.

The campground is located 2 miles below Supai village, between Havasu Falls and Mooney Falls. The campsites are mostly in the shade of cottonwood trees on either side of Havasu Creek. Picnic tables are provided, but no firewood is available at the campground. Cutting any trees or shrubs is prohibited, so be sure to bring a camp stove with you. Spring water is available, and though it's considered safe to drink, we advise treating it first.

**Havasupai Lodge.** General Delivery, Supai, AZ 86435. ☎ **520/448-2111.** 24 rms. A/C. Apr–Oct $80 double; Nov–Mar $50 double. MC, V.

Located in Supai village just past the school, this modern lodge is, aside from the campground, the only accommodation in the canyon. The two-story building features standard motel-style rooms that are lacking only TVs and telephones, neither of which are in demand at this isolated retreat. People come to Havasu Canyon to get away from it all, and the Havasupai Lodge is happy to oblige. The only drawback of this comfortable lodge is that it's 2 miles from Havasu Falls and 3 miles from Mooney Falls. The Havasupai Café, across from the general store, serves breakfast, lunch, and dinner. It's a very casual place, and the prices are high because all ingredients must be packed in by horse.

## NEAR HUALAPAI HILLTOP

**Grand Canyon Caverns Inn.** P.O. Box 180, Peach Springs, AZ 86434. ☎ **520/422-3223.**
48 rms. A/C TV TEL. Summer $46 double; winter $23 double. AE, DISC, MC, V.

If you're planning to hike or ride into Havasu Canyon, you'll need to be at Hualapai
Hilltop as early in the morning as possible. It's a 3- to 4-hour drive to Hualapai
Hilltop from Flagstaff, so you might want to consider staying here, the only lodging for miles around. As the name implies, this motel is built on the site of the Grand
Canyon Caverns, which are open to the public. There's a casual restaurant and cocktail lounge. Facilities include a games room, a gift shop, and a general store with
camping supplies and food. For much of the year, this motel is used by Elderhostel
and stays full.

# 5  Lake Powell & Page

272 miles N of Phoenix; 130 miles E of the Grand Canyon North Rim; 130 miles NE of Grand
Canyon South Rim

Had the early Spanish explorers of Arizona suddenly come upon Lake Powell after
traipsing for months across desolate desert, they would have either taken it for a mirage or fallen to their knees and rejoiced. Surrounded by hundreds of miles of parched
desert land, this artificial lake seems unreal when first glimpsed. Yet real it is, and,
like a magnet, it draws everyone in the region toward its promise of relief from the
heat.

Though construction began on the Glen Canyon Dam in 1960 and was completed in 1963, Lake Powell did not reach capacity until 1980. Today it's a water
playground frequented by boaters, skiers, fisherfolk, and people who come here to
see **Rainbow Bridge,** one of the natural wonders of the world. Rainbow Bridge is
called *nonnozhoshi,* or "the rainbow turned to stone," by the Navajo. It's the largest natural bridge on earth and stretches 278 feet across a side canyon of Lake
Powell.

Construction of the Glen Canyon Dam came about despite the angry outcry of
many who felt that this canyon was even more beautiful than the Grand Canyon and
should be preserved in its natural state. Preservationists lost this battle, and today
houseboats and skiers cruise where birds and waterfalls once filled the canyons with
their songs.

The town of Page, a work camp constructed to house the workers who built the
dam, has now become much more than just a construction camp and, with its many
motels and restaurants, is the best place from which to explore Lake Powell.

## ESSENTIALS

**GETTING THERE**   Page is connected to Flagstaff by U.S. 89. Ariz. 98 leads
southeast onto the Navajo Indian Reservation and connects with U.S. 160 to Kayenta
and Four Corners.

The Page Airport, 1 mile east of town on Ariz. 98, is served by **Scenic Airlines**
(☎ **800/445-8738**) from Las Vegas and **Great Lakes Airlines** (☎ **800/274-0662**)
from Phoenix.

**VISITOR INFORMATION**   For further information on Page and Lake Powell,
contact the **Page/Lake Powell Chamber of Commerce,** 106 S. Lake Powell Blvd.
(P.O. Box 727), Page, AZ 86040 (☎ **520/645-2741;** fax 520/645-3181); or the
**John Wesley Powell Memorial Museum and Visitor Information Center,** 6 N.
Lake Powell Blvd. (P.O. Box 547), Page, AZ 86040 (☎ **520/645-9496;** fax 520/
645-3412).

**GETTING AROUND**　Rental cars are available at the Page Airport from **Budget** (☎ **800/527-0700** or 520/645-3977). Call **Lake Powell Limo/Taxi** (☎ **520/ 645-8540**) if you need a cab.

# GLEN CANYON NATIONAL RECREATION AREA

Until the flooding of Glen Canyon formed Lake Powell, this area was one of the most remote regions in the contiguous 48 states. However, with the construction of Glen Canyon Dam across a stretch of the Colorado River less than a third of a mile wide, this remote and rugged landscape became one of the country's most popular national recreation areas. Today the lake and much of the surrounding land is designated the Glen Canyon National Recreation Area and attracts nearly 4 million visitors each year. The otherworldly setting amid the slick-rock canyons of northern Arizona and southern Utah is a tapestry of colors, the blues and greens of the lake contrasting with the reds and oranges of the surrounding sandstone cliffs. This interplay of colors and vast, desert landscapes easily makes Lake Powell the most beautiful of Arizona's many reservoirs.

Built to provide water for the desert communities of the Southwest and West, **Glen Canyon Dam** stands 710 feet above the bedrock and contains almost 5 million cubic yards of concrete. The dam also provides hydroelectric power, and deep within its massive wall of concrete are huge power turbines. Most visitors to the area are, however, more interested in waterskiing and powerboating than they are in drinking water and power production. Without the dam, however, there would be no lake, so any visit to this area ought to start with a tour of the dam and a stop at the **Carl Hayden Visitor Center** (☎ **520/608-6404**), which is located beside the dam (on U.S. 89 just north of Page) and is open daily from 8am to 5pm (7am to 7pm in summer). Here you can learn about the construction of the dam and then descend into the dam itself for a free self-guided tour (allow 30 to 45 minutes). Keep in mind that dam tours must start at least 1 hour before the visitor center closes. A visit to the dam helps add a bit of perspective to an appreciation of Lake Powell's many recreational pursuits.

More than 500 feet deep in some places, and bound by nearly 2,000 miles of shoreline, Lake Powell is a maze of convoluted canyons where rock walls often rise hundreds of feet straight out of the water. In places, long, winding canyons are so narrow that you can reach out and touch the towering walls on either side of a boat simultaneously. It is this otherworldly meeting of rock and water that has made this lake one of the most popular destinations in the Southwest.

For more information before leaving home, you can contact the **Glen Canyon National Recreation Area,** P.O. Box 1507, Page, AZ 86040 (☎ **520/608-6405** or 520/608-6404). Admission to the national recreation area is $5 per car (pass good for 1 week), and there is also a $5 per day or $10 per week boat fee if you bring your own boat. In addition to the Carl Hayden Visitor Center mentioned above, there is the **Bullfrog Visitor Center,** in Bullfrog, Utah (☎ **801/684-7400**). This visitor center is open daily from 8am to 5pm, but may be closed in winter months.

## BOAT TOURS

There are few roads penetrating the Glen Canyon Recreation Area, so the best way to appreciate this rugged region is by boat. If you haven't got your own boat, you can at least see a small part of the lake on a boat tour. There are a variety of boat tours that depart from **Wahweap Marina** (☎ **800/528-6154** or 520/645-2433). Three times daily, the paddlewheeler *Canyon King* embarks on a 1-hour tour ($10 for adults, $7 for children) that, unfortunately, doesn't really show you much more of the lake than you can see from shore. The *Canyon King* also does sunset ($22.50 for adults,

$19.50 for children) and dinner cruises ($45.50). A better choice for anyone with limited time or finances would be one of the tours to Navajo Canyon ($22 to $28 for adults, $14 to $20 for children). However, to see the most of the lake, opt for the full-day tour to Rainbow Bridge (see below for details).

## WATER SPORTS

While simply exploring the lake's maze of canyons on a narrated tour is satisfying enough for many visitors, houseboating, waterskiing, riding personal watercraft, and fishing are still the most popular activities, and five marinas (only Wahweap is in Arizona) help boaters explore the lake. You can bring your own boat or rent one here. At the **Wahweap Marina** (☎ **800/528-6154** or 520/645-2433) you can rent various types of boats, personal watercraft, and water-skis and head out on your own to have some fun on the water. Rental rates in the summer high season range from $66 for a 16-foot skiff with a 25-horsepower engine up to $275 per day for a 19-foot boat with a 150-horsepower engine. In the low season rates range from $40 to $165 a day. Weekly rates are also available. Small boats and personal watercraft can also be rented from **High Image Marine Center,** 920 Hemlock St. (☎ **520/645-8845**), and **Doo Powell,** 130 Sixth Ave. (☎ **800/350-1230** or 520/645-1230). For information on renting houseboats, see "Houseboating" below.

If roaring engines aren't your speed, you might want to consider exploring Lake Powell in a sea kayak. While afternoon winds can sometimes make paddling difficult, mornings are often quiet. With a narrow sea kayak, you can even explore canyons too small for powerboats. You can rent sea kayaks from **Red Rock Cyclery,** 819 N. Navajo Dr. (☎ **520/645-1479**). A one-person kayak rents for $40 per day and a two-person kayak rents for $45 a day.

While most of Glen Canyon National Recreation Area consists of the impounded waters of Lake Powell, within the recreation area there is also a short stretch of the Colorado River that still flows swift and free. If you'd like to see this stretch of river, try a float trip from Glen Canyon Dam to Lees Ferry. These raft trips are operated by **Wilderness River Adventures** (☎ **800/528-6154** or 520/645-3279) between March and October and cost $44 for adults and $37 for children for a half-day trip. All-day trips are also available ($65 adults, $57 children). Make reservations at least 2 weeks in advance.

If you've got a boat (either your own or a rental), avail yourself of some excellent year-round **fishing.** Smallmouth, largemouth, and striped bass, as well as walleye, catfish, and crappie, are all plentiful. Because the lake lies within both Arizona and Utah, you'll need to know which state's waters you're fishing in whenever you cast your line out, and you'll need the appropriate license. (Also, be sure to pick up a copy of the Arizona and Utah state fishing regulations or ask about applicable regulations at any of the marinas on the lake.) You can arrange licenses to fish the entire lake at **Wahweap Lodge and Marina** (☎ **520/645-2433**), which also sells bait and tackle and can provide you with a bit of advice on fishing this massive reservoir. Other marinas on the lake also sell licenses, bait, and tackle. The best season is March through November, though walleye are most often caught during the cooler months. Throughout the year there are numerous fishing tournaments.

If you'd rather try your hand at catching humongous rainbow trout, try downstream of the Glen Canyon Dam, where cold waters provide ideal conditions for trout to grow big. Unfortunately, there isn't much access to this stretch of river. You'll need a trout stamp to fish for these trophy trout.

If you're just looking for a good place to go for a swim near Wahweap Lodge, take the Coves Loop just west of the marina. Of the three coves, the third one is the best, with a sandy beach. The Chains area, another good place to jump off the rocks and otherwise lounge by the lake, is just outside Page down a rough dirt road just before you reach Glen Canyon Dam. The view underwater at Lake Powell is as scenic as the view above it, and if you're interested in exploring the underwater regions of the canyon, contact **Twin Finn Diving Center** (☎ 520/645-3114), which charges $90 for a 1-day resort diving course. Guided shore dives that include all equipment are $55, and boat dives for up to six people cost $250 for the boat and all equipment.

## HIKING

While most activity within the national recreation area centers around water, the short hike to the **Horseshoe Bend** viewpoint is very worthwhile (be sure to bring your camera). Horseshoe Bend is a huge loop of the Colorado River, and the viewpoint is hundreds of feet above the water on the edge of a sheer cliff. Far below, you can often see people camped at a riverside campsite that is accessible only by boat. It's about one-half mile to the viewpoint from the trailhead, which is located 5 miles south of the Carl Hayden Visitor Center on U.S. 89 just south of milepost 545.

At Lees Ferry, 39 miles from Page at the southern tip of the national recreation area, you'll find three short trails (Cathedral Wash, River Trail, and Spencer Trail), as well as the southern trailhead for the famed **Paria Canyon,** a favorite of canyoneering backpackers. This latter trail is 37 miles long and follows the meandering route of a narrow slot canyon for much of its length. Most hikers start from the northern trailhead, which is in Utah on U.S. 89. At the Carl Hayden Visitor Center, you can also pick up brochures that describe several area day hikes.

# RAINBOW BRIDGE NATIONAL MONUMENT

Roughly 50 miles up Lake Powell from Wahweap Marina and Glen Canyon Dam, in a narrow side canyon of the lake, rises **Rainbow Bridge,** the world's largest natural bridge and one of the most spectacular sights in the Southwest. Preserved in Rainbow Bridge National Monument, this natural arch of sandstone stands 290 feet high and spans 275 feet. Carved by wind and water over the ages, Rainbow Bridge is an awesome reminder of the powers of erosion that have sculpted this entire region into the spectacle it is today.

Rainbow Bridge is accessible only by boat or on foot (13-mile hike minimum), and traveling there by boat is by far the more popular route. **Lake Powell Resorts and Marinas** (☎ 800/528-6154 or 520/645-2433) offers daily half-day ($59.50 for adults, $39.50 for children) and full-day ($83 for adults, $55 for children) boat tours to Rainbow Bridge. The latter tours include box lunches and exploring one or more other major canyons along the way.

Rainbow Bridge National Monument is administered by Glen Canyon National Recreation Area, and information is available from sources mentioned above for the recreation area. For information on hiking to Rainbow Bridge, contact the **Navajo Parks and Recreation Department,** P.O. Box 9000, Window Rock, AZ 86515 (☎ 520/871-6647).

# ANTELOPE CANYON

If you've spent any time in Arizona, chances are you've seen photos of a narrow canyon only a few feet wide. The sandstone walls of the canyon seem to glow with an inner light in these photos, and beams of sunlight slice down through the darkness of this deep slot canyon. Sound familiar? If you have seen such a photo, chances are you were seeing **Antelope Canyon** (also known as Corkscrew Canyon). Located a few miles outside of Page off Ariz. 98 (at milepost 299), this famous photogenic canyon lies on the Navajo Indian Reservation at the end of a rough dirt and sand road. There are currently two options for visiting Antelope Canyon. You can take a 1¹/₂-hour tour with **Lake Powell Jeep Tours** (☎ 520/645-5501) or **Photographic Tours** (☎ 520/645-8579 or 801/675-9109), both of which charge $26.50 per person (children 7 and under are free), or you can drive out to the trailhead and hire a Navajo guide to drive you to the canyon. This latter option will cost you $5 for a visitor's permit and around $10 for the guide to drive you from the highway to the canyon. As we were going to press a group of hikers was killed in a flash flood in Antelope Canyon. Call ahead for information as tours may or may not be operating.

## OTHER AREA OUTDOOR ACTIVITIES & TOURS

The Page area is rapidly becoming known as another of the Southwest's great mountain biking hot spots. **Red Rock Cyclery,** 819 N. Navajo Dr. (☎ 520/645-1479) rents mountain bikes ($25 to $35 per day) and can point you in the direction of rides to fit your abilities.

The 27-hole **Lake Powell National Golf Course,** 400 Clubhouse Dr. (☎ 520/645-2023), is one of the most spectacular golf courses in the state. The fairways wrap around the base of the red sandstone bluff atop which lies the town of Page. In places, walls of eroded sandstone come right down to the greens, and alongside one fairway, water is pumped up the rock to create a waterfall. The views stretch to forever. Greens fees are $60 in the warmer months and tee times can be booked up to 1 week in advance.

The Glen Canyon National Recreation Area covers an immense area, much of it inaccessible by car and only partially accessible by boat. If you'd like to see more of the area than is visible from car or boat, consider taking an air tour with **Scenic Airlines** (☎ 800/245-8668 or 520/645-2494), which offers several air tours of northern Arizona and southern Utah, including flights over Rainbow Bridge, the Escalante River, the Grand Canyon, Canyonlands, Bryce Canyon, Monument Valley, and the Navajo nation. Rates range from $71 to $262.

## MORE AREA ATTRACTIONS

In addition to the two small museums listed below, you might want to check out the **Fatali Gallery,** 40 S. Lake Powell Blvd. (☎ 520/645-3553), where photographer Michael Fatali exhibits his prints of this very scenic region.

**Diné Bí Keyah Museum.** At Big Lake Trading Post, 1501 Hwy. 98. ☎ **520/645-2404.** Free admission. Mon–Fri 5:15am–midnight, Sat–Sun 6am–midnight.

From the hours listed above, you might have already guessed that this isn't your ordinary museum. Located on the second floor of a convenience store/trading post on the outskirts of Page, the tiny museum is a private collection of Indian artifacts. Here, in dusty, poorly lit shelves, you'll find an impressive assortment of Mimbres, Tularosa, and Hohokam pots, some of which date back to the 12th century, as well as many other pots and even some fiber artifacts. Well worth a visit.

**John Wesley Powell Memorial Museum.** 6 N. Lake Powell Blvd. ☎ **520/645-9496.** Free admission; requested donation $1. May–Oct daily 8am–6pm; Nov–Dec 15 and Feb 17–Apr Mon–Fri 9am–5pm. Closed Dec 16–Feb 16.

Lake Powell is named after John Wesley Powell, the one-armed Civil War veteran who led the first expedition through the Grand Canyon. In 1869 Powell and a small band of men spent more than 3 months fighting the rapids of the Green and Colorado rivers in wooden-hulled boats. This small museum is dedicated to the courageous—some said crazy—Powell and his expedition. Besides documenting the Powell expedition with photographs, etchings, and artifacts, the museum displays Indian artifacts from Anasazi pottery to contemporary Navajo and Hopi crafts. The exhibit of fluorescent minerals is particularly interesting, and there are several informative videos that are regularly screened in the museum's small auditorium. The museum also acts as an information center for Page, Lake Powell, and the region, and has a small gift shop.

## HOUSEBOATING

**⊙ Lake Powell Resorts and Marinas.** P.O. Box 56909, Phoenix, AZ 85079-6909. ☎ **800/ 528-6154,** or 602/278-8888 in Phoenix. Fax 602/331-5258. May to mid-Oct $1,499–$4,300 per week; Jan–Apr and mid-Oct to Dec $899–$2,580 per week (3-, 4-, 5-, and 6-night rates also available). AE, DISC, MC, V.

Although there are plenty of hotels and motels in and near Page, the most popular accommodations here are not waterfront hotel rooms but houseboats, which function as floating vacation homes. With a houseboat, which is as easy to operate as a car, you can explore Lake Powell's beautiful red-rock country, far from any roads. No special license or prior experience is necessary, and plenty of hands-on instruction is offered before you leave the marina. Because Lake Powell houseboating is extremely popular with people from all over the world, it's important to make reservations as far in advance as possible, especially if you plan to visit in the summer.

Houseboats range in size from 36 to 59 feet, sleep anywhere from 6 to 12 people, and come complete with hot showers, refrigerator/freezer, heating system (more expensive houseboats also have heat pumps or evaporative coolers), stove, oven, and gas grill. Kitchens come equipped with everything you'll need to prepare meals. The only things you'll really need to bring are bedding and towels.

## WHERE TO STAY
### EXPENSIVE

**⊙ Courtyard by Marriott.** 600 Clubhouse Dr. (P.O. Box 4128), Page, AZ 86040. ☎ **800/ 321-2211** or 520/645-5000. Fax 520/645-5004. 153 rms. A/C TV TEL. Mar–Oct $109–$149 double; Nov–Apr $69–$89 double. AE, CB, DC, DISC, MC, V.

Located at the foot of the mesa on which Page is built and adjacent to the Lake Powell National Golf Course, this hotel is the closest you'll come to a golf resort in this corner of the state and is the top in-town choice. The rooms are larger than those at most motels and there are king-size beds, separate seating areas, dressing areas, and mirrored closet doors. You'll pay a premium for views of the golf course or canyon.

**Dining/Entertainment:** Moderately priced meals are served in a casual restaurant that has a terrace overlooking the distant lake. There's also an adjacent lounge.

**Services:** Room service, valet/laundry service, in-room massage.

**Facilities:** The adjacent 18-hole golf course has great views of the surrounding landscape. There's also an outdoor pool, whirlpool, and exercise room.

**Wahweap Lodge.** 100 Lakeshore Dr. (Mailing address: P.O. Box 56909, Phoenix, AZ 85079). ☎ **800/528-6154,** 520/645-2433, or 602/278-8888 in Phoenix. Fax 602/331-5258. 375 rms, 2 suites. A/C TV TEL. Apr–Oct $123–$149 double, $200 suite; Nov–Mar $80–$95 double, $130 suite. AE, DC, DISC, MC, V.

The Wahweap Marina is a sprawling complex 4 miles north of Glen Canyon Dam on the shores of Lake Powell. As the biggest and busiest hotel in the area, Wahweap features many of the amenities and activities of a resort. The guest rooms are arranged in two long two-story wings. All the rooms have either a balcony or a patio, but only half have lake views. The west wing has the better view (the east wing overlooks the

Navajo coal-fired power plant). This place stays packed with tour groups from around the world and getting a reservation can be difficult.

**Dining/Entertainment:** The Rainbow Room (see "Where to Dine," below) offers fine dining with a sweeping panorama of the lake and desert. The menu is equally divided between American standards and Southwestern fare. A snack bar near the boat ramp provides light meals, snacks, ice cream, and cookies, and a lounge serves cocktails with a view.

**Services:** Room service, boat rentals, boat tours, float trips.

**Facilities:** Two outdoor pools, whirlpool, boat ramp.

## MODERATE

**Best Western Arizonainn.** 716 Rimview Dr. (P.O. Box C), Page, AZ 86040. ☎ **800/826-2718** or 520/645-2466. Fax 520/645-2053. 103 rms, 2 suites. A/C TV TEL. Apr–Oct $85–$105 double, $130 suite; Nov–Mar $44–$70 double, $75 suite. AE, DC, DISC, MC, V.

Perched right at the edge of the mesa on which Page is built, this modern motel has a fine view across miles of desert. Half the rooms have views, and of course these are more expensive. The hotel also offers free coffee in the lobby, an airport shuttle, an outdoor pool with a 100-mile view, a whirlpool, and access to a nearby health club.

**Best Western at Lake Powell.** 208 N. Lake Powell Blvd., Page, AZ 86040. ☎ **800/528-1234** or 520/645-5988. Fax 520/645-2578. 132 rms. A/C TV TEL. May–Oct $59–$135 double; Oct–May $35–$89 double. AE, CB, DC, DISC, MC, V.

This modern hotel lies on the edge of town overlooking Lake Powell and is right next door to the Arizonainn. The rooms are comfortable and modern, and there's a pool with a great view. There's no restaurant on the premises, but breakfast is available. The hotel also offers a free airport shuttle.

**Lake Powell Motel.** U.S. 89 near Wahweap Marina (Mailing address: P.O. Box 56909, Phoenix, AZ 85079). ☎ **800/528-6154,** 520/645-2477, or 602/278-8888 in Phoenix. Fax 602/331-5258. 25 rms. A/C TV TEL. $74–$139.50 double. AE, DC, DISC, MC, V. Closed Nov–Mar. Drive 3 miles west of the Wahweap Marina or 4 miles north of the Glen Canyon Dam on U.S. 89.

Located on a barren hill set back from the lake, the Lake Powell Motel offers an alternative away from the traffic and lights of downtown Page and the bustle of activity at the Wahweap Marina. The accommodations are standard motel rooms with two queen-size beds.

## INEXPENSIVE

**Pension at Lake Powell/International Hostel.** 141 Eighth Ave. (P.O. Box 1077), Page, AZ 86040. ☎ **520/645-3898.** 14 rms, 2 with bath; 50 dormitory beds. May–Oct $30–$35 double without bath, $50–$70 double with bath, $15 dorm bed; Nov–Apr $25 double without bath, $40–$45 double with bath, $12 dorm bed. No credit cards.

Housed in old company apartments built for the construction of the Glen Canyon Dam, this economical lodging offers budget travelers a couple of options. With both a pension offering private rooms and a hostel offering small dorms, this place caters to young travelers, primarily Europeans. The rooms are clean and there's a kitchen available. They even offer free airport pickups.

## CAMPGROUNDS & RV PARKS

There are campgrounds and RV facilities at Wahweap and Lees Ferry in Arizona and at Bullfrog, Hite, and Halls Crossing in Utah. At Wahweap, there are separate campgrounds for tenters and for RVers. Some scrubby trees provide a bit of shade at the tenting campground, but the winds and sun make this a rather bleak spot in summer. However, because of the lake's popularity, these campgrounds stay packed for much of the year. Reservations are not taken.

## WHERE TO DINE

**Butterfield Stage Co.** 704 Rimview Dr. ☎ **520/645-2467.** Main courses $9–$17. AE, MC, V. Daily 6:30am–10pm. STEAKS/AMERICAN.

Large windows take in a view of the desert that's slightly marred by the number of power lines that stretch out from the dam. Still, the sunrise and sunset views are phenomenal. Steaks and seafood are the menu mainstays.

**☼ The Dam Bar & Grille.** 644 N. Navajo Dr. ☎ **520/645-2161.** Reservations recommended in summer. Main courses $9–$20. AE, MC, V. Daily 11am–9pm (10pm in summer). AMERICAN.

Page's first theme restaurant is a warehouse-size space that is designed to conjure up images of the Glen Canyon Dam. Big industrial doors are the first hint that this is more than the usual small-town dining establishment. Inside, cement walls, hardhats, and a big transformer that sends out neon bolts of "electricity" all put you in a dam good mood. In the summer, there's a cook-your-own-steak grill, and at lunch there are often deli-style buffets. Burgers, steaks, and prime rib dominate the menu. There's sometimes live music here in the evening, and the bandstand is surrounded by cement walls cast to look like a dam. There's also a large lounge area and a small outdoor patio overlooking the parking lot. Next door is the affiliated Gunsmoke Theatre, a dinner theater that does Branson-style shows complete with celebrity impersonators (including Elvis).

**Rainbow Room.** In the Wahweap Lodge, at the Wahweap Marina, Lakeshore Dr. ☎ **520/ 645-2433.** Reservations not accepted. Main courses $10–$15. AE, DC, DISC, MC, V. Daily 6am–2:30pm (3pm in summer) and 5–9pm (10pm in summer). AMERICAN/SOUTHWEST.

Because of the sweeping vistas of Lake Powell through the walls of glass (and not necessarily because of the food), the Rainbow Room at the Wahweap Lodge is Page's premier restaurant. However, be prepared for a wait; this place daily feeds busloads of tourists from around the world. The menu features American dishes, such as blackened catfish and Caesar salad, but there are also specials and such dishes as pine nut–crusted trout. If you're heading out on the water for the day, they'll fix you a box lunch.

**Strombolli's Restaurant & Pizzeria.** 711 N. Navajo Blvd. ☎ **520/645-2605.** Main dishes $5.95–$16.95. MC, V. Daily 11am–9pm in summer (closed Sun other months). SOUTHERN ITALIAN.

With its New Orleans–style grillwork and large front terrace, Strombolli's is unmistakable, but it's really nothing fancy. The menu features all the usual southern Italian dishes, but also includes such items as fresh-baked Tuscany bread with basil pesto, spinach, tomatoes, mozzarella, and Parmesan cheese, and several gourmet pizza combinations. We started with a dip of spinach, artichoke hearts, and cheeses, which was a tad on the salty side, but delicious anyway. There are also a good assortment of salads, calzones as big as your head, and water glasses so large they could double as free weights (it's important to drink a lot of liquids out here). The terrace makes a great dining spot on a warm evening, and is popular with families.

**Zapata's.** 614 N. Navajo Dr. ☎ **520/645-9006.** Main courses $7–$13. AE, DC, DISC, MC, V. Mon–Fri 11am–2pm and 5–10pm, Sat–Sun 5–10pm. SONORAN/MEXICAN.

Zapata's is a little place located in the shopping plaza diagonally across from the intersection at the Powell Museum. We popped in here for lunch and were pleasantly surprised by a spicy chile verde burrito and the somewhat milder, though flavorful, chicken enchilada that we ordered. Rice and beans, which are frequently pretty generic in Mexican restaurants, were tasty too. At lunch there are a limited selection of specials for about $6. The crowd here is usually more locals than tourists.

# EN ROUTE TO THE NORTH RIM OF THE GRAND CANYON

Between Page and the North Rim of the Grand Canyon, U.S. 89A crosses the Colorado River at **Lees Ferry** in Marble Canyon. Lees Ferry is the starting point for raft trips through the Grand Canyon, and for many years was the only place to cross the Colorado River for hundreds of miles in either direction. There's also a campground here.

Lees Ferry is legendary among anglers for its trophy trout fishing, and when the North Rim closes and the rafting season comes to an end, about the only folks you'll find up here are fisherfolk and hunters. **Lees Ferry Anglers** (☎ **800/962-9755** or 520/355-2261), located 3 miles west of the bridge at Lees Ferry, is fishing headquarters for the region. Not only do they sell all manner of fly-fishing tackle and offer advice about good spots to try your luck, but they also operate a guide service and rent waders and boats.

Continuing west, the highway passes under the **Vermilion Cliffs,** so named for their deep red coloring. At the base of these cliffs are huge boulders balanced on narrow columns of eroded soil. The balanced rocks give the area a very otherworldly appearance. These cliffs became the focus of area attention in December of 1996 when six California condors were released here in hopes that these endangered birds would reestablish a viable population in this remote location. Along this unpopulated stretch of road are a couple of very basic lodges.

West of Marble Canyon 17 miles, you'll see a sign for **House Rock Ranch.** This wildlife area, managed by the Arizona Game and Fish Department, is best known for its herd of bison (American buffalo). From the turnoff it's a 22-mile drive on a gravel road to reach the ranch.

## WHERE TO STAY

If you don't have a reservation at one of the three lodges at or near the North Rim, you may want to stop at one of the lodges recommended below and continue on to the North Rim the next morning. Lodges near the canyon fill up early if they aren't already fully booked with reservations made months in advance.

**Cliff Dwellers Lodge.** U.S. 89A (HC67–30), Marble Canyon, AZ 86036. ☎ **800/433-2543** or 520/355-2228. Fax 520/355-2229. 21 rms. Apr–Sept $57–$67 double; Oct–Mar $39 double. DISC, MC, V.

To give you some idea of how remote an area this is, the Cliff Dwellers Lodge is marked on official Arizona state maps. There just isn't much else out here, so a single lodge can be as important as a town. The newer, more expensive rooms here are standard motel rooms and have combination bathtub/showers, while the older rooms, in a stone-walled building, have more character but showers only. A small restaurant provides meals. The lodge is close to some spectacular balanced rocks and it's about 11 miles east to Lees Ferry. The views here are great.

**Lees Ferry Lodge.** U.S. 89A (HC67-Box 1), Marble Canyon, AZ 86036. ☎ **520/355-2231.** 9 rms. A/C. $50 double. MC, V.

Located at the foot of the Vermilion Cliffs, $3^1/2$ miles west of the Colorado River, the Lees Ferry Lodge, built in 1929 of native stone and rough-hewn timber beams, is a small place with rustic accommodations. However, the rafters and anglers who stay here don't seem to care much about the condition of the rooms, and besides, the patio seating area in front of all the rooms has fabulous views of the Vermilion Cliffs. Unfortunately the highway is only a few yards away, so traffic noises occasionally disturb the tranquillity. A small dining room provides what's reputed to be the best food for miles around.

**Marble Canyon Lodge.** Marble Canyon, AZ 86036. ☎ **800/726-1789** or 520/355-2225. 60 rms. A/C. $60–$125 double. DISC, MC, V.

Located just 4 miles from Lees Ferry, the Marble Canyon Lodge was built in the 1920s and is popular with rafters preparing to head down the Grand Canyon. The room styles vary considerably in size and age, with some rustic rooms in old stone buildings and other newer motel-style rooms as well. You're right at the base of the Vermilion Cliffs here, and the views are great. There's a cozy restaurant and a trading post (be sure to have some Marble Canyon cake).

## 6 The Grand Canyon North Rim

42 miles S of Jacob Lake; 216 miles N of Grand Canyon Village (South Rim); 354 miles N of Phoenix; 125 miles W of Page/Lake Powell

Although the North Rim is only 10 miles as the raven flies from the South Rim, it's 200 miles as the car drives. Additionally, the North Rim is only open from mid-May to October or early November. There are also far fewer activities on the North Rim than there are on the South Rim (no helicopter or plane rides, no IMAX theater, no McDonald's). For these reasons, most of the millions of people who visit the Grand Canyon annually never make it to this side of the canyon. And that is exactly why quite a few people think the North Rim is a far superior place to visit. If Grand Canyon Village was more human zoo than the wilderness experience you had expected, the North Rim will probably be much more to your liking, though crowds, traffic congestion, and parking problems are not unheard of here either.

At 8,000 feet in elevation, the North Rim is 1,000 feet higher than the South Rim and receives considerably more snow in the winter. The highway south from Jacob Lake is not plowed in winter and consequently the Grand Canyon Lodge closes down.

The North Rim is located on the Kaibab Plateau, which takes its name from the Paiute word for "mountain lying down" and averages more than 8,000 feet high. The higher elevation of the North Rim means that instead of the junipers and ponderosa pines of the South Rim, you'll find dense forests of ponderosa pines, Douglas firs, and aspens interspersed with large meadows. Consequently, the North Rim has a much more alpine feel than the South Rim. This plateau is also home to the unique white-tailed Kaibab squirrel. Keep your eyes open for this large-eared squirrel whenever you're walking in the forest.

### ESSENTIALS

**GETTING THERE**   The North Rim is at the end of Ariz. 67 (the North Rim Parkway), which is reached from U.S. 89A.

Trans Canyon operates a shuttle between the North Rim and South Rim of the Grand Canyon during the months that the North Rim is open. The trip takes 5 hours and the fare is $60 one way and $100 round-trip. Call ☎ **520/638-2820** for more information.

**VISITOR INFORMATION**   For information before leaving home, contact **Grand Canyon National Park,** P.O. Box 129, Grand Canyon, AZ 86023 (☎ **520/638-7888**). You can also check out the canyon on the Web at www.thecanyon.com/nps.

There's an **information desk** in the lobby of the Grand Canyon Lodge, open daily from 8am to 5pm. At the entrance gate you'll also be given a copy of *The Guide,* a small newspaper with information on park activities. There's a separate edition of *The Guide* for each of the two rims.

*Important note:* The North Rim is only open from mid-May to late October. The park admission fee is $20 per car and is good for 1 week.

## EXPLORING THE AREA

While it is hard to beat the view from a rustic rocking chair on the terrace of the Grand Canyon Lodge, the best spots for viewing the canyon are Bright Angel Point, Point Imperial, and Cape Royal. **Bright Angel Point** is the closest to Grand Canyon Lodge, and from here you can see and hear Roaring Springs, which is 3,600 feet below the rim and is the North Rim's only water source. From Bright Angel Point you can also see Grand Canyon Village on the South Rim. At 8,803 feet, **Point Imperial** is the highest point on either rim of the Grand Canyon. A short section of the Colorado River can be seen far below, and off to the east the Painted Desert is visible. However, **Cape Royal** is the most spectacular setting on the North Rim.

Along the 23-mile road to Cape Royal are several scenic overlooks. Across the road from the **Walhalla Overlook** are the ruins of an Anasazi structure, and just before reaching Cape Royal you'll come to the **Angel's Window Overlook,** which gives you a breathtaking view of the natural bridge that forms Angel's Window. Once at Cape Royal, you can follow a trail across this natural bridge to a towering promontory overlooking the valley.

If you'd like to see the North Rim on a guided tour, stop by the tour desk in the lobby of the Grand Canyon Lodge, where you can arrange a 3-hour van tour that stops at the overlooks mentioned above. The cost is $20 for adults and $50 for families.

After simply taking in the views, **hiking along the rim** is the most popular activity. There are quite a few day hikes of varying lengths possible on the North Rim. The shortest is the half-mile paved trail to Bright Angel Point, and the longest is the North Kaibab Trail to Roaring Springs and back, which takes 6 to 8 hours.

If you want to see the canyon from a saddle, contact **Grand Canyon Trail Rides** (☎ **520/638-9875** in summer, or 801/679-8665 in winter), which offers mule rides varying in length from 1 hour to a full day. Prices range from $15 for an hour ride up to $85 for the all-day trip.

## WHERE TO STAY

✪ **Grand Canyon Lodge.** Contact AmFac Parks & Resorts, 14001 E. Iliff Ave., Suite 600, Aurora, CO 80014. ☎ **303/297-2757** or 520/638-2611 (for same-day reservations). Fax 303/297-3175. 209 rms and cabins. $60–$95 double in room or cabin. AE, CB, DC, DISC, MC, V. Closed Nov to mid-May.

Perched right on the canyon rim, this classic mountain lodge is listed on the National Register of Historic Places and is as impressive a lodge as you will find in any national park. The stone-and-log main lodge building has a soaring ceiling and a viewing room set up with chairs facing a wall of glass. On either side of this room are flagstone terraces set with rustic chairs that face out toward the canyon.

The guest rooms vary from standard motel rooms to rustic mountain cabins to comfortable modern cabins. Our favorites are the little cabins, which, though cramped and paneled with dark wood, capture the feeling of a mountain retreat better than any of the other rooms. A few rooms have views of the canyon, but most are tucked back away from the rim.

**Dining/Entertainment:** A large dining hall with two walls of glass serves straightforward American food and is open daily for all three meals. There are also a saloon and a snack bar outside the lodge's front entrance.

**Services:** Tour desk.

**Jacob Lake Inn.** Jacob Lake, AZ 86022. ☎ **520/643-7232.** 11 rms, 33 cabins. May 15–Nov $66–$95 double in room or cabin; Dec–May 15 $55 double in room or cabin. AE, DC, DISC, MC, V.

Located 30 miles north of the entrance to the North Rim, the Jacob Lake Inn consists of motel rooms and rustic cabins. The motel rooms are quite a bit nicer than the cabins, which have old carpets and cramped bathrooms with showers (no tubs). This lodge stays open in winter and is a base for cross-country skiers and snowmobilers.

**Dining/Entertainment:** Just off the lobby is a coffee shop, and adjacent is a more formal dining room. A bakery counter sells delicious cookies and fudge, and the general store sells snacks.

**Facilities:** Gas station, basketball and volleyball courts, playground.

**Kaibab Lodge.** P.O. Box 2997, Flagstaff, AZ 86003. ☎ **800/525-0924** or 520/526-0924. Fax 520/527-9398. 24 rms. May 15–Nov $69–$95 double (multiday ski packages only in winter; rates start at $740 double for 2 nights). DISC, MC, V.

Located 5 miles north of the entrance to the Grand Canyon's North Rim, the Kaibab Lodge was built around 1926 and is situated on the edge of a large meadow where deer can often be seen grazing. The rooms are in small rustic cabins set back in the pines from the main lodge building. Nights here are cool even in summer and a favorite pastime of guests is to sit by the fireplace in the lobby. Although the highway from Jacob Lake is closed by the first big snow, the lodge stays open for much of the winter as a cross-country ski lodge, shuttling skiers in by snowcoach. This remote setting is ideal for cross-country skiing and makes a very quiet retreat.

**Dining/Entertainment:** The lodge's dining room serves all meals, and the kitchen also prepares box lunches.

**Services:** Tour desk, hiking-equipment rentals, mountain-bike rentals, ski lessons, ski tours.

**Facilities:** Gift shop, whirlpool spa.

## CAMPGROUNDS

Located just north of Grand Canyon Lodge, the **North Rim Campground,** with 82 sites and no hookups for RVs, is the only campground at the North Rim. Reservations can be made by calling **DESTINET** (☎ **800/365-2267**). The fee is $15 per site per night.

There are also two campgrounds outside the park in the Kaibab National Forest. These are **DeMotte Park Campground,** which is the closest to the park entrance and has only 25 sites, and **Jacob Lake Campground,** which is 30 miles north of the park entrance and has 50 sites. Both campgrounds charge $10 per night and do not take reservations. You can also camp anywhere in the Kaibab National Forest. So, if you can't find a site in a campground, simply pull off the highway in the national forest and park your RV or pitch your tent.

The **Kaibab Lodge Camper Village,** P.O. Box 498, Jacob Lake, AZ 86022 (☎ **520/643-7804**), is a privately owned campground in the crossroads of Jacob Lake, 30 miles north of the park entrance. This campground has 80 RV sites and 50 tent sites. Rates are $12 to $15 per night for tent sites and $22 per night for RV sites with full hook-ups. Reservations are accepted at least 2 weeks in advance.

# 8

# The Four Corners Region: Land of the Hopi & Navajo

**W**ay up in the northeast corner of Arizona is a spot that's unique in the United States. It's not a canyon or a mountain or an ancient ruin. No, this spot is unusual because here four states—Arizona, New Mexico, Colorado, and Utah—all come together at the same point. But the name Four Corners refers to more than just a spot where you can stand in four states at the same time. The name also applies to the huge surrounding area, including a large piece of northeastern Arizona.

Most of the land in the Four Corners region of Arizona is Navajo and Hopi reservation land, and it's also some of the most spectacular countryside in the state, with majestic mesas, rainbow-hued deserts, gravity-defying buttes, cliffs, and canyons. Among the most spectacular of these are the 1,000-foot buttes of Monument Valley. For years these evocative and colorful monoliths have symbolized the Wild West of cowboys and John Wayne movies.

The Navajo and Hopi peoples who have lived on this land for hundreds of years have adapted different means of surviving in the arid Four Corners region. The Navajo, with their traditional log homes scattered across the countryside, have become herders of sheep, goats, and cattle. The Hopi, on the other hand, have congregated in villages atop mesas and built houses of stone. They farm the floors of narrow valleys at the feet of their mesas in much the same way the indigenous peoples of the Southwest have done for centuries.

These two tribes are, however, only the most recent Native Americans to inhabit what many consider to be a desolate, barren wilderness. The ancient Anasazi left their mark throughout the canyons of the Four Corners region, with cliff dwellings dating from 700 years and more, the most spectacular of those in Arizona being the ruins in Canyon de Chelly and Navajo national monuments. No one is sure why the Anasazi moved up into the cliff walls, but there is speculation that unfavorable growing conditions brought on by drought may have forced them to use every possible inch of arable land. The cliff dwellings were mysteriously abandoned in the 13th century, and with no written record, the disappearance of the Anasazi may forever remain a mystery.

The Hopi, who believe that the Anasazi were their ancestors, have had their villages for centuries on the tops of mesas in northeastern Arizona. They claim that Oraibi, on Third Mesa, is the oldest continuously inhabited community in the United States. Whether or not this is true, several of the Hopi villages are quite old and for this reason they have become tourist attractions. Most of the villages are built on three mesas, known simply as First, Second, and Third Mesa, which are numbered from east to west. These villages have always maintained a great deal of autonomy, which over the years has led to fighting. The appearance of missionaries and the policies of the Bureau of Indian Affairs have also created conflicts among and within villages. Today the Hopi Reservation is completely surrounded by the much larger Navajo Reservation.

Roughly the size of West Virginia, the Navajo Reservation covers an area of 25,000 square miles in northeastern Arizona, as well as parts of New Mexico, Colorado, and Utah. It's the largest Native American reservation in the United States and is home to nearly 200,000 Navajo. Though there are now modern towns with supermarkets, shopping malls, and hotels on the reservation, many Navajo still follow a pastoral lifestyle as herders of goats and sheep. As you travel the roads of the Navajo Reservation, you'll frequently encounter flocks of sheep and goats, as well as herds of cattle and horses. These animals have free range of the reservation and often graze beside the highways.

Unlike the pueblo tribes such as the Hopi and Zuñi, the Navajo are relative newcomers to the Southwest. Their Athabascan language is most closely related to the languages spoken by Native Americans in the Pacific Northwest, Canada, and Alaska. It's believed that the Navajo migrated southward from northern Canada beginning around A.D. 1000, arriving in the Southwest sometime after 1400. At this time the Navajo were still hunters and gatherers, but contact with the pueblo tribes, who had long before adopted an agricultural lifestyle, began to change the Navajo into farmers. When the Spanish arrived in the Southwest in the early 17th century, the Navajo acquired horses, sheep, and goats through raids and adopted a pastoral way of life, grazing their herds in the high plains and canyon bottoms.

The continued use of raids, made even more successful with the acquisition of horses, put the Navajo in conflict with the Spanish settlers who were beginning to encroach on Navajo land. In 1805, the Spanish sent a military expedition into the Navajo's chief stronghold, Canyon de Chelly, and killed 115 people, who, by some accounts, may have been all women, children, and old men. This massacre didn't stop the conflicts between the Navajo and Spanish settlers. In 1846, when this region became part of the United States, American settlers encountered the same problems that the Spanish had. Military outposts were established to protect the new settlers, and numerous unsuccessful attempts were made to establish peace. In 1863, after continued Navajo attacks, a military expedition led by Col. Kit Carson burned crops and homes late in the summer, effectively obliterating the Navajo's winter supplies. Thus defeated, the Navajo were rounded up and herded 400 miles to an inhospitable region of New Mexico near Fort Sumner. This march became known as the Long Walk and had a profound influence on the Navajo. Living conditions at Fort Sumner were deplorable, and the land was unsuitable for farming. In 1868, the Navajo were allowed to return to their homeland.

Upon returning home, and after continued clashes with white settlers, the Navajo eventually settled into a lifestyle of herding. In recent years the Navajo have had to turn to different livelihoods. Though weaving and silver work have become lucrative businesses, the amount of money they garner for the tribe as a whole is not significant. Many Navajo now take jobs as migrant workers, and gas and oil leases on the reservation provide more income.

Though the reservation covers an immense area, much of it is of no value other than as scenery. Fortunately, the Navajo are recognizing the income potential of their

# The Four Corners Region

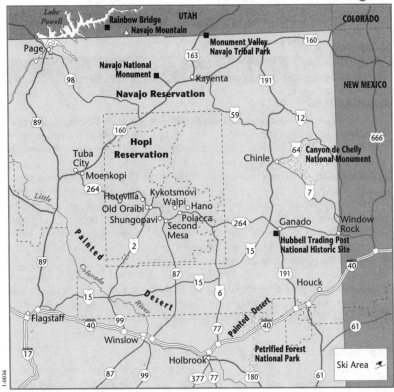

spectacular land. Monument Valley is operated as a tribal park, and there's also a Navajo-owned marina on Lake Powell in Utah.

As you travel the Navajo reservation you may notice small hexagonal buildings with rounded roofs. These are hogans, the traditional homes of the Navajo, and are usually made of wood and earth. The doorway of the hogan always faces east to greet the new day. At the Canyon de Chelly and Navajo National Monument visitor centers you can look inside hogans that are part of the parks' exhibits. If you take a tour at Canyon de Chelly or Monument Valley, you may have an opportunity to visit a hogan that is still someone's home. Most Navajo now live in modest houses or mobile homes, but a family will usually also have a hogan for religious ceremonies.

All over the Navajo Reservation you'll see stalls set up beside the road and at scenic overlooks. Though you might find quality merchandise and bargain prices, you'd do better to confine your purchases to trading posts, museum and park gift shops, and established shops where you receive some guarantee of the quality of the pieces for sale.

The Navajo and Hopi reservations cover a vast area and are laced with a network of good paved roads, as well as many unpaved roads that are not always passable to cars without four-wheel drive. The main things to keep in mind when driving in this area are to keep your car gassed up, since distances are great, and to keep an eye out for livestock on the road, especially at night.

Before taking a photograph of a Navajo, always ask permission. If permission is granted, a tip of $1 or more is expected. Photography is not allowed at all in the Hopi villages. The Navajo Reservation observes daylight saving time, unlike the rest of

Arizona, so remember to set your watch forward an hour if you're visiting in the summer. The Hopi reservation is on Arizona time. Also keep in mind that *alcohol is not allowed on the reservation.*

# 1 The Hopi Reservation

250 miles NE of Phoenix; 67 miles N of Winslow; 100 miles SW of Canyon de Chelly; 140 miles SE of Page/Lake Powell

Completely surrounded by the Navajo Reservation, the Hopi Reservation has at its center the grouping of mesas that are home to the Hopi pueblos. This remote region of Arizona, with its flat-topped mesas and rugged, barren landscape, is the center of the universe for the Hopi peoples.

The handful of villages that together make up the Hopi pueblos are ancient and independent communities that have today been brought together under the guidance of the Hopi Tribal Council. This land has been inhabited by the Hopi and their ancestors for nearly 1,000 years and many aspects of the ancient pueblo culture remain intact. However, much of the Hopi culture is hidden from the view of non-Hopi. Though the Hopi perform elaborate religious ceremonies throughout the year, most of these ceremonies are no longer open to outsiders.

*Important note:* When visiting the Hopi pueblos, remember that you are a guest and your privileges can be revoked at any time. Respect all posted signs at village entrances, and remember that *photographing, sketching, and recording are all prohibited in the villages and at ceremonies.* Also, kivas (ceremonial rooms) and ruins are off-limits.

## ESSENTIALS

**GETTING THERE**    This section of Arizona is one of the state's most remote regions. Distances are great but the highways are generally in good condition. Ariz. 87 leads from Winslow to Second Mesa, while Ariz. 264 runs from Tuba City in the west to the New Mexico state line in the east.

**Amtrak** passenger trains stop in Winslow, 67 miles south of Second Mesa. The train station is on East Second Street. Call ☎ **800/872-7245** for schedule information.

The **Navajo Transit System** (☎ **520/729-4002**) operates a bus service Monday through Friday throughout the Navajo and Hopi reservations with service between the following towns: Farmington, Gallup, and Crown Point (all in New Mexico) and Window Rock, Kayenta, Chinle, and Tuba City. The route between Window Rock and Tuba City stops at several of the Hopi villages, including Second Mesa.

**VISITOR INFORMATION**    For more information before you leave home, contact the **Hopi Tribal Council,** P.O. Box 123, Kykotsmovi, AZ 86039 (☎ **520/734-2441**).

Because each of the Hopi villages is relatively independent, you might want to contact the **Community Development Office** of a particular village for specific information on that village: Bacavi (☎ 520/734-9360), First Mesa (☎ 520/737-2670), Hotevilla (☎ 520/734-9360), Kykotsmovi (☎ 520/734-2474), Mishongnovi (☎ 520/737-2520), Moenkopi (☎ 520/283-8054), and Shipaulovi (☎ 520/737-2570). These offices are open Monday through Friday from 8am to 5pm.

## EXPLORING THE WORLD OF THE HOPI

Start your visit to the Hopi pueblos at the **Hopi Cultural Center,** on Ariz. 264 (☎ **520/734-6650**) in Second Mesa. This museum, motel, and restaurant is the tourism headquarters for the area. Here you can visit the museum and learn about the Hopi culture and its history. Be sure to take notice of signs indicating when villages are open to visitors. The museum is open Monday through Friday from 8am to 5pm and on Saturday and Sunday from 9am to 3pm. Admission is $3 for adults and $1 for children.

Though it's possible to get permission to visit most Hopi villages, the easiest to visit is **Walpi,** on First Mesa. Guided tours of this tiny village are offered daily from about 9:30am to 4pm, and admission is by donation. To sign up for a tour, drive up to the top of First Mesa (in Polacca, take the road that says to First Mesa villages) and continue driving straight through the village at the top of the mesa until you see the **information office** (☎ **520/737-2262** or 520/737-2760) and the signs for the tour. The 40-minute tours are led by young Hopis who will tell you the history of the village and explain a bit about the local culture. Tours usually include a visit to one of the old stone homes.

## THE VILLAGES

**FIRST MESA**    At the foot of First Mesa is **Polacca,** a settlement founded in the late 1800s by Walpi villagers who wanted to be closer to the trading post and school.

At the top of First Mesa is the village of **Walpi,** which was located lower on the slopes of the mesa until the Pueblo Rebellion of 1680 brought on fear of reprisal by the Spanish. The villagers moved Walpi to the very top of the mesa so that they could better defend themselves in the event of a Spanish attack. Walpi looks much like the Anasazi villages of the Arizona canyons, with small stone houses that seem to grow directly from the rock of the mesa top and ladders jutting from the roofs of kivas. The view stretches for hundreds of miles around.

**Sichomovi,** lower down on the mesa, was founded in 1750 as a colony of Walpi, while **Hano,** adjacent to Walpi, was founded by Tewa peoples either seeking refuge from the Spanish or offering aid to the people of Walpi.

**SECOND MESA**    Second Mesa is today the center of tourism in Hopiland, as the Hopi country is called, and this is where you'll find the Hopi Cultural Center.

Villages on Second Mesa include **Shungopavi,** which was moved to its present site after Old Shungopavi was abandoned in 1680 after the Pueblo Revolt against the Spanish.

Below Shungopavi is **Gray Spring.** The Snake Dance is performed here in even-numbered years.

**Mishongnovi,** which means "place of the black man," is named for the leader of a clan that came here from the San Francisco Peaks around A.D. 1200. This village was also abandoned in 1680 and moved to its present location. The Snake Dance is held here in odd-numbered years.

**Shipaulovi** may also have been founded after the Pueblo Revolt of 1680.

**THIRD MESA**    **Oraibi,** which the Hopi claim is the oldest continuously occupied town in the United States, is located on Third Mesa. The village dates from 1150 and, according to legend, was founded by people from Old Shungopavi. A Spanish mission was established in Oraibi in 1629 and the ruins are still visible north of the village.

For centuries Oraibi was the largest of the Hopi villages, but in 1906 a schism occurred over Bureau of Indian Affairs policies and many of the villagers left to form **Hotevilla.** This latter village is considered the most conservative of the Hopi villages and has had frequent confrontations with the federal government.

**Kykotsmovi,** also known as Lower Oraibi or New Oraibi, was founded in 1890 by villagers from Oraibi who wanted to be closer to the school and trading post.

**Bacavi** was founded in 1907 by villagers who had helped found Hotevilla but who later decided that they wanted to return to Oraibi. The people of Oraibi would not let them return, and rather than go back to Hotevilla, they founded a new village.

## A Native American Crafts Primer

The Four Corners region is taken up almost entirely by the Navajo and Hopi reservations, so Native American crafts are ubiquitous here. You'll see jewelry for sale by the side of desolate, windswept roads, Navajo rugs for sale in tiny trading posts, Hopi kachinas being sold out of village homes. If you decide you want to take home a work by a local craftsperson, the information below will help you make an informed purchase.

**Hopi Kachinas**    These elaborately decorated wooden dolls are representations of spirits of plants, animals, ancestors, and sacred places. Traditionally they have been given to children to initiate them into the pantheon of kachina spirits, who play important roles in ensuring rain and harmony in the universe. In recent years kachinas have become popular with collectors of Native American crafts, and Hopi kachina carvers have changed their style to cater to the new market. Older kachinas were carved from a single piece of cottonwood, sometimes with arms simply painted on. This older style of kachina is much simpler and stiffer than the currently popular style that emphasizes action poses and realistic proportions. A great deal of carving and painting goes into each kachina, and prices today are in the hundreds of dollars for even a simple kachina. Currently gaining popularity with tourists and collectors are the *tsuku*, or clown, kachinas, which are usually painted with bold horizontal black and white stripes. The tsukus are often depicted in humorous situations or carrying slices of watermelon.

**Navajo Silver Work**    While the Hopi create overlay silver work from sheets of silver and the Zuñi use silver work simply as a base for their skilled lapidary or stone-cutting work, the Navajo silversmiths highlight the silver itself. Just as rug weaving did not begin until the latter part of the 19th century, silversmithing did not catch on with the Navajo until the 1880s, when Lorenzo Hubbell decided to hire Mexican silversmiths as teachers. When tourists began visiting the area after 1890, the demand for Navajo jewelry increased. The earliest pieces of Navajo jewelry were replicas of Spanish ornaments, but as the Navajo silversmiths became more proficient, they began to develop their own designs. Sand casting, stamp work, repoussé, and file-and-chisel work create the distinctively Navajo jewelry. The squash-blossom necklace, with its horseshoe-shaped pendant, is perhaps the most distinctive Navajo jewelry design. Wide bracelets and concha belts are also popular.

**Hopi Overlay Silver Work**    Overlay silver work has come to be considered the characteristic Hopi style of silver work, but only since World War II have the Hopi been making this sort of jewelry almost exclusively. After the war the GI bill provided the funds for Hopi soldiers to study silversmithing at a school founded by

**ELSEWHERE**    One last Hopi village, **Moenkopi,** is located 40 miles to the west. Founded in 1870 by people from Oraibi, Moenkopi sits in the center of a wide green valley where plentiful water makes farming more reliable. Moenkopi is only a few miles from Tuba City off U.S. 160.

## CULTURAL TOURS

Perhaps the best way to see the Hopi mesas is on a guided small-group tour. With a guide, you will likely learn much more about this rather insular culture than you ever

the famous Hopi artist Fred Kabotie. The overlay process basically uses two sheets of silver, one with a design cut out of it. The two sheets are fused together with heat to form a raised image. Designs used in overlay jewelry are often borrowed from other Hopi crafts such as baskets and pottery, as well as from ancient Anasazi pottery designs. Belt buckles, earrings, bola ties, and bracelets are all popular.

**Hopi Baskets**    Though the Tohono O'odham of the deserts of central and southern Arizona are better known for their basketry, the Hopi also produce beautiful work. Wicker plaques and baskets are made on Third Mesa from rabbit brush and sumac and are colored with bright aniline dyes. Coiled plaques and baskets are made on Second Mesa from dyed yucca fibers. Yucca-fiber sifters are made by plaiting over a willow ring. This style of basket is made throughout the reservation.

**Hopi Pottery**    With the exception of undecorated utilitarian pottery that's made in Hotevilla on Third Mesa, most Hopi pottery is produced on First Mesa. Contemporary Hopi pottery comes in a variety of styles including a yellow-orange ware that's decorated with black-and-white designs. This style is said to have been introduced by the potter Nampeyo, a Tewa from the village of Hano who stimulated the revival of Hopi pottery in 1890. A white pottery with red and black designs is also popular. Hopi pottery designs tend toward geometric patterns.

**Navajo Rugs**    After they acquired sheep and goats from the Spanish, the Navajo learned weaving from the pueblo tribes, and by the early 1800s their weavings were widely recognized as being the finest in the Southwest. The Navajo women primarily wove blankets, but by the end of the 19th century the craft began to die out when it became more economical to purchase a ready-made blanket. When Lorenzo Hubbell set up his trading post, he immediately recognized a potential market in the East for the woven blankets if they could be made heavy enough to be used as rugs. Having great respect for Hubbell, the Navajo adapted his ideas and soon began doing a brisk business. Although today the cost of Navajo rugs, which take hundreds of hours to make, has become almost prohibitively expensive, there are still enough women practicing the craft to keep it alive and provide plenty of rugs for shops and trading posts all over Arizona.

The best rugs are those made with homespun yarn and natural vegetal dyes. However, commercially manufactured yarns and dyes are being used more and more to keep costs down. There are more than 15 regional styles of rugs and quite a bit of overlapping and borrowing. Bigger and bolder patterns are likely to cost quite a bit less than very complex and highly detailed patterns. Navajo rug auctions are held at Crown Point, New Mexico, about 60 miles east of Window Rock.

could on your own. Tour companies also frequently use local guides and stop at the homes of working artisans. This all adds up to a more in-depth and educational visit to one of the oldest cultures on the continent.

Some companies offering Hopi tours include **Sun Tours** (☎ **800/483-4488** or 520/774-7400); **Crossing Worlds,** P.O. Box 171, Young, AZ 85554 (☎ **800/ 350-2693,** or 520/462-3356 in Young, or 520/282-7148 in Sedona); and **Discovery Passages,** 1161 Elk Trail (P.O. Box 630), Prescott, AZ 86303 (☎ **520/ 717-0519**).

## DANCES & CEREMONIES

The Hopi, who long ago adopted a farming lifestyle, have developed the most complex religious ceremonies of any of the Southwest tribes. Masked **kachina dances,** for which the Hopi are most famous, are held from January to July, while the equally well-known Snake Dances are held from August through December.

Kachinas, whether in the form of dolls or as masked dancers, are representative of the spirits of everything from plants and animals to ancestors and sacred places. There are more than 300 kachinas that appear on a regular basis in Hopi ceremonies, and another 200 that appear occasionally. The kachina spirits are said to live in the San Francisco Peaks to the south and at Spring of the Shadows in the east. According to legend, the kachinas lived with the Hopi long ago, but the Hopi people made the kachinas angry, causing them to leave. Before leaving, though, the kachinas taught the Hopi how to perform their ceremonies. Today the kachina ceremonies serve several purposes. Most important, they bring clouds and rain to water the all-important corn crop, but they also ensure health, happiness, long life, and harmony in the universe. The kachina season lasts from the winter solstice until shortly after the summer solstice. These months are marked by various kachina dances and ceremonies, with men wearing the elaborate costumes and masks of whichever kachinas have been chosen to appear. Clowns known as *koyemsi*, *koshares*, and *tsukus* entertain spectators between the more serious dances, with ludicrous and sometimes lewd mimicry, bringing a lighthearted counterpoint to the very serious nature of the kachina dances.

Preparations for the dances take place in the kivas (circular ceremonial rooms) that are entered from the roof by means of a ladder. The kachina dancers often bring carved wooden kachina dolls to village children to introduce them to the various kachina spirits.

Despite the importance of the kachina dances, it's the **Snake Dance** that has captured the attention of many non-Hopi. The Snake Dance is held only every other year in any given village and involves the handling of both poisonous and nonpoisonous snakes. The ceremony takes place over 16 days with the first 4 days dedicated to collecting all the snakes from the four cardinal directions. Later, footraces are held from the bottom of the mesa to the top. On the last day of the ceremony, the actual Snake Dance is performed. Men of the Snake Society form pairs of dancers—one to carry the snake in his mouth and the other to distract the snake with an eagle feather. When all the snakes have been danced around the plaza, they are rushed down to their homes at the bottom of the mesa to carry the Hopi prayers for rain to the spirits of the underworld.

The best way to find out about attending dances or ceremonies is to call the **Community Development Office** of the individual villages (see phone numbers under "Visitor Information"). However, as of press time, most ceremonies and dances have been closed to non-Hopi because of the disrespectful attitude of some visitors. It's doubtful that these ceremonies and dances will again be open to non-Hopis, but it's certainly worth checking.

## SHOPPING

Most visitors come to the reservations to shop for Hopi crafts. There are literally dozens of small shops selling crafts and jewelry of different quality, and some homes have signs indicating that they sell crafts—you never know what you might discover by following such signs. Shops often sell the work of only a few individuals, so you should stop at several to get some idea of the variety of work available.

One of the best places to stop to get a quick education in Hopi art and crafts is **Tsakurshovi** (☎ **520/734-2478**), a tiny shop 1¹/₂ miles east of the Hopi Cultural Center on Second Mesa. This shop has an amazing selection of crafts, old-style kachina dolls, native herbs, coil and wicker plaque baskets, and "Don't Worry Be Hopi" T-shirts. The owners are very friendly and are happy to share their knowledge and expertise with visitors.

If you're in the market for Hopi silver jewelry, stop in at **Hopi Arts and Crafts-Silvercraft** (☎ **520/734-2463**), 100 yards from the Hopi Cultural Center on Second Mesa. This arts-and-crafts cooperative has more than 300 members. The **Honani Crafts Gallery** (☎ **520/737-2238**), at the intersection of Highway 264 and the road up to Second Mesa, sells both silver and the less common gold jewelry.

If you're interested in kachina dolls, be sure to visit the **Monongya Gallery** (☎ **520/734-2344**), a big blue and gray building on Ariz. 264 in Old Oraibi (west of the Hopi Cultural Center). This store usually has one of the largest selections of kachina dolls in the area. At Keams Canyon, almost 30 miles east of the cultural center, you'll find another great place to shop for kachina dolls. Also in Old Oraibi you'll find **Old Oraibi Crafts** (no phone), which sells artwork and crafts based on kachina images. **McGee's Indian Art** (☎ **520/738-2295**) is adjacent to a grocery store and has been a trading post for more than 100 years. There's always an outstanding selection of the best quality kachina dolls here.

# WHERE TO STAY & DINE
## SECOND MESA

**Hopi Cultural Center Restaurant & Motel.** P.O. Box 67, Second Mesa, AZ 86043. ☎ **520/734-2401.** 30 rms. TV TEL. Apr 1–Oct 31 $80 double; Nov 1–Mar 31 $60 double. AE, DISC, MC, V.

Though it isn't much, this is the only lodging for miles around—so be sure you have a reservation before heading up here for an overnight visit. The rooms are comfortable and modern if a bit Spartan. The restaurant serves American and traditional Hopi meals, including piki bread. There's also a museum here.

## TUBA CITY

**Quality Inn Tuba Trading Post, Restaurant & RV Park.** At the junction of U.S. 160 and Ariz. 264 (P.O. Box 247), Tuba City, AZ 86045. ☎ **800/644-8383** or 520/283-4545. 80 rms, 2 suites. A/C TV TEL. May–Oct $90–$135 double, $135 suite; Nov–Apr $75–$105 double, $105 suite. AE, DISC, JCB, MC, V.

If you can't get a room at the Hopi Cultural Center, this is the next nearest acceptable motel and even then, it is 62 miles away from Second Mesa. Located on the Navajo Reservation adjacent to the historic Tuba City Trading Post, the motel offers comfortable, modern rooms. The motel's restaurant serves Mexican and American meals. There's also an RV park here.

## WINSLOW

Though it's nearly 70 miles south of Second Mesa, this is the closest off-reservation town to the Hopi pueblos. Budget chain motels in Winslow include the **Best Western Adobe Inn,** 1701 N. Park Dr. (☎ **520/289-4638**), charging $50 to $68 double; **Comfort Inn,** 520 Desmond St. (☎ **520/289-9581**), charging $52 to $70 double; **Econo Lodge,** 1706 N. Park Dr. (☎ **520/289-4687**), charging $48 to $80 double; and **Super 8 Motel,** 1916 W. Third St. (☎ **520/289-4606**), charging $41 to $57 double. See the appendix for toll-free central reservation numbers.

## 2 The Petrified Forest & Painted Desert

25 miles E of Holbrook; 90 miles E of Flagstaff; 118 miles S of Canyon de Chelly; 180 miles N of Phoenix

Though petrified wood can be found in almost every state, the "forests" of downed logs here in northeastern Arizona are by far the most spectacular. A 27-mile scenic drive winds through the petrified forest and a small corner of the Painted Desert, providing a fascinating high desert experience.

Petrified wood has intrigued people for years and when, in the 1850s, it was discovered scattered like kindling across this section of Arizona, enterprising people began exporting it wholesale to the East. By 1900 so much had been removed that in 1906 several areas were set aside as the Petrified Forest National Monument.

It may be hard to believe when you drive across this arid landscape, but at one time this area was a vast humid swamp. That was 225 million years ago, when dinosaurs and huge amphibians ruled the earth and giant now-extinct trees grew on the high ground around the swamp. Fallen trees were washed downstream and gathered in piles in still backwaters and were eventually covered over with silt, mud, and volcanic ash. As water seeped through this soil, it dissolved the silica in the volcanic ash and redeposited this silica inside the cells of the logs. Eventually the silica recrystallized into stone to form petrified wood.

This region was later inundated with water, and thick deposits of sediment buried the logs ever deeper. Eventually the land was transformed yet again as a geologic upheaval thrust the lake bottom up above sea level. This upthrust of the land cracked the logs into the segments we see today. Eventually wind and water eroded the landscape to create the many colorful and spectacular features of northern Arizona, including the Painted Desert, and the petrified logs were once again exposed on the surface of the land.

Throughout the region you'll see petrified wood in all sizes and colors, natural and polished, being sold in gift stores. This petrified wood comes from private land. No petrified wood, no matter how small, may be removed from Petrified Forest National Park.

### ESSENTIALS

**GETTING THERE**   The north entrance to Petrified Forest National Park is 25 miles east of Holbrook on I-40. The south entrance is 20 miles east of Holbrook on U.S. 180.

There is **Amtrak** passenger service to Winslow, 33 miles west of Holbrook. Call ☎ **800/872-7245** for schedules and rate information.

**VISITOR INFORMATION**   For further information on the Painted Desert or the Petrified Forest, contact the **Petrified Forest National Park,** P.O. Box 2217, Petrified Forest National Park, AZ 86028 (☎ **520/524-6228**). The park is open daily from 8am to 5pm (longer hours in summer), and admission is $10 per car.

For information on Holbrook and the surrounding region, contact the **Holbrook Chamber of Commerce,** 100 E. Arizona St., Holbrook, AZ 86025 (☎ **800/524-2459** or 520/524-2459).

### EXPLORING A UNIQUE LANDSCAPE

Although Petrified Forest National Park has both a north and a south entrance, it is probably better to start at the southern entrance and work your way north. This way, you'll see the most impressive displays of petrified logs early in your visit. The north end of the park is where you'll find Painted Desert overlooks.

The park has two visitor centers, and both have maps and books about the region and issue the free permits necessary to backpack and camp in the park's wilderness areas. The **Rainbow Forest Museum,** at the south end of the park, is open daily from 8am to 5pm (also with longer hours in summer). Exhibits, including letters written by people who had taken pieces of petrified wood and who later felt guilty and returned the stones, chronicle the area's geologic and human history.

The **Painted Desert Oasis Visitor Center** is at the north end of the park and is open daily from 8am to 5pm (longer hours in summer). A 17-minute film here explains the process by which wood becomes fossilized. Connecting the two visitor centers is a 27-mile scenic road with more than 20 overlooks.

Starting at the southern end of the park, there is the **Giant Logs self-guided trail.** This trail starts behind the Rainbow Forest Museum and a booklet explaining the numbered stops is available at the front desk. The trail lives up to its name, with huge logs strewn about the hilly area. Almost directly across the parking lot from the Rainbow Forest Museum is the entrance to the **Long Logs** and **Agate House** areas. On the Long Logs trail you can see more big trees, while at Agate House you will see the ruins of a pueblo built from wood that was turned into colorful agate. Minerals such as iron, manganese, and carbon are what give petrified wood its distinctive colors.

Heading north, you pass by the unusual formations known as **The Flattops.** These structures are caused by the erosion of softer soil deposits from beneath a harder and more erosion-resistant layer of sandstone. The Flattops area is one of the park's wilderness areas. The **Crystal Forest** is the next stop to the north and is named for the beautiful amethyst and quartz crystals that were once found in the cracks of petrified logs. Concern over the removal of these crystals was what led to the protection of the petrified forest.

At the **Jasper Forest Overlook** you can see logs that include petrified roots, while at **Blue Mesa** pieces of petrified wood form capstones over easily eroded clay soils. As wind and water wear away at the clay beneath a piece of stone, the balance of the stone becomes more and more precarious until it eventually comes toppling down. At the **Agate Bridge** stop, the soil has been washed away under a petrified log creating a natural agate bridge.

Erosion has played a major role in the formation of the Painted Desert, and to the north of Blue Mesa you'll see some of the most interesting erosional features of the area. It's quite evident why these hills of sandstone and clay are known as **The Teepees.** The layers of different color are due to different types of soils and stone and to minerals dissolved in the soil.

Human habitation of the area dates from more than 2,000 years, and at **Newspaper Rock** you can see petroglyphs left by generations of Native Americans. At **Puerco Indian Ruins** you can see the homes of the people who made the carvings before the area's abandonment around 1400.

North of Puerco Ruins, the road crosses the Santa Fe Railroad and then I-40. From here to the Painted Desert Visitor Center there are eight overlooks onto the southernmost edge of the **Painted Desert.** Named for the vivid colors of the soil and stone that cover the land here, the Painted Desert is a Technicolor dreamscape of pastel colors washed across a barren expanse of eroded hills. The colors are created by minerals dissolved in the sandstone and clay soils that were deposited during different geologic periods. There's a picnic area at Chinde Point overlook, and at Kachina Point, where you'll also find the **Painted Desert Inn Museum.** From here, there's access to the park's other wilderness area.

At the north end, the **Painted Desert Oasis** provides a full-service cafeteria, and at the south end of the park there's a snack bar serving sandwiches and ice cream.

## A STOP IN HOLBROOK

Though the Petrified Forest National Monument is the main reason for visiting this area, you may also want to stop at the **Navajo County Historical Society Museum** in downtown Holbrook. This old and dusty museum has exhibits on local history, but is most interesting for having the town's old jail cells on display. From June to August, the Holbrook Chamber sponsors Native American dancers Monday through Friday evenings from 7 to 9pm on the lawn in front of the museum. There are also several rock shops in Holbrook where you can buy petrified wood and other fascinating stones. Also here in town (on the north side of I-40) is **McGee's Gallery,** 2114 E. Navajo Blvd. (☎ **520/524-1977**), a Native American crafts gallery with a wide selection of typical crafts at reasonable prices.

### PETROGLYPHS & WESTERN-STYLE FUN

If you're interested in petroglyphs, you may want to schedule a visit to the **Rock Art Canyon Ranch** (☎ **800/524-2459** or 520/288-3260), which is located southwest of Holbrook on part of the old Hashknife Ranch, which was the largest ranch in the country during the late 19th century. Within the bounds of this ranch are hundreds of Anasazi petroglyphs pecked into the rocks of Chevelon Canyon. Ranch visits are more than just a chance to see petroglyphs; they include wagon rides, horseback riding, swimming, and rockhounding. Cowboy lunches and dinners, complete with music and storytelling, are also part of the Rock Art Canyon Ranch experience. Tours are scheduled May 1 through the end of November; a half-day tour costs about $100 minimum for a group of four, and less per person as the size of the group increases.

## WHERE TO STAY

Holbrook is the nearest town to Petrified Forest National Monument. Here, in addition to the unique Wigwam Motel listed below, you'll find several budget chain motels, including the **Comfort Inn,** 2602 E. Navajo Blvd. (☎ **520/524-6131**), charging $41 to $70 double; **Days Inn,** 2601 E. Navajo Blvd. (☎ **520/524-6949**), charging $42 to $60 double; **Motel 6,** 2514 Navajo Blvd. (☎ **520/524-6101**), charging $26 to $36 double; and **Super 8 Motel,** 1989 Navajo Blvd. (☎ **520/ 524-2871**), charging $41 to $50 double.

✪ **Wigwam Motel.** 811 W. Hopi Dr., Holbrook, AZ 86025. ☎ **520/524-3048.** 15 rms. A/C TV TEL. $30 double. MC, V.

Here in Holbrook you can have your chance to sleep in a concrete wigwam. This unique motel was built in the 1940s when unusual architecture was springing up all along famous Route 66. Owned by the same family since it was built, the Wigwam was renovated a few years back. However, you'll still find the original rustic furniture and colorful bedspreads in the small wigwam-shaped buildings. There's also a small museum here at the motel.

## WHERE TO DINE

**Butterfield Stage Co.** 609 W. Hopi Dr. ☎ **520/524-3447.** Main courses $7–$18. AE, MC, V. Oct–Mar daily 4–10pm, Apr–Sept daily 11am–10pm. STEAK/SEAFOOD.

It's natural to assume that finding a decent meal in an out-of-the-way town might be nearly impossible, so the Butterfield Stage Co. is a pleasant surprise. The owners are from the former Yugoslavia, and we're not sure how they got to Holbrook, but we do know that meals here are excellent. The soup and salad bar is always fresh, and there isn't a better espresso or cappuccino for miles around. The tables have historical panels with amusing information to read while waiting for your peppersteak or filet mignon. The restaurant is named for the famous overland stagecoach line that carried the mail from St. Louis to San Francisco in the mid-19th century.

## 3  The Window Rock & Ganado Areas

190 miles E of Flagstaff; 68 miles SE of Canyon de Chelly National Monument; 74 miles NE of Petrified Forest National Park; 91 miles E of Second Mesa

Window Rock, less than a mile from the New Mexico state line, is the capital of the Navajo nation and is named for a huge natural opening in a sandstone cliff just outside town. Today that landmark is preserved as the **Window Rock Tribal Park,** which is located 2 miles north of Ariz. 264. At one time there was a spring at the base of Window Rock, and water from the spring was used by medicine men performing the Tohee Ceremony, a water ceremony intended to bring the rains.

As the Navajo nation's capital, Window Rock is the site of government offices, a museum and cultural center, and a zoo. About a half hour's drive west of Window Rock is the community of Ganado, the location of two historic sites—St. Michael's Mission and the Hubbell Trading Post. Window Rock's motel makes this town a good base for exploring this corner of the reservation.

### ESSENTIALS

**GETTING THERE**  To reach Window Rock from Flagstaff, take I-40 east to Lupton and go north on Indian Route 12.

There is **Amtrak** passenger service to Winslow, south of the reservation. Call ☎ 800/872-7245 for schedules and fares.

The **Navajo Transit System** operates bus service Monday through Friday throughout the Navajo nation with service between the cities of Farmington, Gallup, and Crown Point (all in New Mexico), and Window Rock, Kayenta, Chinle, and Tuba City. Call ☎ 520/729-4002 for schedule information.

**VISITOR INFORMATION**  For more information before visiting, contact the **Navajoland Tourism Department,** P.O. Box 663, Window Rock, AZ 86515 (☎ 520/871-7371 or 520/871-6436).

**SPECIAL EVENTS**  Unlike the village ceremonies of the pueblo-dwelling Hopi, Navajo religious ceremonies tend to be held in the privacy of family hogans. However, there are numerous fairs, powwows, and rodeos held throughout the year, and the public is welcome to attend these. The biggest of these is the **Navajo Nation Fair** (☎ 520/871-6478), held in Window Rock in early September each year. At this fair there are traditional dances, a rodeo, a powwow, a parade, a Miss Navajo Pageant, and arts-and-crafts exhibits and sales. In addition, other important fairs on the Navajo Reservation include the **Shiprock Navajo Fair** at Shiprock, New Mexico, in early October (the most traditional of all Navajo fairs); and the **Western Navajo Fair** at Tuba City, Arizona, in mid-October.

### HUBBELL TRADING POST

Located just outside the town of Ganado, 26 miles west of Window Rock, the **Hubbell Trading Post National Historic Site** (☎ 520/755-3475) is the oldest continuously operating trading post on the Navajo Reservation. The trading post was established in 1876 by Lorenzo Hubbell, who did more to popularize the arts and crafts of the Navajo people than any other person. The trading post includes a small museum, and in the visitor's center you can watch Navajo weavers in the slow process of creating a rug.

The rug room is filled with a variety of traditional and contemporary Navajo rugs. Though it's possible to buy a small 12- by 18-inch rug for around $100, most cost in the thousands of dollars. There are also baskets, kachinas, and several cases of jewelry by Navajo, Hopi, and Zuñi in another room. Glance around the general store and you'll see basic foodstuffs (not much variety here) and bolts of cloth used by Navajo women for sewing their traditional skirts and blouses.

Trading posts have long been more than just a place to trade crafts for imported goods. They were for many years the main gathering spot for meeting people from other parts of the reservation and served as a sort of gossip fence and newsroom. You can tour the grounds on your own or take a guided tour. There's no admission fee. From April to October, hours are daily from 8am to 6pm; in other months, daily 8am to 5pm.

## OTHER SIGHTS

**Navajo Tribal Museum.** W. Ariz. 264, Window Rock (across from the Navajo Nation Inn). ☎ 520/871-6673. Donations welcome. Mon–Sat 9am–5pm.

Sponsored by the Navajo Nation Historic Preservation Society, this new museum and cultural center will contain Navajo artifacts, old photos, and contemporary crafts. They have been in the process of relocating to this new facility and hopefully will be open when you come to visit.

**Navajo Nation Zoo & Botanical Park.** Ariz. 264, Window Rock. ☎ 520/871-6573. Free admission. Daily 8am–5pm. Closed Jan 1 and Dec 25.

Located in back of the Navajo Nation Inn, this zoo and botanical garden features animals and plants that are significant in Navajo history and culture. The zoo includes bears, cougars, and wolves among its small collection. The setting, which includes several sandstone "haystack" rocks, is very striking, and several of the animal enclosures are quite large and incorporate natural rock outcroppings. Also exhibited are examples of different styles of hogans.

**St. Michael's Historical Museum.** St. Michael's, just south of Ariz. 264. ☎ 520/871-4171. Free admission. Memorial Day–Labor Day daily 9am–5pm. Closed the rest of the year.

Located in the town of St. Michael's 4 miles west of Window Rock, this historical museum chronicles the lives and effects of Franciscan friars who started a mission in this area in the 1670s. The museum is in a small building adjacent to the impressive stone mission church.

## A TOUR FROM THE NAVAJO PERSPECTIVE

The best way to understand the Navajo culture is through the eyes of a Navajo. Stanley M. Perry, a Navajo Indian born and raised on the reservation, is a **storyteller** and step-on guide who will accompany you in your vehicle to tour the Window Rock, Canyon de Chelly, and Monument Valley areas. He can be reached at P.O. Box 2381, Window Rock, AZ 86515 (☎ 520/871-2484, best after 7pm). The rate is $100 per day for up to four persons, then rates vary depending on the number in the party.

## SHOPPING

The Hubbell Trading Post, though it is a National Historic Site, is still an active trading post and has an outstanding selection of rugs, as well as lots of jewelry (see above).

In Window Rock, be sure to visit the **Navajo Arts and Crafts Enterprise** (☎ 520/871-4095), which is adjacent to the Navajo Nation Inn and has been operating since 1941. Here you'll find high-quality silver-and-turquoise jewelry, Navajo rugs, sandpaintings, baskets, pottery, and Native American clothing.

## WHERE TO STAY

**Navajo Nation Inn.** 48 W. Hwy. 264 (P.O. Box 2340), Window Rock, AZ 86515. ☎ **800/ 662-6189** or 520/871-4108. Fax 520/871-5466. 54 rms, 2 suites. A/C TV TEL. $72 double; $83 suite. AE, DC, MC, V.

Located in the center of Window Rock, the administrative center of the Navajo Reservation, the Navajo Nation Inn is a modern motel with rustic pine furniture in the guest rooms. The restaurant and coffee shop are open daily from 6am to 9pm serving American and traditional Navajo dishes. The hotel also offers a tour desk.

## WHERE TO DINE

In Window Rock, your best bet for a meal is at the **Navajo Nation Inn.** In Ganado, you can get good, inexpensive cafeteria-style food at **Cafe Sage** (☎ **520/755-3411,** ext. 292 or 294) on the grounds of Ganado's health clinic, which is across Ariz. 264 and half a mile east of the trading post.

## 4 Canyon de Chelly

222 miles NE of Flagstaff; 68 miles NW of Window Rock; 110 miles SE of Navajo National Monument; 110 miles SE of Monument Valley Navajo Tribal Park

It's hard to imagine narrow canyons less than 1,000 feet deep being more spectacular than the Grand Canyon, but in some ways Canyon de Chelly National Monument is just that. Gaze down from the rim of Canyon de Chelly at an ancient Anasazi cliff dwelling as the whinnying of horses and clanging of goat bells drifts up from far below, and you will be struck by the continuity of human existence. For more than 2,000 years people have called these canyons home, and today there are more than 100 prehistoric dwelling sites in the area.

Canyon de Chelly National Monument consists of two major canyons—Canyon de Chelly (which is pronounced *canyon de SHAY* and is derived from the Navajo word *tségi,* meaning "rock canyon") and Canyon del Muerto (Spanish for Canyon of the Dead)—and several smaller canyons. The canyons extend for more than 100 miles through the rugged slick-rock landscape of northeastern Arizona, draining the seasonal runoff from the snowmelt of the Chuska Mountains.

Canyon de Chelly's smooth sandstone walls of rich reds and yellows contrast sharply with the deep greens of corn, pasture, and cottonwood on the canyon floor. Vast stone amphitheaters form the caves in which the ancient Anasazi built their homes, and as you watch shadows and light paint an ever-changing canyon panorama, it's easy to see why the Navajo consider these canyons sacred ground. With mysteriously abandoned cliff dwellings and breathtaking natural beauty, Canyon de Chelly is certainly as worthy of a visit as the Grand Canyon.

From June to the beginning of September there have in the past been interpretive programs here at the national monument. However, these have been curtailed due to budget constraints. Check at the **visitor center** for daily activities, such as ranger-led canyon hikes (these are popular, so be sure to sign up at the visitor center), campfire programs, and natural-history programs, that might still be scheduled.

### ESSENTIALS

**GETTING THERE**   From Flagstaff, the easiest route to Canyon de Chelly is to take I-40 to U.S. 191 to Ganado. At Ganado, drive west on Ariz. 264 and then pick up U.S. 191 again heading north to Chinle. If you're coming down from Monument Valley or Navajo National Monument, Indian Route 59, which connects U.S. 160 and U.S. 191, is an excellent road with plenty of beautiful scenery.

Chinle, 3 miles from the entrance to Canyon de Chelly National Monument, is served by the **Navajo Transit System** (☎ 520/729-4002 for schedules and fares).

**VISITOR INFORMATION**   Before leaving home you can contact **Canyon de Chelly National Monument,** P.O. Box 588, Chinle, AZ 86503 (☎ 520/674-5500). Once at the national monument, your first stop should be at the **visitor center,** open daily May through September from 8am to 6pm (on daylight saving time) and October through April from 8am to 5pm. Park admission is free.

**SPECIAL EVENTS**   The **Central Navajo Fair** is held in Chinle each year in late August.

## ARRANGING YOUR TRIP INTO THE CANYON

In front of the **visitor center** is an example of a traditional crib-style hogan, a hexagonal structure of logs and earth that Navajo use both as a home and as a ceremonial center. Inside, a small **museum** acquaints visitors with the history of Canyon de Chelly, and there's sometimes a silversmith demonstrating Navajo jewelry-making techniques. If you want to drive your own four-wheeler into the canyon, this is where you need to get your permit, and you must hire a guide as well (see below).

Access to the canyons is restricted, and in order to descend into the canyon *you must be accompanied by either a park ranger or an authorized guide,* unless you're on the White House Ruins trail. To hire a **Navajo guide** to lead you into the canyon on foot or in your own four-wheel-drive vehicle is $10 per hour with a 3-hour minimum. Check with the visitor center, which maintains a list of guides.

Another way to see Canyon de Chelly and Canyon del Muerto is from one of the **four- or six-wheel-drive trucks** that operate out of **Thunderbird Lodge** (☎ 800/679/2473 or 520/674-5841). These trucks are equipped with seats in the bed and stop frequently for photographs and to visit ruins, Navajo farms, and rock art. Tours cost $34 per person for a half-day ($25.50 for children 12 and under); all-day tours are $54. Half-day tours leave at 9am and 2pm in summer, at 9am and 1pm in winter; full-day trips leave at 9am and return at 5:30pm (summer only).

There are also two stables offering horseback tours into the canyon. **Justin Tso Horse Rental** (☎ 520/674-5678) charges $8 per hour per person for a horse and $8 per hour per group for a guide. **Twin Trails Tours** (☎ 520/674-8425) charges $35 for a 2-hour ride, $45 for a 3-hour ride, and $70 for a full-day ride.

Jeep tours of Canyon de Chelly with an emphasis on Navajo culture are offered by **Crossing Worlds,** P.O. Box 171, Young, AZ 85554 (☎ 800/350-2693, 520/462-3356 in Young, or 520/282-7148 in Sedona). Tours go to back-country ruins on the reservation to view cliff dwellings and rock art.

## THE RIM DRIVES

A very different view of the canyons is provided by the North and South Rim drives. The North Rim Drive overlooks Canyon del Muerto, while the South Rim Drive overlooks Canyon de Chelly. Each of the rim drives is around 20 miles in each direction, and with stops it can easily take 3 hours to visit each rim.

### THE NORTH RIM DRIVE

The first stop on the north rim is the **Ledge Ruin Overlook.** On the opposite wall, about 100 feet up from the canyon floor, you can see the Ledge Ruin. This site was occupied by the Anasazi between A.D. 1050 and 1275. Nearby, at the **Dekaa Kiva Viewpoint,** you can see a lone kiva (circular ceremonial building). This structure was reached by means of toeholds cut into the soft sandstone cliff wall.

The second stop is at the **Antelope House Overlook.** The Antelope House ruin takes its name from the paintings of antelopes on a nearby cliff wall. It's believed that the paintings were done in the 1830s. Beneath the ruins of Antelope House, archaeologists have found the remains of an earlier pit house dating from A.D. 693. Though most of the Anasazi cliff dwellings were abandoned sometime after a drought began in 1276, Antelope House had already been abandoned by 1260, possibly because of damage caused by flooding. Across the wash from Antelope House, an ancient tomb, known as the Tomb of the Weaver, was discovered in the 1920s by archaeologists. The tomb contained the well-preserved body of an old man wrapped in a blanket of golden eagle feathers and accompanied by cornmeal, shelled and husked corn, piñon nuts, beans, salt, and thick skeins of cotton. Also visible from this overlook is Navajo Fortress, a red sandstone butte that the Navajo once used as a refuge from attackers. A steep trail leads to the top of Navajo Fortress, and through the use of log ladders that could be pulled up into the refuge, the Navajo were able to escape their attackers.

The third stop is at **Mummy Cave Overlook,** named for two mummies that were found in burial urns below the ruins. Archaeological evidence indicates that this giant amphitheater consisting of two caves was occupied for 1,000 years from A.D. 300 to 1300. In the two caves and on the shelf between there are 80 rooms, including three kivas. The central structure between the two caves is interesting because it includes a three-story building characteristic of the architecture in Mesa Verde in New Mexico. Archaeologists speculate that a group of Anasazi migrated here from New Mexico. Much of the original plasterwork of these buildings is still intact and indicates that the buildings were colorfully decorated.

The fourth and last stop on the north rim is at the **Massacre Cave Overlook.** The cave received its name after an 1805 Spanish military expedition killed more than 115 Navajo at this site. The Navajo at the time had been raiding Spanish settlements that were encroaching on Navajo territory. Accounts of the battle at Massacre Cave differ. One account claims that there were only women, children, and old men taking shelter in the cave, though the official Spanish records claim 90 warriors and 25 women and children were killed. Also visible from this overlook is Yucca Cave, which was occupied about 1,000 years ago.

If you continue another 10 miles or so from the end of the North Rim Drive to the community of Tsaile, you can visit the **Hatathli Gallery** at Navajo Community College (☎ **520/724-3311**). This modern art gallery has a small but interesting collection of Navajo art, crafts, and artifacts, old photos, and even a collection of Plains Indian regalia and clothing. The gallery is open Monday through Friday from 9am to noon and from 1 to 4pm, and admission is free.

## THE SOUTH RIM DRIVE

The South Rim Drive climbs slowly but steadily along the south rim of Canyon de Chelly, and at each stop you're a little bit higher above the canyon floor.

The first stop is at **Tségi Overlook.** *Tségi* means "rock canyon" in Navajo, and that's just what you'll see when you gaze down from this viewpoint. A short narrow canyon feeds into Chinle Wash, which is formed by the streams cutting through the canyons of the national monument.

The second stop is at the **Junction Overlook,** so named because it overlooks the junction of Canyon del Muerto and Canyon de Chelly. Visible here is the Junction Ruin, with its 10 rooms and one kiva. The Anasazi occupied this ruin during the great pueblo period, which lasted from around 1100 until the Anasazi disappeared shortly before 1300. Also visible is First Ruin, which is perched precariously on a long narrow ledge. In this ruin are 22 rooms and two kivas.

The third stop, at **White House Overlook,** provides the only opportunity for descending into Canyon de Chelly without a guide or ranger. The White House Ruins Trail descends 600 feet to the canyon floor, crosses Chinle Wash, and approaches the White House Ruins. These buildings were constructed both on the canyon floor and 50 feet up the cliff wall in a small cave. Though you cannot enter the ruins, you can get close enough to get a good look. You're not allowed to wander off this trail, and please respect the privacy of those Navajo living here. It's a 2½-mile round-trip hike and takes about 2 hours. Be sure to carry water. If you aren't inclined to hike the trail, you can view the ruins from the overlook. This is one of the largest ruins in the canyon and contained 80 rooms. It was inhabited between 1040 and 1275. Notice the black streaks on the sandstone walls above the White House Ruins. These streaks were formed by seeping water that reacted with the iron in the sandstone. Iron is what gives the walls their reddish hue. Anasazi artists used to chip away at this black patina to create petroglyphs. Later the Navajo would use paints to create pictographs, painted images of animals, and records of historic events such as the Spanish military expedition that killed 115 Navajo at Massacre Cave. Many of these petroglyphs and pictographs can be seen if you take one of the guided tours into the canyon.

The fourth stop is at **Sliding House Overlook.** These ruins are built on a narrow shelf and appear to be sliding down into the canyon. Inhabited from about 900 until 1200, Sliding House contained between 30 and 50 rooms. This overlook is already more than 700 feet above the canyon floor, with sheer walls giving the narrow canyon a very foreboding appearance.

**Wild Cherry Overlook** and **Face Rock Overlook,** the next two stops, provide further glimpses of the ever-deepening canyon. Here you gaze 1,000 feet down to the bottom of the canyon. The last stop on the south rim is one of the most spectacular: **Spider Rock Overlook.** This viewpoint overlooks the junction of Canyon de Chelly and Monument Canyon, and at this wide spot in the canyon stands the monolithic pinnacle called Spider Rock. Rising 800 feet from the canyon floor, the freestanding twin towers of Spider Rock are a natural monument, a geologic wonder. Across the canyon from Spider Rock stands the similarly striking **Speaking Rock,** which is connected to the far canyon wall.

## SHOPPING

The large **Thunderbird Lodge Gift Shop** (☎ 520/674-5841) in Chinle is well worth a stop while you're in the area. It has a huge collection of rugs, as well as good selections of pottery and plenty of souvenirs. Also here in Chinle, at the junction of U.S. 191 and Indian Route 7, is an outpost of the **Navajo Arts and Crafts Enterprise** (☎ 520/674-5338).

## WHERE TO STAY & DINE

In addition to the motels listed below, there is one other lodging option in the Canyon de Chelly area. **Coyote Pass Hospitality,** P.O. Box 91-B, Tsaile, AZ 86558 (☎ 520/724-3383), operates a very rustic sort of bed-and-breakfast operation. Guests stay in a traditional dirt-floored hogan and receive a traditional breakfast in the morning. For an additional cost, you can arrange dinner for the night of your arrival. Rates are $85 for one person and $10 for each additional person. At the time of making the reservation, guests may also arrange for customized, off-the-beaten path Navajo cultural and historic tours with the hosts.

**Best Western Canyon de Chelly Inn.** 100 Main St. (P.O. Box 295), Chinle, AZ 86503. ☎ **800/528-1234** or 520/674-5875. Fax 520/674-3715. 99 rms. A/C TV TEL. $66–$112 double. AE, CB, DC, DISC, JCB, MC, V.

Located in the center of Chinle, this modern motel is the farthest from the park of the three hotels here in town and should be a last choice. The rooms are medium size to large and have beamed ceilings and coffeemakers. The restaurant is large, and the menu features moderately priced American and Navajo meals. There's also an indoor swimming pool.

**Holiday Inn—Canyon de Chelly.** Indian Rte. 7 (P.O. Box 1889), Chinle, AZ 86503. ☎ **800/ 23-HOTEL** or 520/674-5000. Fax 520/674-8264. 108 rms. A/C TV TEL. Summer $104–$130 double; winter $59–$69 double. AE, CB, DC, DISC, JCB, MC, V.

This is the newest hotel in Chinle and is located between the town and the entrance to Canyon de Chelly National Monument. The hotel is on the site of an old trading post, which is incorporated into the restaurant and gift shop building. The guest rooms all have patios or balconies and big windows and bathrooms, and most face the cottonwood-shaded pool courtyard. The hotel's restaurant serves moderately priced American and Navajo meals. Room service is available when the restaurant is open. Native American dance performances are held some summer evenings here at the hotel.

**✪ Thunderbird Lodge.** P.O. Box 548, Chinle, AZ 86503. ☎ **800/679-BIRD** or 520/ 674-5841. Fax 520/674-5844. 72 rms, 1 suite. A/C TV TEL. $83–$88 double; $152 suite. Lower rates Nov–Mar. AE, DC, DISC, MC, V.

Built on the site of an early trading post at the mouth of Canyon de Chelly, the Thunderbird Lodge is the most appealing of the hotels in Chinle. The pink adobe construction is reminiscent of ancient pueblos, and the guest rooms have rustic furniture and Navajo sandpaintings on the walls. The rooms come in two different sizes, with either two double beds or two queen-size beds. Ceiling fans and air conditioners keep the rooms cool in the hot summer months. The original trading post building now serves as the lodge cafeteria, where American and Navajo meals are served. The lodge also has a tour desk, gift shop, and rug room.

## CAMPGROUNDS

Adjacent to the Thunderbird Lodge is the **Cottonwood Campground,** which doesn't take reservations. In the summer the campground has water and rest rooms, but in the winter you must bring your own water and only portable toilets are available. The next nearest campgrounds are at **Tsaile Lake** and **Wheatfields Lake,** both of which are south of the town of Tsaile on Indian Route 12. Tsaile is at the east end of the North Rim Drive.

# 5 Monument Valley & Navajo National Monument

Monument Valley Navajo Tribal Park: 200 miles NE of Flagstaff, 60 miles NE of Navajo National Monument, 110 miles NW of Canyon de Chelly, 150 miles E of Page
Navajo National Monument: 140 miles NE of Flagstaff; 90 miles E of Page; 60 miles SW of Monument Valley; 110 miles NW of Canyon de Chelly

Nature, in its role as sculptor, has created a garden of monoliths and spires in the north-central part of the Navajo Reservation. You may not be aware of it, but you have almost certainly seen Monument Valley before. This otherworldly landscape has been an object of fascination for years, and has served as backdrop for countless movies, including John Ford's *Stagecoach* (1938) and *Thelma and Louise* (1992), with Susan Sarandon and Geena Davis, as well as for television shows and commercials.

Located 30 miles north of Kayenta just across the Utah state line, Monument Valley is a vast flat plain punctuated by natural cathedrals of sandstone. These huge monoliths rise up from the sagebrush with sheer walls that capture the light of the rising and setting sun and transform it into fiery hues. Evocative names reflect the shapes the sandstone has taken on as the forces of nature have eroded it: the Mittens, Three Sisters, Camel Butte, Elephant Butte, the Thumb, and Totem Pole being some of the most awe-inspiring natural monuments. A 17-mile unpaved loop road winds among these 1,000-foot-tall buttes and mesas.

Human habitation has also left its mark. Within the park there are more than 100 ancient Anasazi archaeological sites, ruins, and petroglyphs dating from before A.D. 1300. The Navajo have been living in the valley for generations, herding their sheep through the sagebrush scrublands, and some families continue to live here today.

Navajo National Monument, though set in a less spectacular landscape, is no less interesting, though for a very different reason. It is here that you will find some of the largest cliff dwellings in Arizona. Located 30 miles west of Kayenta and 60 miles northeast of Tuba City, Navajo National Monument encompasses three of the best-preserved Anasazi cliff dwellings in the region: Betatakin, Keet Seel, and Inscription House. It's possible to visit both Betatakin and Keet Seel, but fragile Inscription House is closed to the public. The name Navajo National Monument is a bit misleading. Although the Navajo people do inhabit the area now, it was the ancient Anasazi who built the cliff dwellings. The Navajo arrived centuries after the Anasazi had abandoned the area.

The inhabitants of Tsegi Canyon were ancestral Hopi and Pueblo peoples known as the Kayenta Anasazi. The Anasazi began abandoning their well-constructed homes around the middle of the 13th century for reasons unknown. Tree rings suggest that a drought in the latter part of the 13th century prevented the Anasazi from growing sufficient crops. However, in Tsegi Canyon there's another theory for the abandonment. The canyon floors were usually flooded each year by spring and summer snowmelt, which made farming quite productive, but in the mid-1200s weather patterns changed and streams running through the canyons began cutting deep into the soil, forming deep, narrow canyons called arroyos, which lowered the water table and made farming much more difficult.

## ESSENTIALS

**GETTING THERE**    From Flagstaff, Navajo National Monument can be reached by taking U.S. 89 north to U.S. 160; Monument Valley Navajo Tribal Park is a bit farther on U.S. 160 and then north on U.S. 163.

The **Navajo Transit System** operates bus service Monday through Friday throughout the Navajo nation with service between the cities of Farmington, Gallup, and Crown Point (all in New Mexico) and Window Rock, Kayenta, Chinle, and Tuba City. Call ☎ **520/729-4002** for schedule information.

**VISITOR INFORMATION**    For more information on Monument Valley, contact **Monument Valley Navajo Tribal Park,** P.O. Box 360289, Monument Valley, UT 84536 (☎ **801/727-3287** or 801/727-3353). The park is open May to September, daily from 7am to 7pm; October to April, daily from 8am to 5pm. Admission is $2.50 for adults, $1 for seniors, and free for children 7 and under. Please note, the National Park Services Golden Eagle Passport isn't valid here because Monument Valley is a private park.

For more information on the national monument, contact **Navajo National Monument,** HC 71, Box 3, Tonalea, AZ 86044-9704 (☎ **520/672-2366**). The park is open daily. There's no lodge at the national monument, but there is a campground that's usually closed in winter. Park admission is free.

## MONUMENT VALLEY NAVAJO TRIBAL PARK

This is big country, and, like the Grand Canyon, is primarily a point-and-shoot experience. Because this is reservation land and people still live in Monument Valley, backcountry or off-road travel is prohibited unless you have a licensed guide. So, basically the only way to see the park is from the overlook at the visitor center, by driving the park's scenic (but very rough) dirt road, or by taking either a four-wheel-drive, horseback, or guided hiking tour.

At the valley overlook parking area in Monument Valley Navajo Tribal Park you'll find a small museum, gift shop, snack bar, campground, and numerous local Navajo guides who offer tours of the park.

If you want to do a four-wheel-drive tour, try **Roland's Navajo Land Tours** (☎ **800/368-2785** or 520/697-3524). Owner Roland Cody Dixon offers three different four-wheel-drive tours of Monument Valley. **Sacred Monument Tours** (☎ **520/691-6199**) also offers jeep tours, as well as hiking and horseback tours.

If you want to see the park on foot, you can arrange a hiking tour through **Fred's Adventure Tours** (☎ **801/739-4294**), **Black's Hiking/Jeep Tours** (☎ **801/ 739-4226**), or **Totem Pole Guided Tours** (☎ **800/345-TOUR** or 801/727-3313).

If nothing but the cowboy thing will do for you in this quintessential Wild West landscape, you've got some options. **Ed Black's Monument Valley Trail Rides** (☎ **800/551-4039** or 801/739-4285) is located near the visitor center and charges $30 for a 1$\frac{1}{2}$-hour ride and $85 to $100 for an overnight ride. **Bigman's Horseback Riding** (☎ **520/677-3219**) is located on the road to the monument entrance.

Another option is to book with **Goulding's Tours,** P.O. Box 360001, Monument Valley, UT 84536-0001 (☎ **801/727-3231**). This company has its office on the edge of the valley at Goulding's Lodge, just a few miles from the park entrance. Half-day tours are $30 for adults and $18 for children 6 and under; full-day tours are $60 for adults and $45 for children 6 and under.

Before leaving the area, you might also want to visit **Goulding's Museum and Trading Post** at Goulding's Lodge. This old trading post was the home of the Gouldings for many years and is set up as they had it back in the 1920s and 1930s. There are also displays about the many movies that have been shot here. The trading post is open daily from 7:30 to 9pm, and admission is by donation.

## NAVAJO NATIONAL MONUMENT

Unlike Monument Valley, a visit to Navajo National Monument requires physical effort. The shortest distance you'll have to walk here is 1 mile, which is the round-trip distance from the visitor center to the Betatakin overlook. However, if you want to actually climb around inside these ruins, you're looking at strenuous day-long or overnight hikes.

Your first stop here should be the visitor center, which has informative displays on the ancestral Pueblo and Navajo cultures, including numerous artifacts from Tsegi Canyon. You can also watch two 20-minute films or a short slide show. The center is open daily from 8am to 5pm (until 6pm in summer when daylight saving time is observed).

**Betatakin,** which means "ledge house" in Navajo, is the only one of the three ruins that can be seen easily. Built in a huge amphitheater-like alcove in the canyon wall, Betatakin was occupied only from 1250 to 1300, and at its height of occupation may have housed 125 people.

A 1-mile round-trip paved trail from the visitor center leads to overlooks of Betatakin. The strenuous 5-mile round-trip hike to Betatakin itself is ranger-led, takes about 6 hours, and involves descending more than 700 feet to the floor of Tsegi Canyon and later returning to the rim. This hike is conducted from May through September and leaves from the visitor center. All hikers are required to carry 2 quarts of water. This hike is very popular, and the number of people allowed is limited to 25 per tour; many people line up at the visitor center an hour or more before the center opens.

**Keet Seel,** which means "broken pieces of pottery" in Navajo, has a much longer history than Betatakin, with occupation beginning as early as A.D. 950 and continuing until 1300. At one point Keet Seel may have housed 150 people.

The 17-mile round-trip hike or horseback ride to Keet Seel is even more strenuous. Hikers may stay overnight at a primitive campground near the ruins. You must carry enough water for your trip since none is available along the trail. Only 20 people a day are given permits to visit Keet Seel, and the trail is only open from Memorial Day to Labor Day.

## WHERE TO STAY & DINE

**Anasazi Inn at Tsegi Canyon.** U.S. 160 (P.O. Box 1543), Kayenta, AZ 86033. ☎ **520/ 697-3793.** Fax 520/697-8249. 57 rms. A/C TV TEL. May–Sept $80–$110 double; Oct–Apr $50– $80 double. AE, CB, DC, DISC, MC, V. Take U.S. 160 west of Kayenta.

Located about halfway between Kayenta and Navajo National Monument, the Anasazi Inn at Tsegi Canyon is a very basic motel surrounded by wilderness, but it's the closest lodging to Navajo National Monument. If your standards aren't too high, this motel should be fine for you. Think of it as a last resort or option to camping. There's a small dining room attached to the motel.

✪ **Goulding's Lodge.** P.O. Box 360001, Monument Valley, UT 84536-0001. ☎ **801/ 727-3231.** Fax 801/727-3344. 62 rms. A/C TV TEL. Mar 15–Oct 15 $92–$128 double; Oct 16– Mar 14 $62–$72 double. AE, DC, MC, V.

This is the only lodge actually located in Monument Valley, and it offers superb views from the private balconies of the guest rooms, which are furnished with Southwestern decor. A restaurant serves Navajo and American dishes, and the views from here are enough to make any meal an event. The hotel also has an indoor pool, tour desk, museum, gift shop, coin laundry, and gas station.

**Holiday Inn—Kayenta.** At the junction of U.S. 160 and U.S. 163 (P.O. Box 307), Kayenta, AZ 86033. ☎ **800/HOLIDAY** or 520/697-3221. Fax 520/697-3349. 160 rms. A/C TV TEL. Mar–Sept $109–$129 double; Oct–Feb $69–$89 double. AE, DC, DISC, MC, V.

Located in the center of Kayenta, 23 miles south of Monument Valley and 29 miles east of Navajo National Monument, this Holiday Inn is very popular with tour groups and is almost always crowded. Though the grounds are dusty and a bit run-down, the rooms are spacious and clean and most have new carpets. We like the poolside rooms best. Part of the motel's restaurant is designed to look like an Anasazi ruin. The menu offers both American and Navajo meals. Room service is available. The hotel also has an outdoor pool and a tour desk.

**Wetherill Inn Motel.** P.O. Box 175, Kayenta, AZ 86033-0175. ☎ 520/697-3231. 54 rms. A/C TV TEL. Apr 15–Oct 14 $98 double; Oct 15–Apr 14 $49.50–$69.50 double. AE, CB, DC, DISC, MC, V.

Located 1 mile north of the junction of U.S. 160 and U.S. 163 and 20 miles south of Monument Valley, the Wetherill Inn Motel offers modern guest rooms with coffeemakers. The hotel has no restaurant or pool, but there's a cafe next door that serves Navajo and American food.

## CAMPGROUNDS

If you're headed to Monument Valley Navajo Tribal Park, you can camp in the park at the **Mitten View Campground** (☎ 801/727-3353), which charges $10 per night per site April to September and $5 October to March, or just outside the park at **Goulding's Monument Valley KOA Campground** (☎ 801/727-3231), which charges $14 to $22 per night.

There's also a free campground at **Navajo National Monument** (☎ 520/672-2366), west of Kayenta. There are only 30 campsites here, plus an overflow area containing about a dozen more (summer only). In summer they're usually full by dark. In winter, the campground is closed.

# DRIVING ON TO COLORADO OR NEW MEXICO: THE FOUR CORNERS MEET

Other attractions you might want to visit while you're in this part of the state include the **Four Corners Monument Navajo Tribal Park** (☎ 520/871-6647), north of Teec Nos Pos in the very northeast corner of the state. This is the only place in the United States where the corners of four states come together. Those states are Arizona, Colorado, Utah, and New Mexico. In the park you'll find a picnic ground and crafts vendors. The park is open daily from 8am to 8pm in summer and 8am to 5pm in winter. Admission is $2.50 per person.

Also in the area, in the community of Teec Nos Pos, you'll find the **Teec Nos Pos Trading Post** (☎ 520/656-3224) and **Foutz Teec Nos Pos Arts and Crafts** (☎ 520/656-3228), both of which have good selections of rugs and other crafts.

# DRIVING ON TO FLAGSTAFF OR THE GRAND CANYON

On the west side of the reservation, in Tuba City, you'll find the **Tuba Trading Post** (☎ 520/283-5441) on the corner of Main Street and Moenave Street. This octagonal trading post was built in 1906 of local stone and is designed to resemble a Navajo hogan. The trading post serves both as a small market and as a store selling Native American crafts. On the western outskirts of Tuba City, on U.S. 160, you'll find **Van's Trading Co.** (☎ 520/283-5343), which has a dead-pawn auction on the 15th of each month at 3pm. This auction provides opportunities to buy older pieces of Navajo silver-and-turquoise jewelry.

West of Tuba City and just off U.S. 160, you can see **dinosaur footprints** preserved in the stone surface of the desert. There are usually a few people waiting at the site to guide visitors to the best footprints. These guides will expect a tip.

The **Cameron Trading Post** (☎ 520/679-2231), 16 miles south of the junction of U.S. 160 and U.S. 89, is also well worth a visit. The large main trading post is filled with souvenirs, but it also has large selections of rugs and jewelry. In the adjacent stone-walled gallery, you'll find museum-quality Native American artifacts (with prices to match). The trading post also includes a motel (see chapter 7 for details).

Between Cameron and Flagstaff, keep an eye out for **Sacred Mountain Trading Post** (☎ 520/679-2255), which though small, has the look and feel of a trading post of 50 years ago. The shelves are full of Navajo pottery.

# 9 Eastern Arizona's High Country

**W**hen most people think of Arizona, they think of deserts and saguaro cacti. But Arizona actually has more mountainous country than Switzerland and more forest than Minnesota—and most of this landscape lies here, in the highlands of eastern Arizona.

In this sparsely populated region, towns with such apt names as Alpine, Lakeside, and Pinetop have become summer retreats for the people who live in the state's low-lying, sun-baked deserts. Folks from Phoenix and its surrounding cities discovered long ago how close the desert was to the cool mountain forests. In only a few hours you can drive up from the cacti and creosote bushes to the meadows and pine forests of the White Mountains.

Dividing the arid lowlands from the cool pine forests of the highlands is the Mogollon Rim (pronounced *MUG-ee-un* by the locals), a 2,000-foot-high escarpment that stretches for 200 miles from central Arizona into New Mexico. Along this impressive wall, the climatic and vegetative change is dramatic. Imagine sunshine at the base and snow squalls at the top and you have an idea of the Mogollon Rim's variety. This area was made famous by Western author Zane Grey who lived in a cabin near Payson and set many of his novels in this scenic, yet often-overlooked part of Arizona. Fans of Zane Grey's novels can follow in the author's footsteps and also visit a small museum dedicated to him.

Trout fishing, hiking, horseback riding, and hunting are the main warm-weather pastimes of eastern Arizona, and when winter weather reports from up north have Phoenicians dreaming about snow (it's true, they really do), many head up this way to the White Mountains for a bit of skiing. Sunrise Park Resort, operated by the White Mountain Apache Tribe, is the state's biggest and busiest downhill ski area, and in the region there are also plenty of cross-country ski trail systems.

A large chunk of this region, 1,664,874 acres to be exact, is Apache reservation land. Recreational activities abound on the reservation, but just remember that the Apache tribe requires visitors to have reservation fishing permits and outdoor recreation permits. Fishing is particularly popular on the reservation, which isn't surprising considering that there are 400 miles of trout streams and 25 lakes stocked with rainbow and brown trout.

Another draw of this region is the chance to experience all four seasons, and unless you live in the desert you may not understand

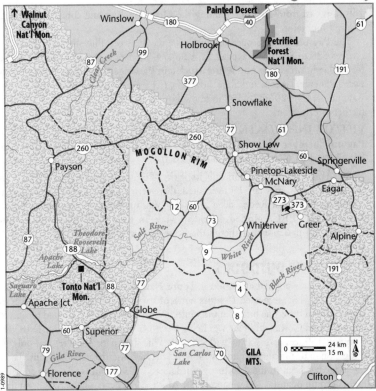

the power of this appeal. There is something deeply reassuring about seeing meadows full of wildflowers in the spring and mountainsides of aspens painted golden in the autumn. Though in the past this region has appealed primarily to family vacationers, as the population of Phoenix has grown, so too has the interest in the eastern highlands. If you have time to explore outside the state's main tourist routes, you'll find that this area has a lot to offer.

## 1 Payson & the Mogollon Rim

94 miles NE of Phoenix; 90 miles SW of Winslow; 90 miles SE of Flagstaff; 100 miles W of Pinetop-Lakeside

Payson, 94 miles from Phoenix and 5,000 feet above sea level, is one of the closest places for Phoenicians to find relief from the summer heat. Summer temperatures are 20° cooler than in the Valley of the Sun, and the surrounding Tonto National Forest provides opportunities for hiking, swimming, fishing, and hunting. It isn't quite high enough to be the mountains, but it certainly isn't the desert. The 2,000-foot-high, 200-mile-long Mogollon Rim is only 22 miles north of town. In recent years, retirees have discovered the nearly perfect climate of Payson. Summer highs are usually in the 80s or 90s while winter highs are usually in the 50°-to-60° range.

## ESSENTIALS

**GETTING THERE**   Payson is 94 miles from Phoenix on Ariz. 87, the Beeline Highway. Ariz. 87 also connects Payson to Winslow, which is 90 miles away. Ariz.

260 runs east from Payson, climbing the Mogollon Rim and continuing into the White Mountains.

The **Payson Express** operates one bus a day between Phoenix and Payson and charges $25 to $35 one-way; call ☎ **520/474-5254** or 602/256-6464 in Phoenix, for further information. The **White Mountain Passenger Line** also offers service between Phoenix, Payson, and Show Low. The fare from Phoenix to Payson is $22 one-way; phone ☎ **520/537-4539** in Show Low or ☎ **602/275-4245** in Phoenix for further information.

**VISITOR INFORMATION**   For more information on Payson, contact the **Payson Chamber of Commerce,** 100 W. Main St. (P.O. Box 1380), Payson, AZ 85547 (☎ **800/672-9766** or 520/474-4515).

**SPECIAL EVENTS**   Payson calls itself the "Festival Capital of the World," and though this claim may be a bit overstated, there certainly are plenty of festivals here. The **World's Oldest Rodeo** takes place each year on the third weekend in August, while another **PRCA Rodeo** is held in May. In June there's the annual **Blues Festival,** and in September there's the **State Championship Old Time Fiddler's Contest.**

## ENJOYING THE OUTDOORS

The area's most popular attraction is **Tonto Natural Bridge State Park** (☎ **520/476-4202**), which is located 15 miles north of Payson on Ariz. 87 and preserves the largest natural travertine bridge in the world. Discovered in 1877 by a gold prospector named David Gowan while he was being chased by Apaches, the bridge is 183 feet high and 150 feet across at its widest point. This state park preserves not only the bridge, but a historic lodge built by Gowan's nephew and the nephew's sons. Today the lodge has been restored to the way it looked in 1927 but is not open for overnight accommodations. Admission to the park is $5 per car. The park is open daily April to October from 8am to 6pm and November to March from 9am to 5pm.

If you want to do some fishing, there are seven lakes nearby atop the Mogollon Rim (several of which are accessed from Forest Road 300); all are well known for their excellent fishing. Stop in at the Payson Chamber of Commerce information center for directions to where the fish might be biting. Anglers might also want to visit the **Tonto Creek Fish Hatchery** (☎ **520/478-4200**), which is off of Ariz. 260 about 17 miles east of Payson (open daily 8am to 4pm).

If you'd like to go horseback riding between Memorial Day and late September, contact **O.K. Corral Stables** (☎ **520/476-4303**) in Pine, which is 14 miles north of Payson on Ariz. 87, or **Don Donnelly Stables** (☎ **520/478-4701**) in Little Green Valley, which is 10 miles east of Payson on Ariz. 260. Rates start around $20 for a 1-hour ride.

In the winter, cross-country skiers will find ski rentals and 30 kilometers of groomed trails at **Forest Lakes Touring Center and Cabins,** 36 miles east of Payson on Ariz. 260 (☎ **520/535-4047**).

The **Highline Trail** is a 51-mile-long hiking trail along the lower slope of the Mogollon Rim. You can find out more about this and other area trails at the **Payson Ranger Station** (☎ **520/474-7900**) on Ariz. 260 at the east end of town (open Monday through Friday 7:45am to 4:30pm). At the ranger station, you can also find out about area trails open to mountain bikes.

## MORE TO SEE & DO

About 2 miles north of town, off of Ariz. 87 on Houston Mesa Road, you can visit the ruins of **Shoofly Village,** in the Tonto National Forest. This village was first occupied nearly 1,000 years ago by peoples related to the Hohokan and Salado cultures and contained 87 rooms. Today only rock foundations remain, but an interpretive trail helps bring the site to life.

To learn a bit more about the history of the area, stop in at the **Museum of the Forest,** 700 Green Valley Pkwy. (☎ **520/474-3483**), which has displays on the region, as well as a special Zane Grey exhibit. The museum, which is located in Green Valley Park, is open Wednesday through Sunday from noon to 4pm and admission is $1.

You'll find more Zane Grey memorabilia at the **Zane Grey Museum,** 408 W. Main St., Suite 8 (☎ **520/474-6243**). This tiny museum is open Monday through Saturday from 10am to 4pm and Sunday from 11am to 2pm, and admission is free.

Other attractions in the Payson area include the small **Payson Zoo,** located less than 7 miles east of town on Ariz. 260 (☎ **520/474-5435**). It's a good place to bring the kids, where they'll see animals from around the world, many of which have appeared in films, TV shows, and commercials. Open daily 10am to 3:30pm in summer; Friday through Wednesday 10am to 3pm in winter. Admission is $4 for adults and $1 for children 12 and under.

If you feel lucky, you can spend some time and money at the **Mazatzal Casino** (☎ **520/474-6044**) a half mile south on Ariz. 87. The casino is run by the Tonto Apaches.

## SCENIC DRIVES

Scenic drives through this region are also among the favorite pastimes of visitors. One of the most popular drives is along the top of the Mogollon Rim on 45-mile-long **Forest Road 300.** Along the route, which clings to the edge of the Mogollon Rim, there are numerous views of the forest far below and plenty of places to stop, including lakes, picnic areas, trailheads, and campgrounds. This is a good gravel road in summer and can be negotiated in a standard passenger car. However, in winter, the road is not maintained. To access the rim road, head east on Ariz. 260 or north on Ariz. 87 for 30 miles and watch for signs.

About 15 miles north of Payson on Ariz. 87, you'll find the village of **Pine** and another 3 miles beyond this, the village of **Strawberry.** Here, in a quiet setting in the forest, you'll find a few antiques and crafts shops, and, in Pine, a small museum that chronicles the history of this area. In Strawberry, on the road that leads west from the center of the village, is the old Strawberry schoolhouse, a restored log building dating from 1885.

Another interesting drive starts in the village of **Strawberry** west of the old Strawberry schoolhouse. If you continue west on this road, you will be on the Fossil Creek Road, a gravel road leading down a deep and spectacular canyon. It's a bit of a hair-raising drive, but if you like views, it's well worth the white knuckles and dust. At the bottom, **Fossil Creek** offers swimming and fishing.

## WHERE TO STAY

**Best Western Paysonglo Lodge.** 1005 S. Beeline Hwy. (P.O. Box 620), Payson, AZ 85541. ☎ **800/772-9766** or 520/474-2382. Fax 520/474-1937. 47 rms. A/C TV TEL. $65–$125 double. Rates include continental breakfast. AE, DC, DISC, MC, V.

Located on the south side of town near the Mazatzal Casino, this is Payson's best motel. The guest rooms feature contemporary furnishings and several have their own fireplaces. The hotel also offers free coffee and cookies, an outdoor pool, and a whirlpool.

**Christopher Creek Lodge.** Ariz. 260 (Star Rte., Box 119), Payson, AZ 85541. ☎ **520/ 478-4300.** 6 rms, 18 cabins. $45–$85 double. MC, V.

Located 21 miles east of Payson on Ariz. 260, the Christopher Creek Lodge is a family-oriented rustic mountain retreat. You can choose between motel-style rooms with sleeping lofts; large spartan creekside cabins complete with full kitchen, woodstove, and sleeping loft; or duplex cabins with woodstoves, sliding glass doors, and picnic tables in the dining areas. All the accommodations are under the trees, and Christopher Creek runs along the edge of the property. For Phoenicians fleeing the heat of summer, this is one of the nearest escapes.

✪ **Kohl's Ranch Lodge.** E. Ariz. 260, Payson, AZ 85541. ☎ **800/331-5645** or 520/478-4211. Fax 520/478-0353. 41 rms, 8 cabins. A/C TV TEL. May 1–Sept 30 $95–$105 double, $180–$205 cabin; Oct 1–Apr 30 $75–$85 double, $150–$175 cabin. AE, DISC, MC, V.

Now under the same management as Los Abrigados resort in Sedona, Kohl's Ranch is 17 miles east of Payson on Ariz. 260 and is surrounded by quiet forests. Situated on the banks of Tonto Creek, this casual, family-oriented resort is an excellent base for exploring the Mogollon Rim region. The lodge's lobby is a towering glass-fronted A-frame with a large stone fireplace and exposed beams. With the new ownership have come much-needed room renovations (and much-less-needed rate hikes). Some of the smaller rooms have fireplaces, as do the cabins.

The dining room gives the impression that you're eating in an old log cabin. There's a lounge in the main lodge and a cowboy bar and pool hall across the parking lot. The hotel also offers horseback riding ($20 for 1 hour, $35 for 2 hours), an outdoor pool, a fitness room, volleyball, horseshoes, bocce ball, a video arcade, and a playground. This is the most comfortable of the region's mountain retreats.

✪ **Majestic Mountain Inn.** 602 E. Ariz. 260, Payson, AZ 85541. ☎ **800/408-2442** or 520/474-0185. 37 rms. A/C TV TEL. $58–$140 double. AE, CB, DC, DISC, MC, V.

Although it is located in town, this motel is built in an attractive, modern mountain-lodge design. There's a large stone chimney and fireplace in the lobby, and several of the deluxe rooms have fireplaces of their own. These deluxe rooms also have tile floors and double whirlpool tubs facing the fireplaces. The standard rooms aren't as spacious or luxurious, but are still quite comfortable. The biggest drawback here is the lack of a pool.

**Pueblo Inn.** 809 E. Ariz. 260, Payson, AZ 85541. ☎ **800/888-9828** or 520/474-5241. Fax 520/472-6919. 32 rms, 7 suites. A/C TV TEL. $49–$59 double; $95–$125 suite. AE, DC, DISC, MC, V.

This pueblo-style motel is on the right as you're heading east out of town on Ariz. 260. The rooms here are modern and clean, and all have refrigerators. Tile accents on the bathroom counters are a nice touch. There's no pool, but there is free morning coffee. The suites, with whirlpool tubs and fireplaces, are particularly comfortable.

## CAMPGROUNDS

East of Payson on Ariz. 260 are several national forest campgrounds, some of which accept reservations, which can be made through the **National Forest Recreation Reservation System** (☎ **800/280-2267**). These campgrounds include (from west to east) Ponderosa Campground, Lower Tonto Creek Campground, Upper Tonto Creek Campground, and Christopher Creek Campground.

## WHERE TO DINE

**Creekside Steakhouse and Tavern.** On Ariz. 260 in Christopher Creek. ☎ **520/478-4557.** Main courses $6.50–$42. MC, V. Sun–Thurs 8am–10pm, Fri–Sat 8am–11pm (from 7am in summer). STEAKS/AMERICAN.

If you're staying out at Kohl's Ranch or in the Christopher Creek area, this log steakhouse is a good bet for breakfast, lunch, or dinner. The wide range of prices listed above is due to the fact that not only does this place serve fried chicken but it also serves filet and lobster tails. Sundays are prime rib day.

**Heritage House Garden Tea Room.** 202 W. Main St. ☎ **520/474-5501.** All items $5–$15. AE, DISC, MC, V. Mon–Sat 11am–8pm. AMERICAN.

Tucked away in the back of this crafts store is a popular ladies' lunch spot and tearoom that now serves dinner also. The short lunch menu features delicious sandwiches and crisp salads, and at dinner there are steaks, seafood, and pasta dishes. However, for many people the real draw here is the dessert tray. There's always a great selection of tempting cakes, cheesecakes, and mousses, as well as respectable cappuccinos and espressos.

**The Oaks Restaurant & Lounge.** 302 W. Main St. ☎ **520/474-1929.** Reservations recommended. Main courses $12–$16. AE, DC, DISC, MC, V. Sun–Thurs 11am–2pm and 5–8pm, Fri–Sat 11am–2pm and 5–9pm. AMERICAN.

Taking its name from the grove of oak trees spreading over it, the Oaks Restaurant is a quiet place for a meal in Payson. The large patio dining area beside the grassy front lawn is a great spot for lunch or dinner on a warm night. The dinner menu is short and to the point: Steaks and seafood, simply prepared, are the mainstays. The Caesar salad is good, as are the various cakes. The lunch menu features a variety of hot and cold sandwiches as well as several salads.

# 2 Pinetop & Lakeside

185 miles NE of Phoenix; 140 miles SE of Flagstaff; 50 miles S of Holbrook; 90 miles NE of Payson

Pinetop and Lakeside, two towns that grew together over the years, are the busiest towns in the White Mountains, with dozens of motels and cabin resorts strung out along Ariz. 260 as it passes through the two towns. At first glance it is easy to dismiss Pinetop-Lakeside as too commercial, what with all the strip malls, budget motels, and old cabin resorts, but these two towns have spent a lot of years entertaining families during the summer months and they still have plenty of things to keep visitors busy. You just have to look a little harder than you might in other White Mountains communities.

With Apache Sitgreaves National Forest on one side of town and the unspoiled lands of the White Mountain Apache Indian Reservation on the other, Pinetop-Lakeside is well situated for anyone who enjoys getting outside. Several lakes with good fishing; nearly 200 miles of hiking, mountain biking, and cross-country ski trails; horseback riding stables; and downhill skiing are all nearby, which makes this area a good base for a visit to the White Mountains. Although summer is the busy season up here, Pinetop-Lakeside becomes a ski resort in the winter. Sunrise ski area is only 30 miles away, and on weekends the town is packed with skiers.

Pinetop-Lakeside is definitely the family destination of the White Mountains, so if you're looking for a romantic weekend or to just get away from it all, you should continue farther into the White Mountains to Greer or Alpine.

## ESSENTIALS

**GETTING THERE** Pinetop and Lakeside are both located on Ariz. 260.

**Great Lakes Aviation** flies several times a day from Phoenix to Show Low. The fare is $83 one way, $141 round-trip. Call ☎ **800/274-0662** for schedule information.

**White Mountain Passenger Lines** has regularly scheduled service to Show Low from Phoenix. The fare is $40 each way. For the schedule, call ☎ **520/537-4539** in Show Low or ☎ **602/275-4245** in Phoenix.

**GETTING AROUND**   Rental cars are available in Show Low from **Enterprise Rent-a-Car** (☎ **520/537-5144**), **Hatch Motor Car Rental** (☎ **520/537-8887**), and **Horne Auto Center Car Rental** (☎ **520/537-5500**).

**VISITOR INFORMATION**   For information on this area, contact the **Pinetop-Lakeside Chamber of Commerce,** 592 W. White Mountain Blvd., Lakeside, AZ 85929 (☎ **520/367-4290**), which has a visitor center that's open daily. For more information on the White Mountain Apache Reservation, contact the **White Mountain Apache Tribe Office of Tourism,** P.O. Box 710, Fort Apache, AZ 85926 (☎ **520/338-1230**).

## ENJOYING THE OUTDOORS

Old forts and casinos aside, it is the outdoors (and the cool weather) that really draws people up here. Fishing, hiking, mountain biking, and horseback riding are among the most popular activities in the Pinetop-Lakeside area.

If you want to saddle up, call **Porter Mountain Stable,** Porter Mountain Road (☎ **520/368-5306**), or **Pinetop Lakes Stables,** Buck Springs Road (☎ **520/369-1000**) for trail rides.

Mountain bikes can be rented at **Mountain Outfitters/The Skier's Edge** (☎ **520/367-6200**) for $16 a day. They also rent downhill and cross-country ski equipment and sell hiking and camping equipment. The store is located next to the Pinetop-Lakeside Chamber of Commerce on Ariz. 260.

In the forests surrounding Pinetop-Lakeside is the 180-mile **White Mountain Trailsystem.** Many of these trails are easily accessible (in fact some are right in town) and are open to hikers and mountain bikers. The trails at **Woodland Lake Park** are among my favorites. The park is located just off Ariz. 260 near the east side of Pinetop and has 6 miles of trails, including a paved trail around the lake. For a panoramic vista of the Mogollon Rim, you can hike the short **Mogollon Rim Nature Walk** off Ariz. 260 on the west side of Lakeside. For another short but pleasant stroll, check out the **Big Springs Environmental Study Area,** which is on Woodland Road in Lakeside. This quiet little preserve encompasses a small meadow through which flows a spring-fed stream. There is often good bird-watching here. You can spot more birds at **Woodland Lake Park** in Pinetop and at **Jacques Marsh,** 2 miles north of Lakeside on Porter Mountain Road. For more information on area trails, contact the **Lakeside Ranger Station** (☎ **520/368-5111**).

If you're up here to catch the big one, you've got plenty of options. Area lakes hold native Apache trout, as well as stocked rainbows, browns, and brookies. This is also the southernmost spot in the United States where you can fish for Arctic graylings. Right in the Pinetop-Lakeside area, try **Rainbow Lake,** which is a block south of Ariz. 260 in Lakeside; **Woodland Lake,** in Woodland Lake Park, which is toward the east end of Pinetop and just south of Ariz. 260; or **Show Low Lake,** which is east of Lakeside and north of Ariz. 260. On the nearby White Mountain Apache Indian Reservation, there is good fishing in **Hawley Lake** and at **Horseshoe Lake,** both of which are east of Pinetop-Lakeside and south of Ariz. 260. Be sure to get your reservation fishing license ($5 per day); they're available at **The Skier's Edge,** 560 W. White Mountain Blvd., Pinetop-Lakeside (☎ **520/367-6200**); **Hon Dah service station,** at the junction of Ariz. 260 and Ariz. 73; and **Hawley Lake Resort** (☎ **520/335-7511**), south of Ariz. 260 between Hon Dah and Sunrise.

Several golf courses in the area are open to the public, including **Concho Valley Country Club** (☎ **520/337-4644**) in Show Low, **Pinetop Lakes Golf Club** (☎ **520/369-4531**) in Pinetop-Lakeside, **Silver Creek Golf Club** (☎ **520/537-2744**) in Show Low, and the **Show Low Country Club** (☎ **520/537-4564**), which is also in Show Low.

## MORE TO SEE & DO

**Fort Apache Historic Park,** in the town of Fort Apache (☎ **520/338-1392**), centers around Old Fort Apache, which, along with the White Mountain Apache reservation, was established in 1870 by the U.S. government. The park, which is located approximately 22 miles south of Pinetop on Ariz. 73, now encompasses almost 300 acres, including more than 20 buildings, prehistoric ruins, petroglyphs, and the **Apache Cultural Center** (☎ **520/338-4625**). The cultural center is openTuesday though Sunday 9am to 4:30pm.

Admission is $2 for adults and 50¢ for children (guided tours available for $5). At press time, a new museum was about to open here at Fort Apache and exhibits from the cultural center were likely going to be moved, and the new facility promises to be a great improvement over the old center. For more information, you can contact the **Fort Apache Office of Tourism** (☎ **520/338-1230**), which is also in the Fort Apache Historic Park.

If you're looking for something to do after dark, you can head out to the **Hon-Dah Casino** (☎ **520/369-0299** or 800/WAY-UP-HI), which is owned and operated by the White Mountain Apache Tribe. It's open daily around the clock and is located at the junction of Ariz. 73 and Ariz. 260, about 4 miles east of Pinetop. A very different sort of entertainment is available at **Theatre Mountain,** on Woodland Road in Lakeside (☎ **520/368-8888**), where melodramas and vaudeville shows are staged.

## WHERE TO STAY
### IN PINETOP

In addition to accommodations listed below, area chain motels include the **Best Western Inn of Pinetop,** 404 S. White Mountain Blvd., Pinetop (☎ **520/367-6667**), charging $60 to $105 double; and the **Econo Lodge,** 458 White Mountain Blvd., Pinetop (☎ **520/367-3636**), charging $59 to $110 double.

✪ **Elk Mountain Lodge.** White Mountain Blvd. (P.O. Box 1254), Pinetop, AZ 85935. ☎ **800/238-3144** or 520/367-0626. Fax 520/367-2606. 4 suites. TV TEL. $129–$149 suite for 2. AE, MC, V.

This modern two-story log building sits right on busy Ariz. 260, but because the rooms face into the pines, you hardly even notice you're in town. In fact the lodge's backyard opens onto the national forest (and black bears sometimes wander out of these woods and onto the inn's porches). The rustic architecture makes this small lodge stand out from the many old cabin resorts and motels that clutter the town. Each large suite has two bedrooms, two bathrooms, and two porches, as well as a full kitchen.

✪ **Sierra Springs Ranch.** H.C. 62, Box 32100, Pinetop, AZ 85935. ☎ **520/369-3900.** Fax 520/369-0741. 9 cabins. $150 cabin for 2; $200 and up for larger cabins. Two-night minimum stay. MC, V.

Located off a gravel road east of Pinetop, the Sierra Springs Ranch is the most upscale property around and is as idyllic a mountain retreat as you'll find in Arizona. Set in a wide clearing in the forest, each of the nine cabins is a little bit different, but all are large and comfortable. Our favorite is the honeymoon cottage, which is built of logs and has a stone fireplace. All the cabins have full kitchens, which make up for the lack of a restaurant on the premises.

On the ranch grounds you'll find a trout pond and meadows, a tennis court, and a walking/jogging path. Fishing gear, tennis racquets, and bicycles are all available for the use of guests. In the recreation room in the main lodge there's a big-screen TV. In winter cross-country skiing and snowmobiling are both popular, while at other times fly-fishing classes attract guests. The largest cabin sleeps 13.

**Whispering Pines Resort.** White Mountain Blvd. (P.O. Box 307), Pinetop, AZ 85935. ☎ **800/840-3867** or 520/367-4386. 33 cabins. $35–$95 double. AE, MC, V.

Situated on 12¹/₂ wooded acres, the Whispering Pines Resort is a rustic family retreat. The cabins have one or two bedrooms; some newer and nicer than others. All have fireplaces so you'll stay cozy and warm even in winter. One of the older cabins is a genuine log cabin with a stone fireplace, and though this isn't one of the better cabins, it does have a rustic appeal that may be suitable for the less finicky traveler. Other, more luxurious cabins have their own saunas. Recreational facilities include a whirlpool, volleyball court, and horseshoe pit; there's also a coin laundry.

## IN LAKESIDE

✪ **Lake of the Woods.** Ariz. 260 (P.O. Box 777), Lakeside, AZ 85929. ☎ **520/368-5353.** 24 cabins, 5 houses. TV. $62–$147 cabin for 2; $81–$263 house for 2. MC, V.

Located on its own private lake right on Ariz. 260, Lake of the Woods is a rustic mountain resort that caters to families. The kids can fish in the lake, play in the snow, or row a boat. The resort also offers a whirlpool, sauna, exercise equipment, table tennis, pool table, shuffleboard, horseshoes, a playground, and coin-operated laundry. The resort's cabins range from tiny to huge, with rustic and deluxe side by side; the smallest sleep two or three while the largest house sleeps 18. Some are on the edge of the lake while others are tucked away under the pines. Several have kitchens and fireplaces. Be sure to request one away from the busy highway.

**The Meadows.** 453 N. Woodland Rd., Lakeside, AZ 85929. ☎ **520/367-8200.** Fax 520/367-0334. 7 rms. $95–$145 double. Rates include full breakfast. AE, DISC, MC, V.

Set just a short distance off the main highway, this combination restaurant and lodge has a quiet and secluded feel to it. The inn is a modern Victorian building with large decks overlooking the "meadows" (actually expansive lawns). The secluded setting is marred only by the sight of a suburban-style housing development on the far side of the lawns. The guest room decor is predominantly done in floral patterns. Perhaps the inn's greatest strength is its dining room, and the fact that a second good restaurant—The Christmas Tree—is just at the end of the driveway.

## CAMPGROUNDS

There are four campgrounds in the immediate Pinetop-Lakeside area, including Show Low Lake, Fool Hollow, Lewis Canyon, and Lakeside. Of these, **Show Low Lake County Park** (☎ 520/537-4126) and **Fool Hollow Lake Recreation Area** (☎ 520/537-3680) are the nicest. There are also numerous campgrounds nearby on the White River Apache Indian Reservation. For information about these campgrounds, contact the **White Mountain Wildlife and Outdoor Recreation Division,** (☎ 520/338-4385) or the **Fort Apache Office of Tourism** (☎ 520/338-1230).

# WHERE TO DINE

In addition to the places mentioned below and a few basic burger and steak places in town, there's **Lauth's Country Store,** on Ariz. 260 at the east end of Pinetop

(☎ **520/367-2161**), where you can get an inexpensive breakfast and a variety of burgers and sandwiches made with applewood-smoked meats. Also, the food at the Hon-Dah Casino gets high praises from locals, but the prices are only cheap if you can resist the temptation to spend some time at the slot machines.

**Charlie Clark's Steak House.** Ariz. 260 at Penrod Ave., Pinetop. ☎ **520/367-4900.** Main courses $10–$20. AE, CB, DC, MC, V. Daily 5–10pm in summer (off-season hours vary).

Charlie Clark's has been serving up thick, juicy steaks since 1938 and is the oldest steakhouse in the White Mountains. Mesquite-broiled steaks and chicken, as well as seafood and prime rib, fill the menu; in the lounge there is off-track betting on horse and dog races broadcast from Phoenix. This has long been a local favorite and is steeped in traditional White Mountains atmosphere. To find Charlie Clark's just look for the building with the buggy, wagon, and fake horse on the roof.

**The Christmas Tree Restaurant.** 455 Woodland Rd., Lakeside. ☎ **520/367-3107.** Reservations recommended on weekends. Main courses $7–$28. DISC, MC, V. Wed–Sun 5–9pm. AMERICAN/CONTINENTAL.

Located in a quiet setting off the main drag, this country restaurant serves good old-fashioned American food as well as a few standard continental offerings. Chicken and dumplings are the specialty of the house, but you can also get a good New York steak accompanied by your choice of seafood. Meals are large and filling and come with everything from pickled beets to Boston clam chowder.

**The Meadows.** 453 N. Woodland Rd., Lakeside. ☎ **520/367-8200.** Reservations recommended. Main courses $13–$21. AE, DISC, MC, V. Mon and Wed–Thurs 5–8pm, Fri–Sat 5–9pm. Lunch served summer only Wed–Mon 10am–2pm. CONTINENTAL/NEW AMERICAN.

Located in a woodland setting, this rambling Victorian-style mansion is casually elegant inside, with dark green carpeting and blond furnishings, and has a large shady deck that wraps around the back. This is the most elegant dining establishment in the area, but don't feel compelled to get too dressed up. The surroundings are as much a part of dinner here as the food. The menu, which changes monthly, focuses on continental favorites with a contemporary twist, such as shrimp and scallops with a chile-cheese sauce served over chile-pepper pasta, or grilled salmon topped with basil pesto. The deck is a charming place for Sunday brunch.

# 3 Greer

51 miles SE of Show Low; 98 miles SE of Holbrook; 222 miles NE of Phoenix

The tiny community of Greer, set in the lush meadows on either side of the Little Colorado River and surrounded by forests, must hold the distinction of being the most picturesque mountain village in Arizona. The elevation of 8,525 feet assures plenty of snow in winter and pleasantly cool temperatures in summer, and together these two factors have turned Greer into a very popular vacation village. In the past few years Greer has begun to take on the appearance of an upscale mountain getaway town and has become quite popular with the wealthy cognoscenti of Phoenix. Modern log homes are springing up all over the valley, but Greer is still free of the sort of strip-mall developments that have forever changed the character of Payson and Pinetop-Lakeside.

The Little Colorado River, which flows through the middle of Greer on its way to the Grand Canyon, is little more than a babbling brook up here, but it's well known for its trout fishing, which is one of the main draws here. Several lakes and ponds in the area also provide good fishing. In winter there are more than 12 miles of cross-country ski trails around Greer, and ice skating, ice fishing, and sleigh rides are also popular activities. Greer also happens to be the closest town to the Sunrise ski area, which is what gives the village its ski resort atmosphere. There are several rustic mountain lodges and a number of rental-cabin operations here.

## ESSENTIALS

**GETTING THERE**    From Phoenix, take U.S. 87 north to Payson and then go east on Ariz. 260, or take U.S. 60 east from Phoenix through Globe and Show Low to Ariz. 260 east. Greer is just a few miles south of Ariz. 260 on Ariz. 373.

**VISITOR INFORMATION**    For information on the Greer area, contact the **Round Valley Chamber of Commerce,** P.O. Box 31, Springerville, AZ 85938 (☎ **520/333-2123**).

## ENJOYING THE OUTDOORS

Winter is one of the busiest seasons in Greer, since it is so close to the **Sunrise Park Resort** ski area (☎ **520/735-7600; 888/804-2779** for snow conditions). Located just off Ariz. 260 on Ariz. 273, this ski area is operated by the White Mountain Apache Tribe. The ski area usually opens in November and receives more than 20 feet of snow per year, though winter thaws and long stretches without snow can make winters here a bit unreliable. There are also snowmaking machines to enhance natural snowfall and lights for night skiing on the weekends. Sunrise is one of the largest ski areas in the Southwest and is the most popular in Arizona. Though there are some good advanced runs here, beginner and intermediate skiers will be in heaven. I've rarely seen so many green runs starting from the uppermost lifts of a ski area—all of which translates into a very family-oriented ski area. Plenty of winter sun makes skiing here almost as pleasant as lounging by the pool down in Phoenix. At the top of 11,000-foot Apache Peak is a day lodge offering meals and a view that goes on forever. There's also a **ski school** (☎ **520/735-7518**) that offers classes for beginners as well as advanced skiers. Lift tickets are $32 for adults and $18 for children.

There are also more than 13.5 kilometers of groomed **cross-country ski trails** at Sunrise. These trails, which begin at the service station at the turn-off for the downhill area, wind their way through forests of ponderosa pines and across high snow-covered meadows. There are also good opportunities for cross-country skiing in Greer, which has 35 miles of developed trails. At 8,500 feet, the alpine scenery here is quiet and serene. You can also go for a sleigh ride in Greer. They're offered by **Lee Valley Outfitters** (☎ **520/735-7454**).

Come summer the cross-country ski trails in Greer become **mountain-bike trails,** and when combined with the nearby **Poll Knoll trail system,** provide mountain bikers with 35 miles of trails of varying degrees of difficulty.

This area offers some of the finest mountain **hiking** in Arizona, and most popular of all the area trails is the trail up 11,590-foot **Mount Baldy,** which is the second-highest peak in Arizona. This peak lies on the edge of the White Mountain Apache Indian Reservation and is sacred to the Apaches. Consequently, the summit is off limits to non-Apaches. The Mount Baldy trail starts at Sheep Crossing, south of Sunrise ski area, and passes through beautiful scenery on the flanks of the mountain.

To explore the Greer area from the back of a horse, contact **Lee Valley Outfitters** (☎ **520/735-7454**), which is located between Greer and Ariz. 260 and offers rides of varying lengths ($18 for 1 hour, $28 for 2 hours, $60 for 4 hours with lunch). They also do hay rides and cookout rides.

The three Greer Lakes—Bunch, River, and Tunnel reservoirs—on the outskirts of town, are popular fishing spots. All three lakes hold brown and rainbow trout. On River Reservoir, try fishing the shallows at the south end. On Tunnel Reservoir, you can often do well fishing from shore, especially if fly-fishing, but there is a boat launch. However, it is Big Lake, south of Greer, that has the biggest fishing reputation around these parts. Fishing is also good on Sunrise Lake, but be sure to get a White Mountain Apache Indian Reservation fishing license (available at the Sunrise service station). If you'd like a guide to take you out for a day of fishing the Arizona high country, contact **Troutback Flyfishing Guide Service,** P.O. Box 344, Springerville, AZ 85938 (☎ **520/333-2371**), which charges $125 per day for one angler and $200 for two anglers. This guiding company also leads llama packtrips into the nearby mountains ($150 per person per day).

**Sunrise Lake,** near the Sunrise ski area, is a popular spot in the summer when boat rentals (including small sailboats) are available.

## A MUSEUM

The **Butterfly Lodge Museum** (no phone), a restored historic cabin built in 1914 was Greer's first museum. Once owned by James Willard Schultz (a writer) and his son Hart Merriam Schultz (a painter), the museum is a memorial to these two unusual and creative individuals who once called Greer home. The museum, which is located just off Ariz. 373 between Ariz. 260 and Greer, is open Memorial Day through Labor Day Friday through Sunday from 10am to 5pm.

## WHERE TO STAY
### MODERATE

✪ **Aspen Meadow Guest Ranch.** P.O. Box 879, Eagar, AZ 85925. ☎ **520/521-0880** or 520/333-2717. 12 cabins. Labor Day–Memorial Day $95 cabin for 2 (meals not included); Memorial Day–Labor Day full guest-ranch experience (with all meals and horseback riding) $750 for half a week for up to 6 people in a cabin (over 6 people add $50 per half week), $1,500 per week for up to 6 people in a cabin (over 6 people add $100 per week). MC, V.

Situated on 160 acres about 10 miles north of Greer on a gravel road, this guest ranch is surrounded by meadows and ponderosa pine forest. Accommodations are in modern log cabins with rustic log furniture and kitchenettes. Meals are taken in the main lodge, which is built of spruce logs and has a cathedral ceiling and massive stone fireplace. Ranch activities include horseback riding, fishing, basketball, volleyball, square dancing, table tennis, and crafts making—plenty to keep the whole family occupied for the duration of a stay at this remote ranch. If you're looking to get away from it all, this is the place.

**Greer Lodge.** 44 Main St. (P.O. Box 244), Greer, AZ 85927. ☎ **520/735-7216.** 8 rms, 7 cabins, 1 house. $120 double; $75–$110 cabin for 2; $280 house. AE, MC, V.

The Little Colorado River, which truly lives up to its name here in Greer, runs right past the deck of this old log lodge. There are a variety of accommodations here including spacious rooms in the main lodge. These rooms all have views of the mountains or river, but those on the second floor tend to get quite a bit of noise from the lobby. If you're seeking quiet, try to get a cabin, most of which have fireplaces and are quite modern. One rustic log cabin sleeps six and has a sleeping loft and fireplace. Only 20 minutes from the Sunrise ski area and with its own trout ponds and section of river, the lodge is popular with both skiers and anglers. The hotel also offers ice skating, croquet, volleyball, horseshoes, a barbecue area, fishing ponds, and cross-country ski trails.

**The Peaks at Greer.** P.O. Box 132, Greer, AZ 85927. ☎ **520/735-7777.** Fax 520/735-7204. 15 rms, 2 suites, 2 cabins. $99–$109 double; $149–$159 suite; $95 cabin for 2. AE, DISC, MC, V.

Located on a hill just past Greer Lodge, this is the most luxurious of Greer's handful of full-service hotels. In the high-ceilinged lobby, there are huge overstuffed chairs in front of the fireplace and exposed log beams overhead. Guest rooms are new and many are quite large. Suites have their own fireplaces, as do the much more rustic cabins which are quite a bit older than the rest of the hotel. The restaurant here is one of the best in town, and there is also a small bar with a big deck and good views.

**○ Red Setter Bed & Breakfast Inn.** P.O. Box 133, Greer, AZ 85927. ☎ **520/735-7441.** Fax 520/735-7425. 9 rms. $120–$160 double. Rates include full breakfast. AE, MC, V.

If you're headed up to the mountains for a romantic weekend getaway, this three-story log lodge should be your first choice. Several of the guest rooms have fireplaces and whirlpool tubs that make them just right for a quiet weekend together. The inn is built on the bank of the Little Colorado River, which is only steps away from the decks of some rooms. Other rooms have vaulted ceilings, some with skylights. If you stay for two nights or more, you'll also receive a complimentary picnic lunch to take with you on an outing. Cases full of antique toys and a game room with old arcade games make this inn fun as well as romantic.

**Snowy Mountain Lodge.** P.O. Box 337, Greer, AZ 85927-0377. ☎ **520/735-7576.** 5 rms, 8 cabins. $69–$85 double; $110–$150 cabin double. Room rates include continental breakfast. Two- to 5-night minimums during weekends in lodge rooms. MC, V.

Set back from the main road down a gravel driveway and shaded by tall pines, the Snowy Mountain Lodge has a very remote yet very comfortable feel about it. The large cabins are perfect for family vacations and come with gas fireplaces, porches, and sleeping lofts. Surrounding the modern log cabins and main lodge building are 100 acres of private forest, so guests have plenty of room to roam. The 1¹/₂-acre trout pond here is one of the largest in the area. The inn also has its own gourmet restaurant, which even serves kangaroo (see "Where to Dine," below, for details).

## INEXPENSIVE

**Cattle Kate's Dining Hall & Boarding House.** P.O. Box 21, Greer, AZ 85927. ☎ **520/735-7744.** 8 rms, 1 suite. $65–$75 double; $115 suite. MC, V.

Consisting of several new log buildings with a classic mountain feel, Cattle Kate's seems to be trying to compete with the nearby Greer Lodge and seems to be doing a respectable job. The rooms, though spartanly furnished in classic Western style, have high ceilings and look out on small trout ponds and the meadows along the Little Colorado River. In the dining hall, a huge elk head hangs over the fireplace and an antler chandelier hangs from the ceiling. The menu features reasonably priced and creative dishes, and in summer, it's possible to dine on the deck overlooking the trout ponds. The only real drawback here is that you are right on the main road through Greer; however, this road is rarely very busy.

**Sunrise Park Hotel.** Hwy. 273, near intersection of Hwy. 260 (P.O. Box 217), McNary, AZ 85930. ☎ **800/55-HOTEL** or 520/735-7676. Fax 520/735-7315. 93 rms, 1 suite. TV TEL. Winter $59–$112 double, $195–$295 suite; summer $50–$70 double, $135 suite. AE, DC, DISC, MC, V. Closed Apr–Memorial Day weekend and Labor Day weekend–Nov.

Located 20 miles outside Greer in McNary, this is the closest lodge to the Sunrise ski area and is only open during the winter and summer seasons. About half the rooms overlook Sunrise Lake, and the suite has a whirlpool tub. The lounge is a cozy place to gather after a day of skiing or hiking, and in the dining room, you'll find filling, if unremarkable, food. The hotel also offers a ski area shuttle bus, tiny indoor swimming pool, indoor and outdoor whirlpools, sauna, volleyball, rental bikes, and video arcade.

**White Mountain Lodge Bed & Breakfast and Cabins.** P.O. Box 143, Greer, AZ 85927. ☎ **520/735-7568.** Fax 520/735-7498. 7 rms, 4 cabins. $54–$75 double; $80–$95 cabin for 2. Two-night minimum on weekends. DC, DISC, MC, V.

Situated on the road into Greer with a view across an open, marshy stretch of the valley, this recently remodeled lodge was built in 1892 and is the oldest building in Greer. Knotty pine throughout gives the lodge a classic feel. Our favorite lodge room has a king-size bed and a view up the valley. However, the cabins, which are perfect for families or two couples, are even more comfortable. One has a stone fireplace and a porch swing.

## CAMPGROUNDS

In the immediate vicinity of Greer, there are three National Forest Service campgrounds on Apache-Sitgreaves National Forest. There are also several campgrounds nearby on the White Mountain Apache Indian Reservation (no reservations accepted). Reservations can be made at the Rolfe C. Hoyer campground 1 mile north of Greer and at the Winn Campground 12 miles southwest of Greer by calling the National Forest Service Campground Reservation line (☎ **800/280-CAMP**). Benny Creek, 2 miles north of Greer, does not take reservations. Because of their proximity to Greer and the Greer lakes, Rolfe C. Hoyer and Benny Creek are the top choices in the area.

# WHERE TO DINE

In addition to the two restaurants mentioned here, the dining rooms at The Peaks at Greer hotel and Cattle Kate's Dining Hall & Boarding House (see "Where to Stay," above) serve some of the best meals in town.

**Greer Lodge.** 44 Main St. ☎ **520/735-7216.** Reservations suggested. Main courses $9–$21. AE, MC, V. Summer daily 7–10:30am, 11am–2:30pm, and 5–9pm. Other seasons Fri 11am–2pm and 5–9pm; Sat–Sun 7–10am, 11am–2pm, and 5–8:30pm. AMERICAN/CONTINENTAL.

You couldn't wish for a prettier location than this one for a meal in the mountains. This multilevel restaurant has walls of glass that look out over a river, meadows, and a trout pond. In the winter there's a cozy fireplace. Unfortunately, meals are not always up to the quality of the view, which really is the main reason to come here. Dinner fare includes various treatments of chicken, lamb, shrimp, and prime rib, including some Southwestern flavorings. The wine list has some reasonably priced wines.

**Snowy Mountain Inn.** North of Greer on Ariz. 373. ☎ **520/735-7576.** Reservations required. Main courses $10–$20. MC, V. Tues–Sun 5–8pm. CONTINENTAL/AMERICAN/AUSTRALIAN.

How often do you find kangaroo on a menu in the United States? Not too often, so it comes as even more of a shock to run across it way out here in little old Greer. The explanation, however, is simple: One of the owners of this combination lodge and restaurant is from down under. You'll also find New Zealand lamb on the menu, and though neither of these meats are always available, you just may luck into a culinary adventure on the night of your visit. To accompany meals here, there is an excellent wine list. The restaurant's decor reflects the owners' global travels. Note: If the restaurant doesn't have any reservations by mid-afternoon, it may not be open that evening.

## 4  Springerville & Eagar

56 miles E of Show Low; 82 miles SE of Holbrook; 227 miles NE of Phoenix

Together, the adjacent towns of Springerville and Eagar constitute the northeastern gateway to the White Mountains. Though the towns themselves are at the foot of the mountains, the vistas from around the two towns take in all of the area's peaks. Springerville and Eagar like to play up their Wild West background, and in fact John Wayne liked the area so much he owned a ranch along the Little Colorado River just west of Eagar. Today large ranches still run their cattle on the windswept plains north of the two towns.

However, it was volcanic activity between 300,000 and 700,000 years ago that gave the land north of Springerville and Eagar its distinctive character. This area is known as the Springerville Volcanic Field, and it is the third largest volcanic field of its kind in the continental United States (the San Francisco Field near Flagstaff and the Medicine Lake Field in California are both larger). The Springerville Volcanic Field covers an area larger than the state of Rhode Island and contains 405 extinct volcanic vents. However, it is the many cinder cones dotting the landscape that give this region such a distinctive appearance. For a brochure outlining a tour of the volcanic field, contact the Round Valley Chamber of Commerce (see "Visitor Information," below).

One other thing you might be curious about is that big dome—the Round Valley Ensphere. This is the only domed high school football stadium in the country.

## ESSENTIALS

**GETTING THERE**  Springerville and Eagar are in the northeast corner of the White Mountains at the junction of U.S. 60, U.S. 180/191, and Ariz. 260. From the Phoenix area, there are two routes: Ariz. 87 north to Payson and then Ariz. 260 east or U.S. 60 east to Globe and then north to Show Low and on to Springerville (alternatively you can take Ariz. 260 from Show Low to Springerville). From Holbrook, take U.S. 180 southeast to St. Johns and U.S. 180/191 south to Springerville. From southern Arizona, U.S. 191 is slow but very scenic.

**VISITOR INFORMATION**  For information on the Springerville and Eagar areas, contact the **Round Valley Chamber of Commerce,** P.O. Box 31, Springerville, AZ 85938 (☎ **520/333-2123**).

## WHAT TO SEE & DO: FROM ANASAZI RUINS TO EUROPEAN ART & ANTIQUES

If you've ever dreamed about working on site as an archaeologist, here in eastern Arizona you can do just that. The **White Mountain Archaeological Center and Raven Site Ruin,** H.C. 30, Box 30, St. Johns, AZ 85936 (☎ **520/333-5857**), operates as a field school and research center on a 5-acre pueblo site where Mogollon and Anasazi artifacts have been found. You can participate on a daily or weekly basis in excavating the site and learning the basics of archaeology. Daily rates are $59 for adults, $37 for children 9 to 17. Children under 9 are not accepted. Also offered are guided hikes and horseback rides through areas rich in petroglyphs. The nearby ruins at **Casa Malpais Archaeological Park,** 318 Main St. (P.O. Box 807), Springerville, AZ 85938 (☎ **520/333-5375**), can also be visited on guided tours costing $4 for adults, $3 for students and seniors, $1 for children 11 and under. The Casa Malpais museum is in downtown Springerville. The archaeological park and museum are open in summer, Monday through Saturday from 9am to 5pm and Sunday from 10am to 4pm. Hours vary the rest of the year.

One other area ruin open to the public is the Rattlesnake Point Pueblo at **Lyman Lake State Park** (☎ 520/337-4441), located 18 miles north of Springerville. On Saturday and Sunday in summer there are guided tours of these Anasazi ruins. Also in the park are petroglyphs dating back to 10,000 B.C. Park admission is $4 per car and tours of the ruins or petroglyphs are $2 per person.

Also in the area are a couple of small museums worth a look if you have the time. The **Reneé Cushman Art Collection** (☎ 520/333-2123) is housed in the L.D.S. Church in Springerville and consists of one woman's personal collection of European art and antiques. Among the works in the collection are an etching attributed to Rembrandt and three pen-and-ink drawings by Tiepolo. The antique furniture dates back to the Renaissance. The museum is open by appointment only.

Local history and old automated musical instruments are the focus of the **Little House Museum** (☎ 520/333-2286), which is located 7 miles west of Eagar on South Fork Road, which is off Ariz. 260. The museum is open May 15 through Labor Day and 90-minute tours are offered Thursday through Sunday at 1:30pm and Friday and Saturday at 11am. In winter, tours are by appointment only. Tours cost $4 for adults and $1.50 for children 12 and under.

If you're interested in fishing, contact **Troutback Flyfishing Guide Service,** in Springerville (☎ 520/333-2371), which charges $125 ($200 for two people) for a day of guided fly-fishing. Alternatively, you can head out to the **X Diamond Ranch,** P.O. Box 791, Springerville, AZ 85938 (☎ 520/333-2286), which maintains a section of the Little Colorado River as a fishing habitat. Half a day here will cost $25 Friday through Monday and $20 Tuesday through Thursday.

**Lyman Lake State Park** (☎ 520/337-4441), 18 miles north of Springerville, is also popular for lake fishing. And if it's high summer and you feel like swimming, this is the place to take a dip, or even plan a day of water-skiing or sailing.

## WHERE TO STAY

**Paisley Corner Bed & Breakfast.** 287 N. Main St. (P.O. Box 458), Eagar, AZ 85938. ☎ **520/333-4665.** 4 rms. $65–$75 double. Rates include full breakfast. MC, V.

This lovingly restored 1910-vintage colonial-revival house in Eagar is one of the most authentic B&Bs I've visited and as such is one of my favorites in the state. By authentic, I mean lots of Victorian antiques and dark color schemes. However, to counterbalance this authenticity, there is a room done up to resemble an old soda fountain, complete with vintage jukeboxes and an old telephone booth in one corner. The inn's kitchen features a 1910 gas stove and looks as though it came straight out of a 1920s Sears and Roebuck catalog—and not just for decoration's sake; this is a fully functional kitchen. Guest rooms on the second floor have antique beds, and two have bathrooms with claw-foot tubs and old pull-chain toilets.

**South Fork Guest Ranch.** P.O. Box 627, Springerville, AZ 85938. ☎ **888/333-3565** or 520/333-4455. 14 cabins. $35–$115 double. Two- to 4-night minimum in summer. MC, V.

Located just a few miles west of Eagar on Ariz. 260 at the confluence of the Little Colorado River and South Fork Creek, this 38-acre guest ranch is a popular summer vacation spot for families looking to get away from it all. The cabins vary from the very basic to much more luxurious with king beds and fireplaces. I like the creekside cabins best. Peace and tranquillity are the stock in trade here with trout fishing a favorite activity of guests. Also on the ranch is Ms. Elle's, serving a surprising variety of good food (see "Where to Dine," below, for details).

## CAMPGROUNDS

**Lyman Lake State Park,** north of Springerville, is a good place to camp, but is very popular in summer. Reservations are not taken, but, except for the July 4th weekend, getting a campsite usually isn't a problem.

## WHERE TO DINE

**Ms. Elle's of South Fork.** At South Fork Guest Ranch, 8 miles west of Eagar off Ariz. 260. ☎ **520/333-4455.** Reservations required. Main courses $10–$16. MC, V. Wed–Mon 5–9pm. Closed Oct–Apr. CONTINENTAL/INTERNATIONAL.

Named after a character on *Dallas,* this restaurant is part of a family-oriented guest ranch. The menu is surprisingly eclectic and includes such dishes as Chinese sesame buns (*cha su bao*), pesto ravioli, smoked pork ribs, poached salmon, and shrimp-and-cheese–stuffed flounder. Desserts are simple and delicious.

**Nancy Jean's Cafe.** 213 N. Main St. ☎ **520/333-5986.** Main courses $5–$6. MC, V. Tues–Sat 7am–3pm. SALADS/SANDWICHES.

This casual breakfast and lunch place is housed in a renovated cottage on the edge of Eagar and does a particularly brisk lunch business. The menu is basic, with a half dozen sandwiches and an equal number of salads, but these are all well made. Daily specials, such as chicken-lime soup and tempting baked goodies round out the offerings here. Weekday breakfasts are basically continental affairs, but the sticky rolls are among the best we've ever had. Saturday breakfast specials include French toast layered with apricot jam and cream cheese.

## 5 The Coronado Trail

If you are *not* prone to car sickness, you may want to take a leisurely drive down the Coronado Trail (U.S. 191). This is one of the most remote and little-traveled paved roads in the state and winds southward from Springerville/Eagar to the Clifton/Morenci area. Because this road is so narrow and winding, it is slow going—the sort of road meant for people who aren't in a hurry to get anywhere anytime soon.

The Coronado Trail is named for the Spanish explorer Francisco Vásquez de Coronado who came to Arizona in the early 1540s in search of gold. Though he never found it, his party did make it as far north as the Hopi pueblos and would have traveled through this region on its march northward from Mexico. Centuries later the discovery of huge copper reserves would make the fortunes of the towns of Clifton and Morenci, which lie at the southern end of the Coronado Trail.

However, it is **Alpine,** at the northern end of the Coronado Trail (27 miles south of the end of Ariz. 260 at the junction of U.S. 180 and U.S. 191), that is the main base for today's explorers, who tend to be outdoor types in search of uncrowded trails and trout streams where the fish are still biting. In Alpine, which is located not far from the New Mexico state line, you'll find a few basic lodges and restaurants and easy access to the region's many trails.

This area is known as the Alps of Arizona, and Alpine's picturesque setting in the middle of a wide grassy valley at 8,030 feet certainly lives up to this image. Alpine is surrounded by **Apache-Sitgreaves National Forest,** which has miles of hiking trails and several campgrounds. In spring wildflowers abound and the trout fishing is excellent. In summer there are forest trails to be hiked. In autumn the aspens in the Golden Bowl on the mountainside above Alpine turn a brilliant yellow, and in winter, there's cross-country skiing and ice fishing in the area.

For more information on this area, contact the **Alpine Area Chamber of Commerce,** P.O. Box 410, Alpine, AZ 85920 (☎ **520/339-4330**).

# ENJOYING THE OUTDOORS

Fall, when the aspens turn the mountainside gold, is probably the single most popular time of year in this area (there are a lot of transplants from up north living in Arizona these days). There are only a few places in Arizona where fall color is worth a drive and this is one of them.

Not far outside Alpine, there is cross-country skiing at the **Williams Valley Winter Recreation Area,** which doubles as a mountain-biking trail system in summer.

Also in Alpine you can play a round of golf at the **Alpine Country Club** (☎ **520/339-4944**), which is 3 miles east of town.

If you're looking for fish to catch, try **Luna Lake,** which is east of Alpine.

The best hiking in the area is the trail up **Escudilla Mountain** just outside Alpine. It is here that you'll see some of the best displays of aspens in the autumn.

Summer or winter, **Hannagan Meadows,** 23 miles south of Alpine, is the place to be. Here you'll find excellent mountain-biking and cross-country ski trails. Hannagan Meadows also provides access to the **Blue Range Primitive Area,** which is popular with hikers.

# WHERE TO STAY & DINE

Between Springerville/Eagar and Clifton/Morenci, there are nearly a dozen National Forest Service campgrounds. One particularly popular spot is **Luna Lake campground** just east of Alpine. The **Hannagan Meadows campground** is also popular, and makes a good base for exploring the Coronado Trail. For information on these campgrounds, contact the Alpine Ranger District (☎ **520/339-4384**).

If you're looking for someplace to eat, you'll find a couple of basic restaurants in Alpine.

**Sprucedale Ranch.** HC 61, Box 10, Alpine, AZ 85920. ☎ **520/333-4984.** 14 cabins. $325 adults per 6-day week, $280 children ages 6–15; $60 per adult daily, $50 per child daily. Children under age 6 receive discounts. Rates include all meals. No credit cards.

Located 14 miles south of Alpine and then 11 miles down gravel Forest Roads 26, 24, and 565, this working horse and cattle ranch is one of the most remote guest ranches in the state. Situated in a small valley at 8,000 feet, the ranch's lodge and cabins are surrounded by ponderosa pines. In addition to horseback riding ($20 per ride) on miles of trails, there's volleyball and basketball. Other ranch activities include hayrides, square dancing, and campfire singalongs, all of which add up to the perfect family vacation. The rustic cabins have wood stoves, and meals are served family style in the log-framed dining room. This place is so remote that it's 25 miles to the nearest store and they use a generator for electricity. Most people stay for a whole week, and daily cabin rentals are not always available.

**Tal-Wi-Wi Lodge.** U.S. 191 (P.O. Box 169), Alpine, AZ 85920. ☎ **520/339-4319.** 20 rms. $61–$95 double. Two-night minimum on weekends in summer. MC, V.

Located 3 miles north of Alpine on U.S. 191, the Tal-Wi-Wi Lodge is the best lodging in Alpine. The deluxe rooms here come with their own hot tub and fireplace, both of which are appreciated on cold winter nights. (Alpine is usually the coldest town in Arizona.) The furnishings in the guest rooms are rustic and comfortable, and the wood-paneled walls and large front porches give the lodge a classic country flavor. The lodge's dining room serves country breakfasts and dinners.

# 10 Tucson

Melding Hispanic, Anglo, and Native American roots, Tucson has become a city with character—aware of its desert setting, confident in its style. Although the city is spawning the same sort of sprawl that has turned Phoenix into a sort of Los Angeles without a beach, advocates for controlled growth are fighting hard to preserve both the city's unique character and its surrounding desert environment. Tucson has also managed to breathe life into its downtown area both by preserving several historic districts and by turning the inner city into an arts district.

Founded by the Spanish in 1775, Tucson is built on the site of a much older Native American village. The city's name comes from the Pima Indian word *chukeson,* which means "spring at the base of black mountain," a reference to the peak now known simply as "A Mountain." From 1867 to 1877 Tucson was the territorial capital of Arizona, but eventually the capital was moved to Phoenix. Consequently, Tucson did not develop as quickly as Phoenix and holds fast to its Hispanic and Western heritage.

Tucson supports a very active cultural life, with symphony, ballet, opera, and theater companies, and many festivals celebrating aspects of local life. However, it's the city's natural surroundings that set Tucson apart. Four mountain ranges ring the city, and in those mountains and their foothills are giant saguaro cacti, an oasis, one of the finest zoos in the world, a ski area, and miles of hiking and horseback-riding trails. Understandably, the Tucson lifestyle is oriented toward the outdoors.

History, culture, and nature are the major attractions, but with its mild, sunny climate and mountain vistas, Tucson is a natural for resorts. Maybe it doesn't have as many world-class resorts as the Valley of the Sun yet, but those in Tucson definitely boast the finer views.

## 1 Orientation

Not nearly as large and spread out as Phoenix and the Valley of the Sun, Tucson is small enough to be convenient, yet large enough to be sophisticated. The mountains ringing the city are bigger and closer than those of Phoenix, and the desert is equally close.

### ARRIVING

**BY PLANE**   Located 6 miles south of downtown, **Tucson International Airport** (☎ 520/573-8100) is served by many airlines, including **Aero México** (☎ 800/237-6639), **America West** (☎ 800/235-9292), **American** (☎ 800/433-7300), **Continental** (☎ 800/525-0280), **Delta** (☎ 800/221-1212), **Northwest** (☎ 800/225-2525), **Southwest** (☎ 800/435-9792), and **United** (☎ 800/241-6522).

At the airport you'll find car-rental desks, regularly scheduled shuttle vans to downtown, and taxis. In the baggage-claim area are two **visitor information centers** where you can pick up brochures about Tucson and reserve a hotel room if you haven't done so already.

Many resorts and hotels in Tucson provide airport shuttle service and will pick you up and return you to the airport either for free or for a competitive fare, so check with your hotel. **Arizona Stagecoach** (☎ 602/889-1000) operates a daily 24-hour van service to downtown Tucson and the foothills resorts. You'll find their vans outside the center of the baggage-claim area. Fares range from $12 to downtown up to $21 to the foothills resorts. To return to the airport, it's best to call at least a day before your scheduled departure.

You'll also find taxis waiting in the same area or you can call **Courier Cab** (☎ 520/624-6455), or **Allstate Cab** (☎ 520/798-1111). A taxi to downtown costs around $16, and to the resorts about $28 to $38.

**Sun Tran** (☎ 520/792-9222), the local public transit, operates a bus service to and from the airport, though you'll have to make a transfer to reach downtown. The bus at the airport is no. 25 (ask for a transfer when you board); at the Roy Laos Transit Center you should transfer to no. 16 for downtown. The fare is 75¢. Route 25 from the airport operates daily Monday through Friday between about 6:30am and 7:30pm, on Saturday between about 8am and 7pm, and on Sunday between about 9am and 7pm. Departures are every hour.

**BY CAR**   **I-10,** the main east-west interstate across the southern United States, passes through Tucson as it swings north to Phoenix. **I-19** connects Tucson with the Mexican border at Nogales. **Arizona 86** heads southwest into the Papago Indian Reservation and **U.S. 89** leads north toward Florence and eventually connects with **U.S. 60** into Phoenix.

If you're headed downtown, take the Congress Street exit off I-10. If you're headed for one of the foothills resorts north of downtown, you'll probably want to take the Ina Road exit.

**BY TRAIN**   Tucson is served by **Amtrak** passenger rail service (☎ 800/872-7245 in the United States and Canada). The *Sunset Limited,* which runs between Miami and Los Angeles, stops in Tucson. The **train station** is at 400 E. Toole Ave. (☎ 520/623-4442) in the heart of downtown Tucson and is within walking distance of the Tucson Convention Center, El Presidio Historic District, and a few hotels. You'll find taxis waiting to meet the train.

**BY BUS**   **Greyhound Lines** (☎ 800/231-2222 or 520/792-3475) connects Tucson to the rest of the United States through its extensive system. The bus station is at 2 S. Fourth Ave., across the street from the Hotel Congress in the Downtown Arts District.

## VISITOR INFORMATION

The **Metropolitan Tucson Convention and Visitors Bureau (MTCVB),** 130 S. Scott Ave., Tucson, AZ 85701 (☎ 800/638-8350, 888/2-TUSCON, or 520/624-1817), is an excellent source of information on Tucson and environs. If you are visiting Tucson after May of 1998, the visitor center should be in its new facility at 525 W. Congress St. (just off I-10), with the main MTCVB offices located at 555 W. Congress St. The MTCVB's Web site is at **http://www.arizonaguide.com/visittucson**. You can contact them before leaving home or stop at their visitor

# Tucson at a Glance

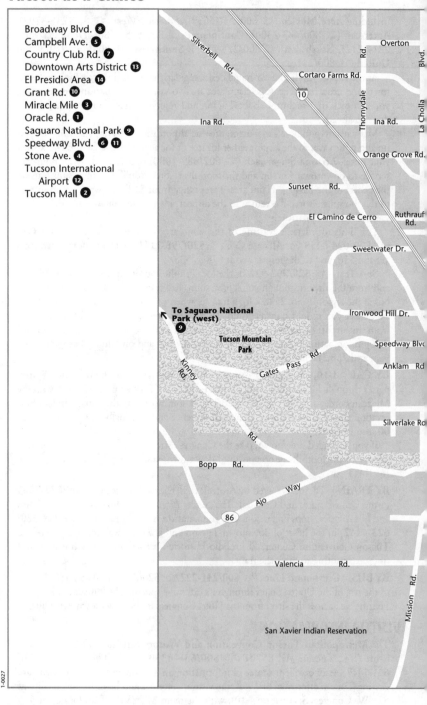

Silverbell Rd.

Overton

Cortaro Farms Rd.

Rd.

Blvd.

10

Thornydale

La Cholla

Ina Rd.

Ina Rd.

Orange Grove Rd.

Sunset Rd.

El Camino de Cerro

Ruthrauf Rd.

Sweetwater Dr.

Ironwood Hill Dr.

**To Saguaro National
Park (west)
9**

**Tucson Mountain
Park**

Speedway Blvd

Anklam Rd

Kinney Rd.

Gates Pass Rd.

Silverlake Rd

Rd.

Bopp Rd.

Ajo Way

86

Valencia Rd.

Mission Rd.

San Xavier Indian Reservation

1-0027

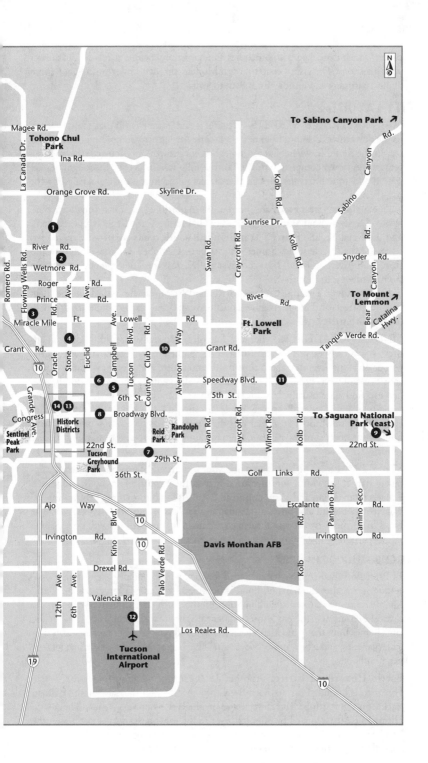

center, which is stocked with brochures and has helpful people at the desk to answer your questions. The visitor center is open Monday through Friday from 8am to 5pm and on Saturday and Sunday from 9am to 4pm.

## CITY LAYOUT

**MAIN ARTERIES & STREETS**   Tucson is laid out on a grid that's fairly regular in the downtown areas but becomes less orderly the farther you go from the city center. In the foothills, where Tucson's most recent growth has occurred, the grid system breaks down completely because of the hilly terrain. Major thoroughfares are spaced at 1-mile intervals, with smaller streets filling in the squares created by the major roads.

The **main east-west roads** are (from south to north) 22nd Street, Broadway Boulevard, Speedway Boulevard, Grant Road (with Tanque Verde Road as an extension), and Ina Road/Skyline Drive. The **main north-south roads** are (from west to east) Miracle Mile/Oracle Road, Stone/Sixth Avenue, Campbell Avenue, Country Club Road, and Alvernon Road. **I-10** cuts diagonally across the Tucson metropolitan area from northwest to southeast.

In **downtown Tucson,** Congress Street and Broadway Boulevard are the main east-west streets and Stone Avenue, Fourth Avenue, and Sixth Avenue are the main north-south streets.

**FINDING AN ADDRESS**   Because Tucson is laid out on a grid, finding an address is relatively easy. The zero (or starting) point for all Tucson addresses is the corner of Stone Avenue, which runs north and south, and Congress Street, which runs east and west. From this point, streets are designated either north, south, east, or west. Addresses usually, but not always, increase by 100 with each block, so that an address of 4321 East Broadway Boulevard should be 43 blocks east of Stone Avenue. In the downtown area, many of the streets and avenues are numbered, with numbered streets running east and west and numbered avenues running north and south.

**STREET MAPS**   The best way to find your way around Tucson is to pick up a detailed map at the visitor information center at the airport, or at the Metropolitan Tucson Convention and Visitors Bureau (see "Visitor Information," above) for $2. The visitors bureau also offers a free map in the *Tucson Official Visitors Guide.* The maps handed out by car-rental agencies are not very detailed, but will do for some purposes. Local gas stations also sell detailed maps.

### NEIGHBORHOODS IN BRIEF

**El Presidio Historic District**   Named for the Spanish military garrison that once stood on this site, the neighborhood is bounded by Alameda Street on the south, Main Avenue on the west, Franklin Street on the north, and Church Avenue on the east. El Presidio was the city's most affluent neighborhood in the 1880s, and many large homes from that period have been restored and now house restaurants, arts-and-crafts galleries, and a bed-and-breakfast inn. The Tucson Museum of Art anchors the neighborhood.

**Barrio Histórico District**   Another 19th-century neighborhood, the Barrio Histórico is bounded on the north by Cushing Street, on the west by the railroad tracks, on the south by 18th Street, and on the east by Stone Avenue. The Barrio Histórico is characterized by Sonoran-style adobe row houses that directly abut the street with no yards, a style typical in Mexican towns. Although a few restaurants and art galleries dot the neighborhood, most restored buildings serve as offices. This is still a borderline neighborhood where restoration is a slow, ongoing process, so try to avoid it late at night.

**Armory Park Historic District** Bounded by 12th Street on the north, Stone Avenue on the west, 19th Street on the south, and Second Avenue and Third Avenue on the east, the Armory Park neighborhood was Tucson's first historic district. Today this area is undergoing a renaissance but isn't yet an entirely safe place to wander after dark.

**Downtown Arts District** This neighborhood encompasses a bit of the Armory District, a bit of El Presidio District, and the stretch of Congress Street and Broadway Boulevard west of Toole Avenue. Home to galleries, boutiques, nightclubs, and hip cafes, it's Tucson's liveliest neighborhood on weekends of Downtown Saturday Night activities. Other nights it's the realm of the young and the homeless.

**Fourth Avenue** Running from University Boulevard in the north to Ninth Street in the south, Fourth Avenue is Tucson's hippest shopping district (although a little run-down and not tending upward as one would expect). Businesses cater to University of Arizona students with boutiques selling ethnic clothing and shops offering handcrafted items from around the world. Twice a year, in spring and fall, the street is closed to traffic for a colorful street fair. With plenty of bars and restaurants, this street sees a lot of after-dark foot traffic that keeps it pretty safe.

**The Foothills** Encompassing a huge area of northern Tucson, the foothills contain the city's most affluent neighborhoods. Elegant shopping plazas, modern malls, world-class resorts, golf courses, and expensive residential neighborhoods are surrounded by hilly desert at the foot of the Santa Catalina Mountains.

# 2 Getting Around

## BY CAR

Unless you plan to stay by the pool or on the golf course, you'll probably want to rent a car. See "Getting Around," in chapter 3, for details on renting a car in Arizona. Luckily, rates are fairly economical, especially if you can skip the collision-damage waiver. At press time, Budget was charging $145 per week or $21 per day for a compact car with unlimited mileage in Tucson.

The **rental-car agencies** below have offices at Tucson International Airport: **Alamo** (☎ 800/327-9633), **Avis** (☎ 800/331-1212), **Budget** (☎ 800/527-0700), **Dollar** (☎ 800/800-4000), **Hertz** (☎ 800/654-3131), and **National** (☎ 800/227-7368). Several companies have offices in other parts of the city as well, so be sure to ask if they have a more convenient location for pickup or drop-off of your car.

Downtown Tucson is still a relatively easy place to find a parking space, and parking fees are low. There are two huge parking lots at the south side of the Tucson Convention Center, a couple of small lots on either side of the Tucson Museum of Art (one at Main Avenue and Paseo Redondo, south of El Presidio Historic District, and one at the corner of Council Street and Court Avenue) where it will cost you $2 to park for up to 12 hours, and parking garages beneath the main library and El Presidio Park. You'll also find plenty of metered parking on the smaller downtown streets. Almost all Tucson hotels and resorts provide free parking.

Lanes on several major avenues in Tucson change direction at rush hour to facilitate traffic flow, so pay attention to signs hung over the street. These tell you the time and direction of traffic in the lanes.

## BY PUBLIC TRANSPORTATION

**BY BUS**   Operating over much of the Tucson Metropolitan area, **Sun Tran** (☎ **520/792-9222**) public buses cost only 75¢ for adults, 50¢ for students, 30¢ for senior citizens, and are free for children 5 and under.

Bus stops are marked by signs that provide information on which buses stop there, the major streets they serve, and their final destinations. The **Downtown-Ronstadt Transit Center,** at the corner of Congress Street and Sixth Avenue, is served by nearly 30 regular and express bus routes to all parts of Tucson.

Monthly bus passes and 20-ride coupon booklets are available.

The bus system does not extend to such tourist attractions as the Arizona-Sonora Desert Museum, Old Tucson, Saguaro National Park, or the foothills resorts, and consequently is of limited use to visitors.

**BY TROLLEY**   Though they don't go very far, the restored electric streetcars of **Old Pueblo Trolley** (☎ **520/792-1802**) provide a fun way to get from the Fourth Avenue shopping district to the University of Arizona. The trolleys operate on Friday from 6pm to midnight, on Saturday from 10am to midnight, and on Sunday from noon to 6pm. The fare is $1 for adults and 50¢ for children 6 to 12; Children under 5 ride free. All-day passes are $2.50 for adults and $1.25 for children.

## BY TAXI

If you need a taxi, you'll have to phone for one. **Yellow Cab** (☎ **520/624-6611**) and **Allstate Cab** (☎ **520/798-1111**) provide service throughout the city. Fares start at $1.10, and after that it's $1.50 per mile. Although distances in Tucson are not as great as those in Phoenix, it's still a good 10 or more miles from the foothills resorts to downtown Tucson, so expect to pay at least $10 for any taxi ride. Most resorts offer or can arrange taxi service to the major tourist attractions around Tucson.

Shoppers should keep in mind that several Tucson shopping malls offer free shuttle service from hotels and resorts. Be sure to ask at your hotel before paying for a ride to a mall.

## ON FOOT

Downtown Tucson is compact and easily explored on foot. Many old streets in the downtown historic neighborhoods are narrow and much easier to appreciate if you leave your car in a parking lot. On the other hand, several major attractions, including the Arizona–Sonora Desert Museum, Old Tucson Studios, Saguaro National Park, and Sabino Canyon, require quite a bit of walking, often on uneven footing, so be sure to bring a good pair of walking shoes.

## FAST FACTS: Tucson

**American Express**   The local American Express representative in the Tucson area is Bon Voyage Travel, with 10 offices. One is located at 3375 N. Campbell Ave., at Ft. Lowell Rd. (☎ **520/795-8991**), open Monday through Friday from 8:30am to 5:30pm.

**Baby-sitters**   Most hotels can arrange a baby-sitter for you, and many resorts feature special programs for children on weekends and throughout the summer. If your hotel can't help, call **A-1 Messner Sitter Service** (☎ **520/881-1578**), which will send a sitter to your hotel.

**Car Rentals**   See "Getting Around," earlier in this chapter.

**Climate**   See "When to Go," in chapter 3.

**Dentist**   Call the **Arizona State Dental Association** (☎ **800/866-2732**) for a dentist referral.

**Doctor**   Call the **Tucson Medical Center** (☎ **800/230-CARE**) for a doctor referral. Or for answers to health questions, dial **Nurse on Call** (☎ **520/544-2000**).

**Emergencies**   For fire, police, or medical emergency, phone ☎ **911.**

**Eyeglasses**   **Alvernon Optical** has several stores around town where you can have your glasses repaired or replaced. Locations include 440 N. Alvernon Way (☎ **520/327-6211**), 7043 N. Oracle Rd. (☎ **520/297-2501**), and 7123 E. Tanque Verde Rd. (☎ **520/296-4157**).

**Hospitals**   The **Tucson General Hospital** is at 3838 N. Campbell Ave. (☎ **520/318-6300**); the **Tucson Medical Center** is at 5301 E. Grant Rd. (☎ **520/327-5461**); and the **University Medical Center** is at 1501 N. Campbell Ave. (☎ **520/694-0111**).

**Information**   See "Visitor Information" in "Orientation," earlier in this chapter.

**Lost Property**   If you've lost something and you don't know where, try the **Tucson Police Department Found-Recovered Property office** (☎ **520/791-4458**). If you lost something at the airport, call ☎ **520/573-8156**; if you lost something on a Sun Tran bus, call ☎ **520/792-9222.**

**Newspapers/Magazines**   The *Arizona Daily Star* is Tucson's morning daily and the *Tucson Citizen* is the afternoon daily. The *Tucson Weekly* is the city's weekly news-and-arts journal; it's published on Thursday. The **Crescent Smoke Shop Newsstand,** 216 E. Congress St. (☎ **520/622-1559**) and 7037 E. Tanque Verde Rd. (☎ **520/296-3102**), carries newspapers and magazines from all over the country.

**Pharmacies**   Walgreens has stores all over Tucson. Call ☎ **800/WALGREENS** for the Walgreens pharmacy that's nearest you or that's open 24 hours a day.

**Photographic Needs**   **NuArt Photo,** at 7090 N. Oracle Rd. (☎ **520/797-2493**), and El Con Mall, 3601 E. Broadway Blvd. (☎ **520/327-7062**), can supply camera needs or repairs.

**Police**   In case of an emergency, phone ☎ **911.**

**Post Office**   The main Tucson post office is at 141 S. Sixth Ave. (☎ **800/297-5543**), open Monday through Friday from 8:30am to 5pm and on Saturday from 9am to noon.

**Radio**   KXCI (91.3 FM) has an eclectic mix of programming and is a favorite with local Tucsonians, while KUAT (90.5 FM) has all-classical programming and is a good station for news.

**Safety**   Tucson is surprisingly safe for a city of its size. However, the Downtown Arts District isn't all that lively after dark and you should be particularly alert in this area if you're down here for a performance of some sort. An exception is on the nights of Downtown Saturday Night festivities. Just to the south of downtown Tucson lies a poorer section of the city that's best avoided after dark unless you are certain of where you're going. Otherwise, take the same precautions you would in any other city.

When driving, be aware that many streets in the Tucson area are subject to flooding when it rains. Heed warnings about possible flooded areas and don't try to cross a low area that has become flooded. Find an alternative route instead.

**Taxes**    In addition to the 5% state sales tax, Tucson levies a 2% city sales tax. Car-rental tax is 5%. The hotel room tax is 9.5%.

**Taxis**    See "Getting Around," earlier in this chapter.

**Television**    You can get Channels 4 (NBC), 6 (PBS), 9 (ABC), 11 (Fox), 13 (CBS), 14 (Independent), 18 (Independent), and 52 (Independent). Several other stations broadcast in Spanish.

**Transit Information**    For information on Sun Tran public buses, phone ☎ **520/792-9222.**

**Weather**    Phone ☎ **520/881-3333** for the local weather forecast.

## 3  Accommodations

Though Phoenix still holds the title of "Resort Capital of Arizona," Tucson is also rapidly becoming known as a resort destination, and this city's resorts boast much more spectacular settings than comparable resorts in Phoenix and Scottsdale. Also, as far as nonresort accommodations go, Tucson has a wider variety of accommodations than Phoenix. This is due in part to the fact that several historic neighborhoods around Tucson are becoming home to bed-and-breakfast inns. The presence of several guest ranches within a 20-minute drive of Tucson also adds to the city's diversity of accommodations. Business and budget travelers are well served with downtown all-suite and conference hotels and budget chain motels.

If you're looking to stay in a bed-and-breakfast inn while in Tucson, you can contact several agencies. The **Arizona Association of Bed and Breakfast Inns,** P.O. Box 7186, Phoenix, AZ 85011 (☎ **800/284-2589**), has several members in Tucson. **Old Pueblo Homestays,** P.O. Box 13603, Tucson, AZ 85732 (☎ **800/333-9776** or 520/790-0030; fax 520/790-2399), will book you into one of its many homestays in the Tucson area (or elsewhere in the state); as will **Mi Casa-Su Casa,** P.O. Box 950, Tempe, AZ 85280-0950 (☎ **800/456-0682** or 602/990-0682); **Bed & Breakfast Southwest Reservation Service,** 6916 E. Mariposa St., Scottsdale, AZ 85251 (☎ **602/947-9704;** fax 602/994-5967); and **Arizona Trails Bed & Breakfast Reservation Service,** P.O. Box 18998, Fountain Hills, AZ 85269-8998 (☎ **888/799-4284** or 602/837-4284; fax 602/816-4224).

At the more expensive hotels and resorts, summer room rates, usually in effect from May to September or October, are roughly half what they are in winter. Temperatures usually aren't unbearable in May or September, which makes these good times to visit. Hotels change their rates on different dates, so always ask when rates go up or down.

Most hotels also offer special packages, weekend rates, various discounts, and free accommodations for children, so it also helps to ask when you reserve. Also keep in mind that nearly all hotels have no-smoking and wheelchair-accessible rooms.

In the following listings, price categories are based on the rate for a double room (with tax included) in high season (most resorts and hotels charge the same for a single or double room) and are as follows: "Very Expensive," more than $250 per night; "Expensive," $150 to $250 per night; "Moderate," $80 to $149 per night; and "Inexpensive," under $80 per night. Keep in mind, however, that these are what hotels call "rack rates." Various discounts are often available that will reduce these rates, so be sure to ask if there are any specials or discounted rates available.

# DOWNTOWN & THE UNIVERSITY AREA
## EXPENSIVE

✪ **Arizona Inn.** 2200 E. Elm St., Tucson, AZ 85719. ☎ **800/933-1093** or 520/325-1541. Fax 520/881-5830. 66 rms, 15 suites, 2 houses. A/C TV TEL. Mid-Jan to late May $165–$215 double, from $210 suite; late May to mid-Sept $82–$100 double, from $110 suite; mid-Sept to mid-Dec $115–$156 double, from $178 suite; mid-Dec to mid-Jan $134–$175 double, from $196 suite. AE, MC, V.

If you're searching for the old Arizona but still demand modern levels of comfort and service, then look no further. This classically elegant lodging, which opened in 1930, is one of the only historic inns in Arizona and the most unique resort in Tucson. Perhaps the most telling example of this resort's classic atmosphere is the large high-ceilinged library lounge where guests can sit back with a newspaper or good book and relax in grand style. The ever-peaceful and immaculately groomed grounds are a welcome oasis from hectic city life, and include a swimming pool surrounded by a flower-scented private courtyard.

Guest rooms are in pink stucco buildings surrounded by mature gardens, and are individually decorated, often with furniture made more than 60 years ago by disabled World War I veterans hired to furnish the lodge when it first opened. Although the bathrooms are small and have their original fixtures, the guest rooms themselves are often very spacious, and most suites have private patios or enclosed sunporches, as well as sitting rooms. Some also have fireplaces.

**Dining/Entertainment:** The inn's main dining room is a casually elegant hall with French doors leading to a dining terrace. Continental cuisine is served at dinner. The lounge is filled with greenery and Audubon prints, and a pianist performs in the evening.

**Services:** Concierge, room service.

**Facilities:** Outdoor pool, two tennis courts, croquet court.

**Doubletree Tucson.** 445 S. Alvernon Way, Tucson, AZ 85711. ☎ **800/222-TREE** or 520/881-4200. Fax 520/323-5223. 295 rms, 11 suites. A/C TV TEL. Mid-Jan to mid-Apr $139–$174 double, $250–$375 suite; mid-Apr to mid-May and mid-Sept to mid-Dec $99–$134 double, $175–$250 suite; mid-May to mid-Sept $69–$100 double, $150–$225 suite; mid-Dec to mid-Jan $79–$114 double, $150–$225 suite. AE, DC, DISC, MC, V.

Located directly across the street from the Randolph Park municipal golf course, the Doubletree is midway between the airport and downtown Tucson. Although the hotel does a lot of convention business and sometimes feels quite crowded, the gardens, with their citrus trees and roses, are almost always tranquil. The rooms are divided between a nine-story building that offers views of the valley and a two-story building with patio rooms overlooking the quiet garden and pool area. All rooms are comfortably appointed with contemporary furnishings.

**Dining/Entertainment:** The Cactus Rose Restaurant serves Southwestern cuisine, and the Javelina Cantina, a more lively place, serves Mexican food and mega-margaritas. There's also a quieter lobby lounge.

**Services:** Room service, valet/laundry service.

**Facilities:** Outdoor pool, whirlpool, exercise room, three tennis courts, boutiques, car-rental desk.

**Marriott University Park Hotel.** 880 E. Second St., Tucson, AZ 85719. ☎ **800/228-9290** or 520/792-4100. Fax 520/881-4100. 250 rms. A/C TV TEL. Jan–Apr $139–$169 double; May–Sept $69–$110 double; Oct–Dec $99–$129 double. AE, CB, DC, DISC, MC, V. Self parking $5, valet parking $7.

This new nine-story atrium hotel is located in the heart of the university district only a block from campus, which means it's a convenient choice if you're interested in the

# Tucson Accommodations

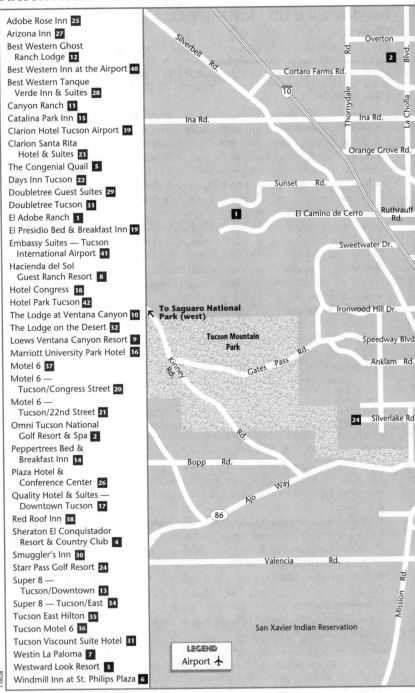

1-0028

312

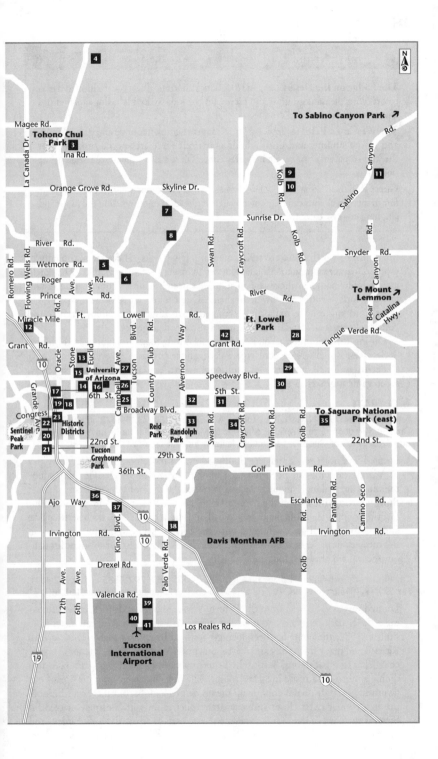

**Family-Friendly Hotels**

**The Lodge on the Desert** *(see p. 318)*   This economical and old-fashioned desert resort offers pleasant grounds and plenty for the kids to do, including table tennis, a pool, shuffleboard, and croquet.

**The Westin La Paloma** *(see p. 321)*   Kids get their own lounge and games room, and in the summer and during holiday periods there are special programs for the kids so parents can have a little free time. There's also a great waterslide in the pool area.

**Guest Ranches** *(see p. 327)*   Tucson has several guest ranches, most of which are family-oriented. Kids can play cowboy to their heart's content, riding the range and singing songs by campfire.

museums, of which there are several within a few blocks. There are also plenty of espresso bars, cheap restaurants, and a brewpub in the immediate vicinity. The hotel's atrium lobby has an artificial stream running through it, and a combination restaurant and lounge with a Southwestern theme. Guest rooms are for the most part quite large, and some have balconies. Irons and ironing boards, hair dryers, and coffeemakers are all standard here. There's also a concierge floor.

**Dining/Entertainment:** You'll find a casual dining room and lounge in the lobby.

**Services:** Room service, concierge, valet/laundry service.

**Facilities:** Small outdoor pool, whirlpool, sauna, exercise room, business center, video game room, gift shop.

## MODERATE

**Adobe Rose Inn.** 940 N. Olsen Ave., Tucson, AZ 85719. ☎ **800/328-4122** or 520/318-4644. Fax 520/325-0055. 5 rms. A/C TV. Mid-Dec to May $95–$115 double; June–Aug $65–$75 double; Sept to mid-Dec $75–$85 double. Rates include full breakfast. AE, DISC, MC, V.

Located in a quiet residential neighborhood only a few blocks from the University of Arizona campus, this B&B has the feel of a little adobe village. The pink adobe buildings are strikingly angular. As you step through the front door, almost the first thing you see is the blue of the swimming pool outside a large picture window. Our favorite room is right off the entrance hall and has a brick floor, beehive fireplace, and colorful stained-glass windows. For extra privacy, you can opt for the room in the cottage out back. In addition to the pool, there's a hot tub. Furnishings throughout the inn are of peeled lodgepole pine logs.

**Catalina Park Inn.** 309 E. First St., Tucson, AZ 85705. ☎ **800/792-4885** or 520/792-4541. Fax 520/792-0838. 6 rms. A/C TV TEL. $90–$115 double. Rates include full breakfast. MC, V.

Located just a few blocks from the Fourth Avenue shopping district and overlooking a shady park, this bed-and-breakfast inn has the look of a Mediterranean villa. Built in 1927, the home has been lovingly restored by owners Mark Hall and Paul Richard and many interesting and playful touches enliven the classic interior (a crystal chandelier in a bathroom, beautifully lit display cases in the living room, a formal dining room, and a rustic breakfast room). The huge basement room is one of our favorites. Not only does it conjure up the inside of an adobe, but there's a whirlpool tub in a former cedar closet and a separate toilet room with a display of colorful Fiesta ware. Two of the rooms are in a separate cottage across the back garden, and these offer more contemporary styling than rooms in the main house. Two upstairs rooms have balconies.

✪ **El Presidio Bed & Breakfast Inn.** 297 N. Main Ave., Tucson, AZ 85701. ☎ **800/349-6151** or 520/623-6151. Fax 520/623-3860. 3 suites. TEL. $95–$110 double. Two-night minimum in winter season. Rates include full breakfast. No credit cards.

Built in 1886, El Presidio is a merger of Victorian and adobe architectural styles and is only steps away from the Tucson Museum of Art, Old Town Artisans, and Janos, one of Tucson's best restaurants. Owners Patti and Jerry Toci spent many years restoring the old house, and today it's a little oasis with lush gardens, fountains, and a courtyard filled with birds. The guest rooms are arranged around the courtyard, and two of the three suites have little kitchens. All are decorated with antiques and original art. In addition to the filling breakfast in the sunroom, there are complimentary drinks, fruit, and treats in the afternoon and evening.

**Peppertrees Bed & Breakfast Inn.** 724 E. University Blvd., Tucson, AZ 85719. ☎ **800/348-5763** or 520/622-7167. Fax 520/622-5959. 3 rms, 2 guest houses. A/C. $98 double; $165 suite. Rates include full breakfast. MC, V.

Located only a few blocks from the University of Arizona campus, this casual B&B is housed in several buildings, one of which is a brick Victorian cottage that dates from 1905. A couple of rooms have Victorian furnishings, while another is decorated with African art. The two guest houses feature comfortable modern furniture. As you might guess, the inn is popular with the families of students going to school here, but the location is also convenient if you plan to spend much time downtown.

**Quality Hotel & Suites—Downtown Tucson.** 475 N. Granada Rd., Tucson, AZ 85701. ☎ **800/446-6589** or 520/622-3000. Fax 520/623-8922. 297 rms, 10 suites. A/C TV TEL. Late Jan to Apr $89–$129 double; May–Oct $49 double; Nov to late Jan $69–$79 double. AE, CB, DC, DISC, MC, V.

Pink stucco walls, red-tile roofs, and arched windows give this convenient downtown hotel a classic Spanish colonial flavor. Located just off I-10 and only a few blocks from El Presidio Historic District and the Tucson Museum of Art, this is a good choice for conventioneers, but also for anyone who wants to be close to Tucson's past and its arts district. The guest rooms are comfortable enough, but be sure to request one away from the freeway. The Olympic-size pool is the hotel's best feature. There's a restaurant on the premises and a complimentary airport shuttle.

### INEXPENSIVE

In addition to the inexpensive hotels listed below, you'll find dozens of budget chain motels along I-10 as it passes through downtown Tucson. Among the better choices are **Days Inn Tucson,** 222 S. Freeway (Exit 258; ☎ **520/791-7511**), charging $48 to $125 double; **Motel 6—Tucson/Congress Street,** 960 S. Freeway (Exit 258; ☎ **520/628-1339**), and **Motel 6—Tucson/22nd Street,** 1222 S. Freeway (Exit 259; ☎ **520/624-2516**), both charging $38–$49 double; and **Super 8—Tucson/Downtown,** 1248 N. Stone St. (Exit 257; ☎ **520/622-6446**), charging $42 to $90 double. See the appendix for a list of toll-free numbers.

✪ **Best Western Ghost Ranch Lodge.** 801 W. Miracle Mile, Tucson, AZ 85705. ☎ **800/456-7565** or 520/791-7565. Fax 520/791-3898. 83 rms. A/C TV TEL. Jan–Apr $52–$110 double; May–June and Nov to early Jan $52–$75 double; July–Oct $39–$68 double. AE, CB, DC, DISC, MC, V.

Although Miracle Mile was once Tucson's main drag, today it's looking a bit shabby. One exception is the Ghost Ranch, which opened back in 1941 and was for many years one of Tucson's desert resorts catering to northern visitors who stayed for the winter. If you're looking for affordable Old Tucson, this is it. Situated on 8 acres, the lodge has a justly famous cactus garden, orange grove, and extensive lawns that together create an oasis atmosphere. The guest rooms have all been recently refurbished but still have a bit of Western flavor to them, with beamed ceilings, painted brick walls, and patios covered by red-tile roofs.

The lodge's dining room serves Southwestern-style meals and offers dining on a poolside patio or inside with a view of the Santa Catalina Mountains. Facilities at the Ghost Ranch include a small pool, a whirlpool, and a games room.

✪ **Clarion Santa Rita Hotel & Suites.** 88 E. Broadway Blvd., Tucson, AZ 85701. ☎ **800/ 622-1120** or 520/622-4000. Fax 520/620-0376. 163 rms, 8 suites. A/C TV TEL. $69–$139 double; $89–$225 suite. Rates include continental breakfast. AE, DISC, MC, V.

Located almost across the street from the convention center and around the corner from the arts district and El Presidio Historic District, this high-rise hotel is surprisingly inexpensive for such an excellent location. In 1996 the hotel underwent a complete renovation that extended from the lobby to the guest rooms. Marble floors and paneled walls now greet guests as they enter the lobby, and in the guest rooms, you might find such highly appreciated touches as ergonomic office chairs, hair dryers, coffeemakers, refrigerators, microwaves, and irons and ironing boards. Local calls are also free here.

The hotel's Cafe Poca Cosa is a wildly painted cafe that serves some of the best Mexican food in town. The hotel offers complimentary breakfast and evening cocktails. Facilities include saunas and a surprisingly pleasant little pool in a lushly landscaped patio area.

✪ **Hotel Congress.** 311 E. Congress St., Tucson, AZ 85701. ☎ **800/722-8848** or 520/622-8848. Fax 520/792-6366. 40 rms. TEL. $31–$45 double. Student discount available. $11 per person in shared hostel rooms. AE, MC, V.

Located in the heart of Tucson's Downtown Arts District, the Hotel Congress once played host to John Dillinger. Today it operates as a youth hostel and budget hotel. Conveniently located near the Greyhound and Amtrak stations, this hotel is popular with students and European backpackers. Although the hotel is far from luxurious, the lobby has been restored to its original Southwestern elegance. The guest rooms get a lot of hard use and aren't in great shape, but the young crowd that stays here doesn't seem to mind. Some bathrooms have bathtubs only and others have showers only. There's a popular cafe off the lobby, as well as a properly Western bar. At night the Club Congress is a popular (read loud) dance club. Guests can pick up free earplugs at the front desk if they want to sleep through the noise. Loads of atmosphere and a very happening nightlife scene make this a great choice for the young and financially challenged.

**Plaza Hotel & Conference Center.** 1900 E. Speedway Blvd., Tucson, AZ 85719. ☎ **800/ 843-8052**, 800/654-3010 in Arizona, or 520/327-7341. Fax 520/327-0276. 150 rms, 1 suite. A/C TV TEL. Dec–May $65–$115 double; June–Aug $39–$79 double; Sept–Nov $89 double; year-round $125–$250 suite. AE, CB, DC, MC, V.

Though this seven-story hotel is quite plain looking, it's conveniently located across the street from the University of Arizona campus and a 5-minute drive from downtown. The upper rooms on the north side offer the best views, so try to get one of these. There's a casual cafe dining room in the lobby, as well as a lobby sports bar. A pool, whirlpool, and access to a nearby health club round out the offerings here. Although this hotel sees a lot of hard use by partying college students, there are plans to renovate the rooms.

# EAST TUCSON
## MODERATE

**Best Western Tanque Verde Inn & Suites.** 7007 E. Tanque Verde Rd., Tucson, AZ 85715. ☎ **800/528-1234** or 520/298-2300. Fax 520/298-6756. 89 rms, 2 suites. A/C TV TEL. Jan–Mar $85–$130 double, $139 suite; Apr–May and Oct–Dec $75–$100 double, $89–$109 suite; June–Sept $50–$65 double, $79 suite. Rates include continental breakfast. AE, CB, DC, DISC, MC, V.

Though it looks rather stark from the outside, the Tanque Verde Inn is surprisingly pleasant inside. This modest motel is built around four tranquil and lushly planted garden courtyards that have bubbling fountains and tile benches. Most rooms are quite large, and some have kitchenettes. There's no restaurant on the premises, but numerous excellent restaurants are nearby. The inn provides complimentary evening cocktails and health club privileges, as well as free local phone calls. Facilities include a pool, whirlpool, and coin-operated laundry.

**Bienestar Bed & Breakfast.** 10490 E. Escalante Rd., Tucson, AZ 85730. ☎ **520/290-1048.** Fax 520/290-1367. 1 rm, 1 suite. Oct 1–May 31 $85 double, $125 suite; June 1–Sept 30 $62 double, $93 suite. DISC, MC, V.

Located way out on the east side of Tucson, this contemporary home is set amid spacious grounds, complete with stables (if you happen to be traveling with your horses), and is convenient to the east unit of Saguaro National Park. The hillside setting provides far-reaching views of mountains and valley, and the desert landscaping gives the inn a solid sense of place. Friendly innkeepers with a holistic bent have provided a refreshingly tranquil lodging. Entered through a small courtyard garden with a fountain, the inn is built in an open Southwestern style. Outside there is a pool and a whirlpool spa. The suite is of course the accommodation of choice and is absolutely huge. It has a complete entertainment center, a beautiful big bathroom with a little garden patio area, two fireplaces, and a custom-made dream-catcher bed. The smaller room is equally comfortable; its bathroom is across the hall, though it's designated for this room only. Breakfasts feature natural foods, including organic coffee, and eggs from free-range hens.

**Doubletree Guest Suites.** 6555 E. Speedway Blvd., Tucson, AZ 85710. ☎ **800/222-TREE** or 520/721-7100. Fax 520/721-1991. 304 suites. A/C TV TEL. Feb–Apr $133–$147 double; May–Sept $74–$89 double; Oct–Jan $96–$103 double (lower rates for advance-purchase bookings). Rates include full breakfast (discounts available for guests not wanting breakfast). AE, CB, DC, DISC, MC, V.

With surprisingly reasonable rates throughout the year, this all-suite hotel is a good choice both for those who need plenty of space and those who want to be in the eastside business corridor. The five-story brick building is arranged around two long courtyards, one of which has a small pool and whirlpool. The lobby is small but attractively decorated in contemporary Southwestern style. The guest rooms also feature contemporary furnishings and the glass blocks over the wet bars add a vaguely art deco touch. All rooms have refrigerators and coffeemakers and at press time, microwaves, irons, and ironing boards were being added.

**Dining/Entertainment:** The hotel restaurant's menu has enough variety to satisfy most people who are just looking for an easy meal. The cookies you get at check-in are reason enough to stay!

**Services:** Room service, complimentary cocktail hour, valet/laundry service.

**Facilities:** Pool, whirlpool, exercise room, access to nearby health club and tennis courts.

**Hotel Park Tucson.** 5151 E. Grant Rd., Tucson, AZ 85712. ☎ **800/257-7275** or 520/323-6262. Fax 520/325-2989. 81 rms, 135 suites. A/C TV TEL. Jan–Mar $89–$155 double, $109–$159 suite; Apr–May and Sept–Dec $69–$139 double, $79–$149 suite; June–Aug $65–$79 double, $69–$89 suite. Rates include full breakfast. AE, CB, DC, DISC, MC, V.

Recently renovated, this eastside business hotel has mostly large suites and offers the same sort of amenities as other nearby all-suite hotels. The rooms should all have been redone by the time you arrive and will feature Southwestern styling. All have refrigerators and irons and ironing boards. Several rooms are also specially designed for women travellers.

**Dining/Entertainment:** The Ranchers Club of Arizona is one of the best reasons to stay here, and what you save on room rates, you can spend on this restaurant's superb steaks. There is also a very large and lively sports bar, one of the most popular in the city.

**Services:** Room service, shopping shuttle, valet/laundry service.

**Facilities:** Medium-sized outdoor pool, exercise room, whirlpool, steam room, sauna, car-rental desk.

✪ **The Lodge on the Desert.** 306 N. Alvernon Way (P.O. Box 42500), Tucson, AZ 85733. ☎ **800/456-5634** or 520/325-3366. Fax 520/327-5834. 37 rms. A/C TV TEL. Nov–May $92–$118 double; June–Oct $58–$82 double. Rates include continental breakfast. AE, CB, DC, DISC, MC, V.

A sort of poor man's Arizona Inn, The Lodge on the Desert offers the same adobe-style buildings in a garden compound shaded by palms and orange and eucalyptus trees. This older resort, popular with families who have been staying here for years, is still owned by the same family that founded it in 1936. The lodge's greatest draw is its old-world charm and mix of hacienda and pueblo styling. The beautiful manicured lawns and flower gardens offer a lush and relaxing retreat. Several guest rooms are housed in buildings made of adobe blocks, and some have beamed ceilings or fireplaces. Larger rooms have Mexican-tile floors rather than carpeting, and one room has a private swimming pool.

All meals are served in the lodge's dining room, one section of which has a fireplace and a bench built into the adobe wall. Among the lodge's other features are a pool with a view of the Santa Catalina Mountains, a shuffleboard court, table tennis, a croquet court, and a library.

**Smuggler's Inn.** 6350 E. Speedway Blvd. (at Wilmot), Tucson, AZ 85710. ☎ **800/525-8852** or 520/296-3292. Fax 520/722-3713. 121 rms, 28 suites. A/C TV TEL. Jan–Mar $99–$119 double, $125–$135 suite; Apr to early May $83–$119 double, $125 suite; early May to Sept $56–$63 double, $96 suite; Oct–Dec $66–$73 double, $96 suite. AE, CB, DC, DISC, MC, V.

The Smuggler's Inn is a very comfortable and economically priced hotel built around an attractive garden and pond, and the neatly trimmed lawns and tall palm trees give the garden a tropical look. The guest rooms are spacious and all have modern furnishings and a balcony or patio; a recent renovation has kept them all in good shape. Guest rooms include such features as bathroom phones, coffeemakers, and video games on the TVs. The inn's restaurant sports a Caribbean nautical theme, though the menu doesn't reflect this. There's also a cocktail lounge. The inn offers room service, a complimentary morning newspaper, and golf and health club privileges. Its facilities include a pool, whirlpool, and putting green.

**Tucson East Hilton.** 7600 E. Broadway Blvd., Tucson, AZ 85710. ☎ **800/648-7177** or 520/721-5600. Fax 520/721-5696. 232 rms, 9 suites. A/C TV TEL. Jan 1–Mar 31 $119–$178 double, $250 suite; Apr–May and Oct–Dec $89–$154 double, $225 suite; June 1–Sept 30 $69–$99 double, $200 suite. AE, DC, DISC, MC, V.

Located in the east-side business corridor, this is a high-rise hotel with unobstructed views across the valley. The lobby is large and bright and the view through the seven-story wall of glass serves as the focal point. Most rooms have been recently remodeled, but even those that haven't still look good. All the rooms have computer jacks and most have coffeemakers and hair dryers. There are floors for frequent Hilton customers as well as concierge floors with extra amenities. Some of the suites have large sundecks.

**Dining/Entertainment:** A casual restaurant serves international contemporary cuisine with a hint of Southwestern flavoring, and has an outstanding view of the mountains. There's also an adjacent lounge.

**Services:** Room service, complimentary shuttle to within 3 miles, children's programs.

**Facilities:** Outdoor pool, whirlpool, access to nearby health club, tennis courts nearby.

**Tucson Viscount Suite Hotel.** 4855 E. Broadway Blvd., Tucson, AZ 85711. ☎ **800/ 527-9666** or 520/745-6500. 215 suites. A/C TV TEL. Oct–May $99–$145 double; June–Sept $79–$99 double. Rates include full breakfast. AE, CB, DC, DISC, MC, V.

This all-suite business hotel is centrally located in east Tucson only a few minutes from downtown and is the most upscale and service oriented of the east-side all-suites. The suites, which feature a mix of contemporary and classic furnishings, are arranged around a four-story garden atrium in which breakfast is served. Some suites have refrigerators or microwaves. Large windows let sunshine flood the bedrooms.

**Dining/Entertainment:** Breakfast and complimentary afternoon cocktails are served in the atrium. For more formal dining there's the Oxford Club Restaurant. Wilbur's is a sports bar named after the University of Arizona mascot.

**Services:** Concierge, room service, shopping shuttle.

**Facilities:** Outdoor pool, whirlpool, sauna, exercise room, car-rental desk.

# THE FOOTHILLS
## VERY EXPENSIVE

**The Lodge at Ventana Canyon.** 6200 N. Clubhouse Lane, Tucson, AZ 85750. ☎ **800/ 828-5701** or 520/577-1400. Fax 520/577-4063. 49 suites. A/C TV TEL. Jan–Apr $260–$475 double; May $225–$375 double; June–Sept $125–$235 double; Oct–Dec $225–$425 double. AE, MC, V.

Golf is the name of the game at this country club–style resort, which underwent a $5 million renovation a couple of years ago. Any avid golfer will want to make this (or Loew's Ventana Canyon Resort, which shares the two courses) their first choice in Tucson. However, even the nongolfer will be impressed by the spectacular setting at the foot of the rugged Santa Catalina Mountains. Small size combined with big-resort amenities—including 12 tennis courts and good exercise facilities—are what make this gated retreat so appealing. The accommodations are in spacious suites, most with walls of windows so you can enjoy the views from the comfort of your room. Furnishings are modern Mission-style, and all suites include small kitchens and large bathrooms with oversize tubs (sometimes old-fashioned footed tubs), two sinks, and separate changing rooms. Some also have balconies, cathedral ceilings, and spiral stairs that lead to sleeping lofts.

**Dining/Entertainment:** The dining room, a few steps from the lobby, offers fine dining with a view of the Santa Catalinas. Drinks are served in two lounges, and there's also a poolside snack bar.

**Services:** Concierge, room service, golf and tennis lessons, massages, baby-sitting, valet/laundry service, complimentary daily newspaper, free shuttle to Loews Ventana Canyon Resort.

**Facilities:** The two 18-hole golf courses designed by Tom Fazio are among the most dramatic in the state, and the third hole on the Mountain Course is one of the most photographed holes in the West. Twelve tennis courts, pool, whirlpools, exercise room, aerobics room, steam rooms, saunas, beauty salon, and pro shop round out the facilities here.

✪ **Loews Ventana Canyon Resort.** 7000 N. Resort Dr., Tucson, AZ 85750. ☎ **800/234-5117** or 520/299-2020. Fax 520/299-6832. 371 rms, 27 suites. A/C TV TEL. Jan 1 to late May $295–$395 double, $750–$2,400 suite; late May to early Sept $135–$165 double, $215–$1,235 suite; early Sept to Dec 31 $235–$325 double, $600–$2,085 suite. AE, CB, DC, DISC, ER, JCB, MC, V.

For breathtaking scenery, fascinating architecture, and superb resort amenities (including two excellent golf courses and a recently expanded full-service spa), no other Tucson resort can compare with Loews Ventana Canyon. The Santa Catalina Mountains rise up in rugged contrast to the genteel comforts of this haven of luxury, while outside the grand entrance lie a small lake and the golf course. Despite its many amenities, the resort is firmly planted in the desert and uses desert plants in much of its landscaping. Of particular appeal is a short nature trail that leads to a cascading waterfall. Flagstone floors in the lobby and tables with boulders for bases give the resort's public rooms a rugged but luxurious appeal. Spectacular setting aside, most guests come to avail themselves of the two golf courses, tennis courts, other sports facilities, and the spa.

The guest rooms are designed to impress. Beds angle out from corners and drapes hang from headboards. Private balconies overlook either the city lights or the mountains, and some rooms have fireplaces. The bathrooms are designed for convenience and comfort, with tiny TVs, hair dryers, telephones, travertine floors, and bathtubs built for two.

**Dining/Entertainment:** The Ventana Room is one of the finest restaurants in Tucson and serves new American cuisine amid views of the city lights (see "Dining" below). The casual Canyon Cafe offers a view of the waterfall and less expensive meals. For lakeside terrace dining there's the newly remodeled and expanded Flying V with large decks overlooking the golf course and city lights, and by the pool, there's a snack bar with a pleasantly varied menu. The lobby lounge serves afternoon tea and then becomes an evening piano bar.

**Services:** Concierge, 24-hour room service, valet/laundry service, free shopping shuttle, massages.

**Facilities:** Two outstanding Tom Fazio–designed 18-hole golf courses, two pools with mountain views, whirlpools, eight lighted tennis courts, croquet court, health spa (including a lap pool, aerobics room, exercise machines and free weights, steam rooms, saunas, and full assortment of spa treatments and services), beauty salon, bike rentals, car-rental desk, tour desk.

**Omni Tucson National Golf Resort & Spa.** 2727 W. Club Dr. (off Magee Rd.), Tucson, AZ 85742. ☎ **800/528-4856** or 520/297-2271. Fax 520/297-7544. 167 rms. A/C MINIBAR TV TEL. Mid-Jan to Mar $240–$310 double; Apr–May $150–$200 double; June to mid-Sept $80–$145 double; mid-Sept to mid-Jan $130–$200 double. AE, CB, DC, MC, V.

As its name implies, golf is the driving force behind most stays at this boutique resort in the foothills of north Tucson, and if you haven't got your own set of clubs, you might feel out of place here. However, the full-service health spa is one of the best in Arizona and makes this a great place for some serious stress reduction. A new pool and tennis complex has made the resort appealing to families as well.

The guest rooms here are mostly in two-story buildings and all are spacious and have their own patio or balcony. Hand-carved doors and Mexican hand-painted tile counters in the bathrooms give the rooms a Spanish colonial feel, though furnishings have a classically modern Mediterranean style. For our money, the rooms here (other than the least expensive ones) are the best and most luxurious in Tucson. For convenience there are two sinks and large dressing areas in all the rooms.

**Dining/Entertainment:** A clublike gourmet dining room serves good regional American fare, while a second restaurant, downstairs from the lobby, serves reasonably priced Southwestern fare. A lobby lounge provides distant views of the Santa Catalina Mountains, and an upscale, club-like sports bar looks out over the golf course.

**Services:** Concierge, 24-hour room service, valet/laundry service, in-room massage.

**Facilities:** Excellent 27-hole golf course (many times the site of PGA Tour events); four lighted tennis courts; two pools; basketball and volleyball courts; pro shop; mountain-bike rentals; and full-service health spa with exercise machines, free weights, an aerobics room, steam rooms, saunas, whirlpools, and numerous skin and body treatments.

✪ **Sheraton El Conquistador Resort & Country Club.** 10000 N. Oracle Rd., Tucson, AZ 85737. ☎ **800/325-7832** or 520/544-5000. Fax 520/544-1228. 428 rms, 100 suites. A/C MINIBAR TV TEL. Late Dec to late Apr $230–$310 double, $290–$1,200 suite; late Apr to late May $165–$265 double, $210–$1,200 suite; late May to early Sept $100–$125 double, $130–$1,200 suite; early Sept to late Dec $190–$240 double, $240–$1,200 suite. AE, CB, DC, DISC, ER, JCB, MC, V.

Located 14 miles north of downtown and with the Santa Catalina Mountains rising up behind it, this resort boasts one of the most spectacular settings in the state. The majority of the guest rooms are built around a central courtyard with a large pool and manicured lawns. However, this area is often taken over by conventions and those seeking peace and quiet may want to opt for a room in the separate casitas area, which has its own pool. If you're a golfer, though, you're not likely to get much rest at the resort, since it boasts three courses to keep you busy. Nongolfers have plenty of options, too, including 31 tennis courts, racquetball courts, and two health clubs.

The guest rooms feature Southwestern-influenced contemporary furniture, including TV armoires reminiscent of old Mexican cabinets. All rooms have computer jacks, coffeemakers, hair dryers, and a balcony or patio, and there are fireplaces in most suites. The bathrooms are spacious.

**Dining/Entertainment:** The White Dove, a small, contemporary dining room, serves French-influenced cuisine. In the lively Mexican restaurant strolling mariachis entertain, while in the steakhouse cowboy vittles and music are the order of the day. A casual cafe offers patio dining and moderate prices. The country club's restaurant capitalizes on its outstanding view and serves continental and Southwestern dishes.

**Services:** Concierge, 24-hour room service, valet/laundry service, shopping shuttle, baby-sitting, massages, horseback riding, children's programs.

**Facilities:** Three golf courses (45 holes total), 31 lighted tennis courts, seven indoor racquetball courts, four pools, whirlpools, sauna, two health clubs, jogging paths, volleyball and basketball courts, rental bikes, car-rental desk, tour desk.

**Westin La Paloma.** 3800 E. Sunrise Dr., Tucson, AZ 85718. ☎ **800/937-8461** or 520/742-6000. Fax 520/577-5878. 487 rms, 41 suites. A/C MINIBAR TV TEL. Jan 1 to late May $325–$416 double, from $495 suite; late May to early Sept $109–$215 double, from $310 suite; early Sept to Dec 31 $265–$365 double, from $445 suite. AE, CB, DC, DISC, ER, JCB, MC, V.

La Paloma (The Dove) sits in the middle of Tucson's prestigious foothills neighborhoods and offers sweeping panoramas from its hilltop perch. The mission-revival architecture in a sunset pink gives the resort a timeless feel, and the golf course, which surrounds the resort, offers great views of both the city and the Santa Catalinas. The resort's associated country club, with tennis courts and extensive exercise facilities, also keeps active guests busy. A recent remodel has given the lobby a very classic look, sort of reminiscent of a Bogart movie, with gold tones throughout, beautiful large wicker chairs, and a multicolored hardwood floor in the adjacent lounge. The renovation also added a 170-foot waterslide and a new pool and poolside landscaping, making this an even better choice for families now.

Guest rooms are situated in 27 low-rise buildings and were all renovated a few years ago; they now sport desert hues and Western art. The bathrooms are extremely spacious, with separate tubs and showers, two sinks, telephones, and bathrobes.

**Dining/Entertainment:** New American cuisine is highlighted in the formal clubhouse dining room, while a dining room with views of the mountains provides a more casual setting. In early 1997, a new tropical-theme cantina and brewpub (one of the few in Tucson) opened in its own hacienda near the hotel's massive portico. Snack bars are convenient to tennis and golf. There's also a swim-up bar and grill. The lobby lounge provides great views and evening piano music. Golfers have their own bar at the 19th Hole.

**Services:** Concierge, 24-hour room service, valet service, massages, day-care center, shopping shuttle.

**Facilities:** 27-hole golf course, three swimming pools (one for adults only), waterslide, 12 tennis courts, racquetball court, three whirlpools, golf and tennis pro shops, volleyball and croquet courts, bike rentals, children's lounge and game room, shopping arcade, beauty salon offering spa services, health club with exercise machines, aerobics room, and steam room.

## EXPENSIVE

✪ **Westward Look Resort.** 245 E. Ina Rd., Tucson, AZ 85704. ☎ **800/722-2500** or 520/297-1151. Fax 520/297-9023. 244 rms. A/C MINIBAR TV TEL. Mid-Jan to late Apr $159–$339 double; late Apr to May $129–$209 double; June to late Sept $69–$139 double; late Sept to early Jan $139–$219 double. AE, CB, DC, DISC, ER, JCB, MC, V.

Opened in 1929 as a dude ranch, the Westward Look has since become one of Tucson's most reasonably priced resorts, and has been undergoing quite a bit of renovation in the past few years. If you aren't a golfer but do enjoy resort amenities, this is one of your best Tucson choices. Offering quiet, traditional luxury in the foothills of the Santa Catalina Mountains, the resort is surrounded by desert and attracts a varied clientele. There is no golf course here, but guests enjoy tennis courts, a fitness center, jogging trails, and a full-service health spa. The guest rooms, all of which were recently renovated, are quite large and have private patios or balconies and coffeemakers and hair dryers. Spanish colonial–style furnishings with an antique look give rooms here a classic, Southwestern flavor. Many also have exposed-beam ceilings and great views of the city.

**Dining/Entertainment:** The Gold Room restaurant features walls of glass that provide sweeping views of Tucson and serves reliably excellent continental cuisine. A casual bar and grill, with live music on weekends, benefits from the same views.

**Services:** Concierge, room service, valet/laundry service, in-room massages, tennis lessons, horseback riding, guided hikes, baby-sitting. Exercise, tai chi, and yoga classes are also offered through the Wellness Center

**Facilities:** Three pools, eight lighted tennis courts, three whirlpools, basketball and volleyball courts, horseshoe pits, jogging trail, pro shop, a recently renovated and expanded fitness center, Wellness Center (health spa), rental bikes, tour desk.

## MODERATE

✪ **Hacienda del Sol Guest Ranch Resort.** 5601 N. Hacienda del Sol Rd., Tucson, AZ 85718. ☎ **800/728-6514** or 520/299-1501. 25 rms, 5 suites, 3 casitas. A/C TV TEL. Dec 1–May 31

$115–$155 double, $195–$210 suite, $245–$285 casita; June 1–June 30 and Sept 1–Nov 30 $75–$95 double, $150–$170 suite, $185–$225 casita; July 1–Aug 31 $70–$80 double, $125–$140 suite, $165–$175 casita. Rates include continental breakfast. AE, MC, V.

Hacienda del Sol is not for everyone. Let me make that perfectly clear right now. If you need carpeting and central air, a concierge and 24-hour room service, don't even consider this place. If, on the other hand, you want to stay in the foothills at a historic lodge that was once a guest ranch (and later a private girls' school) and that exudes the sort of Old Tucson atmosphere only available at a couple of other lodgings, then this may be your place. The basic rooms are not fancy, but their rustic Spanish colonial furnishings give them an old-world air that we find especially engaging. These particular rooms are in the lodge's oldest buildings, which are set around courtyards and surrounded by mature desert gardens. If you prefer more modern, spacious, and comfortable accommodations, opt for a suite. If, on the other hand, you want loads of space and the chance to stay where Katherine Hepburn and Spencer Tracy may have once stayed, then ask for a casita.

**Dining/Entertainment:** At press time, the resort's dining room was just about to open, with views over the foothills and large terraces for alfresco dining. Expect creative Southwestern flavors. There will also be a full lounge adjacent to the dining room.

**Services:** Horseback riding, nature walks, massages.

**Facilities:** The small pool has a great view of the Santa Catalinas and is the focus of most guest activity. Also available are tennis and croquet courts and a whirlpool.

**Windmill Inn at St. Philip's Plaza.** 4250 N. Campbell Ave., Tucson, AZ 85718. ☎ **800/547-4747** or 520/577-0007. Fax 520/577-0045. 122 suites. A/C TV TEL. Jan 21–Apr 20 $115–$150 double; Apr 21–May 31 and Sept 15–Jan 20 $97–$107 double; June 1–Sept 14 $65–$75 double. Rates include continental breakfast. AE, DC, DISC, MC, V.

Located in St. Philip's Plaza, which has several great restaurants and an array of upscale shops, this hotel offers both a good location and spacious accommodations. All the rooms are suites and have couches, work desks, two TVs, three telephones (one in the bathroom), double vanities, wet bars, small refrigerators, and microwaves. Basically there's everything to make the business traveler or vacationer comfortable for a long stay, and local phone calls are free.

**Facilities:** Pool, whirlpool, lending library, complimentary use of bicycles.

### INEXPENSIVE

**The Congenial Quail.** 4267 N. Fourth Ave., Tucson, AZ 85705. ☎ **520/887-9487.** 2 rms (with shared bath), 1 cottage. $65–$80 double; $100 cottage. Two-night minimum. Rates include full breakfast. MC, V. Closed June–Aug.

Located just south of River Road between Oracle Road and Campbell Avenue, this 1940s ranch house sits on almost 3 acres of desert where there are indeed many quails scurrying about. Yet the cottage is my favorite room here. It's set off a bit from the main house and has its own private yard. This and the other two rooms all come with lots of books—science fiction and mysteries in the cottage, American writers in one room, and children's books in the other. Breakfasts offer flavors of the Southwest such as homemade tequila marmalade and muffins made with mesquite bean flour. The huge Tucson Mall is only blocks away.

# WEST OF DOWNTOWN
## EXPENSIVE

**El Adobe Ranch.** 4630 N. El Adobe Ranch Rd., Tucson, AZ 85745. ☎ **520/743-3525.** Fax 520/743-3525. 5 casitas. Oct 1–May 1 $175 double; May 2–Sept 30 $110 double. Rates include continental breakfast. AE, MC, V.

Sort of a cross between a bed-and-breakfast and a guest ranch, this unusual lodging offers seclusion amid saguaros and accommodations in contemporary Southwestern casitas. Staying here is a bit like having your own contemporary house in the desert with Saguaro National Park and the Tucson mountains for your backyard. Of course such a setting isn't for everyone. The road in isn't paved and it's 20 minutes or so to the nearest good restaurant, but if you came to Tucson expecting to stay in the desert, this will definitely fit the bill. The casitas all have their own kitchens, and you'll find fireplaces in both the bedrooms and the living rooms. A pavilion is designed to accommodate groups (such as weddings and family reunions) and has a big barbecue grill and an outdoor fireplace.

**Starr Pass Golf Resort.** 3645 W. Starr Pass Blvd., Tucson, AZ 85745. ☎ **800/503-2898** or 520/670-0500. Fax 520/670-0590. 105 rms and suites. A/C TV TEL. Jan 1–Apr 15 $169–$289 suite, $439 2-bedroom casita; Apr 16–May 31 $109–$159 suite, $249 2-bedroom casita; June 1–Sept 30 $89–$139 suite, $189 2-bedroom casita; Oct 1–Dec 31 $139–$229 suite, $339 2-bedroom casita. AE, DISC, MC, V.

Located off West 22nd Street 3 miles west of I-10, Starr Pass is Tucson's newest golf resort and is the closest one to downtown. It's also the most economically priced in the city. The resort's centerpiece, the Starr Pass Golf Course, is a championship course that in the past has hosted Tucson's PGA tournament. This is a small resort, so you won't find the sort of service you get at Tucson's bigger resorts, but on the other hand, you won't pay nearly as much either.

Accommodations here are in privately owned Santa Fe–style casitas that can be broken down into a master suite and a standard hotel-style room or that can be rented as two-bedroom units. The master suites are the larger and more comfortable style of room and have fireplaces, washers and dryers, full kitchens with Mexican tile floors, wrought-iron breakfast-bar stools and bed frames, and a general South-western styling throughout. Bathrooms are large and have separate showers and tubs. The smaller rooms are a bit cramped and much less lavish in their appointments.

**Dining/Entertainment:** The dining room here looks out over the golf course and surrounding hills and serves a mix of continental and Southwestern dishes at very reasonable prices.

**Services:** Valet/laundry, baby-sitting. Note that room service is not available here.

**Facilities:** The championship 18-hole golf course is best known for its 15th hole, which plays through a narrow pass that was once the route of a stagecoach. In addition, there's a large pro shop, outdoor pool (surrounded by a rather stark patio area), exercise room, two tennis courts, whirlpool spa, hiking/biking trails.

## MODERATE

✪ **Casa Tierra.** 11155 W. Calle Pima, Tucson, AZ 85743. ☎ **520/578-3058.** Fax 520/578-3058. 3 rms. Sept 1–Dec 15 $75–$85 double; Dec 16–May 31 $85–$95 double. Rates include a full vegetarian breakfast. No credit cards. Closed June–Aug.

If you've come to Tucson to be in the desert and you really want to be a *part* of the desert, then there's no doubt about where you should stay. Casa Tierra, a modern adobe home surrounded by 5 acres of cactus and palo verde, is situated on the west side of Saguaro National Park and has fabulous views of a landscape full of saguaros. There are also stunning sunsets and views of the mountains to the north. The owners are a young couple who built this home to look as if it has been here since the days when the area was under Spanish rule. Surrounding a central courtyard with a desert garden is a covered seating area where guests congregate. The rooms open off this covered patio and have queen-size beds, brick floors, and private patios. The outdoor whirlpool spa makes a perfect stargazing spot at night. There is also a rental house available for long-term stays.

# NEAR THE AIRPORT

## MODERATE

**Best Western Inn at the Airport.** 7060 S. Tucson Blvd., Tucson, AZ 85706. ☎ **800/528-1234** or 520/746-0271. Fax 520/889-7391. 149 rms. A/C TV TEL. Jan–Mar $78–$134 double; Apr–May $65–$95 double; June to mid-Sept $55–$89 double; mid-Sept to Dec $60–$90 double. Rates include continental breakfast. AE, CB, DC, DISC, MC, V.

If you're the type who likes to get as much sleep as possible before getting up to catch a plane, this motel right outside the airport entrance will get you absolutely the most sleep. There's no place closer. The one drawback is, unfortunately, the airport noise. You do, however, get a great range of amenities here at surprisingly reasonable rates. In addition to the buffet breakfast, evening beer and wine and late-night snacks are also complimentary. The rooms are comfortable and have small refrigerators and hair dryers. The restaurant and the lounge assure that guests don't go hungry or thirsty. There's a small courtyard pool and a whirlpool, as well as a fitness room and a tennis court.

**Clarion Hotel Tucson Airport.** 6801 S. Tucson Blvd., Tucson, AZ 85706. ☎ **800/526-0550** or 520/746-3932. Fax 520/889-9934. 191 rms. A/C TV TEL. Jan–Apr $105–$150 double; May to mid-Sept $75–$120 double; mid-Sept to Oct $90–$135 double; Nov–Dec $85–$130 double. Rates include a full breakfast. AE, CB, DC, DISC, MC, V.

Located just outside the airport exit, this low-rise hotel provides convenience and some great amenities, including a nightly complimentary cocktail reception and late-night snacks. The rooms are generally quite large, and the "king" rooms are particularly comfortable. The poolside rooms, in addition to being convenient for swimming and lounging, also have small refrigerators.

**Dining/Entertainment:** The restaurant offers moderately priced meals in casual surroundings and the menu is rather eclectic. There's also an adjacent lounge.

**Services:** Concierge, room service, valet service, complimentary airport shuttle, shopping shuttle.

**Facilities:** Pool, whirlpool, exercise room.

**Embassy Suites—Tucson International Airport.** 7051 S. Tucson Blvd., Tucson, AZ 85706. ☎ **800/262-8866** or 520/573-0700. Fax 520/741-9645. 204 suites. A/C TV TEL. Jan–May $134 double; June–Sept $89 double; Oct–Dec $114 double. Rates include full breakfast. AE, CB, DC, DISC, MC, V.

This all-suite hotel is conveniently located just outside the airport exit, and offers spacious suites that all have kitchenettes, two phones, and two TVs. The courtyard pool area is attractively landscaped, which makes this a great (if a bit noisy) escape at the end of the day.

**Dining/Entertainment:** A restaurant serves simple, moderately priced meals, and in the lounge you'll find a big-screen TV and pool table. Complimentary evening cocktails and hors d'oeuvres are served.

**Services:** Room service, complimentary airport shuttle, valet/laundry service.

**Facilities:** Outdoor pool, whirlpool, fitness center, business center, guest laundry, car-rental desk.

## INEXPENSIVE

There are numerous budget motels near the Tucson Airport. These include the **Red Roof Inn,** 3700 E. Irvington Rd. (Exit 264 off I-10; ☎ **520/571-1400**), charging $43 to $99 double; **Motel 6,** 755 E. Benson Hwy. (Exit 262 off I-10; ☎ **520/**

622-4614), charging $35 to $45 double; **Motel 6,** 1031 E. Benson Hwy. (Exit 262; ☎ 520/628-1264), charging $35 to $45 double; and **Super 8—Tucson/East,** 1990 S. Craycroft Rd. (Exit 265 off I-10; ☎ 520/790-6021), charging $46 to $99 double. See the appendix for a list of toll-free numbers.

## SPAS

**Canyon Ranch.** 8600 E. Rockliff Rd., Tucson, AZ 85750. ☎ **800/726-9900** or 520/749-9000. Fax 520/749-1646. 180 rms. A/C TV TEL. Mid-Sept to mid-June 4-night package from $3,160–$5,460 double; mid-June to mid-Sept 4-night package from $2,440–$3,380 double. Rates include all meals and a variety of spa services and programs. AE, DISC, MC, V. No children under 14.

Canyon Ranch is one of America's premier health spas, and offers the sort of complete spa experience that's only available at a few places around the country (and then only to those who can afford it). On staff are doctors, nurses, psychotherapists and counselors, fitness instructors, tennis and racquetball pros, and massage therapists. There are a variety of spacious and very comfortable accommodations. So that guests are assured of a tranquil visit, children under 14 are not allowed, with the exception of infants in the care of nannies (baby-sitting services are not available).

**Dining/Entertainment:** Three gourmet low-calorie meals are served daily with options for total daily caloric intake. Because this is a health spa, no alcoholic beverages are served.

**Services:** Health and fitness assessments; health, nutrition, exercise, and stress-management consultations, seminars, presentations, and evaluations; fitness classes and activities; massage therapy; herbal and aroma wraps; facials, manicures, pedicures, haircuts, and styling; private sports lessons; makeup consultations; cooking demonstrations; art classes; concierge.

**Facilities:** 62,000-square-foot spa complex that includes seven gyms, aerobics and strength-training rooms, squash and racquetball courts, yoga/meditation room, saunas, steam rooms, inhalation rooms, whirlpools, cold plunges, private sunbathing areas, and skin care and beauty salons. Additional facilities include four pools (one indoors), eight tennis courts, and a basketball court.

**Miraval.** 5000 E. Via Estancia Miraval, Catalina, AZ 85739. ☎ **800/232-3969** or 520/825-4000. Fax 520/792-5870. 90 rms, 16 suites. A/C MINIBAR TV TEL. Oct 1–May 31 $800–$920 double, $1,100–$1,300 suite for 2; June 1–Sept 30 $540–$630 double, $930–$1,100 suite for 2. Rates include all meals and a variety of spa services and programs. AE, DC, MC, V.

Focusing on what it calls "life balancing," Miraval is Arizona's newest full-service health spa resort. Rather than emphasizing facials and mud baths, however, it focuses on stress management, self-discovery, and relaxation. To this end, activities at the all-inclusive resort include meditation, tai chi, and yoga, but for more active types, there is also hiking, mountain biking, and rock climbing (on an outdoor climbing wall). Of course such desert classics as horseback riding, tennis, volleyball, and swimming are also available. However, staying busy isn't really the objective here; learning a new way of living your life is the ultimate goal at Miraval.

Throughout the resort, Southwestern styling predominates and lots of original art hangs on the walls. However, no amount of art can equal the views of the Santa Catalina Mountains to be had from restaurants, terraces, and almost anywhere on the grounds. Guest rooms, many of which also have mountain views, are done in a Southwestern style and have very large bathrooms that, for the most part, have showers but no tubs.

**Dining/Entertainment:** With two restaurants and two snack lounges, no one need fear going hungry here. Unlike at many other health spas, your caloric intake is not restricted, and to make a point of this, Miraval lays out an extraordinarily lavish buffet lunch. However, rest assured that everything served here is healthy as well as delicious.

**Services:** In addition to activities mentioned above, Miraval offers lifestyle management workshops, fitness/nutrition consultations, cooking demonstrations, exercise classes, an "equine experience" program, massage, skin care and facials, and a confidence-building course. Airport transfers are also included in the rates.

**Facilities:** Two exercise pools and a three-tiered leisure pool surrounded by waterfalls and desert landscaping are among the most popular facilities here, but you'll also find a superbly equipped exercise room, rock climbing wall, tennis courts, volleyball court, riding stables, whirlpool spas, saunas, steam rooms.

# GUEST RANCHES

**Lazy K Bar Ranch.** 8401 N. Scenic Dr., Tucson, AZ 85743. ☎ **800/321-7018** or 520/744-3050. Fax 520/744-7628. 19 rms, 4 suites. A/C. $185–$275 double; $225–$300 suite. Three-night minimum. Rates include all meals. AE, DISC, MC, V.

Homesteaded in 1933 and converted to a dude ranch in 1936, the Lazy K Bar Ranch covers 160 acres adjacent to Saguaro National Park. There are plenty of nearby hiking and riding trails, and if you have a hankering for city life, it isn't difficult to reach downtown (20 minutes away). The guest rooms vary in size and comfort level. The newest are the most comfortable, with exposed brick walls and sliding glass doors that open onto patios. The ranch-oriented activities at the Lazy K include horseback riding twice daily, hayrides, lunch rides, cookouts, and square dances. There are also nature walks and talks and weekly excursions to the Arizona–Sonora Desert Museum.

**Dining/Entertainment:** Meals are served family style in a dining room that features Mexican tile floors and an open-pit fireplace. The food is hearty American ranch style with cookouts some nights. Each evening there's a happy hour at the ranch's BYOB bar.

**Services:** Complimentary airport transfer, Sunday shuttle to the Arizona–Sonora Desert Museum, horseback riding and lessons.

**Facilities:** Pool, whirlpool, two tennis courts, volleyball and basketball courts, horseshoe pits, stables, mountain bikes.

✪ **Tanque Verde Ranch.** 14301 E. Speedway Blvd., Tucson, AZ 85748. ☎ **800/234-DUDE** or 520/296-6275. Fax 520/721-9426. 71 rms. A/C TEL. Mid-Dec to Apr $280–$365 double; May–Sept $225–$280 double; Oct to mid-Dec $235–$310 double. Rates include all meals. AE, DISC, MC, V.

Far and away the most luxurious guest ranch in Tucson, the Tanque Verde, founded in the 1880s, is very popular with both Americans and Europeans who come to live their cowboy dreams in the Old West. The ranch, which still has some of its original buildings, borders both Saguaro National Park and the Coronado National Forest, which assures plenty of room for guided horseback rides. In addition to riding, the bird watching here is excellent (more than 220 species have been seen on the ranch) and birders are well served. There are also nature trails, wildlife viewing ramadas, and a nature center with displays of live snakes and other desert critters. The guest rooms are spacious and comfortable, but don't expect a TV here—ranch policy encourages guests to participate in various activities. Many rooms have fireplaces and patios, and the bathrooms are large.

**Dining/Entertainment:** The large dining room, which overlooks the Rincon Mountains, sets impressive buffets. There are also breakfast horseback rides, poolside luncheons, and cookout rides. An old foreman's cabin now houses a cantina.

**Services:** Complimentary riding and tennis lessons, evening lectures and performances, nature hikes, children's programs, baby-sitting, complimentary airport shuttle with four-night stay.

**Facilities:** Indoor and outdoor pools, riding stables, five tennis courts, exercise room, saunas, whirlpool, horseshoes, basketball and volleyball courts, tennis pro shop, rodeo arena, nature trails. There is also a Desert Interpretive Center where guests can learn more about the region. There are also plans to add a second pool (with lap lanes) and a whirlpool with a waterfall.

**White Stallion Ranch.** 9251 W. Twin Peaks Rd., Tucson, AZ 85743. ☎ **888/977-2624** or 520/297-0252. Fax 520/744-2786. 20 rms, 10 suites. Oct 1–Dec 15 $212–$236 double, $254–$282 suite; Dec 16–May 31 $234–$274 double, $296–$334 suite. Rates include all meals. Weekly rates available. Four-night minimum stay in winter. No credit cards. Closed June–Sept.

Set on 3,000 acres of desert just over the hill from Tucson, the White Stallion Ranch is perfect for those who crave wide-open spaces. Operated for more than 30 years by the True family, this spread has a more authentic ranch feel than any other guest ranch in the area. Two fast rides and two slow rides are offered daily, and a petting zoo keeps kids entertained. The guest rooms vary considerably in size and comfort from the tiny, Spartan single rooms to suites with beamed ceilings, ceiling fans, modern bathrooms, and patios.

**Dining/Entertainment:** All meals, mostly traditional and familiar American fare, are served family style in the main dining room, which is housed in a 90-year-old building. There's also an honor bar with cowhide stools and a longhorn steer head on the wall.

**Services:** Airport pickup, hayrides, guided nature walks and hikes, car-rental desk; tours available at additional charge.

**Facilities:** Outdoor pool, indoor hot tub, two tennis courts, basketball and volleyball courts, nature trails, rental bikes, games room.

# 4 Dining

A few years back, Tucson's mayor declared the city the Mexican restaurant capital of the universe. Though Mexico City might want to contest that claim, it isn't far off the mark. There's historic Mexican at El Charro Cafe, nouveau Mexican at Café Poca Cosa, Mexico City Mexican at La Parilla Suiza, family-style Mexican at Casa Molina, and upscale Mexican at La Placita Cafe. If you like Mexican food, you'll be in heaven; if you don't, there are dozens of other restaurants serving everything from the finest French cuisine to innovative American to Italian to Southwestern.

Be sure to take one of your first meals here in a Southwestern restaurant. This cuisine can be brilliantly creative, and after trying it you may want *all* your meals to be Southwestern style. Keep in mind, however, that Southwestern cuisine tends to be a bit pricey. If you're in town during the summer, be on the lookout for early-bird dinners and summer sampler plates such as those served at Janos.

## DOWNTOWN & THE UNIVERSITY AREA
### EXPENSIVE

✪ **Arizona Inn.** 2200 E. Elm St. ☎ **520/325-1541.** Reservations recommended. Main courses $5–$11 at lunch; $18–$24 at dinner. AE, MC, V. Mon–Sat 7–10am, 11:30am–2pm, and 6–10pm; Sun 7–10am, 11am–2pm (brunch), and 6–10pm. SOUTHWESTERN.

Opened in 1930, the Arizona Inn is one of the state's first resorts, and the dining room has established itself as a consistently excellent restaurant with reasonable prices. The rose-pink stucco pueblo-style buildings of the resort are surrounded by neatly manicured gardens that have aged gracefully, and it's a treat to dine on the terrace overlooking the garden and croquet lawn. The menu is not extensive, but every dish, such as mesquite-smoked quail with candied chile pecans and apple dressing, is perfectly prepared. Flavors are predominantly Southwestern, with hints of Continental. The fixed-price dinner, which changes daily, is a good value at $21. A live guitarist entertains in the dining room Friday and Saturday year-round, but if you're in the mood for a lighter meal, the bar patio is open until midnight. Lunches tend toward a wide variety of salads and sandwiches.

✪ **Janos.** 150 N. Main St. ☎ **520/884-9426.** Reservations highly recommended. Main courses $22–$32; 5-course tasting menu $55 ($85 with wines); summer sampler $13–$15. AE, DC, MC, V. Winter Mon–Sat 5:30–9pm; summer Tues–Sat 5:30–9pm (closes earlier or later than 9pm, depending on bookings). SOUTHWESTERN/REGIONAL.

Across the courtyard from the Tucson Museum of Art, and located in one of El Presidio Historic District's beautifully restored old adobe homes, is one of Tucson's best restaurants. Janos owes its popularity as much to its setting as to its stellar cuisine. This is a spot for the well-heeled to dine before attending the theater or to celebrate a special occasion, and is at once traditional and contemporary. The menu changes both daily and seasonally, and the wine list is award-winning. Chef Janos shows his enthusiasm in creating dishes such as a colorful appetizer of roasted beets, green lip mussels, orange sections, and asparagus with walnut-oil vinaigrette, and dramatically presented entrees such as tournedos of salmon and corncakes garnished with smoked salmon, and roast venison chop rubbed with chile-lime paste and pumpkin seeds and served with a wild mushroom tortilla casserole. At least one vegetarian entree with sophisticated embellishments appears on the menu nightly.

Even those on a limited budget can enjoy Janos in the summer, when an amazingly low-priced sampler menu represents one of the best values in Tucson. One last thing—Janos will be moving in the summer of 1998 to a location as yet unknown, so call to be sure of the address.

## MODERATE

**B&B Café.** 330 S. Scott Ave. ☎ **520/792-2623.** Reservations recommended. Main courses $4–$7.50 at lunch; $15 2-course prix-fixe dinner. AE, MC, V. Tues–Sat 11am–3pm. Also open for dinner on nights of Arizona Theatre Company performances, which frequently is Tues–Sun at 5:30pm or 6:30pm depending on the performance time. DANISH/INTERNATIONAL.

Located inside the Temple of Music and Art, this chic little cafe is more than just someplace to get a bite before the show. It's also a popular downtown lunch spot and a great place to just hang out over an espresso. While salads and open-face sandwiches are the specialty at lunch, dinners take the form of a two-course Danish smorgasbord, with the likes of dover sole on Swiss chard with a mustard sauce appearing recently. Personally, I like the appetizers and desserts best. In the former category, you might encounter pâté campagne or herring. In the latter category, the tiramisu is excellent.

✪ **Café Magritte.** 254 E. Congress St. ☎ **520/884-8004.** Reservations recommended for dinner. Main courses $6–$11. AE, DISC, MC, V. Tues–Thurs 11am–11pm, Fri–Sat 11am–midnight, Sun 4–11pm. INTERNATIONAL.

The Café Magritte is a cubbyhole of the surreal in a downtown neighborhood that in recent years has experienced a cultural renaissance, becoming the young, hip, and artistic part of town. Shoulder to shoulder with galleries, nightclubs, and curious boutiques, this trendy cafe serves up inexpensive, creative meals amid a thoroughly urban atmosphere, with changing works of cutting-edge art by local artists. One of the best dishes we've had here lately was the Sonoran tortellini with red-pepper cream sauce, crowned with feta cheese and roasted red peppers. You'll also find live music

# Tucson Dining

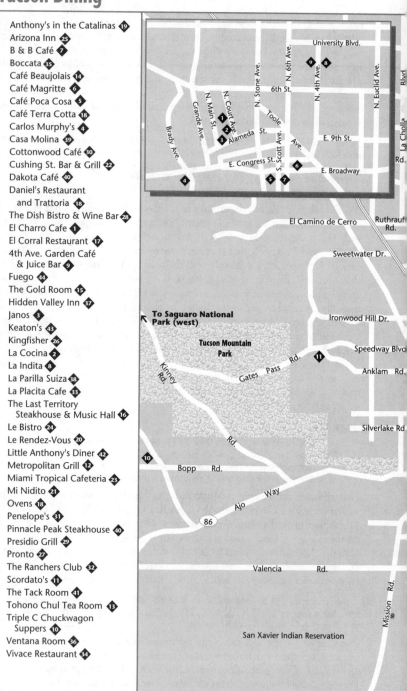

1-0029

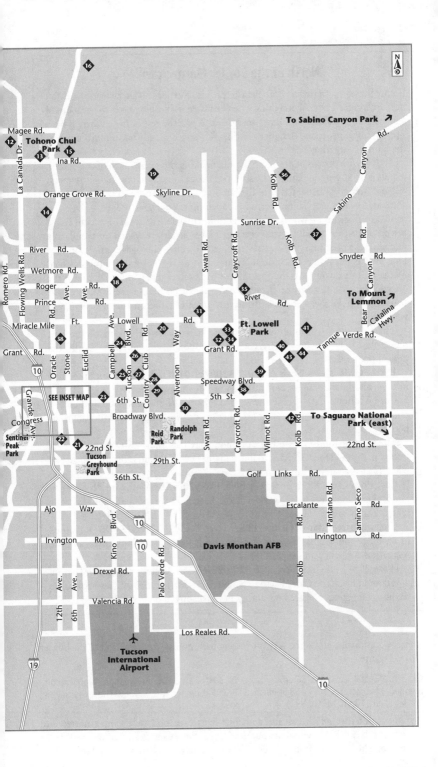

## North of the Border Margaritaville

Jimmy Buffet may have had a problem keeping his flip flops on after a few margaritas, but he certainly knew a good thing when he tasted it. Nothing takes the heat out of a hot desert day like an icy, limey margarita. While the rest of the country is busy sipping single malts and designer martinis, Tucson is quietly becoming a north of the border margaritaville.

Today, with dozens of premium tequilas making their way north of the border, tequila is no longer something to be slammed back as quickly as possible with enough salt and lime to hide the flavor of the liquor. Salt and lime are still the perfect accompaniment to tequila, but there is a much more enjoyable way to arrange this trio—as a margarita—which, with the addition of a dash of orange liqueur (Triple Sec or Cointreau), produces the perfect drink for the desert. When the tequila in a margarita is a premium *reposado* (rested or aged), 100% blue agave tequila, and the lime juice is fresh squeezed instead of from a bottle (or worse still, a prepackaged margarita mix), you have the makings of the perfect maragarita. Of course the question of on the rocks or frozen is a matter of personal taste; we prefer our margaritas on the rocks. It allows the flavors to better express themselves. And, yes, with salt.

The following are some restaurants and bars that we think make the best margaritas in Tucson and where you, too, can ponder the question, "Is this the perfect margarita?"

**Barrio Grill,** 135 S. Sixth Ave. (☎ 520/629-0191). Best selection of tequilas in town and limey/orangey margaritas. A real downtown scene.

**Casa Molina,** 6225 E. Speedway Blvd. (☎ 520/886-5468). Long the most popular margaritas in Tucson, strong. They go well with the cheap Mexican meals here. No pretension.

**The Cottonwood Cafe,** 60 N. Alvernon Way (☎ 520/326-6000). Big selection of premium tequilas, rich and limey margaritas. Cool building, great patio, so what if it has a bit of a suburban feel.

**Café Poca Cosa,** 88 E. Broadway Blvd. (☎ 520/622-6400). Great food, great atmosphere, and you never wonder if the bartender forgot the tequila in your margarita.

**Cushing Street Bar & Grill,** 343 S. Meyer Ave. (☎ 520/622-7984). Housed in a vintage adobe building, this place positively oozes old Tucson style, and the margaritas come in pint glasses.

**¡Toma!,** 311 N. Court Ave. (☎ 520/622-1922). Another downtown favorite next door to El Charro Cafe, Tucson's famous *carne seca* restaurant. These margaritas are just plain good, and are best during Friday happy hour.

here occasionally, and some very interesting bathrooms—a surreal doff of the bowler to Magritte.

✪ **Café Poca Cosa.** 88 E. Broadway Blvd. ☎ **520/622-6400.** Reservations highly recommended. Main courses $6.50–$8 at lunch, $11–$15 at dinner. MC, V. Mon–Thurs 11am–9pm, Fri–Sat 11am–10pm. MEXICAN.

This is not just *any* Mexican food, but Mexican food that's imaginative and different, created by owner-chef Suzana Davila. Poca Cosa is located on the ground floor of a downtown hotel, where it's a surprise to find this atmosphere of rich red-and-purple walls and Mexican/Southwestern artwork. The cuisine here—which has been compared to the dishes dreamed up in *Like Water for Chocolate*—consists of creations such as beef marinated in tequila and then grilled, and chicken with a green mole (pronounced *MOLE-ay)* sauce made with pistachios. The menu changes daily—you never know what the offerings will be, but there is always something wonderful to try, accompanied by tasty rice and beans. The service staff is courteous and friendly and will recite the menu for you in both Spanish and English.

There's another (smaller) Café Poca Cosa downtown at 20 S. Scott St., open for breakfast and lunch Monday through Friday from 7:30am to 2pm.

**Carlos Murphy's.** 419 W. Congress St. ☎ **520/628-1958.** Main courses $6–$15. AE, DISC, MC, V. Sun–Thurs 11am–10pm, Fri–Sat 11am–11pm. BAJA MEXICAN.

If you think you made a wrong turn and ended up at the train station instead of Carlos Murphy's, you're right—and you're wrong. It is, make that *was,* the train station, but now it's a cavernous Mexican restaurant with a sense of humor, which kids will certainly appreciate. To the left inside the restaurant is Carlos's sports bar, and the walls everywhere are covered with old posters and photographs. Folks come here to fill up on red-hot chicken wings with blue-cheese dressing, or sizzling fajitas made with sirloin, chicken, shark, shrimp, or veggies. Sunday through Thursday, a child accompanied by an adult who purchases a meal can get a meal from the children's menu and pay just a penny for each pound of the child's weight.

✪ **The Dish Bistro & Wine Bar.** 3200 E. Speedway Blvd. (at the Rumrunner). ☎ **520/326-1714.** Reservations highly recommended and accepted Tues–Sat after 3pm. Main courses $14–$19, smaller dishes $6–$13. AE, MC, V. Tues–Sat 5–10pm. NEW AMERICAN.

Located in the rear of The Rumrunner Wine and Cheese Co. (and also part of the same operation), this tiny, minimalist restaurant is brimming with urban chic. On a busy night, the space could be construed as either cozy or crowded, so if you like it more on the quiet side, come early. The chef has a well-deserved reputation for daring, and turns out such dishes as smoked salmon cakes with corn, sweet peppers, and thyme aioli; colorful and well-composed salads; and Italian-influenced pasta dishes such as lemon-pepper linguine with scallops, shrimp, and green beans in a vanilla-seafood broth, topped with fried tomatoes. Naturally, the wine list is also great, and the servers, who are well-informed about the menus, will be happy to help you choose a bottle. We like the ice cream sandwich for dessert, made with the homemade ice cream of the day.

✪ **El Charro Cafe.** 311 N. Court Ave. ☎ **520/622-1922.** Reservations recommended for dinner. Main courses $5.50–$16. AE, DISC, MC, V. Mon–Thurs 11:30am–3pm and 5–9pm, Fri 11am–3pm and 5–10pm, Sat noon–10pm, Sun noon–9pm. SONORAN MEXICAN.

El Charro, located in an old stone building in El Presidio Historic District, claims to be Tucson's oldest family-operated Mexican restaurant. A front porch has been glassed in for a greenhouselike dining area overlooking the street, and there's also dining downstairs. Look at the roof of El Charro as you approach, and you might see a large metal cage containing beef drying in the sun. This is the main ingredient in *carne seca,* El Charro's well-known specialty (like beef jerky), which is oft copied but never duplicated at other Mexican restaurants around town. You'll rarely find carne seca on a Mexican menu outside Tucson, so indulge in it while you're here. *A warning:* The cafe can be packed at lunch, so arrive early or late.

Other El Charro Cafe branches can be found in the Tucson International Airport (☎ **520/573-8222**) and at 6310 E. Broadway (☎ **520/745-1922**). The family also runs the adjacent ¡Toma!, a colorful bar/cantina next door.

**Kingfisher.** 2564 E. Grant Rd. ☎ **520/323-7739.** Reservations recommended on weekends. Main courses $6.50–$11 at lunch, $15–$19 at dinner. AE, CB, DISC, MC, V. Mon–Fri 11am–midnight, Sat–Sun 5pm–midnight. SEAFOOD.

If you're serious about seafood, head for the Kingfisher. It's upscale and a bit noisy with strains of jazz, its dark walls hung with colorful pieces of contemporary art. But you don't come here to look at the art; you come here to enjoy a wide selection of appetizers, sandwiches, and main dishes that use the freshest seafood, artfully accented with other imaginative ingredients. You may have difficulty deciding whether to begin with Umpqua Bay oysters (there's a full-service raw bar), bay scallop ceviche, or the delicately smoked red trout—so why not tackle them all? Fans of Southern seafood will appreciate the cornmeal-crusted catfish, which comes with hush puppies, and pan-fried soft shell crabs, which rarely makes it onto menus west of the Mississippi. Meat eaters as well as vegetarians will find items on the menu.

**La Cocina.** 186 N. Meyer Ave. (downtown at Old Town Artisans). ☎ **520/622-0351.** Reservations recommended for dinner. Main courses $7–$9 at lunch, $9–$16 at dinner. AE, DISC, MC, V. Daily 11am–3pm; Thurs–Sat 5–9:30pm. SOUTHWESTERN.

This is a great place for a patio lunch or dinner under the trees in historic Old Town, surrounded by beautiful gardens with lots of flowers (you will be competing with other tourists for a table). There's lots of shopping opportunities as well in the surrounding Old Town Artisans complex. Lunch offerings include sandwiches and salads, and for dinner you can start out with black-bean chili with mesquite beef or gazpacho, then move on to an entree of grilled halibut or filet mignon.

**Le Bistro.** 2574 N. Campbell Ave. ☎ **520/327-3086.** Reservations recommended for dinner. Main courses $5–$8 at lunch, $8–$17 at dinner. AE, DISC, MC, V. Mon–Fri 11am–2:30pm and 5–10pm, Sat–Sun 5–10pm. FRENCH/EUROPEAN.

Etched mirrors, lace, and live trees full of twinkling lights set the scene for some casual bistro cuisine. European specialties include the likes of duck pâté, roast quail, and bouillabaisse. I like the blackened sea scallops, myself. Salads here are quite good, there are dozens of choices for wine, and prices across the board are reasonable. On the extravagant side is the showcase of desserts, with names such as Tuxedo (a double-chocolate mousse), Opera (a creation with hazelnut and mocha crème), and Bombe (a chocolate-covered mountain of cream puffs) which frequently stops passersby dead in their tracks. We've come here to sit in the bar for a glass of wine and to share one of these rich, decadent desserts.

**Presidio Grill.** 3352 E. Speedway Blvd. ☎ **520/327-4667.** Reservations recommended. Main courses $6.50–$10 at lunch, $9–$18 at dinner. AE, MC, V. Mon–Thurs 11am–10pm, Fri–Sat 11am–midnight, Sun 10am–10pm. Late-night menu Sun–Thurs 10pm–midnight. AMERICAN REGIONAL.

This ever-trendy restaurant, modern in both cuisine and interior design, is located in Rancho Center, along busy Speedway Boulevard. Whether you want pizza, pasta, or something from the grill, the dishes here show a variety of international influences. One of my favorite salads is the one with wilted greens, smoked chicken, fried shallots, tortilla strips, and Thai lime vinaigrette dressing. Sunday breakfast is served from 10am to 1pm, when you can choose from the long menu which includes many breakfast items. Lunchtime during the week the restaurant is usually packed, so make a reservation if possible. A good selection of wines and liquors can be found here.

## INEXPENSIVE

**Cushing Street Bar & Grill.** 343 S. Meyer Ave. at Cushing St. (across from the Tucson Convention Center). ☎ **520/622-7984.** Reservations recommended. Main courses $7–$12. AE, DISC, MC, V. Daily 11am–midnight (bar open until 1am). NEW AMERICAN.

A renovation has restored this historic adobe building located at the edge of the old Barrio neighborhood. Formerly a bar, it's more of a restaurant now, with saltillo tile floors, adobe walls, old-fashioned wooden chairs, and other antique touches. A patio in the courtyard is classically stark and a private place to have lunch. We like the spicy and flavorful blackened scallops and Gorgonzola cheese or blackened tuna. Unbattered Poblano chiles stuffed with chorizo sausage in a red-pepper sauce were flavorful and visually rich. An assortment of burgers, sandwiches, pastas, and a late-night menu provide plenty of other choices along the same vein. But I'd save room for a cocktail like the big 1-pint margaritas or the homemade chocolate desserts, which are reason enough to come here. This place is popular with retirees as well as a 30-to-40-year-old crowd—maybe it's the swing and jazz music. Parking is available on site.

**La Indita.** 622 N. Fourth Ave. ☎ 520/792-0523. Main courses $4–$7. DISC, MC, V. Mon–Fri 11am–9pm, Sat–Sun 6–9pm. REGIONAL MEXICAN.

It's just a little family-run business serving Tohono-Tarascan Mexican-style food, but the home cooking here is cheap and authentic. House and daily specials such as chiles rellenos, chicken mole, and chicken enchiladas with green sauce are all popular. There are also plenty of vegetarian dishes such as spinach-and-nut enchiladas and mushroom tacos.

**Miami Tropical Cafeteria.** 1045 E. Sixth St. ☎ 520/623-8020. Main courses $3–$5. No credit cards. Mon–Sat 11am–9pm. CUBAN.

The Miami Tropical sits on a hot treeless street but is an oasis for Cuban cuisine, and, with just a few tables in a storefront near the University of Arizona, it really does seem like a Cuban restaurant straight out of Miami. The cheerful proprietor will dish you up a daily special from the steam table, a heaping dish of chicken seasoned with olives, garlic, and bay leaves, or pork with achiote and onions, accompanied by black beans and rice. The Cuban sandwich is a meat- and cheese-filled baguette, pressed and warmed on the grill. We tried an exotic juice that we couldn't quite identify, but equally delicious if not more familiar drinks such as *tamarindo* and fruit shakes of mango, papaya, and *guanabana* can be had.

**Pronto.** 2955 E. Speedway Blvd. ☎ 520/326-9707. Soups, salads, and sandwiches $2.50–$6. MC, V. Mon–Thurs 11am–9pm, Fri–Sat 11am–10pm, Sun 4–9pm. INTERNATIONAL.

This restaurant is a good example of what can be done to recycle a fast-food establishment. It still retains the walk-up counter, but now boasts an international menu and hip decor. Come here if you want your food fast, good, and cheap. You can get not only burgers and lots of other sandwiches, but favorites such as vegetarian lasagne, pizza, chicken satay, and penne with chicken and Gorgonzola cream sauce. There's also a kids' menu with items like macaroni and cheese for $1.50.

# EAST TUCSON
## EXPENSIVE

✪ **Le Rendez-Vous.** 3844 E. Fort Lowell Rd. (at Alvernon Way). ☎ 520/323-7373. Reservations highly recommended. Main courses $8–$11 at lunch, $15–$26 at dinner. AE, DC, DISC, MC, V. Tues–Fri 11:30am–2pm; Tues–Sun 6–10pm. FRENCH.

Le Rendez-Vous has become legendary among Tucson's foodies for its phenomenal duck à l'orange. Consequently, patrons are almost exclusively locals who return again and again for the duck, mussels cooked in white wine, and the ultimate spinach salad. If it's hot out, cool off with a bowl of creamy vichyssoise. If you're inclined to expand your own culinary horizons, you won't go wrong with the veal sweetbreads with Dijon mushrooms. You might expect such rich and savory fare to be served amid rarefied elegance, but instead Le Rendez-Vous is housed in an unpretentious little stucco cottage. The waiters are dressed in black tie, but aside from this little concession, the atmosphere is strictly bistro. When the pastry cart comes around, try one of the tempting, airy desserts.

**Penelope's.** 3071 N. Swan Rd. ☎ **520/325-5080.** Reservations recommended. Main courses $7–$10 at lunch, $13–$22 at dinner; 6-course fixed-price dinner $29.50 without wine, $42.50 with wine. MC, V. Tues–Fri 11:30am–2pm; Tues–Sun 5:30–8pm. FRENCH.

Penelope's, located in a converted 1910 house with a small garden and country French decor, is a favorite place with the older Tucson set. On our last visit, dinner began with a half dozen escargots followed by a choice of chilled cucumber or onion soup. There was a choice of four dishes including scallops with white wine, herbs, and shallots, and filet mignon with a red wine sauce. This was followed by salad and cheese courses, and then a choice from an assortment of pastries and other desserts. For those who want to include wine with their meal, there are appropriately chosen selections for each course and each dish. If you can't afford dinner, stop by for lunch.

**The Ranchers Club.** In the Hotel Park Tucson, 5151 E. Grant Rd. ☎ **520/321-7621.** Reservations recommended. Main courses $8–$17 at lunch, $17–$64 at dinner. AE, CB, DC, MC, V. Mon–Fri 11:30am–2pm; Mon–Sat 5:30–10pm. STEAK/SEAFOOD.

There's no question as to where to get the best steak in Tucson—The Ranchers Club. But before you saddle up the palomino and trot over, be sure you're prepared for the hefty tab. And if you're offended by stuffed animal heads, you might want to pass it by as well. The Ranchers Club glorifies the Old West with its decor of old saddles, chaps, and steer horns, while antiques and brocade chairs lend the dining room a touch of elegance.

Hefty aged prime beef is grilled over aromatic mesquite, hickory, sassafras, and cherrywood fires, adding subtle flavors to the meats. About 20 sauces and condiments, such as horseradish cream, wild mushroom sauce, and red-pepper chutney, are offered to complement the meat. Seafood is also offered, grilled over the special woods, which lend it extra flavor.

## MODERATE

✪ **Cottonwood Café.** 60 N. Alvernon Way. ☎ **520/326-6000.** Reservations recommended especially for weekends. Main courses $6–$9 at lunch, $11–$19 at dinner. AE, DC, DISC, MC, V. Mon–Thurs 11:30am–2:30pm and 5:30–11pm, Fri–Sat 11:30am–2:30pm and 5:30–12pm, Sun 11:15am–2:30pm (brunch) and 5:30–11pm. SOUTHWESTERN.

Very bold flavors here attract all types and ages, making this one of Tucson's most popular new Southwestern restaurants. It's big, with a lush and relaxing ambience created by fawn-colored walls, purple accents and soft dramatic lighting. We tried the Zuni roll, with smoked turkey, scallions, havarti cheese, and boar bacon in a flour tortilla with raspberry chipotle sauce, which was complex and delicious, and chicken diablo, sort of a very spicy chicken fajita with a smoky jalepeño flavor. Fish, in the form of Sonoran seafood paella and grilled shrimp, are done well. Portions are generous and wine prices moderate. A large selection of tequilas, especially blue agave tequilas, make this a good place to try a margarita, perhaps on the palm-shaded patio. A late-night menu goes until about 11pm earlier in the week and until about midnight later in the week.

**Dakota Café.** 6541 E. Tanque Verde Rd. (at Traildust Town near the Pinnacle Peak Steakhouse). ☎ **520/298-7188.** Reservations recommended on weekends, especially for the patio. Main courses $6–$9 at lunch, $8–$17 at dinner. AE, MC, V. Mon–Thurs 11am–9pm, Fri–Sat 11am–10pm. INTERNATIONAL.

A bold paint job and halogen lighting are an unexpected surprise at this mock cow town location. The decor and creative dishes have been luring a more sophisticated crowd to what was once strictly a family-outing spot. We started our meal with fruity apricot iced tea (very refreshing on a hot day) and tempura coconut shrimp with chutney marmalade. The grilled Ahi tuna sandwich with herbed aioli and pickled ginger was tasty and well textured, and came with a generous side of pasta salad. I can also recommend the chicken Caesar salad. The food here is hearty yet inventive enough to try on a regular basis, and vegetarians will find many non-meat choices on the menu. Prices are reasonable, and the comfortable atmosphere adds even greater value.

**Fuego.** 6958 E. Tanque Verde Rd. ☎ **520/886-1745.** Reservations recommended. Main courses $12–$22. AE, MC, V. Daily 5–10pm, late menu Fri–Sat 10–11pm, brunch Sun Oct–May 11am–2pm. NEW AMERICAN/SOUTHWEST.

The name of the game here is Sunday brunch. Although the menu is tempting at dinner (and don't get me wrong, dinnertime is also a fine time to be here), it doesn't have the visual impact of a panoramic buffet that includes fresh berries and fruits; salads; cheeses; chilled shrimp and oysters; hot entrees of ancho chile lamb, seared salmon, and enchiladas; chocolate-dipped strawberries; and myriad cakes and tarts, all for a reasonable price of about $17 (children $9). The restaurant is small and pleasantly decorated with earth tones. Other possible selections at dinner include contemporary Southwest preparations of seafood, veal, ostrich, pasta, and a limited selection of vegetarian dishes, along with a wine list that includes many regional wines.

**Keaton's.** 6464 E. Tanque Verde Rd. ☎ **520/721-1299.** Reservations recommended on weekends. Main courses $7.50–$19. AE, DISC, MC, V. Sun–Thurs 11am–10pm, Fri–Sat 11am–10:30pm. NOUVELLE AMERICAN.

Both the crunchy sourdough and zucchini breads here are so good, I nearly forgot to save room for my meal. But fortunately I still had the appetite for my mesquite-grilled salmon with cucumber-yogurt relish. Several salmon dishes are featured on the nightly specials menu, but various cuts of beef, barbecued pork ribs, and pasta dishes are also done well, as is the Cajun chicken Caesar salad tossed with a classic, well-balanced dressing. The restaurant is fairly roomy and sophisticated, and the lighting and booths are cozy, a comfortable spot for conversation with friends. A summertime early-bird menu, served Monday through Thursday from 3 to 6pm, is a very good deal. Keaton's is also responsible for the delicious food served at the restaurants at the Arizona–Sonora Desert Museum.

Another Keaton's is at 7401 N. La Cholla Blvd. (☎ **520/297-1999**).

**✪ Vivace Restaurant.** 4811 E. Grant Rd. ☎ **520/795-7221.** Reservations recommended. Main courses $10–$19. DC, MC, V. Mon–Thurs 11:30am–9pm, Fri–Sat 11:30am–10pm, Sun 5–9pm. NORTHERN ITALIAN.

Run by the same folks who gave Tucson Scordato's restaurant, this Italian restaurant serves reasonably priced creative dishes in a casual but upscale setting in a shopping plaza. The restaurant can be noisy at times, owing to its popularity—the crowd is mixed, both young and old. First, crusty bread comes with a basil-infused olive oil. Then, one of the possible appetizers is a large luscious antipasto platter for two containing garlicked spinach, mequite-grilled asparagus, *caponata* (eggplant relish), ham, and goat cheese. The dish was visually appealing and tasted as good as it looked. The bustling wait staff doesn't waste time in getting your order from the open kitchen to you. Pasta dishes, such as penne with sausage and roasted pepper sauce, come served on a very large dish. Salads are generous, the wine list is good and reasonable, and the waitperson will recite a long litany of desserts: mango sorbet, crème brûlée, and the lightest ever flourless chocolate cake.

## INEXPENSIVE

**Casa Molina.** 6225 E. Speedway Blvd. (near the northwest corner with Wilmot Rd.). ☎ **520/ 886-5468.** Reservations recommended. Dinners $11–$17. AE, DC, DISC, MC, V. Daily 11am– 10pm. MEXICAN.

For years this has been Tucson's favorite family-run Mexican restaurant. You can't miss it—just watch for the larger-than-life-size bull and bullfighter in front. Casa Molina sports a festive atmosphere, and is usually abuzz with families, groups, and couples. The margaritas are some of the best in town, and the carne seca (sun-dried beef) shouldn't be missed. Lighter eaters will enjoy a layered topopo salad made with tortillas, refried beans, chicken, lettuce, celery, avocado, tomato, and jalapeños. The food is good and the service is efficient; the only complaint here is that prices are a little on the high side for Mexican cookery. The patio is pleasant in almost any weather.

Other locations include 3001 N. Campbell Ave. (☎ **520/795-7593**) and 4240 E. Grant Rd. (☎ **520/326-6663**).

**La Parilla Suiza.** 5602 E. Speedway Blvd. ☎ **520/747-4838.** Main courses $6–$13. AE, DISC, MC, V. Sun–Thurs 11am–10pm, Fri–Sat 11am–11pm. MEXICAN.

Most Mexican food served in the United States is limited to Sonoran style, originating just south of the border. However, the cuisine of Mexico is nearly as varied as that of China, and the meals served at La Parilla Suiza are based on the style popular in Mexico City, where most of the chain's restaurants are located. This is why I like this place so much—eating here is like eating at a restaurant in Mexico. Many menu items are sandwiched between two flour tortillas, much like a quesadilla, but the charcoal broiling of meats and cheeses lends the sandwiches special status. Fried green scallions with lime is a favorite appetizer.

There's another La Parilla Suiza at 2720 N. Oracle Rd. (☎ **520/624-4300**).

**Little Anthony's Diner.** 7010 E. Broadway Blvd. (in back of the Broadway Shopping Plaza). ☎ **520/296-0456.** Burgers and sandwiches $4–$5.50. MC, V. Mon–Thurs 11am–10pm, Fri 11am–11pm, Sat 8am–11pm, Sun 8am–10pm. AMERICAN.

This is a place for kids, although big kids like us also enjoy the 1950s music and decor. The staff is good with children, and there's a video-games room and a rocket ship outside to ride. How about a jailhouse rock burger or hound dog hot dog with a tower of onion rings? Daily specials and bottomless soft drinks make feeding the family fairly inexpensive. Beer and wine are also served, and Wednesday through Saturday after 5pm there's a DJ along with the dinner. The gaslight melodrama theater next door makes a perfect night out for the family.

## THE FOOTHILLS
### EXPENSIVE

**Anthony's in the Catalinas.** 6440 N. Campbell Ave. ☎ **520/299-1771.** Reservations highly recommended. Main courses $8–$13 at lunch, $18–$30 at dinner. AE, DC, MC, V. Mon–Fri 11:30am–2:30pm and 5:30–10pm, Sat–Sun 5:30–10pm. SOUTHWESTERN/CONTINENTAL.

If you head north on Campbell Avenue up into the foothills of the Catalinas, you'll reach a modern hacienda-style building overlooking the city. Anthony's exudes Southwestern elegance from the moment you drive under the portico and let the valet park your car. The waiters are smartly attired in tuxedos and the guests are almost as well dressed. Quiet classical music plays in the background, and the lights of the city below twinkle through the window of the main dining room. In such a rarefied atmosphere you'd expect only the finest meal, and that's what you get. Grilled quail and mesquite-smoked duck breast is a fitting beginning, followed by lamb Wellington, baked in puff pastry with pâté and prosciutto. At 72 pages, the wine list may be the most extensive in the city. The pastry cart may tempt you, but, if it's available, don't miss out on the best part of a meal: the day's soufflé (order early).

**Boccata.** In River Center, 5605 E. River Rd. ☎ **520/577-9309.** Reservations recommended. Main courses $12–$23. AE, MC, V. Sun–Thurs 5:30–9pm, Fri–Sat 5–10pm. INTERNATIONAL/ NEW AMERICAN.

You'll find this casually elegant restaurant at the back of the River Center complex in the foothills. Large windows frame the panoramic view of Tucson in the valley below, while marble floors, rich colors, and works of contemporary art add the finishing touches. The menu changes seasonally, and a recent menu included such temptations as crayfish cakes made with just a hint of creole fire; honey- and saffron-glazed pork tenderloin with savory bread pudding; and penne ciao bella, made with grilled chicken, artichoke hearts, pine nuts, roasted peppers, and a cream sauce of white wine, shallots, carrots, Gorgonzola, and chives. Save room for dessert. The profiteroles au chocolat—cream puffs filled with vanilla ice cream and topped with chocolate sauce and whipped cream—are absolutely heavenly.

**✪ Daniel's Restaurant & Trattoria.** In St. Philip's Plaza, 4340 N. Campbell Ave. ☎ **520/ 742-3200.** Reservations recommended. Main courses $17–$27. AE, DC, MC, V. Daily 5–10pm. NORTHERN ITALIAN.

The elegant, art deco atmosphere here translates into a good place for business meetings or a romantic setting for an evening out (you might want to dress up a bit). But what stands out most is the contemporary northern Italian cuisine, which varies from simple to complex preparations. Service is attentive but non-intrusive—a basket of bread that appears as soon as you're seated includes fresh baked focaccia and breadsticks with herb-flavored olive oil. For an appetizer, we recommend the intriguing flavors of salmon gravlox layered with cream cheese and shaved sweet potato, garnished with capers and red onion. No less extravagant, a seafood risotto is accented with lemon and dill, and a fennel garlic wine sauce. The pastry chef has a creative flair with chocolate, so save room for the warm chocolate truffle cake and vanilla-bean gelato. An outstanding wine list contains about 200 selections (Italian wines are emphasized), with about 30 wines by the glass—and there's a satisfying number in the lower price ranges. A single-malt scotch list offers many choices.

**The Gold Room.** In the Westward Look Resort, 245 E. Ina Rd. ☎ **520/297-1151.** Reservations recommended. Main courses $9–$16 at lunch, $16–$29 at dinner. AE, DC, DISC, MC, V. Mon–Sat 7–10:30am, 10:30am–2:30pm, and 5:30–10pm; Sun 7–10:30am, 10:30am–2pm (jazz buffet brunch), and 5:30–10pm. SOUTHWESTERN.

For more than 20 years the Gold Room has been one of the best hotel dining rooms in Tucson. Located in the Westward Look Resort, which opened in 1929 as a dude ranch, the Gold Room is a tastefully casual restaurant featuring Southwestern ranch decor that includes stucco walls, viga beams in the ceiling, and large comfortable booths. There are views of the city through two walls of glass and a terrace for alfresco dining. Despite the casual decor, the place settings are elegant and the service is very professional. There's a distinct seafood slant to the hors d'oeuvres list, including crab cakes, salmon, and oysters in various guises. Although it's possible to order classics such as filet mignon and roast rack of lamb, our personal favorite on a recent visit was the grilled buffalo medaillons with blackberry zinfandel espresso bean sauce. Lunch prices are less expensive, but the restaurant is most remarkable at night when the cityscape of Tucson twinkles below.

**✪ The Tack Room.** 2800 N. Sabino Canyon Rd. ☎ **520/722-2800.** Reservations recommended. Main courses $25–$35. AE, CB, DC, DISC, JCB, MC, V. May to mid-Jan Tues–Sun 6– 10pm; mid-Jan to Apr daily 6–10pm. SOUTHWESTERN/AMERICAN.

The Tack Room is the city's most prestigious restaurant, housed in an older Southwestern-style hacienda with an atmosphere of casual elegance in which a bevy of tuxedoed waiters attends to your every need. The longtime staff have had the opportunity to hone their professional service to a high art, and made us feel pampered. From the time we sat down to the little bites of marinated salads that appeared on the table to the moment the last bit of chocolate was savored from the bottom of our crème brûlée, the service was attentive and discreet. We could recite a list of all the tastes we experienced, but will recall just a few, in the plump guaymas shrimp subtly seasoned with orange and cilantro, salmon with papaya salsa perfectly grilled (crusty on top and moist on the inside), and crispy yet succulent duck, topped with pistachios and sitting on a pile of not-too-sweet fig-and-orange chutney. Coffee came with a condiment tray that included whipped cream and crumbled Belgian chocolate. Of course, you'll pay for all this, but this dining experience leaves you truly satisfied.

✪ **Ventana Room.** In Loews Ventana Canyon Resort, 7000 N. Resort Dr. ☎ **520/299-2020.** Reservations highly recommended. Jacket requested for men. Main courses $18–$36; chef's 5-course tasting menu $55 without wine, $75 with wine. AE, CB, DC, MC, V. Sun–Thurs 6–9pm, Fri–Sat 6–10pm. NOUVELLE AMERICAN.

With the spectacular setting and waterfall at the head of Ventana Canyon, it would be worth eating at the Ventana Room even if the food weren't so good. *Ventana* means "window" in Spanish, and the views are emphasized here, whether of the canyon waterfall or the twinkling lights of the city in the valley far below. The ethereal strains of a harp set the mood.

The menu, which changes daily, is not long, but its memorable quality compensates. Venison, lamb, veal, and quail make regular appearances; on our last visit, grilled venison with dried cherry-barley "risotto" and cabernet wine sauce was especially appealing. With such creations as prickly pear Charlotte, an elegant layered mousse, you might not want to let the dessert cart pass you by.

## MODERATE

**Café Terra Cotta.** In St. Philip's Plaza, 4310 N. Campbell Ave. (at River Rd.). ☎ **520/577-8100.** Reservations recommended. Main courses $11–$22. AE, DC, DISC, MC, V. Sun–Thurs 11am–10pm, Fri–Sat 11am–11pm. Closes a half-hour earlier in summer. SOUTHWESTERN.

Located in the upscale St. Philip's Plaza shopping center, Café Terra Cotta is one of Tucson's most highly acclaimed restaurants, and although the food usually is good, we have found it uneven at times. A casual atmosphere and creative Southwestern cooking is a combination that appeals to trendy Tucsonians, who stop by for dinner at the restaurant or to pick up gourmet food to go. A large brick oven is used to make imaginative pizzas. How about a pie with rosemary grilled chicken, feta cheese, black olives, crushed chiles, and roasted garlic? With salads, small plates, and main dishes as well, it's often very difficult to make a choice, but we can recommend the grilled eggplant and portabello sandwich with red bell peppers, basil, and goat cheese on focaccia. For dessert, I like Divine Madness with espresso ice cream.

**La Placita Cafe.** In the Plaza Palomino, 2950 N. Swan Rd. ☎ **520/881-1150.** Reservations recommended on weekends. Main courses $6–$15. AE, DISC, MC, V. Mon–Sat 11:30am–2:30pm and 5–9:30pm, Sun 5–9:30pm. MEXICAN.

The Plaza Palomino is an upscale, modern shopping center in northern Tucson, and La Placita is a rather upscale Mexican restaurant. The decor is pastel with a few Mexican crafts on display, not your usual garish Mexican hacienda design. The

## 👪 Family-Friendly Restaurants

**Pinnacle Peak Steakhouse** *(see p. 343)*   Dinner here is a Wild West event, with an entire Western town outside and a carousel. Kids love it.

**Carlos Murphy's** *(see p. 333)*   Situated in Tucson's former train station, this trendy Mexican place has walls that are covered with old posters and photographs. Sunday through Thursday, a child accompanied by an adult who purchases a meal can get a meal from the children's menu and pay just a penny per pound of the child's weight

**Hidden Valley Inn** *(see p. 342)*   It's a false-fronted cowtown in bright colors with an authentic dance hall and stable which are the dining rooms. Kids will love the miniature action dioramas of funny Western scenes.

**Little Anthony's Diner** *(see p. 338)*   This is a place for kids, although big kids like us also enjoy the 1950s music and decor. The staff is good with children, and there's a video-games room and a rocket ship outside to ride. The gaslight melodrama theater next door makes a perfect night out for the family.

varied menu includes not only dishes from around Mexico, but also some gringo fare. There are all the usual tacos, enchiladas, burritos, tostadas, and tamales, but you'd do well to try one of the special dinners. Mole Oaxaqueño is my favorite. It's served in a spicy chocolate-based sauce.

**Metropolitan Grill.** 7892 N. Oracle Rd. ☎ 520/531-1212. Reservations recommended weekends. Main courses $6–$13 at lunch, $7–$16 at dinner. AE, DC, DISC, MC, V. Sun–Thurs 11am–10pm, Fri–Sat 11am–10:30pm. NEW AMERICAN/SOUTHWESTERN.

This huge restaurant in the Plaza Escondida shopping mall attracts many types (and lots of them) from young to old. An underlying buzz of conversation fills the monstrous space, but the noise is not obnoxious. You'd want to come here either to be seen, or to get a good meal at a fairly inexpensive price, the latter of which I suspect is what attracts most of the patrons. The formula here has three elements: a woodburning oven that cranks out pizzas, mesquite-grilled seafood and meats, and spit-roasted chicken, pork, and beef. Sounds like a winning plan to me.

**Ovens.** At St. Philip's Plaza, corner of Campbell Ave. at River Rd. ☎ 520/577-9001. Reservations recommended. Main courses $8–$18. AE, DC, MC, V. Mon–Thurs 11am–9:30pm, Fri–Sat 11am–10pm, Sun 4:30–9:30pm. INTERNATIONAL.

There's just about anything you can think of on this extensive menu, from blackened Cajun meat loaf to a moo shu calzone. Don't get me wrong—I can look at a menu for a long time and get vicarious pleasure from the seemingly infinite choices, but what I finally settled on was a wood-fired pizza with a salad on top, consisting of grilled eggplant, fresh spinach, pine nuts, and a lemon-herb vinaigrette. And don't touch that herbed bread with the buttery olive oil—the servings are huge. The patio here is quite popular and fills up quickly, so if you want to get a seat outside, come early for mealtime. Wine prices tend to be on the high side.

## INEXPENSIVE

**☻ El Corral Restaurant.** 2201 E. River Rd. ☎ 520/299-6092. Reservations not accepted. Complete dinner $7–$12. AE, DC, DISC, MC, V. Mon–Fri 5–10pm, Sat–Sun 4:30–10pm. STEAKS.

Owned by the same folks who brought you Tucson's Pinnacle Peak Steakhouse, El Corral is another inexpensive steakhouse, and very popular with retirees and families. The restaurant doesn't accept reservations, so expect long lines. The hacienda building has flagstone floors and wood paneling that make it dark and cozy, while outside in the bright sunlight a cactus garden flourishes. In keeping with the name, there's a traditional corral fence of mesquite branches around the restaurant parking lot. Prime rib is the house specialty, but there are also steaks, pork ribs, chicken, and burgers for the kids.

**Tohono Chul Tea Room.** 7366 N. Paseo del Norte (1 block west of the corner of Ina and Oracle rds. in Tohono Chul Park). ☎ **520/797-1711.** Reservations not accepted. Main courses $4.50–$9. AE, MC, V. Daily 8am–5pm. SOUTHWESTERN.

Located on a 37-acre preserve in a brick territorial-style building, this restaurant makes a nice place for an outing because it's in a park landscaped with desert plants and has an adjoining gift shop. Outdoor patios surrounded by natural vegetation and plenty of flowers in pots are a place for animal and bird watching. For breakfast, there's a fritatta of the day or scrambled-egg enchiladas, or light fare such as croissants. Lunch selections include chipotle-glazed chicken breast or a grilled veggie sandwich. And there's a kids' menu. The gift shop is packed with Mexican folk art, nature theme toys, household items, T-shirts, and books. For a description of the park, see "Parks, Gardens & Zoos" under "Seeing the Sights."

## WEST TUCSON

**Scordato's.** 4405 W. Speedway Blvd. ☎ **520/792-3055.** Reservations highly recommended. Main courses $15–$21. AE, DISC, MC, V. Tues–Sat 5–9pm, Sun 4–9pm. ITALIAN.

It's a long way out to Scordato's, but that doesn't bother the loyal clientele who enjoy the setting near Saguaro National Park. The restaurant looks a bit like a lost Italian villa searching for the Mediterranean coast, with saguaros standing next to cypresses out front. Inside, plush carpets, comfortable brocade chairs, and big windows allow diners to enjoy desert views in comfort. Despite the crystal chandeliers and tapestries on the walls, you don't have to dress up for dinner here, where you'll find both families and business types. The menu contains many tempting choices, although it's difficult to move beyond the variety of veal dishes. Veal stresa is our favorite—it's stuffed with prosciutto and mozzarella and then sautéed in marsala and white-wine sauce. For an appetizer, we like the scampi sauté. The extensive wine list will satisfy the wine connoisseur.

## DINING WITH A VIEW

Virtually all the foothills resorts offer dining with a view, including the **Ventana Room** and the **Gold Room,** both discussed above. Outside the foothills resorts, there are many additional choices. **Anthony's in the Catalinas, Boccata, Scordato's,** and **The Tack Room** offer superb views of the city's twinkling lights or the jagged mountains surrounding the valley. These restaurants are all listed above.

## COWBOY STEAKHOUSES

**Hidden Valley Inn.** 4825 N. Sabino Canyon Rd. ☎ **520/299-4941.** Reservations not accepted. Main courses $6–$19. MC, V. Daily 11am–10pm. STEAK.

Kids will love this place. It's a false-fronted cowtown in bright colors. Inside, there's a very authentic dance hall and stable which are the dining rooms, and the Red Garter Saloon which is, yup, a saloon. The most amusing feature is about a dozen miniature action dioramas of funny Western scenes. This steakhouse is the kind of place where people come to celebrate a family birthday and inevitably leave with large doggie bags. Cowpuncher-size steaks and barbecued ribs are the main attraction, although there are also some seafood and chicken choices.

✪ **L'il Abner's Steakhouse.** 8500 N. Silverbell Rd. ☎ **520/744-2800.** Reservations accepted Fri–Sat. Main courses $11–$22. MC, V. Sun–Thurs 5–10pm, Fri–Sat 5–11pm. Take I-10 to the Cortaro Farms Rd. exit, then go west on Cortaro Farms Rd. and north on Silverbell Rd. STEAKS.

This steakhouse, which used to be an old stagecoach stop, is almost as rustic as in the days of the Wild West. The steaks are cooked over a mesquite fire and eaten (with all the beans, bread, and salsa your heart desires) at picnic tables. Friday and Saturday nights are extra-lively with country music and dancing.

**Pinnacle Peak Steakhouse.** 6541 E. Tanque Verde Rd. ☎ **520/296-0911.** Reservations not accepted. Main courses $5–$13. AE, DC, DISC, MC, V. Winter Mon–Thurs 5–10pm, Fri–Sun 4:30–10pm; summer daily 5–10pm. STEAKS.

Located in the Trail Dust Town, a Wild West–themed shopping and dining center, the Pinnacle Peak Steakhouse specializes in family dining in a fun cowboy atmosphere. Be prepared for crowds—this place is very popular with tour buses. Stroll the wooden sidewalks past the opera house and saloon to the grand old dining rooms of the Pinnacle Peak Steakhouse. You'll be surprised at the authenticity of the restaurant, which really does resemble a dining room in Old Tombstone or Dodge City.

**Triple C Chuckwagon Suppers.** 8900 W. Bopp Rd. ☎ **800/446-1798** or 520/883-2333. Reservations recommended. Complete meal $14 adults, $7 children. DISC, MC, V. Dec–Apr daily dinner at 7pm and show at 8pm. Closed May–Nov. Take Ariz. 86 west to San Joaquin Rd. WESTERN.

This restaurant is located on an old cattle ranch. Dinner, which consists of cowboy fare such as barbecued beef or chicken and baked beans is dished up chuck-wagon style (in a serving line), and there are nightly Western-music performances.

## QUICK BITES, CAFES & COFFEEHOUSES

A student hangout near the University of Arizona, **Café Paraíso,** 820 E. University Blvd. (☎ **520/624-1707**), has a shady and cool patio, easy chairs, and delectable pastries, salads, and sandwiches. **Cuppuccinos,** 3400 E. Speedway Blvd. (☎ **520/323-7205**), bills itself as a Seattle-style coffeehouse, and **The Epic Café,** 745 N. Fourth Ave. (☎ **520/624-6844**), is a good hangout place with wild artwork, delicious pastries, soups, salads, and sandwiches. Look for the mural out front. **The Pink Motel,** 3266 E. Speedway Blvd. (☎ **520/318-3500**), is both a cafe and a wacky shrine to vintage kitsch. Here you can sip a latte and listen to a jukebox with the most eclectic selections in town.

With choices from chocolate chip to white chocolate/macadamia nut, **Stacia's Bakery Café,** 3022 E. Broadway Blvd. (☎ **520/325-5549**), has the most delectable cookies in Tucson and also does breakfast and lunch. And you can't beat the cheap breakfast specials on darn good bagels at **The Bagelry,** 5319 E. Speedway Blvd. (☎ **520/322-0223**), 2707 E. Broadway Blvd. (☎ **520/795-0929**), and 2575 N. Campbell Ave. (☎ **520/881-6674**). When we need a quick lunch, we dart over to **Baggins Gourmet Sandwiches** for a delicious sandwich. They have seven locations, three of which are at Kolb Road and Speedway Boulevard (☎ **520/290-9383**), Campbell Avenue and Ft. Lowell Road (☎ **520/327-1611**), and Church Avenue and Pennington Street (☎ **520/792-1344**). Call for the one nearest you. The best pizza in town can be had at **Magpies Gourmet Pizza,** at Speedway Boulevard and Swan Road (☎ **520/795-5977**), Broadway Boulevard and Pantano Road (☎ **520/751-9949**), and two other locations. **Reay's Ranch Markets** is a good place to get picnic supplies. They have organic fruit, delicious baked goods, cheese, meats, and wine, the kind of things you'd expect from a specialty market. They're located at 3360 E. Speedway Blvd. (☎ **520/795-9844**) or 7133 N. Oracle Rd. (☎ **520/297-5394**).

## 5 Seeing the Sights

### THE TOP ATTRACTIONS

While there are plenty of interesting things to see and do all over the Tucson area, anyone interested in the desert Southwest or the cinematic Wild West should head over to the western edge of the city immediately. Here is not only the west section of Saguaro National Park (with the biggest and best stands of saguaro cactus), but also the Arizona–Sonora Desert Museum (one of Arizona's most popular attractions) and Old Tucson Studios (film site for hundreds of westerns over the years). Together these three make a great day's outing.

#### THE TUCSON AREA'S (MOSTLY) NATURAL WONDERS

✪ **Arizona–Sonora Desert Museum.** 2021 N. Kinney Rd. ☎ **520/883-2702** or 520/883-1380. Admission $8.95 adults, $1.75 children 6–12, free for children 5 and under. Oct–Feb daily 8:30am–5pm; Mar–Sept daily 7:30am–6pm. From downtown Tucson, go west on Speedway Blvd., which becomes Gates Pass Rd., and follow the signs.

Don't be fooled by the name. This is a zoo, and it's one of the best in the country. Don't be surprised to find yourself spending more hours here than you intended. The Arizona–Sonora Desert Museum is located 14 miles west of Tucson between Tucson Mountain Park and Saguaro National Park West.

The Sonoran Desert is the arid region that encompasses much of central and southern Arizona as well as parts of northern Mexico. In this desert are not only arid lands but also forested mountains, springs, rivers, and streams. The full spectrum of Sonoran Desert life—from plants to insects to fish to reptiles to mammals—is on display in natural settings. There are black bears and mountain lions, beavers and otters, frogs and fish, tarantulas and scorpions, prairie dogs and javelinas (peccaries). In addition, there's a simulated cave with exhibits on prehistoric desert life. Our favorite exhibit is an aviary holding a dozen species of hummingbird. The tiny birds buzz past your ears and stop only inches in front of your face. A separate aviary contains many other bird species. Docents explain everything from the life cycle of the saguaro cactus to the feeding habits of the tarantula. Two restaurants, Ironwood Terraces (cafeteria-style) and the Ocatillo Cafe (a sit-down restaurant), serve excellent food and are well worth a stop.

**Saguaro National Park.** East district visitor center, 3693 S. Old Spanish Trail. ☎ **520/733-5100.** West district visitor center, 2700 N. Kinney Rd. ☎ 520/733-5158. $4 per car (charged on the east section only). Park open daily 7am–sunset; visitor centers daily 8:30am–5pm.

The saguaro cactus has been called the monarch of the desert and is the quintessential symbol of the American desert. Coyotes, foxes, squirrels, and javelinas all eat the sweet fruit and seeds of the saguaro, as have for centuries the Tohono O'odham.

Since 1933 the two sections of Saguaro National Park have protected the saguaro and all the other inhabitants of this section of the Sonoran Desert. The west section is the more popular because of its proximity to both the Arizona–Sonora Desert Museum and Old Tucson Studios. In the area near the Red Hills Information Center is a water hole that attracts wild animals, which you're most likely to see at dawn, dusk, or at night. The east section of the park contains an older area of forest at the foot of the Rincon Mountains. This section is popular with hikers because most of it has no roads. There's also a visitor center here. Both sections have loop roads, nature trails, hiking trails, and picnic grounds.

To reach the west section, take Speedway Boulevard west from downtown Tucson (it becomes Gates Pass Boulevard); to reach the east section, take Speedway Boulevard east, then head south on Freeman Road to Old Spanish Trail.

○ **Sabino Canyon.** 5900 N. Sabino Canyon Rd. ☎ **520/749-2861.** Free admission. Sabino Canyon tram ride, $5 adults, $2 children 3–12, free for children 2 and under; Bear Canyon tram ride, $3 adults, $1.25 children 3–12, free for children 2 and under. Park: daily dawn–dusk. Sabino Canyon tram rides, daily 9am–4:30pm; Bear Canyon tram rides, daily 9am–4pm (both trams more limited in summer). Take Grant Rd. east to Tanque Verde Rd., continuing east; at Sabino Canyon Rd., turn north and watch for the sign.

Located in the Santa Catalina Mountains of Coronado National Forest, Sabino Canyon is a desert oasis that has attracted people and animals for thousands of years. These days it is the chance to splash and swim in the canyon's waterfalls and pools that attracts most visitors. However, for those who prefer just to gaze at the beauty of crystal-clear water flowing over rock, there's a narrated tram ride through the lower canyon leaving frequently every day. There are also many trails and picnic tables. Moonlight tram rides take place three times each month between April and December ( ☎ **520/749-2327** for reservations). The Bear Canyon tram is used by hikers heading to the picturesque Seven Falls, which are at the end of a 2.2-mile hiking trail. Bring at least 1 quart of water per person.

**Colossal Cave Mountain Park.** 22 miles east of Tucson off I-10, Vail. ☎ **520/647-7275.** Admission $6.50 adults, $5 children 11–16, $3.50 children 6–10, free for children 5 and under. Mar 16–Sept 15 Mon–Sat 8am–6pm, Sun and holidays 8am–7pm; Sept 16–Mar 15 Mon–Sat 9am–5pm, Sun and holidays 9am–6pm.

Colossal Cave may once have served as a bandit hangout. Today, tours through the cave combine a bit of history with a bit of geology. This is a dry cave, where the stalactites, stalagmites, and other formations are no longer actively growing. The 45-minute tours of the cave cover about half a mile, and the temperature is a comfortable 70° to 72°F.

## HISTORIC ATTRACTIONS BOTH REAL & REEL

○ **Old Tucson Studios.** 201 S. Kinney Rd. ☎ **520/883-0100.** Admission $14.95 adults, $9.45 children 4–11 (Pima County residents $12.95 adult and $8.95 children). Winter daily 9am–7pm, summer daily 10am–6pm. Closed Thanksgiving and Dec 25. Take Speedway Blvd. west, continuing in the same direction when it becomes Gates Pass Blvd., and turn left on S. Kinney Rd.

Despite the name, this is not the historic location of the old city of Tucson—it's a Western town originally built as the set for the 1939 movie *Arizona*. In the years since then, Old Tucson has been used during the filming of John Wayne's *Rio Lobo, Rio Bravo,* and *El Dorado;* Clint Eastwood's *The Outlaw Josey Wales;* Kirk Douglas's *Gunfight at the O.K. Corral;* Paul Newman's *The Life and Times of Judge Roy Bean;* and, more recently, *Tombstone* and *Geronimo.*

Today, however, Old Tucson is far more than just a movie set. In addition to serving as a site for frequent film, TV, and advertising productions (call ahead to find out if any filming is scheduled), it has become a Wild West theme park with diverse family-oriented activities and entertainment. Throughout each day there are staged shoot-outs in the streets, stunt shows, cancan performances, medicine shows, and other performances. There are also train rides, stagecoach rides, kiddie rides, a circus act, video games, restaurants, and gift shops.

A fire destroyed much of Old Tucson in early 1995 and many of the original buildings were lost. However, the town has since been rebuilt. Though it isn't quite

# Tucson Attractions

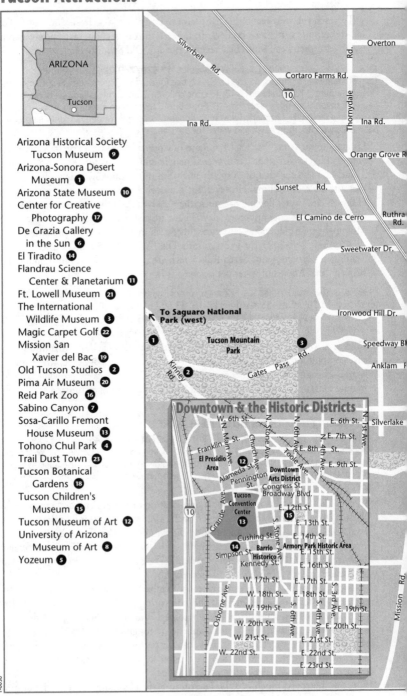

Arizona Historical Society
Tucson Museum ⑨
Arizona-Sonora Desert
Museum ①
Arizona State Museum ⑩
Center for Creative
Photography ⑰
De Grazia Gallery
in the Sun ⑥
El Tiradito ⑭
Flandrau Science
Center & Planetarium ⑪
Ft. Lowell Museum ㉑
The International
Wildlife Museum ③
Magic Carpet Golf ㉒
Mission San
Xavier del Bac ⑲
Old Tucson Studios ②
Pima Air Museum ⑳
Reid Park Zoo ⑯
Sabino Canyon ⑦
Sosa-Carillo Fremont
House Museum ⑬
Tohono Chul Park ④
Trail Dust Town ㉓
Tucson Botanical
Gardens ⑱
Tucson Children's
Museum ⑮
Tucson Museum of Art ⑫
University of Arizona
Museum of Art ⑧
Yozeum ⑤

1-0030

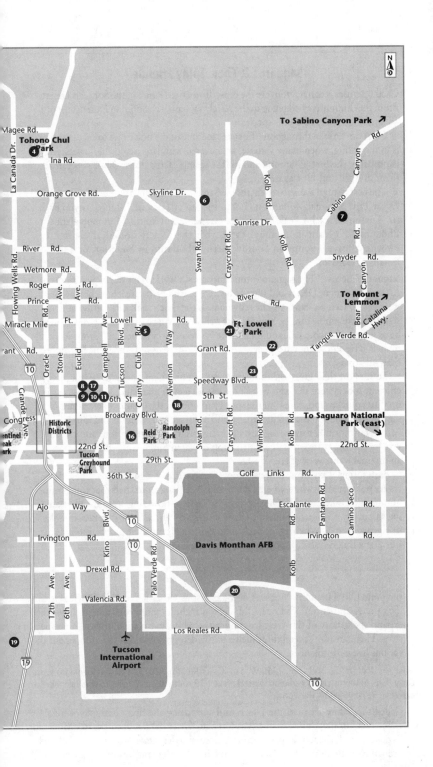

## Saguaros & Their Spiny Friends

Cacti (cactuses is correct, too) are the most distinctive feature of the Sonoran Desert. From the diminutive hedgehog to the stately saguaro, the Sonoran Desert supports an amazing variety of cactus species.

Cacti can be seen throughout the state, and one of the best times to cactus-watch is in the spring, when many varieties are covered with large, colorful flowers. May is probably the best all-around month for seeing cactus flowers, but you can see them in April and June as well.

The best natural areas to see cactus are Saguaro National Park (outside Tucson), Organ Pipe National Monument (100 miles west of Tucson), Sabino Canyon Park (in Tucson), Picacho Peak (near Casa Grande), and South Mountain Park (in Phoenix). To learn more about cacti, visit the Desert Botanical Garden in Phoenix, Boyce Thompson Southwestern Arboretum in Superior, or Tucson Botanical Gardens.

**Saguaro Cactus**   The saguaro (pronounced *sa-HWAH-ro*) is the largest cactus of Arizona's Sonoran Desert and grows nowhere else on earth. Reaching heights of as much as 50 feet, saguaros are the redwoods of the desert, and often grow in dense stands that resemble forests. Saguaros are a slow-growing cactus; a 10-year-old may be as little as 6 inches tall, and it can take 75 years for a saguaro to sprout its first branch. The oldest-known saguaros are around 200 years old, and some have more than 40 arms.

To support their great size in such an arid environment, saguaros have a highly efficient root system that can be as large as 100 feet in diameter. These roots soak up water quickly and store it in the spongy interior of the cactus. The exterior of a saguaro is pleated so that it can expand and contract as it takes up and loses water. After a rainstorm, a mature saguaro can weigh as much as seven tons and can survive for up to 2 years without another drop of water. Supporting this great mass is an internal framework of sturdy ribs.

Each spring, waxy white flowers sprout from the tips of saguaro arms. These flowers are pollinated by white-winged doves and lesser long-nosed bats that come from hundreds of miles away in Mexico just for saguaro flowering season. Other animals that rely on saguaros include gila woodpeckers and elfowls that nest in holes in saguaro trunks. When a bird pecks a hole into a saguaro, the cactus responds by forming a tough scab around the interior of the hole.

the same Old Tucson it once was, it looks just as old as it ever did (movie sets can look pretty authentic). The new Old Tucson includes more educational shows that explain the history of the West from both the white and Native American perspectives. There are also several multimedia and video presentations to complement the various live performances.

**Mission San Xavier del Bac.** 1950 W. San Xavier Rd. ☎ **520/294-2624.** Free admission. Daily 8am–5:30pm (closes earlier in winter). Take I-19 south about 9 miles to the Valencia Rd. exit (Exit 92) and follow the signs.

Called the White Dove of the Desert and considered the finest example of mission architecture in the United States, Mission San Xavier del Bac incorporates Moorish, Byzantine, and Mexican Renaissance architectural styles into a single beautiful church. Brilliantly white in the desert sun, the church serves the residents of the surrounding

The Tohono O'odham people, natives of the Sonoran Desert, have long relied on saguaro cactus fruit as an important food source, and in fact the Tohono O'odham year begins with the saguaro harvest. The Saguaro fruit, with its red, seedy pulp, is made into a wine that's used in traditional ceremonies.

**Organ Pipe Cactus**   This close relative of the saguaro takes its name from its many trunks, which give it the appearance of an old pipe organ. The organ pipe cactus is even more frost sensitive than the saguaro and lives only in an area 100 miles west of Tucson on either side of the Mexican border. This population of stately cacti has also been preserved in a national monument.

**Barrel Cactus**   When mature, these cacti look much as their name implies and can be confused with young saguaros. However, the barrel cactus can be distinguished by its fishhook-shaped spines which are usually yellow or red in color. This is the cactus that for years has been touted as a source of life-giving water to anyone lost in the desert. The liquid in this cactus's spongy interior is actually quite bitter and foul tasting. However, the same spongy pulp, when cooked in sugar water, becomes very tasty.

**Cholla Cactus**   The cholla (pronounced *CHOI-yah*) is the most dreaded of all the Arizona cacti. Its spines are long, plentiful, sharp, and brittle. To brush up against a cholla is to know certain pain. Here in Arizona, there are several species of this cacti, most of which resemble small trees. They go by such graphic names as jumping cholla, which is said to throw pieces of its spiny branches at unwary passersby; teddy bear cholla, which is so covered with spines that it looks fuzzy; and the chain fruit cholla, on which fruit hang in fragile, spiny chains. The chollas are favored nesting spots of cactus wrens and doves. Give chollas a wide birth.

**Prickly Pear Cactus**   This is one of the largest and most widespread families of cacti and can be found throughout the United States, not just in the desert. They are also among the most commercially important cacti. The flat stems or pads (known as *nopales* in Spanish) of one species are used in Mexican cooking and can be found both fresh and canned in markets in Arizona. The fruit of prickly pears is also edible and is relished by both humans and animals. Here in Arizona, it's possible to find prickly pear jams and jellies, as well as prickly pear ice cream.

San Xavier Indian Reservation. Although a church had existed near here as early as 1700, the existing structure was built between 1783 and 1797. Why only one church tower was completed is a mystery, but you'll immediately notice the missing dome of the right-hand tower. The building is constructed of adobe brick, and faded murals cover the walls. A statue of St. Francis Xavier, the mission's patron saint, is to the left of the ornate main altar. For the past few years the mission has been undergoing restoration, and much of the elaborate interior decoration has taken on a new luster. A small hill just east of the church not only affords an interesting view of the church but is also the site of a replica of the famous grotto in Lourdes, France. The mission is an active Roman Catholic church. Masses are held Tuesday through Friday at 8:30am, on Saturday at 5:30pm, and on Sunday at 8am, 9:30am, 11am, and 12:30pm.

# MORE TO SEE & DO
## ART MUSEUMS

In addition to the museums and galleries listed below, you need only look around you as you drive through Tucson to see some of the city's most memorable art. Tucson abounds in outdoor murals and public art. For handouts and maps that will help you locate some of these art works, stop by the **Tucson/Pima Arts Council,** 240 N. Stone Ave. (☎ 520/624-0595), which is located 1 block north of the Tucson-Pima Library in downtown Tucson. The Farmer John Meats mural at 1102 W. Grant Rd. and the Truly Nolan bee mural at 3620 E. Speedway Blvd. are a couple of our favorites.

**Tucson Museum of Art & Historic Block.** 140 N. Main Ave. ☎ 520/624-2333. Admission $2 adults, $1 students and seniors, free for children 12 and under; free for everyone Tues. Mon–Sat 10am–4pm, Sun noon–4pm. Closed Mon June–Aug and all national holidays. All downtown-bound buses.

The Tucson Museum of Art is situated in a large modern building surrounded by historic adobes and a spacious plaza frequently used to display sculptures. The museum boasts an excellent collection of pre-Columbian art representing 3,000 years of life in Mexico and Central and South America, and a large collection of Western art depicting cowboys, horses, and the wide-open spaces of the American West. In addition, the museum always hosts temporary exhibitions, such as the annual "American Women Artists and the West."

**۞ The University of Arizona Museum of Art.** Park Ave. and Speedway Blvd. ☎ 520/621-7567. Free admission. Labor Day to mid-May Mon–Fri 9am–5pm, Sun noon–4pm; mid-May to Labor Day Mon–Fri 10am–3:30pm, Sun noon–4pm. Closed major holidays. Bus: 1.

This collection is more extensive and diverse than what you'll find at the Tucson Museum of Art. It includes European and American works from the Renaissance to the 20th century, notably by Tintoretto, Rembrandt, Piranesi, Picasso, O'Keeffe, Warhol, and Rothko. Another attraction is the *Retable of Ciudad Rodrigo,* which consists of 26 paintings from 15th-century Spain and was originally placed above a cathedral altar. The museum also has an extensive collection of 20th-century sculpture that includes more than 60 clay and plaster models and sketches by Jacques Lipchitz. From mid-November 1997 through January 1998, there will be a Rodin sculpture exhibit here. Other upcoming shows include Tucson Modern Artists and outdoor bronze sculptures.

**۞ Center for Creative Photography.** East of the corner of Park Ave. and Speedway Blvd. ☎ 520/621-7968. Free admission. Mon–Fri 11am–5pm, Sun noon–5pm. Bus: 1, 4, 5, 9X, 102, or 103.

Have you ever wished you could see an original Ansel Adams print up close, or perhaps an Edward Weston or a Richard Avedon? You can at the Center for Creative Photography. Originally conceived by Ansel Adams, the center now holds more than 500,000 negatives, 200,000 study prints, and 60,000 master prints by the world's greatest photographers, making it one of the best and largest collections in the world. Although the center mounts excellent photography exhibits year-round, it's also a research facility that preserves the complete photographic archives of various photographers, including Adams. Prints may be examined in a special room. It's highly recommended that you make an appointment and decide beforehand whose works you'd like to see. You're usually limited to two photographers per visit.

**De Grazia Gallery in the Sun.** 6300 N. Swan Rd. ☎ 520/299-9191. Free admission. Daily 10am–4pm.

## ❓ Did You Know?

- The University of Arizona was established in Tucson to appease the citizenry after the territorial capital was moved to Phoenix.
- Mount Lemmon, named for the woman who first climbed it, is the site of the southernmost ski area in the continental United States.
- Tucson is the sunniest city in the country.
- The Sonoran Desert is the only place in the world where the saguaro cactus grows, and Saguaro National Park outside Tucson has the greatest concentration of these plants.
- Singer Linda Ronstadt is part of a Tucson family very active in local politics; a public bus station is named for one of the Ronstadts.
- There are more astronomical observatories within a 50-mile radius of Tucson than in any other area of comparable size in the world.

Southwestern artist Ettore "Ted" De Grazia is a Tucson favorite son, and his gallery, set in an adobe home in the foothills, is a Tucson landmark. De Grazia is said to be the most reproduced artist in the world because many of his impressionistic images are found on greeting cards from the 1950s to 1960s and numerous other places. Connected to the gallery is a small adobe chapel that De Grazia built in honor of the missionary explorer Fr. Eusebio Kino. No original works are for sale, but there are many reproductions and other objects with De Grazia images.

### HISTORY MUSEUMS & LANDMARK BUILDINGS

In addition to the museums and buildings listed below, downtown Tucson has a couple of historic neighborhoods, which are described in the "Walking Tours" section below. Among the more interesting buildings are those maintained by the Tucson Museum of Art and located on the block surrounding the museum. These restored homes date from between 1850 and 1907 and are all built on the former site of the Tucson presidio.

**La Casa Cordova,** the oldest house on the block, is one of the city's earliest. It serves as a Mexican Heritage Museum. During the Christmas holiday season, the Casa Cordova contains a traditional *Nacimiento*, a Mexican folk art depiction of the nativity. Scenes from the Bible and the history of Latin America are all rolled up into one miniature landscape full of angels, greenery, and Christmas lights.

The **Leonardo Romero House** is now part of the museum's art school, the **Stevens House** is home to Janos, one of the best restaurants in Tucson (which will be moving out in the summer of 1998), and the **Fish House** contains the museum's Western art collection. A map and descriptive brochures about the houses are available at the museum's front desk. Free guided tours of the historic block are available.

**Arizona Historical Society Tucson Museum.** 949 E. Second St. ☎ **520/628-5774.** Free admission or by donation. Mon–Sat 10am–4pm, Sun noon–4pm. Closed major holidays. Bus: 1, 4, 5, 9X, 102, or 103.

As Arizona's oldest historical museum, this repository of all things Arizonan is a treasure trove for the history buff. If you've never explored a real mine, you can do the next best thing by looking at the museum's full-scale reproduction of an underground mine tunnel. You'll also see an assayer's office, miner's tent, stamp mill, and blacksmith's shop in the mining exhibit. "Transportation through the years" is another interesting exhibit, with silver-studded saddles of Spanish ranchers, steam locomotives that opened Arizona to the world, and "horseless carriages" that revolutionized life in the Southwest. The museum has a research library and a good gift shop.

**Arizona State Museum.** On the University of Arizona campus, University Blvd. and Park Ave. ☎ 520/621-6302. Free admission. Mon–Sat 10am–5pm, Sun noon–5pm. Closed major holidays. Bus: 1, 4, 5, 9X, 102, or 103.

Founded in 1893, the Arizona State Museum houses an extensive collection of artifacts from prehistoric and contemporary Native American cultures of the Southwest. A Paleo-Indian exhibit displays 12,000-year-old spear points that were found embedded in the bones of mammoths, now long extinct, and a large exhibit covers the Hohokam, an ancient farming culture that lived in the desert and built extensive networks of irrigation canals until it disappeared mysteriously around 1450. Across the street in the North Building, an exhibit explores the lifestyles and cultural traditions of Indians living in Arizona today. Excellent temporary exhibits are regularly scheduled here.

**Sosa-Carillo-Frémont House Museum.** 151 S. Granada Ave. (between Broadway Blvd. and Cushing St.). ☎ 520/622-0956. Free admission. Wed–Sat 10am–4pm. Closed all major holidays. All downtown-bound buses.

Located on the shady grounds of the modern Tucson Convention Center, the Sosa-Carillo-Frémont House is a classic example of Sonoran-style adobe architecture. Originally built in 1858 as a small adobe house, the structure was enlarged after 1866. In 1878 it was rented to territorial governor John Charles Frémont, who had led a distinguished military career as an explorer of the West. The building has been restored in the style of this period, with the living room and bedrooms opening off a large central hall known as a *zaguán*. All rooms are decorated with period antiques. The flat roof is made of pine beams called *vigas,* covered with saguaro cactus ribs, and topped by a layer of hard-packed mud.

**Ft. Lowell Museum.** 2900 N. Craycroft Rd. ☎ 520/855-3832. Free admission. Wed–Sat 10am–4pm. Closed all major holidays.

Located in Fort Lowell Park on the site of a former cavalry outpost, this museum chronicles the history of life at the fort. Some of the ruins of the original fort can still be seen. Before it was a fort, this site was a Hohokam village, and artifacts uncovered from archaeological digs around the surrounding park lands are also on display.

## SCIENCE & TECHNOLOGY MUSEUMS

**Flandrau Science Center & Planetarium.** Cherry Ave. and University Blvd. ☎ **520/621-STAR** or 520/621-4515. Admission to exhibits $3 adults, $2 children. Telescope viewing free. Planetarium $5 adults, $4.50 seniors and students, $4 children 3–12. Daytime Mon–Fri 9am–5pm, Sat–Sun 1–5pm; evenings Wed–Thurs 7–9pm, Fri–Sat 7pm–midnight. Telescope viewing Wed–Sat 7–10pm. Closed major holidays. Bus: 1 or 9.

Located on the campus of the University of Arizona, the Flandrau Planetarium offers stargazers a chance to learn more about the universe. The planetarium theater presents programs on the stars as well as very popular laser shows set to music. Exhibit halls contain a mineral collection and hands-on science exhibits for people of all ages. On clear nights, you can gaze through the planetarium's 16-inch telescope. (Arizona has become a magnet for stargazers, and several famous telescopes are near Tucson. See "Side Trips from Tucson," later in this chapter, for information on the Kitt Peak National Observatory.)

## ⭐ Frommer's Favorite Tucson Experiences

**Visiting the Arizona–Sonora Desert Museum.** One of the world's finest zoos, the museum focuses exclusively on the animals and plants of the Sonoran Desert of southern Arizona and northern Mexico.

**Taking a Full-Moon Desert Hike.** There's no better time to explore the desert than at night (when the desert comes alive) under a full moon. Drive to the east or west section of Saguaro National Park for your hike.

**Making the Drive to Mount Lemmon.** From the desert, the road twists and turns up into the Santa Catalina Mountains, with cactus and palo verde gradually replaced by pine and juniper. You'll have breathtaking views of Tucson along the way.

**Taking in Downtown Saturday Night.** On the first and third Saturday of each month Tucson's Downtown Arts District abounds in open art galleries, boutiques, crafts shops, street performers, and free entertainment in hip cafes.

**Spending a Day in Tubac.** As the first European settlement in what would later become Arizona, Tubac has a long history now complemented by dozens of arts and crafts studios, galleries, and shops.

**Spending Time in Sabino Canyon.** Biking, hiking, swimming, birding—Sabino Canyon has it all. The canyon, carved by a creek that flows for most of the year, is an oasis in the desert. Though popular with both locals and tourists, it still offers delightful opportunities for escaping the city.

**Bird Watching in Madera Canyon.** Located south of the city in the Santa Rita Mountains, this canyon attracts many species of birds, some of which can only be seen in a handful of other spots in the United States. Even if you're not into birding, there are hiking trails and lots of shade here.

**The International Wildlife Museum.** 4800 W. Gates Pass Rd. ☎ **520/617-1439** or 520/629-0100. Admission $5 adults, $3.75 seniors and students, $1.50 children 6–12, free for children 5 and under. Daily 9am–5pm. Take Speedway Blvd. west from downtown.

This castlelike building on the road that leads to the Arizona–Sonora Desert Museum is a natural-history museum filled with stuffed animals in lifelike poses and surroundings. Animals from all over the world are displayed.

**Pima Air Museum.** 6000 E. Valencia Rd. ☎ **520/574-9658** or 520/574-0646. Admission $6 adults, $5 seniors and military, $3 children 10–17, free for children 9 and under. Daily 9am–5pm. Closed Thanksgiving and Dec 25. Take the Valencia Rd. exit from I-10 and then drive east 2 miles to the museum entrance.

Located just south of Davis Monthan Air Force Base, reachable from I-10, the Pima Air Museum displays more than 200 aircraft covering the evolution of American aviation. This is one of the largest collections of historic aircraft in the world. A 20,000-square-foot building houses part of the collection, though most of the aircraft are outside. The collection includes replicas of the Wright brothers' 1903 Wright Flyer and the X-15, the world's fastest aircraft. World War II bombers and later jet fighters are popular attractions.

**Titan Missile Museum.** Duval Mine Rd., Green Valley (Exit 69 from I-19). ☎ **520/625-7736.** Admission $6 adults, $5 seniors, $3 children 10–17, free for children 9 and under. May 1–Oct 31 Wed–Sun 9am–5pm; Nov 1–Apr 30 daily 9am–5pm. Closed Thanksgiving and Dec 25.

Operated by the Pima Air Museum and located south of Tucson in the retirement community of Green Valley, this museum is a deactivated intercontinental ballistic missile (ICBM) silo and is the only such museum in the world. Tours lead you down into the silo itself so you can get a firsthand look at what it would be like to have your finger on the button. Advance reservations are recommended.

## PARKS, GARDENS & ZOOS

See " The Tucson Area's (Mostly) Natural Wonders" at the beginning of this section for full details on the Arizona–Sonora Desert Museum, the region's premier zoo.

**Agua Caliente County Park.** 4002 N. Soldier Trail. ☎ **520/740-2680.**

Located way out in the northeast corner of Tucson, this park is a spring-fed oasis in the desert. And though not quite natural (the area has been altered by people over the years), the large pond here is fed by a natural warm spring and is one of the best bird-watching spots in the city of Tucson. You'll also see lots of turtles and fish. Tables in the shade of tall palms and other trees make this a great spot for a picnic. To find the park, follow Tanque Verde Road east 6 miles from the intersection with Sabino Canyon Road and turn left onto Soldier Trail. Watch for signs.

**Reid Park Zoo.** Lake Shore Lane and 22nd St. (between Country Club Rd. and Alvernon Way). ☎ **520/791-4022.** Admission $3.50 adults, $2.50 seniors, 75¢ children 5–14, free for children 4 and under. Daily 9am–4pm. Closed Dec 25. Bus: 14.

Although small and overshadowed by its neighbor, the Arizona–Sonora Desert Museum, the Reid Park Zoo is an important breeding center for several endangered species. Among the animals in the zoo's breeding programs are giant anteaters, white rhinoceroses, tigers, ruffed lemurs, and zebras. There's also a good playground at the park here. A new South American exhibit was scheduled to open in late 1997.

✪ **Tucson Botanical Gardens.** 2150 N. Alvernon Way. ☎ **520/326-9686.** Admission $4 adults, $3 seniors, free for children under 12. Daily 8:30am–4:30pm. Closed Jan 1, July 4, Thanksgiving, and Dec 24–25. Bus: 11.

These gardens form an oasis of greenery in suburban Tucson. On the 5½-acre grounds are several small gardens, including a cactus garden, that not only have visual appeal but are also historic and educational. If you live in the desert, you'll benefit from a visit when you learn about harvesting rainfall for the desert garden and designing a water-conserving landscape. The sensory garden stimulates all five senses, while in another garden traditional Southwestern crops are grown for research purposes. In the greenhouse, you'll see "useful" plants from the tropical forest. There's a gift shop here as well.

**Tohono Chul Park.** 7366 N. Paseo del Norte. ☎ **520/575-8468.** Admission by suggested donation, $2. Grounds, daily 7am–sunset. Exhibit house, Mon–Sat 9:30am–5pm, Sun 11am–5pm. Tea Room, Oct to mid-April daily 8am–5pm, mid-April to Sept daily 8am–8pm.

Though this public park is fairly small, it provides an excellent introduction to the plant and animal life of the desert. You'll see a forest of cholla cactus and a garden of small and complex pincushion cactus. The park includes an ethnobotanical garden; a garden for children that encourages them to touch, listen, and smell; a demonstration garden; natural areas; an exhibit house for art displays; a tea room that is great for breakfast, lunch, or afternoon tea; and a very good gift shop.

## ESPECIALLY FOR KIDS

In addition to the museums listed below, two of the greatest places to take kids in the Tucson area are the Arizona–Sonora Desert Museum and Old Tucson Studios.

## The Shrine That Stopped a Freeway

The southern Arizona landscape is dotted with roadside shrines, symbols of the region's Spanish and Roman Catholic heritage. Most are simple crosses decorated with plastic flowers and dedicated to people who have been killed in auto accidents. However, one shrine in particular stands out from all the rest. It is Tucson's El Tiradito (The Castaway), which is dedicated to a sinner and not too long ago stopped a freeway.

El Tiradito, located on South Granada Avenue at West Cushing Street, is the only shrine in the United States dedicated to a sinner buried in unconsecrated soil. Several stories tell of how this shrine came to be, but the most popularly accepted tells of a young shepherd who fell in love with his mother-in-law some time in the 1880s. When the father-in-law found his wife in the arms of this young man, he shot the son-in-law. The young shepherd stumbled from his in-laws' house and fell dead beside the dusty street. Because he had been caught in the act of adultery and died without confessing his sins, his body could not be interred in the church cemetery, so he was buried where he fell.

The people of the neighborhood soon began burning candles on the spot to try to save the soul of the young man, and eventually people began burning candles in hopes that their own wishes would come true. They believed that if the candle burned through the night their prayers would be answered. The shrine eventually grew into a substantial little structure, and in 1927 was dedicated by its owner to the city of Tucson. In 1940 the shrine became an official Tucson monument.

However, such status was not enough to protect the shrine from urban renewal, and when the federal government announced that it would level the shrine when it built a new freeway through the center of Tucson, the city's citizens were outraged. Their activities and protest led the shrine to be named to the National Register of Historic Places. Thus protected, the shrine could not be destroyed, and the freeway was moved a few hundred yards to the west.

To this day, devout Catholics from the surrounding neighborhood still burn candles at the shrine that stopped a freeway.

Kids will also get a kick out of the tram ride at Sabino Canyon, the Reid Park Zoo, the International Wildlife Museum, Flandrau Science Center & Planetarium, and the Pima Air Museum. All are described in detail above.

They'll also enjoy **Trail Dust Town,** a Wild West–themed shopping and dining center at 6541 E. Tanque Verde Rd. It has a full-size carousel, and there's a mini-golf course next door. If the kids are into miniature golf, another course that we really like is **Magic Carpet Golf,** 6125 E. Speedway Blvd. (☎ **520/885-3691**). Putt balls under and around a sphinx, a skull, a giant Easter Island head, and a huge snake.

**Tucson Children's Museum.** 200 S. Sixth Ave. ☎ **520/792-9985.** Admission $5 adults, $4 seniors, $3 children 3–16, free for children 2 and under; free for everyone on the third Sun of each month. Wed–Fri 9am–5pm, Sat 10am–5pm, Sun noon–5pm. Closed Jan 1, Easter Sunday, Thanksgiving, Dec 25. All downtown-bound buses.

This museum is located in the old Carnegie Library in downtown Tucson and is filled with hands-on activities that are fun and educational. Exhibits change every year or so, but have included a doctor's office, a fire station, and a bubble factory. Weekends generally include special performances and programs.

**Yozeum.** 2900 N. Country Club Rd. ☎ **520/322-0100.** Free admission. Tues–Fri 9am–5pm, Sat 9am–1pm. Bus: 17.

If you were ever a kid (and I guess we all were at one time or another), you must have had a yo-yo, and chances are it was a Duncan yo-yo. Can you imagine the collection of yo-yos the Duncan family must have had? Well, you don't have to imagine—come see for yourself. Not only is this yo-yo museum the Duncan family collection, but it's also a factory outlet for a nearby yo-yo factory.

## SPECIAL EVENTS

Because of the excellent weather year-round, Tucson hosts numerous outdoor festivals, celebrations, and events. Many are free and are held downtown and in the city's parks. See the "Arizona Calendar of Events" in chapter 3 for complete details.

One favorite free event is **Downtown Saturday Night,** a year-round celebration of the Downtown Arts District held on the first and third Saturday of each month. From 7 to 10pm on these nights, the district—which includes East Pennington Street, East Congress Street, and East Broadway Boulevard between Fourth Avenue and Stone Avenue—comes alive with art gallery openings, music performances on the street and in cafes, and late-evening shopping. For more information, call the **Tucson Arts District Partnership** (☎ **520/624-9977**). You'll also hear live music if you wander over to the Old Town Artisans crafts market in El Presidio Historic District. So popular have these events become that sometimes there are performances and tours going on all day long on these Saturdays.

## WALKING TOUR 1
## El Presidio Historic District

**Start:** The Fish House.
**Finish:** Pima County Courthouse.
**Time:** Three hours.
**Best Times:** Weekends, when restaurants aren't packed at lunch.
**Worst Times:** Summer, when it's just too hot to do any walking.

Tucson has a long and varied cultural history, which is most easily seen on a walking tour of the downtown historic districts.

Start your tour at the corner of Alameda Street and Main Avenue. With your back to the modern high-rise office buildings of downtown Tucson, you'll be facing El Presidio Historic District, which is named for the Presidio of San Augustín del Tucson (1775), the Spanish garrison that once stood here to protect the San Xavier del Bac Mission from the Apaches. For many years this was the heart of Tucson. No original building still stands, but those you'll see date from the mid-19th century. The building directly in front of you is the:

**1.** **Fish House,** 120 N. Main Ave., built in 1868 in the Sonoran architectural style and named for Edward Nye Fish, a local merchant. Today this building houses the Western art collection of the Tucson Museum of Art.

Next along Main Avenue is the:

**2.** **Stevens Home,** 150 N. Main Ave. Together with the Fish House, this was the cultural heart of Tucson in the latter 19th century. It now houses Janos, one of Tucson's best restaurants. Next door is the:

# Walking Tour 1—El Presidio Historic Dictrict

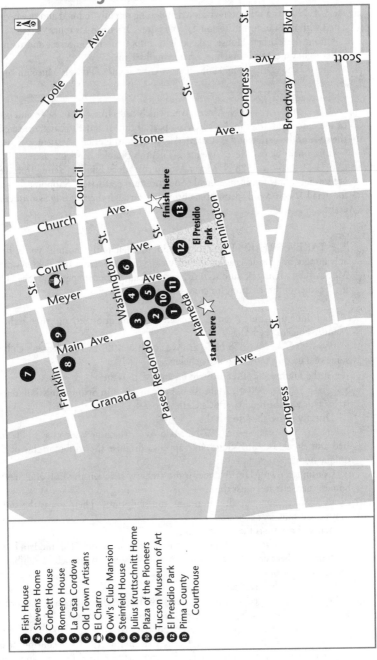

1. Fish House
2. Stevens Home
3. Corbett House
4. Romero House
5. La Casa Cordova
6. Old Town Artisans
7. El Charro
8. Owl's Club Mansion
9. Steinfeld House
10. Julius Kruttschnitt Home
11. Plaza of the Pioneers
12. Tucson Museum of Art
13. El Presidio Park
14. Pima County
    Courthouse

start here
finish here
El Presidio Park

3. Corbett House, a mission revival–style building recently restored and newly decorated with mission furniture and Tiffany lamps. It's open for tours.

From the Corbett House, take a right onto Washington Street and then another right onto Meyer Avenue, where you'll see the:

4. Romero House. Built in 1868, it now contains the Tucson Museum of Art School.

Next door is:

5. La Casa Cordova, 175 N. Meyer Ave., which dates from about 1848 and is one of the oldest buildings in Tucson. As a part of the art museum, it's furnished in the style of the period and is dedicated as a Mexican Heritage Museum.

Diagonally across Meyer Avenue is Tucson's premier crafts market:

6. Old Town Artisans, 186 N. Meyer Ave. In this adobe building dating from 1862 are several rooms full of handmade Southwestern crafts (see "Shopping," below, for details). You could spend hours browsing through the amazing assortment of crafts.

☕ **TAKE A BREAK**    If you started your tour late in the morning you're probably hungry by now, so head up Court Avenue to **El Charro Cafe,** Tucson's oldest Mexican restaurant. Be sure to order carne seca, the house specialty. (See "Dining," earlier in this chapter, for complete information.)

Continue up Court Avenue, turn left on Franklin Street, and then right on Main Avenue to reach the:

7. Owl's Club Mansion, 378 N. Main Ave., built in 1901 as a gentlemen's club for some of Tucson's most eligible bachelors.

At the southwest corner of Franklin and Main is the:

8. Steinfeld House, 300 N. Main Ave., built in 1899 in Spanish mission–revival style. This was the original Owl's Club.

Directly across the street is the:

9. Julius Kruttschnitt House, 297 N. Main Ave., which now serves as El Presidio Bed and Breakfast Inn. Victorian trappings disguise the adobe origins of this unique home.

Continue down Main Avenue to the archway between the Fish and Stevens homes, turn left, and cross the:

10. Plaza of the Pioneers, with fountains and sculptures. The plaza is the site of summer-evening jazz concerts.

Across the plaza is the entrance to the:

11. Tucson Museum of Art (see above for complete information). This modern building houses collections of pre-Columbian and Western art, as well as exhibits of contemporary works.

Cross Alameda Street to:

12. El Presidio Park, once the parade ground for the presidio and now a shady gathering spot for everyone from the homeless to downtown office workers.

Just to the east of the park is the very impressive:

13. Pima County Courthouse, 155 N. Church St. Built in 1928, the courthouse incorporates Moorish, Spanish, and Southwestern architectural features, including a colorful tiled dome. A portion of the original presidio wall is in a glass case on the second floor.

## WALKING TOUR 2
# The Barrio Histórico & Downtown Arts District

**Start:** The Tucson Convention Center.
**Finish:** Hotel Congress.
**Time:** Four hours.
**Best Times:** Daytime, when there are people on the street and it's safer to walk around.
**Worst Times:** After dark or in the summer heat.

When the Tucson city council decided to raze its historic districts in the name of urban renewal, members didn't realize that the old homes in the neighborhood were actually worth saving as an important part of Tucson's history and culture. About half of the downtown was razed before the voices for preservation and restoration were finally heard. And if it had not been for the activism of the residents of the Barrio Histórico, Interstate 10 would now run right through much of this area.

Lying just to the east of the Tucson Convention Center, the Congress Street commercial neighborhood is now the heart of the Downtown Arts District and is home to several galleries, eclectic boutiques, and cafes.

Start your tour at the:

1. **Tucson Convention Center,** a sprawling complex that includes a sports arena, grand ballroom, concert hall, theater, pavilions, meeting halls, gardens, and craft and souvenir vendors. Near the fountains in the center of the complex is the historic:

2. **Sosa-Carillo-Frémont House,** 151 Granada Ave., an adobe structure built in the 1850s and later the home of territorial governor John C. Frémont (see above for complete information).

   Walk back to Church Avenue and across the street you'll see:

3. **St. Augustine Cathedral.** The entrance is from Stone Avenue, so walk around to the front. Above the door you'll see a statue of St. Augustine and symbols of the Arizona desert—the horned toad, the saguaro, and the yucca.

   From the south side of the cathedral, walk a block east on Corral Street and you'll be facing the back of the:

4. **Carnegie Library,** which now houses the Tucson Children's Museum (see "Especially for Kids," above, for complete information).

   Walk around to the front, then back 1 block toward St. Augustine's, turn left, and you'll come to the:

5. **Temple of Music and Art,** 330 S. Scott Ave. It was built in 1927 as a movie and stage theater, and is the home of the Arizona Theatre Company (see "Tucson After Dark," later in this chapter, for complete information).

☕ **TAKE A BREAK**   Housed within the Temple of Music and Art complex is an excellent little cafe popular both with downtown businesspeople and artists. The **B&B Cafe** serves imaginative sandwiches and salads and delicious pastries. Or, for lunch in a historic adobe, visit the **Cushing Street Bar & Grill** at 343 S. Meyer Ave. at Cushing Street (across from the Tucson Convention Center) by turning right on 14th Street, which then becomes Cushing Street, the northern edge of the Barrio Histórico District. The grill is decorated with saltillo tile floors and antiques and serves Southwestern and new American food in a jazzy atmosphere.

# Walking Tour 2—Barrio Historico & Downtown Arts District

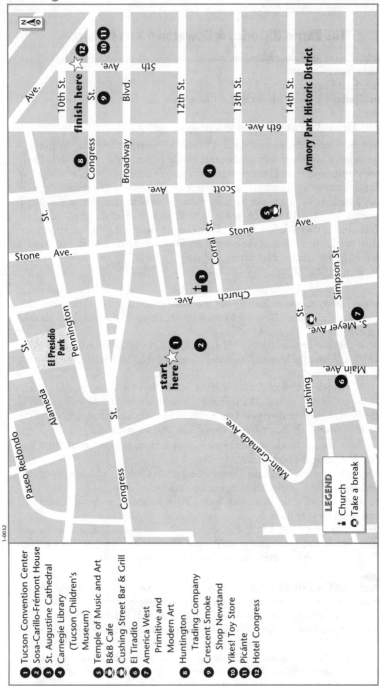

**LEGEND**
✝ Church
☕ Take a break

1 Tucson Convention Center
2 Sosa-Carillo-Frémont House
3 St. Augustine Cathedral
4 Carnegie Library (Tucson Children's Museum)
5 Temple of Music and Art
   B&B Cafe
6 Cushing Street Bar & Grill
   El Tiradito
7 America West Primitive and Modern Art
8 Huntington Trading Company
9 Crescent Smoke Shop Newstand
10 Yikes! Toy Store
11 Picánte
12 Hotel Congress

1-0032

After your rest, turn right on 14th Street (if you haven't already), which becomes Cushing Street in 1 block, and then walk another block. You'll be on the northern edge of the Barrio Histórico District, with its 150 adobe row houses, which is the largest collection of 19th-century Sonoran-style adobe architecture preserved in the United States.

Continue another block west to Main Avenue and turn left. On the far side of the street stands:

**6.** El Tiradito. This is the only shrine in the United States dedicated to a sinner buried in unconsecrated soil. People still light candles here in hope of having their wishes come true (for complete information, see "The Shrine That Stopped a Freeway," a boxed feature earlier in this chapter).

Wander awhile through the Barrio Histórico District admiring the Sonoran-style homes that are built right out to the edge of the street. Many of these homes sport colorfully painted facades, signs of the ongoing renovation of this neighborhood.

Before leaving the Barrio, you may want to stop in at:

**7.** America West Primitive and Modern Art, 363 S. Meyer Ave. Not only will you get a glimpse inside one of these buildings, but the collection of art for sale in this gallery is fascinating.

From here, head back up S. Meyer Avenue, turn right on Cushing Street, left on Church Avenue, and then turn right on Congress Street. As you walk along this street, you'll see many interesting shops and art galleries, including the:

**8.** Huntington Trading Company, 111 E. Congress St., specializing in Mexican and Native American art.

Cross the street, and in the next block, you'll come to the:

**9.** Crescent Smoke Shop Newsstand, 216 E. Congress St., an old-fashioned smoke shop with cigars, magazines, and newspapers from all over the country.

In the next block is:

**10.** Yikes! Toy Store, 302 E. Congress St., a wacky toy store filled with rubber dinosaurs, plastic spiders, and other inexpensive, offbeat items that appeal as much to adults as they do to children.

Next door is:

**11.** Picánte, 306 E. Congress St., which has a plethora of Hispanic-themed icons and accessories, including milagros (charms) and Day of the Dead skeletons.

Just before the end of Congress Street, you'll come to the:

**12.** Hotel Congress, 311 E. Congress St. The famous gangster John Dillinger stayed here shortly before he was captured. The Congress Hotel was renovated several years ago and now houses a youth hostel and budget hotel. Be sure to look around the lobby.

## 6 Organized Tours

To get a thorough overview of Tucson, you can take a $6^1/_2$-hour tour with **Old Pueblo Tours** (☎ **520/795-7448**). The tour includes visits to A Mountain, the downtown historic districts, De Grazia's Gallery in the Sun, the Arizona Historical Society Tucson Museum, and Mission San Xavier del Bac. The tour is $40 for adults and $15 for children 16 and under.

The costumed tour leader at **Tours of Tucson** (☎ **520/884-4560** or 520/325-2450) tells stories from the perspective of a saloon keeper who lived in Tucson during the 1870s. The 2-hour bus adventure is $25 per person.

**Tucson Tours** (☎ 520/297-2911) offers 1¹/₂-hour guided city tours for $15. The tours head up to the top of A Mountain for an overview of the city, then visit the three downtown historic districts and the University of Arizona. The same company also offers a shuttle service to the Arizona–Sonora Desert Museum and Old Tucson Studios, and tours to Mission San Xavier del Bac, Bisbee, Tombstone, Nogales, and Sedona.

To learn more about the history of Tucson, see if you can attach yourself to one of Ken Scoville's **Old Pueblo Walking Tours** (☎ 520/323-9290), tours of the downtown area that include a photo and map packet (he usually does tours for groups). Mr. Scoville has a wealth of knowledge about the city and can make the historic districts come alive. These 2-hour tours cost $10 and are offered November to May or on request; call for a reservation first.

If you'd like to learn more about people who lived in the Tucson area hundreds of years ago, take a tour with the **Center for Desert Archaeology** (☎ 520/881-2244 or 520/885-6283). A nonprofit educational and research organization, it can take you to view petroglyphs near Tucson and ruins of the Hohokam people in Catalina State Park. Tours cost $40 for a half day and $70 for a full day.

You can also play at being an archaeologist for a day at the **Old Pueblo Archaeology Center,** P.O. Box 40577, Tucson, AZ 85717-0577 (☎ 520/798-1201), which is excavating the Sabino Canyon Ruin. A day-long program includes an orientation, a tour of the ruin site, 4 to 5 hours of excavation, and time in the lab. The 1-day program is $69, and a 3-day program is $189. They also have a special archaeology program for children.

If you want to get out into the wilds or crave a taste of pioneer history, **High Desert Convoys** (☎ 800/93-TOURS or 520/323-3386) will take you out on one of their tours in four-wheel-drive WWII vehicles. They offer trips to Buenos Aires National Wildlife Refuge, an excursion to a ghost town, a trip to some remote petroglyphs, and a tour that includes a hike to a cave. Prices range from $45 to $75.

For an aerial perspective on Tucson and its surrounding mountains, try **Papillon Helicopters** (☎ 520/573-6817), which charges $80 per person for a half-hour flight and $160 per person for a 1-hour flight.

# 7 Outdoor Pursuits

**BALLOONING**    **Balloon America** (☎ 520/299-7744) offers breakfast flights over the foothills of the Santa Catalina Mountains with free pickups at selected resorts. The ballooning season runs only from October to June. Flights cost $135 per person, with a champagne toast at the end. **Southern Arizona Balloon Excursions** (☎ 520/624-3599) offers similar flights at about $125 per person as well.

**BIKING**    You can explore the Arizona backcountry with a rental mountain bike from the helpful folks at **Full Cycle,** 3232 E. Speedway Blvd. ☎ 520/327-3232. Rates are $20 per day or $35 for a 3-day holiday period. **Bargain Basement Bike,** 428 N. Fremont Ave., near the university (☎ 520/628-1015), or **Broadway Bicycles,** 140 S. Sarnoff Dr. (☎ 520/296-7819), rent mountain bikes for about $18 to $33 per day.

Places for biking include the **Rillito River Park,** a 4-mile trail that runs along the riverbed between Campbell Avenue and La Cholla Boulevard; and the **Santa Cruz River Park,** from West Grant Road to 29th Street, 4 miles with a view of the Santa Cruz River. But the best place for biking in Tucson is in **Sabino Canyon** (see "Seeing the Sights," above), where bicycles are allowed after 5pm and before 9am every day except Wednesday and Saturday.

If you'd prefer to go out on a **guided mountain bike ride,** Tucson Bicycles (☎ **520/577-7374**) accommodates all levels of riders. Half-day trips start at $65 and full-day trips start at $125 per person (includes use of bicycle and equipment).

Half-day and full-day mountain-bike trips within a 50-mile radius of Tucson are offered by **Arizona Offroad Adventures,** P.O. Box 3339, Tucson, AZ 85722 (☎ **800/689-BIKE** or 520/882-6567). They also sell a **mountain-biking map** of the Tucson area for $12 (available by mail). It covers the Santa Catalina, Santa Rita, Rincon, and Tucson Mountains.

**BIRD WATCHING** Southern Arizona has some of the best bird watching in the country, and though the best spots are south of Tucson, there are a few places around the city that birders will enjoy seeking out. **Agua Caliente County Park,** at the corner of Soldier Trail and Roger Road in the northeast corner of the city, is just about the best place to see birds in the city. The year-round warm springs here are a magnet for dozens of species, including waterfowl, great blue herons, black phoebes, soras, and vermilion flycatchers. Other good places include **Sabino Canyon Recreation Area** and the path to the waterfall at **Loews Ventana Canyon Resort.** However, the best area bird watching is in **Madera Canyon,** which is south of the city. See "Side Trips from Tucson," below, for details.

**GOLF** Although there aren't quite as many golf courses in Tucson as in Phoenix, this is still a golfer's town.

In addition to the public links, there are numerous resort courses that allow nonguests to play. Perhaps the most famous of these courses are the two 18-hole courses at **The Lodge at Ventana Canyon,** 6200 N. Clubhouse Lane (☎ **520/577-2115**). These Tom Fazio–designed courses offer challenging desert target-style play that is nearly legendary. The third hole on the Mountain Course here is one of the most photographed holes in the west. However, as famous as Ventana Canyon courses are, it is the 27-hole **Omni Tucson National Golf Resort and Spa,** 2727 W. Club Dr. (☎ **520/297-2271** or 520/575-7540), a traditional course, that is perhaps more familiar to golfers—as the site of the annual Tucson Open. The **Sheraton El Conquistador Resort and Country Club,** 10555 N. La Cañada Dr. (☎ **520/544-1800**), with two 18-hole courses and a nine-hole course, offers stunning (and very distracting) views of the Santa Catalina Mountains. At the **Westin La Paloma Resort and Country Club,** 3660 E. Sunrise Dr. (☎ **520/299-1500**), golfers will find 27 holes designed by Jack Nicklaus. At **Starr Pass Golf Resort,** 3645 W. Starr Pass Blvd. (☎ **520/670-0300**), players are seduced by the deceptively difficult 15th hole that plays right through the narrow Starr Pass.

There are also many other public courses around town. The **Raven Club at Sabino Springs,** 9777 E. Sabino Greens Dr. (☎ **520/749-3636**), a relative newcomer to the Tucson golf scene, incorporates stands of cactus and rocky outcroppings into the course layout. One of the most recent additions to the Tucson golf scene is **The Golf Club at Vistoso,** 955 W. Vistoso Highlands Dr. (☎ **520/797-7900**). Although a new course, it features a traditional, very playable design.

Greens fees at these clubs vary with the season, but expect to pay around $120 for 18 holes in winter, much less in summer. For last-minute tee-time reservations, contact **Stand-by Golf** (☎ **520/882-2665**).

Tucson Parks and Recreation operates five municipal golf courses, of which the **Randolph North** and **Dell Urich,** 600 S. Alvernon Way (☎ **520/325-2811**), are the premier courses. The former is the site of the Welch's/Circle K LPGA Open, and the latter was recently remodeled. Other municipal courses include **El Rio,** 1400 W. Speedway Blvd. (☎ **520/623-6783**); **Silverbell,** 3600 N. Silverbell Rd. (☎ **520/743-7284**); and **Fred Enke,** 8251 E. Irvington Rd. (☎ **520/296-8607**). Greens fees for 18 holes range from $16.50 in summer to $26.50 in winter. Golf carts are available for $16.

**HIKING**    Tucson is nearly surrounded by mountains, most of which are protected as city and state parks, national forest land, or as national park. Within these areas are hundreds of miles of hiking trails.

**Saguaro National Park** flanks Tucson on both the east and west with units accessible off Old Spanish Trail east of Tucson and past the end of Speedway Boulevard west of the city. In these areas you can observe Sonoran Desert vegetation and wildlife and hike among the huge saguaro cacti for which the park is named.

**Tucson Mountain Park,** also at the end of Speedway Boulevard, is adjacent to Saguaro National Park and preserves a similar landscape.

**Sabino Canyon,** off Sabino Canyon Road, is Tucson's most popular recreation area. A cold mountain stream here cascades over waterfalls and forms pools that make great swimming holes. The most popular trail is the 4¹/₂-mile-long Seven Falls Trail, which follows Bear Canyon deep into the mountains.

**Catalina State Park,** 11570 N. Oracle Rd. (☎ **520/628-5798**), is set on the rugged northwest face of the Santa Catalina Mountains, between 2,500 and 3,000 feet high. Hiking trails beginning in the park lead into the Pusch Ridge Wilderness. Romero Pools are a refreshing destination for a day hike. Admission to the park is $4. There are also horseback-riding stables adjacent to the park, and within the park there is an ancient Hohokam ruin.

The **Mount Lemmon Recreation Area,** at the end of the Catalina Highway, is set amid high alpine forests on this 8,250-foot mountain. The cool air at this elevation makes this a popular summertime retreat.

**HORSEBACK RIDING**    If you want to play cowboy or just go for a leisurely ride through the desert, there are plenty of stables around Tucson where you can saddle up. In addition to renting horses and providing guided trail rides, all the stables below also offer sunset rides with cookouts. Though reservations are not always required, they're a good idea. You can also opt to stay at a guest ranch and do almost as much riding as your muscles can stand.

**Pusch Ridge Stables,** 13700 N. Oracle Rd. (☎ **520/825-1664**), is adjacent to Catalina State Park and Coronado National Forest. Rates are $20 for 1 hour, $35 for 2 hours, and $30 for a 1¹/₂-hour sunset ride.

**El Conquistador Stables** (☎ **520/742-4200**) and **Walking Wind Stables** (☎ **520/742-4422**) are both at 10811 N. Oracle Rd. at Catalina State Park. Rates are $15 for 1 hour, $28 for 2 hours, and $23 for a 1¹/₂-hour sunset ride. Reservations are required.

**Desert-High Country Stables,** 6501 W. Ina Rd. (☎ **520/744-3789**), is located 2 miles west of I-10 and offers a variety of rides in the Tucson Mountains and Saguaro National Park West. Rates range from $15 for 1 hour to $60 for a full day. Reservations are requested.

If just riding the range isn't enough for you and you really want to do the city slicker thing, then you need to contact **Rocky Mountain Cattle Moo-vers** (☎ **800/826-9666** or 520/682-2088) and sign on for a cattle drive. These aren't genuine cattle drives, but you will be movin' them doggies up the trail a piece. Prices range from $80 for a breakfast cattle drive to $170 for an all-day cattle drive.

**IN-LINE SKATING**    You can rent in-line skates at **Peter Glen's,** 5626 E. Broadway Blvd. (☎ **520/745-4514**), for $6 per 3 hours or $12 per day, including protective equipment. Good places to skate include Reid Park, the University of Arizona Campus, the Rillito River Wash between North Campbell Avenue and North Oracle Road, and the Udall Center on Tanque Verde Road near the Sabino Canyon turnoff.

**JOGGING**   **McCormick Park,** 2950 N. Columbus Blvd., has a 1-mile jogging course, and **Fort Lowell Park,** 2900 N. Craycroft Rd., has a 1½-mile course. Both are open from sunup to sundown.

**ROCK CLIMBING**   Tucson's premier climbing spot is high up on the Mount Lemmon Highway at a windy viewpoint that offers excellent climbing and totally awesome views of Tucson spread out far below. If you want to take a class or go out with a guide, contact **impulse!** (☎ **800/X-IMPULSE** or 520/888-6880), which charges $99 for an all-day class.

Whether you're a novice or a more experienced climber, **Venture Up** (☎ **602/ 955-9100**) will take you out rock climbing or rappelling in the Tucson area or other places around Arizona. It's $185 per person per day for private guiding, which includes all equipment.

**SKIING**   One hour (35 miles) from Tucson, **Mount Lemmon Ski Valley** (☎ **520/ 576-1321**) offers 15 slopes for experienced downhill skiers as well as beginners. This is the southernmost ski area in the continental United States, and at times there's insufficient snow for good skiing. Be sure to call ahead before driving up. The ski season runs from December to April. Lift tickets are $27 for adults, $12 for children. Half-day rates are $22 for adults, $10 for children.

**SWIMMING**   See "Seeing the Sights," earlier in this chapter, for Sabino Canyon, a terrific place to splash around in a crystal-clear pool.

**TENNIS**   Tucson boasts more than 220 public tennis courts, many lighted for night playing. The **Randolph Tennis Center,** 50 S. Alvernon Way (☎ **520/791-4896**), convenient to downtown, offers 25 lighted courts. During the day court time is $1.50 per person; at night it's $4.50 per court. Many of the city's hotels and resorts provide courts for guest use.

**WHITE-WATER RAFTING**   The desert may seem like a strange place to think about rafting, but within 3½ hours of the city, there are two raftable rivers with enough white water to keep the casual paddler happy. **Chandelle Ski and Travel** (☎ **800/242-6335** or 520/577-1824) offers trips on the Gila River 60 miles north of Tucson. This is a Class II stretch of river and trip prices for a half-day run $59 per person, including lunch.

# 8 Spectator Sports

For most sporting events, call the numbers in the listings below for ticket information. However, tickets for special sporting events at the **Tucson Convention Center Arena** are sold by Dillard's department store box offices (☎ **800/638-4253**).

**BASEBALL**   The **Colorado Rockies** (☎ **520/327-9467**) pitch spring-training camp in March at Hi Corbett Field, 900 S. Randolph Way, in Reid Park (at South Country Club Road and East 22nd Street). Tickets are $4 to $28; to order, call ☎ **800/388-ROCK.** In March of 1998, The Chicago White Sox and the Arizona Diamondbacks will be playing at Tucson's new sports complex, due to be finished in 1997.

This is also where you can watch the **Tucson Toros** (☎ **520/325-2621**), the Milwaukee Brewers AAA team in the Pacific Coast League. The season runs from April to August, and tickets are $4 to $8 for adults and $3 for children 6 to 16, free for children 5 and under.

**FOOTBALL**   The **University of Arizona Wildcats** (☎ **520/621-2287**), a PAC-10 team, play at the U of A's Arizona Stadium, and between Christmas and New Year's Day each year, two of the nation's top NCAA teams play each other in the Copper Bowl game.

**GOLF TOURNAMENTS** In mid-March, women golfers compete for big prizes at the **Welch's/Circle K LPGA Championship** (☎ 520/791-5742), which is held at the Randolph North Golf Course. The **Tucson Chrysler Classic** (☎ 800/882-7660), Tucson's main PGA tournament, is held in mid-February (February 16 to 22, 1998) at the Omni Tucson National Golf Resort and Spa.

**GREYHOUND RACING** Greyhounds race year-round at **Tucson Greyhound Park,** 36th Street at Fourth Ave.; take Exit 261 off I-10 (☎ 520/884-7576). Admission ranges from $1.25 for general admission to $3 for the clubhouse.

**HORSE RACING** Rillito Park, on First Avenue between River and Limberlost roads (☎ 520/322-9291), was the birthplace of quarterhorse racing and has now been restored for both quarterhourse and thoroughbred racing. The season is weekends anywhere from October to March (as yet undetermined) and admission is $2 to $3, children free.

**TENNIS TOURNAMENTS** The **CIGNA Healthcare Celebrity Tennis Classic** (☎ 520/623-6165) takes place at the Randolph Tennis Center at Randolph Park in mid- to late April, when more than 40 celebrity tennis players take on local tennis players.

**WILDFLOWER VIEWING** Blooming time varies from year to year, but April and May are good times to view native wildflowers in the Tucson area. We love seeing the saguaro cacti in bloom. Good places to view these massive cacti and other wildflowers in bloom are in Saguaro National Park and Sabino Canyon.

# 9 Day Spas

If you'd rather opt for a massage than a round on the links, consider spending a few hours at a day spa. While full-service health spas can cost $400 to $500 or more per person per day, for less than $100, you can avail yourself of a spa treatment or two (massages, facials, seaweed wraps, loofah scrubs, and the like) and maybe even get to spend the day lounging by the pool at some exclusive resort. Spas are great places to while away an afternoon if you couldn't get a tee time at that golf course you wanted to play or if it happens to be raining (which, believe it or not, it sometimes does here in Tucson). While spas in general still cater primarily to women, the spas mentioned below also have special programs for men.

Our favorite day spa is at **Loews Ventana Canyon Resort,** 7000 N. Resort Dr. (☎ 800/234-5117 or 520/299-2020), which has recently opened a luxurious new spa in the Catalina foothills. Soothed by the scent of aromatherapy, you can treat yourself to herbal wraps, mud body treatments, seaweed body masks, different styles of massage, specialized facials, steam and dry saunas ($45 to $125), and complete beauty salon services. With any body treatment you can also use the spa's fitness facilities and pool for the day.

For an equally luxurious day at the spa, you can opt to visit the **Omni Tucson National Golf Resort & Spa,** 2727 W. Club Dr. (☎ 520/575-7559), off Magee Road in the northwestern foothills. Services and prices here are comparable to those at Loew's, and once again, with any body treatment or massage, you have full use of the spa's facilities.

With four locations around the Tucson area, **Gadabout Day Spa** offers the opportunity to slip a relaxing visit to a spa into a busy schedule. Mud baths, facials, and massages as well as hair and nail services are available. You'll find Gadabout at the following locations: St. Philip's Plaza, 1990 E. River Rd. (☎ 520/577-2000); 393 E. Grant Rd. (☎ 520/885-0000); Rancho Center, 3382 E. Speedway Blvd. (☎ 520/

**325-0000**), and Canyon Ranch, 8600 Rockcliff Rd. (☎ **520/749-1002**). Body treatments and massages range in price from $50 to $110.

## 10 Shopping

Tucsonians have a very strong sense of their place in the Southwest, and this is reflected in the city's shopping scene. Southwestern clothing, food, crafts, furniture, and art abound (often at reasonable prices), as do shopping centers built in a Southwestern architectural style.

Although Tucson is overshadowed by Scottsdale and Phoenix, the city provides a very respectable diversity of merchants. Its population center has moved steadily northward for some years, so it is in the northern foothills that you'll find most of the city's large enclosed shopping malls as well as expensive shops selling the best-quality merchandise.

There are also plenty of new, hip, and unusual shops in downtown Tucson. On Fourth Avenue, between Congress Street and Speedway Boulevard, are more than 100 shops, galleries, and restaurants in the **North Fourth Avenue historic shopping district.** The buildings here were built in the early 1900s, and a drive to keep the neighborhood humming has helped maintain Tucson's downtown vitality. Through the underpass at the south end of Fourth Avenue is Congress Street, the heart of the **Downtown Arts District.** Here you'll find numerous galleries specializing in contemporary art, avant-garde boutiques, and a few trendy eating establishments. However, neither of these neighborhoods seems to be catching on very fast with Tucson shoppers, and they continue to be a bit seedy.

**El Presidio Historic District** around the Tucson Museum of Art is the city's center for crafts shops. Here are Old Town Artisans and the Tucson Museum of Art museum shop. The **"Lost Barrio"** on the corner of Southwest Park Avenue and 12th Street (a block off Broadway) is a good place to look for Mexican imports and Southwestern-style home furnishings at good prices. Stores include Rústica, Vaqueros de los Artes, Magellan Trading, and Colonial Frontiers.

### ANTIQUES

In addition to the shops listed below, you'll find concentrations of antiques shops along Speedway Boulevard between Swan and Craycroft roads and along Grand Road between Tucson Boulevard and Alvernon Way.

**Antique Center.** 5000 E. Speedway Blvd. ☎ **520/323-0319.**

This mall has 90 dealers and claims to be the largest antiques mall in southern Arizona. For sale are all manner of collectibles and antiques, including Aunt Jemima figures, old radios and telephones, and lots of copper and glassware collectibles.

**F. L. Wright.** 316 E. Congress St. ☎ **520/622-3350.**

Mission-revival and arts-and-crafts furnishings, as exemplified by the simple oak furniture of the Stickley company, have been all the rage for several years now, and here in this store you'll find the largest selection of such furniture in the city.

### ART

**Americas.** 6420 N. Campbell Ave. (corner of Skyline Dr. and N. Campbell Rd.). ☎ **520/529-7002.**

Located right below Anthony's restaurant, this very small shop specializes in very expensive Native American artifacts such as pots, baskets, beaded moccasins, Navajo rugs, and antique kachinas.

**America West Primitive & Modern Art.** 363 S. Meyer Ave. (in the Old Barrio). ☎ **520/623-4091.**

Although this gallery specializes in works by Native Americans, you'll also find pre-Columbian art and pieces from Africa, Oceania, and Asia. This is museum-quality work. An appointment is requested, but drop-ins are also welcome.

**Eleanor Jeck Galleries.** 4280 N. Campbell Ave. (at River Rd. in St. Philip's Plaza). ☎ **520/299-2139.**

Featuring brilliant and whimsical contemporary paintings, this gallery also carries art glass, sculpture, painted furniture, large-format ceramics, and art jewelry.

**El Presidio Gallery.** 7000 E. Tanque Verde Rd. (at Santa Fe Sq.). ☎ **520/733-0388.**

This is one of Tucson's premier galleries and deals primarily in traditional paintings of the Southwest, although some contemporary works are also available. A second location is at St. Philip's Plaza, 4340 N. Campbell Ave. (☎ **520/529-1220**).

✪ **Etherton Gallery.** 135 S. Sixth Ave. ☎ **520/624-7370.**

For more than 20 years this gallery has been presenting Tucson with some of the finest new art to be found in this city, including contemporary and historic photographs. They aren't afraid to present work with strong themes. The Etherton Gallery also has exhibition space upstairs from the B&B Café at the Temple of Music and Art

✪ **Philabaum Gallery.** 711 S. Sixth Ave. ☎ **520/884-7404.**

Visitors can stop by Tom Philabaum's glass studio and watch vases, perfume bottles, and bowls being blown, then browse the gallery full of lovely art glass pieces by Philabaum and other artists from around the country.

## BOOKS

**The Book Mark.** 5001 E. Speedway Blvd. ☎ **520/881-6350.**

This plain-looking storefront doesn't hint at what lies behind it. What you'll find are densely packed shelves of books and books piled on the floor. The huge selection includes many books by local authors.

✪ **Coyote's Voice.** 16 S. Eastbourne Ave. (at Broadway Blvd. and Country Club Rd.). ☎ **520/327-6560.**

Located in the Broadway Village, Coyote's Voice specializes in books on and by Hispanic writers, Mexican fiction and history, and Southwestern architecture. It has an active schedule of readings and signings by regional authors.

**Settlers West Book & Print Gallery.** 3061 N. Campbell Ave. ☎ **520/323-8838.**

An impressive selection of books about the West, both for adults and children, is the main attraction here, but there are also lots of interesting Western-themed prints.

## CRAFTS

✪ **Berta Wright Gallery.** In the Foothills Mall at the corner of Ina Rd. and La Cholla Blvd. ☎ **520/742-4134.**

A rich assemblage of imported crafts including Huichol beadwork, Southwestern and Mexican jewelry, sculpture, figurines, and a smattering of ethnic clothing are all selected by the scrutinizing eye of Berta Wright. She also carries Soleri bells from the foundry at Cosanti in Scottsdale.

**Obsidian Gallery.** 4340 N. Campbell Ave. (at River Rd. in St. Philip's Plaza). ☎ **520/577-3598.**

Contemporary crafts by artists of national renown fill this gallery. You'll find luminous art glass, unique jewelry (including designs by Thomas Mann), imaginative ceramics, and much more.

✪ **Old Town Artisans.** 186 N. Meyer Ave. ☎ **800/782-8072** or 520/623-6024.

Housed in a restored 1850s adobe building covering an entire city block of El Presidio Historic District are 15 rooms brimming with the best of Southwestern arts and crafts. You'll find traditional and contemporary designs by more than 400 artisans.

**Pink Adobe Gallery.** 222 E. Congress St. ☎ **520/623-2828.**

This contemporary crafts gallery sells works produced by artists from all over the United States. On a recent visit there were hand-tinted photos, painted-tin folk art, ceramics, one-of-a-kind pieces of furniture, and cases full of unique jewelry. There is a second Pink Adobe in La Plaza Shoppes, 6538 E. Tanque Verde Rd. ( ☎ **520/298-5995**).

**Tucson Museum of Art Shop.** 140 N. Main Ave. ☎ **520/624-2333.**

The museum's gift shop offers a colorful and changing selection of Southwestern arts and crafts, mostly by local and regional artists.

## FASHIONS
See also "Western Wear," below.

### For Both Men & Women
**The Buffalo Exchange.** 2001 E. Speedway Blvd. ☎ **520/795-0508.**

It's fun to visit The Buffalo Exchange and browse through racks of resale and new clothing at fairly reasonable prices. You'll find a very large selection of things recently in style. There's another Buffalo Exchange at 7045 E. Tanque Verde Rd. ( ☎ **520/885-8392**).

### For Men
**Franklin's.** 5420 E. Broadway Blvd. ☎ **520/747-0680.**

From business suits to casual attire such as Hawaiian shirts, this place offers good quality and is a favorite spot for local guys to shop.

**Individual Man.** In St. Philip's Plaza, 4320 N. Campbell Ave. ☎ **520/577-2121.**

Unique ties, silk and other natural-fiber shirts, and cotton slacks are colorful and casual, with styles by American and Italian designers.

### For Women
**Jasmine.** 423 N. Fourth Ave. ☎ **520/629-0706.**

Natural fibers, including washable silks and some hand-loomed fabrics are the specialty here. There are plenty of styles to browse from on the crowded racks, from classic to exotic. There are Southwestern accessories and jewelry to go with the clothes. A second shop is at 3025 N. Campbell Ave. ( ☎ **520/323-1771**).

**Maya Palace.** In Plaza Palomino, 2960 N. Swan Rd. ☎ **520/325-6411.**

This small shop features lushly ethnic but very wearable women's clothing in natural fabrics. A second shop is at El Mercado de Boutiques, 6332 E. Broadway Blvd. ( ☎ **520/748-0817**).

**Nicole Miller.** 4380 N. Campbell Ave. (at St. Philip's Plaza). ☎ **520/577-9843.**

One of the many small shops that are extensions of Nicole Miller in New York, you'll find here a limited selection of whimsical sportswear or dressy items for a special event.

✪ **Rochelle K.** In The Plaza at Williams Centre, 5350 E. Broadway Blvd. ☎ **520/745-4600.**

With everything from the latest in the little black dress to casual and drapey silks and linens, Rochelle K attracts a well-heeled clientele. There are also beautiful accessories and jewelry.

**The Strand.** In Plaza Palomino, 2920 N. Swan Rd., no. 118. ☎ **520/322-5114.**

This very small boutique features a limited selection of dresses and casual sportswear in fabrics suited to the Tucson climate.

### For Children

**Angel Threads.** In Broadway Village, 3050 E. Broadway. ☎ **520/326-1170.**

From denims to cute-as-a-button dresses, the color-coordinated outfits here are absolutely heavenly—or at least that's what mothers and grandmothers seem to think.

## GIFTS/SOUVENIRS

**B&B Cactus Farm.** 11550 E. Speedway Blvd. ☎ **520/721-4687.**

This plant nursery is devoted exclusively to cacti and succulents. The store can pack your purchase for traveling or can ship it anywhere in the United States. The farm is worth a visit just to see the amazing variety of cacti on display. It's a good place to stop on the way to or from Saguaro National Monument East.

**Picánte.** 306 E. Congress St. ☎ **520/622-8807.**

There's a lot of things to look at and buy in this tiny shop, which has a plethora of Hispanic-theme icons and accessories, including *milagros* (charms), Day of the Dead skeletons, Mexican crosses, jewelry, and greeting cards. She also has a nice selection of clothing made from ethnic fabrics.

**Tohono Chul Gift Shop and Tea Room.** 7366 N. Paseo del Norte (1 block west of the corner of Ina and Oracle rds. in Tohono Chul Park). ☎ **520/797-1711.**

This gift shop is packed with Mexican folk art, nature theme toys, household items, T-shirts, and books. Combined with the restaurant and Tohon Chul Park, which is landscaped with desert plants, this makes a nice place for an outing. For a description of the park, see "Parks, Gardens & Zoos" under "Seeing the Sights."

## JEWELRY

**Beth Friedman Jewelry.** 186 N. Meyer Ave. ☎ **520/622-5013.**

Located in the Old Town Artisans complex, this shop sells jewelry from Southwestern tribes and international designers. She also carries some extravagant cowgirl getups in velvet, lace, and denim.

✪ **Turquoise Door.** In St. Philip's Plaza, 4330 N. Campbell Ave. (at River Rd.). ☎ **520/299-7787.**

The Southwestern contemporary jewelry here is among the most stunning in the city and is made with opals, diamonds, lapis lazuli, amethyst, and the ubiquitous turquoise. There are also baskets, sculptures, bronzes, and rugs. Another location is at 5675 N. Swan Rd. (☎ **520/299-7551**).

**The Turquoise Land.** In Park Mall, 5870 E. Broadway Blvd. ☎ **520/745-1383.**

Masses of Indian turquoise-and-silver jewelry at reasonable prices make this a good stop for anyone looking to accessorize à la Southwest.

## MALLS/SHOPPING CENTERS

**Broadway Village.** Broadway Blvd. and Country Club Rd.

Broadway Village is the oldest shopping center in Tucson, as evidenced by the lettering painted on the brick walls. Stacia's Cafe and Coyote's Voice Bookstore, along with other small shops, are housed here.

**El Con Mall.** 3601 E. Broadway Blvd. ☎ **520/795-9958.**

With more than 170 establishments, including major department stores, theaters, and restaurants, this is Tucson's oldest regional shopping mall.

**Plaza Palomino.** 2970 N. Swan Rd. ☎ **520/795-1177.**

This small shopping plaza is built in the style of a Spanish hacienda with a courtyard and fountains, and is home to some of Tucson's little boutiques, specialty shops, galleries, and restaurants. They provide a courtesy hotel shuttle (☎ **520/444-1630**).

**✪ St. Philip's Plaza.** 4280 N. Campbell Ave. (at River Rd.). ☎ **520/529-2775.**

This yupscale Southwestern-style shopping center includes three excellent restaurants, a luxury beauty salon, and numerous shops and galleries, including Bahti Indian Arts and Turquoise Door jewelry.

**The Tucson Mall.** 4500 N. Oracle Rd. ☎ **520/293-7330.**

The foothills of northern Tucson have become shopping center central, and this is the largest of the malls. You'll find more than 200 merchants in this busy two-story skylit complex.

## MEXICAN & LATIN AMERICAN IMPORTS

In addition to the shops mentioned below, the **"Lost Barrio"** on the corner of Southwest Park Avenue and 12th Street (a block off Broadway) is a good place to look for Mexican imports and Southwestern-style home furnishings at good prices.

**Antigua de Mexico.** 7037 N. Oracle Rd. (in the Casa Adobes Plaza). ☎ **520/742-7114.**

This is a place for big household items (many of which are made in Mexico), such as oversized ceramics and painted plates, wooden and wrought-iron furniture, and punched-metal-framed mirrors and frames. Smaller items include crucifixes and candlesticks.

**La Buhardilla, "The Attic."** 2360 E. Broadway Blvd. ☎ **520/622-5200.**

Okay, so you just cashed in your place in California, you bought a big house, and you need some sizeable furniture to fill up all that space. Buhardilla has it—the hand-carved Spanish Baroque furniture is big, carved wood doors are 10 feet high, and there are larger-than-life-sized carvings of angels and archangels. There are also Latin American arts and crafts pieces to accessorize all that furniture.

**Rusticos de Mexico.** 4664 E. Speedway Blvd. (at Swan Rd.). ☎ **520/327-4053.**

This small shop contains low to mid-end rustic Southwestern and neo-colonial furniture.

## NATIVE AMERICAN ARTS & CRAFTS

**Bahti Indian Arts.** In St. Philip's Plaza, 4300 N. Campbell Ave. ☎ **520/577-0290.**

Family owned for more than 40 years, this store sells fine pieces—jewelry, baskets, sculpture, paintings, books, weavings, kachina dolls, Zuñi fetishes, and much more.

**✪ Huntington Trading Company.** 111 E. Congress St. ☎ **520/628-8578.**

Grotesque and humorous Yaqui masks glare at you from the walls of this store specializing in American and Mexican tribal arts and crafts. There are also Tohono

O'odham and Tarahumara baskets, Huichol bead sculptures, Casas Grandes and Oaxacan pottery, and paintings and sculptures by various artists. An affiliated store, the Sonora Trading Co., is located in Tubac in the Plaza Antigua on Tubac Road (☎ 520/398-9016).

✪ **Indian Territory.** 5639 N. Swan Rd. (on the northwest corner with Sunrise Dr.). ☎ **520/ 577-7961.**

Despite the location in the foothills in a shopping plaza, it's a bit like an old museum in here, with hardwood floors and antique display cases full of Plains and Southwest Indian arts and crafts and regalia. Though much of the store is devoted to new works, you'll also find rare old pieces such as beaded gauntlets and moccasins. Get owner Neil Hicks to take you on a tour of some of the amazing pieces here, but don't come on Monday—the store is closed.

**J Mark Sublette Medicine Man Gallery.** In Santa Fe Square, 7000 E. Tanque Verde Rd. ☎ **520/722-7798.**

Collectors of old Navajo rugs seem to agree that this rug shop has the best and biggest selection in the city and perhaps even the entire state. There are also Mexican and other Hispanic textiles, Acoma pottery, and other Indian crafts.

**The Kaibab Shops.** 2841 N. Campbell Ave. ☎ **520/795-6905.**

This store has been in business for almost 50 years and offers one of the best selections of Native American arts and crafts in Tucson. You can also find high-quality jewelry, Mexican pottery, home furnishings, glassware, kachinas, and antique *retablos*.

✪ **Morning Star Traders.** 2020 E. Speedway Blvd. (next door to the Plaza Hotel). ☎ **520/ 881-2112.**

With hardwood floors and a museumlike atmosphere, this store features museum-quality goods in the way of antique Navajo rugs, kachinas, furniture, and a huge selection of old Native American jewelry. This just may be the best store of its type in the entire state.

A newly opened adjoining shop carries an astounding selection of antique Spanish mission and Mexican furniture, as well as WPA, Mennonite, and South American pieces.

**Silverbell Trading.** In Casas Adobes Plaza, 7007 N. Oracle Rd. ☎ **520/797-6852.**

Not your usual run-of-the-mill crafts store, this shop carries unique items that the shopkeeper has obviously sought out. Small items such as stone Navajo corn maidens, Zuñi fetishes, and animals carved from sandstone caught our eye.

## OUTDOOR EQUIPMENT

**Bob's Bargain Barn.** 2330 N. Country Club Rd. (south of Grant Rd.). ☎ **520/325-3409.**

From that last-minute camping necessity to lightweight desert clothing to a major purchase like hiking boots, Bob's has what you need at good prices.

**Summit Hut.** 5045 E. Speedway Blvd. ☎ **520/325-1554.**

For top-name equipment and outdoor clothing, this store is hard to beat.

## TOYS

✪ **Yikes!** 300–302 E. Congress St. ☎ **520/622-8807.**

If you love wild and wacky toys that are as fun for adults as they are for kids, you won't want to miss Yikes!, which has a huge selection of rubber bugs, lizards, snakes, and frogs, as well as yo-yos, marbles, wind-up toys, and other absurd playthings.

## WESTERN WEAR

**Arizona Hatters.** 3600 N. First Ave. ☎ **520/292-1320.**

Arizona Hatters carries important names in cowboy hats, from Stetson to Bailey to Tilles. They do custom fitting and shape the hat to the wearer's head and face. You'll also find fancy beaded hatbands, shirts, and belts here.

**The Corral Western Wear.** 4525 E. Broadway Blvd. (just west of Swan Rd.). ☎ **520/322-6001.**

Standard cowboy gear and accoutrements for the more flamboyant wrangler such as turquoise cowboy hats and brightly colored cowboy boots are stocked here. This is the oldest Western-wear store in Tucson.

**Western Warehouse.** 3030 E. Speedway Blvd. ☎ **520/327-8005.**

If you want to put together your Western-wear ensemble under one roof, this is the place. It's the largest Western-wear store in Tucson and can deck you out in jeans, hats, boots, and Native American jewelry. There are also branches at 3719 N. Oracle Rd. (☎ **520/293-1808**) and 6701 E. Broadway Blvd. (☎ **520/885-4385**).

# 11  Tucson After Dark

Tucson after dark is a much easier landscape to negotiate than the vast cultural sprawl of the Phoenix area. Instead of having numerous performing arts centers all over the suburbs as in the Valley of the Sun, Tucson has a more centralized nightlife scene. The **Downtown Arts District** is the center of all the action, with the Temple of Music and Art, the Tucson Convention Center Music Hall, a small avant-garde theater, and several nightclubs. The **University of Arizona campus,** only a mile away, is another hot spot for entertainment.

The best place to look for entertainment listings is in the *Tucson Weekly.* Here you'll find thorough listings of concerts, theater and dance performances, and club offerings. The newspaper is free and can be picked up in convenience stores and record stores, among other places. For information on the current week's music performances on the University of Arizona campus, call the **MusiCall hotline** (☎ **520/621-2998**).

## THE CLUB & MUSIC SCENE
### MARIACHI MUSIC

Tucson is the mariachi capital of the United States, and no one should visit without spending at least one evening listening to some of these strolling minstrels. Luckily, there are at least two restaurants in town that feature mariachi music several nights each week.

**El Mariachi Restaurant.** 106 W. Drachman St. ☎ **520/791-7793.** No cover.

Although the view of the stage is better and the music is just as good, El Mariachi just doesn't have the atmosphere you'll find at La Fuente. The band International Mariachi America performs Wednesday through Sunday night (closed Monday and Tuesday) and the menu features steaks, shrimp, and Mexican food in the $10-to-$18 range. Shows are at 7 and 8:30pm. Reservations are recommended.

**La Fuente.** 1749 N. Miracle Mile. ☎ **520/623-8659.** No cover.

La Fuente is the largest Mexican restaurant in Tucson and serves up good food, but what really draws the crowds is the live mariachi music 5 nights a week. The music starts after 6pm Wednesday through Sunday (closed Monday and Tuesday), and if you just want to listen and not have dinner, you can hang out in the lounge.

## COUNTRY

**Cactus Moon Café.** 5470 E. Broadway Blvd. (on the east side of town at the corner of Craycroft Rd.). ☎ **520/748-0049.** Cover $3–$5.

A younger to middle-aged crowd frequents this large and glitzy nightclub for some Top 40 and rock, but mostly for country music (free dance lessons are offered just about nightly), drink specials, and Friday and Sunday buffets.

**The Maverick.** 4702 E. 22nd. St. (at Swan Rd.). ☎ **520/748-0456.** Cover Fri–Sat $2.

This country-and-western place is tiny and much more personable than Texas-sized The Stampede, which as far as a lot of people are concerned makes The Maverick a much more fun place to go dancing. Basically it attracts an older crowd, but there's usually a mix of people. Live bands play Tuesday through Sunday nights.

**The Stampede.** 4385 W. Ina Rd. ☎ **520/744-7744.** Cover $3–$5.

This country-music club used to be a bowling alley, and since the conversion it has the biggest and best dance floor in Tucson. In fact, there's an acre of floorboard for all you two-steppers. The crowd is mixed ages, and dance lessons are available. Drink specials and live music round out the bill. Closed Sunday through Tuesday.

## ROCK, JAZZ & BLUES

**Berky's Bar.** 5769 E. Speedway Blvd. ☎ **520/296-1981.** Cover Fri–Sat $3 after 8:30pm.

There's live blues wailing here 7 nights a week in a dark and smoky bar.

**Berky's on Fourth.** 424 N. Fourth Ave. ☎ **520/622-0376.** Cover free–$3.

This downtown Berky's outpost strays a bit from the blues format to bring in the occasional alternative rock band. Although the club is big and open, it can still get crowded.

**Chicago Bar.** 5954 E. Speedway Blvd. ☎ **520/748-8169.** Cover Wed–Sat $3.

Transplanted Chicagoans love to watch their home teams on the TVs at this neighborhood bar, but there's also live music nightly. Sure, blues gets played a lot, but so do reggae and jazz and about everything in between.

**✪ Club Congress.** 311 E. Congress St. ☎ **520/622-8848.** Cover $1–$15.

Just off the lobby of the restored Hotel Congress (now a youth hostel), Club Congress is one of Tucson's main alternative-music venues and a good choice for dancing. There are usually a couple of nights of live music each week.

## A COMEDY CLUB

**Laffs Comedy Caffè.** The Village, 2900 E. Broadway Blvd. ☎ **520/323-8669.** Cover Wed, Thurs, and Sun $5, Fri–Sat $8.

This stand-up comedy club has local comedians and professional comedians from around the country performing Wednesday through Sunday nights. They have a full bar and a full menu.

## DANCE CLUBS/DISCOS

**The Cage.** 5851 E. Speedway Blvd. ☎ **520/885-3030.** Cover $3.

The youngish crowd here turns out for the drink specials, pounding industrial and techno rock, and the 10-foot video screen. It's very casual and very big.

**The Outback.** 296 N. Stone Ave. ☎ **520/622-4700.** Cover $2–$5.

It's big, it's loud, it's crowded, it's Outback! No place else in town can compete with this club for sheer variety of dance space. There are no less than four club areas under one roof.

# THE BAR, LOUNGE & PUB SCENE
## BARS

**Barrio Grill.** 135 S. Sixth Ave. ☎ **520/629-0191.**

This is *the* place to sample tequilas, whether by the shot (with or without lime and salt) or in a margarita. A couple of dozen tequilas are available, including *reposado* (rested), *anejo* (aged), and blue agave tequilas. The Barrio Grill has also won kudos for its interior design, so perch on one of the artist-created bar stools, sip a tequila, and soak in the atmosphere. Popular with downtown professionals and the art crowd.

**The Bum Steer.** 1910 N. Stone Ave. ☎ **520/884-7377.**

This huge red barn is a hit with the college crowd and has stuff hanging from every inch of wall and ceiling space in the joint. There's a volleyball court out back for those who want to pretend this is the beach.

**¡Toma!** 311 N. Court Ave. ☎ **520/622-1922.**

Located in El Presidio Historic District and owned by the family who operates El Charro Cafe next door, this cafe has a humorous and festive atmosphere with a Mexican hat fountain/sculpture in the courtyard. Happy hour is Friday from about 4 to 7pm, and mariachi or other Latin-inspired music happens Friday and Saturday nights.

## LOUNGES

**The Arizona Inn.** 2200 E. Elm St. ☎ **520/325-1541.**

If you're looking for a quiet and comfortable scene, the piano music in the Audubon Lounge at the Arizona Inn is sure to soothe your soul. The gardens here are beautiful.

**Cascade Lounge.** In Loews Ventana Canyon Resort, 7000 N. Resort Dr. ☎ **520/299-2020.**

This is Tucson's ultimate piano bar. With a view of the Catalinas and a caviar happy hour, the plush lounge is perfect for romance or relaxation at the start or end of a night on the town.

**Presidio Grill.** 3352 E. Speedway Blvd. ☎ **520/327-4667.**

With its hip contemporary decor, Presidio Grill attracts a young upscale crowd. Though best known as one of the city's premier restaurants, the lounge is a great place for a cocktail.

## PUBS

**Breckenridge Brewery.** 1980 E. River Rd. (at River Rd. and Campbell Ave. in St. Philip's Plaza). ☎ **520/577-0800.**

This cavernous brewpub in an upscale shopping plaza may be more glitz than local pub, but their motto—"Life's too short to drink cheap beer!"—leaves no question about what the priority is here.

**Gentle Ben's Brewing Co.** 865 E. University Blvd. ☎ **520/624-4177.**

Gentle Ben's, located a block away from the university, is Tucson's favorite microbrewery, with daily food and drink specials. The crowd is young and active.

**Habaneros Tropical Cantina & Brewery.** In the Westin La Paloma resort, 3800 E. Sunrise Dr. ☎ **520/742-6000.**

At press time this was the newest brewpub to open in Tucson and was done up in the let's-party Mexican cantina style. They usually have four or so of their own brews on tap. You'll find Habaneros in a separate building just outside the resort's portico.

## COCKTAILS WITH A VIEW

Just about all the best vistas in town are at foothills resorts, but luckily they don't mind sharing with nonguests. In addition to those listed below, the lounge at Anthony's in the Catalinas has a great view. See "Dining," earlier in this chapter, for details.

**Desert Garden Lounge.** In the Westin La Paloma, 3800 E. Sunrise Dr. ☎ **520/742-6000.**

If you'd like a close-up view of the Santa Catalina Mountains, head over to the Desert Garden Lounge, where there's live jazz or classical music and Southwestern decor.

✪ **Flying V Bar & Grill.** In Loews Ventana Canyon Resort, 7000 N. Resort Dr. ☎ **520/299-2020.**

If you can't afford the lap of luxury, you can at least pull up a chair next to the large waterfall at this popular resort watering hole. The view over the golf course to the lights of Tucson far below is one of the best in the city. The Flying V has recently been redesigned and has more deck space and a new menu—you might want to consider a light meal here as well.

**Lookout Lounge.** In the Westward Look Resort, 245 E. Ina Rd. ☎ **520/297-1151.**

The Westward Look is one of Tucson's oldest resorts and took to the hills long before it became the fashionable place to be. The nighttime view of twinkling city lights and stars is unmatched. There's live music Thursday through Saturday nights.

## SPORTS BARS

**Famous Sam's.** 3620 N. First Ave. ☎ **520/292-0314.**

With 10 branches around the city, Famous Sam's keeps a lot of Tucson's sports fans happy. Other convenient locations include 1830 E. Broadway Blvd. (☎ **520/884-0119**), 7930 E. Speedway Blvd. (☎ **520/290-9666**), and 4801 E. 29th St. (☎ **520/748-1975**).

**Trophies.** In the Hotel Park Tucson, 5151 E. Grant Rd. ☎ **520/323-6262.**

On weekends and any time there's an Arizona sports team playing, this place gets packed. If you want some sports camaraderie, check it out.

## GAY & LESBIAN BARS

**Ain't Nobody's Bizness.** 2900 E. Broadway Blvd. ☎ **520/318-4838.**

This bar, located in a mall, has a couple of pool tables and a dance floor and caters to lesbians and their friends (including gay men).

**Hours.** 3455 E. Grant Rd. ☎ **520/327-3390.**

With a pool table and dance floor, this casual neighborhood bar is one of Tucson's most popular gay and lesbian hangouts, but straight people come here too.

**IBT's.** 616 N. Fourth Ave. ☎ **520/882-3053.**

Located near Wingspan, Tucson's gay and lesbian community center, IBT's is one of the most popular gay dance bars in town. It's always an interesting crowd here.

**Boom Booms.** 2520 N. Oracle Rd. ☎ **520/623-6969.**

This bar caters to the entire gay community and is a place where gay, lesbian, and bisexual people meet. Some nights are given over to country-and-western music or social mixes. There are pool tables and dart boards, and no cover charge unless a live band is playing.

# THE PERFORMING ARTS

To a certain extent, Tucson is a clone of Phoenix when it comes to the performing arts. Three of Tucson's major performance companies—the Arizona Opera Company, Ballet Arizona, and the Arizona Theatre Company—spend half their time in Phoenix. This means that whatever gets staged in Phoenix also gets staged in Tucson. This city does, however, have its own symphony, and Tucson manages to sustain a diversified theater scene as well, with more experimental theater getting staged here.

The best way to purchase tickets in Tucson is directly from the company's box office, but tickets to many concerts and theater performances are also available at **Dillard's** department store box offices or by calling the Dillard's telephone reservation line (☎ **800/638-4253**). Tickets to Tucson Convention Center events may be available by calling the TCC box office (☎ **520/791-4266**). **Ticketmaster** (☎ **520/321-1000**) also sells tickets to some Tucson performances. Sales outlets are at Foley's, 3435 E. Broadway Blvd., and 4470 N. Oracle Rd.

## CLASSICAL MUSIC, OPERA & DANCE

The **Tucson Symphony Orchestra** (☎ **520/792-9155** for information or 520/882-8585 for tickets), which performs at the Tucson Convention Center Music Hall, 260 S. Church Ave., is the oldest continuously performing symphony in the Southwest; tickets run $12 to $26.

Opera fans can catch the **Arizona Opera Company** (☎ **520/293-4336**), performing at the Tucson Convention Center Music Hall, 260 S. Church Ave. Tickets go for $14 to $56. This company performs both in Phoenix and Tucson.

Tucson's dance scene is dominated by **Ballet Arizona** (☎ **888/322-5538**), which splits its season between Tucson and Phoenix. Productions usually include well-known ballets as well as new works by regional choreographers, and performances are at different venues around town, including the Tucson Convention Center. Most tickets are $17 to $41.

## THEATER

Tucson doesn't have a lot of theater companies, but what few there are stage a surprisingly diverse sampling of both classic and contemporary plays.

**Arizona Theatre Company (ATC)** (☎ **520/622-2823**), which performs at the Temple of Music and Art, 330 S. Scott Ave., splits its time between here and Phoenix and is the state's top professional theater company. Each season sees a mix of comedy, drama, and Broadway-style musical shows; tickets cost about $18 to $32.

If you enjoy new works by unknown playwrights, check the schedule of **Theatre Congress,** 125 E. Congress St. (☎ **520/623-7852**), a company that often stages plays by local playwrights. This company also has late shows on Friday and Saturday nights. Tickets cost $7 to $10.

For even more experimental theater, there's the **Invisible Theatre,** 1400 N. First Ave. (☎ **520/882-9721**), a tiny theater in a converted laundry building that has been home to Tucson's most experimental theater for 25 years (they also do Off-Broadway shows and musicals). Tickets here go for $10 to $15.

The West just wouldn't be the West without good old-fashioned melodramas, and the **Gaslight Theatre,** 7010 E. Broadway Blvd. (☎ **520/886-9428**), is where evil villains, stalwart heroes, and defenseless heroines pound the boards in Tucson. You can boo and hiss, cheer and sigh as the predictable stories unfold on stage. It's all great fun for kids and adults. Tickets are $12.95 for adults, $10.95 for students and senior citizens, and $6 for children. Performances are Wednesday through Sunday at 7pm, Friday and Saturday at 9:30pm, and Sunday at 3pm.

## PERFORMING ARTS CENTERS & CONCERT HALLS

Tucson's largest performance venue is the **Tucson Convention Center Music Hall,** 260 S. Church Ave. (☎ **520/791-4266**). It's the home of the Tucson Symphony Orchestra and is where the Arizona Opera Company and Ballet Arizona usually perform when they're in town. This hall also hosts many touring companies. The box office is open Monday through Saturday from 10am to 6pm; tickets run $10 to $75.

However, the **Temple of Music and Art,** 330 S. Scott Ave. (☎ **520/622-2823** or 520/884-8210), a restored historic theater dating from 1927, is the centerpiece of the Tucson theater scene. The 605-seat Alice Holsclaw Theatre is the Temple's main stage, but there's also the 90-seat Cabaret Theatre. You'll also find an art gallery, a gift shop, and a restaurant here. Free tours of the Temple of Art and Music are given on Saturday mornings. The box office is open Monday through Friday from 10am to 6pm, on Saturday from 11am to 6:30pm, and on Sunday from noon to 3:30pm. Tickets range from about $7 to $37.

Located on the campus of the University of Arizona, **Centennial Hall,** at University Boulevard and Park Avenue (☎ **520/621-3341**), is one of Tucson's main venues for touring national musical acts, international performance companies, and Broadway shows. A large stage and excellent sound system permit large-scale productions. The box office is open Monday through Friday from 10am to 5pm, Saturdays during the season from noon to 5pm, and $1^1/2$ hours before curtain time. Tickets go for about $18 to $45.

The **Center for the Arts,** Pima Community College (West Campus), 2202 W. Anklam Rd. (☎ **520/884-6986** or 520/884-6988), is another good place to check for performances. It offers a wide variety of shows, including the occasional name act, with tickets priced at $4 to $30.

## OUTDOOR VENUES & SERIES

Between April and October, Tucsonians head to Reid Park's **DeMeester Outdoor Performance Center,** at Country Club Road and East 22nd Street (☎ **520/791-4079**), for performances under the stars. This amphitheater is the site of performances by the Parks and Recreation Community Theatre and other production companies, as well as frequent music performances.

The **Tucson Jazz Society** (☎ **520/743-3399**), which manages to book a few well-known jazz musicians each year, sponsors different outdoor music series at various locations around the city including St. Philip's Plaza shopping center. Over the course of the year they present around 40 concerts. Tickets are $10 to $23.

There are also various outdoor concert series downtown throughout the year. These include the Brown Bag lunch series at La Placita Village in the convention center complex and various other locations, and Downtown Saturday/Downtown Saturday Night performances. Check in the *Tucson Weekly* for details.

## FILM

**Cineplex Odeon Catalina Cinema.** 2320 N. Campbell Ave. ☎ **520/881-0616.** Tickets $7 adults, $4 children 3–11 and seniors. Special matinee prices.

Not only do they show both currently popular and independent films here, but the decor is very cool and so's the air-conditioning.

**The Loft Cinema.** 3233 E. Speedway Blvd. ☎ **520/795-7777.** Tickets $6 adults, $3.75 students and seniors, $3.75 before 5pm daily.

If *Star Wars* wasn't your idea of the best movie ever made, this is the place for you. The screen here is one of the largest around, just right for watching one of the new independent or foreign releases.

## CASINOS

**Casino of the Sun.** 7406 S. Camino de Oeste. ☎ **800/344-9435** or 520/883-1700.

Located 15 miles southwest of Tucson and operated by the Pascua Yaqui tribe, this is southern Arizona's largest casino and offers slot machines, "live" video blackjack, keno, bingo, and a card room.

**Desert Diamond Casino.** 7350 S. Nogales Hwy. ☎ **520/294-7777.**

Operated by the Tohono O'odham tribe and located only 3 miles away from Mission San Xavier del Bac, this casino offers the same variety of slot and video poker machines found at other casinos in the state. A card room, bingo, and keno round out the options here.

## 12 Side Trips from Tucson

## NORTH OF TUCSON

For a day's excursion, you can combine a visit to Biosphere 2 with some hiking or horseback riding in Catalina State Park.

**Biosphere 2 Visitor Center.** Ariz. 77, mile marker 96.5. ☎ **800/828-2462** or 520/ 896-6200. Admission $12.95 adults, $6 children 6–17, free for children 5 and under. Discounts for students and seniors. Daily 8am–5pm. Closed Dec 25. Take Oracle Rd. north out of Tucson and continue north on U.S. 89 and Ariz. 77 until you see the Biosphere sign.

For 2 years, beginning in September 1991, four men and four women were locked inside this airtight, 3-acre greenhouse in the desert 35 miles north of Tucson near the town of Oracle. During their tenure in Biosphere 2 (earth is considered Biosphere 1) they conducted experiments on how the earth, basically a giant greenhouse, manages to support all the planet's life forms. Though there are no longer people living in Biosphere 2, similar experiments continue to be undertaken. In addition, this giant science project is a major tourist attraction.

Tours of the facility are offered daily, including a tour of the interior of Biosphere 2. You can learn about the project at an orientation center and then take a guided tour which includes the Ocean Viewing Gallery, the test module, Biome Ecology Laboratories, and multi-media presentations. An interactive display area provides entertainment for children. Whether you see it as science or a tourist attraction, there's plenty to see and do. Also on the grounds are a hotel, restaurant, cafe, bookstore, and gift shop.

## WEST OF TUCSON

**Kitt Peak National Observatory.** Off Ariz. 86. ☎ **520/318-8726** or 520/318-8000. Free admission, $2 donation suggested. Stargazing program $35 adults; $25 students, seniors, and children under 18. Daily 9am–4pm and evening hours (call for reservation). Closed Jan 1, Thanksgiving, and Dec 24–25. Take Ariz. 86 southwest from Tucson; in about 40 miles you'll see the turnoff for Kitt Peak.

Southern Arizona likes to brag about how many sunny days it has each year, and the nights are just as clear. The starry skies have lured more astronomical observatories to the Tucson vicinity than to any other region of the world, and southern Arizona has come to be known as the "Astronomy Capital of the World." The largest of the astronomical observatories here is the famous Kitt Peak National Observatory.

Located in the Quinlan Mountains, 56 miles southwest of Tucson, the observatory sits atop 6,882-foot Kitt Peak. The lack of lights in the surrounding desert makes the night sky here as brilliant as anywhere on earth.

There are five major telescopes operating at Kitt Peak, including the McMath telescope, the world's largest solar telescope. This telescope's system of mirrors channels an image of the sun deep into the mountain before reflecting it back up to the observatory where scientists study the resulting 30-inch-diameter image. The 158-inch Mayall telescope features a 30,000-pound quartz mirror and is used for studying distant regions of the universe.

Guided tours are given daily at 10am, 11:30am, 1pm, and 2:30pm. There's also a visitor center and museum. For an evening of stargazing, call for a reservation and to purchase tickets; a box meal is included in the price. There's no restaurant at the observatory, but there is a picnic area.

## SOUTH OF TUCSON: SPECTACULAR BIRD WATCHING

Located in the Coronado National Forest about 40 miles south of Tucson, **Madera Canyon National Forest Recreation Area** (☎ **520/281-2296**) is one of southern Arizona's prime bird-watching spots. Because of the year-round water to be found here, Madera Canyon attracts a surprising variety of bird life, and in recent years has also been attracting a surprising number of bird-watchers as well. Avid birders flock to this canyon from around the country in hopes of spotting more than a dozen species of hummingbirds, an equal number of flycatchers, warblers, tanagers, buntings, grosbeaks, and many rare birds that are not found in any other state.

However, before birding became a hot activity, this canyon was popular with families looking for a way to escape the heat down in Tucson. The shady picnic areas and trails still get a lot of use by those who don't carry binoculars.

If you're heading out here for the day, arrive early—parking is very limited. To reach Madera Canyon, take Exit 39 from I-19; from the exit, it's another 12 miles southeast. Admission is a suggested $2 donation and the canyon is open daily from dawn to dusk. There's a $5 camping fee.

### WHERE TO STAY

**Santa Rita Lodge Nature Resort.** HC 70, Box 5444, Sahuarita, AZ 85629. ☎ **520/625-8746.** 8 rms, 4 cabins. $68 double in the lodge, $78 double in cabins. AE, MC, V.

Located in the shade of Madera Canyon, this lodge is used almost exclusively by bird-watchers, and natural history programs and guided bird walks are offered. The rooms and cabins are large and fairly comfortable.

# Southeastern Arizona

# 11

Southeastern Arizona, roughly defined as the land between the Mexican border and Interstates 8 and 10 and between New Mexico and Interstate 19, is a part of Arizona that's being discovered rapidly. Much of the region lies about a mile above sea level, which means that the climate in this region is far more temperate than in most of the state. As a result, thousands of people have been retiring here in recent years. Although Tucson is the only major city in this region, there are many small historic towns.

In the past few years, not only retirees but bird watchers have discovered this corner of the state. The mountains of southeastern Arizona are home to more than a dozen species of hummingbirds, as well as many other species of birds that are found nowhere else in the United States. Additionally, the area along the San Pedro River provides a habitat for many other rare bird species.

A century ago, however, it was gold and silver, and not the climate or the birds, that lured prospectors and fortune seekers to what was then considered a godforsaken wasteland. Tombstone, "the town too tough to die," was the most infamous of the region's mining towns, but others such as Bisbee, which has recently become a popular weekend destination, survived long after the mines shut down in Tombstone.

Giant saguaro cacti cover the slopes of the Sonoran Desert throughout much of southeastern Arizona, though numerous mountain ranges also rise up above the desert. Cacti give way to pines in the cool mountains, where passing clouds bring snow and rain. Narrow canyons and broad valleys, fed by the rain and snow melting on the high peaks, provide habitats for birds and other wildlife unique to the region.

Many of the high valleys between the mountain ranges receive enough rain to support some of the best grasslands in the country. This is prime grazing land, and huge ranches have sprawled across the landscape for more than a century.

Perhaps because of this prime ranchland, it was here that much of America's now-famous Western history took place. Wyatt Earp and the Clantons shot it out at Tombstone's O.K. Corral, Doc Holliday played his cards, and Cochise and Geronimo staged the last Indian rebellions. Cavalries charged. Prospectors searched for the motherlode. Today, ghost towns litter the landscape of southeastern

Arizona, and the ghosts of the past are kept alive by people searching for a glimpse of the Wild West.

The very first Spanish expedition into the American Southwest, led by Francisco Vásquez de Coronado in 1540, marched up the San Pedro River valley past present-day Sierra Vista, where a national memorial commemorates his unfruitful search for the Seven Cities of Cibola. These cities were rumored to be filled with gold and precious jewels, but all Coronado found were simple Indian pueblos. Nearly 150 years later Fr. Eusebio Francisco Kino would found a string of Jesuit missions across the Pimeria Alta, a region that would later become northern Mexico and southern Arizona. Converting the Indians and building mission churches, Father Kino left a long-lasting mark on this region. Today two of the missions founded by Father Kino—San Xavier del Bac (see chapter 10 on Tucson) and San José de Tumacacori (see the section on Amado, Tubac, and Tumacacori, below)—still stand.

Native Americans still make their homes here in southern Arizona, and the Papago Indian Reservation covers a vast expanse south of Casa Grande and west of Tucson. This reservation belongs to the Tohono O'odham tribe (formerly known as the Papagos). Well known for their basketry, the Tohono O'odham also sponsor one of the largest annual Native American festivals in the country. The **O'odham Tash** is held each February in Casa Grande and attracts dozens of tribes who participate in rodeos, parades, arts-and-crafts exhibits, and dance performances. Near Willcox, the Amerind Foundation, one of the state's finest museums dedicated to the cultures of Southwest peoples, provides insightful exhibits on indigenous culture.

## 1  Amado, Tubac & Tumacacori

45 miles S of Tucson; 21 miles N of Nogales; 84 miles W of Sierra Vista

Located in the fertile valley of the Santa Cruz River 45 miles south of Tucson, Tubac and Tumacacori together sum up the early experiences of the Spanish, who were the first Europeans to settle in this region. Established in 1691 by Father Eusebio Francisco Kino, Tumacacori was one of the first Spanish missions in what would eventually become Arizona. At that time, Tubac was a Pima village, but by the 1730s, the Spanish had begun settling here in the region they called Pimeria Alta. After a Pima uprising in 1751, Spanish forces were sent into the area to protect the settlers and, in 1752, Tubac became a presidio (fort). Between 1752 and the present, seven different flags have flown over Tubac, including those of Spain, Mexico, the United States, the New Mexico Territory, the Confederacy, the U.S. Territory of Arizona, and the state of Arizona.

Though the European history of this area dates from more than 300 years, the area's human habitation actually dates far back into prehistory. Archaeologists have found evidence that there have been people living along the nearby Santa Cruz River for nearly 10,000 years. The Hohokam dwelt in the area from about A.D. 300 until their mysterious disappearance around 1500, and when the Spanish arrived around 200 years later, it was the Pima people that they found inhabiting this region.

Tubac's other claim to fame is as the site from which Juan Bautista de Anza III, the second commander of the presidio, set out in 1775 to find an overland route to California. De Anza led 240 settlers and more than 1,000 head of cattle on this grueling expedition, but the group did finally reach the coast of California and founded the settlement of San Francisco. One year later, the garrison was moved from Tubac to Tucson, and, with no protection, settlers moved away from the area. Soldiers were once again stationed here beginning in 1776, but lack of funds caused the closure of the presidio when, in 1821, Mexican independence brought Tubac under a new flag.

# Southeastern Arizona

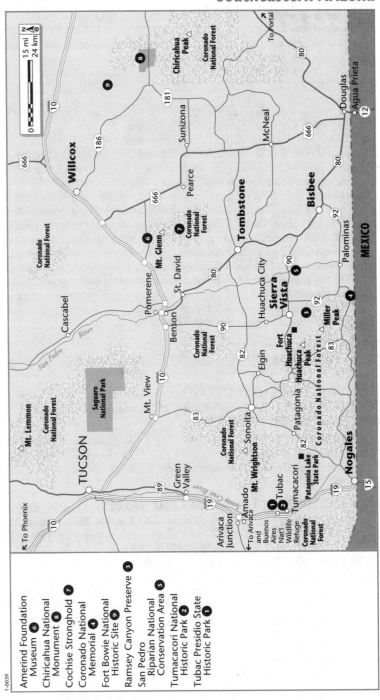

Amerind Foundation Museum ⑥
Chiricahua National Monument ⑧
Cochise Stronghold ⑦
Coronado National Memorial ④
Fort Bowie National Historic Site ⑨
Ramsey Canyon Preserve ③
San Pedro Riparian National Conservation Area ⑤
Tumacacori National Historic Park ②
Tubac Presidio State Historic Park ①

1-0039

383

---

**Impressions**

*It has a melancholy appearance. The walls of the church still stand, no roof, and only the upright piece of the cross. It looks desolate indeed.*
              —A traveler named Hays, upon seeing the ruins of Tumacacori in 1849

---

It was not until this region became U.S. territory that settlers returned to the area, and by 1860, Tubac was the largest town in Arizona.

Today, Tubac is one of Arizona's largest arts communities. The town's old buildings house more than 80 shops selling fine arts, crafts, and unusual gifts, and although some are touristy, others are gems worth seeking out. This concentration of shops, artists' studios, and galleries makes Tubac one of southern Arizona's most popular destinations, and a small retirement community is beginning to develop in the area. After visiting Tubac Presidio State Historic Park and Tumacacori National Monument to learn about the area's history, you'll probably want to spend some time browsing through these interesting shops. Keep in mind, however, that many of the local artists leave town during the summer, so it's best to visit on weekends then. The busy season is from October to May, and during these months shops are open daily.

The tiny community of Amado is the site of a couple of good restaurants, an inn, and an interesting collection of shops in a garden setting. However, one of Amado's most interesting attractions is an abandoned building that was built in the shape of a giant cow skull. It's on the west side of I-19 at Exit 48.

## ESSENTIALS

**GETTING THERE**   Amado, Tubac, and Tumacacori are all due south of Tucson on I-19.

**VISITOR INFORMATION**   For further information about Tubac and Tumacacori, contact the **Tubac Chamber of Commerce,** P.O. Box 1866, Tubac, AZ 85646 (☎ 520/398-2704).

**SPECIAL EVENTS**   The **Tubac Festival of the Arts** is held each year in February. Artists from all over the country participate. In October, on the weekend nearest to the 23rd, **De Anza Days** commemorate Capt. Juan Bautista de Anza's 1775 trek to found San Francisco.

## ART & HISTORY IN THE SANTA CRUZ VALLEY

**Tumacacori National Historical Park.** Frontage Rd. ☎ **520/398-2341.** Admission $2 per person, free for children 16 and under. Daily 8am–5pm. Closed Thanksgiving and Dec 25. Take I-19 to Exit 29; you'll find Tumacacori 3 miles south of Tubac.

We in the United States often forget our Spanish heritage, but these mission ruins are a silent reminder of the role that Spanish missionaries played in settling the Southwest. The Tumacacori mission was founded by Jesuit missionary and explorer Fr. Eusebio Francisco Kino in 1691 to convert the Pima people. Much of the old adobe mission church still stands, and the Spanish architectural influence can readily be seen. A small museum contains exhibits on mission life and the history of the region.

On weekends Native American and Mexican craftspeople give demonstrations of indigenous arts. The **Tumacacori Fiesta,** a celebration of Indian, Hispanic, and Anglo cultures, is held the first weekend of December.

**Tubac Presidio State Historic Park.** Presidio Dr. ☎ **520/398-2252.** Admission $2 adults, $1 children 7–14, free for children 6 and under. Daily 8am–5pm. Closed Dec 25.

The Tubac Presidio has a long and fitful history. Though the Tumacacori mission was founded in 1691, it was not until 1752 that the Tubac Presidio was established in response to a Pima uprising. In 1775 the presidio's military garrison was moved to Tucson and, with no protection from raiding Apache, most of Tubac's settlers also left the area. A military presence was reestablished in 1787, but after Mexican independence in 1821, insufficient funds led to the closing of the presidio. Villagers once again abandoned Tubac because of Apache attacks. After the Gadsden Purchase, Tubac became part of the United States and was again resettled.

Though little but buried foundation walls remains of the old presidio, Tubac Presidio State Historic Park has exhibits that explain the history of the presidio. There are displays on the Spanish soldiers, Native Americans, religion, and contemporary Hispanic culture in southern Arizona. Also on the grounds is the old Tubac School, which was built in 1885 and is the oldest schoolhouse in Arizona.

From October through March on Sundays between 1 and 4pm, there are living history presentations here. Among the characters you'll meet are Spanish soldiers, settlers, and friars.

**Tubac Center of the Arts.** Plaza Rd. ☎ **520/398-2371.** $1 donation suggested. Early Sept to early June Tues–Sat 10am–4:30pm, Sun 1–4:30pm. Also open Mon 10am–4:30pm late Nov to Mar. Closed early June to early Sept.

Tubac is an arts community, and this Spanish colonial building serves as its center for cultural activities. Throughout the season there are workshops, traveling exhibitions, juried shows, an annual craft show, theater and music performances, and a gift shop.

## SHOPPING

With so many shops and with people having such varied tastes, it is hard to recommend specific stops in the Tubac area. But if you want to take home the flavor of the area, stop in at **The Chile Pepper** (☎ **520/398-2921**) on Tubac Road in downtown Tubac for gourmet foods with a Southwestern accent. Down near Tumacacori National Historical Park, you'll find all things hot (chiles, hot sauces, salsas) arranged on the shelves of the **Santa Cruz Chile and Spice Co.** (☎ **520/398-2591**), which is a combination store and packing plant. There's also an amazing assortment of familiar and obscure spices for sale. In the back, you can see various herbs being prepared and packaged. The shop is closed on Sunday.

Our favorite art galleries and artisan's studios are scattered around this region. In Amado, at Exit 48 off I-19, you'll find the **Glaspy Raku Studio** (☎ **520/398-2725**) in the Amado Territory shops. The **Sonora Trading Company** (☎ **520/398-9016**), in Plaza Antigua on Tubac Street in downtown Tubac, is another interesting shop and is associated with the Huntington Trading Company in Tucson. Some of the most interesting fine art in Tubac is found at the **Karin Newby Gallery,** Mercado de Baca, 19 Tubac Rd. (☎ **520/398-9662**). Across the road from Tumacacori National Historical Park, you'll find **Kim Yubeta Designs** (☎ **520/398-9583**), where you can see beautiful ethnic jewelry creations that draw on many different influences.

## ENJOYING THE OUTDOORS

Linking Tubac with Tumacacori is the 4½-mile-long **Anza Trail,** which follows the Santa Cruz River for much of its route and passes through forests and grasslands. This trail is part of the Juan Bautista de Anza National Historic Trail, which stretches from Nogales to San Francisco. Along the trail is an excavation of part of the Spanish colonial settlement of Tubac. However, bird watching is the most popular activity along the trail. An interesting way to see this trail is on horseback rides offered by **Rex Ranch** (☎ **520/398-2696**), which charges $45 for a 2-hour horseback ride.

If golf is more your speed, you can play a round at the **Tubac Golf Resort** (☎ **520/398-2021**), just north of Tubac off East Frontage Road. Greens fees range from $22 to $47.

## WHERE TO STAY

**Amado Territory Inn.** P.O. Box 81, Amado, AZ 85645. ☎ **520/398-8684.** 9 rms. Dec–Mar $95–$125 double; Apr–Nov $65–$95 double. Rates include full breakfast. MC, V.

This modern inn just off I-19 in the crossroads of Amado is built in the territorial style and succeeds in capturing the feel of old Arizona ranch houses. A spacious high-ceilinged lobby has a big leather couch in front of the fireplace—welcome warmth on cool winter nights. Guest rooms are furnished in a mix of reproduction East Coast antiques and Mexican rustic furnishings, much the way homes would have been furnished in Arizona 100 years ago. While a bit spartan, the rooms have plenty of character, and those on the second floor have balconies with views across the farm fields of the Santa Cruz Valley. Breakfast is served in a sunny breakfast room and there's a flagstone patio out back under the mesquite trees. Next door, there's a similarly designed restaurant affiliated with the inn.

**Rex Ranch.** P.O. Box 636, Amado, AZ 85645. ☎ **800/547-2696** or 520/398-2914. Fax 520/398-8229. 17 rms and casitas. Oct–May $120–$135 double, $225 casita; June–Sept $105 double, $205 casita. Rates include deluxe continental breakfast. AE, MC, V.

The Spanish colonial styling and Southwestern flavor of this inn make it a good choice for anyone seeking peace and quiet and plenty of pampering. Located 6 miles north of Tubac in the community of Amado, it's housed in beautiful renovated adobe buildings and is surrounded by rose and Japanese gardens. A pool and whirlpool spa provide options for relaxing any time of year, and massages are available. A restaurant, located in the original ranch house on the premises, provides an option for those who don't want to drive to find dinner. Horseback riding, mountain biking, and historic walking tours can be arranged.

**Tubac Golf Resort.** 1 Otero Rd. (P.O. Box 1297), Tubac, AZ 85646. ☎ **800/848-7893** or 520/398-2211. 16 rms, 16 casitas. A/C TV TEL. $69–$125 double; $87–$169 casita. AE, MC, V.

The Tubac Golf Resort is built on the Otero Ranch, which, in 1789, became the first Spanish land grant in the Southwest. The old ranch stables, which now house the resort's restaurant, are the ranch's oldest buildings and date from the turn of the century. Red-tile roofs and brick archways remind you that this was once a Spanish hacienda. The guest rooms come in two sizes, but all have brick walls and shuttered windows. The casitas have two patios, tile bathroom counters, beamed ceilings, and beehive fireplaces.

The dining room, in the old ranch stables, has booths that resemble horse stalls, and the menu focuses on mesquite-broiled steaks and seafood. A wall of glass looks out from the lounge to the golf course and mountains beyond. Facilities include an 18-hole golf course (used in the film *Tin Cup*), a swimming pool, and a pro shop.

**Tubac Secret Garden Inn.** 13 Placita de Anza (P.O. Box 1561), Tubac, AZ 85646. ☎ **520/398-9371.** 2 rms. $79–$89 double. Rates include continental breakfast. No credit cards.

Located down a short dirt lane in the heart of Tubac, this casual inn is surrounded by a huge yard that is set with sculptures and secret garden nooks. It's all very surprising, given the location, and makes an excellent retreat after a day of shopping. The house is of an unusual Spanish-influenced construction (designed to resemble the town of Alamos, Mexico), and rooms are simply furnished (one room has a Murphy bed). If you have an artistic bent or are a gardener, this is a good choice.

**Valle Verde Ranch Bed & Breakfast.** ¼ mile south of Tubac on E. Frontage Rd. (P.O. Box 157), Tumacacori, AZ 85640. ☎ **520/398-2246.** 3 rms, 2 casitas. TV. $80–$95 double; $100–$135 casita. Rates include full breakfast (in rooms) and continental breakfast (in casitas). No credit cards.

Built in 1937, this mission-revival ranch house fairly jumps out of the brown landscape with its pink walls and blue trim. The interior of the main house is straight out of a 1940s Hollywood movie, and its cool darkness is well appreciated on hot afternoons. European furnishings predominate in the guest rooms. In one of the casitas you'll find a whirlpool bath, but if you don't stay in that particular one, you can still relax in the inn's main outdoor whirlpool spa. Though it is only a quarter mile out of town, this inn feels as though it is miles away from civilization.

## WHERE TO DINE

A couple of the best restaurants in the area are the dining rooms of the Tubac Golf Resort and the Rex Ranch. See "Where to Stay," above, for details.

**Amado Café.** 3001 E. Frontage Rd., Amado (Exit 48 off I-19). ☎ **520/398-9211.** Lunch $5–$10, dinner main courses $11–$14. MC, V. Tues–Sun 11:30am–3pm, Tues–Sat 5–8pm. Closes for lunch an hour earlier in summer. GREEK/AMERICAN.

There aren't a lot of dining options out here, so this restaurant in a handsome territorial-style building just off the highway is a welcome addition to the community. The best part of the experience here is to sit out back on the rustic flagstone patio, listen to the gurgling fountain, and contemplate the view of the mountains in the distance. The menu includes sandwiches, salads, and more filling fare such as meatloaf or prime rib. Because the family who owns the restaurant is Greek, there are several Greek-influenced choices such as Greek salad, a gyro sandwich, and lamb shanks. Four-berry tart, carrot cake, and baklava are selections that came by on the dessert tray.

**Cow Palace.** 28802 S. Nogales Hwy. (Exit 48 off I-19). ☎ **520/398-2201.** Main courses $7–$18. DISC, MC, V. Daily 8am–9pm. STEAKS.

Located across I-19 from the Amado Café (see above), this long red building has a steer on the roof which signals its status as an institution for steak in southern Arizona. Another claim to fame is that John Wayne frequented the place. Inside, there are plenty of deer heads and wagon wheels, and a Wild West bar. You can get your three squares here, from chorizo and eggs for breakfast, to salads and burgers for lunch, to sizzling steaks for dinner. A couple of alternatives to steak include fried shrimp or fried chicken.

## A SIDE TRIP FOR FABULOUS BIRD WATCHING

If you are a bird watcher, you'll definitely want to make the trip over to **Buenos Aires National Wildlife Refuge,** P.O. Box 109, Sasabe, AZ 85633 (☎ 520/823-4251), which is about 28 miles from Tubac. To get to the refuge, first head north to Arivaca Junction and then drive west on a winding but paved two-lane road. The refuge begins just outside the small community of Arivaca.

Your first stop should be at **Arivaca Cienaga,** a quarter mile east of Arivaca. *Ciénaga* is a Spanish word for marsh. This particular marsh is fed by seven springs that provide year-round water and consequently attract an amazing variety of bird life. This is one of the few places in the United States where you can see a gray hawk. Vermilion flycatchers are also common here. A boardwalk leads across the marsh.

Other good birding spots within the refuge include **Arivaca Creek,** 2 miles west of Arivaca, and **Aguirre Lake,** a half mile north of the refuge headquarters and visitor center, which is located off Ariz. 286 north of Sasabe. The visitor center is also a good place to spot one of the refuge's rarest birds, the masked bobwhite quail. These quail disappeared from Arizona in the late 19th century but have been reintroduced in the refuge. Other birds you might spot outside the visitor center include Bendire's thrasher, Chihuahuan ravens, canyon towhees, and green-tailed towhees. Other wildlife in the refuge includes pronghorn antelopes, javelinas, coatimundis, white-tailed deer, mule deer, and coyotes.

The visitor center is open daily from dawn to dusk. There is also a refuge information center in Arivaca, though this center is only open when volunteers are available to staff it.

There are guided bird walks between October and April on the first Saturday of each month. Call for details; reservations are requested. There is primitive camping within the refuge at more than 100 designated spots along rough gravel roads. Look for the brown campsite signs, and bring water. There is also good mountain biking on these roads. If you're looking for a strenuous hike, try the **Mustang Trail,** which has its trailhead 2 miles west of Arivaca. The trail climbs up from Arivaca Creek into the surrounding dry hills and makes for a 5-mile round-trip hike.

If you enjoy scenic drives and don't mind gravel roads, you won't want to pass up the opportunity to drive the Ruby Road through Coronado National Forest to **Peña Blanca Lake** and **Nogales.** This road winds its way slowly through the mountains just north of the Mexican border, passing Arivaca Lake and the privately owned ghost town of Ruby before reaching picturesque Peña Blanca Lake, where there are a couple of campgrounds and the paved road picks up again.

## WHERE TO STAY

✪ **Rancho de la Osa.** P.O. Box 1, Sasabe, AZ 85633. ☎ **800/872-6240** or 520/823-4257. Fax 520/823-4238. 14 rms, 4 suites. $250 double, $325 suite (3- to 4-night minimum stay). Rates include all meals. MC, V.

Steeped in history and hard up against the Mexican border, this ranch dates from roughly 200 years ago and was one of the last Spanish haciendas in the United States. The adobe buildings, painted in bright colors, have the look of a quiet village down in old Mexico, and the remote location further enhances this feeling. It's a long way to civilization from here, so kick back and relax. Although horseback riding is the traditional favorite activity, in recent years, the ranch has begun attracting birdwatchers due to its proximity to Buenos Aires National Wildlife Refuge. A swimming pool and whirlpool are refreshing after long days riding the range on the ranch's purebred quarterhorses. Guest rooms are in sun-baked adobe buildings and all have fireplaces and rustic Southwestern styling. Meals are gourmet Southwestern fare, and the lounge has a liquor license so there's no need to bring your own.

## 2 Nogales

175 miles S of Phoenix; 63 miles S of Tucson; 65 miles W of Sierra Vista

Situated on the Mexican border, the twin towns of Nogales, Arizona, and Nogales, Sonora, Mexico (known jointly as Ambos Nogales), form a bustling border town. All day long U.S. citizens cross into Mexico to shop for bargains on hand-crafted items and duty-free imports from around the world, while Mexican citizens cross into the United States to buy products not available in their own country. Nogales is also the busiest produce port in the world. During the harvest season more than 700 truckloads of produce cross into the United States from Mexico per day.

## ESSENTIALS

**GETTING THERE**   Nogales is the last town on I-19 before the Mexican border. Arizona 82 leads northeast from town toward Sonoita and Sierra Vista.

**Citizens/Grayline Bus** has service between Nogales and Tucson. There's also bus service from Mexico. The bus station is at 35 N. Terrace Ave. Call ☎ **520/287-5628** for schedules and rates.

**VISITOR INFORMATION**   For further information on Nogales, contact the **Nogales–Santa Cruz County Chamber of Commerce,** Kino Park, Nogales, AZ 85621 (☎ **520/287-3685**).

## WHAT TO SEE & DO

Most people who visit Nogales, Arizona, are here to cross the border to Nogales, Mexico. The favorable exchange rate makes shopping in Mexico very popular with Americans, though most of the items for sale in Mexico are actually cheaper in Tucson. Many people now cross the border specifically to purchase prescription drugs, and pharmacies line the streets near the border crossing.

If you'd like to learn more about the history of this area, stop by the **Pimeria Alta Historical Society,** at the corner of Grand Avenue and Crawford Street (☎ **520/287-4621**), near the border crossing in downtown Nogales. The historical society maintains a small museum, library, and archives on this region of northern Mexico and southern Arizona, which was once known as Pimeria Alta. It's open Friday from 10am to 5pm, Saturday from 10am to 4pm, and Sunday from noon to 4pm. Admission is by donation.

**Bazaar de Mexico** at 18 Terrace St. (☎ **520/287-5253**), diagonally across from the bus station, has an interesting selection of Mexican folk art.

Just a couple of miles outside Nogales on the road to Patagonia, you'll see signs for the **Arizona Vineyard Winery** (☎ **520/287-7972**). You may not think of Arizona as wine country, but the Spanish began growing grapes and making wine as soon as they arrived in the area several centuries ago. You can taste free samples of white burgundy, Grand Canyon White, Road Runner White, Desert Dust, and Rattlesnake Red, among others.

As you can probably guess, Nogales, Mexico, is a typical border town filled with tiny shops selling Mexican crafts and souvenirs, and dozens of restaurants serving simple Mexican food. Some of the better deals are on wool rugs, which cost a small fraction of what a Navajo rug will cost, but are not nearly as well made. Pottery is another popular buy. Our personal favorite items are the ceramic sinks and the handblown drinking glasses and pitchers.

All the shops and restaurants in Nogales, Mexico, are within walking distance of the border, so unless you're planning to continue farther into Mexico, it's not a good idea to take your car across the border. There are numerous pay parking lots and garages on the U.S. side of the border where your car will be secure for the day. If you should take your car into Mexico, be sure to get Mexican auto insurance before crossing the border—your U.S. auto insurance is not valid. There are plenty of insurance companies set up along the road leading to the border.

Most shops and restaurants in Nogales, Mexico, accept U.S. dollars. You may bring back $400 worth of merchandise duty free, including 1 liter of liquor (if you are 21 or older).

## WHERE TO STAY

In addition to the golf resort listed below, you'll find numerous budget chain motels in Nogales, including the **Best Western Time Motel,** 921 N. Grand Ave.,

---

## Tumbleweed: An Undesirable Alien

The first ones snuck into the country with a load of wheat from Russia. Farmers unwittingly helped these new aliens move around the country, and before anyone realized it an invasion was under way. Though there are several species of plants that go by the name of tumbleweed, it's the Russian thistle (*Salsola kali* var. *tenuifolia*) that has become the bane of farmers and the mainstay of many a Western movie.

Able to live on next to no water, these scruffy annual plants, which grow to about 3 feet in diameter, colonize in seemingly any soil, no matter how bad. After maturing and setting up to 50,000 seeds per plant, they die down and become dry and brittle. The first strong wind can snap their weakened stems and send a tumbleweed rolling off across the landscape.

With good winds and with miles of treeless plains, tumbleweed has traditionally had plenty of room to roam. But the West is no longer as wide open as it once was. Fences crisscross the land, and when tumbleweeds meet fences they pile up into deep drifts. Sometimes the wind fills gullies with these wayward plants, and the unfortunate homesteader who happened to build his house out of the wind, sometimes found his abode buried beneath many feet of thorny tumbleweeds. These days it's drivers on interstate highways who more often have unfortunate encounters with these rolling plants. Tumbleweeds trapped under cars have been known to catch fire from the heat of a muffler or an inopportune spark.

---

Nogales (☎ **520/287-4627**), charging $36 to $56 double; **Motel 6,** 141 W. Mariposa Rd. (☎ **520/281-2951**), charging $36–$40 double; and **Super 8 Motel,** 547 W. Mariposa Rd. (☎ **520/281-2242**), charging $45 to $56 double.

**Rio Rico Resort & Country Club.** 1069 Camino Caralampi, Rio Rico, AZ 85648. ☎ **800/288-4746** or 520/281-1901. Fax 520/281-7132. 180 rms, 15 suites. A/C TV TEL. $110–$150 double; $170–$600 suite. AE, CB, DC, DISC, MC, V.

Located a few miles north of Nogales, Rio Rico is the site of a secluded and little-known golf resort that has undergone extensive renovations the past few years and hopes to siphon off a bit of Tucson's resort business. For now, however, guests tend to be golfing senior citizens contemplating a move to this area. The hotel is built atop a low hill, and all the guest rooms have excellent views over the golf course and desert (third floor rooms have the best views). The resort's dining room sports Southwestern decor and features great views and primarily Italian dishes. The adjacent lounge offers the same views. The resort also offers horseback riding, a Mexico shopping shuttle, an 18-hole golf course, Olympic-size pool, whirlpool, sauna, exercise room, four tennis courts, and pro shop.

## WHERE TO DINE

✪ **La Roca Restaurant.** Calle Elias 91, Nogales, Mexico. ☎ **(52) 631/2-08-91.** Main courses $7–$14. MC, V. Daily 11am–midnight. MEXICAN.

La Roca is as unexpected a restaurant as you're ever likely to find in a border town. Built into a cliff and cool as a cave, the restaurant conjures up images of colonial Mexico. White-jacketed waiters provide a level of professional service found only in the most expensive restaurants north of the border. Folk art and large paintings in the spacious rooms seem to make the interior glow, and at night the place is lit with candles ensconced on the stone walls. The Guaymas shrimp and chicken mole are our longtime favorites. The shrimp are reliably succulent, and the mole sauce is a brilliantly flavorful balance between chile and chocolate. Don't miss the margaritas—small but zesty with lime and full of tequila.

To find La Roca, walk through the border checkpoint, continue 100 feet or so, cross over the railroad tracks on your left, and continue walking away from the border. Within a block, you'll see a narrow street angling toward the big rock wall to your left. The restaurant is about 100 feet down this street.

**Las Vigas Steak Ranch.** 180 W. Loma St. ☎ **520/287-6641.** Main courses $5–$6 at lunch, $6–$11 at dinner. MC, V. Tues–Fri 10am–10pm, Sat–Sun 8am–10pm. Head down Grand Ave. toward the border; before you get to downtown Nogales, watch for Arroyo Blvd., which forks to the right; Las Vigas is just past the fork. STEAKS/SONORAN MEXICAN.

This is a Western-style building with a covered sidewalk in front and old photos of Mexican men and women inside. Antiques on the walls give Las Vigas a very rustic feel, and a G-gauge model train chugs around the dining room. Meals are inexpensive and filling, and there are daily specials during the week. Steaks are accompanied by a salad bar, beans, baked potato, and tortillas. Breakfast comes both Mexican and Western-style.

**Mr. C's Supper Club.** 282 W. View Point Dr. (off Mariposa Rd.). ☎ **520/281-9000.** Reservations recommended. Main courses $9–$25. DISC, MC, V. Mon–Sat 11:30am–11pm. Closed holidays. CONTINENTAL.

Located atop a hill on the north side of town, Mr. C's is Nogales's best restaurant. The menu leans heavily toward fresh fish dishes, with the day's menu written over the salad bar. There are fat Guaymas shrimp, escargots, salmon, and tender steaks. Early diners can take advantage of the early-bird specials for $7 to $13.

## 3 Patagonia & Sonoita

Patagonia: 171 miles SE of Phoenix; 60 miles SE of Tucson; 50 miles SW of Tombstone; 19 miles NW of Nogales

The two small communities of Patagonia and Sonoita have become a favorite weekend getaway for Tucsonians. The mild climate, bed-and-breakfast inns, and wineries are the main attractions for many. However, it's Sonoita Creek that manages to attract visitors from all over the country. This creek is one of only a few in the region that flows throughout the year, and consequently attracts an amazing variety of birdlife and bird watchers.

Most people heading out to explore the Patagonia-Sonoita wine country have heard about the area's excellent restaurants and are looking forward to dining at a few of these establishments. However, be forewarned that the best restaurants, including Karen's, Er Pastaro, Marie's, and The Ovens of Patagonia, are closed on Monday and Tuesday. Bird watchers should also take note that the Patagonia–Sonoita Creek Sanctuary is also closed on Monday and Tuesday.

### ESSENTIALS

**GETTING THERE**    Sonoita is at the junction of Ariz. 83 and Ariz. 82. Patagonia is 12 miles southwest of Sonoita on Ariz. 82.

**VISITOR INFORMATION**    For further information on Patagonia and Sonoita, contact the Patagonia Community Association, **Patagonia Visitors Center,** P.O. Box 241, Patagonia, AZ 85624 (☎ **520/394-0060**). The visitor center is located in the center of town at 315 McKeown Ave., in the building with the espresso shop, art gallery, and bookstore.

# BIRD WATCHING, WINE TASTING & OTHER AREA ACTIVITIES

Patagonia, 18 miles north of Nogales on Ariz. 82, is a historic old mining and ranching town 4,000 feet up in the Patagonia Mountains. Surrounded by higher mountains, the little town has for years been popular with film and television crews. Among the films that have been shot here are *Oklahoma, Red River, A Star Is Born,* and *David and Bathsheba.* Television programs filmed here have included *Little House on the Prairie, The Red Badge of Courage,* and *The Young Riders.* Today, however, bird watching and tranquillity draw people to this remote town.

The **Patagonia–Sonoita Creek Sanctuary** is a nature preserve owned by the Nature Conservancy and protects a mile and a half of Sonoita Creek riparian (riverside) habitat, which is important to migratory birds. More than 250 species of birds have been spotted on the preserve, which makes this a very popular spot with birders from all over the world. Among the rare birds that may be seen here are 22 species of flycatchers, kingbirds, and phoebes, and the Montezuma quail. A forest of cottonwood trees, some of which are 100 feet tall, lines the creek and is one of the best examples of such a forest left in southern Arizona. At one time forests such as this grew along all the rivers in southern Arizona. The sanctuary is located just outside Patagonia on a dirt road that parallels Ariz. 82. Hours are Wednesday to Sunday from 7:30am to 4pm. If the reserve should be closed when you visit, you are welcome to bird along the road bordering the preserve.

Avid birders will also want to visit the BLM's **Empire-Cienaga Resource Conservation Area** (☎ 520/722-4289), which has grasslands, wetlands, and oak forests. This is a good place to look for the rarely seen gray hawk. Access is off Ariz. 83 10 miles north of Sonoita.

**Patagonia Lake State Park** (☎ 520/287-6965), a popular boating and fishing lake formed by the damming of Sonoita Creek, is 11 miles south of Patagonia. The lake is 2¹/₂ miles long and is stocked in the winter with trout; bass, crappie, bluegill, and catfish also live in the lake. Park facilities include a picnic ground, a campground, and a swimming beach.

Sonoita proper is little more than a crossroads with a few shops and restaurants. Surrounding the community are miles of rolling grasslands that are primarily cattle ranches. However, recent years have seen the planting of several wine vineyards in the area and the Sonoita area is slowly becoming Arizona's wine country. The **R. W. Webb Winery** (☎ 520/762-5777) is the most accessible of the area's wineries and is located 27 miles north of Sonoita at Exit 279 off I-10. In the ghost town of Elgin, you'll find the **Village of Elgin Winery** (☎ 520/455-9309), and 3 miles south of Elgin, **Sonoita Vineyards** (☎ 520/455-5893) on Canelo Road. In Patagonia, the **Santa Cruz Winery** (☎ 520/394-2888) is located at 315 McKeown Ave, in the same building as the Patagonia Visitors Center.

# WHERE TO STAY
## IN PATAGONIA

**Circle Z Ranch.** Patagonia, AZ 85624. ☎ **888/854-2525** or 520/394-2525. 8 rms, 6 cottages. $246–$324 double; $610–$750 cottage (sleeping 4–6 people). Three-night minimum. Lower weekly rates, special long-weekend rates, and lower rates for ages 18 and under. Rates include all meals and horseback riding. No credit cards.

Located on Ariz. 82 between Nogales and Patagonia, this guest ranch has been in business since 1925, and is the oldest working cattle ranch in Arizona. Over the years it has served as a backdrop for numerous movies and TV shows including *Gunsmoke* and John Wayne's *Red River.* The 6,000-acre ranch on the banks of Sonoita Creek is bordered by the Nature Conservancy's Patagonia–Sonoita Creek Sanctuary,

Patagonia State Park, and the Coronado National Forest. Miles of trails and a remuda of nearly 80 ranch-bred horses assure everyone of getting in plenty of riding in a variety of terrains from desert hills to grasslands to the riparian forest along the creek. The adobe cabins, some of which are stuccoed and some of which have their adobe blocks exposed, provide that authentic ranch feel that is appreciated by guests hoping to find a genuine bit of the Old West. There is a wide variety of accommodation styles, including large cottages for families. Kids get to eat with the wranglers and there's also a special kids' cantina complete with video games, jukebox, and a pool table.

**Duquesne House.** 357 Duquesne St. (P.O. Box 772), Patagonia, AZ 85624. ☎ **520/ 394-2732.** 3 suites. $70 double. No credit cards.

This funky old adobe building with a long shady porch across the front was built at the turn of the century as a miner's boarding house and has been renovated and converted into a B&B. Each guest room has its own entrance off the front porch, and all have sitting rooms and bedrooms. My favorite room has an ornate woodstove and clawfoot bathtub. At the back of the house is a screened porch that overlooks the garden and a fish pond. The owner of the B&B also owns a local art gallery, and artists will feel right at home here.

**Stage Stop Inn.** 303 W. McKeown St. (P.O. Box 777), Patagonia, AZ 85624. ☎ **520/ 394-2211.** 43 rms. $60 double. MC, V.

Though nothing fancy, this small hotel in the center of town is large enough that it usually has a few rooms available. Furnishings are motel basic, but there's a small pool in the courtyard if you happen to be there in the heat of summer. A bit of Western styling adds a touch of character to the lobby, where you'll usually find information on local attractions and activities.

## IN SONOITA

**The Vineyard Bed & Breakfast.** 92 S. Los Encinos Rd. (P.O. Box 1227), Sonoita, AZ 85637. ☎ **520/455-4749.** 3 rms, 1 casita. $75 double, $85 casita. Rates include full breakfast. No credit cards.

Set atop a hill just south of Sonoita, this B&B is in a pink adobe ranch house that was built in 1916. There are expansive views from the property, and though the vineyards for which the inn is named haven't been doing too well, there are plans to replant. No matter, there are plenty of other vineyards and wineries in the area for oenophiles to visit. The sweeping views of plains and mountains are the biggest selling point of this inn, so if you're looking for high, wide, and handsome, this is it. The house itself has an unpretentious farm/ranch feel. The casita is well worth the little extra it costs and has its own patio and Saltillo tile floors. During the summer, you can cool off in the inn's small pool.

# WHERE TO DINE
## IN PATAGONIA

**Marie's European Cuisine.** 340 Naugle Ave. ☎ **520/394-2812.** Main courses $10–$14. MC, V. Wed–Fri 5–9pm, Sat 4–9pm, Sun 1–7pm. EUROPEAN.

In the center of Patagonia behind a wall there are a few tiled tables and colorful chairs with a "secret garden" kind of feeling. Dinners here, cooked by Marie, are European style chicken, lamb, pork loin, and spinach pie. This is a small two-person operation, so be prepared to relax.

**The Ovens of Patagonia.** 292 Naugle St. (Ariz. 82). ☎ **520/394-2483.** Main courses $9– $13. AE, MC, V. Wed–Sun 11am–2:30pm, Thurs–Sun 5–9pm. CUBAN/MEXICAN/BAKERY.

Also in "downtown" Patagonia, this cafe has a casual atmosphere with watercolors on the walls and picnic tables out front. The specialties here are Cuban-influenced dishes such as chicken with *sofrito* sauce (a combination of prosciutto ham, garlic, and chiles), or portobello mushrooms marinated in *mojito,* a dressing of garlic, lime, and onion, then topped with oregano, chiles, and pine nuts and oven roasted. There are also muffins, breads, stuffed focaccias, and the like, but Ovens is most famous for their key lime pie and key lime cheesecake.

## IN SONOITA

In addition to the restaurants mentioned below, **The Grasslands Café** (☎ 520/455-4770), a casual restaurant and bakery at 3119 Ariz. 83, and **Café Sonoita,** 3280 Ariz. 82 (☎ 520/455-5278) are both dining options. Café Sonoita is open for lunch on Monday.

**Er Pastaro.** 3084 Ariz. 82. ☎ **520/455-5821.** Reservations not accepted. Main courses $12–$13. No credit cards. Wed–Sun 4–9pm. Closed mid-June to mid-Sept. ROMAN ITALIAN.

This restaurant is situated on Ariz. 82, but when you walk through the door, the cuisine and the service at Er Pastaro ("the pastamaker") will convince you that you've gone to Italy. People come from all over Arizona for this dining event, primarily, as the name implies, a pasta experience. Penne pasta with fried eggplant, tomato sauce, and basil, or with vodka, hot pepper, and cream are both simple, but powerfully flavored. When owners Giovanni Schifano and his wife Karin go to Malta each summer, they pick wild capers, pickle them, and use them in the pastas and salads that appear here; Karin brings back the best Italian sausages and hams. The wine list is composed of Italian wines and prices are quite reasonable. A tree-shaded patio in back is a popular spot on hot evenings.

✪ **Karen's Wine Country Café.** 3266 Ariz. 82. ☎ **520/455-5282.** Reservations recommended. Main courses $7–$9 at lunch, $14–$18 at dinner. Chef's wine dinner $34.50. MC, V. Wed and Sun 11am–4pm, Thurs 11am–8pm, Fri–Sat 11am–9pm. SOUTHWESTERN.

With crisp blue and white tablecloths and wrap-around windows, this bright room looks out on panoramic rangeland that, framed by the windows, seems almost surreal. The view is of the Empire Cienaga Ranch, a grassland ringed by mountain ranges—you might see antelope grazing here. And inside, instead of dusty, beer-drinking cowboys, there are well-dressed urbanites sipping wine and grazing on focaccia. You can order such dishes as shrimp quesadilla, grilled chicken glazed with honey-jalapeño sauce, or rack of lamb with tomato and mint chutney. Salads are good and liberally dosed in vinaigrette dressing (which is a specialty here, along with local jams and jellies, all available for purchase). This being wine country, local wines are available and highlighted in the chef's wine dinner.

## 4 Sierra Vista & the San Pedro Valley

189 miles SE of Phoenix; 70 miles SE of Tucson; 33 miles SW of Tombstone; 33 miles W of Bisbee

At 4,620 feet above sea level, surrounded by deserts and mountains, Sierra Vista is blessed with the perfect climate—never too hot, never too cold. However, because it's a long way from any population centers and is not on an interstate, few people know about Sierra Vista. If it weren't for the U.S. Army's Fort Huachuca, it's likely that no one would have ever settled here, but when Camp Huachuca (later to become Fort Huachuca) was founded in 1877, the seeds of Sierra Vista were sown. Today, however, retirees, free from the necessity of living where there are jobs available, have discovered the climate and settled down here.

Though the town itself is modern and has very little character, the surrounding countryside has much to offer. Within a few miles' drive of town are a national conservation area, a national memorial, and a Nature Conservancy preserve. No other area of the United States attracts more attention from birders, who come for the 300 bird species in southeastern Arizona. With its many inexpensive motels, Sierra Vista makes a good base for exploring all of this region.

## ESSENTIALS

**GETTING THERE**    Sierra Vista is located at the junction of Ariz. 90 and Ariz. 92 about 35 miles south of I-10.

**America West** has regular flights from Phoenix to the Fort Huachuca Airport (also called the Sierra Vista Airport), 2100 Airport Dr. Call ☎ **800/235-9292** for schedules and fares.

**VISITOR INFORMATION**    For further information on Sierra Vista, contact the **Sierra Vista Chamber of Commerce,** 21 E. Wilcox Dr., Sierra Vista, AZ 85635 (☎ **800/288-3861** or 520/458-6940). Follow the signs for Visitor Information/ Chamber of Commerce.

## CAVERNS TO MAKE CARLSBAD ENVIOUS

**Kartchner Caverns State Park.** Off Ariz. 90, 10 miles south of Benson. ☎ **602/542-4174.** Call for admission prices.

These caverns, discovered in 1974 and kept secret for 14 years to protect them, are among the largest and most beautiful caverns in the country. Currently Arizona State Parks expects to have the caverns open to the public some time in 1998. The park will include a campground and there are plans for an exhibit hall and multimedia presentation as well. These caverns are likely to become one of the biggest attractions in southern Arizona.

## BIRD WATCHING HOT SPOTS

In addition to the birding hot spots listed below, there are two other spots in the area that serious birders should not miss. **Garden Canyon,** on Fort Huachuca, has 8 miles of trails, and 350 species of birds have been sighted. There are also Indian pictographs along one of the trails through the canyon. This is a good place to look for elegant trogons and Mexican spotted owls. Get directions to Garden Canyon at the fort's front gate where you must show your license and vehicle registration and proof of vehicle insurance. The canyon is sometimes closed due to military maneuvers, so be sure to check with the **Fort Huachuca Wildlife Office** (☎ 520/533-7083) before heading out here. The canyon is open to the public Wednesday through Friday from 11am to 7pm and on Saturday and Sunday from 10am to 6pm.

South of Ramsey Canyon, you'll find **Carr Canyon,** which has a road that climbs up through the canyon to some of the higher elevations in the Huachuca Mountains. This is a good place to look for buffbreasted flycatchers, red crossbills, and red-faced warblers.

**San Pedro Riparian National Conservation Area.** Ariz. 90. ☎ **520/458-3559.** Free admission.

Located 8 miles east of Sierra Vista, the San Pedro Riparian National Conservation Area is a rare example of a natural riverside habitat. Over the past 100 years the Southwestern landscape has been considerably altered by the human hand. Most deleterious of these changes has been the loss of 90% of the region's free-flowing year-round rivers and streams that once provided water and protection to myriad plants, animals, and even humans. Fossil findings from this area indicate that people were living along this river 11,000 years ago. At that time this area was not a desert but a swamp, and the San Pedro River is all that remains of this ancient wetland (today there isn't much water on the surface because most of the river water has flowed underground since an earthquake a century ago). The conservation area is particularly popular with birders, who have a chance of spotting more than 300 species of birds here. Also living in this region are 80 species of mammals, 14 species of fish, and 40 species of amphibians and reptiles.

There are three main parking areas for the conservation area at the bridges over the San Pedro River on Ariz. 92, Ariz. 90, and Ariz. 82. This last parking area is at the ghost town of Fairbank. At the Ariz. 90 parking area, the San Pedro House, a 1930s ranch, operates as a visitor center and bookstore. It's open daily from 9:30am to 4:30pm.

✪ **Ramsey Canyon Preserve.** Ariz. 92. ☎ **520/378-2785.** $5 suggested donation (free for Nature Conservancy members). Mar–Oct daily 8am–5pm; Nov–Feb Mon–Fri 9am–5pm, Sat–Sun 8am–5pm. Closed Thanksgiving, Christmas, and New Year's Day.

A buzzing fills the air in Ramsey Canyon, but it's not mosquitoes; it's the buzzing of curious hummingbirds. Wear bright red clothing when you visit this preserve and you're certain to attract the curious little avian dive bombers, which will mistake you for the world's largest flower. Located 5 miles south of Sierra Vista off Ariz. 92, this wildlife preserve is owned by the Nature Conservancy and is internationally known as home to 14 species of hummingbirds—more than anywhere else in the United States.

Covering only 280 acres, the preserve is situated in a wooded gorge in the Huachuca Mountains. A short nature trail leads through the canyon, with an explanatory guidebook that points out the reasons for and difficulties in preserving Ramsey Canyon; a second trail leads higher up the canyon. There are guided walks as well. Ramsey Creek is a year-round stream, a rarity in this region, and attracts a wide variety of wildlife, including bears, bobcats, and nearly 200 species of birds.

Because the preserve has become very popular and has only a few parking spaces, we recommend calling ahead to make a parking reservation 2 to 3 days in advance of your visit, if possible. Otherwise, parking is first come, first served. April and May are the busiest times of year here and August and May are the best times to see hummingbirds. To avoid parking problems, you can stay in a cabin at the preserve (see "Where to Stay," below, for details).

**Coronado National Memorial.** Montezuma Canyon Rd. ☎ **520/366-5515.** Free admission. Daily 8am–5pm.

About 20 miles south of Sierra Vista is a 5,000-acre memorial dedicated to Francisco Vásquez de Coronado, the first European to explore this region. Coronado, leading more than 700 people, left Compostela, Mexico, on February 23, 1540, in search of the fabled Seven Cities of Cibola. These cities were said to be rich in gold and jewels, and Coronado had dreams of becoming wealthy from his expedition. Coronado led his band of weary men and women up the valley of the San Pedro River sometime between 1540 and 1542. The forested Montezuma Pass, in the center of the memorial, is situated at 6,575 feet and provides far-reaching views of Sonora, Mexico, to the south, the San Pedro River to the east, and several mountain ranges and valleys to the west. A visitor center tells the story of Coronado's fruitless quest for riches, and features a wildlife observation area where you might see some of the memorial's 140 or more species of birds.

# A FORT, A RAILROAD & A BOOKSTORE

**Fort Huachuca Museum.** Inside the Fort Huachuca U.S. Army base, Grierson Rd. ☎ **520/ 533-5736.** Free admission. Mon–Fri 9am–4pm, Sat–Sun 1–4pm.

Fort Huachuca, an army base located at the mouth of Huachuca Canyon northeast of Sierra Vista, was established in 1877 and, though it has been closed a couple of times, is still active today. The buildings of the old post have been declared a National Historic Landmark and one is now a museum dedicated to the many forts that dotted the Southwest in the latter part of the 19th century. One of the most interesting aspects of the exhibits is quotes by soldiers which give an idea of what it was like to serve in the Southwest in the latter half of the 19th century. Near the museum stands a row of Victorian officers' quarters. Also nearby is the U.S. Army Military Intelligence Museum.

The **B Troop,** 4th Regiment, U.S. Cavalry (Memorial) is one of Sierra Vista's claims to fame. The original B Troop was formed in 1855 and saw action at Little Big Horn. To celebrate the horseback days of the cavalry, the new B Troop memorial was formed. The troop of about 30 members, who dress in the blue-and-gold uniforms of the 1880s, has made appearances across the country, including at the Tournament of Roses Parade, and can often be seen right here in Sierra Vista. Phone ☎ 520/533-2622 to find out if they'll be riding while you're in town.

**San Pedro & Southwestern Railroad.** 796 E. Country Club Dr., Benson. ☎ **520/ 586-2266.** Tickets for the 3$^1$/2-hour rides are $27.95 round-trip for adults, $24.73 for seniors, and $18.28 for children kindergarten–12th grade. To reach the train depot, take I-10 east to Exit 303 in Benson, drive through town and take U.S. 80 south 1 mile, and then turn left on Country Club Dr. Call ahead for the current schedule. Reservations required.

Railroad buffs and anyone else who wants to see the San Pedro River valley from a different perspective may want to check out this train excursion which runs between Benson and the ghost town of Charleston. Along the route the train passes ghost towns, the ruins of a Spanish outpost, stamp mill ruins, and abandoned ranches. Much of the trip is within the San Pedro Riparian National Conservation Area. In addition to desert scenery, the historical narration provides fascinating background on this region, including stories from Tombstone's glory days.

✪ **Singing Wind Bookshop.** ☎ **520/586-2425.** See text below for directions.

Located far off the beaten path down a dirt road outside the town of Benson, this remarkable bookstore is the brainchild of Winifred Bundy, who, with her late husband, began the business 20 years ago with only a couple of shelves of books. Now the inventory is well into the thousands and although the emphasis is on the Southwest, almost any category you can think of, plus fiction and children's books, can be found. Despite the shop's remote location on Bundy's ranch, it attracts book lovers from around the world. To reach Singing Wind Bookshop, take Exit 304 from I-10 in Benson. Drive north 2$^1$/4 miles and take a right (east) at the black mailbox full of buckshot holes. Drive to the end, opening and closing the green gate.

# WHERE TO STAY

## IN BENSON

**Skywatcher's Inn.** c/o 420 S. Essex Lane, Tucson, AZ 85711. ☎ **520/745-2390** in Tucson or 520/596-7906 in Benson. 2 rms with private bath, 1 rm with shared bath. $75 double with shared bath, $85 double with private bath. Rates include full breakfast. MC, V.

This has to be the most unusual lodging in the state of Arizona. Situated on the grounds of the privately owned Vega-Bray Observatory, an amateur observatory with six telescopes and a planetarium, the inn provides visitors with a chance to observe both the night sky and the sun through the observatories telescopes. Although experienced amateur astronomers can rent the facilities for $35 per night, inexperienced guests should opt for one of the astronomer-assisted programs, which range in price from $70 to $150 per night per group. The observatory also includes a small science and astronomy museum, and on the grounds there are two ponds and a 1 1/2-mile nature trail that provide good bird-watching opportunities. The inn is located 4 miles outside Benson; call for directions.

## IN SIERRA VISTA

In addition to the moderately priced Sierra Vista hotel listed below, you'll find numerous budget chain motels in Sierra Vista. These include the **Motel 6,** 1551 E. Fry Blvd. (☎ **520/459-5035**), charging $35 to $36 double; and **Super 8 Motel,** 100 Fab Ave. (☎ **520/459-5380**), charging $47 to $52 double. See the appendix for toll-free numbers.

**Windemere Hotel & Conference Center.** 2047 S. Hwy. 92, Sierra Vista, AZ 85635. ☎ **800/ 825-4656** or 520/459-5900. Fax 520/458-1347. 149 rms, 3 suites. A/C TV TEL. $66–$96 double; $150–$195 suite. Rates include full breakfast. AE, CB, DC, DISC, JCB, MC, V.

This modern three-story motel on the south side of town is one of Sierra Vista's best lodgings and one of the closest motels to Ramsey Canyon. However, it still seems much more popular with conventions than with avid bird watchers. The guest rooms feature contemporary furnishings, coffeemakers, large closets, and plenty of counter space in the bathrooms. There's a casual restaurant, a lounge, an outdoor pool, and a whirlpool. The hotel also offers room service, complimentary evening cocktails, and access to a health club.

## IN HEREFORD

**Casa de San Pedro.** 8933 S. Yell Lane, Hereford, AZ 85615. ☎ **520/366-1300.** Fax 520/ 366-0701. 10 rms. $95 double. Rates include full breakfast. MC, V.

Built with bird-watching tour groups in mind, this modern inn is set on the west side of the San Pedro River on 10 acres of land that border the river. While the setting doesn't have as much historical character as that of the San Pedro River Inn (see below), the rooms are large, modern, hotel-style accommodations. Built in the territorial style around a courtyard garden, the inn has a large common room where birders gather to swap tales of the day's sightings. This is by far the most upscale inn in the region.

✪ **Ramsey Canyon Inn Bed & Breakfast.** 31 Ramsey Canyon Rd., Hereford, AZ 85615. ☎ **520/378-3010.** Fax 520/378-0487. 6 rms, 2 cottages. $90–$105 double (including full breakfast); $105–$125 cottage for 2 to 4. No credit cards.

Located just outside the gates of the Nature Conservancy's Ramsey Canyon Preserve, the Ramsey Canyon Inn is a pleasant B&B that offers less rustic accommodations than are available in the preserve. Located on both sides of Ramsey Creek, the inn has rooms in the main building and small cabins that are reached by a footbridge over the creek. Hummingbird feeders set up on the inn's front porch attract 14 species of hummers throughout the year.

A large country breakfast is served in the morning, and in the afternoon you're likely to find a fresh pie made with fruit from the inn's orchard. Breakfast is not included in the cottage rates because they have their own kitchens.

**Ramsey Canyon Preserve.** 27 Ramsey Canyon Rd., Hereford, AZ 85615. ☎ **520/378-2785.** 6 cabins. $80–$90 cabin for 2. AE, MC, V.

Located on the banks of Ramsey Creek within the Nature Conservancy's preserve, these very basic cabins stay filled most of the year with avid bird watchers. Each cabin is different, but all have kitchens where you can fix your own meals. There are also patio chairs and barbecue grills. If you're used to roughing it, these cabins should be fine for you. You can be out birding at dawn and dusk when the birds are most active. If you're planning to visit during April, May, or August, you should make a reservation at least a year in advance. You can bring your own food, but there are also restaurants within 5 miles of the preserve.

**San Pedro River Inn.** 8326 S. Hereford Rd., Hereford, AZ 85615. ☎ **520/366-5532.** 4 cottages. $85–$95 double. Rates include continental breakfast. No credit cards.

With the character of a small guest ranch, this inn is a casual place that will please avid birders who prefer old Arizona character or spotless modern accommodations. Located on the east side of the San Pedro Riparian National Conservation Area, the four cottages here are set beneath huge old cottonwood trees. Surrounding the grounds are acres of grasslands and expansive vistas. All the cottages, which are rather eclectically furnished, have kitchens so you can do your own cooking.

### CAMPGROUNDS

You'll find two Coronado National Forest campgrounds—Reef Townsite and Ramsey Vista—in Carr Canyon south of Sierra Vista off Ariz. 92. On Fort Huachuca there a few campsites and a rustic cabin available in Garden Canyon. To reserve a site or the cabin, contact the **Sportsmen Center** (☎ **520/533-7085**) on base.

## WHERE TO DINE

Because Sierra Vista is home to a military base and many of the servicemen have Asian wives, the town supports quite a number of good Asian restaurants, with an emphasis on Chinese and Japanese cuisine.

**Bunbuku.** 297 W. Fry Blvd. ☎ **520/459-6993.** Main courses $6–$15. MC, V. Mon–Sat 11am–2:30pm and 4:30–9pm. JAPANESE.

Serving decent Japanese meals, this place is packed at lunch when everyone from the base heads into town to eat, but at dinner there's usually no problem getting a seat. *Katsu donburi* (pork cutlets), *yakitori* (chicken on a skewer), tempura, sushi, and sashimi are all available. Prices at lunch are quite low.

**The Outside Inn.** 4907 S. Ariz. 92. ☎ **520/378-4645.** Reservations recommended on weekends. Main courses $5–$7 at lunch, $11–$18 at dinner. AE, MC, V. Mon–Fri 11am–1:30pm and 5–9pm, Sat 5–9pm. STEAKS/SEAFOOD/ITALIAN.

Located south of town just north of the turnoff for Ramsey Canyon, The Outside Inn is a culinary oasis in southern Arizona. Outside, the Inn is a country cottage in the midst of malls; inside, it's a casual place with a bright, tile-floored main dining room and a patio area. The dinner menu includes such well-prepared fare as salmon baked in parchment and chicken topped with prosciutto ham and fontina cheese. The lunch menu offers a variety of salads and sandwiches.

## 5 Tombstone

181 miles SE of Phoenix; 70 miles SE of Tucson; 24 miles N of Bisbee

"The town too tough to die" is today one of Arizona's most popular tourist attractions, though we'll leave it up to you to decide whether the town deserves its reputation (either as a tough town or as a tourist attraction). Although the name

Tombstone alone would be enough to interest most visitors, this old mining town's claim to fame is that of the Wild West—"cowboys and Indians" and the cavalry. It was here in Tombstone that a livery stable known as the O.K. Corral once stood. When Wyatt Earp, his brothers Virgil and Morgan, and Doc Holliday took on the outlaws Ike Clanton and Frank and Tom McLaury on October 26, 1881, the ensuing gun battle sealed the fate of this town.

Tombstone was named by Ed Schieffelin, a silver prospector who had been warned against venturing into this region, which at the time was home to Apache tribes who were fighting to preserve their homeland. Schieffelin was warned that the land would be his tombstone, so when he discovered a mountain of silver here, he named it Tombstone. Within a few years Tombstone was larger than San Francisco. Between 1880 and 1887 an estimated $37 million worth of silver was mined here. Such wealth created a sturdy little town, and as the Cochise County seat of the time, Tombstone boasted a number of imposing buildings, including the county courthouse, which is now an Arizona state park. In 1887 the silver mines were flooded by an underground river. Despite attempts to pump the water out, the mines were never reopened, and the population rapidly dwindled.

Today the historic district consists of both original buildings that went up after the town's second fire and newer structures built in keeping with the architectural styles of the time. Most of them house souvenir shops and restaurants, which should give you some indication that this place is a classic tourist trap, but kids (and adults raised on Louis L'Amour and John Wayne) love it, especially when the famous shootout is reenacted.

## ESSENTIALS

**GETTING THERE**   From Tucson, take I-10 east to Benson, from which U.S. 80 heads south to Tombstone. From Sierra Vista, take Ariz. 90 north to Ariz. 82 heading east.

**VISITOR INFORMATION**   Contact the **Tombstone Office of Tourism,** P.O. Box 917, Tombstone, AZ 85638 (☎ **800/457-3423**). There's also a **visitor information center** on the corner of Allen Street and Fourth Street that's run by the Tombstone Chamber of Commerce (☎ **520/457-9317**).

**SPECIAL EVENTS**   Tombstone's biggest annual celebrations are **Territorial Days,** held the first weekend of March; **Wyatt Earp Days,** held Memorial Day weekend; and **Helldorado Days,** held in late October. The latter celebrates the famous gunfight at the O.K. Corral and includes countless shoot-outs in the streets, mock hangings, a parade, and contests.

## GUNSLINGERS & SALOONS: IN SEARCH OF THE WILD WEST

As portrayed in novels, movies, and TV shows over the years, the shoot-out has come to epitomize the Wild West, and nowhere is this great American phenomenon more glorified than here in Tombstone, where the star attraction is the famous **O.K. Corral.** Located on Allen Street near the corner of Third Street, the O.K. Corral, site of a brief gun battle, has taken on mythic proportions over the years despite the brevity of the shoot-out that took place here. Today fans of Western lore flock to this site as if on pilgrimage. Inside the corral, you'll find life-size figures set up in the spots where all the famous gunslingers are thought to have been standing when the fight took place. Admission is $2.50. Next door you'll find **Tombstone's Historama,** a sort of multimedia affair that rehashes the well-known history of Tombstone's "bad old days."

However, you need not settle for static figures and dioramas. All over Arizona there are regular reenactments of gunfights, with the sheriff in his white hat always triumphing over the bad guys in black hats, and nowhere else in the state are there so many modern-day gunslingers entertaining so many people with their blazing six-guns. On the first and third Sunday of each month at 2pm, inside the O.K. Corral, the Wild Bunch performs a live reenactment of the famous shoot-out. However, there are always plenty of other opportunities around town to watch the good guys and the bad guys shoot it out. The Boothill Gunslingers knock each other down Monday through Saturday at 2pm, the Tombstone Cowboys have it out Monday through Saturday at high noon and 4pm, and at Six Gun City on the corner of Fifth and Toughnut streets, there are shootouts Tuesday through Sunday at 11:30am and 1:30 and 3pm. The Vigilantes blaze away at 2pm on the second, fourth, and fifth Sundays of the month. Expect to pay around $3 for any of these shows.

When the smoke cleared in 1881, three men lay dead. They were later carted off to the **Boot Hill Graveyard** on the edge of town. The cemetery is open to the public and is entered through a gift shop on U.S. 80 just north of town. The graves of Clanton and the McLaury brothers, as well as those of others who died in gunfights or by hanging, are well marked.

When the residents of Tombstone weren't shooting each other in the streets, they were likely to be found in the saloons and bawdy houses that lined Allen Street. The most famous of these is the **Bird Cage Theatre,** so named for the large cagelike cribs that hang from the ceiling. These velvet-draped cages were used by prostitutes to ply their trade. The town's other famous drinking and gambling emporium is the **Crystal Palace,** at the corner of Allen Street and Fifth Street. The high-ceilinged saloon, built in 1879, has been completely restored and is a hangout for costumed members of the Wild Bunch, the local group that stages the Sunday shoot-out at the O.K. Corral.

Tombstone has long been a tourist town, and its streets are lined with souvenir shops; however, there are also several small museums scattered around town. At the **Rose Tree Inn Museum,** at Fourth and Toughnut streets, you can see what may be the world's largest rose bush (actually more of a tree). The shrub is indeed impressive as it sprawls across an arbor and covers 8,000 square feet. Inside the museum you'll see antique furnishings from Tombstone's heyday in the 1880s.

The most imposing building in town is the **Tombstone Courthouse State Park,** at the corner of Third and Toughnut streets. Built in 1882, the courthouse is now a state historic park and museum, containing artifacts, photographs, and newspaper clippings chronicling Tombstone's lively past. In the courtyard, the gallows that once ended the lives of outlaws and bandits still stands.

At the **Tombstone Epitaph Museum,** on Fifth Street between Allen and Fremont streets, you can inspect the office of the town's old newspaper. To see what life was like for the common folk in the old days, pay a visit to the **Pioneer Home Museum,** on Fremont Street (U.S. 80) between Eighth and Ninth streets.

Of the dozens of shops in town, one that stands out is **G. F. Spangenberg,** 17 S. Fourth St. (☎ 520/457-9229), a gun shop dealing in antique and modern six-shooters, as well as other guns, holsters, and the sundry necessities of the cowboy life. This is the town's most authentic shop and has been in business since 1880. One other shop well worth a visit is the **Tombstone Smithy,** 600 E. Fremont St. (☎ 520/457-3303), where a wide variety of Western-theme ironwork is crafted.

You can take historic tours by stagecoach or covered wagon with **Tombstone Stagecoach Lines,** located across the street from the visitor's center (☎ 800/355-5628 or 520/457-3191), or with **Old Tombstone Historical Tours,** next to the Birdcage Theater (☎ 520/457-3018).

# WHERE TO STAY

**Adobe Lodge Motel.** 505 Fremont St. (P.O. Box 718), Tombstone, AZ 85638. ☎ **888/457-2241** or 520/457-2241. 20 rms. A/C TV TEL. $50–$125 double. AE, DISC, MC, V.

Located in the heart of Tombstone only a block off historic Allen Street, the Adobe is a small motel with clean, no-frills rooms. If you prefer being close to the historic district, where you can walk back to your room after dinner or a nightcap, this is a good choice. The more expensive rooms are quite large and easily sleep four people.

**Best Western Lookout Lodge.** U.S. 80 West (P.O. Box 787), Tombstone, AZ 85638. ☎ **800/652-6772** or 520/457-2223. 40 rms. A/C TV TEL. $54–$81 double. Rates include continental breakfast. AE, CB, DC, DISC, MC, V.

The biggest and most comfortable motel in Tombstone is located 1 mile north of town. Stone walls, porcelain doorknobs, Mexican tiles in the bathrooms, and old-fashioned "gas" lamps give the spacious rooms an Old West feel, and all overlook the Dragoon Mountains. The rooms come with king- or queen-size beds. In summer the pool is very welcome after a long hot day.

**Priscilla's Bed & Breakfast.** 101 N. Third St. (P.O. Box 700), Tombstone, AZ 85638. ☎ **520/457-3844.** 3 rms with shared bath, 1 suite with private bath. $55 double without bath; $69 double suite with bath. Rates include full breakfast. AE, CB, DC, JCB, MC, V.

Located 2 blocks from the O.K. Corral, this small Victorian farmhouse has been completely restored and is set behind its original white picket fence. Built in 1904, the home reflects a less notorious period of Tombstone's past, a time when lawyers could build houses such as this. Lace curtains hang in the windows and, throughout the house, oak trim and oak furniture set a Victorian mood.

**Silver Nugget Bed & Breakfast.** 520 E. Allen St. (P.O. Box 268), Tombstone, AZ 85638. ☎ **520/457-9223.** 3 rms with shared bath, 1 rm with private bath. $45 double with shared bath, $65 double with private bath. Rates include continental breakfast. MC, V.

While the rooms at this inn upstairs from a souvenir shop are fairly plain, the second-floor veranda overlooking busy Allen Street can't be beat. From the rockers on the porch you can watch the stagecoaches roll by, spy on gunslingers in the street below, and generally keep tabs on the comings and goings in this historic town. One room is done up with angels, one sports a John Wayne theme, and one is filled with clown images.

# WHERE TO DINE

**Don Teodoro's Mexican Restaurant.** 15 N. Fourth St. ☎ **520/457-3647.** Reservations recommended on weekends. Main courses $5–$10. MC, V. Daily 6–10:30am; Sun–Thurs 11am–9pm, Fri–Sat 11am–10pm. SONORAN MEXICAN.

I heard the sweet strains of a guitar wafting through Tombstone, and followed the sound to Don Teodoro's, a little restaurant with a real south-of-the-border ambiance. We dined on the patio, and the experience as a whole was slightly better than the food, which consisted of adequately prepared dishes such as burritos, chile relleno, and carne asada. What I really enjoyed was the Sonoran-style enchilada, a thick corn tortilla covered with enchilada sauce and jack cheese; the tortilla soup was okay, but too salty. Without a lot of choices for dining in Tombstone, this is one of the better places. For breakfast, there's choices from huevos rancheros to omelets.

**OK Café.** 220 E. Allen St. (corner of Third and Allen sts.). ☎ **520/457-3980.** Main courses $4–$7. Credit cards not accepted. Tues–Sun 7am–2pm. AMERICAN.

Sure it's touristy, since it's on the main drag in Tombstone, but we really enjoy the buffalo burgers (also served as lunch specials with potato and vegetable). Along with buffalo burgers, you'll also find ostrich and veggie burgers, and of course hamburgers, as well as chicken and BLTs. It's also a good place for breakfast—the service is bustling and the people are friendly.

## 6 Bisbee

205 miles SE of Phoenix; 94 miles SE of Tucson; 24 miles NW of Douglas

Arizona has a wealth of ghost towns that boomed on mining profits but then quickly went bust when the mines played out. Between 1880 and 1975 the mines in Bisbee produced $6.1 *billion* worth of metals. When the Phelps Dodge Company shut down its copper mines here, Bisbee nearly went the way of other abandoned mining towns. But because it's the county seat of Cochise County, it was not fated to disappear into the desert dust. And since the town stopped growing in the early part of this century, it's one of the best-preserved turn-of-the-century towns anywhere in the Southwest. Old brick buildings line the narrow winding streets of the old section of town. Television and movie producers have discovered these well-preserved streets and in recent years Bisbee has doubled as New York City, Spain, Greece, Italy, and, of course, the Old West.

The rumor of silver in "them thar hills" is what first attracted prospectors to the area in 1877, and within a few years the diggings attracted the interest of some San Francisco investors, among them Judge DeWitt Bisbee, for whom the town is named. However, it was copper and other less-than-precious metals that would make Bisbee's fortune. With the help of outside financing, large-scale mining operations were begun in 1881 by the Phelps Dodge Company. By 1910 the population had climbed to 25,000 and Bisbee was the largest city between New Orleans and San Francisco. The town boasted that it was the liveliest spot between El Paso and San Francisco— and the presence of nearly 50 saloons and bordellos along Brewery Gulch backed up the boast.

Tucked into a narrow valley surrounded by red hills a mile high in the Mule Mountains, Bisbee today has a very cosmopolitan air. Many artists now call the town their home, and urban refugees have been dropping out of the rat race to restore the town's old buildings and open small inns, restaurants, and art galleries. Between the rough edges left over from its mining days and this new cosmopolitan atmosphere, Bisbee is rapidly becoming one of Arizona's most interesting towns.

*A word of warning:* If you think dining at good restaurants is an integral part of any vacation, you might want to avoid visiting Bisbee on a Monday or Tuesday. On these days, the town's best restaurants—High Desert Inn and Café Roka—are closed.

### ESSENTIALS

**GETTING THERE**    Bisbee is on U.S. 80, which begins at I-10 in the town of Benson, 45 miles east of Tucson.

**VISITOR INFORMATION**    For further information on Bisbee, contact the **Bisbee Chamber of Commerce,** 7 Main St. (P.O. Box BA), Bisbee, AZ 85603-0560 (☎ **520/432-5421**).

**SPECIAL EVENTS**    Each year, Bisbee puts on the Vuelta de Bisbee bicycle race, Mule Mountain Marathon, and Mile High Chili Cookoff, all in April; a soap box derby on the Fourth of July; Brewery Gulch Days in August; a Poetry Festival in September; a Gem and Mineral Show in October; and a Fiber Arts Festival and Historic Homes tour in November. Ask the Bisbee Chamber of Commerce for specific information.

# EXPLORING THE TOWN

At the Bisbee Chamber of Commerce visitor center, located in the middle of town, you can pick up walking-tour brochures that will lead you past the most important buildings and sites in town. There's parking available around the downtown area.

Your first stop should be the **Bisbee Mining and Historical Museum,** 5 Copper Queen Plaza (☎ 520/432-7071), which is housed in the 1897 Copper Queen Consolidated Mining Company office building. This small museum features an exhibit on the history of Bisbee and other exhibits that change annually. The museum is open daily from 10am to 4pm, and admission is $3 for adults, $2.50 for seniors, and free for anyone 17 and under.

For another look at early life in Bisbee, visit the **Muheim Heritage House,** 207B Youngblood Hill (☎ 520/432-7071), which was built between 1902 and 1915 and has an unusual semicircular porch. Inside is period furniture. You'll find the historic home up Brewery Gulch. The Muheim House is open Friday through Monday from 10am to 4pm (Thursday through Monday from 10am to 5pm in summer), and a $2 donation is suggested.

On the second floor of the **Copper Queen Library,** across the street from the visitor center, are some great old **photographs** which give a pretty good idea of what the town looked like within the last century.

If you climb up to the top of **OK Street,** there's a path that will take you up to a hill above town for an excellent panorama of the jumble of old buildings. Atop this hill are numerous small colorfully painted shrines built into the rocks and filled with candles, plastic flowers, and pictures of the Virgin Mary. It's a steep climb on a rocky, very uneven path, but the views and the fascinating little shrines make it well worth the effort. After you've seen the old town, you might want to drive out to the Warren district, where the wealthier citizens of Old Bisbee built their homes.

You can also see what it was like to work inside one of Bisbee's copper mines by taking one of the **Queen Mine Tours** (☎ 520/432-2071). You can choose either the underground Queen Mine tour or the surface mine and historic tour. Tours are offered daily from 9am to 3:30pm. Underground Queen Mine tours cost $8 for adults, $3.50 for children 7 to 11, $2 for children 3 to 6; surface mine and historic tours cost $7 per person; children under 3 are free. You'll find the ticket office and mine just south of the Old Bisbee business district at the U.S. 80 interchange.

If you're interested in a personally guided tour of the area, **Mary's Walking Tours** originate at 39 Shearer St., Old Bisbee.

If you have an interest in the plants of the desert, stop by **Arizona Cactus's Botanical Garden,** which is located at Arizona Cactus and Succulent Research, 8 S. Cactus Lane (☎ 520/432-7040), 6 miles south of Bisbee at Bisbee Junction. Guided tours are available. This serene oasis is surrounded by handmade adobe walls which enclose gardens containing hundreds of types of high desert plants.

Bisbee's population of artists, writers, and other creative souls demand an active cultural life, so throughout the year you can enjoy classical music performances, gallery exhibits, comedy nights, theater performances, and that old Western standby, the melodrama. Just by strolling around town on the weekends, you are likely to come upon art gallery openings. **Bisbee Repertory Theatre** stages contemporary drama, comedy, and classics. For performance and ticket information, call ☎ 520/432-3786.

There are lots of interesting shops and galleries in Bisbee—all you have to do is walk around to explore—but there are a couple of places we especially like. **Optimo Custom Hat Works,** 47 Main St. (☎ 520/432-4544) sells Panama hats woven by hand in Ecuador and custom fitted with finesse. The hats sold here range in price from about $20 for a low-grade model to several thousand dollars for a grade 20 "fino fino" (but many are priced in-between this range). **The Firehouse Gallery,** 6 Naco Rd. (☎ **520/432-1224**), is located, wouldn't you know, in the large old firehouse. Here you'll find local and "global" art. Other shops worth mentioning include **55 Main,** at 55 Main St. (☎ **520/432-4694**), with handmade lamps and garden sculpture, and **Write on Paper,** 76 Main St. (☎ **520/432-7916**), featuring objects made from beautiful paper.

# WHERE TO STAY

## MODERATE

**Copper Queen Hotel.** 11 Howell Ave. (P.O. Drawer CQ), Bisbee, AZ 85603. ☎ **800/ 247-5829** or 520/432-2216. Fax 520/432-4298. 45 rms. TV TEL. $69–$100 double. AE, DC, MC, V.

Located in the center of Bisbee, the Copper Queen Hotel was built just after the turn of the century by the Copper Queen Mining Company. At that time Bisbee was a booming mining town and the "Queen" played hostess to such notables as Teddy Roosevelt and Gen. "Black Jack" Pershing.

The atmosphere here is casual and authentic. The old safe behind the check-in desk has been there for years, as has the oak rolltop desk. Spacious halls, with their own lounges, lead to guest rooms furnished with antiques. Rooms vary considerably in size, the smallest being quite cramped. And while most have been renovated and are quite attractively furnished, there are still some that need to be refurbished. Ask for a renovated room.

The hotel's dining room, through swinging screen doors off the lobby, serves Continental and Southwestern fare, and out front there's a terrace for alfresco dining. And what would a mining-town hotel be without its saloon? For cooling off, there's even a swimming pool.

✪ **High Desert Inn.** 8 Naco Rd. (P.O. Box 145), Bisbee, AZ 85603-9998. ☎ **800/281-0510** or 520/432-1442. Fax 520/432-1410. 6 rms. A/C TV TEL. $60–$85 double. DISC, MC, V.

Though small, this is Bisbee's most luxurious hotel and is housed in the former Cochise County Jail (ca. 1901). The guest rooms vary in size, but all feature high ceilings, new carpets, and contemporary furnishings including wrought-iron headboards on the beds. The small bathrooms have lace shower curtains and modern fixtures. The inn's dining room is one of the best restaurants in town.

## INEXPENSIVE

✪ **Bisbee Grand Hotel.** 61 Main St. (P.O. Box 825), Bisbee, AZ 85603. ☎ **800/421-1909** or 520/432-5900. 8 rms, 3 suites. $55–$78 double; $95–$110 suite. DISC, MC, V.

The Bisbee Grand Hotel is the sort of place you'd expect Wyatt Earp and his wife to patronize. At street level there's a historic saloon with a high pressed-tin ceiling and an 1880s back bar from Tombstone. Upstairs are beautifully decorated turn-of-the-century guest rooms. The Oriental Suite has a ceiling fan, an incredibly ornate Chinese wedding bed, a claw-foot tub, and a skylight, and the Victorian Suite has a red-velvet canopy bed. Other rooms, though smaller, are equally attractive and sport their own themes, and while they all have private bathrooms, some of these are not in the room but rather across the hall. For 1890s atmosphere, this inn can't be beat.

**The Clawson House atop Castle Rock.** 116 Clawson Ave. (P.O. Box 454), Bisbee, AZ 85603. ☎ **800/467-5237** or 520/432-5237. 1 rm with private bath, 2 rms with shared bath. $55 double with shared bath, $75 double with private bath. Rates include full breakfast. AE, DISC, MC, V.

Set high atop Castle Rock and overlooking all of Bisbee, this 1895 home was originally built for the manager of the Copper Queen Mine. Today this inn is filled with antiques and its location makes it one of the sunniest inns in Bisbee. The spacious grounds are also the most attractive inn gardens in town. The owners of this inn also own the Main Street Inn right in the heart of Bisbee's business district. This latter inn is slightly cheaper and is not as attractively furnished, but it puts you right in the thick of things. The Clawson House is a steep 10-minute walk from downtown.

**The Inn at Castle Rock.** 112 Tombstone Canyon Rd. (P.O. Box 1161), Bisbee, AZ 85603-2161. ☎ **800/566-4449** or 520/432-4449. Fax 520/432-7868. 15 rms. $55–$88 double. Rates include full breakfast. MC, V.

This funky B&B right on the main road into Bisbee was built in 1890 as a miners' boarding house. Today the bright-red two-story inn, with verandas on both floors, is a warren of casually furnished small rooms affecting such themes as a sultan's harem. A shady patio, bar, and dining room serving French and Flemish dinners add to the appeal of this unusual place. Most unusual of all is the flooded mine shaft in the middle of the dining room! Definitely not for everyone, this inn attracts a young and artistic clientele who appreciate the owners' unusual sense of style.

**School House Inn Bed & Breakfast.** 818 Tombstone Canyon (P.O. Box 32), Bisbee, AZ 85603. ☎ **800/537-4333** or 520/432-2996. 9 rms. $50–$70 double. Rates include full breakfast. AE, DC, DISC, MC, V.

Located on a hillside overlooking Bisbee, this old schoolhouse dates back to 1918. The original hardwood floors still creak underfoot, and the bathrooms date from when the building was converted into apartments. The rooms on the front side of the B&B have the best views, and all the rooms are fairly comfortable. The rooms are filled with an eclectic mix of antique and newer furniture. On warm days, breakfast is served on the terrace beneath a big, old shade tree.

## WHERE TO DINE

In addition to the restaurants listed below, the dining room of The Inn at Castle Rock (see above) offers excellent meals amid unusual surroundings.

**Café Cornucopia.** 14 Main St. ☎ **520/432-3364.** Sandwiches, juices, and smoothies $3–$6. No credit cards. Sat–Tues 11am–6pm. DELI/JUICE BAR.

Every town should have an atmospheric juice bar, and luckily there's one in Bisbee. Not only do they serve intoxicating smoothies such as Raz-ma-taz, a concoction of raspberry, pineapple, and lemon, but salads, quiche of the day, sandwiches on delicious homemade bread (the special is meat loaf), and homemade pies and cookies are also available.

✪ **Café Roka.** 35 Main St. ☎ **520/432-5153.** Reservations recommended. Main courses $11–$17. MC, V. Wed–Sat 5–9pm. CONTEMPORARY ITALIAN.

Ask almost anyone in southern Arizona where to eat in Bisbee, and this is where they'll send you. Café Roka offers good value, as well as imaginatively prepared food. Every main course comes with a soup, salad, and sorbet, and the presentation is quite elegant. You'll find an interesting mix of locals and out-of-towners here having dinner or sitting at the bar in the middle of the room. It's all very sophisticated and a surprising find in out-of-the-way Bisbee. On the menu you'll find the likes of white corn–and–pine nut risotto cakes and roast duck in a sauce of cranberries, honey, and merlot. Local artists display their works here.

**High Desert Inn Restaurant.** 8 Naco Rd. ☎ **520/432-1442.** Reservations recommended. Main courses $12–$15. DISC, MC, V. Thurs–Sat 5:30–9pm. INTERNATIONAL.

Along with Café Roka, this is the most upscale restaurant in Bisbee. It's housed in what was formerly a courthouse—the back patio used to be the jail cells. In a genteel, romantically lit ambiance, you may dine here on food that draws its inspiration from around the globe, created by a chef transplanted from New York City. Such dishes as roasted rosemary chicken, baked brie and goat cheese with sliced green apple, and baked filet of salmon with coarse grain mustard, sautéed leeks, and saffron rice showed up on a recent menu.

**Ironman Café.** 203 Tombstone Canyon Rd. ☎ **520/432-2552.** Sandwiches, desserts $3–$6. No credit cards. Fri–Mon 8am–2pm. DELI.

This little cafe has tables on a small patio where you can sit, have an espresso or a smoked-turkey sandwich, and watch cars and trucks chug up and down the canyon. It's a little bit out of town and most popular with locals. Desserts and baked goods are a specialty.

**Stenzels.** 207 Tombstone Canyon Rd. ☎ **520/432-7611.** Reservations recommended. Main courses $3–$7 at lunch, $9–$17 at dinner. MC, V. Thurs–Fri 11:30am–2pm, Thurs–Tues 5:30–10pm. SEAFOOD/STEAKS.

It may seem strange to think about fish in the middle of the desert, but seafood is the primary attraction in this small cafe. Inside, it's a homey atmosphere with only a few tables. This is a three-person operation—the cook, the waitress, and the dishwasher—so service may be slow, but the food is worth the wait. Mr. Stenzel turns out carefully prepared fish dishes which can be sautéed, grilled, baked, or blackened to your liking, and large and juicy steaks. Dinners come with lightly cooked vegetables, red beans and rice, or potato. Don't let the outer appearance of Stenzels put you off—the meals are quite good.

## BISBEE AFTER DARK

Once home to more than 50 saloons, Bisbee still has a handful of authentic Old West saloons clustered along Brewery Gulch. One such bar is the **Stock Exchange Bar,** at 15 Brewery Gulch (☎ 520/432-9924), with a stock board from the 1920s. However, the **Bisbee Grand Saloon,** at 57 Main St. (☎ 520/432-5900), is the most upscale and appealing of the town's drinking establishments and boasts a bar from Tombstone.

## 7 Cochise Country

Willcox: 192 miles SE of Phoenix; 81 miles E of Tucson; 74 miles N of Douglas

This is the land that Apache chief Cochise once called home and that he and his men fought hard to keep. The region's high plains attracted cattle ranchers early on, and to this day ranching is a mainstay of the local economy. Today it's the spectacular scenery of the Chiricahua and Dragoon mountains that lure many visitors. Others come to add to their bird-watching life lists.

In the southern part of this region lies the town of Douglas, which is an important gateway to Mexico. Unless you're heading to Mexico, there aren't many reasons to visit Douglas. But if you do find yourself passing through town, be sure to stop in at the historic Gadsden Hotel (see page 411 for more information).

Just across the border from Douglas is Agua Prieta, Sonora, where Pancho Villa lost his first battle. Whitewashed adobe buildings, old churches, and sunny plazas provide a contrast to Douglas. Curio shops and Mexican restaurants abound. A rough map of Agua Prieta is available at the Douglas Chamber of Commerce, 1125 Pan American Ave., Douglas, AZ 85607 (☎ 520/364-2477).

# ESSENTIALS

**GETTING THERE**   Willcox is located on I-10, with Ariz. 186 heading southeast toward Chiricahua National Monument.

**VISITOR INFORMATION**   For more information on this area, contact the **Willcox Chamber of Commerce and Agriculture,** 1500 N. Circle I Rd., Willcox, AZ 85643 (☎ **520/384-2272**).

**SPECIAL EVENTS   Wings Over Willcox,** a festival celebrating the return to the area of more than 12,000 sandhill cranes and other migratory birds, takes place in January. For information, contact the Willcox Chamber of Commerce and Agriculture (☎ **520/384-2272**).

# NATURAL AREAS & BIRD WATCHING

Sea Captain, China Boy, Duck on a Rock, Punch and Judy—these may not seem like appropriate names for landscape features, but **Chiricahua National Monument** (☎ **520/824-3560**) is no ordinary landscape. These gravity-defying rock formations—called "the land of the standing-up rocks" by the Apache and the "wonderland of rocks" by the pioneers—are the equal of any of Arizona's many amazing rocky landmarks. Rank upon rank of monolithic giants seem to have been turned to stone as they marched across the forested Chiricahua Mountains. Big Balanced Rock and Pinnacle Balanced Rock threaten to come crashing down at any moment. Formed about 25 million years ago by a massive volcanic eruption, these rhyolite badlands were once the stronghold of renegade Apache. If you look closely at Cochise Head peak, you can even see the famous chief's profile.

Within the monument are a campground, picnic area, visitor center (open daily from 8am to 5pm), many miles of hiking trails, and a scenic drive that provides views of many of the most unusual rock formations. Admission is $6 per vehicle. To reach Chiricahua National Monument, take Ariz. 186 southwest from Willcox for about 30 miles and watch for the signs.

The Chiricahuas are still an important haven, but now they're a refuge for nature. The climate is just right for many species of birds, mammals, and plants normally found only in Mexico. To the east of the monument, on the far side of the Chiricahuas, is **Cave Creek Canyon,** one of the most important bird-watching spots in America. It's here that the colorful, elegant trogon reaches the northern limit of its range. Other rare birds that have been spotted here include sulfur-bellied flycatchers and Lucy's, Virgina's, and black-throated gray warblers. To reach Cave Creek Canyon in summer you can drive over the Chiricahuas from the national monument on graded gravel roads. However, in the winter you'll have to drive around the mountains, which entails going south to Douglas or north to I-10.

Another great bird-watching spot in this region is the **Willcox sewage-recycling ponds** area just past the golf course on the south side of town, where bird-watchers can see a wide variety of waterfowl including avocets and sandhill cranes. To find the ponds, head south out of Willcox on Ariz. 186, turn right onto Rex Allen, Jr., Drive at the sign for the golf course, and go past the golf course. Between October and March, as many as 12,000 sandhill cranes gather in the Willcox area, and in January, the town holds a Wings over Willcox celebration of these majestic birds.

Across the Sulphur Springs Valley from the Chiricahuas is **Cochise Stronghold,** a rugged section of the Dragoon Mountains that's almost as spectacular as Chiricahua National Monument. Here you'll find hiking trails, a campground, and a picnic area. A hike among the incredible rock formations is an opportunity to muse on the history of this area.

The Apache peoples first moved into this region of southern Arizona sometime in the early 16th century. They pursued a hunting and gathering lifestyle that was supplemented by raiding neighboring tribes for food and other booty. When the Spanish arrived in the area, the Apache acquired horses and became even more efficient raiders. They attacked Spanish, Mexican, and eventually American settlers, and despite repeated attempts to convince them to give up their hostile way of life, the Apache refused to change. Not long after the Gadsden Purchase of 1848 made Arizona U.S. soil, more people than ever before began settling in the region. The new settlers immediately became the subject of Apache raids, and eventually the U.S. Army was called in to put an end to the attacks.

By the mid-1880s only Cochise and Geronimo and their Chiricahua Apache were continuing to attack settlers and fight the U.S. Army. Cochise used this rugged section of the Dragoon Mountains as his hideout, and managed to elude capture for years because the granite boulders and pine forests made it impossible for the army to track Cochise and his followers. Cochise eventually died and was buried at an unknown spot somewhere in the area now called Cochise Stronghold.

Also north of Willcox, at the end of a 30-mile-long gravel road, lies the **Muleshoe Ranch Cooperative Management Area** (☎ **520/586-7072**), a Nature Conservancy preserve that contains seven perennial streams. These streams support endangered aquatic life as well as riparian zones that attract a large number of bird species. To reach the ranch, take Exit 340 off I-10 and go south and take a right on Bisbee Avenue and then another right onto Airport Road. After 15 miles watch for a fork in the road and take the right fork. If the road is dry, it is usually passable in passenger cars. The ranch is open daily from 8am to 5pm and overnight accommodations are available by reservation in casitas.

## HISTORIC SITES & A MUSEUM NOT TO MISS

**Fort Bowie National Historic Site.** Off Ariz. 186. ☎ **520/847-2500.** Free admission. Ranger station, daily 8am–5pm; grounds, daily dawn–dusk. Closed Christmas. Drive southeast from Willcox on Ariz. 186, and after about 20 miles, watch for the signs; it's another 6 miles up a dirt road and then a $1^1/_2$-mile hike to the fort.

The Butterfield Stage, which carried mail, passengers, and freight across the Southwest in the mid-1800s, followed a route that passed through the heart of Apache territory in the Chiricahua Mountains. Fort Bowie was established in 1862 near the mile-high Apache Pass to protect the slow-moving stage as it traversed this difficult region. It was from Fort Bowie that federal troops battled Geronimo until the Apache chief finally surrendered in 1886. Today there's little left of Fort Bowie but some crumbling adobe walls.

**Slaughter Ranch State Park.** ☎ **520/558-2474.** Admission $3 adults, children free. Wed–Sun 10am–3pm. From Douglas, go east on 15th St., which runs into Geronimo Trail; keep going east.

About 15 miles east of Douglas on a gravel road is the verdant San Bernardino Valley. In 1884, former Texas Ranger John Slaughter bought the valley and turned it into a cattle ranch, one of the finest in the West. Slaughter later went on to become the sheriff of Cochise County and helped rid the region of the unsavory characters who had flocked to the many mining towns of this remote part of the state. Today the ranch is a National Historic Landmark and has been restored to its turn-of-the-century look. Long shady porches, whitewashed walls, and dark green trim give the ranch a well-manicured look, while inside, antique furnishings present a picture of a very comfortable life.

✪ **Amerind Foundation Museum.** ☎ **520/586-3666.** Admission $3 adults, $2 seniors and children 12–18, free for children 11 and under. Sept–May daily 10am–4pm; June–Aug Wed–Sun 10am–4pm. Closed major holidays. See the text below for directions.

It may be out of the way and difficult to find, but this museum is well worth seeking out. Established in 1937, the Amerind Foundation is dedicated to the study, preservation, and interpretation of prehistoric and historic Indian cultures. To that end the foundation has compiled the nation's finest private collection of archaeological artifacts and contemporary items. There are exhibits about the dances and religious ceremonies of the major Southwestern tribes, including the Navajo, Hopi, and Apache, and exhibits that contain archaeological artifacts amassed from the numerous Amerind Foundation excavations over the years. Many of the pieces came from right here in Texas Canyon. Other exhibits contain fascinating ethnology displays, including amazingly intricate beadwork from the Plains tribes, a case full of old Zuñi fetishes, Pima willow baskets, old kachina dolls, 100 years of Southwestern tribal pottery, and Navajo weavings. The art gallery contains works by 19th- and 20th-century American artists, such as Frederic Remington, whose works focused on the West. The museum store is small but has a surprisingly good selection of books and Native American crafts and jewelry.

The Amerind Foundation is located 64 miles east of Tucson in the heart of Texas Canyon, a small but rugged canyon strewn with huge rounded boulders. To reach the museum, take the Triangle T-Dragoon exit (Exit 318) from I-10 between Benson and Willcox. There's no museum sign on the highway so you must pay attention. The museum entrance is 1 mile east.

## MORE TO SEE & DO

If you're a fan of old-time singing cowboys, you may want to visit Willcox's **Rex Allen Museum,** 155 N. Railroad Ave. (☎ 520/384-4583). It was Rex Allen who made famous the song "Streets of Laredo." The museum houses Rex Allen memorabilia and a Cowboy Hall of Fame exhibit. Each year in October, Willcox celebrates Rex Allen Days. The museum is open daily from 10am to 4pm, and admission is $2 per person, $3 per couple, or $5 per family.

If you want to learn more about the history and geology of southeastern Arizona, stop by the **Museum of the Southwest,** a small museum housed in the same buildings as the Willcox Chamber of Commerce Visitor Center at 1500 N. Circle I Rd. (☎ **520/384-2272**). The museum is located just off the interstate at the Rex Allen Drive exit (Exit 340) and is open Monday through Saturday from 9am to 5pm and on Sunday from 1 to 5pm. Admission is free.

Right next door, you'll find **Stout's Cider Mill** (☎ **520/384-3696**), off I-10 at Exit 340. It makes delicious concoctions with apples, including cider, cider floats, cidersicles, apple cake, and the biggest (and contender for the best) apple pie in the world here. They're open daily 8am to 6pm.

While in the Willcox area, you can visit the **Kokopelli Winery,** southeast of town at 961 N. Haskell Ave. (☎ **520/384-3800**), which makes several distinctive and very reasonably priced wines. The tasting room is open Saturday and Sunday from noon to 5pm. Call for directions and to be sure they'll be open.

The town of Douglas abounds in old buildings, and though not many of them are restored, they hint at the diverse character of this community. At the **Douglas Chamber of Commerce,** 1125 Pan American Ave., Douglas, AZ 85607 (☎ **520/364-2477**), you can pick up a map to the town's historic buildings.

If you'd like to hire a guide to show you this corner of the state, contact **Apacheland Custom Tours** (☎ 520/826-3087), run by Jerry Dobers. He will shuttle you around the area and fill you in on the region's colorful history.

# WHERE TO STAY

## In Douglas

✪ **Gadsden Hotel.** 1046 G Ave., Douglas, AZ 85607. ☎ **520/364-4481.** Fax 520/364-4005. 150 rms, 6 suites. A/C TV TEL. $34–$65 double; $70–$85 suite. AE, DC, MC, V.

There aren't many reasons to stay in the quiet border town of Douglas; this hotel is about it. Built in 1907, the Gadsden bills itself as "the last of the grand hotels," and its listing on the National Register of Historic Places backs up that claim. The marble lobby, though dark, is a classic. Vaulted stained-glass skylights run the length of the ceiling, and above the landing of the wide Italian marble stairway is a genuine Tiffany stained-glass window. Though the carpets in the halls are well worn, many of the rooms have been renovated and refurnished in various styles. The bathrooms are, however, a bit worse for the wear. The lounge is a popular local hangout, with more than 200 cattle brands painted on the walls. The dining room serves Mexican and American food, and there's also a coffee shop.

## In the Pearce Area

✪ **Grapevine Canyon Ranch.** P.O. Box 302, Pearce, AZ 85625. ☎ **800/245-9202** or 520/826-3185. Fax 520/826-3636. 3 cabins, 9 casitas. Mar–May and Sept–Nov $300 cabin for 2, $340 casita for 2; Dec–Feb and June–Aug $260 cabin for 2, $300 casita for 2. Rates include all meals. Two-night minimum summer and winter, 3-night minimum spring and fall. AE, DISC, MC, V.

This ranch is located in the Dragoon Mountains about 35 miles southwest of Willcox and can be either a quiet hideaway where you can enjoy the natural setting or a place to experience traditional ranch life—horseback riding, rounding up cattle, mending fences. The comfortably furnished small cabins (with only showers in their bathrooms) and larger casitas (with combination baths) are set under groves of manzanita and oak trees, and there are decks where you can view wildlife and the night sky. There's a swimming pool, and if you don't care to go horseback riding, complimentary sightseeing is included.

**Sunglow Guest Ranch.** HCR 1 Box 385, Turkey Creek Rd., Pearce, AZ 85625. ☎ **520/824-3334.** 13 rms, 1 house. $50–$85 double; $110–$140 for 4 in house. DISC, MC, V.

Located in the western foothills of the Chiricahua Mountains roughly 40 miles southeast of Willcox, this remote and tranquil ranch is surrounded by Coronado National Forest. A small lake lies just downhill from the ranch buildings and rising up behind this lake are the peaks of the Chiricahuas. Back in the 1880s Sunglow was a logging boom town, but all that remains today is an adobe cottage said to have been the home of outlaw Johnny Ringo's girlfriend. Today the old adobe building is the ranch's dining hall. A reproduction of an old mission church serves as a recreation hall and lounge. Guest rooms are all quite large and have kitchenettes, and most also have wood stoves. However, you won't find TVs or telephones in the rooms. This guest ranch is much less structured than so many others in the state, and consequently rates are also much lower. Horseback riding is an additional $10 per hour for guests. There's also a flock of emus here at the ranch, but many guests are much more interested in the many species of wild birds that can be seen on the ranch and in the nearby hills. Meals are available if arranged in advance ($30 per person per day). Daily maid service is not provided.

In association with another nearby ranch, Sunglow can arrange multiday ranch-to-ranch horseback-riding vacations. You'll spend a lot of miles in the saddle on one of these trips, so you'll need to be a fairly competent horseback rider. Trips cost $150 per person per day.

## IN PORTAL

**Portal Peak Lodge, Portal Store & Cafe.** P.O. Box 364, Portal, AZ 85632. ☎ **520/ 558-2223.** Fax 520/558-2473. 16 rms. A/C TV. $65 double. AE, DISC, MC, V.

This birders' lodge is located behind the general store and cafe in the hamlet of Portal, which lies just east of the Chiricahua Mountains and Cave Creek Canyon, a nesting area for the rare elegant trogon. The guest rooms are fairly new and face each other across a wooden deck. All have two double beds and coffeemakers. Meals are available in the adjacent cafe.

## IN WILLCOX

Budget chain motels are the only options in Willcox. These include the **Best Western Plaza Inn,** 1100 W. Rex Allen Dr. (☎ 520/384-3556), charging $59 to $99 double; **Days Inn,** 724 N. Bisbee Ave. (off I-10 at Exit 340; ☎ **520/384-4222**), charging $46 to $80 double; and **Motel 6,** 921 N. Bisbee Ave. (off I-10 at Exit 340; ☎ **520/384-2201**), with rates of $35 double.

## CAMPGROUNDS

Campgrounds in the area include one at **Chiricahua National Monument** (☎ 520/ 824-3560) and several others not far from there in the **Coronado National Forest** (☎ **520/670-4552**) on the road to Portal. There is also a small campground at Cochise Stronghold. For national forest campground reservations, call **National Forest Recreation Reservations** (☎ **800/280-2267**).

# WHERE TO DINE
## IN WILLCOX

**Historic Saxon House.** 308 S. Haskell Ave. (Bus. Rte. 10). ☎ **520/384-4478.** Reservations recommended on weekends. Main courses $7–$14. MC, V. Call for hours. STEAKS/SEAFOOD.

The Saxon house is a former home of Henry Saxon, a cowboy rancher who used it as his "city house" during the 1920s. Period furnishings and racehorse photos add to the sense of history here. The menu is simple and straightforward, with traditional favorites such as lasagna, shrimp scampi, and steaks. At press time, the restaurant was closed for repairs. Call to see if they have reopened.

## IN SUNIZONA

**Frontier Pizza and Café.** U.S. 191 (1/4 mile north of Ariz. 181). ☎ **520/824-3202.** Reservations not necessary. Main courses $4–$7. DISC, MC, V. Daily 6am–8pm. AMERICAN.

Because it's located out in the middle of nowhere, with nothing much else around except a grocery store, the food at this restaurant is surprisingly good. The place is frequented by locals and travelers who order the chili burger with mild green chiles, chicken-fried steak, or pizza. A big draw here are the baked goods, especially the pies. Some are better than others—we like the strawberry-rhubarb with crumbly topping. The folks here are very friendly and willing to chat if they're not busy.

## IN DOUGLAS

**The Grand Café.** 1119 G Ave. ☎ **520/364-2344.** Reservations not necessary. Main courses $5–$14. MC, V. Daily 10am–10pm. SONORAN MEXICAN.

The most interesting part of this cafe is the flamboyant interior and the Marilyn Monroe pictures all over the walls. On the whole, the food is Sonoran Mexican, interspersed with several Italian dishes. I like the chicken mole, if it's available, with an appetizer of grilled green onions. There are plenty of the familiar enchiladas, tacos, fajitas, and steak choices on the menu, as well as *pozole*, a chile stew with hominy and beef or pork. The guacamole had cottage cheese in it, which seemed rather strange. As a bonus, you may catch one of the owners doing theatrical impersonations.

## NORTH TOWARD PHOENIX: THE SAFFORD AREA & MOUNT GRAHAM

Roughly 50 miles north of Willcox, off U.S. 191, lie the Pinaleno Mountains and 10,717-foot **Mount Graham** in a unit of Coronado National Forest. Mount Graham has for decades been a favorite summer vacation spot for desert dwellers. Its cool heights offer respite from the heat. Campgrounds and hiking trails provide places to stay and activities while on the mountain. However, in recent years, Mount Graham has been at the center of a controversy over the construction of an astronomical observatory (partly operated by the Vatican). The mountaintops of southern Arizona have long been popular places to build high-powered telescopes, but when the University of Arizona decided to build a telescope on top of Mount Graham, they located it smack in the middle of the last remaining habitat of 400 endangered Mount Graham red squirrels. No amount of protesting was able to stop the construction of the telescope and it is yet to be seen what impact it will have on the red squirrels. However, in the spring of 1996, a devastating forest fire on the flanks of Mount Graham killed numerous squirrels and showed just how tenuous the red squirrel's lease on life is here in the Pinaleno Mountains.

Not far from the turn-off for Mount Graham, you'll find **Roper Lake State Park** (☎ 520/428-6760), which has a hot spring in the campground and a swimming beach on the lake. There's also good bird watching here and at the nearby Dankworth Ponds (where you'll also find another hot spring). You'll find the park off U.S. 191 south of Safford about 6 miles (and the ponds another 2 miles farther south). In Safford itself, **Discovery Park,** 1651 32nd St. (☎ 520/428-6260), is an interesting stop for both kids and adults. This science park includes the Gov Aker Observatory (open Wednesday through Monday from noon to 9pm), which provides opportunities for exploring the heavens. There are also plans to add other science-oriented attractions within the park.

For more information on the Safford area, contact the **Graham County Chamber of Commerce,** 1111 Thatcher Blvd., Safford, AZ 85546 (☎ 520/428-2511).

# 12 Western Arizona

They call it Arizona's West Coast, and for good reason. Separating Arizona from California and Nevada are 340 miles of Colorado River waters, and for most of this distance, the river has been dammed to form a string of lakes—Lake Havasu, Lake Mohave, and Lake Mead. Because of convolutions of the landscape, these lakes offer thousands of miles of shoreline. In some ways Arizona's West Coast is better than the Pacific coast of California. Though there aren't any waves, the weather and the water are warmer, the fishing is some of the best in the country, and water sports of all types are extremely popular.

In addition to the lakefront resorts, hotels, and campgrounds on all three lakes, there are also houseboats, which are perfect for family or group vacations. When you find a remote cove, the best fishing, or the most spectacular views, you can just anchor for a few days. You can even houseboat to the London Bridge on Lake Havasu.

A hundred years ago, rugged individuals ventured into this sun-baked landscape hoping to strike gold in the mountains. Some did hit pay dirt, and mining towns flourished briefly, only to be abandoned when the gold played out. Today, Oatman is the most famous of these towns, though it has a few too many people (and wild burros) to be a true ghost town. People are still venturing into this region in hopes of striking it rich, but now they head for the casinos in the boomtown of Laughlin, Nevada, just across the Colorado River from Bullhead City, Arizona.

## 1 Kingman

90 miles SE of Las Vegas; 180 miles SW of Grand Canyon Village; 150 miles W of Flagstaff; 30 miles E of Laughlin

Though Lt. Edward Fitzgerald Beale, leading a special corps of camel-mounted soldiers, passed through this area in 1857, Kingman was not founded until 1882, by which time the railroad had already arrived in this region. Gold and silver were discovered in the nearby mountains in the 1870s, and mining successfully continued well into the 1920s, until the mines eventually became unprofitable and were abandoned.

During the 1930s, Kingman was a stop on the road to the promised land of California, as tens of thousands of unemployed people followed U.S. 66 from the Midwest to Los Angeles. The old Route 66 has since been replaced by I-40, but the longest-remaining stretch

# Western Arizona

0    37 km
     23 mi

N

Grand Canyon
National Park

Las
Vegas

*Lake
Mead*

Lake Mead National
Recreation Area

The
South Cove

Meadview

Grand

Havasupai
Indian
Reservation

*River*

Hoover
Dam

Lake Mead National
Recreation Area

Canyon

*Colorado*

93

Hualapai Indian
Reservation

Dolan Springs

*Lake
Mohave*

Chloride

Valentine

66

Seliseman

Seligman

66

Hackberry

40

68

Laughlin

Bullhead
City

Kingman

Oatman

95

40

Yucca

Hualapi Indian Res.

Prescott

89

Wikieup

National

93

Forest

Lake Havasu City

97

Prescott

*Lake
Havasu*

Alamo Lake
State Park

Hillside

93

CALIFORNIA

*River*

Parker

Congress

Yarnell

*Colorado*

Bouse

Aguila

71

Wickenburg

95

72

Wenden

Circle City

89

Quartzite

60

Hope

Ehrenberg

10

Sun City

Kofa
National
Wildlife
Refuge

Wintersburg

95

Arlington

Buckeye

Painted Rocks
State Park

85

Gila Bend
Indian Reservation

Sentinel

Gila Bend

Dome

Dateland

Tacna

8

Yuma

85

San Luis

Barry M. Goldwater Airforce Range

Ajo

1-1308

## Get Your Kicks on Route 66

It was the Mother Road, the Main Street of America, and for thousands of Mid-westerners devastated by the dust bowl days of the 1930s, Route 66 was the road to a better life. On the last leg of its journey from Chicago to California, Route 66 meandered across the vast empty landscape of northern Arizona.

Officially dedicated in 1926, Route 66 was the first highway in America to be uniformly signed from one state to the next. Less than half of the highway's 2,200-mile route was paved, and in those days the stretch between Winslow and Ashfork was so muddy in winter that drivers had their cars shipped by railroad between those two points. By the 1930s, however, the entire length of Route 66 had been paved, and the westward migration that characterized the Great Depression was under way.

The years following World War II saw Americans take to Route 66 in unprecedented numbers, but this time for a different reason. Steady jobs, a new prosperity, and reliable cars made travel a pleasure, and Americans set out to discover the West—many on the newly affordable family vacation. Motor courts, cafes, and tourist traps sprang up along its length, and these businesses turned to increasingly more eye-catching signs and billboards in order to lure passing motorists. Neon lights abounded, looming out of the dark Western nights on lonely stretches of highway.

By the 1950s, Route 66 just couldn't handle the amount of traffic it was seeing. With President Eisenhower's initiation of the National Interstate Highway System, Route 66 was eventually replaced by a four-lane divided highway. Many of the towns along the old highway were bypassed, and motorists stopped frequenting such roadside establishments as Pope's General Store and the Oatman Hotel. Many closed, and others were replaced by their more modern equivalents. Some, however, have managed to survive, and they appear along the road like strange time capsules from another era, vestiges of Route 66's legendary past.

The **Wigwam Motel** is my personal favorite Route 66 landmark. For many miles out from the town of Holbrook, billboards along I-40 beckon weary motorists with the chance to sleep in a wigwam. The wigwams in question (ca. 1940) are made of concrete and still contain many of their original furnishings. Also in Holbrook are several rock shops with giant signs—and life-size concrete dinosaurs—that date from Route 66 days. Nighttime here comes alive with vintage neon.

Continuing west, between Winslow and Flagstaff, you'll find a landmark that even made it into *Forrest Gump*. The Twin Arrows truck stop, now little more than an old cafe just off the Interstate, has as its symbol two giant arrows constructed from telephone poles.

Flagstaff, the largest town along the Arizona stretch of Route 66, became a major layover spot. Motor courts flourished on the road leading into town from the east. Today this road has been officially renamed Route 66 by the city of Flagstaff, and many of the old motor courts remain. Though you probably wouldn't want to

of the old highway runs between Kingman and Ash Fork. Over the years old Route 66 has taken on legendary qualities. Today people come from all over the country searching for pieces of this highway's historic past.

Remember Andy Devine? No? Well, Kingman is here to tell you all about its squeaky-voiced native-son actor. Devine starred in hundreds of short films and

stay in many of these old motels, their neon signs were once beacons in the night for tired drivers. Downtown Flagstaff has quite a few shops where you can pick up Route 66 memorabilia, and the first weekend in June, the town stages a **Route 66 Festival,** complete with a classic car show.

About 65 miles west of Flagstaff begins the longest remaining stretch of old Route 66. Extending for almost 100 miles from Ashfork to Kingman, this lonely blacktop passes through some of the most remote country in Arizona. There are no real towns to speak of along this stretch, but in the community of Seligman you'll find the **Snow Cap Drive-In,** a classic burger joint with some outrageous decor. You can't miss it. You might also want to stop in at Angel's Barber Shop and Pope's General Store.

After leaving Seligman, the highway passes through such waysides as Peach Springs, Truxton, Valentine, and Hackberry. Before reaching Peach Springs, you'll come to **Grand Canyon Caverns,** once a near-mandatory stop for families traveling Route 66. At Valle Vista, near Kingman, the highway goes into a curve that continues for 7 miles. Some people claim it's the longest continuous curve on a U.S. highway.

After driving through the wilderness west of Seligman, Kingman feels like a veritable metropolis, and its bold neon signs once brought a sigh of relief to the tired and the hungry. Today there are dozens of modern motels in Kingman, but our favorite is the **Quality Inn** on Andy Devine Avenue. The lobby here is filled with Route 66 memorabilia, and a breakfast room is done up like a 1950s malt shop. **Mr. D'z Route 66 Diner,** a modern rendition of a 1950s diner (housed in an old gas station/cafe), serves burgers and blue plate specials and usually has a few classic cars parked out front. Each April, Kingman is the site of the **Route 66 Fun Run Weekend.** This is also the headquarters of the **Historic Route 66 Association of Arizona** (☎ 520/753-5001), which at press time was in the process of renovating an old powerhouse to serve as a Route 66 museum. Difficulties with funding have delayed the opening of this museum, but be sure to ask about it if you're passing through town. The museum will be about 200 yards east of the present information center on West Andy Devine Avenue on the west side of town.

The last stretch of Route 66 in Arizona heads southwest out of Kingman through the rugged Sacramento Mountains. This stretch of original 66 passes through **Oatman,** once almost a ghost town after the local mining industry collapsed and the new interstate pulled money out of town. Today mock gunfights and nosy wild burros (watch out, they bite) entice motorists to stop, and shops playing up Route 66 heritage line the wooden sidewalks.

Dropping down out of the mountains, the road once crossed the Colorado River on a narrow metal bridge. The bridge is still there, but now it carries a pipeline instead of traffic, and cars must return to the bland I-40 to continue their journey into the promised land of California.

features in the silent-screen era, but he's perhaps best known as cowboy sidekick Jingles on the 1950s TV Western *Wild Bill Hickok.* In the 1960s, he played Captain Hap on the popular program *Flipper.* Devine died in 1977, but here in Kingman his memory lives on—in a room in the local museum, on an avenue named after him, and, every October, when the town celebrates Andy Devine Days.

# ESSENTIALS

**GETTING THERE**   Kingman is on I-40 at the junction with U.S. 93 from Las Vegas. One of the last sections of old Route 66 (Ariz. 66) connects Kingman with Seligman, Arizona.

**America West Express** flies between Phoenix and Kingman Airport. One-way tickets start around $113. Call ☎ **800/235-9292** for fare and schedule information.

There is **Amtrak** passenger service to Kingman from Chicago and Los Angeles. The train stops along Andy Devine Avenue downtown. Phone ☎ **800/872-7245** for fares and schedules.

**VISITOR INFORMATION**   For more information about Kingman, contact the **Kingman Area Chamber of Commerce,** 333 W. Andy Devine Ave. (P.O. Box 1150), Kingman, AZ 86402-1150 (☎ **520/753-6106**) or the **Historic Route 66 Association of Arizona** (☎ **520/753-5001**) is at the same address. The chamber of commerce is open Monday through Friday from 8am to 5pm and Sunday from 10am to 3pm. By the time you visit Kingman, both of these organizations may have already moved 200 yards east of their present location to a renovated powerhouse that dates from 1907.

## EXPLORING THE KINGMAN AREA

There isn't much to do in Kingman, but while you're in town, you can learn more about local history at the **Mohave Museum of History and Arts,** 400 W. Beale St. (☎ **520/753-3195**). There's also plenty of Andy Devine memorabilia on display. The museum is open Monday through Friday from 9am to 5pm and on Saturday and Sunday from 1 to 5pm. Admission is $2. After touring the museum, take a drive or a stroll around downtown Kingman to view the town's many historic buildings. At the Mohave Museum of History and Arts, you can pick up a map of the town's historic buildings.

If you're interested in historic homes, you can tour the **Bonelli House,** 430 E. Spring St., a two-story stone home that was built in 1915 and is now furnished much as it may have been when it was constructed. The house is open to the public Thursday through Monday from 1 to 5pm, but before heading over to the Bonelli House, check at the Mohave Museum of History and Arts to see if there will be a guide to show you around the historic home. Admission is by donation.

A new **Route 66 museum** is also under construction in a renovated powerhouse on Andy Devine Avenue. This same building will also house the Kingman Area Chamber of Commerce when construction is completed. Be sure to ask about this new museum if you're interested in the history of the Mother Road.

If you're interested in old trains, check out the **1927 steam engine** that's the focal point of Locomotive Park on Andy Devine Avenue across from the Chamber of Commerce visitors center. This engine was Kingman's last operating steam engine.

When you're tired of the heat and want to cool off, head southeast of Kingman to **Hualapai Mountain Park,** on Hualapai Mountain Road (☎ **520/757-0915**), which is at an elevation of 7,000 feet and offers picnicking, hiking, camping, and rustic rental cabins that were built in the 1930s by the Civilian Conservation Corp.

## GRAND CANYON WEST

Kingman also serves as a sort of gateway to the little-visited west end of the Grand Canyon. However, access is over dirt roads that are not passable after rains. If, on the other hand, you are seeking a Grand Canyon experience without the crowds, consider the drive out to Grand Canyon West, which is reached by turning off U.S. 93

northwest of Kingman and following signs for Dolan Springs and Meadview. About 21 miles beyond Dolan Springs, turn right onto the dirt road signed for Grand Canyon West. Another 21 miles down this road brings you to the Hualapai Indian Reservation (and a bit of paved road again) and the Quartermaster Viewpoint over the Grand Canyon. Because this is Hualapai land, you'll have to pay a $7 entry fee.

If you'd like to see more of this area, you'll have to join the guided bus tour that leaves from Grand Canyon West daily throughout the year. These tours stop at two additional overlooks and include a barbecue lunch. For more information on these tours, contact **Grand Canyon West** (☎ **520/699-0269**) or **Hualapai Enterprises** (☎ **520/769-2419**). No reservations are accepted, so it's a good idea to arrive around 9am when Grand Canyon West opens (if coming from Kingman leave yourself at least 1¹/₂ hours to get here). Helicopter flights down into the canyon are also offered from Grand Canyon West with fares ranging from $30 to $70. Unlike South Rim helicopter flights, which stay thousands of feet above the canyon, these chopper flights actually go down into the canyon.

## GHOST TOWNS OF THE KINGMAN AREA

Located 30 miles southwest of Kingman on what was once Route 66 is the busy little ghost town of **Oatman.** Founded in 1906 when gold was discovered here, Oatman quickly grew into a lively town of 12,000 people, and was an important stop on Route 66—even Clark Gable and Carole Lombard once stayed here. However, when the U.S. government closed down many of Arizona's gold-mining operations in 1942 because gold was not essential to the war effort, Oatman's population plummeted. Today there are fewer than 250 inhabitants, and the once-abandoned old buildings have been preserved as a ghost town. The historic look of Oatman has attracted filmmakers for years, and among the movies filmed here was *How the West Was Won.*

One of the biggest attractions of Oatman is its population of almost-wild burros. These animals, which roam the streets of town begging for handouts, are descendants of burros used by gold miners. Be careful—they bite!

On weekends there are staged shoot-outs in the streets and dancing to Western music in the evening. Special events include bed races in January, a Fourth of July high noon sidewalk egg fry, a Labor Day burro biscuit toss, and a December Christmas bush festival. Saloons, restaurants, and a couple of very basic hotels provide food and lodging if you decide you'd like to stay in Oatman for a while. For more information, contact the **Oatman Chamber of Commerce,** P.O. Box 423, Oatman, AZ 86433 (☎ **520/768-6222**).

**Chloride,** yet another almost-ghost town, is located about 20 miles northwest of Kingman. The town was founded in 1862 when silver was discovered in the nearby Cerbat Mountains, and is named for a type of silver ore that was mined here. By the 1920s, there were 75 mines and 2,000 people in Chloride. When the mines shut down in 1944, the town lost most of its population. Today there are about 300 residents.

Much of the center of the town has been preserved as a historic district and includes the oldest continuously operating post office in Arizona, the old jail, the Silverbelle Playhouse, and the Jim Fritz Museum. Many of the downtown buildings now serve as studios and shops for artists and craftspeople.

On the first and third Saturday of each month, Chloride comes alive with **staged gunfights** in the streets and an afternoon **vaudeville show** at the Tennessee Saloon. On the first Saturday of May, the town celebrates **Old Miners' Day** with a parade, shoot-outs, melodramas, music, and dancing.

Chloride's biggest attractions are the **Chloride murals,** which were painted by Western artist Roy Purcell in 1966. The murals are painted on the rocks on a hillside just outside of town. To find the murals, drive through town on Tennessee Avenue and continue onward after the road turns to dirt. The murals are about a mile outside of town. You'll also find old petroglyphs created by the Hualapai tribe on the hillside opposite the murals.

For more information about Chloride, contact the **Chloride Chamber of Commerce,** P.O. Box 268, Chloride, AZ 86431 (☎ **520/565-2204**).

## WHERE TO STAY

In addition to the motel and bed-and-breakfast inn listed below, most of the budget chain motels have lodgings in Kingman. These include the **Days Inn—Kingman,** 3023 E. Andy Devine Ave. (☎ **520/753-7500**), charging $50 to $70 double; **Motel 6,** 3351 E. Andy Devine Ave. (☎ **520/757-7151**), charging $35 double; and **Super 8 Motel,** 3401 E. Andy Devine Ave. (☎ **520/757-4808**), charging $45 double. See the appendix for toll-free numbers.

✪ **Brunswick Hotel.** 315 E. Andy Devine Ave., Kingman, AZ 86401. ☎ **520/753-4944.** 3 rms with private bath, 12 rms with shared bath, 8 suites. $25 double with shared bath, $65 double with private bath; $85–$95 suite. AE, DISC, MC, V.

At press time, the historic Brunswick Hotel, built in 1909 and located in downtown Kingman, had just reopened after a complete renovation. The imposing tufa stone building dates to the days when the railroad was the lifeblood of this town, and inside you'll find rooms furnished with antiques and vintage character from those days. In addition to including breakfast in most room rates, the hotel was planning to open a full-service restaurant in the fall of 1997.

**Quality Inn—Kingman.** 1400 E. Andy Devine Ave., Kingman, AZ 86401. ☎ **800/228-5151** or 520/753-4747. 98 rms. A/C TV TEL. $49–$74 double. Rates include continental breakfast. AE, CB, DC, DISC, MC, V.

Andy Devine Avenue used to be the famous Route 66, and this motel, located 2 miles south of I-40, cashes in on the fame of the former highway with antique gas pumps and other Route 66 memorabilia in the motel lobby and a breakfast room done up like a 1950s soda shop. The rooms here are a bit cramped but are clean and have coffeemakers and two sinks in the bathrooms. The hotel also offers an outdoor pool, whirlpool, sauna, and fitness room.

## WHERE TO DINE

**DamBar & Steak House.** 1960 E. Andy Devine Ave. ☎ **520/753-3523.** Main courses $9–$20. AE, MC, V. Daily 4–10pm. STEAK.

It's hard to miss the DamBar—just watch for the steer on the roof of a rustic wooden building as you drive along Andy Devine Avenue. Inside, the atmosphere is very casual, with sawdust on the floor and wooden booths. Mesquite-broiled steaks are the name of the game here (locals claim they're the best in town), but there's mesquite-broiled chicken as well.

**Mr. D'z.** 105 E. Andy Devine Ave. ☎ **520/718-0066.** Sandwiches $3–$7; blue plate specials $7–$9. AE, DISC, MC, V. Tues–Sun 10am–8pm. AMERICAN.

This 1990s version of the vintage diner is where car buffs traveling Route 66 like to stop, probably because of the good burgers and the highly polished vintage cars in the parking lot. You can get a Corvette burger and a root beer float and punch in a few classic tunes on the jukebox. Blue plate specials include meatloaf and turkey plates, with gravy of course. The retro lunch counter and pink-and-turquoise booths are loads of fun.

✪ **Portofino Ristorante Italiano.** 318 Oak St. ☎ **520/753-7504.** Main courses $7.50–$14. MC, V. Tues–Fri 11am–2pm; Tues–Sat 5–9pm, Sun 5–8pm. ITALIAN.

Housed in an old territorial-style cottage in the historic section of downtown Kingman, this friendly Italian restaurant is our favorite spot in Kingman for a meal. Displays of cheeses, wines, and liqueurs around the restaurant lend an authentic and rustic feel to the dining room, and once you peruse the menu, you'll know you're in for a meal the likes of which you won't find for many, many miles around. You might start with grilled sausage and tomato or eggplant marinated in garlic oil. From there you can move on to a selection from the long pasta menu (penne with smoked salmon and arugula or maybe farfalle with baby artichokes) or the short selection of filling main courses. Of course, there's tiramisu with which to finish things off.

## 2  Lake Mead National Recreation Area

30 miles SE of Las Vegas; 70 miles NW of Kingman; 256 miles NW of Phoenix

Constructed between 1931 and 1935, Hoover Dam was the first major dam on the Colorado River, and by providing huge amounts of electricity and water to Arizona and California, it set the stage for the phenomenal growth that this region has experienced in the second half of this century. However, Lake Mead, the massive reservoir impounded by Hoover Dam's gargantuan cement wall, provides far more than just water and power. As the focal point of Lake Mead National Recreation Area, it is one of Arizona's (and Nevada's) favorite aquatic playgrounds. Every year more than 8 million people visit this national recreation area to boat, ski, fish, swim, and camp on both Lake Mead and Lake Mohave. This latter lake, impounded by Davis Dam, is much smaller than Lake Mead but also lies within the boundaries of the national recreation area, which encompasses parts of both Arizona and Nevada.

### ESSENTIALS

**GETTING THERE**   U.S. 93, which runs between Las Vegas and Kingman, crosses over Hoover Dam. Traffic back ups at the dam can be horrendous. You can easily get stuck for an hour just trying to get across the dam. Several small secondary roads lead to various marinas on the lake. There are also many miles of unpaved roads within the recreation area. If you have a high-clearance vehicle or four-wheel drive, these roads can take you to some of the least visited shores of the two lakes.

**VISITOR INFORMATION**   For more information, contact the **Lake Mead National Recreation Area,** 601 Nevada Hwy., Boulder City, NV 89005-2426 (☎ **702/ 293-8906** or 702/294-3523) or stop by the **Alan Bible Visitor Center,** between Hoover Dam and Boulder City, Nevada. The telephone area code for Nevada is 702.

### DAM, LAKE & RIVER TOURS

At 726 feet from bedrock to the roadway atop it, **Hoover Dam** is the highest concrete dam in the western hemisphere. It tapers from a thickness of 660 feet at its base to only 45 feet thick at the top. **Lake Mead,** the reservoir formed by Hoover Dam, is 110 miles long, has more than 550 miles of shoreline, and is the largest artificial lake in the United States. U.S. 93 runs right across the top of the dam, and there's a visitor center here that chronicles the dam's construction. The dam, which has a visitors center with exhibits on the construction, is open to the public daily from 8:30am to 5:30pm (closed Thanksgiving and Christmas). Two different guided tours of the dam are offered. The basic tours last 35 minutes and cost $6 for adults, $5 for seniors, and $2 for children ages 6 to 16. These tours leave every 10 minutes. The "Hardhat Tour," a more behind-the-scenes tour, lasts an hour and leaves every 30 minutes. This tour costs $25, but you get to keep the hard hat that you wear during the tour.

If you'd like to find out more about why Lake Mohave is there for you to play in, stop by the **Davis Dam** for a free self-guided tour. The dam is just north of Bullhead City and is open to the public daily from 7:30am to 3:30pm.

If you'd rather take a tour of the lake than a tour of the dam, that can be arranged too. **Lake Mead Cruises** (☎ **702/293-6180**) offers a variety of paddlewheeler cruises around the lake on the *Desert Princess.* There is a terminal right at Hoover Dam that makes these cruises very convenient. Day tours last 1³/₄ hours and are $17 for adults and $7 for children ages 2 to 11. There are also breakfast cruises ($21 adults and $10 children), dinner cruises ($29 adults and $15 children), and dinner-and-dancing cruises ($43).

One of the most interesting ways to see a remote section of Lake Mohave is to take a kayak trip with **Back Bay Canoes & Kayaks,** 1450 Newberry Dr., Bullhead City (☎ **520/758-6242** or 888/KAYAKEN), which offers half-day trips through Black Canyon (just below Hoover Dam) to Willow Beach. Trips cost $50 per person. **Black Canyon Raft Tours** (☎ **702/293-3776**) offers 3-hour motorized raft trips down this same stretch of the river. Trips cost $65 (includes lunch). This is an easy float trip rather than a white-water run.

## OUTDOOR RECREATIONAL OPTIONS

Swimming, fishing, water-skiing, sailing, windsurfing, and powerboating are the most popular activities within Lake Mead National Recreation Area. On Arizona shores, there are designated swimming beaches at Katherine Landing and Temple Bar. Picnic areas can be found at these two areas and also at Willow Beach on Lake Mohave and more than half a dozen spots on the Nevada side of Lake Mead.

**Fishing** for monster striped bass (up to 50 pounds) is one of the most popular activities on Lake Mead, and while Lake Mohave's striped bass may not reach these awesome proportions, fish in the 25-pound range are not uncommon and are definitely braggable. However, largemouth bass and even rainbow trout are also plentiful within the national recreation area's waters due to the diversity of habitats. Try for big rainbows in the cold waters that flow out from Hoover Dam through Black Canyon and into Lake Mohave. Trout are stocked during winter and spring in several places around both Lake Mead and Lake Mohave. To fish from shore you'll need a fishing license from either Arizona or Nevada (depending on which shore you're fishing from). To fish from a boat, you'll need a license from one state and a special use stamp from the other.

The fishing season for striped bass starts around the beginning of April when the water starts to warm up. If you don't have your own boat, try fishing from the shore of Lake Mohave near Davis Dam, where the water is deep. Anchovy pieces work well as bait, but be sure to put some shot on your line to get it down to the depths where the fish are feeding. You can get bait, tackle, and fishing tips at the **Lake Mohave Resort marina** at Katherine Landing.

In Arizona, **marinas** can be found at Katherine Landing on Lake Mohave (just outside Bullhead City), near the north end of Lake Mohave at Willow Beach (best access for trout angling), and at Temple Bar on Lake Mead. There is also a boat ramp at South Cove, north of the community of Meadview at the east end of Lake Mead. This latter boat ramp is the closest to the Grand Canyon end of Lake Mead. On the

Nevada side of Lake Mohave, you'll find a marina at Cottonwood Cove, and on the Nevada side of Lake Mead, you'll find marinas at Boulder Beach, Las Vegas Bay, Callville Bay, and Echo Bay. These marinas offer resorts, restaurants, general stores, campgrounds, and boat rentals. At both **Temple Bar** (☎ **520/767-3211**) and **Lake Mohave Resort** (☎ **520/754-3245**), you can rent ski boats, fishing boats, and patio boats for between $60 and $225 per day. Personal watercraft are also available and rent for $50 an hour or $250 a day.

Despite the area's decided water orientation, there's also quite a bit of mountainous desert here, land that's home to bighorn sheep, roadrunners, and other wild animals. This land was also once home to several indigenous tribes who left reminders of their presence in petroglyphs.

The best place to see **petroglyphs** is at Grapevine Canyon, which is due west of Laughlin, Nevada, in the southwest corner of the national recreation area. To reach Grapevine Canyon, take Nev. 163 west from Laughlin to milepost 13 and turn right on the marked dirt road. From the highway, it's about 1 1/2 miles to the turn-off for the parking area. From here it is less than a qarter mile to the petroglyph covered jumble of rocks at the mouth of Grapevine Canyon. Covering the boulders here are thousands of cryptic symbols, as well as ancient illustrations of bighorn sheep. To see these petroglyphs, you'll have to do a lot of scrambling, so wear sturdy shoes (preferably hiking boots). There are also some small springs here.

For information on other **hikes,** contact any of the ranger stations within the national recreation area (Katherine Landing, Cottonwood Cove, Temple Bar, Las Vegas Bay, Callville Bay, Echo Bay, or Overton Beach).

## WHERE TO STAY
### HOUSEBOATS

**Seven Crown Resorts.** P.O. Box 16247, Irvine, CA 92623-9801. ☎ **800/752-9669.** A/C. $1,050–$2,550 per week. DISC, MC, V.

Why pay extra for a lake-view room when you can rent a houseboat that always has a 360° water view? There's no better way to explore Lake Mead than on one of these floating vacation homes. You can cruise for miles, tie up at a deserted cove, and have a wilderness adventure with all the comforts of home. Houseboats come complete with full kitchens, air-conditioning, and room to sleep up to 14 people. The scenery here isn't quite as spectacular as on Lake Powell, Arizona's other major houseboating lake.

### RESORTS

**Lake Mohave Resort.** Katherine Landing, Bullhead City, AZ 86430. ☎ **800/752-9669** or 520/754-3245. 52 rms. A/C TV TEL. $60–$83 double. MC, V, DISC.

Just up Lake Mohave from Davis Dam and only a few minutes outside Bullhead City, the Lake Mohave Resort is an older motel, but the huge rooms are ideal for families on vacation. About half the rooms have limited views of the lake, which is across the road from the motel. Tail O' the Whale, the resort's nautical-theme restaurant and lounge, overlooks the marina where giant carp loll just below the surface waiting for people to feed them. The resort also offers boat rentals, a convenience store, and a tackle-and-bait store.

**Temple Bar Resort.** Temple Bar, AZ 86443. ☎ **800/752-9669** or 520/767-3211. 22 rms with private bath. A/C TV TEL. $43–$89 double. DISC, MC, V.

Though basically just a motel, the Temple Bar Resort has a wonderfully remote setting that will have you thinking you're on vacation in Baja California. With a beach right in front of the motel, great fishing nearby, and 40 miles of prime skiing waters extending out from the resort, this place makes an excellent getaway. Directly across from Temple Bar is the huge Temple monolith from which this area gets its name. A restaurant and lounge overlook the lake and provide economical meals. The resort offers ski rentals, powerboat rentals, shuffleboard, bocce, horseshoes, and a convenience store. Four of the rooms here are very basic fishing cabins that share shower rooms and toilets.

The same company that operates this resort also operates two others on the Nevada side of the lake. Contact the above toll-free number for more information.

## CAMPGROUNDS

In Arizona, there are campgrounds at Katherine Landing on Lake Mohave and at Temple Bar on Lake Mead. Both of these campgrounds have been heavily planted with trees so they provide some semblance of shade during the hot, but popular, summer months. In Nevada, you'll find campgrounds at Cottonwood Cove on Lake Mohave and at Boulder Beach, Las Vegas Bay, Callville Bay, and Echo Bay on Lake Mead.

RV sites are available at Lake Mohave Resort (☎ **520/754-3245**) and Cottonwood Cove (☎ **702/297-1464**) on Lake Mohave and at Temple Bar Resort (☎ **520/ 767-3211**), Callville Bay Resort (☎ **702/565-8958**), Echo Bay Resort (☎ **702/ 394-4000**), Lakeshore Trailer Village (☎ **702/293-2540**), and Overton Beach Resort (☎ **702/394-4040**).

## 3 Bullhead City & Laughlin, Nevada

30 miles W of Kingman; 216 miles NW of Phoenix; 60 miles N of Lake Havasu City

You may find it difficult at first to understand why anyone would ever want to live in Bullhead City. According to the U.S. Weather Service, this is the hottest town in the country, with temperatures regularly topping 120°F during the summer. However, to understand Bullhead City, you need only gaze across the Colorado River at the gambling mecca of Laughlin, Nevada, where the slot machines are always in action and the gaming tables are always as hot as the air outside (well, sometimes). Laughlin, Nevada, is the southernmost town in Nevada and is therefore the closest place to Phoenix to do some serious gambling. This makes Bullhead City one of the busiest little towns in Arizona.

Laughlin is a perfect miniature of Las Vegas. High-rise hotels loom above the desert like so many glass mesas. Miles of neon lights turn night into day. Acres of asphalt are always covered with cars and RVs as hordes of hopeful gamblers go searching for Lady Luck. Cheap rooms and cheap meals lure people into spending on the slot machines what they save on food and a bed. It's a formula that works well. Why else would anyone endure the heat of this remote desert?

## ESSENTIALS

**GETTING THERE**   From Phoenix, take U.S. 60, which becomes U.S. 93, northwest to I-40. From Kingman, take Ariz. 68 west to Bullhead City.

The Bullhead City–Laughlin Airport is in Bullhead City and is served by **America West Express** (☎ **800/235-9292**).

There are also shuttle bus services operating between Laughlin and the Las Vegas airport. For information or a reservation, call **Super Shuttle** (☎ **800/801-8687** or 520/704-9000) or **Best-Way Shuttle** (☎ **800/248-9744** or 520/758-1220), both of which charge around $20 one-way.

**VISITOR INFORMATION**   For more information on Bullhead City and Laughlin, Nevada, contact the **Bullhead Area Chamber of Commerce,** 1251 Ariz. 95, Bullhead City, AZ 86429 (☎ 520/754-4121).

**GETTING AROUND**   Car rentals are available in Bullhead City/Laughlin from **Avis** (☎ 800/831-2847 or 520/754-4686), **Budget** (☎ **800/499-4888,** 520/754-3362, or 702/299-9200), **Enterprise** (☎ **800/325-8007** or 520/758-4441), and **Hertz** (☎ **800/654-3131** or 520/754-4111). **Citizens Area Transit (CAT)** provides public bus service within Laughlin. The fare is $1.50. There is also a shuttle service that operates between casinos in Laughlin, or you can hire a **Stardust Limo** for $10 (look for these limos outside casinos). Free ferries shuttle gamblers back and forth across the river from Bullhead City to Laughlin. There is also **water taxi service** (☎ 702/298-6828) between casino hotels. The fare is $2 one-way and $3 round-trip from the Riverside to Harrah's.

## CASINOS & OTHER INDOOR PURSUITS

Laughlin is a very popular weekend destination for Phoenicians and other Arizonans, who have limited gambling in their own state. The casinos of Laughlin are known for having liberal slots—that is, the slot machines pay off frequently. There's also keno, blackjack, poker, craps, off-track betting, and sports betting. If you want to learn how to play a game that requires a bit more thinking than slot machines, you can take a lesson in poker, blackjack, or craps at most of the casinos. All the hotels in Laughlin offer live entertainment of some sort, including an occasional headliner (Roy Clark, The Doobie Brothers, Wayne Newton, The Mills Brothers), but gambling is still the main event after dark as far as most people are concerned.

If you'd like to learn more about the history of this area, visit the **Colorado River Museum,** 355 Hwy. 95, Bullhead City (☎ **520/754-3399**), which is located half a mile north of the Laughlin Bridge. The museum is open April to June, September, and October Tuesday to Saturday from 9:30am to 2:30pm; November to March daily 9:30am to 2:30pm; closed July and August. Admission is free.

## OUTDOOR ACTIVITIES & TOURS
### BOAT TOURS

If you'd like to get away from the noise of the casinos and see a bit of the Colorado River, there are daily cruises on two paddlewheelers. The *Little Belle* and the *Fiesta Queen* (☎ 800/228-9825 or 702/298-1047) charge $10 for adults and $6 for children and leave from docks at the Edgewater and Gold River hotels. A tour boat also operates out of the **Riverside Resort & Casino** (☎ **800/227-3849, ext. 5770** or 702/298-2535, ext. 5770) and charges these same fares. Alternatively, you could opt for a more luxurious cruise from **Harrah's** (☎ **800/74-BEACH** outside Nevada, or 702/298-6828 ) on a modern blue-water yacht. These cruises cost only $12.95 for adults and $7.95 for children age 12 and under. One other option is to take a jet-boat tour through the scenic Topock Gorge with **Desert Recreation** (☎ **702/298-6828**). These trips leave from the Harrah's Casino dock and cost $40 per person. At press time, the Flamingo Hilton was also in the process of adding a tour-boat dock.

### WATER SPORTS

If you want to get wet during your boat tour, try **London Bridge Watercraft Tours** (☎ **800/732-3665** or 520/453-8883), which leads 80-mile Sea-Doo tours down the Colorado River to Topock Gorge. On these adventurous trips, you ride on a personal watercraft, which is equivalent to a motorcycle for the water. Tours are $139 per person if there are two of you and $199 if there is only one person going.

If you'd rather just rent a personal watercraft yourself and play around a bit on the river, there are rental kiosks along the waterfront behind the casinos, as well as other rental shops in Bullhead City. Try **Del Rio Beach Club,** 2900 S. Casino Dr. (☎ **800/74-BEACH** outside Nevada, or 702/298-6828) in Laughlin, or **Wet 'n Wild,** 1159 Hwy. 95, Bullhead City (☎ **520/754-9453**), and **Riverfront Water Sports,** 1631 Hwy. 95, Bullhead City (☎ **800/342-3667** outside Arizona, or 520/763-5333).

If you'd like to do some guided kayak paddling, contact **Back Bay Canoes & Kayaks,** 1450 Newberry Dr., Bullhead City (☎ **888/KAYAKEN** or 520/758-6242), which offers half-day and multi-day kayak trips through both Black Canyon (just below Hoover Dam) and Topock Gorge (south of Bullhead City). Prices start at $50 per person.

If you're looking for someplace to put your own boat in the water, you'll find **boat ramps** at the Bullhead City Chamber of Commerce, Davis Camp, and Katherine Landing on the Arizona side and at Avi and Fisherman Landing (north of the Riverside Hotel) on the Nevada side.

## FISHING

If you're interested in doing a little fishing and want to have a guide show you some local hot spots, contact **Chet's Fishing Guide Service** (☎ **520/754-7111**), which is operated by Chet Moreland, or **Desert Recreation** (☎ **702/298-6828**), which operates out of Harrah's Casino. For information on fishing in the nearby Lake Mohave, see the "Lake Mead National Recreation Area" section of this chapter.

## GOLF

In Laughlin, golfers can play a round at the scenic and challenging **Emerald River Golf Course** (☎ **702/298-0061**), which is 2 miles south of Harrah's. Greens fees range from $50 to $60. In Bullhead City, try the **Desert Lakes Country Club** (☎ **520/768-1000**) 15 miles south of town off Ariz. 95 on Joy Lane in Fort Mohave. Greens fees range from $45 to $50. There are also three nine-hole courses near Bullhead City. These include **Riverview Resort & Golf Club,** 2000 E. Ramar Rd. (☎ **520/763-1818**), **Chaparral Country Club,** 1260 E. Mohave Dr. (☎ **520/758-6330**), and **Willow Spring Golf Course,** 8011 Hwy. 95, Mohave Valley (☎ **520/768-4414**).

## SCENIC TOURS

Topock Gorge is a 15-mile stretch of the Colorado River that is bordered by the **Havasu National Wildlife Refuge** (☎ **619/326-3853**) and is only accessible by boat. With multicolored cliffs rising up from the river, the gorge is one of the most scenic stretches of the lower Colorado River. **Bird watching** is excellent both in Topock Gorge and in more accessible sections of Havasu National Wildlife Refuge north of the community of the I-40 bridge over the Colorado. The refuge is a wintering area for many species of waterfowl.

## SKYDIVING

Looking for more excitement? How about skydiving? **Air Mel's Mohave Valley Skydiving Center** (☎ **520/346-3483**) at the Eagle Airport in Fort Mohave (4 miles north of Needles on Ariz. 95) offers tandem and traditional static-line jumps that take the gamble out of skydiving. Jumps start at $150.

# WHERE TO STAY & DINE
## IN BULLHEAD CITY

Bullhead City has numerous budget chain motels, including the **Days Inn,** 2200 Karis Dr. (☎ **520/758-1711**), charging $48 to $97 double; **Econo Lodge,** 1717

Ariz. 95 (☎ **520/758-8080**), charging $32 to $125 double; and **Motel 6,** 1616 Ariz. 95 (☎ **520/763-1002**), charging $24 to $34 double.

## IN LAUGHLIN, NEVADA

Laughlin, Nevada, currently has 10 huge hotel-and-casino complexes, 8 of which are right on the west bank of the Colorado River (the 9th is across the street from the river, and the 10th is on the river but several miles south of town). All offer incredibly cheap rooms to lure potential gamblers. In addition to huge casinos with hundreds (even thousands) of slot machines and every sort of gaming table, these hotels all have several restaurants each (with ridiculously low prices in at least one restaurant, which usually has long lines), bars and lounges (usually with live country or pop music nightly), swimming pools, video arcades for kids, ferry service to parking lots on the Arizona side of the river, valet parking, room service, car-rental desks, airport shuttles, gift shops, and gaming classes. The only real difference between most of these places is the theme each has adopted for its decor.

✪ **Avi Hotel & Casino.** 10000 Aha Macav Pkwy. (P.O. Box 77011), Laughlin, NV 89029-7011. ☎ **800/284-2946** or 702/535-5555. 301 rms, 29 suites. A/C TV TEL. Sun–Thurs $19–$25 double, Fri–Sat $35–$55 double; $50–$99 suite (rates higher on holidays and special events). AE, DISC, MC, V.

Located several miles south of the main Laughlin casino strip, this sprawling hotel/casino boasts the largest beach on this stretch of the Colorado. The wide expanses of grass that surround the hotel and the relatively remote location on the Fort Mojave Indian Reservation make this a welcome alternative to the glitz of the Laughlin strip.

While gambling is still the main event here, the location lends this hotel a much more resortlike and vacation-oriented feel. Don't bother opting for the riverview room upgrades; they don't have much in the way of views. Suites, however, are large and are good values.

**Colorado Belle Hotel & Casino.** 2100 S. Casino Dr., Laughlin, NV 89028. ☎ **800/477-4837** or 702/298-4000. 1,238 rms, 8 suites. A/C TV TEL. Sun–Thurs $17–$32 double, Fri–Sat $35–$55 double; $75–$120 suite. AE, CB, DC, DISC, MC, V.

Nevada gambling casinos and hotels have always been given over to Disneyesque flights of fancy when it comes to architectural themes, and Laughlin is no exception. The Colorado Belle is built to resemble a Brobdingnagian paddle-wheel riverboat, complete with smokestacks and eight-story paddle wheels. Of course the guest rooms are all done in nautical themes as well.

**Edgewater Hotel & Casino.** 2020 S. Casino Dr. (P.O. Box 30707), Laughlin, NV 89028. ☎ **800/677-4837** or 702/298-2453. 1,450 rms, 4 suites. A/C TV TEL. Sun–Thurs $17–$32 double, Fri–Sat $36–$51 double; $120 suite. AE, CB, DC, DISC, MC, V.

Riverfront rooms here are slightly more expensive than other rooms, but there really isn't an expensive room in the house. The Edgewater is one of the largest of the Laughlin hotels and is conveniently located right in the middle of all the action. The riverfront walk behind the hotel can connect you to other casinos.

**Flamingo Hilton.** 1900 S. Casino Dr., Laughlin, NV 89029. ☎ **800/FLAMINGO,** or 702/298-5111. 2,000 rms, 30 suites. A/C TV TEL. Sun–Thurs $17–$29 double, Fri–Sat $29–$99 double; $150–$325 suite. AE, CB, DC, DISC, MC, V.

Two shimmering glass towers reflect all the neon in Laughlin at night and make the Flamingo impossible to miss. This is pure unadulterated glitz à la Las Vegas. The guest rooms are attractively decorated and feature modern furnishings. For upgraded amenities, opt for a Flamingo room on one of the upper floors. The suites are huge (though pricey by Laughlin standards).

**Golden Nugget.** 2300 S. Casino Dr., Laughlin, NV 89029. ☎ **800/950-7700** or 702/298-7222. Fax 702/298-7111. 300 rms, 4 suites. A/C TV TEL. Sun–Thurs $21–$65 double, Fri–Sat $35–$95 double; $150 suite. AE, CB, DC, DISC, MC, V.

Here in the lobby of the Golden Nugget, the desert is turned into the jungle, with lush plantings of tropical plants and waterfalls. Tarzan's Lounge and Jane's Grill also reflect this jungle theme.

**Gold River Resort & Casino.** 2700 S. Casino Dr. (P.O. Box 77700), Laughlin, NV 89029. ☎ **800/835-7903** or 702/298-2242. 1,003 rms, 13 suites. A/C TV TEL. Sun–Thurs $16–$45 double, Fri–Sat $40–$70 double; $200–$300 suite. AE, CB, DISC, MC, V.

This high-rise hotel is done up to look like an old mine building with a copper roof and open beams. Often, the Gold River has the lowest room rates in town. You'll also find a health spa here (fee charged).

✪ **Harrah's Laughlin.** 2900 S. Casino Dr., Laughlin, NV 89028. ☎ **800/447-8700** or 702/298-4600. 1,657 rms and minisuites. A/C TV TEL. Sun–Thurs $16–$40 double, Fri–Sat $35–$65 double; $140–$180 minisuite. AE, CB, DC, DISC, MC, V.

This is one of the biggest and glitziest of the Laughlin hotels, and it sits on the bluff at the south end of town. The hotel even has its own sand beach, which gives it an advantage over other Laughlin hotels. There are also boat rentals, a health club, and two pools. The hotel is done up in a Mexican hacienda style throughout.

**Pioneer Hotel & Gambling Hall.** 2200 Casino Dr. (P.O. Box 29664), Laughlin, NV 89029. ☎ **800/634-3469** or 702/298-2442. 414 rms and minisuites. A/C TV TEL. Sun–Thurs $16–$60 double, Fri–Sat $25–$60 double; $75 minisuite. AE, CB, DC, DISC, MC, V.

This smaller (by Laughlin standards) hotel is done up to resemble an old Western town, and in true Las Vegas fashion, features a giant, waving neon cowboy. Many of the rooms are quite close to the water. Most rooms are motel style (you can park outside your door). There are nice gardens along the water side of the hotel.

**Ramada Express.** 2121 S. Casino Dr. (P.O. Box 77771), Laughlin, NV 89029. ☎ **800/243-6846** or 702/298-4200. 1,501 rms, 48 suites. A/C TV TEL. Sun–Thurs $17–$25 double, Fri–Sat $39–$59 double; $65–$125 suite. AE, DC, DISC, MC, V.

This is the only hotel in Laughlin that isn't on the water. The hotel sports a railroad theme and is designed to resemble a turn-of-the-century railway station. There's even a small train that provides free rides around the grounds. The hotel has tennis courts and a locomotive-shaped swimming pool. Last season the hotel was doing a 1940s/World War II theme with big band music, a military equipment display, and various nostalgic diversions.

**Riverside Resort Hotel & Casino.** 1650 S. Casino Dr. (P.O. Box 500), Laughlin, NV 89029. ☎ **800/227-3849** or 702/298-2535. 1,405 rms, 124 suites. A/C TV TEL. Sun–Thurs $19–$49 double, Fri–Sat $46–$99 double; $69–$129 suite (rates higher during holidays and special events). AE, CB, DC, DISC, MC, V.

This is Don Laughlin's original Laughlin casino and hotel, and it offers as many entertainment and dining options as you'll find under any one roof in Laughlin. The guest rooms are spacious and modern. Be sure to check out Don Laughlin's Classic Car Collection of more than 70 vehicles and the impressive collection of antique slot machines. There's also a big whirlpool here and two swimming pools, one of which has a short water slide. A multiplex movie theater offers an alternative to gambling (well, sort of; not all the movies are winners).

## CAMPGROUNDS

You'll find a campground on the bank of the Colorado at **Davis Camp County Park** (☎ 520/754-4606), just north of the Bullhead City–Laughlin bridge on the Arizona side of the river. Rates range from $8 to $15 for campsites, and full hook-ups are available. There are also a campground and an RV park at Lake Mohave Resort at Katherine Landing (see the "Lake Mead National Recreation Area" section of this chapter for details). Right in Laughlin, you'll find the **Riverside RV Park** (☎ **800/ 227-3849** or 702/298-2535), which is across the street from the Riverside Resort Hotel. In fact, all the hotels in Laughlin have plenty of RV parking areas.

## WHERE TO DINE

The dozens of inexpensive casino hotel restaurants are usually the top choice of visitors to Laughlin and Bullhead City. However, here's a much more low-key option:

**Señor Shrimp.** 1852 Ariz. 95, Bullhead City. ☎ **520/763-3535.** Fish and shrimp tacos $1.50– $4.75, dinners $6.25–$8.95. No credit cards. Daily 10:30am–9pm.

This hole-in-the-wall on the south side of Bullhead City looks as though it was picked up and moved here from a beach in Baja California (cable spool tables out front), which is just what the owner wants you to think when you order up a plate-load of tasty fish tacos. Tortilla chips come with an unusual spicy tuna dip.

# 4  Lake Havasu & the London Bridge

200 miles NW of Phoenix; 60 miles S of Bullhead City; 61 miles S of Kingman; 150 miles S of Las Vegas

Once upon a time London Bridge really was falling down, but that was before Robert McCulloch, founder of Lake Havasu City, hit upon the brilliant idea of buying the bridge and having it shipped to his under-touristed little town in the middle of the Arizona desert. Today the London Bridge sits like a mirage on the banks of Lake Havasu. An unlikely place for a bit of British heritage, true, but Lake Havasu City and the London Bridge have become the second-most-popular tourist destination in Arizona (only the Grand Canyon attracts more visitors).

Lake Havasu was formed in 1938 by the building of the Parker Dam, but it wasn't until 1963 that the town of Lake Havasu City was founded by McCulloch. Not too many people were keen on spending time out in this remote corner of the desert, where summer temperatures are often over 110°F. Despite its name, Lake Havasu City was little more than an expanse of desert with a few mobile homes on it. It was then that McCulloch began looking for ways to attract more people to his little city on the lake. His solution proved to be a stroke of genius.

In recent years, Lake Havasu City has become very popular with college students across Arizona, especially during spring break. The city is sort of a Fort Lauderdale in the desert, and businesses cater primarily to young partiers. Be prepared for a lot of noise if you are here on a weekend or during a holiday.

## ESSENTIALS

**GETTING THERE**   From Phoenix, take I-10 west to Ariz. 95 north. From Las Vegas, take U.S. 93 south to Kingman, then I-40 west to Ariz. 95 south.

**America West Express** (☎ **800/235-9292**) has regular flights to Lake Havasu. Round-trip fares start around $120.

The **Havasu/Vegas Express** (☎ **800/459-4884** or 520/453-4884) operates a shuttle van between Lake Havasu City and Las Vegas. One-way fare is $49.

**VISITOR INFORMATION**   For more information on this area, contact the **Lake Havasu City Visitors & Convention Bureau,** 314 London Bridge Rd., Lake Havasu City, AZ 86403 (☎ **800/242-8278** or 520/453-3444).

**GETTING AROUND**   Taxi service is available from **City Transit Service** (☎ **520/453-7600**). Car rentals are available from **Budget** (☎ **800/527-0700,** 520/453-3361, or 520/764-2277) and **Enterprise Rent-a-Car** (☎ **800/325-8007** or 520/453-0033).

# LONDON BRIDGE

In the mid-1960s, the British government decided to sell the London Bridge, which was indeed falling down—or, more correctly, sinking—into the Thames River because of too much heavy car and truck traffic. McCulloch and his partner paid $2,460,000 for the famous bridge and had it shipped 10,000 miles to Long Beach, California, and then trucked it to Lake Havasu City. Reconstruction of the bridge was begun in 1968, and the grand reopening was held in 1971. Oddly enough, the 900-foot-long bridge was not built over water. It connected only desert to more desert on a peninsula jutting into Lake Havasu. It wasn't until after the bridge was rebuilt that a 1-mile-long channel was dredged through the base of the peninsula, thus creating an island offshore from Lake Havasu City.

The London Bridge has a long history, though the bridge that now stands in Arizona is not very old by British standards. The first bridge over the Thames River in London was probably a pontoon bridge built by the Romans in A.D. 43. However, the first written record of a London Bridge comes from the mention of a suspected witch being drowned at the bridge in 984. In 1176, the first stone bridge over the Thames was built. They just don't build 'em like that bridge anymore—it lasted for more than 600 years but was eventually replaced in 1824 by the bridge that now stands in Lake Havasu City.

At the base of the bridge you'll find **English Village,** which is done up in proper English style and has shops, restaurants, and a waterfront promenade. It's here that you'll find several cruise boats and small-boat rental docks.

# LAND, RIVER & LAKE TOURS

There are several companies offering different types of boat tours on Lake Havasu. **Bluewater Charters** (☎ **520/855-7171**) offers jet-boat tours that leave from the London Bridge and spend 2 hours cruising up the Colorado River to the Topock Gorge, a scenic area 25 miles from Lake Havasu City. The tours are $25 for adults, $23 for seniors, $12 for children 6 to 12, and free for children 5 and under. **World Jet Boat Tours** (☎ **888/505-3545** or 520/505-3545) offers similar trips that go all the way to Laughlin. The round-trip fare to Laughlin is $49 for adults and $30 for children 12 and under.

*Miss Havasupai* **Boat Tours** (☎ **520/855-7979**), which leaves from the Island Fashion Mall near Shugrue's restaurant, provides a more leisurely 45-minute narrated pontoon-boat tour of the island that was formed when the London Bridge was built. Tours are $12 for adults, $10 for seniors, $6 for children age 9 to 14, and free for children 8 and under.

You can also cruise on the *Dixie Belle* (☎ **520/855-0888** or 520/453-6776), a small replica paddle-wheel riverboat. Cruises are $12 for adults, $11 for seniors, $5 for children 6 to 12.

One of the most interesting and beautiful boat tour destinations is Copper Canyon, a flooded canyon 9 miles from Lake Havasu City. The *Kon Tiki,* a pontoon boat berthed at English Village, makes the trip regularly and charges $10 for adults, $9 for seniors, and $4 for children 6 to 12.

If you want to get wet during your boat tour, try **London Bridge Watercraft Tours** (☎ **800/732-3665** or 520/453-8883), which leads 50-mile Sea-Doo tours up

Lake Havasu and the Colorado River to Topock Gorge. On these adventurous trips, you ride on a personal watercraft, which is equivalent to a motorcycle for the water. Tours are $109 per person if there are two of you and $169 if there is only one person going.

For a more leisurely trip through the beautiful and rugged Topock Gorge, where you're likely to see bighorn sheep and ancient petroglyphs, contact **Western Arizona Canoe and Kayak Outfitter** (☎ 520/855-6414), which offers guided canoe and kayak trips. Trips start at $39 per person (mention this book and you'll get a 15% discount). **Jerkwater Canoe Company,** P.O. Box 800, Topock, AZ 86436 (☎ 520/768-7753), arranges more than half a dozen canoe trips of varying lengths. They provide canoes, paddles, life jackets, maps, and shuttles to put-in and take-out points, but no guide (the maps make it easy for you to find your own way). Rentals are $35 for 1 day, $50 for 2 days, and $62 for 3 days. The most popular trips are through the Topock Gorge and Black Canyon. Some trips also include overnight campground fees or a bunkhouse bed-and-breakfast (and lunch) stay for $80.

If you'd like to explore the desert surrounding Lake Havasu City, you can arrange a four-wheel-drive tour through **Outback Off-Road Adventures** (☎ 520/680-6151), which charges $65 for a half-day tour and $130 for a full-day tour.

If you happen to be in town on the second Saturday of the month, you could also join a guided hike led by the **Lords and Ladies Club** (☎ 520/855-3341) of Lake Havasu City.

## WATER SPORTS

While the London Bridge is what made Lake Havasu City, these days water sports on 45-mile-long Lake Havasu are the area's real draw. Whether you want to go for a swim, take a leisurely pedalboat ride under the London Bridge, go parasailing, or spend the day water-skiing, there are plenty of places to arrange to get wet.

The best beach in the area is the **London Bridge Beach,** in a county park behind the Island Inn Resort off West McCulloch Boulevard. This park has a sandy beach, lots of palm trees, and views of both the London Bridge and the distant desert mountains. There are also picnic tables and a snack bar, which make this park a great place to spend the whole day. There are also beaches at **Windsor Beach State Park,** 2 miles north of the London Bridge; **Lake Havasu State Park,** just south of town; and **Cattail Cove State Park,** 15 miles south of Lake Havasu City.

The cheapest way to get out on the water in Lake Havasu also happens to involve the greatest expenditure of energy. At the **Fun Center** (☎ 520/453-4386) in the English Village you can rent pedalboats and aqua cycles for $10 to $12 an hour. If kayaking or canoeing is more your style, contact **Western Arizona Canoe and Kayak Outfitter** (☎ 520/855-6414), which rents canoes and kayaks on the lake for $15 to $25 a day.

If you didn't bring your own boat, you can rent one at **Resort Boat Rentals,** in the English Village beside the bridge (☎ 520/453-9613 or 520/855-7171). They offer half- and full-day rentals of ski, pontoon, and Nordic boats. Rental rates start at $45 an hour for a pontoon boat or runabout. They also rent water-skiing equipment for $25 a day. Boats are also available at **Lake Havasu Marina,** 1100 McCulloch Blvd. (☎ 520/855-2159), and at **Havasaki,** 1693 Industrial Blvd. (☎ 800/333-2125 or 520/855-0028).

Two- and three-passenger Waverunners are available from **Arizona Jet Ski Rentals,** 655 Kiowa Ave. (☎ 800/393-5558 or 520/453-5558), and the **Water Sport Center,** Nautical Inn Resort, 1000 McCulloch Blvd. (☎ 520/855-2141, ext. 429). Rates range from $45 to about $55 an hour. Waverunners are also available at the

Fun Center in English Village, and from **River Rat Wave Runner,** 475 London Bridge Rd., #2 (☎ 800/824-5253 or 520/855-4600), and **Arizona Aquatics,** 1535 El Camino Way (☎ 520/680-4151).

If you want to learn to water-ski, contact **Havasu Adventures Water Ski School,** 1425 McCulloch Blvd. (☎ 520/855-6274) or the above-mentioned Water Sport Center.

How about a bit of parasailing? You can get airborne at the above-mentioned Fun Center or Water Sport Center at the Nautical Inn Resort. Either place charges $35 to $45 for about 10 minutes.

If your main reason for getting out on the water is so you can catch some fish, you'll likely come away from a visit to Lake Havasu with plenty of fish stories to tell. Striped bass, also known as stripers, are the favorite quarry of lake waters. These fish have been known to reach almost 60 pounds here, so be sure to bring the heavy tackle. Largemouth bass in the 2- to 4-pound range are also fairly common here, and giant channel catfish of up to 35 pounds have been caught in Topock Marsh. The best fishing starts in mid-spring when the water begins to warm up, but there is also good winter fishing. If you want a guide to take you out, contact Jim Ocker's **Sundance Fishing** (☎ 520/680-1873). Expect to pay around $100 for a day of fishing (additional anglers are $50) for stripers or largemouth bass.

## GOLF

And what would an Arizona desert community be without its golf courses? Lake Havasu City has four, all of which are open to the public. Panoramic views are to be had from each of the courses here, and there's enough variety to accommodate golfers of any skill level.

**London Bridge Golf Club,** 2400 Club House Dr. (☎ 520/855-2719), with two 18-hole courses, is the area's premier championship course. Greens fees start at $60 (with cart) for the West Course and $25 (without cart) for the East Course. For advance tee-time reservations at this course, call **American Golf** (☎ 800/GO-TRY-18). The **Havasu Island Golf Course,** 1000 McCulloch Blvd. (☎ 520/855-2131), is a par-60, 4,012-yard executive course with lots of water hazards. Greens fees for 18 holes are $19 without a cart and $27 with a cart. The nine-hole **Queens Bay Golf Course,** 1477 Queen's Bay Rd. (☎ 520/855-4777), at the London Bridge Resort, is the most accessible and easiest of the area courses. With a $14 greens fee, it's also the cheapest in town.

Golfers also won't want to miss the **Emerald Canyon Golf Course,** 72 Emerald Canyon Dr., Parker (☎ 520/667-3366), which is about 30 miles south of Lake Havasu City. This county-owned public course is the most spectacular course in the region and plays through rugged canyons and past red-rock cliffs, from atop which there are views of the Colorado River. One hole even has you hitting your ball off a cliff to a green 200 feet below you! Greens fees range from $24 on weekdays in summer to $35 daily in fall, winter, and spring.

## WHERE TO STAY
### HOUSEBOATS

**Havasu Springs Resort.** Rte. 2, Box 624, Parker, AZ 85344. ☎ 520/667-3361. Mar 1–Sept 9 $1,855–$2,432 per week; Sept 10–Feb 28 $1,166–$1,690 per week. No credit cards.

One of the most popular ways to enjoy Lake Havasu is on a rented houseboat. You can spend your days motoring from one good fishing or swimming hole to the next, and there are beaches and secluded coves where you can drop anchor and stay for days. If you feel like doing a bit of sightseeing or shopping, you can cruise right up to the London Bridge. Houseboats come in four sizes, with the large boats providing much more luxury. Boats sleep 10 to 12 people and are very popular with families.

## HOTELS & MOTELS

**Bridgeview Motel.** 101 London Bridge Rd., Lake Havasu City, AZ 86403. ☎ **520/855-5559.** Fax 520/855-5564. 37 rms. A/C TV TEL. $35–$50 double ($90–$116 on holidays). MC, V.

If you're just looking for a clean and inexpensive place to stay, this motel fits the bill and offers a view of the bridge. It's also quiet here (usually) and there's a small pool.

**Island Inn Resort.** 1300 W. McCulloch Blvd., Lake Havasu, AZ 86403. ☎ **800/243-9955** or 520/680-0606. Fax 520/680-4218. 117 rms, 2 suites. A/C TV TEL. Mar 1–Oct 31 $65–$95 double, $130–$180 suite; Nov 1–Feb 28 $49–$59 double, $98 suite. AE, DC, DISC, MC, V.

This is one of the newest hotels in Lake Havasu City, and is located across the London Bridge from downtown. Though it's not right on the water, the Island Inn is close to one of the area's best public beaches. This hotel tends to be more popular with an older crowd than many in town and is relatively quiet even on busy weekends. The rooms are large and Spartan, though they do have big TVs. Most rooms have balconies, and those on the upper floors have the better views (and higher prices). You'll find a restaurant and lounge in the lobby, and there is often live music in the lounge. Facilities include an outdoor pool and a whirlpool.

✪ **London Bridge Resort.** 1477 Queens Bay, Lake Havasu City, AZ 86403. ☎ **800/624-7939** or 520/855-0888. Fax 520/855-9209. 170 rms, 17 suites. A/C TV TEL. Sun–Thurs $49–$99 double, $119–$219 suite; $79–$159 double, Fri–Sat $149–$269 suite. Higher rates on holidays. AE, DC, DISC, MC, V.

It doesn't take much to figure out that this resort was built after the London Bridge made its historic move to the Arizona desert. Merrie Olde England was once the theme here, with Tudor half-timbers jumbled up with turrets, towers, ramparts, and crenellations. However, England is giving way to the tropics and the desert as the resort strives to please its young, partying clientele (who tend to make a lot of noise and have left the hotel looking much the worse for wear). Though the bridge is just out the hotel's back door, and a replica of Britain's gold State Coach is inside the lobby, guests seem more interested in the three pools, the tropical-theme outdoor nightclub, and the Mexican cantina. Even the dining room now serves Southwestern food. The rooms are large, but all, including those with views, have small windows. In addition to the three pools, recreational options here include an executive golf course, tennis courts, whirlpools, and a beach.

## CAMPGROUNDS

There are several lakefront campgrounds, both public and private, in the Lake Havasu City area. **Crazy Horse Campgrounds,** 1534 Beachcomber Blvd., Lake Havasu City, AZ 86403 (☎ **520/855-4033**), has more than 600 RV spaces and a mile of waterfront. It's popular both with RVing retirees and partying college students and stays packed on weekends and holidays.

Much quieter but no less busy are the area's public campgrounds, including **Windsor Beach State Park** (☎ **520/855-2784**), 2 miles north of the bridge; **Lake Havasu State Park** (☎ **520/855-7851**), which stretches south from the south end of town; and **Cattail Cove State Park** (☎ **520/855-1223**), which is 15 miles south of Lake Havasu City. Campsite rates range from $10 to $15. In addition to sites in these campgrounds, there are 200 boat-in campsites within Lake Havasu and Cattail Cove state parks.

# WHERE TO DINE

If you'd like a bit of entertainment with your meal, consider an evening at the **Drury Lane Repertory Players' Dinner Theatre** at the London Bridge Resort (☎ 520/453-9466). Shows are held at regular intervals throughout the year, and ticket prices range from $19 to $22.

✪ **Chico's Tacos.** In the Basha's Center, 1641 McCulloch Blvd. ☎ **520/680-7010.** Main courses $1.75–$5. No credit cards. Sun–Thurs 10:30am–9pm, Fri–Sat 10:30am–10pm. MEXICAN.

This Mexican fast food place is a great place for a quick, cheap bite to eat. The carne asada and chicken carbón are excellent, and there's a fresh salsa bar for you to do your own doctoring of your meal. Be forewarned that the burritos are big and messy!

✪ **City of London Arms Pub & Restaurant.** 422 English Village. ☎ **520/855-8782.** Reservations recommended. Main courses $8–$17. AE, DISC, MC, V. Sun–Thurs 7am–10pm, Fri–Sat 7am–11pm. PUB FARE/STEAKS.

A British pub atmosphere reigns here, with a Tudor-style interior and fish-and-chips, steak-and-mushroom pie, and bangers and mash on the menu. It's a cool retreat from the blazing sun, and kind of an odd place in which to find oneself (since this *is* the desert). But take heart—if you desire something non-British, they also serve seafood, steaks, and pasta. For dessert, we wouldn't pass up the trifle, and yes, they have imported British beers and Guiness stout, served cold since this is the desert. At press time, the restaurant was adding a brewpub and beer garden as well.

**Shugrue's.** 1425 McCulloch Blvd. ☎ **520/453-1400.** Reservations recommended. Main courses $12–$20. AE, MC, V. Daily 11am–3pm and 5–10pm. STEAK/SEAFOOD.

Located just across the London Bridge from the English Village shopping complex, Shugrue's seems to be popular as much for its view of the London Bridge as it is for its food. The large restaurant has been built so that most diners get a view of the bridge. In addition to the seafood, prime rib, and Mexican dishes, there's a short list of pastas. Dieters and those who like to save room for dessert may want to choose from the menu of lighter fare.

**Versailles.** 357 S. Lake Havasu Ave. ☎ **520/855-4800.** Reservations recommended. Main courses $9–$25. AE, MC, V. Mon–Thurs 4–9pm, Fri–Sat 4–10pm. Closed Mon June–Aug. CONTINENTAL.

This building looks a little shabby on the outside but the inside is surprisingly elegant, if not a little fussy—definitely not the kind of place to come wearing your favorite torn jeans and tank top. The view from the dining room overlooks the highway and the lake beyond, while a sophisticated bar is a comfortable spot to try a selection from the long wine list. An oversized menu full of traditional choices offers such dishes as escargots with garlic sauce, surf and turf, veal marsala, frogs' legs with herb butter, and coquilles St. Jacques. Live organ music creates a lounge ambience on Saturday evenings.

# DRIVING DOWN TO YUMA
## THE PARKER AREA

About 16 miles south of Lake Havasu City stands the **Parker Dam,** which holds back the waters of Lake Havasu. Beginning just above the dam and stretching south to the town of Parker is one of the most beautiful stretches of the lower Colorado River. Just before you reach the dam, you'll come to the **Bill Williams National Wildlife Refuge,** which preserves the lower reaches of the Bill Williams River. This refuge offers some of the best bird watching in western Arizona. Keep your eyes out for vermilion flycatchers, Yuma clapper rails, soras, Swainson's hawks, and white-faced ibises.

Continuing south, you'll come to a dam overlook and the Take-Off Point boat launch, where you can also do some fishing from shore. If you're interested, there are free self-guided tours of **Parker Dam** Monday through Friday between 8am and 5pm. Below the dam, the river becomes narrow and red-rock canyon walls close in. Though this narrow gorge is lined with mobile home parks, the most beautiful sections have been preserved in two units of **Buckskin Mountain State Park,** 54751 Ariz. 95, Parker, AZ 85344 (☎ 520/667-3231). Both units—Buckskin Point and River Island—have campgrounds ($15 at Buckskin and $12 at River Island) as well as day-use areas ($7) that include river beaches and hiking trails leading into the Buckskin Mountains. In this area is the spectacular Emerald Canyon Golf Course (see "Golf" above for details).

South of this area, the highway leaves the banks of the river and the scenery becomes far less memorable. However, in the town of Parker, you might want to stop at the **Colorado River Indian Tribes Museum,** Second Street and Mohave Road (☎ 520/669-9211, ext. 335), which is south of downtown Parker on the outskirts of town. The museum is dedicated to preserving the history of several of the Colorado River's tribes. Included here is a large collection of Chemehuevi baskets, as well as pottery, beadwork, and jewelry. The museum is open Monday through Friday from 8am to 5pm with a lunch closure from noon to 1pm. Admission is free. To find the museum, follow signs to the hospital and then go 1.3 miles farther on Mohave Road. Not far from this museum, you'll find the **Ahakhav Tribal Preserve** (☎ 520/669-8831), a backwater of the Colorado River, where you can rent canoes for $25 per person per day. Call for reservations.

If you didn't already lose all your money in Laughlin, you can try again in Parker at the **BlueWater Casino,** Moovalya Plaza, 119 W. Riverside Dr. (☎ 520/669-7777), which is an enterprise of the Colorado River Indian Tribes.

## THE QUARTZSITE AREA

The population of the desert community of **Quartzsite** swells tremendously each winter with the annual influx of RVing retirees, and from early January to mid-February the community is the site of 11 gem-and-mineral shows that attract more than a million rock hounds. Among these shows is the **Quartzsite Pow Wow,** which is held the first weekend in February and is the largest gem-and-mineral show in the world. If you're passing through during these months, you might want to check out one of these shows. The town, which is little more than a crossroads for much of the year, sprouts thousands of vendor stalls as flea markets and the like are erected along the main streets. A variety of interesting food makes this a great place to stop for lunch or dinner. For more information, contact the **Quartzsite Chamber of Commerce,** P.O. Box 85, Quartzsite, AZ 85346 (☎ 520/927-5600).

For information on parking your RV in the desert outside Quartzsite, contact the **Bureau of Land Management,** Yuma District Office, Yuma Resource Area Office, 3150 Winsor Ave., Yuma, AZ 85365 (☎ 520/726-6300). Alternatively, you can get information and camping permits at the Long-Term Visitor Area entrance stations just south of Quartzsite on U.S. 95.

Also in Quartzsite is **Hi Jolly's Last Camp,** the pyramid-shaped stone monument and tomb of Hadji Ali (Hi Jolly), the Syrian camel driver who tended the camels of the U.S. Army's experimental camel corps from 1856 to 1864. You'll find the monument at the west end of town off Main Street, and though it's not particularly impressive, it commemorates a fascinating desert experiment of the 19th century.

There are only three places in Arizona where palm trees grow wild, and if you'd like to visit one of these spots, watch for the Palm Canyon turnoff 18 miles south of Quartzsite. Palm Canyon lies within the boundaries of the **Kofa National Wildlife Refuge,** which was formed primarily to protect the desert bighorn sheep that live here in the rugged Kofa Mountains. The palms are 8 miles off U.S. 95 in a narrow canyon a short walk from the end of the well-graded gravel road, and though there are only a couple of dozen of them, the hike to see them provides an opportunity to experience these mountains up close. Keep your eyes peeled for desert bighorn sheep. Incidentally, the Kofa Mountains took their name from the King of Arizona Mine. For maps and more information, contact the **Kofa National Wildlife Refuge,** 356 W. First St., Yuma (☎ **520/783-7861**).

## 5 Yuma

180 miles SW of Phoenix; 180 miles E of San Diego; 240 miles W of Tucson

Though you may never have heard of Yuma, Arizona, it was once one of the most important towns in the Southwest. Known as the Rome of the Southwest, all roads led to Yuma Crossing—the shallow spot along the Colorado River where Yuma was founded. The Quechan tribe, Spanish missionaries and explorers, Kit Carson and his mountain men, '49ers heading for the goldfields of California, pioneers, and soldiers all passed through this narrows. Despite its location in the middle of the desert, Yuma was also a busy port town when shallow-draft steamboats began traveling up the Colorado River from the Gulf of California in the 1850s. From here, during the Apache wars of the 1870s and 1880s, military supplies were transported overland to the many forts and camps throughout the Southwest. When the railroad pushed westward into California in the 1870s, it also passed through Yuma. Even today I-8, which connects San Diego with Tucson and Phoenix, crosses the Colorado at Yuma.

Hotter than Phoenix, Yuma often records summer temperatures in excess of 120°F, and the U.S. Weather Service says that Yuma is the sunniest city in the United States. Yuma is gloriously warm and sunny in the winter and has become the winter home of tens of thousands of "snowbirds" (visitors from up north), who drive their RVs from as far away as Canada.

## ESSENTIALS

**GETTING THERE**    Yuma is on I-8, which runs from San Diego, California, to Casa Grande, Arizona.

The Yuma Airport is at 2191 32nd St. and is served by **America West Airlines** (☎ **800/235-9292**), **Skywest Airlines** (☎ **800/453-9417**), and **United Express** (☎ **800/241-6522**).

There's **Amtrak** passenger service to Yuma from Los Angeles and New Orleans. The station is on Gila Street. Phone ☎ **800/872-7245** for fares and schedules.

**Greyhound** buses also stop in Yuma. The station is at 170 E. 17th Place (☎ **520/ 783-4403**).

**VISITOR INFORMATION**    For more information about Yuma, contact the **Yuma Convention and Visitors Bureau,** 377 Main St. (P.O. Box 11059), Yuma, AZ 85366 (☎ **520/783-0071**).

**GETTING AROUND**    For a taxi, call **Yuma City Cab** (☎ **520/782-0111**). Rental cars are available in Yuma from **Avis** (☎ **520/726-5737**), **Budget** (☎ **800/ 227-3678** or 520/344-1822), **Enterprise** (☎ **520/344-5444**), and **Hertz** (☎ **520/ 726-5160**).

# HISTORIC SITES

**Yuma Crossing State Historic Park.** 221 N. Second Ave. (Fourth Ave. and the Colorado River). ☎ **520/783-4771.** Admission $3 adults, $2.50 seniors, $2 children 6–17, free for children 5 and under. Daily 10am–5pm. Closed Dec 25.

In 1865, Yuma Crossing, the narrow spot in the Colorado River where the town of Yuma sprang up, became the site of the military's Quartermaster Depot. Yuma was a busy river port during this time, and after supplies shipped from California were unloaded, they went to military posts throughout the region. When the railroad arrived in Yuma in 1877, the Quartermaster Depot began losing its importance in the regional supply network. By 1883 the depot had been closed. Today the depot's large wooden buildings have been restored, and though they are now set back from the current channel of the Colorado River, it's easy to imagine being stationed at this hot and dusty outpost in the days before air-conditioning. Exhibits tell the story of those who lived and worked at Yuma Crossing, and a short video documents the town's story. There are also costumed guides on hand to answer questions about the depot and its role in Arizona history.

**Yuma Territorial Prison State Historic Park.** 1 Prison Hill Rd. ☎ **520/783-4771.** Admission $3 adults, $1 children 13–17, free for children 12 and under. Daily 8am–5pm. Closed Dec 25.

Yuma is one of the hottest places in the world, so it comes as no surprise that the Arizona Territory chose this bleak spot for a prison (although there is a nice view of the confluence of the Gila and Colorado rivers from Prison Hill). The prison first closed its doors on convicts in 1876 but operated for only 33 years before being replaced by a larger prison. Despite the stone walls (albeit thick ones) and iron bars, this prison was considered a model penal institution in its day. It even had its own generating plant for electricity and a ventilation system. The prison museum has some interesting displays, including photos of many of the 3,049 men and 29 women who were incarcerated at Yuma over the years. After the prison was shut down, the building served as a high school and as housing for the homeless during the Depression.

**Arizona Historical Society Century House Museum.** 240 S. Madison Ave. ☎ **520/782-1841.** Free admission. Tues–Sat 10am–4pm.

If you'd like to find out more about pioneer life in Yuma, stop by this territorial-period home, which is full of historical photographs and artifacts and is surrounded by lush gardens and aviaries full of exotic birds. Adjacent to the museum is the Garden Cafe, an excellent lunch spot.

**Quechan Indian Museum.** Indian Hill Rd. ☎ **619/572-0661.** Admission $1. Mon–Fri 8am–noon and 1–5pm.

Cross the river to California to find displays of tribal arts and crafts and historic photos and artifacts covering both the past and present of the Quechan culture. The Quechan were one of eight tribes living and farming along the Colorado River when the Spanish first arrived in this region in 1540.

# DOWNTOWN YUMA

Historic downtown Yuma isn't exactly a bustling place, and it doesn't abound in historic flavor, but the south-of-the-border atmosphere is well worth a visit. Huge well-shaped ficus trees provide deep shade, and at the center of the shopping district is a plaza similar to those found in towns all over Mexico. One of the best reasons to visit Main Street is to pay a visit to the **301 Main/Yuma Fine Arts Center,** 301 Main St. (☎ **520/783-2314**), which often stages surprisingly provocative and imaginative art shows. Funky and inexpensive craft and antiques shops occupy an occasional store-front. An alleyway of shops off Main Street (at 224 Main St., across from Lutes Casino) has a potpourri of small tourist-oriented stores.

## CAMELS, DATES & DESERT TOURING

A hundred years ago there used to be camels wandering the deserts near here. No, they weren't native camels, they were just some the army turned loose after an experimental camel corps was disbanded. Today there are still camels in Yuma at the **Saihati Camel Farm,** 15672 S. Ave. 1E (☎ **520/627-2553**), which keeps a large camel herd, as well as other interesting desert wildlife. Guided tours are offered October to May (reservations recommended), Monday through Saturday at 10am and 2pm and on Sunday at 2pm. Admission is $3.

Just as much a part of this desert as camels, are date gardens. Dates are among the most ancient of cultivated tree crops and were grown in the Middle East as many as 5,000 years ago. Right in Yuma, you'll find **Ehrlich's Date Garden,** 868 Ave. B (☎ **520/783-4778**), which sells nearly a dozen varieties of organically grown dates, as well as organic oranges. Prices are incredibly low and the old-fashioned fruit stand is open daily from 9am to 5pm.

Another unusual farmstand worth visiting is **The Peanut Patch,** 4322 E. County 13th St. (☎ **520/726-6292**), located way out on the east side of town past the Marine Corps Air Station. As the name implies, this place specializes in peanuts, but they also sell lots of other quality produce from around the area, including dates and citrus fruits. The shop is open October through May, Monday through Saturday from 9am to 5pm. Tours are offered Tuesday, Wednesday, Friday, and Saturday at 10am.

The Colorado River has been the life blood of the Southwestern desert for centuries, and today there's a wealth of history along its banks. **Yuma River Tours,** 1920 Arizona Ave. (☎ **520/783-4400**), operates narrated jet-boat tours of varying lengths between Yuma and the Imperial Wildlife Refuge to the north. Along the way, you'll learn about the homesteaders, boatmen, Native Americans, and miners who relied on the Colorado River. Tours cost $25 to $69. This company also offers jeep tours of the area. Alternatively, you can take a 3-hour paddle-wheel trip on the *Colorado King I* (☎ **520/782-2412**). Tours are $25 to $35 for adults and $15 for children 12 and under.

While the river was the reason for Yuma's existence, it was the railroad that finally forced the town to abandon its connection to the Colorado. Today, you can ride the rails on the historic **Yuma Valley Railway** (☎ **520/783-3456**), which offers 22-mile excursions along the Colorado River between October and May. Along the way you may spot birds and other wildlife on the banks of the river, and you'll get views of Mexico across the river and rich agricultural lands on this side. Passengers ride in a 1922 Pullman coach pulled by either a 1941 Whitcombe diesel or a 1952 Davenport-Beshler diesel-electric engine. Fares are $10 for adults, $9 for seniors, and $5 for children ages 4 to 16. There are also picnic and steak runs.

If you're a bird-watcher, an angler, or a canoeist you'll want to spend some time along the Colorado River north of Yuma. Here you'll find the **Imperial and Cibola national wildlife refuges,** with their lakes and marshes. Plenty of bird species, good fishing and canoeing, and several campgrounds make this a popular area. For more information on this area contact the **Bureau of Land Management (BLM),** Yuma District Office, Yuma Resource Area Office, 3150 Winsor Ave., Yuma, AZ 85365 (☎ **520/726-6300**).

If you're interested in doing some horseback riding, make a reservation at **U Ride 'Um Cowboy,** 1120 Berryman Rd., Bard, CA (☎ **520/785-3819** or 619/

572-0426), which charges $20 for a 1-hour ride. Breakfast, lunch, and dinner rides are also available.

Yuma is also well known among rock hounds. Within 80 miles of here are numerous **gem fields** where it's possible to search for such interesting minerals and semiprecious stones as garnet, tourmaline, magnetite, jasper, rhyolite, pyrite, agate, and chalcedony roses. Contact the Yuma Convention and Visitors Bureau for information on getting to some of these gem fields.

## GOLF

Golf courses cater to the "snowbirds" who descend on this area every winter. The **Mesa del Sol Golf Resort,** 10583 Camino del Sol (☎ 520/342-1283), off I-8 at the Fortuna Road exit, is the most challenging local course open to the public. On the other hand, the **Desert Hills Municipal Course,** 1245 W. Desert Hills Dr. (☎ 520/341-0644), has been rated the best municipal course in the state. Other area courses include the **Arroyo Dunes Golf Course,** 32nd Street and Avenue A (☎ 520/726-8350); and the **Cocopah Bend RV Resort,** 6800 Strand Ave. (☎ 520/343-1663). The nine-hole Ironwood Public Golf Course, 2945 W. Eighth St. (☎ 520/343-1466), has recently been redesigned and is worth a round if you're only in the mood for a quick nine holes.

## WHERE TO STAY
### MODERATE

**Best Western Inn Suites Hotel.** 1450 S. Castle Dome Ave., Yuma, AZ 85365. ☎ **800/922-2034** or 520/783-8341. Fax 520/783-1349. 166 studios and suites. A/C TV TEL. Jan 1 to mid-Apr $89–$159 double; mid-Apr to early Sept $59–$99 double; early Sept to Dec 31 $69–$129 double. Rates include continental breakfast. AE, DC, DISC, MC, V.

If you've come to Yuma to escape the cold weather up north and want to enjoy some active sports, this hotel may be just what you're looking for. They've got a pool, whirlpool, exercise room, and tennis courts, and there's a golf course nearby. The rooms are divided between studios and one- and two-bedroom suites; all have microwave ovens, coffeemakers, refrigerators, and hair dryers. P.J.'s Poolside Café serves breakfast, sandwiches, snacks, and cocktails. The hotel also offers complimentary afternoon cocktails.

**La Fuente Inn.** 1513 E. 16th St., Yuma, AZ 85365. ☎ **800/841-1814** or 520/329-1814. Fax 520/343-2671. 96 rms, including 46 suites. A/C TV TEL. Jan–Apr $60–$70 double, $75–$85 suite; May–Dec $50–$70 double, $60–$80 suite. Rates include continental breakfast. AE, DC, DISC, MC, V.

Conveniently located just off the Interstate at 16th Street, this appealing hotel is done in Spanish colonial style with red-tile roof, pink stucco walls, and a fountain out front. In the lobby the theme is continued with rustic furnishings and a tile floor. French doors open onto the pool terrace and a large courtyard, around which the guest rooms are arranged. These rooms feature modern motel furnishings. Suites offer much more space and are well designed. The hotel also offers complimentary newspapers, evening happy hour, whirlpool, fitness room (and use of a nearby fitness center), coin laundry, and poolside gas barbecue grills.

**Shilo Inn Hotel.** 1550 S. Castle Dome Rd., Yuma, AZ 85365-1702. ☎ **800/222-2244** or 520/782-9511. Fax 520/783-1538. 134 rms, 10 suites. A/C TV TEL. $79–$105 double; $125–$250 suite. AE, CB, DC, DISC, MC, V.

Located on the edge of town overlooking farmland and desert, the Shilo Inn is Yuma's most luxurious hotel, and the neatly manicured gardens provide an oasis of greenery in this dry landscape. The bright guest rooms have comfortable chairs, couches, and patios, as well as microwaves, refrigerators, and VCRs. In the tile bathrooms you'll find plenty of counter space and a hair dryer. The hotel's more expensive rooms are those with a view of the desert. For long-term stays, there are also suites with kitchenettes. The hotel's spacious dining room offers both indoor and terrace dining, and to one side of the dining room is a lounge that often has live music on weekends. The hotel also offers complimentary newspaper and coffee, room service, a large pool, whirlpool, exercise room, sauna, and steam room.

## INEXPENSIVE

In addition to numerous older budget motels, Yuma has several newer budget chain motels. These include the **Airport Travelodge,** 711 E. 32nd St. (☎ 520/726-4721), charging $44 to $69 double; **Days Inn,** 1671 E. 16th St. (☎ 520/329-7790), charging $54 to $89 double; **Motel 6,** 1445 E. 16th St. (☎ 520/782-9521), charging $32 to $44 double; **Super 8,** 1688 S. Riley Ave. (☎ 520/782-2000), charging $50 to $61 double. See the appendix for toll-free numbers.

# WHERE TO DINE

✪ **The Garden Cafe.** 250 Madison Ave. ☎ **520/783-1491.** Main courses $4–$8. AE, MC, V. Tues–Fri 9am–2:30pm, Sat–Sun 8am–2:30pm. SANDWICHES/SALADS.

In back of the Century House Museum you'll find Yuma's favorite breakfast and lunch cafe. Set amid quiet terraced gardens and large aviaries full of singing birds, the Garden Cafe is a cool retreat from Yuma's heat. On the hottest days, misters spray the air with a gentle fog that keeps the gardens cool. There's also an indoor dining area. The menu consists of various well-constructed sandwiches, daily special quiches, salads, and rich desserts. Pancakes with lingonberry sauce are a breakfast specialty. On Sunday there's a brunch buffet.

**Hunter Steakhouse.** 2355 S. Fourth Ave. ☎ **520/782-3637.** Reservations recommended. Main courses $10–$19. AE, MC, V. Mon–Fri daily 11am–2pm; Mon–Thurs 4:30–9:30pm, Fri–Sat 4:30–10pm, Sun 3:30–9pm. STEAKS/SEAFOOD.

This dark and comfortable steakhouse has long been a Yuma favorite. While the restaurant is particularly popular for its $10 early-dinner specials, it's hard to pass up such offerings as top sirloin with whiskey-and-peppercorn sauce or prime rib served in combination with salmon, shrimp, or swordfish. Just be sure to save room for a towering mudd pie or creamy Bailey's Irish Cream mousse.

✪ **Lutes Casino.** 221 Main St. ☎ **520/782-2192.** Main courses $2.75–$4. No credit cards. Mon–Sat 9am–9pm, Sun 10am–6pm. BURGERS/SANDWICHES.

You won't find any slot machines or poker tables at Lutes Casino anymore, but back in the 1920s when this place opened, gambling was legal in Arizona. Today it's a dark and cavernous pool hall and the state's only domino parlor, but it's better known as a family restaurant serving the best hamburgers in town. You don't need to see a menu—just walk in and ask for a special, or *especial* (this is a bilingual joint). What you'll get is a combination of a cheeseburger and a hot dog. Then cover your special with Lute's own secret-recipe hot sauce to make it *truly* special.

**Mandarin Palace.** 350 E. 32nd St. ☎ **520/344-2805.** Main courses $7.25–$25; lunches $5.75–$7. AE, CB, DC, DISC, MC, V. Sun–Thurs 11am–10pm, Fri–Sat 11am–11pm. CHINESE.

Yuma doesn't seem the sort of town to support a palace, but that's exactly what this Chinese restaurant seems to be. It's big and elegant, and you'll probably be greeted by a host in a tuxedo. The prices seem a bit high for a Chinese restaurant, but you get plenty of choices that on the whole are fairly well done, including smoked tea duck, lobster in black-bean sauce, and a number of Szechuan dishes.

## HEADING EAST: A DETOUR TO ORGAN PIPE NATIONAL MONUMENT

Located roughly midway between Yuma and Tucson, and 70 miles south of I-8, lies one of Arizona's least visited and most remote national monuments. **Organ Pipe Cactus National Monument** is a preserve for the rare organ pipe cactus. This massive cactus resembles the saguaro in many ways, but instead of forming a single main trunk, it forms many trunks, some 20 feet tall, that resemble organ pipes.

Two well-graded one-way gravel roads loop through the park. The Puerto Blanco Drive is a 53-mile loop, while the Ajo Mountain Drive is only 21 miles long. On the Puerto Blanco Drive, you'll pass **Quitobaquito Spring,** which was relied on by Native Americans and pioneers as the only reliable source of water for miles around. This large spring offers great bird-watching opportunities, but cars are subject to break-ins (a Mexican highway is only 100 yards from the parking lot). Quitobaquito Springs can also be reached at the end of a 15-mile two-way section of the Puerto Blanco Drive. Guides available at the park's visitor center explain natural features of the landscape along both the loop roads. There are also a number of hiking trails along both of these roads.

Inside the park there's only one campground (although non-vehicle camping is allowed in the backcountry with a permit).

For more information, call ☎ **520/387-6849.** Admission to the park is $4 per car; camping fees are $8 per night. The visitor center is open daily from 8am to 5pm.

This is a rugged region with few towns or services. To the west lies the inaccessible Cabeza Prieta Wildlife Refuge and the Barry M. Goldwater Air Force Range (a bombing range), and to the east lies the large Papago Indian Reservation. The only services and motels in the area are to be found in Ajo. This former company town was built around a now-abandoned copper mine, and the downtown plaza has the look and feel of a Mexican town square. There are tall palm trees, arched and covered walkways, and a Mexican restaurant. On a hot day, the ice cream parlor here does a booming business. Be sure to gas up your car before leaving Ajo.

North of Ajo 42 miles, you'll find more lodging options in the town of Gila Bend, which has several chain motels. While in Gila Bend, you may want to stop in at the **Gila Bend Museum,** 644 W. Pima St. (☎ **520/683-2002**), where you can learn about the area's historic and prehistoric past. If you're interested in petroglyphs, you might want to drive 23 miles northwest from Gila Bend (take Exit 102 off I-8) to **Painted Rocks Park,** where you'll find an extensive concentration of petroglyphs, as well as a free campground and picnic area operated by the Bureau of Land Management (BLM). Also in the Gila Bend area is the world's tallest saguaro; ask at the museum for directions.

# Appendix: Useful Toll-Free Numbers & Web Sites

## LODGINGS

**Best Western International, Inc.**
800/528-1234 in North America
800/528-2222 TDD

**Clarion Hotels**
800/CLARION in Continental U.S. and Canada
800/228-3323 TDD
http://www.hotelchoice.com/cgi-bin/res/webres?clarion.html

**Comfort Inns**
800/228-5150 in Continental U.S. and Canada
800/228-3323 TDD
http://www.hotelchoice.com/cgi-bin/res/webres?comfort.html

**Courtyard by Marriott**
800/321-2211 in Continental U.S. and Canada
800/228-7014 TDD
http://www.courtyard.com

**Days Inn**
800/325-2525 in Continental U.S. and Canada
800/325-3297 TDD
http://www.daysinn.com/daysinn.html

**Doubletree Hotels**
800/222-TREE in Continental U.S. and Canada
800/528-9898 TDD

**Econo Lodges**
800/55-ECONO in Continental U.S. and Canada
800/228-3323 TDD
http://www.hotelchoice.com/cgi-bin/res/webres?econo.html

**Fairfield Inn by Marriott**
800/228-2800 in Continental U.S. and Canada
800/228-7014 TDD
http://www.marriott.com/fairfieldinn/

**Hampton Inn**
800/HAMPTON in Continental U.S. and Canada
800/451-HTDD TDD
http://www.hampton-inn.com/

**Hilton Hotels Corporation**
800/HILTONS in Continental U.S. and Canada
800/368-1133 TDD
http://www.hilton.com

**Holiday Inn**
800/HOLIDAY in Continental U.S. and Canada
800/238-5544 TDD
http://www.holiday-inn.com/
**Howard Johnson**
800/654-2000 in Continental U.S. and Canada
800/654-8442 TDD
http://www.hojo.com/hojo.html
**Hyatt Hotels and Resorts**
800/228-9000 in Continental U.S. and Canada
800/228-9548 TDD
http://www.hyatt.com
**ITT Sheraton**
800/325-3535 in Continental U.S. and Canada
800/325-1717 TDD
**La Quinta Motor Inns, Inc.**
800/531-5900 in Continental U.S. and Canada
800/426-3101 TDD
**Marriott Hotels**
800/228-9290 in Continental U.S. and Canada
800/228-7014 TDD
http://www.marriott.com
**Quality Inns**
800/228-5151 in Continental U.S. and Canada
800/228-3323 TDD
http://www.hotelchoice.com/cgi-bin/res/webres?quality.html
**Radisson Hotels International**
800/333-3333 in Continental U.S. and Canada
**Ramada Inns**
800/2-RAMADA in Continental U.S. and Canada
http://www.ramada.com/ramada.html
**Red Roof Inns**
800/843-7663 in Continental U.S. and Canada
800/843-9999 TDD
http://www.redroof.com
**Residence Inn by Marriott**
800/331-3131 in Continental U.S. and Canada
800/228-7014 TDD
http://www.marriott.com/lodging/resinn.htm
**Rodeway Inns**
800/228-2000 in Continental U.S. and Canada
800/228-3323 TDD
http://www.hotelchoice.com/cgi-bin/res/webres?rodeway.html
**Super 8 Motels**
800/800-8000 in Continental U.S. and Canada
800/533-6634 TDD
http://www.super8motels.com/super8.html
**Travelodge**
800/255-3050 in Continental U.S. and Canada

# Index

# WHEREVER YOU TRAVEL, *H*ELP IS NEVER FAR AWAY.

From planning your trip to providing travel assistance along the way, American Express® Travel Service Offices are always there to help you do more.

---

## *Arizona*

Flagstaff Travel (R)
508 North Humphreys
Flagstaff
602/774-9104

American Express Travel Service
6900 East Camelback Road
Camelview Plaza
Phoenix
602/949-7000

American Express Travel Service
2508 East Camelback Road
Biltmore Fashion Park
Phoenix
602/468-1199

Ford's World Travel (R)
15414 N. 99th Avenue
Sun City
602/933-8295

Century Travel (R)
4361 E. Broadway
Tucson
520/795-8400

Bon Voyage Travel (R)
4747 B. East Sunrise Drive
Tucson
520/299-6618

Bon Voyage Travel (R)
6482 N. Oracle Road
Tucson
520/297-7338

Bon Voyage Travel (R)
925 E. University Boulevard
Tucson
602/622-5842

## do more

**Travel**

http://www.americanexpress.com/travel

**American Express Travel Service Offices are found in central locations throughout Arizona. For the office nearest you, call 1-800-AXP-3429.**